RAVES FROM THE PRESS

"The Worldwide Adventure TravelGuide is the best organized and most comprehensive such publication we've seen . . ."
—*MOTORLAND/CSSA*

"The variety of trips outlined should whet the appetite of anyone with the spirit of adventure . . ."
—*FAIRBANKS DAILY NEWS*

"The Worldwide Adventure TravelGuide is a gold mine for $9.95. Not only for real adventurers but also for armchair dreamers. . . . Whatever your dream, the Guide will offer you some details about who will help fulfill it."   —*SAN DIEGO EVENING TRIBUNE*

"If the lengthening days of winter into spring have made you think of taking down your 10-speed bicycle and of getting out the backpack gear from a closet corner, then this is for you."   —*THE NEW YORK TIMES*

"The book is actually a directory of adventure travel information for people who want to do something besides visit an area and who dislike being shepherded about like sheep by a tourist guide."   —*THE SCRANTON TRIBUNE*

"More than 2,000 'adventures' are outlined in a new 600-page paperback that will prove useful to anyone who spends his or her spare time on a bicycle, in a canoe or jumping out of airplanes . . ."
—*THE HUNTSVILLE TIMES*

AND PRAISE FROM OUR READERS

Your adventure TravelGuide is fantastic! I think I've been waiting for it all my life. I'd go into more of a rapture about it were I not about to leave for a trip . . . and time is limited. Great work!"
    —ELLEN SEIDMAN
    Plainsboro, New Jersey

"Just received the first edition of Worldwide Adventure TravelGuide. I can't put it down. I am truly impressed with the great amount of work and coordination that went into compiling such a fantastic guide. You open the world of adventure through your publication . . ."
    —JOYCE E. GORDON
    Beaverton, Oregon

"Congratulations on your Worldwide Adventure TravelGuide. An excellent job of pulling a tremendous amount of information together for us who love the call of adventure. It is an excellent reference book."
    —LANCE FIELD, *President,*
    International Backpackers Assn.

"We believe that the adventuresome spirit has come into its own, and that your publication will aid those newcomers and seasoned adventurers alike in planning new and exciting things to do."
    —JUDY FITZPATRICK
    Hilliard, Florida

"The TravelGuide is a fantastic compendium of sources of adventure trips . . . and my only regret is that I don't have more free time because I usually get stirred up so much that I want to just take off . . ."   *STEVE NUSSBAUM*
    Houston, Texas

1979 WORLDWIDE Adventure TravelGuide ©

PUBLISHED BY THE

AMERICAN ADVENTURERS ASSOCIATION

SEATTLE, WASHINGTON

To order additional copies of the 1979 Worldwide Adventure TravelGuide (or to place advance orders for the 1980 edition), contact

AMERICAN ADVENTURERS ASSOCIATION
Suite 301, 444 NE Ravenna Blvd.
Seattle, WA 98115, USA

1979 WORLDWIDE ADVENTURE TRAVELGUIDE

Bob Citron, *Executive Editor & Publisher*
Constance Balint, *Editor*
Kristin Tregillus, *Managing Editor*
Kris Fulsaas, *Production Editor*
Knute Berger, Christian Kallen, *Associate Editors*
Barbara L. Sleeper, *Senior Editor*
Douglas Honig, Kevin Gaery, *Copy Editors*
Nicholas H. Allison, Donn Cave, Judy Frostega,
Philip Haldeman, Gordon Hardy, Beth Healy, Rick
Hermann, Joan Kerr, Ruth Stanbrough, *Writers*
Dawn Heathers, Liz Heath, *Typesetting*
Carol A. Baker, *Photography Editor*
Elizabeth Watson, Carolyn
Linville, *Design & Production*
Craig Sternagel, *Advertising Manager*
Lynette Klein, Steven Maris, Sarah Pape,
Steve Rees, Kim Salzwedel, *Advertising Staff*

American Adventurers Association

Bob Citron, *Founder and President*
Barbara L. Sleeper, *Vice President
and Treasurer*
S. Scot Litke, *Membership Director*
Claudia Mirchel, *Executive Assistant*
Sandy Halladay, *Promotion Assistant*
Howard Baldwin, Donn Cave, Beth
Healy, Kyle Kittoe, Lynn Knight,
Dora Lange, Eric Lindh, *Membership Services*
Maggie Riester, Sally Schaake, *Business Office*
Richard K. Citron, *Legal Counsel*
James B. Kobak, *Business Advisor*

Cover: A backpacker hikes along the timberline of Washington's Mt. Rainier. Photograph by Bob Citron.

International Standard Book Number 394-737-23-7
International Standard Serial Number 0148-2300.
Library of Congress Number LC-78-24748.

Distributed in the United States
by Random House, Inc. and in
Canada by Random House of Canada, Ltd.
Printed in the USA.

First Printing Feb. 1979: 30,000 copies.

About the American Adventurers Association

Today more than 2,000 organizations in the world offer the opportunity for members of the general public to join some 6,000 different adventure trips—ranging from backpacking the Appalachian Trail to bicycle touring in Vermont, bush flying in the Yukon, river rafting the mighty Colorado, scuba diving with great white sharks off Australia's Great Barrier Reef, trekking in the Nepalese Himalayas, climbing in the Peruvian Andes, observing wildlife from elephant-back in Kaziranga, India, or working with anthropologists, archaeologists and naturalists on dozens of nature trips and field research expeditions that you can join as a paying participant. Adventure travel is booming —already more than two million people join adventure trips each year.

The American Adventurers Association was founded in 1976 because we felt that there was a growing need to develop an association of members who were tied together by an abiding interest in adventure travel. We knew there was a lack of readily available information on who was doing what, where, when, and how. We realized there was no focal point, no international repository, no data center, where information on adventure travel could easily be obtained.

At the outset the association had ambitious goals. We hoped to become the world center for adventure travel information, to keep our fingers on the pulse of the international adventure travel industry, to set standards for adventure trips, to evaluate adventure travel organizations, and to develop a series of first-class publications that would be exciting, educational, and environmentally concerned.

In the past two years the association has become *the* worldwide clearinghouse for information on adventure trip opportunities open to public participation, and it has developed a worldwide constituency of hundreds of organizations, businesses, and institutions that organize adventure trips and adventure travel programs. The association has also established an adventure trip evaluation program to evaluate individual trips with regard to their cost, environmental impact, and adventurous desirability; trip operators are evaluated with regard to their experience, reliability and responsibility (both to the participants and to the environment).

Our most exciting achievements are our publications. *Adventure Travel Newsletter* is the most quoted source of adventure travel information published today. *Adventure Travel* magazine has been described as "the most beautiful travel magazine ever published." And our annual *Worldwide Adventure TravelGuide* is "the most comprehensive and authoritative source of adventure trip information available anywhere."

The association has now grown to more than 10,000 members, and during its first year of publication *Adventure Travel* magazine reached a paid circulation of 70,000 and a total circulation of more than 100,000 copies a month. *Adventure Travel Newsletter* now has a circulation of 10,000 and, in this, its second edition, the *Worldwide Adventure TravelGuide* had a printing of 30,000 copies.

The book that you are holding in your hands represents a full year of exhaustive work by a very dedicated team of people. We hope you enjoy using it, not just to titillate your fancies for adventure, but to actually plan, schedule, and participate *in your own adventure*. This book is to help you make your dream come true!

Bob Citron
Founder and President
American Adventurers Association
February 1979

How to Use the TravelGuide

You hold in your hand a passport to adventure. In 32 different chapters are listed some 3,000 opportunities for adventure travel. Many long hours of research, writing, editing, checking and rechecking have gone into this, the second *Worldwide Adventure TravelGuide*. It is the most comprehensive directory of adventure trips open to public participation ever published. While the extensive listings of this material may make the guide seem impenetrable, it is in fact designed for quick reference.

The *TravelGuide* is divided into four major sections—for Land Adventures, Air Adventures, Water Adventures and Underwater Adventures. Each section includes an overview of the range of possible trips for each activity. Each section is further divided into activities offered within that medium. For instance, under Air Adventures you will find Ballooning, Soaring, Flying, Hang Gliding, Parasailing and Parachuting.

The trip descriptions within each section give a run-down of the highlights of every trip including its itinerary, requirements, level of experience needed, location, duration, dates, and cost. Addresses and phone numbers of organizations which run the trips are listed so you can contact them directly for additional information or to make your reservation.

Finally, each activity is divided into geographic regions. All seven continents are used for these divisions, as well as marine areas such as the Caribbean, Pacific, Atlantic and Indian oceans, and the cultural region of the Middle East. These areas are then further broken down into individual countries. In the case of North America—Mexico, Canada and the United States—sections are also listed by states or provinces.

At the end of most activities within the *TravelGuide* is a Resource addendum which names clubs, associations, rental agencies and consultants involved in each activity, so you can write to them for further information. There are also two useful indexes to the *TravelGuide*. One lists the type of trip by geographical area (e.g., Nepal, river rafting) and the other lists the trips by the operators who run them. If you wish to go on a horsepacking trip in Colorado, for example, Index I lists a) Colorado, and b) the pages where horsepacking trips in that state can be found. If you wish to find out what trips are run by a specific organization, Index II lists a) the name of the organization and b) the pages on which their trips are described. An appendix lists the organizational members of the American Adventurers Association, who represent every aspect of the adventure travel field.

For additional information on any particular trip write to the trip operator or contact us at the American Adventurers Association if you are a member. We hope you have many hours of pleasure thumbing through this *TravelGuide*, savoring the trip descriptions and vicariously participating in some of the world's most exciting adventures. But most of all, we hope you go on them and explore the world of adventure. □

CONTENTS

Note: *(M)* at the end of many of the write-ups in the *Adventure TravelGuide* indicates that the trip operators involved are members of the American Adventurers Association.

The Spirit of Adventure

From the summit, the world spreads out beneath you, majestic in its asymmetrical beauty. Distant peaks form a ring of snow-capped challenges inviting further exploration, silhouetted against the clear, blue sky. Or maybe a thousand miles away, a hammerhead shark glides like a shadow 20 feet beneath you. You subconsciously hold your breath lest the bubble and rasp of the regulator prompt the beast to investigate more closely. Or perhaps you are walking into a small New Guinea village, high above the forested canyons, and from the looks of surprise, curiosity and excitement you know that these people may never have seen anyone from outside their highlands before. Each moment seems intensified; each sensation rings with clarity; each sound, sight and scent directly connects you with the world around you. This is adventure travel. You could be climbing in the Rockies, diving in the Caribbean, or exploring the cultures of Papua New Guinea. Yes—you *could* be.

Sometimes it may seem that all the great discoveries have been made. The Age of Exploration has come and gone, the Everests and Matterhorns have been climbed, the Amazon has been investigated from its source to its delta. But have you made these discoveries for yourself? Have you sailed those seas, climbed those mountains or explored those rivers? Each discovery waits to be made anew on adventure trips all over the world. Whether you climb, sail, dive, ski or soar, each adventure brings home to you the true meaning of discovery—a gaining of new insight into yourself, as well as the world around you. You cannot read about it, watch it on television or hear it from a friend. You have to do it yourself.

Within the pages of this book, there are 3,000 adventure trips in 32 different activities which take place in 50 states and 114 countries on every continent and ocean of the world. There are trips for every budget, from a $3 ski tour in Wisconsin to an $8,000 around-the-world cruise—even free trips by bicycle or foot. You can sail, dive, or kayak on the water; climb, ski or dogsled on land; or hang glide, parachute or balloon in the air. You could have a lifetime of experience behind you and still find something that you have never done before. Or you could be barely old enough to read, filled with the wonder of being alive, willing to try anything. Curiosity is the keynote, excitement is the reward. And adventure the opportunity. □

Land Adventures

MOUNTAINEERING

From hill climbs in Vermont to assaults on major peaks in the Himalayas, mountaineering offers a wide range of challenges. At its best it combines physical strength with mental agility. The balance between body and mind—and the fullness of spirit it creates—is often reward enough for the mountaineer. Yet there always remains the climax of the climbs, the final spectacle from the summit.

Rock climbing is one of the more popular types of mountaineering, and it has its own advocates, terminology and equipment. Where a mountaineer may try to reach the summit as soon as possible by the most direct route, a rock climber may not be interested in the top at all. Instead, a particularly satisfying face or outcropping might be climbed again and again for the skills it involves. Ice climbing, with crampons and other specialized equipment, turns rock climbing into a year-round sport, and is becoming increasingly popular in its own right.

All of the major ranges in the world, and many of the smaller ones, are visited each year by teams of climbers of varying levels of skill. You don't have to be a professional mountaineer on a major expedition to climb some of these peaks yourself: outfitters and guides on six continents offer complete, exciting and often surprisingly economical climbing trips. Little or no experience is needed to make an overnight ascent of Mt. Rainier (14,410 feet) in Washington, or even to climb Mt. Kilimanjaro (19,340 feet) in Tanzania on a five-day trip.

If your skills have advanced, perhaps through one of the many climbing schools in places such as the Tetons, the Rockies, or the Great Smoky Mountains, you might want to test yourself against some of the great mountains of the world. Each year, one commercial group takes on an unclimbed summit in the Himalayas, prepared with skis for an unusual descent. And several operators tackle the volcanic peaks of central Mexico, Popocatepetl (17,887 feet) and Orizaba (18,851 feet). Even the highest peak in North America, Mt. McKinley—or Denali, as the native Alaskans call it—can be climbed to its 20,320-foot summit.

Mountaineering is a rigorous activity and not without danger. Frostbite, hypothermia, acute mountain sickness and avalanches can strike the expert as well as the novice, so you should go with a reputable guide service. But danger cannot be excluded from human experience. In fact, testing one's limits against the unforgiving heights is what makes mountaineering so rewarding. □

Using crampons and an ice ax, a climber carves a vertical route up the side of a crevasse on Mt. Rainier in Washington. (Keith Gunnar)

MOUNTAINEERING

AFRICA

Tanzania

Research Expedition: A new program to East Africa aims to develop research projects for future expeditions. The 5-week trip for up to 12 participants provides training in mounting and carrying out a mountaineering expedition. Several peaks are climbed, including Mt. Maru and Mt. Kilimanjaro. Expedition members cover diverse ecological zones ranging from the desert areas of the Northern Frontier District of Kenya to the tropical rain forests of Tanzania. The group also visits the East African Outward Bound Mountain School and numerous game parks, where research projects are developed in wildlife conservation. Participants are young people ages 16 to 24. **Cost:** $550. **When:** July, August. **Contact:** Expedition Training Institute, Inc., P.O. Box 171, Prudential Ctr. Sta., Boston, MA 02199, USA; phone (617)922-0577. *(M)*

Climbing Kilimanjaro: Uhuru Peak, the highest point on the African continent at 19,340 feet, is the goal of a 5-day trip up Mt. Kilimanjaro. Beginning at Marangu, trip participants hike 10 miles through coffee and banana plantations to an altitude of 9,000 feet. The following day the group hikes another 10 miles before resting to adjust to the altitude. On the third day, climbers push on to a hut above the vegetation line at 15,000 feet, where the glaciers at the Kilimanjaro range become visible. That night, while the scree is still frozen, the group begins the final ascent,

Climbing the sheer face of an ice wall tests a mountaineer's expertise; many mountaineering trips offer instruction on ice as well as rock. (Carol Baker)

reaching the summit about 6 hours later. Familiarity with mountaineering is recommended and participants should be in good physical condition for this strenuous trip. **Cost:** $104 to $140 includes guide, porters, meals, hut and park fees. **When:** Year-round. **Contact:** Kibo Hotel, P.O. Box 102, Marangu, Tanzania; phone 4 Marangu.

ASIA

Hong Kong

Hong Kong Climbing: A non-profit mountaineering association offers a 30-day course in mountaincraft training for adults. The course provides comprehensive training in many aspects of mountaineering, including orienteering and map use, leadership, rock climbing, rope handling, and mountain rescue and survival. Instruction on selection, care and improvisation of equipment, plus an introduction to environmental education are also part of the course. Instruction, which includes 10 lecture sessions, takes place outside Hong Kong on weekends. The course is strenuous, so good health is essential for participants. **Cost:** $450 includes roundtrip transportation from Hong Kong, equipment. **When:** Year-round except August. **Contact:** Hong Kong Mountaineering Association, P.O. Box 20519, Hennessy Rd. P.O., Hong Kong.

India

Ascending an Unclimbed Peak: Experienced mountaineers can join the annual attempt of an unclimbed mountain in the Himalayas. The exact location for the 44-day expedition has not yet been decided.

The 1978 climb was a difficult rock and ice peak at 21,000 feet in the Kishtwar Himalayas between the Great Himalaya Range and the Pir Panjal Range. The 1977 expedition made a successful ascent of 21,000-foot Berthartoli in the Garwhal Himalaya. **Cost:** $2,495 includes meals, guides, accommodations. **When:** June, July. **Contact:** Mountain Travel Inc., 1398 Solano Ave., Albany, CA 94706, USA; phone (415)527-8100.   *(M)*

Pakistan

K-2 Base Camp Expedition: A strenuous 36-day trek takes participants from Skardu to the base camp of the 1978 American K-2 assault. Group members must be in excellent physical condition and prepared for delays, last-minute route changes and other obstacles. The approach route is rugged, crossing rivers on woven vine bridges, traversing steep landscape scars and following the extremely uneven, unstable surface of the Baltoro Glacier. Travel is by jeep from Skardu to the village of Dassu (8,150 feet) in the Karakoram foothills. The first week of walking is extremely tough, passing through Chakpo and Chongo, along high ridges and across the Baltoro Glacier, which creaks and cracks constantly. The twelfth day brings trekkers to Concordia at the confluence of the Godwin-Austen and Baltoro glaciers, a spot surrounded by Gasherbrum IV at 26,810 feet and 5 other summits over 26,000 feet. The next day the group reaches K-2 base camp, where 3 days are spent watching climbers through binoculars and talking to expedition members. The return trip provides views of Chogolisa at 25,110 feet, the Golden Throne at 23,989 feet, Hidden Peak at 26,470 feet and the Duke of Abruzzi Glacier. **Cost:** $2,805 includes meals, accommodations, equipment, porters, guides. **When:** June. **Contact:** REI Adventure Travel, 1525 11th Ave., Seattle, WA 98122, USA; phone (206)322-7800. *(M)*

AUSTRALASIA

New Zealand

Mt. Cook Mountain Climbing: Experienced alpine guides are available to lead parties and individuals on trips and climbs of 1 day or longer within Mt. Cook and Westland national parks. The high safety margins afforded by guided climbing enable people to visit areas and tackle climbs they might not otherwise attempt. Private guides may also be hired for hut trips and mountaineering instruction. Maximum group numbers are determined by the nature of the expedition and competence of the participants. **Cost:** $12 to $38 depending on number of persons per guide. **When:** October to April. **Contact:** Alpine Guides (Mt. Cook) Ltd., Mt. Cook National Park, P.O. Box 20, Mt. Cook, New Zealand; phone 809.

Ski Mountaineering Course: Proficiency in and appreciation of mountaineering with skis are learned in the Mt. Cook National Park of New Zealand. Members must be fit, familiar with general mountaineering techniques, skilled in soft snow techniques (stem turn or better) and prepared to ski at times with a 40-pound pack. For 7 days participants are based in high mountain huts where they become familiar with roped skiing, winter training and survival, glacier negotiation and bivouacs. Instructors are 10-year veterans accredited by the Federated Mountain Clubs of New Zealand. **Cost:** $130 includes food, accommodations. **When:** September. **Contact:** Alpine Guides (Mt. Cook) Ltd., Mt. Cook National Park, P.O. Box 20, Mt. Cook, New Zealand; phone 809.

Mountaincraft Instruction: Six-day courses designed to meet individual needs of climbers begin on Sunday afternoon and end the following Saturday night. The courses are based at a headquarters near Franz Joseph Glacier, where facilities for rock climbing, ice climbing and river crossing are close at hand. Participants spend 2 or 3 days in high camps learning snow climbing, glacier travel, crevasse rescue, avalanche awareness and mountain survival. Groups are divided into parties of similar abilities, and a ratio of 4 course members to 1 instructor is maintained. **Cost:** $100 includes food, accommodations, instruction. **When:** December, January. **Contact:** Mountain Guides, P.O. Box 30, Franz Josef Glacier, Westland, New Zealand.

Courses for Aspiring Mountaineers: A choice of 6 different skiing and mountaineering courses lasting an average of 8 days is offered in the West Matukituki Valley of Mt. Aspiring National Park. The courses cover the complete range of mountain wilderness skills, from

alpine pass crossing for the bush-walker to rock climbing, ice climbing and skiing alpine terrain. Instruction covers all of the necessary skills, including ice ax and crampon use, snowcave and igloo construction, crevasse rescue, weather and avalanche observation, party self-reliance and improvised rescue techniques. Good physical condition and some outdoor experience are necessary. **Cost:** $155 includes transportation from Wanaka, accommodations, gear, food, instruction. **When:** November through February. **Contact:** Mountain Recreation, P.O. Box 204, Wanaka, Central Otago, New Zealand.

CANADA

Alberta

Canadian Rockies Mountaineering Program: A 3-week training and climbing program takes place in the Moat Lake area of the Tonquin Valley. The main camp at 6,400 feet is reached via a 14-mile trail up Meadow Creek. The large number of guides present insures a high

Inching up exposed rock in the Canadian Rockies, a climber is safely harnessed and roped in case he should take a fall. (Canadian Youth Hostels Association)

instructor-to-participant ratio for a 1-week training period. The next one or two weeks are spent on daily climbs suited to the experience of participants. A high camp is established in the Geikie Meadows at 7,200 feet from where a high-level traverse may be made over Para Pass and down to the Wates-Gibson hut at 6,200 feet. A food cache is established at the hut, and from here mountaineers may climb McDonnell, Simon or Bennington peaks. **Cost:** $475 for 2 weeks, $700 for 3 weeks. **When:** July. **Contact:** The Alpine Club of Canada, P.O. Box 1026, Banff, AB Canada T0L 0C0; phone (403)762-3664.

Rocky Mountain Climbing Instruction: Weekend and week-long courses teach students the fundamentals and intermediate techniques of rock climbing. The courses are based in youth hostels in the Rockies, with climbs chosen to vary with conditions and group ability. At Ribbon Creek Hostel, intermediate students learn to lead, put in their own placements, and plan and prepare trips. At Hilda Creek Hostel, students with previous experience may brush up their skills at a snow and ice school, while a beginners climbing week at Eisenhower Youth Hostel helps participants refine their techniques on snow and rock. **Cost:** From $30 for a weekend to $125 for 1 week. **When:** May to August. **Contact:** Canadian Hostelling Association, North West Region, 10922 88th Ave., Edmonton, AB Canada T6G 0Z1; phone (403)433-4696.

Boulder Camp Climbing Courses: The granite spires and wild glaciers of the Canadian Rockies provide the training ground for participants in any of several mountaineering courses. Staying at a large mountain hut at Boulder Camp at 7,400 feet, students learn and practice rock and ice climbing techniques. Week-long sessions are available to climbers from beginner to advanced, and include ascents of Bugaboo Spire, East Ridge Marmolata, Howser North and South Towers and Snowpatch Spire. The difficulty of the climbs depends on the needs and abilities of the groups and prevailing weather conditions. Towering 10,000 feet high in remote parts of the Rockies, peaks such as Mt. Robson, Mt. Tupper and Rogers Peak may be climbed. A 2-day climb to Mt. Victoria is also available to serious mountaineering enthusiasts. **Cost:** $30 to $365 depending on type and duration of trip includes accommodations, meals, guide. **When:** June to September. **Contact:** Canadian Mountain Holidays Ltd., P.O. Box 1660, Banff, AB Canada T0L 0C0; phone (403)762-4531.

Schooling at Columbia Icefields: Individuals with some prior climbing experience participate in a series of 2-day snow and ice schools in the Canadian Rockies outside of Banff. On the first day climbers traverse steep snow slopes, glissade, and use ice ax and crampons while practicing crevasse rescue on the Columbia Icefields. After the day's mountaineering, participants make camp at a convenient location on the icefields. On the second day climbers ascend Mt. Athabasca at 11,400 feet, returning to Banff by early evening. **Cost:** $45 includes

Special winter mountaineering equipment is used during a 10-day seminar in a remote area of British Columbia. (Northern Lights Alpine Recreation)

instruction only. **When:** June to September. **Contact:** Canadian Mountain Holidays Ltd., P.O. Box 1660, Banff, AB Canada T0L 0C0; phone (403)762-4531.

Teenage Mountaineering Program: From a base camp 30 miles south of Banff in the British Military Range, 3 different programs instruct young people 13 to 18 in mountaineering skills. The basic program begins with a session about ropes, knots, safety and equipment handling, and includes some easy climbs to apply these techniques. Pace setting, route safety, equipment use, crevasse rescue and snow cave construction are practiced during longer climbs and 3-day trips on the Robson Glacier and surrounding peaks. Once out in the mountains, everyone shares in the preparation of supplies, equipment, food and itinerary. Program II includes tougher routes with less orientation, and participants are encouraged to lead. Program III is a 1-week trip for experienced climb-

ers based in Banff, including climbs of Eisenhower, Louis and Yamnuska mountains. **Cost:** $525 for Program I, $550 for Program II includes meals, guides, equipment use; $250 for Program III includes transportation, guides. **When:** July. **Contact:** High Horizons, P.O. Box 1166, Banff, AB Canada T0L 0C0; phone (403)762-2868. *(M)*

Canadian Rockies Mountain Programs: Three different week-long programs for adults cover backpacking, mountaineering and intermediate and advanced climbing in the mountains outside of Banff. Starting at Sunshine Village, an alpine backpacking journey proceeds to Mt. Assiniboine, Matvel and Spray Lakes, continues up the Spray River to reach Burstall Lakes. From a base camp in the Burstall Lakes area, beginning mountaineering is taught according to individual ability. Included is instruction in compass orientation, pace setting, trip planning, botany and basic survival knowledge. In addition to rock and ice climbing instruction, the week includes climbs of some of the local peaks. The intermediate/advanced group climbs several of the classic routes on such peaks as Eisenhower, Louis Tower, Edith, Tuncle and Tower of Babel. There is a maximum of 3 participants with each guide on these outings. **Cost:** $200 to $250 includes instruction, guides, meals (food extra in advanced/intermediate climbing). **When:** July, August. **Contact:** High Horizons, P.O. Box 1166, Banff, AB Canada T0L 0C0; phone (403)762-2868. *(M)*

British Columbia
Arctic Mountaineering Seminar: A 10-day mountaineering seminar is held on one of the largest icefields in the interior ranges of British Columbia. Designed for the intermediate/advanced mountaineer experienced in general glacier travel, the seminar covers high-altitude glacier camping, igloo and snow cave construction, navigation and route-finding, itinerary planning, crevasse rescue and high-angle ice climbing techniques. Camp is established in the center of a large glacier system whose icefalls and neve slopes provide challenging terrain during practice and on actual ascents. Each participant has the chance to lead a summit climb during the seminar. Trip members use a special mountaineering

snowshoe for transportation or, if all members have the proper experience and equipment, the trip may be undertaken on skis. The weather may be harsh, so trip members should be prepared to face trying conditions. **Cost:** $275 includes guide, instruction; transportation, all equipment, food extra. **When:** April to June. **Contact:** Northern Lights Alpine Recreation, Box 399, Invermere, BC Canada V0A 1K0; phone (604)342-6042. *(M)*

Winter Climbing on Waddington: Mt. Waddington, the highest peak in the Coast Mountains of British Columbia at 13,147 feet, was once called Mystery Mountain for its remoteness. A 29-day introduction to mountaineering offers participants a chance to camp on Mt. Waddington's Tiedemann Glacier and possibly make a summit attempt. The party gathers at a lodge in Strathcona Provincial Park, on the northern part of Vancouver Island, for a week of preparation and training before being airlifted onto the glacier to establish base camp. At this point the expedition leaders make a decision, based mainly on the weather, whether or not a summit attempt will be made. If not, participants spend time rock climbing on Mt. Tiedemann and exploring many surrounding smaller peaks and glaciers. After 3 weeks on the mountain the party returns to Strathcona Park by air. **Cost:** $800 includes air transportation to and from the mountain, food, most equipment, instruction, guide. **When:** September. **Contact:** Strathcona Park Lodge, Outdoor Education Society, Box 2160, Campbell River, BC Canada V9W 5C9; phone

Campbell River radiophone operator.

EUROPE

England
Climbing Crags and Walking Fells: Six participants join 2 or 3 guides on a 35-day trip climbing and hiking through England, Scotland and Wales. The group flies from New York to London, where the group begins its sightseeing and rock climbing. Climbing sites include Almscliffe, a gritstone crag in Yorkshire, the Isle of Skye in the Inner Hebrides, the Carn Dearg Buttress at Ben Nevis and Tremadoc. At Wasdale Head the group makes a technical rock climb up Napes Needle, and climbers who are able climb the Centurian route on the Carn Dearg Buttress, one of Britain's most challenging big wall climbs. Also on the itinerary are Stonehenge, Liverpool, Edinburgh and London. Some backpacking and climbing experience is preferred but not required for making the trip; the age for participants is 15 to 21. **Cost:** $1,830 includes airfare from New York. **When:** July. **Contact:** North Country Mountaineering, Inc., P.O. Box 951, Hanover, NH 03755, USA; phone (603)643-3299. *(M)*

Sea Cliff Climbing: Groups of 6 to 10 mountaineers receive 14 days of climbing instruction on the sea cliffs of southwest Britain and Wales. After meeting in London, participants drive to West Penwith in Cornwall from where they receive training at Chairladder, Devon, Snowdonia and Anglesey. Experienced instructors accompany

Students catch their breath while listening to instructions between climbs in the Alps.
(Paulina C. Van Spronsen)

groups, with a ratio of 1 instructor for every 2 students. Accommodations vary from inns and huts to tents. **Cost:** $980 includes accommodations, some meals. **When:** April. **Contact:** Palisade School of Mountaineering, P.O. Box 694, Bishop, CA 93514, USA; phone (714)935-4330.

Llanberis Mountaineering Courses: A hostel on the summit of Llanberis Pass serves as base for climbing and mountaincraft courses. Participants spend a weekend, 7 days or 11 days climbing on nearby cliffs. A course in high-altitude climbing traverses long mountain routes, usually ending on a 3,000-foot peak in Snowdonia. The mountaincraft course provides a general introduction to safe movement over the mountains and includes map and compass work, navigation, route planning, weather, equipment, food and clothing, mountain rescue and rock climbing. With a maximum of 3 pupils to each instructor, rock climbing courses are offered on beginning, intermediate and advanced levels. Beginning climbers concentrate on

learning good rope management and on training good seconds. Intensive intermediate courses include varied climbs with a focus on belaying, prussicking and self-help techniques. Advanced students improve skills by attempting some very difficult climbs. **Cost:** $46 for the weekend, $132 for 7 days, $196 for 11 days includes meals, accommodations, guides, instruction. **When:** January to November. **Contact:** YHA Adventure Holiday, Trevelyen House, St. Albans, Herts., Great Britain; phone St. Albans 55215.

France

Introduction to the Alps: From a base camp over 4,700 feet above sea level in the French Alps, a course for novice mountaineers presents the basics of climbing on both rock and ice. Over a 2-week period groups of 6 to 10 learn increasingly difficult means of travel in the Alps, from high-level alpine walking in valleys to basic glacial and snow walking using ice ax and crampons. An ascent of 12,399-foot Mt. Pourri is optional. From the summit are views of the mountains of France,

Italy and Switzerland, including the Mont Blanc area to the north. Each individual decides how far to advance in the course of instruction. Base camp is in 2- or 3-person tents. **Cost:** $332 includes transportation from London, food, insurance. **When:** July, August. **Contact:** Peter Barnes, 5 Kingarth Ave., Seaburn, Sunderland SR6 8DN, Great Britain.

Scotland

The Crags of Ben Nevis: Summer and winter mountaineering is taught in 1-week courses in Loch Eil for climbers of all levels of experience. Climbers start with the local crags of Poldubh with over 100 routes of all grades, then go up the cliffs of Ben Nevis, Glen Coe and Glen Etive among many others. The basic course involves map work, navigation, basic rope techniques and simple rock climbing, followed by an expedition. There are evening films and lectures on topics such as first aid, meteorology and leadership. A more advanced winter course is offered that emphasizes difficult navigation problems and snow-holing expeditions. Both courses are designed to accommodate individual needs. **Cost:** $116 to $135 includes accommodations. **When:** February, March, May, June, August, September. **Contact:** Outward Bound Loch Eil, Achdalieu, Ft. William, Inverness-shire, Great Britain; phone Corpach 320. *(M)*

Switzerland

Swiss Alpine Schooling: Sidelen Hut, near Andermatt, is the base for a 6-day training course in alpine techniques. The course starts on Sunday evening with a climb to the hut at 8,556 feet for supper. The next day, beginners as well as students with some knowledge of climbing receive instruction in knots, belaying, step cutting and use of crampons. Later in the week participants embark on short climbing tours of grades 3 and 4 to gain confidence and self-sufficiency in alpine situations. Climbers work in small groups, with individual instruction given whenever possible. **Cost:** $303 includes guides, lodging, some meals. **When:** May to September. **Contact:** Alpine Sportschule Gotthard, 6490 Andermatt, Switzerland; phone (044)6 77 33.

Helvetian Mountaineering: Courses designed to suit both absolute beginners and alpinists of intermediate level are given in the Alps. Participants begin the 16-day course with training and acclimatization on lower peaks. Instruction in rope, ax and crampon techniques is given on glaciers, and participants progress to safe movement and control instruction on higher mountains. Every 2 or 3 days in the mountains are followed by a rest day in town. A base camp is located near the village of Zermatt, where accommodations are in 2-person tents. Zermatt is surrounded by several 13,000-foot peaks, and climbs may include the Matterhorn, the Dom and the Monte Rosa. **Cost:** $331. **When:** July, August. **Contact:** Don Morrison Mountaineering, 343 London Rd., Sheffield SR 4NG, Great Britain; phone (0742)56018.

Alpine Climbing School: Courses for beginning, intermediate and advanced climbers are offered in the Alps. Instruction in rock and ice climbing is given by a staff of climbers experienced in both Alpine and Himalayan mountain environments. Over 100 climbing routes in the area near Leysin offer ample opportunity for instruction at all levels of climbing capabilities. The standard introductory class lasts 6 days, as does the intermediate course, which includes climbs in the Mont Blanc area or the Swiss Valaisian Alps. Advanced courses are by arrangement. Lodging is at a mountain club for international travelers, with bunk accommodations and communal dining. Instruction is in English. **Cost:** $161 for standard, $172 for intermediate course. **When:** June through September. **Contact:** International School of Mountaineering, Club Vagabond, 1854 Leysin, Switzerland; phone (025)6-23-21. *(M)*

MEXICO
Puebla

Volcano Climbing: The goals of a 14-day trip are the ascents of Citlaltepec, Popocatepetl and Ixtaccihuatl, some of the highest peaks in North America. No prior climbing experience is required and anyone in reasonably good shape should find the climbs satisfying, challenging and successful. Mexico City is the starting point for the expedition, with transportation provided straight into the backcountry. Instruction on the use of crampons, ropes and ice axes takes place during acclimatization to the altitude. The first summit attempted is Ixtaccihuatl, followed by the neighbor-

ing crest of Popocatepetl. While much of the time is spent in the mountains, there are many opportunities to spend time in the surrounding pastures and meadows and explore the markets and cantinas in the villages. After a rest in town, the group heads for Orizaba, a small village near the base of Citlaltepec, also known as the Pico de Orizaba. The top of the volcano affords one of the most spectacular views in Mexico. **Cost:** $585 from Mexico City includes equipment, meals, transportation. **When:** December, January. **Contact:** Hondo Rast and Co., P.O. Box 231, Hamilton, MT 59840, USA; phone (406)363-3440. *(M)*

Mountain Ascents: Eight-day trips are available for beginning and intermediate climbers who wish to climb 3 Mexican peaks—Orizaba, Ixtaccihuatl and Popocatepetl. The program includes technical instruction in snow and ice climbing. The peaks are ascended by moderate routes, with most encampments in huts. Before each climb participants stay in towns at 7,000 and 8,000 feet for acclimatization where they may visit the ruins of Aztec, Olmec and Toltec civilizations. For advanced climbers, more demanding routes are available on Orizaba and Ixtaccihuatl after conditioning sessions

The seracs of a complex icefall offer difficult route-finding problems on the Coleman Icefall of Mt. Baker in Washington. (Mt. Baker Guide Service)

on Popocatepetl. Each climbing group has 6 to 10 members and 2 instructors. **Cost:** $240 includes transportation within Mexico, accommodations, food, equipment, instructor-guides. **When:** November to March. **Contact:** Mt. Baker Guide Service, 1212 24th St., Bellingham, WA 98225, USA; phone (206)671-1505. *(M)*

Two Peaks: A group of up to 15 climbers assembles in Mexico City to make summit assaults on 2 peaks: Popocatepetl and Pico de Orizaba. Popocatepetl, at 17,887 feet, is the second highest mountain in Mexico and is located only a day's drive from Mexico City. Following the ascent the party returns to Mexico City to regroup for the Pico de Orizaba climb. At 18,800 feet the peak is the third highest in the western hemisphere and the climbing is more challenging than on Popocatepetl. Costs for all transportation within Mexico and food and lodging in Mexico City are pooled; climbers are responsible for

their own meals while on the climbs. **Cost:** On request. **When:** Winter. **Contact:** Rainier Mountaineering, 201 St. Helens, Tacoma, WA 98402, USA; phone (206)627-6242, summer 569-2227.

Aztec Ascent: Trip members are required to be in top physical condition for an 11-day climb up the still-active volcano Popocatepetl in central Mexico. An exploration of the Aztec pyramids, museums and markets in Mexico City helps acclimatize the group for the ascent. Time is spent at a base lodge which affords further time for acclimatization and the opportunity to learn basic mountaineering and glacier technique. Participants climb over lava beds to Popocatepetl's snow clad summit, then approach a second peak, Orizaba, by jeep. Several traditional Indian villages are seen along the route. Although inactive, Orizaba is somewhat higher than Popocatepetl. **Cost:** $575 from Mexico City. **When:** November. **Contact:** Wind Over Mountain, Box

1380, Telluride, CO 81435, USA; phone (303)728-3651.

MIDDLE EAST
Israel
Sinai Climbers Camp: Rock climbers are offered year-round challenges on steep granite mountains in the southern Sinai. Trips begin with a flight or an overland ride by jeep to Santa Katarina in the high desert. From a base camp that provides meals and a range of accommodations, guides transport climbers past water-filled gorges to climbing sites. The mountains provide the special features associated with granite climbing: long crack and chimney systems, delicate face and corner climbing and classic overhangs. Typical routes offer medium to difficult climbs of 660 to 1,300 feet, and walls of 2,000 feet can be found. The camp staff arranges camel rentals and the services of Bedouin guides as needed, maintains contacts with military authorities and coordinates rescue operations when necessary. Guides are familiar with the geology, archaeology and culture of the Sinai Peninsula. **Cost:** $60 to $100 for transportation from Tel-Aviv or Elat to Santa Katarina; $10 to $15 a day for room and board; $4 a day for excursions by foot and camel to climbing areas. **When:** Year-round. **Contact:** Haron-Sinai Tours Division, c/o Neot Hakikar, 28 King David St., Jerusalem, Israel; phone (02) 221624.   *(M)*

SOUTH AMERICA
Bolivia
Climbers' Camp: Experienced

mountaineers are given the opportunity to share costs and planning on a climbing trip to the Cordillera Real. The 25-day expedition assembles in La Paz for planning and acclimatization, and after 3 days the group departs for a quick, fairly easy climb of Nevado Chacaltaya at 17,350 feet. The following day, after a drive to Zongo Pass, participants set up a base camp at 17,000 feet and climb to a high camp for an assault on the summit of Huayna Potosi at 19,924 feet. This is followed by a drive to Zorata and a hike into the Illampu Range base camp. From this point trip members may climb Illampu itself, either by the usual glacier route or by new routes on rock and ice. Also accessible are a number of virgin peaks ranging in height from 8,000 to 10,000 feet. Except at high bivouacs, all food is prepared by a team of cooks. **Cost:** $860 includes transportation from La Paz, most food, porters, cooks, accommodations in La Paz, some equipment. **When:** May. **Contact:** Andean Outfitters, P.O. Box 4547, Aspen, CO 81611, USA; phone (303)925-3371.   *(M)*

Peru
Cordillera Blanca Expeditions: Par-

ticipants travel through the Cordillera Blanca on 2 trips lasting 10 days each. Members of 1 expedition meet at Huaraz and begin hiking at Cachipampa, following a trail that leads up the Quebrada Santa Cruz. After crossing Union Pass into the forests of Huaripampa, hikers descend the Quebrada Llanganuco. Along the hike the group passes near 5 mountains all over 19,500 feet high. The second trip follows the same route in reverse, but includes options for climbing Nevado Pisco (18,764 feet) and Parish (17,963 feet). Guided hikes are scheduled for non-climbers while veteran mountaineers with some glacier climbing experience may attempt the higher peaks. **Cost:** $440 for first trip, $690 for second trip includes food, guide, accommodations. **When:** June to August. **Contact:** Andean Outfitters, P.O. Box 4547, Aspen, CO 81611, USA; phone (303)925-3371. *(M)*

Climbing Peruvian Peaks: Lasting from 3 to 4 weeks, a climbing trip begins with a flight from Miami to Lima. From Lima participants travel to Huaraz and are transferred by truck to the trailhead for a 2-day hike with pack animals to the base camp at 13,500 feet. The peaks surrounding Quebrada Honda, from Copapamparaju at 17,250 feet to Palcaraju at 20,704 feet, range in difficulty from high-altitude hikes to moderate or difficult climbs. After climbing a number of mountains in this area, capable high-

A long traverse of snow and rock awaits climbers in Peru's Cordillera Blanca. Andean Outfitters offers two 10-day trips in the region. (Keith Gunnar)

altitude climbers can join the party climbing the 22,205-foot Nevado de Huascaran, up the west side via the Garganta. Or participants may choose to spend their time in the Quebrada Honda camping, hiking and sightseeing, or in and around Huaraz, Machupicchu and other areas of interest. **Cost:** $1,000 includes roundtrip airfare from Miami. **When:** July. **Contact:** Iowa Mountaineers, 30 Prospect Pl., P.O. Box 163, Iowa City, IA 52240, USA; phone (319)337-7163. *(M)*

UNITED STATES

Classic Climbs: Climbers ages 15 to 21 can increase their standard of climbing by two grades or more in the course of a 42-day trip across America. The climbing begins in North Conway, New Hampshire with a review of basic climbing techniques, after which the group moves west to the Black Hills of South Dakota to climb the Needles for a week. Participants learn to lead climbs on the rock spires that made Needles a mecca for climbers. Next the group travels to Grand Teton National Park, where trip members climb the Middle Teton and several routes on Symmetry Spire, as well as attempt ascents of Grand Teton by several routes. The group also learns techniques for climbing on snowfields and glaciers and takes a whitewater trip through the Snake River Canyon. The trip finishes at Eldorado Springs, Colorado where participants climb in Eldorado Canyon. The group consists of 8 participants, preferably with some technical climbing experience, and 4 staff

members. **Cost:** $1,395 from North Conway. **When:** July. **Contact:** North Country Mountaineering, Inc., P.O. Box 951, Hanover, NH 03755, USA; phone (603)643-3299. *(M)*

Climbing Eastern Cliffs: A 31-day trip enables young people ages 14 to 19 to practice rock climbing skills in northeastern mountains as well as engage in backpacking and cycling. Students learn basic rock climbing techniques on the 2,000-foot-high white cliff faces of the Shawangunk Mountains just west of the Hudson River. Participants then travel to the White Mountains of New Hampshire to climb the smooth granite of White Horse Ledge and to backpack part of the Appalachian Trail. Proceeding to Maine, participants again don their mountaineering gear to climb sea cliffs in Acadia National Park, in addition to doing more hiking. A ferry ride across the Bay of Fundy brings participants to Nova Scotia for a bicycle trip along the rugged shorelines, white beaches and mountains. The trip begins and ends in Poughkeepsie. **Cost:** $935 includes transportation, meals. **When:** July. **Contact:** Wilderness Bound, Ltd., RD 1, Box 365, Highland, NY 12528, USA; phone (914)691-2377. *(M)*

Alaska
Mountaineering the Brooks Range: Backpackers undertake a 30-day trip above the Arctic Circle to the massive mountain range that extends across Alaska. Departing from Fairbanks, participants are flown by bush plane over 200 miles into the interior of the Brooks

A student plans his moves while pausing over thin air. A rappel down a rock face is one of the more enjoyable aspects of a rock climb. (Mountain People School)

Range. Climbs are attempted and some glaciers are explored, with special attention given to the interests and abilities of the group. Members of the party are 16 years or older and need not have had past mountaineering experience since instruction is provided in general mountaineering tech-niques. **Cost:** $995 includes transportation from Fairbanks. **When:** July to August. **Contact:** Hondo Rast and Co., P.O. Box 231, Hamilton, MT 59840, USA; phone (406)363-3440. *(M)*

McKinley Ascent: Mt. McKinley is known as Denali, the great one, to natives in the region. The mountains's 20,320-foot summit is the goal for mountaineers on a 20- to 30-day expedition. From Talkeetna, a bush pilot provides transportation to the base camp at 7,300 feet on the southeast fork of the Kahiltna Glacier. En route to the South Peak, 7 camps are established along the West Buttress before the final push to the summit, the highest point in North America. The ascent is led by an experienced professional guide. Anyone considering the climb should have experience in glacier travel. **Cost:** $1,100 from Talkeetna includes transportation, food, group equipment, guide. **When:** May to July. **Contact:** Rainier Mountaineering, Inc., 201 St. Helens, Tacoma, WA 98402, USA; phone (206)627-6242, summer 569-2227.

California

Rock Climbing in the Sierra Nevadas: A 2-day class in rock climbing takes place in Tahoe National Forest, part of the Sierra Nevadas. This is not a beginners' class, but participants need only a little experience to qualify. Instruction is given in the use of chocks, nuts and natural runners that preserve the rock; techniques covered are belaying, rappelling and climbing on vertical and overhanging rock. Emphasis is placed on such nonphysical aspects of climbing as awareness and judgment. Each day's class meets in San Rafael in the morning and returns in late afternoon. **Cost:** $25 includes transportation to and from San Rafael, equipment, instruction. **When:** On request. **Contact:** Mountain People School, 157 Oak Spring Dr., San

Anselmo, CA 94960, USA; phone (415)457-3664.   *(M)*

Avalanche and Mountaineering Medicine Seminar: Two 3-day courses offer a chance to learn about the more hazardous aspects of mountaineering. One course teaches useful information about avalanches—what the signs are, how to avoid slidepaths and what to do in rescuing victims. Snow work is supplemented by films, and the course's 4 instructors cover weather, route-finding, hazard evaluation and rescue. The other course emphasizes knowledge and preparedness essential for handling winter emergencies. It is designed for those with some first aid experience who plan winter camping or

climbing in unsupervised areas. Among the topics discussed are preventive medicine, shock, hypothermia, frostbite, altitude sickness and trauma. A handbook of the weekend's seminar has been prepared for future reference. **Cost:** $125 for each course. **When:** January, February. **Contact:** Royal Gorge Nordic Ski Resort, P.O. Box 178, Soda Springs, CA 95728, USA; phone (916)426-3793.   *(M)*

From Chocks to Nuts: All the basics of rock climbing as well as more advanced techniques are covered in 2- to 5-day courses and a climb in Yosemite Valley. The beginning and intermediate courses explain and demonstrate use of chocks, nuts and runners as well as familiarize students with belay and rappel systems, lead climbing psychology and proper protection. An advanced seminar in Yosemite's Tuolumne Meadows is highlighted by a 2-day ascent of the Royal Arches Route. **Cost:** $30 for beginning and intermediate classes, $65 for Yosemite seminar and climb includes technical equipment. **When:** March to October. **Contact:** Sports & Trails, Inc., 1491 W. Whittier Blvd., La Habra, CA 90631, USA; phone (213)694-2164.

Colorado

Climbing Rocks over Boulder: Sunny weather and climbs that range from very easy to very difficult make the Boulder area an excellent site for a climbing guide service. Participants can choose from the granite of Boulder Canyon, the sandstone of the Flatirons and the variety and challenge of Eldorado Canyon for either half-day or full-day climbs. If climbers do not have a particular route in mind, guides make suggestions depending on how difficult and how long a climb is desired; climbing varies from easy in the sandstone of the Third Flatiron to the 5.9 rating of T-2, which challenges climbers with 9 leads of high-angle face climbing. By arrangement, guide service can be provided in other parts of the world such as the Alps and the Dolomites. **Cost:** $30 to $45 for half-day, $45 to $65 for full-day climb includes all equipment. **When:** Year-round. **Contact:** The Bob Culp Climbing School, 1329 Broadway, Boulder, CO 80302, USA; phone (303)442-8355.

Rock Climbing and Mountaineering Course: Beginning with a 3-day orientation expedition into the mountains to learn navigation, mountain campcraft and emergency medical aid, participants receive intensive instruction in mountaineering and rock climbing for a total of 23 days. The 6-day introduction to rock climbing begins on easy pitch slabs and progresses to multi-pitch climbs on 600-foot rock faces. Fourteen days are then spent in the mountains of Colorado climbing several 14,000-foot peaks. Snow and ice climbing, belaying on snow, glissading, self-arrest and the construction of emergency snow shelters are among the subjects taught. Students have numerous opportunities to make decisions in the planning of mountain expeditions and should be capable of leading technical rock climbs at the end of the course. In addition to overnight bivouacs, each mountaineer makes a 2-day solo climb.

The June course is recommended for those interested in more intensive snow and ice climbing and separate courses are offered for different age groups. Academic credit is available. **Cost:** $575 from Crested Butte includes transportation, meals, guides, instruction, accommodations, equipment. **When:** June to August. **Contact:** Challenge/Discovery, The Wilderness Center, Box 229, Crested Butte, CO 81224, USA; phone (303)349-5432. *(M)*

Guided Climbs in the Rockies: Ascents of varying lengths are made in the alpine tundra, snowfields, and steep-walled cirques of Rocky Mountain National Park. The multi-pitch climbs along Lumpy Ridge, with an elevation ranging from 8,000 to 10,000 feet, serve as a good conditioner for the higher peaks which offer summits as high as 14,000 feet. Participants can arrange trips with guides ranging from easy mountaineering climbs to involved multi-day ascents. **Cost:** $50 to $125 per day, plus $15 for overnights. **When:** Year-round. **Contact:** Fantasy Ridge, P.O. Box 2106, Estes Park, CO 80517, USA; phone (303)586-5391.

Updating Ice Climbing: Instruction in the new techniques and equipment that have changed the nature of ice climbing is offered in 5-day courses in the Colorado Rockies. Individually oriented instruction covers techniques ranging from the basic French technique for low-angle ice climbing to the method of setting up safe hanging belays on vertical ice with no ledges. Each

course ends with a guided ascent of a multi-pitch ice climb. **Cost:** $200 includes room and board, tuition, some equipment. **When:** February, March. **Contact:** International Alpine School, Eldorado Springs, CO 80025, USA; phone (303)494-4904. *(M)*

San Juan Mountaineering School: Teenagers spend 5 or 6 weeks learning mountaineering and river running skills in the San Juan Mountains. Enrolled in separate programs, girls and boys establish base camp at a ranch on the border of the Mt. Wilson Primitive Area from where they take backpacking trips of 3 to 10 days. Base camp provides acres of aspen and spruce, a rope course and high country lakes that are warm enough to

swim in. A combination of backpacking, technical rock climbing instruction, survival training, hikes along the Continental Divide, whitewater river rafting and exploration of desert and Indian country is designed to develop self-confidence and an understanding of nature. Students over the age of 15 who have had previous camping and climbing experience may enroll in a guide school that offers a more sophisticated and technical approach to leadership training. **Cost:** $850 for 5-week boys' program, $950 for 6-week girls' program includes transportation from Telluride, equipment, instruction, meals, accommodations. **When:** June to August. **Contact:** Telluride Mountaineering School, Box 67, Telluride, CO 81435, USA; phone (303)925-3603. *(M)*

Idaho

Rockface Seminars: Participants engage in 1-, 2- and 6-day seminars in the Sawtooth Mountains covering various mountaineering skills. Rock I is a basic course designed for the rank amateur; techniques such as belaying, rope handling and rappelling are discussed and practiced. Rock II is a more advanced course in which skills such as slab, face and crack climbing are explored. Both courses are 1-day ventures. The 2-day projects involve participants in alpine snow and ice climbing; techniques for anchoring, knots, glissading, self-arrest, belaying and rappelling are practiced. The course is designed for mountaineers who wish to augment their skills. Climbers who elect to take the 6-day seminar learn basic skills as well as more advanced techniques including route selection, trip planning, bivouacking and group organization. A summit climb concludes the seminar. **Cost:** $18 for Rock I, $20 for Rock II, $35 for Alpine, $125 for 6-day seminar. **When:** June to August, or by arrangement. **Contact:** Sawtooth Mountaineering, 5200 Fairview Ave., Boise, ID 83704, USA; phone (208)376-3731.

Iowa

Basic Rock Climbing Course: Intensive instruction in the essentials of rock climbing is provided in a 7-day course in Devil's Lake State Park. Skilled mountaineers teach climbers the fundamental principles of the sport: balance climbing, friction, jam and opposition techniques, belays and practice falls, suspension traverse and other skills. Evening lectures are held to discuss such topics as route selection, weather and equipment. No prior experience is necessary, but participants should be in good shape. **Cost:** $100. **When:** May, June. **Contact:** Iowa Mountaineers, 30 Prospect Pl., P.O. Box 163, Iowa City, IA 52240, USA; phone (319)337-7163. *(M)*

New Hampshire

Introduction to Mountaineering: A maximum of 8 participants receive instruction from 4 guides in the basics of technical rock climbing and mountaineering. Designed for beginning to intermediate climbers, the 15-day course aims to build self-confidence by respecting the needs of each student. After meeting in Hanover, the group travels by van to White Horse Ledge to spend 2 days learning friction

Participants learn a number of essential techniques—such as the friction climbing demonstrated here—from North Country Mountaineering. (Webster)

climbing, rope handling, knots, rappelling, belaying, placing of protection, movement in rope teams, emergency descending techniques and route-finding. A week of climbing in the Mt. Washington Valley area includes ascents of the Pinnacle in Huntington Ravine on Mt. Washington, and Sliding Board, Wedge and Standard on White Horse Ledge. Students move on to the Franconia Notch region for a second week of climbs. **Cost:** $550 from Hanover includes guides, instruction, meals, equipment. **When:** August. **Contact:** North Country Mountaineering, Inc., P.O. Box 951, Hanover, NH 03755, USA; phone (603)643-3299.

(M)

Oregon

Northwest Climbing Seminars: Ice climbing, rock climbing, mountain medicine and rescue, and advanced mountaineering are taught in outdoor seminars usually lasting 3 to 5 days. There are 2 ice climbing courses: one teaches basic skills for the novice entering the sport, and the other covers more advanced techniques for climbing extremely steep ice faces and waterfalls, concluding with a north face ascent of Mt. Hood. The rock climbing seminars are likewise divided into a basic course, held on volcanic formations in Smith Rock State Park in central Oregon, and an advanced seminar, held on granite in Leavenworth in central Washington. The mountain medicine and rescue seminar is designed to evaluate and treat the critically injured, control of hemorrhage, splinting, frostbite and cold injury. It ends with a climb of Mt. Hood and a simulated rescue from its slopes. An advanced mountaineering seminar is also planned; held in a moving camp in the Washington Cascades, the course teaches route selection, rope fixing and jumaring techniques, expedition logistics, expedition medicine and equipment planning. At the close of the seminar members ascend a difficult ice route in the Cascades. **Cost:** $200 to $300. **When:** June, July, August.

Contact: Lute Jerstad Adventures, P.O. Box 19527, Portland, OR 97219, USA; phone (503)244-4364.
(M)

Virginia

On the Rocks: Rock climbing instruction for all levels of skill is offered in Great Falls Park near Vienna. A basic rock climbing course provides a half-day of instruction and introduction to climbing equipment in a "hands on" session. The use of hand- and footholds, correct belay technique,

Glancing upward at the slopes of Mt. Adams, a guide prepares to pick a safe route over Rusk Glacier in Washington. (Mt. Adams Wilderness Institute)

moderate rappels and safety are covered. The intermediate and advanced courses are continuations of the basic course, covering more advanced techniques such as jamming and chimney climbing, overhangs and face climbing. Another course presents the concept of aid climbing as a method of handling pitches of extreme free-climbing difficulty. Private instruction allows the student to choose specific areas of interest. Guided trips offer a challenging climbing experience for intermediate and advanced climbers in areas such as Seneca Rocks and the Shawangunks. **Cost:** $20 for each course. **When:** Year-round. **Contact:** Geneva Spur Ltd., 1109 Lakewood Dr., Vienna, VA 22180, USA; phone (703)281-3316. *(M)*

Washington

Climbing Instruction in the Pacific Northwest: A team assault on Mt. Adams, at 12,276 feet the second-highest peak in the Pacific Northwest, is the ultimate test for students of 8- and 12-day mountaineering and wilderness travel programs. Through intensive individualized instruction, students experience actual climbing situations, backpacking and camping in remote alpine wilderness and learning to interpret the mountain environment. Students gradually build a framework of knowledge and experience for the strenuous ascent that culminates the preliminary learning sessions. Weather permitting, the climb to the summit is made by way of Mazama Glacier and a camp at 8,300 feet. A wide variety of alpine meadows, crystal-clear lakes, recent lava flows, cinder cones and icefalls challenge the climbers. Students, who must be at least 18 years old, rappel from wood or metal bollards on the demanding mountain faces. Awesome precipices provide the chance to practice crevasse rescue, rappelling, belaying, and crampon and snow anchor techniques. **Cost:** $350 for 8 days, $450 for 12 days includes food, climbing gear, tents, transportation from Portland. **When:** June to July. **Contact:** Mt. Adams Wilderness Institute, Flying L Ranch, Glenwood, WA 98619, USA; phone (509)364-3511 or 364-3488. *(M)*

Northwest Snow and Ice Climbing: A 6-day program in the Cascade Mountains provides comprehensive instruction in the skills required for difficult alpine ascents. Instruction is broken down into 3 segments, each including an overnight stay on a mountain and an ascent by an alpine route. Meeting at Glacier Ranger Station, mountaineers proceed to Mt. Baker or Mt. Shuksan for instruction. Students learn a hybrid climbing technique that combines aspects of the French and German approaches to snow and ice as well as belaying techniques and the use of specialized equipment. The curriculum includes glissade skiing, use of ice axes, crampon techniques, ice hammers and direct-aid climbing with jumars, ascenders and prussiks. The curriculum can be adapted to meet the needs of both beginning and advanced climbers. **Cost:** $125 to $155 includes instruction, guide service, technical equipment. **When:** May to December. **Contact:** Mt. Baker Guide Service, 1212 24th

St., Bellingham, WA 98225, USA; phone (206)671-1505. *(M)*

Rainier's Summit: A day-long snow climbing school serves as the introduction and prerequisite for an overnight climb of 14,410-foot Mt. Rainier. The snow climbing school, held daily during the climbing season, teaches most of the basic techniques: rope travel, knots, self and team arrest, and cramponing. After completing the course, participants should be eligible to make the summit climb. This is an excellent introductory climb and is held frequently throughout the summer. Some equipment may be rented at the Paradise Guide House, where the climb begins. Transportation is available from Seattle. **Cost:** $25 for snow climbing school, $75 for summit climb, includes instruction, food, group equipment, guide. **When:** May to October. **Contact:** Rainier Mountaineering, 201 St. Helens, Tacoma, WA 98402, USA; phone (206)627-6242, summer 569-2227.

Snow and Ice Climbing: A course combining evening lectures, weekend practice sessions and a summit climb of Mt. Rainier is designed to fit into the schedules of working people. The 3 evening lectures take place on Wednesday nights in Seattle. Topics covered include equipment, snow travel, ice climbing and crevasse rescue. On weekend field trips, participants practice ice ax self-arrest techniques and crevasse rescue. The third field trip is a summit climb of Mt. Rainier combining all the snow and ice climbing skills learned in the course. The course is taught by guides of Rainier Mountaineering, Inc. **Cost:** $125. **When:** April, May. **Contact:** REI Adventure Travel, Inc., 1525 11th Ave., Seattle, WA 98122, USA; phone (206)322-7800. *(M)*

Wyoming
Rock Climbing Instruction: Three-day rock climbing sessions teach climbers of varied skill levels basic climbing techniques and the use and protection of equipment. Grand Teton National Park provides a scenic learning environment for the programs. Basic courses cover fundamentals on moderate-angle rock, use of rope for protection in belaying and anchoring, and rappelling. The intermediate course covers high-angle climbing and more extensive rappelling, and the advanced course is oriented to special techniques for difficult climbs. **Cost:** $20 for basic course, $25 for intermediate, $35 for advanced. **When:** June to September. **Contact:** Exum Mountain Guide Service and School of American Mountaineering, Moose, WY 83012, USA.

Climbing Camps and Classes: A variety of climbing instruction programs is available in the rugged terrain of the Grand Tetons and Wyoming Rockies. Participants in 8-day climber camps stay overnight

Students can become familiar with equipment and learn skills from glissade skiing to direct-aid climbing during a 6-day Mt. Baker Guide Service program in Washington.
(Elizabeth Watson)

Mountaineering can mean hard work and long hours. NOLS offers a comprehensive 32-day course in the Teton and Wind River ranges of Wyoming, geared to the serious climbing student. (National Outdoor Leadership School)

in mountaineering tents and study either basic, intermediate or technical ice climbing or mountain photography. Special camps for fathers and sons, women only or entire families may be arranged. A sequence of day-long classes limited to 4 students covers beginning to advanced mountaineering skills, with an ascent of a 600-foot wall serving as the finale for advanced students. A day-long snow school teaches the navigation of steep snow passes in the mountains. A guide service for expeditions of climbers' own choosing is also available. **Cost:** $365 to $465 for camp, $22 to $40 for classes, $48 to $58 a person for guide service. **When:** Year-round. **Contact:** Jackson Hole Mountain Guides, Teton Village, WY 83025, USA; phone (307)733-4979.

Climbing Instruction: A 32-day course in mountaineering is offered in the Beartooth, Wind River and Grand Teton ranges. Participants 18 years of age and older practice climbing, protection placement, snow travel techniques and peak ascents. The course also develops skills in snow and ice climbing as well as talus climbing and weather conditions. The packs are heavy and the climbs are rigorous so that participants may end up exemplary mountaineers. **Cost:** $815. **When:** June to August. **Contact:** National Outdoor Leadership School, Box AA, Lander, WY 82520, USA; phone (307)332-4381.

Gannett Peak Winter Ascent: Harsh weather conditions make an 11-day climb of Wyoming's highest mountain, 13,804-foot Gannett Peak, an ideal training ground for advanced winter skiing and technical mountaineering. The climb, an expedition training series for Mt. McKinley, is taxing but not technically difficult. Climbers should be in strong physical condition, be intermediate alpine or nordic skiers, and have some experience with climbing, camping and rope handling. **Cost:** $315 includes equipment, most meals, accommodations. **When:** December. **Contact:** Skinner Brothers Mountaineering, Box B, Pinedale, WY 82941, USA; phone (307)367-2270. *(M)*

Wind River Rock Running: Nine students and 3 instructors embark on a 30-day climbing and hiking excursion through the Wind River Range. Starting in the Bridger Wilderness, the group backpacks to Big Sandy Lake, Arrowhead Lake and the Cirque of the Towers, where they learn wilderness travel, map reading, route-finding and weather prediction. Emphasis is placed upon proper rock climbing technique, including rope handling, friction and slab climbing, rappelling and high-angle rock climbing. After resupplying, climbers take the second part of the course in the Glacier Primitive Area of Shoshone National Forest. Students backpack into camp along the glaciers of Sacajawea, Fremont and Gannett peaks, where they receive instruction in snow climbing, glacier travel and rescue procedures. The course ends with an extended climb on one of the major peaks in the area. **Cost:** $1,060 by land from Poughkeepsie, $1,307 by air from New York City. **When:** July. **Contact:** Wilderness Bound, Ltd., RD 1, Box 365, Highland, NY 12528, USA; phone (914)691-2377. *(M)*

Technical Climbing Camp: Seven-day courses in mountain climbing are given in the Beartooth Range, northeast of Yellowstone National Park. Participants begin by familiarizing themselves with equipment, then learn rappelling and belaying techniques, selection of anchors and high-altitude bivouac. In addition to demonstrating the physical aspects of technical climbing, instructors emphasize the importance of a proper mental attitude when climbing in high-altitude environments. An intermediate course introduces navigation and elementary rescue techniques. **Cost:** $325 includes transportation from Billings, food, equipment. **When:** July to September. **Contact:** Yellowstone Wilderness Guides, Box 446, Red Lodge, MT 59068, USA. *(M)*

RESOURCES
Clubs and Associations

Adirondack Mountain Club
RD 1, Ridge Rd.
Glen Falls, NY 12801, USA
Phone (518)793-7737

Alpine Club
74 S. Audley St.
London W1Y 5FF, Great Britain

Alpine Club of Canada
Box 1026
Banff, AB Canada T0L 0C0

Alpine Club of Peru
Las Begonias 630
Lima 27, Peru

American Alpine Club
113 E. 90th St.
New York, NY 10028, USA
Phone (212)722-1628

American Hiking Society
1255 Portland Pl.
Boulder, CO 80303, USA

Appalachian Mountain Club
5 Joy St.
Boston, MA 02105, USA
Phone (617)523-0636

Appalachian Trail Conference
P.O. Box 236
Harpers Ferry, WV 25425, USA
Phone (304)535-6331

Arizona Mountaineering Club
1241 E. Manhattan
Tempe, AZ 85281, USA

Austrian Alpine Club
Wilhelm-Greil Str. 15
Innsbruck, Austria

British Mountaineering Council
Crawford House, Precinct Ctr.
Manchester U., Booth St. E.
Manchester M13 9RZ, Great Britain

Bruce Trail Association
33 Hardale Crescent
Hamilton, ON Canada L8T 1X7

Camping Club of Great Britain
and Ireland
11 Lower Grosvenor Pl.
London SW1, Great Britain

Canadian Hostelling Association
P.O. Box 3010 S.
Halifax, NS Canada P6A SL2

Chicago Mountaineering Club
2901 S. Parkway
Chicago, IL 60016, USA

Colorado Mountain Club
2530 W. Alameda Ave.
Denver, CO 80219, USA
Phone (303)922-8315

Czechoslovak Alpine Club
Na Porici 12
Prague 1, Czechoslovakia

Dartmouth Mountain Club
23 Robinson Hall
Hanover, NH 03755, USA

Desert Trail Association
P.O. Box 589
Burns, OR 97720, USA

Federation Francaise de la Montagne
7 rue la Boetie
Paris 8e, France

Federation of Mountaineering Clubs
7 Sorbonne, Ardilea Estate
Dublin 14, Ireland

German Alpine Association
Praterinsel
Munich 22, Germany

Green Mountain Club
P.O. Box 94
Rutland, VT 05701, USA
Phone (802)223-3463

Hong Kong Mountaineering Association
P.O. Box 20519
Hennessey Rd. Post Office, Hong Kong

International Backpackers Association
P.O. Box 85
Lincoln Center, ME 00458, USA
Phone (207)794-6062

Italian Alpine Club
Via Ugo Foscolo 3
Milan, Italy

Kenya Mountain Club
P.O. Box 45741
Nairobi, Kenya

Mazamas
909 NW 19th
Portland, OR 97209, USA
Phone (503)227-2345

Mountain Bothies Association
3 Greenfoot
Mealsgate, Carlisle CA5 IDF
Great Britain

Mountain Club of East Africa
P.O. Box 66
Moshi, Tanzania

Mountain Rescue Society
P.O. Box 67
Seattle, WA 98111, USA

Mountaineering Council of Scotland
11 Kirklee Quadrant
Glasgow G12 OTS, Great Britain

Mountaineering Club of Alaska
P.O. Box 2037
Anchorage, AK 99501, USA

Mulanje Mountain Club
P.O. Box 240
Blantyre, Malawi

National Trails Council
c/o Open Lands Project
53 W. Jackson Blvd.
Chicago, IL 60604, USA
Phone (312)427-4258

Newcastle Bushwalking Club
c/o Union Bldg.
Newcastle Tech., Maitland Rd.
Tighes Hills, NSW 2297, Australia

New England Range Rider Association
274 Bishops Terrace
Hyannis, MA 02601, USA

New York-New Jersey Trail Conference
15 E. 40th St.
New York, NY 10016, USA
Phone (212)722-1628

North Country Trail Association
P.O. Box 100
Chester, ME 04458, USA

Northwest Mountaineering Club
10922 88th Ave.
Edmonton, AB Canada

Norwegian Alpine Club
c/o Wilhelmsen
Roald Amundsensgt. 5
Oslo, Norway

Pacific Crest Trail Conference
P.O. Box 1907
Santa Ana, CA 92702, USA

Polish Alpine Club
Sienkiewicza 12/439
Warsaw, Poland

Rideau Trail Association
Box 15
Kingston, ON Canada K7L 4V6

Scottish Youth Hostels Association
7 Glebe Crescent
Stiring FK8 2JA, Great Britain

South African Mountain Club
P.O. Box 164
Cape Town, South Africa

South West Way Association
Kynance, 15 Old Newton Rd.
Kinskerswell, Newton Abbot
Devonshire, Great Britain

Spanish Mountaineering Federation
Barquillo 19
Madrid 4, Spain

Swiss Alpine Club
Swiss Center, 1 New Coventry St.
London W1, Great Britain

Tennessee Trails Association
P.O. Box 4913
Chattanooga, TN 37405, USA

Thames Valley Trail Association
403 Lansing Ave.
London, ON Canada N6K 2J2

Union Internationale des
Associations d'Alpinisme
Waaghausgasse 18
Bern, Switzerland

Voyageur Trail Association
Box 66
Sault Ste. Marie, ON Canada B3J 366

Yugoslav Alpine Club
Postni Predal
Ljubljana, Yugoslavia

SKIING

A stillness has settled over the valley. Nothing moves, no sounds are heard, no color is to be seen other than the green of pines beneath the clinging whiteness of the snow. Then a skier poles himself up over the rise at the head of the valley, a bright red knapsack strapped to his back. He breathes the icy air for a moment, then plants his poles, takes a few steps and schusses rapidly down the slope, gaining speed as he goes, cutting parallel tracks in the pristine snow.

Cross-country skiing is one of the fastest-growing adventure travel sports around, and it's no wonder. Developed over the past hundred years in Norway, where skiing is not a sport but daily transportation, it is now available within a couple hours of many cities in the United States. Developed trail systems and even cross-country "lodges" have sprung up in the Cascades, the Rockies, the Alleghenies and elsewhere. Schooling of only a few hours, offered at many places from Vermont to California, is often sufficient to allow you to take off for the far reaches of the forest.

Organized ski touring groups offer a diverse choice of skiing opportunities in some of the most scenic ski terrain in the world. Professional guides and instructors can take you into the beautiful regions of Yellowstone National Park in midwinter, for dreamlike visits to such sites as Upper Geyser Basin. Even more exotic locations are visited by trip operators, such as San Carlos de Bariloche in Argentina, for several weeks of skiing near the Nahuel Huapi National Park; or two weeks in Norway, birthplace of cross-country skiing, where you can ski alongside reindeer herds in Rondane National Park.

But adventure skiing is more than just cross-country; for the downhill fanatic, remote regions can be reached in a new offshoot of ski touring— heli-skiing. Participants are flown by helicopter to fresh, deep powder high in the wilderness, where they can spend the day skiing to their heart's delight until the copter lifts them back to their lodges. And for the truly adventurous, treks into areas such as the Trisul Basin in the Garhwal Himalayas of India offer the unforgettable experience of climbing a peak 22,000 feet high for an exhilarating ski descent of well over a mile back to base camp.

The challenges of the sport are matched only by the exhilarating range of possibilities currently open to the skier. But whether you're taking off on a downhill run at 20,000 feet or just wandering through the trails in a nearby county park, skiing remains first and foremost a pleasure—as fun as a fall in fresh powder. □

Ski touring can be enjoyed after learning only a few basic skills, which is partly why this winter activity is increasing in popularity. (Keith Gunnar)

SKIING

ANTARCTICA

Bottom of the World: Experienced skiers spend 3 to 6 months exploring Antarctica. Participants cross the continent on skis, pulling provision sleds behind them as they travel a total of 500 to 2,000 miles. No supply caches are used, and after the initial flight to Antarctica no airplane contact is maintained. Participants should expect very cold conditions, even though snowfall is minimal. Planning for the journey has taken more than 2 years. **Cost:** On request. **When:** October, 1979. **Contact:** Cooperative Wilderness Adventures, University of Oregon, Outdoor Program, Erb Memorial Union, Rm. 23, Eugene, OR 97403, USA.

ASIA

India

Skiing in Kashmir: Based at Gulmarg, a village on the slopes above the Vale of Kashmir, participants on a 14-day trip encounter a wide range of snow conditions and grades of difficulty as they ski the surrounding area. Hanging glaciers and the peaks of the Pir Panjal Range form a backdrop for skiers at the lower elevations where pine forests and snow-covered meadows are part of the terrain. Instruction in both downhill skiing and cross-country touring is offered, and more adventurous journeys through the sparsely populated region can be arranged for experienced skiers. **Cost:** $1,497 to $1,864 includes roundtrip airfare from Australia or New Zealand, hotel accommodations, most meals. **When:** January. **Contact:** Ausventure, P.O. Box 54, Mosman, N.S.W. 2088, Australia; phone 960-1677. *(M)*

Trisul Basin Ski Expedition: An unusual 36-day expedition in the Garhwal Himalayas combines a mountaineering ascent of Mrigthuni at 22,620 feet or Trisul at 23,360 feet with a 7,000-foot ski run from the summit to base camp. The trip begins with a trek up the Rishi Gorge and over the Dharansi Pass, passing Dunagiri at 23,184 feet, Changabang at 22,520 feet and Bethartoli at 21,000 feet before turning up the Trisul Nala to a base camp at 15,000 feet. About 10 days are spent climbing above base camp for the summit attempt. The ascent, though not technically difficult, requires strong basic mountaineering skills; the descent on skis is challenging and recommended for those with advanced or very strong intermediate skills. **Cost:** $2,495 includes equipment, food, porters, guide. **When:** May. **Contact:** Mountain Travel Inc., 1398 Solano Ave., Albany, CA 94706, USA; phone (415)527-8100. *(M)*

ATLANTIC

Greenland

Ski Touring with Dogsled Escort: A 10-day cross-country skiing trip above the Arctic Circle begins in Holsteinsborg with a 10-mile training tour before setting out across the open country. Averaging about

Cold, clear and windless conditions make for excellent cross-country ski travel. Level terrain is usually welcome, too. (Elizabeth Watson)

20 miles a day, participants ski across plains and frozen lakes, through valleys, and up steep snowbanks in alpine areas. Supplies are carried on dogsleds which accompany the expedition. Skiers, who camp in 4-person tents, should be prepared for temperatures as low as -5°F. The trip ends in Sondre Stromfjord with time set aside for relaxation. Group size is limited to 12 participants, who should bring ski touring equipment and sleeping bags. **Cost:** $627 includes food, transportation from Holsteinsborg, guides, tents. **When:** March, April. **Contact:** Preben Schleimann, Box 9, DK-3911 Holsteinsborg, Greenland.

AUSTRALASIA

New Zealand

Alpine Skiing Adventure: The large glaciers of New Zealand's Central Alps provide the setting for daily skiing trips. Uphill transport is by ski plane. Tasman Glacier, Murchison Glacier and Annette Plateau offer 2,600 to 3,600 feet of vertical skiing. During the descent about 1 hour is needed for carrying equipment and walking out of various stopping points. On other trips mountain huts are used as bases, where a maximum of 8 members with 2 guides insures a high safety margin. Mountaincraft skills are learned en route. Applicants must be strong intermediate soft-snow skiers or better, of above-average fitness, and prepared to climb and ski with packs of up to 30 pounds. Some mountaineering background is desirable. **Cost:** $170 includes food, accommodations, guides for 7 days; $21 to $50 for various day runs. **When:** September to October. **Contact:** Alpine Guides (Mt. Cook) Ltd., Mt. Cook National Park, P.O. Box 20, Mt. Cook, New Zealand; phone 809.

High Mountain Helicopter Skiing: Jet helicopters transport skiers to the high mountains of the Ohau Range bordering Mt. Cook National Park. Guided groups of 6 to 8 ski down slopes of 9,900 vertical feet for a full day. Groups ski different runs according to their ability, though everyone should be intermediate to expert in skill. It is more important to be able to turn with confidence in untracked snow than to manage perfect parallels. Standard downhill skis and boots are used, although shorter ski lengths are recommended. The guide skis with a pack of emergency and survival equipment and briefs the party on mountain safety, helicopter procedure and the use of avalanche transceivers. **Cost:** $60 a day includes helicopter, guides, use of transceivers. **When:** September to October. **Contact:** Alpine Guides (Mt. Cook) Ltd., Mt. Cook National Park, P.O. Box 20, Mt. Cook, New Zealand; phone 809.

CANADA

Alberta

Ski Mountaineering Camps: A variety of week-long ski camps in western Canada is provided for both ski mountaineering and cross-country skiing. These include helicoptering into and skiing out from the Slocan Chief cabin in the Kokanee area, suitable for ski mountaineering or cross-country; a trip into the Coast Range for both types of skiing; helicoptering into and skiing out from Berg Lake chalet near Robson, primarily for downhill touring; skiing to and from the Skoki area, primarily for cross-country; and a New Year's trip into Eremite/Tonquin for both types of skiing. The trips' accommodations vary from prepared meals and beds to shared chores on lower-budget trips. Ski trips to Oregon's Mt. Hood and to Norway are also available, as are expeditionary trips for experienced mountaineering skiers. **Cost:** On request. **When:** December to April. **Contact:** The Alpine Club of Canada, P.O. Box 1026, Banff, AB Canada T0L 0C0; phone (403)762-3664.

Cariboo Helicopter Skiing: Skiing spots in the Cariboo Range are reached by helicopter from the town of Valemount. Participants stay in a hotel there, traveling by 11-passenger helicopter to nearly inaccessible ski slopes high in the Cariboos. The skiing may be on glaciers or open slopes or among trees. A 5-day and a 7-day package are offered, and these may be extended on a daily rate. It is possible to ski as much as 30,000 vertical feet

in a day, but the average is about 13,000. Participants need to be strong advanced skiers, in good shape and able to handle any kind of snow. **Cost:** $575 to $650 for 5 days, $795 to $900 for 7 days, depending on season includes accommodations, food, use of helicopter, guides. **When:** December to April. **Contact:** Canadian Mountain Holidays Ltd., P.O. Box 1660, Banff, AB Canada T0L 0C0; phone (403)762-4531.

Touring in the Canadian Rockies: Cross-country skiers and ski touring enthusiasts have the opportunity to explore the countryside while spending a week at a remote cabin in the Canadian Rockies. Participants gather in Banff, drive to a drop-off point and ski in on the trips, some of which are suited to alpine skiing and some to cross-country. One of several available cabins is used, at either Little Yoho, Assiniboine, the northern Selkirks, Robson, Eremite, Hooker, Mummery or Bow Emerald; the selection is made according to season. A week of cross-country skiing out of Banff/Lake Louise is also offered, as are individual or group private lessons in either type of skiing. Custom guided trips may also be arranged, and equipment rental is available. **Cost:** $230 to $345 for skiing weeks, depending on location, includes food, accommodations, transportation to and from the trailhead, guide; private lessons from $9. **When:** February to April. **Contact:** Canadian Mountain Holidays Ltd., P.O. Box 1660, Banff, AB Canada T0L 0C0; phone (403)762-4531.

Deep Powder Skiing: Skiers who have maneuvered on the steeper slopes at Aspen, St. Moritz, Whistler and places of like terrain may join a week-long helicopter skiing experience in the Cariboo and Monashee mountain ranges. Skiers meet at the town of Blue River, 1,800 feet above sea level, and board a helicopter for one of numerous landing sites located at elevations between 8,000 and 9,000 feet or Mt. Cheadle at 10,500 feet. Divided only by the narrow valley of the Thompson River and the Yellowhead Highway, the 2 ranges are located in a snow belt where reliable powder and packed skiing conditions await participants. Ski runs vary in steepness and length, ranging from a gentle glacier run to a 5,300-foot vertical drop. Runs sometimes begin in deep soft powder and end in an area of trees, making it necessary to cross some creeks to get to the helicopter pickup point. Instruction is available for skiers with little experience in deep powder snow. English, German, French and some Italian are spoken by guides. **Cost:** $1,065 includes a week of helicopter transport, meals, accommodations. **When:** January to April. **Contact:** Cariboo Helicopter Skiing Ltd., Box 1824, Banff, AB Canada T0L 0C0; phone (403)762-4171.

Skiing in the Canadian Rockies: Mt. Assiniboine, the "Matterhorn of Canada," is the setting for a variety of both downhill and cross-country skiing trips. Participants arrive from the Banff area by helicopter. Lodging is provided at an isolated chalet situated in the meadows at 6,800 feet on the shore of Magog Lake. Another trip is provided at the alpine retreat of Skoki located in the Slate Mountains, also part of the Canadian Rockies and opposite Mt. Temple's 4,000-foot north wall. Skiers of all interests and abilities can be accommodated on both ski tours. **Cost:** $375 for 1 week. **When:** Winter months. **Contact:** Royal Gorge Nordic Ski Resort, P.O. Box 178, Soda Springs, CA 95728, USA; phone (916)426-3793.

British Columbia

Cross-Country Skiing at Whistler Mountain: Weekend, midweek or daily instruction programs in cross-country ski touring are available to guests of the Whistler Hostel. Students begin with an introduction to ski equipment, control on skis and snow conditions given near the hostel. Participants may then proceed deeper into the snow-clad valleys and ridges of the mountain terrain; in addition, they may travel to remote, open snow fields by helicopter for a week-long skiing experience through miles of wilderness. **Cost:** $90 to $300 includes instruction, food, accommodations, helicopter transportation. **When:** January to March. **Contact:** Canadian Hostelling Association, Pacific Region, 10-1557 W. Broadway, Vancouver, BC Canada V6J 1W6; phone (604)736-2674.

Advanced Glacier Skiing: A small group skis the high mountain glaciers near Invermere for a week. A hike of approximately 6 miles brings skiers to a base camp where they may enjoy skiing on glaciers with vertical descents of up to 3,500 feet over 4 miles. After the downhill runs, skiers may engage in such activities as climbing practice, hiking, photography or resting and relaxing. All uphill transportation is by foot, so participants should be in good physical condition. Some instruction is necessary for this type of skiing, and skiers are taught skills such as knots, prussiking, self-arrest, crevasse rescue and roped skiing. The trip is open to intermediate or better skiers who have had some camping and hiking experience. **Cost:** $150 a week. **When:** May, June. **Contact:** Northern Lights Alpine Recreation, Box 399, Invermere, BC Canada V0A 1K0; phone (604)342-6042.   *(M)*

Guided Touring in the Rockies: Kootenay National Park, the Purcell Range and other areas of the southern Canadian Rockies are the location of ski touring experiences of 2 to 7 days. Accompanied by a guide and instructor, skiers tour the entire day, eating lunch on the trail and returning for the evening to home-cooked meals at a mountain lodge. Skiing in a small group, participants can receive instruction at any time during the trip, or a whole day may be set aside for instruction. The levels of physical and technical difficulty can be arranged to accommodate all group members, and participants may make use of the guide service as they wish. Skiers travel on unmarked trails that are well known to the guide. Participants can also spend time soaking in the nearby pools of Fairmont and Radium hot springs. **Cost:** $40 a day depending on length of stay includes meals, guide, instruction, lodging. **When:**

On 2- to 7-day trips offered by Northern Lights Alpine Recreation, skiers forge new trails through untouched areas of the southern Canadian Rockies. (Arnor Larson)

Winter. **Contact:** Northern Lights Alpine Recreation, Box 399, Invermere, BC Canada V0A 1K0; phone (604)342-6042. *(M)*

Purcell Range Ski Touring: Forty miles wide and 150 miles long, the Purcell Range is a large tract of wilderness that includes the 325,000-acre Purcell Wilderness Conservancy, St. Mary's Alpine Park and the famous Bugaboos. On skiing trips in the range participants may see moose, elk, mountain goats, caribou, lynx, wolverines and snowshoe hares as well as winter birds. Log cabins heated by wood stoves are provided for overnight stays. From the cabins group members take day tours into nearby alpine basins and valleys where summits of the surrounding peaks attain heights of 8,500 to 10,000 feet. The day trips provide choices ranging from skiing in gentle terrain to deep powder runs on steeper slopes. Daily outings are tailored to individual ability. Options are also available for overnight trips to high mountain huts. **Cost:** $35 a day from Kimberley includes accommodations, food, guides. **When:** December to March. **Contact:** Ptarmigan Tours, 255 Wallinger, Kimberley, BC Canada V1A 1Z2; phone (604)427-3510.

Chilcotin Cross-Country: Log cabins with wood-burning stoves and kerosene lamps provide accommodations for groups of 2 to 6 people during ski trips in and around the Chilcotin Valley. There are several packed and marked trails for novice and intermediate skiers, and miles of virgin snow on the logging roads. The average snow depth is 2 to 3 feet. Guides are available for a variety of trips, and participants are expected to bring all their own equipment. The road into the area is all-weather gravel, covering 60 miles to the ski area from Williams Lake. **Cost:** On request. **When:** Winter months. **Contact:** TH Guest Ranch, Hanceville, BC Canada V0L 1K0; phone (604)394-4263.

Ontario

Algonquin Nordic: Instruction in cross-country skiing is offered on a weekend basis. Starting from the Sheldon Valley Resource Center 70 miles northwest of Toronto, participants travel through the Sheldon Valley and in Dufferin County Forest, receiving instruction from members of the Canadian Association of Nordic Ski Instructors. Subjects covered include lessons in basic skiing, trail skiing and waxing, with films and auxiliary activities such as snowshoeing, nature touring, orienteering and winter hiking for a change of pace. Meals and accommodations are in rural hostels. **Cost:** $75 includes food, accommodations, instruction. **When:** January, February. **Contact:** Algonquin Waterways Wilderness Trips, 271 Danforth Ave., Toronto, ON Canada M4K 1N2; phone (416)469-1727.

EUROPE

Finland

Scandinavian Ski School: Skiers begin a 6-day ski trip with a flight from Helsinki to Kuusamo, where they may take a sauna before spending the night at a hotel. The next day participants continue to Rukatunturi, a winter resort which is part of a 2,000-square-mile wilderness area bordering the Soviet Union. Here instruction in skiing and lectures on ski equipment are given. Downhill skiing, skiing competitions and rides on reindeer sleighs are also available. The trip ends with a return flight to Helsinki. **Cost:** $345 to $378 includes roundtrip airfare from Helsinki, accommodations. **When:** January to April. **Contact:** Globaltravel Ltd., Yrjonkatu 8A, 00120 Helsinki 12, Finland; phone 171 202.

Lapland Ski Trek: Cross-country skiers explore the Saariselka fell area of Finland on an 8-day trip. After the trip from Helsinki to Ivalo, by train and bus or by plane, participants spend 4 days traveling about 12 miles a day, staying overnight in modest huts. Most of the area is treeless and the slopes are generally of moderate difficulty. Participants should be in good physical condition and willing to share the cooking. **Cost:** $450 by air from Helsinki; $362 by bus and train. **When:** February to April. **Contact:** Globaltravel Ltd., Yrjonkatu 8A, 00120 Helsinki 12, Finland; phone 171 202.

France

Cross-Country Skiing in the Alps: For 7 days skiers tour through the French Alps near St. Veran. Participants proceed at their own pace on the many miles of marked trails near the Italian border. On day trips, skiers can travel through the Cottian Alps to mountain villages to visit local residents. Participants stay at a lodge in St. Veran where skiing and snowshoeing instruction is available. **Cost:** $130 includes equipment, accommodations, meals. **When:** December to April. **Contact:** Terres d'Aventure, 5 rue St. Victor, 75005 Paris, France; phone 033-63-51.

Norway

Skiing the Norse Way: Norway provides many schools and touring routes for winter ski enthusiasts. The climate of the country is varied, from the sunny south coast up to the northernmost province beyond the Arctic Circle, with most terrain suitable for day and night skiing. The main concentration of ski centers is in the mountain ranges along the 2 principal railroads between Oslo and Bergen and between Oslo and Trondheim, with many also available in the province of Telemark. Many towns and villages provide floodlighting for evening runs on ski trails. Instruction is available in the art of ski waxing, as well as ski maneuvering and safety procedures. Norwegian ski schools operate at Beitostolen, Geilo, Oslo, Rauland, Rjukan, Tretten, Tyin, Vinstra and Voss. **Cost:** On request. **When:** Winter months. **Contact:** Norwegian and Swedish National Tourist Offices, 75 Rockefeller Plaza, New York, NY 10019, USA; phone (212)582-2802.

Scandinavian Touring Trails: Advanced and beginning skiers can join a 15-day cross-country ski trip to Norway. After a brief stay in Oslo, skiers hop a train to Lillehammer for 5 days of gliding along hundreds of miles of maintained trails. Skiers can remain in the hotel area for low-level ski paths or take a bus to high mountain trails, including the one on Nordseter-Sjusjoen that offers adventurers 12 miles of downhill skiing via a restored medieval farm village. The next 5 days find participants skiing above timberline and staying at an alpine hotel. Returning to Oslo, skiers can explore the city or ski the hundreds of miles of greenbelt surrounding it. At the Holmenkollen Festival, an international event, the group sees the finest nordic skiers compete and all have a chance to enter Holmenkollmarsjen, a family-style cross-country race with a huge smorgasbord lunch at the halfway point. Skiers observe the giant ski jump competition along with 70,000 other spectators before returning to Seattle. **Cost:** $975 from Seattle includes accommodations, guide, most meals, transportation. **When:** February. **Contact:** REI Adventure Travel, Inc., 1525 11th Ave., Seattle, WA 98122, USA; phone (206)322-7800. *(M)*

Nordseter Ski Touring: Two weeks are spent skiing remote areas of Norway in late winter. The first skiing is done in the area of Lillehammer, on the great municipal ski track system and in the nearby mountains of Nordseter. The trip then moves on to Rondane National Park, where skiers travel from hut to hut, trying out new trails and watching for wildlife, including the frequently sighted wild reindeer. **Cost:** $1,150 includes food, transportation within Norway, accommodations. **When:** March. **Contact:** Royal Gorge Nordic Ski Resort, P.O. Box 178, Soda Springs, CA 95728, USA; phone (916)426-3793. *(M)*

Skiers may make relaxed tours across open country or attempt difficult high alpine traverses in Switzerland. Alpine Sportschule Gotthard offers a 7-day touring course on the lower slopes of the Alps. (Swiss Nat'l. Tourist Office)

Viking Ski Trips: Both the experienced skier and the novice take part in a 2-week trip in Norway. Two members of a Norwegian hiking club guide a small group of skiers on daily excursions and overnight tours. Skiers can learn Norwegian touring techniques from the guides as well. Club huts or lodges provide base camp for the touring party in at least 3 areas—Finse, Hardangervidda on the Oslo-Bergen railroad, Gjendesheim in the Jotunheimen mountains and Rondvassbu in the rolling Rondane National Park. The trip is led by a guide from the United States and leader approval is required for participation. **Cost:** On request. **When:** March. **Contact:** Sierra Club Outing Dept., 530 Bush St., San Francisco, CA 94108, USA; phone (415)981-8634.

Switzerland

Ski Touring from Galenstock: Participants take a 7-day course in European ski touring. From the foot of the Galenstock, groups climb a peak in the Furka area, just east of the famous Jungfrau range.

After a day of instruction and practice, groups return to their hut, where slide shows and lectures are used to teach snowcraft, avalanche safety, navigation, weather and first aid. Three levels of touring are available: easy touring, including visits to Winerhorn, Kleines Buelenhorn, Kleines Furkahorn, Tiefenstock and Stotzigen Firsten; intermediate touring, with a more intensive treatment of the above; and high-alpine tours, which include further instruction in glacier knowledge, crevasse rescue, rope work and uses of crampons and ax. **Cost:** $352. **When:** January to April. **Contact:** Alpine Sportschule Gotthard, 6490 Andermatt, Switzerland; phone (044) 6 77 33.

PACIFIC

Hawaii

Schussing and Sailing in the Pacific: More than 13,000 feet above the surf, participants ski for 2 days on the slopes of Mauna Kea, the tallest island mountain in the world, as part of an 8-day trip in Hawaii. Skiing from the top of a Hawaiian volcano, participants can expect runs of one-half to one mile with vertical drops of 500 to 1,000 feet. Skiers are in blue skies above the clouds 80 percent of the time but storms may blow up suddenly, dropping temperatures from 50° to 15°F. Jeeps return participants to the summit after runs and also take them back to cabins at the 6,700-foot level for the night. The sailing portion of the trip begins at Kaanapali beach on Maui. Adventurers sail 16-foot Hobi Cats and can receive instruction if desired. Car rental is included, so participants may want to see more of Maui by taking trips to Haleakala volcano, the lush Hana coast, Seven Sacred Pools, the Iao Needle or the old whaling town of Lahaina. The group sails on larger boats to the neighboring islands of Lanai and Molokai. **Cost:** $489 includes transportation from Seattle, guide, accommodations, meals. **When:** February. **Contact:** REI Adventure Travel, Inc., 1525 11th Ave., Seattle, WA 98122, USA; phone (206)322-7800. *(M)*

SOUTH AMERICA

Argentina

Andean Ski Touring: A 3-week trip to the eastern slope of the Argentine Andes provides an opportunity for ski touring during the middle of the northern hemisphere summer. Group members fly from California to San Carlos de Bariloche, a small city about 500 miles south of Santiago, Chile. Skiing can be done either on the new municipal track system or in the surrounding Nahuel Huapi National Park, about

the size of Yellowstone. The trip is suitable for all levels of cross-country skiers. **Cost:** $1,775 includes transportation from Los Angeles or New York, food, accommodations, guide. **When:** July. **Contact:** Royal Gorge Nordic Ski Resort, P.O. Box 178, Soda Springs, CA 95728, USA; phone (916)426-3793. *(M)*

Chile

Summer Skiing: Located at an altitude of 10,000 feet, Portillo offers a variety of natural ski slopes. A 2-week program begins in Santiago, followed by a week of skiing in Portillo and finally 6 days in Lima. In the mountains it snows considerably between June and September, and in September and October the fields are covered with powder and hard snow. A hard base of 18 feet and 2 to 4 inches of powder cap await skiers. **Cost:** On request. **When:** June to October. **Contact:** Traveling Taj, Inc., 420 Lexington Ave., Suite 2609, New York, NY 10017, USA; phone (212)687-3717.

UNITED STATES

Alaska

Arctic Skiing: Two different ski touring trips out of Bettles are offered in Alaska's remote Brooks Range, one in the Gates of the Arctic area and the other in the Arrigetch Peaks. The first begins with a flight to a base camp on the North Fork of the Koyukuk River, making day trips to Gates of the Arctic and Mt. Doonerak. After a few days skiers travel up Ernie Creek, accompanied by dogsleds, to the Arctic Divide. Time is al-

After easing over a rise, a lone skier starts the downhill run; ski touring can offer solitary moments away from crowded slopes. (Keith Gunnar)

lowed for frequent side trips, explorations and summit ascents if desired. Finally, after reaching Ernie Pass, skiers follow the Anaktuvuk River back to Anaktuvuk Pass, returning to Bettles by air. Participants in the Arrigetch trip are flown to a base camp site near Arrigetch Valley and from that base make exploration trips with day packs. The area is rich with remnants of glacier activity. Return to Bettles is by air. **Cost:** $400 for Gates of the Arctic trip; $450 for Arrigetch trip includes transportation to and from Bettles,

food, equipment, guide. **When:** March, April. **Contact:** Sourdough Outfitters, Bettles, AK 99726, USA; phone (907)692-5252.   *(M)*

Touring the Nizina Valley: A ski touring trip through the Nizina River Valley is assisted by a dog team which hauls the equipment. The 10-day trip covers about 40 miles, a pace which allows time for in-depth exploration of the countryside. Emphasis is placed on observation and interpretation of trail signs, plant identification, watching for wildlife, studying geological formations and awareness of human impact on the area. Bands of sheep and goats are commonly seen on the lower south slopes, and a careful stalk often yields good photos. The party, which is limited to 5 participants and 2 guides, flies into and out of the area from either Glenallen or Anchorage. **Cost:** $750 includes food, sled service, group equipment, guide. **When:** March. **Contact:** Wrangell Mt. St. Elias Outfitters, Dan Creek, Via Glenallen, AK 99588, USA. *(M)*

Arizona

Grand Skiing: A 15-day cross-country ski journey into the Grand Canyon region departs from Silverton, Colorado. Following 3 days of instruction and orientation, participants ski up Bear Creek to learn winter camping skills. After returning to Silverton, the main part of the journey begins: a trip along the Grand Canyon's north rim for 7 days. The terrain is flat and easy, and affords spectacular views of the canyon in winter. The trip is suitable for all levels of skill and experience. **Cost:** $350 includes food, transportation from Silverton, instruction, guide. **When:** December. **Contact:** San Juan Alpine Tours, Box 457, Silverton, CO 81433, USA.

California

Touring Tahoe: Three ski touring centers in the north Lake Tahoe area offer an interconnecting network of groomed trails and other services for the cross-country skier. The centers are located at Squaw Valley, close to the Pacific Crest Trail; over Lake Tahoe near Burton Creek; and at Alpine Meadows, near Ward Valley. Each offers instruction, equipment rental, guided trips, lodging and food, and each has particular facilities and services. Finnish saunas are featured at Squaw Valley, for example, or multi-lingual instruction is available at Alpine Meadows. The centers also operate several remote, wood-heated mountain huts which can be reached by skis on 2-day trips. Finally, for those interested in ski mountaineering, special courses are offered in avalanche safety, mountaineering techniques and related skills. **Cost:** On request. **When:** November to April. **Contact:** Squaw Valley Mountaineering Center, Box 2288, Olympic Valley, CA 95730, USA; phone (916) 583-4316.

Yosemite Ski Touring: The snow meadows of Yosemite provide the setting for a variety of cross-country ski touring and survival programs designed for skiers of beginning to advanced skill. A 1-day introductory class demonstrates equipment, waxing techniques, single and double poling, strides, uphill skiing and simple downhill turns. A more advanced 2-day course instructs students in simple techniques of reading and handling rough terrain, more difficult downhill turns and other aspects of the sport. In addition, a 1-day touring survival course prepares skiers for unexpected catastrophes in the wilderness. During the course participants learn how to make a simple no-tool shelter, how to conserve body heat and energy, how to "stay found," how to successfully orienteer and how to apply first aid methods. School classes and tours depart from Yosemite National Park. **Cost:** $40 to $75 includes food, guide, instruction. **When:** June and by arrangement. **Contact:** Yosemite Mountaineering, Yosemite National Park, CA 95389, USA; phone (209)372-4611, ext. 244.

Colorado

Rocky Mountain Ski Touring Classes: Cross-country skiing classes in the Rockies cover beginning techniques to advanced skills such as stem christie, stem turn, parallel turn, telemark turn and powder skiing. A guide service is available for overnight ski tours and moonlight skiing. **Cost:** $7 to $10 for 2-hour classes, $10 to $20 for day and overnight tours, $17 an hour for private lessons. **When:** Winter months. **Contact:** Breckenridge Ski Touring School, P.O. Box 1058, Breckenridge, CO 80424, USA; phone (303)453-2368.

Winter Skills in the Rockies: Cross-country skiing and winter survival are taught in the Elk Mountains during 2- and 5-day trips. On the 5-day trip, courses begin at Crested Butte with instruction in the basic techniques of skiing, progressing to the more advanced downhill telemark turns in knee-deep powder. During the tour into the mountains and valleys, short field sessions are conducted on avalanche precautions and prediction, snow shelters and basic navigation. The first 2 days are based in Crested Butte with day-long treks into the mountains, and the remaining 3 days are spent on an extended ski tour into the higher Elk Mountains north of Crested Butte. The 2-day weekend trips are planned for skiers with limited time. **Cost:** $100 for 2 days, $200 for 5 days. **When:** December to March. **Contact:** Challenge/Discovery, Box 229, Crested Butte, CO 81224, USA; phone (303)349-5432. *(M)*

Tennessee Pass Winter Survival: Eighty hours of instruction are offered during an 8-day cross-country skiing and winter survival camp on Tennessee Pass northwest of Leadville, Colorado. Taught by 4 experienced instructors, participants learn cold weather survival techniques such as building survival shelters, detecting avalanche slopes and conditions, treating hypothermia and route finding. Clothing, equipment, pacing and rhythmic breathing, and expedition behavior are also discussed. Instruction in cross-country skiing is enhanced by the fine alpine skiing conditions in the heart of the Collegiate Range. Special tents and equipment allow for comfortable living regardless of temperature on the 10,500-foot Tennessee Pass. A certificate of training is issued to each person completing the course. University credit is available. **Cost:** $178. **When:** January. **Contact:** Iowa Mountaineers, 30 Prospect Pl., P.O. Box 163, Iowa City, IA 52240, USA; phone (319)337-7163. *(M)*

Idaho

Sawtooth Ski Huts: Ski tours designed to fill the needs of skiers from beginner to expert are offered in the Sawtooth Mountains. A series of ski huts is located in an isolated wilderness where no motorized vehicles are allowed. The huts are from 5 to 11 miles apart. Planned tours are geared to the abilities of individual skiers and to the time they wish to spend at each hut. The terrain is varied to provide each skier with the type of touring he or she likes best, from flat meadows to 1,500-foot powder bowls. Each hut is warm and roomy, offering comfortable bunks and wood stoves. **Cost:** On request. **When:** Winter. **Contact:** Leonard Expeditions, P.O. Box 98, Stanley, ID 83278, USA; phone (208)774-3656.

(M)

Idaho by Snow: Winter ski touring and snowshoeing trips of 3 to 5 days begin in Salmon and give campers the opportunity to explore wilderness backcountry while practicing snow skills. The trips are not basically instructional courses; rather, they aim at letting group members experience the diverse terrain and solitude of mountain country in winter. In addition, participants can gain broader expertise in cross-country winter travel methods, menu planning, avalanche danger recognition and fundamental snow camping techniques as they travel through the Idaho wilderness. Skiers should be in good physical condition for any of the trips and must provide proper outfitting. Both tents and snow shelters are used for overnight stops. **Cost:** $180 to $300 includes most camping gear. **When:** February, March. **Contact:** Wilderness River Outfitters and Trail Expeditions, P.O. Box 871, Salmon, ID 83467, USA; phone (208)756-3959.

Mountains are not the only place where ski touring can be enjoyed. An open field in the Swiss cathedral town of Einsiedeln provides young skiers with a taste of cross-country travel. (Swiss Nat'l. Tourist Office)

Maine

Skiing through Forests: Six miles of marked and maintained trails pass through scenic forested land, providing gentle terrain used exclusively for ski travel. Most trails are 2-way, though some require more experience and are one-way only. The trails ascend to approximately 300 feet above the valley. Open spots permit excellent views of the valley, the ski village and the surrounding mountains. The area is located near Andover, and accommodations are available in town, about 20 minutes from the ski site. **Cost:** On request. **When:** Winter months. **Contact:** Akers Ski, Inc., Dept. CT, Andover, ME 04216, USA; phone (207)392-4582.

Minnesota

North Star Ski Trips: Members of the North Star Ski Touring Club may join a wide array of weekend cross-country ski trips originating at various points in Minnesota. The events include clinics and trips to nearby states as well. A racing and touring clinic at the Environmental Learning Center near Isabella includes accommodations at dorms, food and a well-marked trail system. In addition, members may ski around Anderson Lakes and through Tierney's Woods during a day-long ski trip. At Bemidji participants may ski at both Buena Vista and Bemidji state parks. All 50 trips are scheduled for the winter season. North Star Club membership is required. **Cost:** On request. **When:** Winter months. **Contact:** North Star Ski Touring Club, P.O. Box 15144, Commerce Sta., Minneapolis, MN 55415, USA.

Montana

Flint Creek Copter Skiing: Participants spend a day to a week heli-skiing in the Anaconda-Pintlar and Flint Creek mountain range area which receives over 400 inches of snow each winter. From a lodge at an elevation of 7,000 feet on Cable Mountain, skiers are transported by helicopter to deep powder regions where experienced guides take groups across untouched trails and wilderness. Intermediate and advanced skiers with no deep powder experience find the area a perfect place to be introduced to the sport. Lodging is available in either cabins or a hostel. Instruction and equipment rental are also available. **Cost:** $140 a day includes accommodations, meals, transportation. **When:** December to March. **Contact:** High Powder Mountaineering, Southern Cross, Anaconda, MT 59711, USA; phone (406)563-7630.

New Hampshire

Winter Skills for Women: A 10-day course teaches winter camping and ski mountaineering to women 30 and older. The course seeks to provide a sense of personal accomplishment and self-knowledge in addition to introducing participants to survival skills. Skills taught include camping in sub-zero temperatures, snowshoeing, ski mountaineering, fire building, and map and compass navigation. A canoeing course is also scheduled for May. **Cost:** $325 includes equipment, instruction. **When:** February. **Contact:** Dartmouth Outward Bound Center, Box 50, Hanover, NH 03755, USA.

Moose Mountain Cross-Country:
Skiers arrive at a lodge that was
built in the late 1930s when skiing
was in its infancy in the United
States. The lodge is a rustic building high on the western side of
Moose Mountain, built mostly from
logs and stone gathered from the
surrounding forests and fields. The
original tow ropes have disap-
peared, and the lodge now appeals
to those who wish to explore the
mountains and forests on quiet
trails. There are many miles of trails
starting from the lodge, some of
which connect with the Appalachian Trail and Dartmouth Outing
Club trails for extended trips. There
are trails for all levels of ability—
from high ridge trails with views of
the White and Green mountains to
long schusses through open meadows or pine-covered trails following meandering brooks. Skating is
sometimes possible on a beaver
pond near the lodge. Equipment
may be rented. **Cost:** $24 a day
includes accommodations, meals.
When: Winter months. **Contact:**
Moose Mountain Lodge, Etna, NH
03750, USA; phone (603)634-3529.

Winter Wanderings: The rolling
terrain and scattered stands of
hardwood, pine and spruce in rural
New Hampshire reward beginning
skiers and stimulate more advanced enthusiasts with a good
variety of cross-country trails.
Trips, either on skis or snowshoes,
are self-guided and last as long as
participants wish to roam the terrain. Some of the more scenic
routes include Valley Trail and the
Wapack Trail, which runs from Mt.
Watatic to North Pack Monadnock
across an open slope first cleared by
the Civilian Conservation Corps in
1932. The northern exposure and
high elevation in this area produce
a long winter season, with skiing
possible through April. Skiers can
stay overnight or simply stop for
lunch at a warming hut deep in the
woods near the center of the trail
complex. Lessons and rentals are
available. **Cost:** $2 trail use fee, $3
for lessons, $3 for lodging. **When:**
December to April. **Contact:** Windblown, New Ipswitch, NH 03071,
USA; phone (603)878-2869.

New York

Nature Study Ski Tours: While
skiing for 5 days in the northern
Adirondack Mountains, participants gain an increased understanding of the natural world. Led
by 2 guides, participants learn
about the flora and fauna in the
area, the history of the forest, and
the calls of wintering birds, as well
as wilderness skills. Beginning and
experienced skiers find excellent
skiing conditions on miles of
snow-covered paths, old forest
roads, open meadows and thickly
iced lakes. Participants explore the
nearby 18,000-acre St. Regis Canoe
Area, a part of the Adirondack
Forest Preserve. Skiers may silently
come upon many kinds of wildlife
including deer, bobcats, bears,
foxes, coyotes, otters, minks, fisher
and pine martens, beavers, and
many of the 25 to 30 species of birds

*The promise of trackless snow, sunshine and vistas of snowy peaks are some of the reasons
why people take to cross-country skiing in the winter. (Keith Gunnar)*

that winter in the Adirondacks. Fireside evening programs feature distinguished Adirondack writers, photographers, ecologists, conservationists or historians discussing subjects such as geology and conservation. Toward the end of the week there is an optional ski and snowshoe climb of 2,800-foot St. Regis Mountain. Equipment rental and instruction are available. **Cost:** $325 includes roundtrip transportation from Saranac Lake, guides, instruction, equipment use, meals, accommodations. **When:** December to March. **Contact:** Adirondack Ski Tours, Box 934, Saranac Lake, NY 12983, USA; phone (518)891-1080.

Ohio

Park and Lakes Cross-Country: Cross-country beginners or enthusiasts can take lessons and tours at North Chagrin Metro Park and Shaker Lakes in Ohio or travel to New York for a weekend of skiing in Allegheny State Park. Beginners learn to ski in a 1-day lesson in North Chagrin. Following the lesson participants should be comfortable with the diagonal stroke, the standard for cross-country skiing. Skiers who have mastered the basics of cross-country and yearn for more rugged terrain can take the advanced course, in which students learn the telemark, uphill climbing, advanced waxing and skiing through woods. For both courses skiers bring a packed lunch to eat on the trail. Evening cross-country skiing lessons at a beginning level are offered for 3 hours on weekday evenings at Shaker Lakes. Miles of groomed and ungroomed trails await skiers in Allegheny State Park. For one weekend skiers stay at the park in heated cabins with fireplaces and ski independently or take advantage of tours and lessons offered by instructors. All group members take turns cooking and cleaning during the weekend. **Cost:** $9 to $12 includes lesson, skis; $49 for weekend includes skis, cabin, food. **When:** December to February. **Contact:** Wilderness Trails, 728 Prospect Ave., Cleveland, OH 44115, USA; phone (216)696-5222.

Oregon

Summer Racing School: Instruction is offered on Mt. Bachelor near Bend, Oregon in 7-day courses covering junior racing, intercollegiate racing, coaching or learning to ski. In the junior racing course, skiers with minimum strong parallel ability learn either beginning or advanced techniques. Young people ages 9 to 16 are welcome. The intercollegiate program places special emphasis on college coaching and racing concerns. Coaching clinics for aspiring racing instructors involve coaching philosophy, techniques and equipment care, selection and maintenance. The learning-to-ski program provides a week of further instruction for skiers of average ability. Accommodations are at a ski lodge. **Cost:** $360 for racing program, intercollegiate program, coaching clinics; $450 for learn-to-ski program. **When:** May, June. **Contact:** Bob Beattie Summer Ski Camps. P.O. Box 4580, Aspen, CO 81611, USA; phone (303)925-7864.

Ski Lessons for Women: Women can learn to ski via a series of lessons and cross-country trips de-

A fast downhill traverse is one way to experience the powder snow of the Uintas in northern Utah. (Utah Travel Council)

signed for and by women. A 6-lesson package combines classroom instruction in Portland with skiing sessions on Mt. Hood, culminating in a full-day ski tour. Women may bring children over 6 to join them on ski lessons taken either on a daily basis or for a whole weekend. Skiers may also enjoy weekend cross-country trips on Mt. Hood or at Spirit Lake near Mt. St. Helens, and a week-long snow camping trip. **Cost:** $7 a day for adults, $10 a day for women and child for lessons; $35 to $60 for weekend trips includes camping equipment, food, lodging. **When:** January to April. **Contact:** Keep Listening, Box 446, Sandy, OR 97055, USA; phone (503)622-3895.

Winter Touring: Cross-country ski trips of 1 to 4 days travel through the winter landscapes of southern Oregon. The trips take place either in the vicinity of Crater Lake or around Sky Lakes. The trips may be tailored to any level of skier: fast-moving trips that cover a good deal of ground are offered for experienced skiers, and for beginners the trips may include instruction and appropriate pacing. Skiers may either camp out or stay overnight in lodges. **Cost:** $150 for 4-day trip includes equipment, food, transportation, guide. **When:** Winter months. **Contact:** Rogue River Outfitters, 8890 Rogue River Hwy., Grants Pass, OR 97526, USA; phone (503)582-1672. *(M)*

Utah

Winter Skiing Expedition: Guides instruct participants in a variety of wilderness skills on outings of varying lengths through the scenery around the High Uintas Range, the Kaibab Plateau overlooking Grand Canyon, the 10,000-foot Markagunt Plateau at Cedar Breaks and the Aquarius Plateau with vistas across Kaiparowits and into Colorado. Participants ski while sleds pulled by dogs carry equipment. Large white-walled miner's tents warmed by wood-burning stoves are used during the 2-day to 2-week outings. Groups are kept to a maximum of 10 people. **Cost:** On request. **When:** On request. **Contact:** Gypsy Wind Expeditions, 16601 Estralita Dr., Sonora, CA 95370, USA.

Tavaputs Plateau Ski Touring: Gradual sloping landscape provides skiers with an opportunity to explore a wide territory from a base lodge on the crest of the Tavaputs Plateau. The western rim of Desolation Canyon may be skied, where the Green River flows more than 5,000 feet below the trail. Five-day tour experiences cover the wide expanses of scenery available in the area. The plateau itself merges with the Wasatch Mountains in the west, and on the north descends by wooded slopes into the Uinta Valley. Several parks and wild forest areas are located on its summit. On the south it ends in a great escarpment which descends into Castle Valley. The southern escarpment presents a large facade, from 2,000 to 4,000 feet high, cut by canyons and cliffs. Accommodations are available in the lodge or in individual cabins. **Cost:** On request.

Utah's deep snow is renowned among serious skiers. Hondoo Rivers and Trails offers trips of varying lengths throughout the state. (Utah Travel Council)

When: Winter. **Contact:** Hondoo Rivers and Trails, P.O. Box 377, Ferron, UT 84523, USA; phone (801)384-2961. *(M)*

Vermont

Inn to Inn Ski Touring: Accompanied by guides, cross-country skiers cover 35 miles while traveling to 4 country inns in northern Vermont. Skiers meet at Long Run Lodge in Lincoln to begin the journey. Luggage is transported by jitney to the next night's lodging while skiers traverse the spine of the Green Mountains. For the second night ski tourers stay at the classic Chipman House in the mountain valley town of Ripton. From the Middlebury Snow Bowl in Ripton the trail winds around the west face of Worth Mountain until it descends to the Sucker Brook Trail. A long downhill run brings participants to the Blueberry Hill Farm to spend the night. On the next day skiers circle Hogback Mountain, then descend west into rolling terrain and hemlock forests to follow a long gradual downhill to the final evening's stay at Churchill House Inn. The skiers eat country foods from around the world while staying in the farmhouses and inns. Participants should be intermediate or better in touring skills. **Cost:** $192 from Lincoln includes transportation, luggage jitney, meals, accommodations, guide. **When:** Winter months. **Contact:** Blueberry Hill, Goshen, VT 05733, USA; phone (802)247-6735.

New England Ski Touring: Cross-country skiers have access to 22 miles of trails in the Green Mountains while staying at a 19th-century inn. On day trips participants ski by ponds and through meadows on trails marked for the novice, intermediate and expert skier. Winter wildlife is abundant in the area and skiers occasionally see coyotes. Guide services, instruction and rental equipment are available at the inn, which is located along the Vermont Ski Touring Trail. **Cost:** $8 a day includes ski equipment. **When:** January to March. **Contact:** Churchill House Inn, RFD #3, Rt. 73E, Brandon, VT 05733, USA; phone (802)247-3300. *(M)*

New England Winter Sports: A ski touring center in the northeast corner of Vermont provides skiers and non-skiers alike with 850 acres of historic New England farmland for winter sports. About 25 miles of trails are available for ski touring, and other possible activities include sleigh riding, fishing, biking, hiking and horseback riding. Lessons, rentals and a special ski dorm are available, in addition to the main lodge and restaurant; Burke Mountain Alpine Ski Area is only 5 minutes away. **Cost:** $2 adult, $1 child daily for ski tour pass; $25 for season pass. **When:** December to

February. **Contact:** Darion Inn, Box 12A, East Burke, VT 05832, USA; phone (808)626-9332.

Green Mountain Idyll: Both summer and winter recreational activities are available to resort guests in the Vermont mountain country between Mt. Mansfield and the village of Stowe. In winter participants can learn cross-country ski techniques in touring courses or set off on a network of cleared trails through the woods. Downhill skiing is also available at Mt. Mansfield and Spruce Peak. The countryside has a different mood in the summer, and visitors can explore it on foot or horseback, taking advantage of the resort's stable of horses, riding courses and guided trail rides. Five-day packages which combine lodging and either horseback riding or ski touring are also available. **Cost:** $30 to $48 for lodging; $180 to $260 for skiing and riding packages. **When:** Year-round. **Contact:** Edson Hill Manor, Rt. 1, Stowe, VT 05672, USA; phone (802)253-7371.

Ski Tips: Participants learn basic ski techniques in a weekend of skiing. Short trips over flat fields and gentle bumps follow each session of instruction. Small hills and trails provide more advanced terrain as competence increases. Students learn how to fall, slide, step turn and snowplow, as well as how to handle a variety of short tours. A special series of instruction is scheduled for those 50 years of age or older. Accommodations are provided at a farmhouse lodge in Gassetts near Chester. **Cost:** $98 for weekends, $239 for full weeks.

When: January to March. **Contact:** Hike-Skitour Vermont, RFD 1, Chester, VT 05143, USA; phone (802)875-3631 or 875-3613.   *(M)*

Skiing the Green and White Mountains: Depending on the season, a number of activities are offered at the Killington Center including mountain climbing, skiing, camping and tennis. Killington's 4 mountains have 60 trails and 13 lifts. In summer, programs of instruction in camping and climbing include guided trips in the White Mountains of New Hampshire and the Green Mountains of Vermont. Canoeing expeditions are possible, and competition freestyle skiing camps allow basic training or upgrading of skiing skills. **Cost:** $38 to $345 depending on activity, length of stay. **When:** Year-round. **Contact:** Killington Adventure, Killington, VT 05751, USA; phone (802)422-3333.   *(M)*

Cross-Country Skiing in New England: Complete facilities are provided for the cross-country skier on a variety of guided and self-guided trips near a mountain lodge in New England. The trail system spreads across 100 acres around Kent Lake and the surrounding hills, offering a variety of terrain for all levels of ability. Rental or new equipment is available, along with an instruction program that teaches the beginner basic techniques in 1 or 2 days, or helps polish the style of the advanced skier. Fifteen miles of groomed trails and many mapped woodland trails are available, as well as nighttime guided trips. **Cost:** $89 for 5 days includes accommodations, some meals. **When:**

For as little as $28, prospective cross-country skiers can take a 3-lesson package from Mountainholm Touring Center in the Cascade Range. (Carol Baker)

Winter; guided tours by arrangement. **Contact:** Mountain Meadows Ski Touring Center, Killington, VT 05751, USA; phone (802)775-7077.

(M)

Washington

Cascade Racing Camp: A ski racing training camp is held during the summer months at Crystal Mountain in Washington's Cascade Mountains. Located near Mt. Rainier, Crystal Mountain rises 6,830 feet with a slope descent of 2,800 feet. The objective of the camp is to train serious racers of all ages in the basic and refined techniques of ski racing. The participants are chairlifted to Green Valley for 5 hours of training each day of the 5-day training course and are taught dual and giant slalom runs, bump training and dual-start gate training. Some of the training is videotaped for

immediate replay of the individual skier's technique. Camp capacity is limited to 90 per session. **Cost:** $200 for all training and lodging; $110 without lodging. **When:** June. **Contact:** Don Lyon Summer Race Camp, 1802 Harding, Enumclaw, WA 98022, USA; phone (206)633-2312.

Methow Valley Tour: Skiers lodge at a mountain hut, inns and motels on a 5-day cross-country tour through the Methow Valley in the North Cascades. Luggage is carried from inn to inn by car while members ski a high route with a small day pack. On the first day the group skis to a hut overlooking the entire valley; after spending the night there, participants set off downhill into Winthrop, a town with an aura of the Old West. The next 2 days are spent at a lodge where group members can enjoy 30 miles of maintained trails and a hot pool. Skiers traverse the Methow Trail on the final day, winding through forests, meadows and open hillsides on the way back into Twisp, the trip's starting point. **Cost:** $195 includes lodging, meals, guide. **When:** December to April. **Contact:** Liberty Bell Alpine Tours, Mazama, WA 98833, USA; phone (509)996-2250.

Cascade Cross-Country: Cross-country ski touring and lessons are offered in the Cascade Mountains east of Seattle. One package, designed to raise the beginner to an advanced intermediate status, consists of dry-land equipment sessions plus lessons held on 3 consecutive weeks. Prospective par-

Liberty Bell and Sun Mountain Lodge offer trips that allow skiers breathtaking views of the mountains of Washington. (Carol Baker)

ticipants are welcome to try out cross-country skiing on Sundays before committing themselves to lessons. Night skiing by moonlight and special midweek and weekend packages are also available. **Cost:** $28 for 3-lesson package, $10 for Sunday tryouts, $60 for full weekend, $38 for midweek. **When:** December to February. **Contact:** Mountainholm Touring Center, Easton, WA 98925, USA; phone (509)656-2346.

North Cascade Ski Touring: A mountain lodge is the base for a number of ski trails above the Methow Valley area bordering the Okanogan National Forest. Over 30 miles of trails which are specially designed, marked, mapped and maintained are crossed in a combination of walking and sliding on skis using special equipment. This type of skiing gives participants the opportunity to break through snow-locked forests, mountains and lakes to see country seldom visited during the winter months. Short, easy tours are available as well as challenging trips into the backcountry. The lodge is constructed of wood and stone, offering a warm winter atmosphere. Full instruction in cross-country skiing is available. **Cost:** On request. **When:** Winter months. **Contact:** Sun Mountain Lodge, P.O. Box 1000, Winthrop, WA 98862, USA; phone (509)996-2211.

Wisconsin

Skiing on Blackhawk Ridge: On bluffs overlooking the Wisconsin River Valley, skiers may traverse 13 miles of trails on primary paths and 25 miles of interconnecting side trails along the 650-acre Blackhawk Ridge. A 2-mile trail, meandering over the tops of the bluffs, is excellent for beginners while a 3-mile trail, illuminated for night touring, covers a steeper route. A 7½-mile loop crosses even more varied terrain, providing challenges for the experienced skier. On the demanding trails, the difficult areas can be bypassed by beginners. The trails lead through stands of oak, hickory, maple, elm and pine. Snowshoeing is also available. **Cost:** $2 to $3 for trail use. **When:** Winter months. **Contact:** Blackhawk Ridge, P.O. Box 92, Sauk City, WI 53583, USA; phone (608)643-3775.

Indianapolis Ski Weekends: Roundtrip transportation from Indianapolis is provided on 5 weekend cross-country ski trips to Wisconsin and Michigan. The nordic experiences vary in location, degree of difficulty and type of accommodations used. Motel accommodations are provided for skiers on the least physically demanding trips, one through the rolling hills of Michigan's Egypt Valley and the other on the Scuppernong section of the Ice Age Trail in Wisconsin. Participants camp out in Wisconsin's glaciated Kettle Moraine State Forest and in Michigan's 6,000-acre Allegan State Game area. In Nicolet National Forest, participants ski through virgin timber on an expedition covering over 60 miles. Groups are composed of no more than 8 people to maximize individual attention and minimize impact on delicate ecosystems. **Cost:** $59 to $89 includes transportation from Indianapolis, accommodations. **When:** December to March. **Con-**

tact: Eco-Expeditions, 726 E. 65th St., Indianapolis, IN 46220, USA; phone (317)255-3319.

Ski Touring the Green Lake Trails: Marked routes used exclusively for ski touring are categorized for beginners, intermediates and experts. Plenty of level land accentuated by gentle slopes typifies the beginning trails, while intermediate trails offer stands of pine, oak, maple and cherry on terrain with some short advanced slopes. "Expert" trails include parts of other trails plus challenging steep sections along the Green Lake shoreline. The area around the ski center itself is noted for its scenic woods, nature trails, stone fences, old estate farms, tall towers and panoramic views of the lake. **Cost:** $3 includes use of trails, ski lodge, warming shelter, medical insurance. **When:** Winter. **Contact:** Green Lake Chamber of Commerce, Box 78-W, Green Lake, WI 54941, USA; phone (414)294-3231.

Wyoming

Jackson Hole Heli-Skiing: An experienced mountain pilot takes groups of 7 skiers to a variety of isolated runs surrounding the Jackson Hole Valley. Alpine skiers board a helicopter in Teton Village or Jackson for a ride up to peaks in the backcountry of the Wyoming Rockies. Participants ski routes never before taken and have access to more than 500 square miles of terrain in 4 mountain ranges. Extended backcountry ski tours can be arranged. All guides are trained in first aid and avalanche detection. **Cost:** $35 for initial ride, $15 for additional runs. **When:** January to May. **Contact:** High Mountains Helicopter Skiing, Box 2217, Jackson, WY 83001, USA; phone (307)733-3274. **(M)**

Jackson Hole Touring: Skiers are invited to spend a half-day or a full day touring the terrain in and around Grand Teton National Park. Pioneers first used the ski touring method in the area as a way of traveling through the deep snows of Wyoming winters. Today experienced guides take skiers through the wilderness and protected regions of the Grand Tetons. Tours include private, advanced and powder skiing as well as ski mountaineering. Overnight and extended tours for winter camping may be made by arrangement. **Cost:** $13 to $25 includes equipment. **When:** November to March. **Contact:** Rick Horn Wilderness Expeditions, Box 471, Jackson Hole, WY 83001, USA.

Yellowstone Ski Touring: Guides offer a mixture of tours and instruction lasting a week to skiers with the skills of advanced novice or above. The trip from Bozeman, Montana to Yellowstone begins with a bus ride to West Yellowstone. From there participants travel by snow coach to the Old Faithful Snow Lodge. Based at the lodge, skiers take a series of tours into the surrounding area. Upper Geyser Basin, Cascades of the Fire Hole and Fountain Paint Pot are on the itinerary as skiers glide out to see the extensive geothermal activity and abundant wildlife. Sometimes the touring party is accompanied by local elk. Skiers find that Yellowstone in winter provides a sharp contrast to the people-filled national park in the summertime.

Cost: $295 from Bozeman includes transportation, guides, accommodations, meals. **When:** January. **Contact:** Royal Gorge Nordic Ski Resort, P.O. Box 178, Soda Springs, CA 95728, USA; phone (916)426-3793. *(M)*

Touring the Tetons: Ski touring trips of varying lengths begin at Jackson Hole and go either to the Bridger-Teton National Forest or the Gros Ventre Mountain Range. Day-long and 5-day trips are scheduled. The trips are designed for either advanced or relatively inexperienced skiers; a certified guide provides instruction at various ability levels. Beneath 10,000-foot peaks, participants traverse snow-covered forests and ski near rivers covered with ice. Wildlife is frequently seen in the region, including moose, elk, deer and mountain goats. The ski trips are not on a fixed schedule; the outfitter takes any group of 3 or more at their convenience. Other services include climbing instruction and backcountry outfitting during the warmer months. **Cost:** $20 to $185 depending on length of trip includes camping equipment, meals, guide. **When:** December to April. **Contact:** Wilderness Expeditions, Box 1533, Jackson, WY 83001, USA; phone (307)733-3595.

Geyser Touring: Cross-country ski enthusiasts spend from 5 to 7 days touring the countryside and wilderness of Yellowstone National Park. Beginning in West Yellowstone, Montana, participants drive to Old Faithful Geyser, don their skis and tour the local basin area, including Grotto Geyser, Castle Geyser and Old Faithful itself. The next day is spent wandering in the areas of Biscuit Basin, Sapphire Pool, Morning Glory Pool, Hillside Springs, Mystic Falls and the Little Firehole River. The third day opens with a trip to Mallard Lake and continues to favorite animal haunts. The next day skiers head out to Lone Star Geyser Basin and the surrounding area. Participants visit Midway Geyser Basin on the fifth day and for those on the 7-day trip, day 6 provides an extended tour to Madison Plateau, Summit Lake and Hot Springs. The seventh day involves an exploration of the Black Sand Geyser area. **Cost:** $275 for 5 days; $350 for 7 days includes instruction, guides, lunches, lodging, transportation. **When:** December to February. **Contact:** The Wilderness Institute, 333 Fairfax, Denver, CO 80220, USA; phone (303)393-0400. *(M)*

Yellowstone Park Ski Touring: A number of trails are available during the Yellowstone off-season for those wishing to explore the park's terrain. A guest ranch with log cabin facilities is the base from which skiers set out cross-country. The North Fork trail begins at the ranch and follows the north fork of the Gallatin River into the Spanish Peaks Primitive Area. Views on the way in are spectacular, and there are moose, coyotes, pine martens, snowshoe hares and mountain sheep. Another trail, the Upper Geyser Basin, starts at Old Faithful and winds through a geothermal area with close views of elk and bison. It is a 5-mile trip with cut-offs available for those who want a shorter trip. The Lone Star Geyser

Trail also begins at Old Faithful and climbs 500 feet to Lone Star Geyser, which erupts approximately every 3 hours. The trail goes through densely wooded hillsides and is steep in places. The loop is 9 miles and is suitable for intermediate and advanced skiers. **Cost:** $243 to $374 depending on occupancy includes cabin accommodations, meals, transportation to trail heads. **When:** Winter months. **Contact:** Yellow-stone Nordic, Lone Mountain Guest Ranch, Box 145, Big Sky, MT 59716, USA; phone (406)995-4644.

Yellowstone Touring: Skiers are offered twice-daily ski lessons as well as private guide service through the high, flat plateau country of Yellowstone National Park. Because the winter weather blocks off normal traffic, cross-country enthusiasts have the park to them-

Five- or 7-day Wilderness Institute ski tours of Yellowstone's geysers and thermal springs take skiers into a wonderland of snow and billowing steam. (Elizabeth Watson)

selves during the colder months, along with all its wildlife, meadow and forestlands, the geysers and bubbling steam-pools. Complete rental service is available, as are maintenance work, binding work and wax jobs. Lessons last 2 hours, and private guide service is available for the entire day. **Cost:** $5 for instruction, $31 to $52 for private guide. **When:** December to March. **Contact:** Yellowstone Park Co., Yellowstone National Pk., WY 82190, USA; phone (307)344-7311.

RESOURCES

Clubs and Associations

Adirondack Mountain Club
172 Ridge St.
Glenfalls, NY 12801, USA
Phone (518)793-7737

Club Washington
411 N. Washington St., Suite 302
Alexandria, VA 22314, USA
Phone (703)836-2000

Green Mountain Club
Box 94

Rutland, VA 05701, USA
Phone (802)223-3463

Jackson Ski Touring Foundation
Jackson, NH 03846, USA
Phone (603)383-9355

National Hiking and Ski Touring Assn.
P.O. Box 7421
Colorado Springs, CO 80933, USA

Nordic Ski Club of Anchorage
P.O. Box 3301
Anchorage, AK 99501, USA

Northern Pacific Sports and Recreation
P.O. Box 2317
Renton, WA 98055, USA
Phone (206)235-0808

North Star Ski Touring Club
P.O. Box 15144, Commerce Sta.
Minneapolis, MN 55415, USA

Ski Club of Great Britain
118 Eaton Sq.
London SW1W 9AF, Great Britain

Ski Touring Council
West Hill Rd.
Troy, VT 05868, USA
Phone (802)744-2472

United States Ski Touring Association
1726 Champa St., Suite 300
Denver, CO 80202, USA
Phone (303)825-9183

Viking Ski Club
Box 57
Morin Heights, PQ Canada

SNOWSHOEING

When the nomads crossed the Bering Straits landbridge between Asia and Alaska thousands of years ago, they brought with them the materials of their Asian culture: stone-cutting tools, skin shelters, and in all probability, snowshoes. Snowshoes may well be the world's oldest method of winter travel—they were used prehistorically in both Mongolia and North America, and the same basic "bearpaw" design which links the two continents has changed little over the centuries. Firm, pliable branches and tough bark or leather were necessary to make these cumbersome-looking contraptions, but no better design has ever been developed for walking on snow.

The advantages of the snowshoe are as valid now as they were 6,000 years ago. They allow you to walk on snow cover by distributing your weight over a larger surface area than that of a foot alone. Thus, although the snow may be deep and powdery, with snowshoes remote streams become accessible for fishing, quiet lodgepole pine groves for camping and spectacular vistas for sightseeing all winter long.

Some of the most scenic mountain areas in North America are the locations for snowshoe adventure trips during the winter and early spring months. Places like the Kootenays in southeast British Columbia, Lake Timagami in Ontario, the Gunflint Trail in Minnesota and the Green Mountains of Vermont are among the regions where snowshoers can enjoy the quiet solemnity of the wilderness in winter, under the guidance of experienced local outfitters.

An organized winter camping trip can be informative as well as beautiful. Animal track recognition and observation of elk herds and wintering swans highlight a 2-day program on Vancouver Island. Instruction in snow shelter construction is featured at a weekend workshop in New Hampshire. And a 5-day program to view the wildlife and geothermal phenomena in Yellowstone National Park is led by a professional outdoor photographer who helps sharpen your eyes and skills.

Whether you traverse the Jura Mountains in France, take night trips in upstate New York, or even head out on your own from your nearest winter ski lodge, you can thank the Asian nomads for that ancient invention which makes your pleasure possible. □

Skiers and non-skiers alike enjoy one of the world's oldest means of travel to explore snowbound areas like Mt. Rainier. Snowshoers can learn to recognize animal tracks on Vancouver Island, construct snow shelters in New Hampshire and photograph wildlife in Yellowstone. (Carol Baker)

SNOWSHOEING

CANADA

British Columbia

Mountain Touring from a Remote Cabin: For 1 or 2 weeks, the Kootenays in southeastern British Columbia provide participants with snowshoe touring through alpine bowls, wooded trails and meadows leading to secluded mountain lakes. Participants make home base in a small log cabin near the timberline 13 miles from the nearest dwelling. Campers with nordic skis, considerable skiing experience and some mountaineering experience can take the more difficult alpine route to the "Hermitage." Skiers take 3 days to reach the cabin and camp en route, crossing 2 passes and an extensive area of alpine country. Whether taking the high alpine route or the snowshoe route, skiers with the necessary equipment and experience can undertake a series of ascents giving an introduction to ski and winter mountaineering. **Cost:** $140 a week includes guide, lodging, instruction; food, equipment, transportation extra. **When:** December to April. **Contact:** Northern Lights Alpine Recreation, Box 399, Invermere, BC Canada V0A 1K0; phone (604)342-6042. *(M)*

EUROPE

France

Cross-Country in the Juras: A 7-day snowshoeing journey through the Jura mountains traverses forested mountain passes during the winter months. After a rendezvous at the train station near Morez, the group drives to Vathay for an introduction to snowshoeing. The next day brings a warm-up trip of 6 miles into the forests of Furet and another night at Vathay. Distances covered in the following days vary from 5 to 8 miles with overnights in Gralet and Manthiere among other places. At the final destination of Bellegarde, travelers board a train to return home. For those who do not wish to cross the country on snowshoes, a farm in the Queyras serves as a home base for skiing and snowshoeing. With lodging provided dormitory-style, outdoor enthusiasts may receive instruction in both cross-country skiing and snowshoeing. Minimum stay is one week. **Cost:** $170 for 7-day trip, $187 for farm stay includes meals, accommodations, equipment, guides, instruction. **When:** January to March for 7-day trip; December to April for farm stay. **Contact:** Terres d'Aventure, 5, rue St. Victor, 75005 Paris, France; phone 033-63-51.

UNITED STATES

California

Snowshoeing and Winter Survival Class: Two days in the Sierra Nevadas provide an opportunity to learn the basics of winter survival and camping. Leaving by bus from San Rafael early on a Saturday, students cover theoretical and preparatory aspects en route and then snowshoe in to camp. While striking camp, students learn the basics of camping and snow cave construction. On Sunday morning,

Snowshoers traverse alpine slopes in the Kootenays of Canada to reach secluded lakes on a Northern Lights Alpine Recreation trip. (Arnor Larson)

participants take a snowshoe walk, then break camp and head back out. **Cost:** $35 covers transportation, camp equipment, snowshoes, food, guide. **When:** Most winter weekends. **Contact:** Mountain People School, 157 Oak Spring Dr., San Anselmo, CA 94960, USA; phone (415)457-3664. *(M)*

Colorado

Wilderness Snowshoeing: Both novice and experienced snowshoe enthusiasts broaden their knowledge of winter environments and snowshoeing techniques in separate 5-day courses offered near Vail, Colorado. Both courses are based in a cabin on land adjacent to the Holy Cross Wilderness Study Area. In the novice course, stu- dents tour each day through forests of lodgepole pine and return at night to the cabin for meals, discussions and sleep. The advanced course also begins at the cabin, but on the second day the group leaves for an extended tour of the vicinity, camping in tents along the way. The exact itinerary is left open so that travel may be adjusted to the participants' abilities. Additional winter mountain travel courses are scheduled when enough people are interested. **Cost:** $190 a course includes snowshoes and winter camping equipment, meals, instructors, cabin accommodations. **When:** February, April. **Contact:** University of the Wilderness, 29952 Dorothy Rd., Evergreen, CO 80439, USA; phone (303)674-4695. *(M)*

DOGSLEDDING

The only sounds are the hiss of the sled's runners and the excited, eager panting of the huskies. The terrain appears level, but you feel all the bumps beneath your sled over the miles of snow and ice. Balancing and turning by shifting your weight, you have a constant struggle to keep the sled in line behind the dog teams. The harness does not have reins, so the dogs depend on your verbal commands—"Gee!" you shout, and the dogs turn right; "Haw!" and they arc back to the left. Mushing over frozen lakes, through forested portages and across windswept valleys, you pit your stamina and the endurance of the dogs against the unrelenting conditions that have challenged Eskimos for centuries.

Dogsledding may seem like a thing of the past, but it still plays a part in the lifestyle of the Canadian Northwest, Alaska, Greenland and the northern states. Today you can take dogsled trips lasting from an afternoon ride to an 18-day expedition. Helping in all aspects of the sled dog experience, working directly with the musher (or dogsled driver), you can learn to drive the team, break a trail with snowshoes, and even build an igloo and survive in sub-zero temperatures. The romance associated with the days of the Klondike Gold Rush, of the fur traders of the Northwest Territories, of the Eskimo hunters of the Arctic can be relived.

Perhaps nowhere else is dogsledding as exciting as it is in races. Local, national and even international competitions attract scores of participants as well as onlookers. The most famous of these is the annual Iditarod Trail Race, which runs 1,100 miles between Anchorage on the south shore of Alaska to Nome, midway up the state's west coast. You can sign up for a 9-day trip over this same Iditarod Trail or go on other Alaskan expeditions—to explore the region around Mt. McKinley National Park in winter, or cross the Arctic Divide in the Brooks Range during early spring.

Closer to home for many of us, shorter dogsledding trips are available in the Colorado Rockies or in the frozen lakes area of Minnesota near the Canadian border. But for some people, the most exciting location for a dogsled trip would be Greenland. That great expanse of snow and ice over two miles thick plays host to 1-week to 18-day dogsled expeditions leaving from Denmark, Great Britain or New York. You may not come close to duplicating the feat of Naomi Uemura, who recently crossed down the length of the world's largest island after dogsledding to the North Pole, but the few days you spend in the white north with a team of intelligent huskies will be time spent living as part of a legend. □

A dogsledding race recaptures the excitement of the Klondike gold rush. Dogsledding still plays a part in the backcountry of Alaska, Canada and Greenland. (Maine Dept. of Economic Development)

DOGSLEDDING

ATLANTIC

Greenland

Spring Travel in the Arctic: An exploratory overnight camp and some short day trips on frozen fjords introduce participants to the art of dogsledding and arctic living. Based on Greenland's east coast, trip members spend 18 days on 2 to 3 sledding expeditions lasting several days each. Sledders traverse steep-sided fjords and travel through mountainous areas to the settlements of Angmagssalik and Kungmiut. Also included in the itinerary is a boat trip to offshore pack ice to spot polar bears. **Cost:** $3,019 includes roundtrip airfare from London, meals, lodging. **When:** March, April. **Contact:** Explore Beyond Ltd., 1 Ludgate Circus Bldgs., London EC4M 7LQ, Great Britain; phone 01-248-9082 or 01-236-4395; or Adventure Center, 5540 College Ave., Oakland, CA 94618, USA; phone (415)654-1879.

(M)

Northern Lights Expedition: Hardy travelers journey for 18 days along the west coast of Greenland. Starting from New York, participants fly to Denmark, then to the expedition base of Jakobshavn via a helicopter ride from Sondre Stromfjord. After 2 or 3 days at the Hvide Falk Hotel the group sets out by dogsled, traveling north. The itinerary is governed by weather conditions, but one goal of the 18-day trip is the

Dogsledders mush over Greenland's frozen fjords on expeditions lasting from 1 day to several days. (Explore Beyond Ltd.)

A dogsledder in British Columbia commands huskies with calls of "gee" to turn right, "haw" to left and "whoa" to stop. (Keith Gunnar)

Jakobshavn Glacier, an extraordinary ice floe that moves at 3 feet an hour and discharges millions of tons of ice into the sea daily. Participants spend most of their time on the sleds but are expected to help the Eskimo drivers on steep inclines whenever necessary. On day 14 the group returns to Jakobshavn for another couple of nights before retracing its flights back to Sondre Stromfjord, Copenhagen and New York. Participants in good condition should enjoy the challenges and rigorous activities involved in dogsledding wintry terrains. **Cost:** $2,450 plus airfare. **When:** March. **Contact:** Hanns Ebensten Travel Inc., 55 W. 42nd St., New York, NY 10036, USA; phone (212)354-6634.

CANADA

British Columbia

North to Alaska: For 8 days a small group lives and travels like early Alaskan prospectors and trappers. They begin at Whitehorse in the Yukon Territory and drive 110 miles to Lake Atlin where the retired early-day lake steamer *Tarahne* is beached and many vintage buildings are still in use. Participants reach the base camp at Antler Bay by ski plane. The next day participants learn about dogsledding and

familiarize themselves with equipment. After practicing on short runs, the group makes a 15-mile trek to Llewellyn Glacier, part of the 1,500-square-mile Juneau Icefield, where some survival techniques are taught. On returning to Antler Bay individuals unhitch and feed their team before enjoying dinner in the log cabin. Then participants choose their own itinerary before returning to Atlin on an overnight sledding trek which allows everyone to experience the feeling of long-distance travel. On arrival, the Atlin Inn provides travelers with modern conveniences. The trip ends with an exploration of the ghost town of Discovery and a drive back to Whitehorse. **Cost:** $940. **When:** April. **Contact:** Special InteresTours, P.O. Box 37, Medina, WA 98039, USA; phone (206)455-1960. *(M)*

EUROPE

Finland

Reindeer Run-down: Travelers spend 4 days north of the Arctic Circle exploring the Lapp region of Finland by snow-scooter, ski and reindeer sled. The reindeer safari starts in Lulea in northern Sweden, about an hour from Stockholm by

Lapp guides accompany a caravan of reindeer and sleighs on a journey above the Arctic Circle.
(Finland National Tourist Office)

air, and includes activities such as reindeer sledding on frozen lakes, dinner and an overnight stay in a Lapp hut, and a ceremony where group members are presented with reindeer "driver's licenses" by their Lapp hosts. Hotels along the way offer group members a chance to relax with a sauna or swim in a heated pool. **Cost:** On request. **When:** Until the end of April. **Contact:** SAS Ski Desk, 1120 Fourth Ave., Seattle, WA 98101, USA; phone (206)682-5250.

UNITED STATES

Alaska

Arctic Dog Team Trek: The Iditarod Trail stretches over 1,000 miles from Anchorage to Nome, and a 14-day trip spends 9 days on the trail. After one day each in Anchorage and Nome for sightseeing, travelers begin the trip on cross-country skis, snowshoes or foot, accompanied by 2 dog teams which carry the supplies, led by experienced drivers. The route crosses the pack ice of Norton Sound, the taiga and the vast Alaskan tundra, ending about 100 miles away at White Mountain from where participants are flown back to Nome by ski plane. Participants may help with dog mushing and fish for Alaska king crab. Nights are spent in trappers' cabins, tents and igloos built with the help of Eskimo guides. Wildlife likely to be seen includes wolves, reindeer, walruses and seals; temperatures drop as low as -20°F. As this is a rugged trip, participants should be in top shape and familiar with camping in winter conditions. **Cost:** $1,200 includes food, accommodations including hotels in cities, equipment, transportation, guides. **When:** March. **Contact:** Mountain Travel Inc., 1398 Solano Ave., Albany, CA 94706, USA; phone (415)527-8100.

(M)

Dogsledding the Iditarod Trail: Traveling as the Eskimos have for centuries, participants set off from Anchorage on dogsledding treks in the Alaskan wilderness. On trips of varying lengths group members learn from experienced mountaineers the arts of subsistence living and arctic survival. The route along the Iditarod Trail is illuminated by the aurora borealis. Trips are planned with the resources and skills of participants in mind. **Cost:** On request. **When:** January to March. **Contact:** Otis B. Driftwood Adventures Unlimited, 8701 Kathleen, Anchorage, AK 99502, USA.

Arctic Dogsledding: A 10-day dogsledding trip travels near the Arctic Circle in wintertime. Beginning at the village of Anaktuvuk Pass in the Brooks Range, participants travel up the Anaktuvuk River. At its head, the route crosses the Arctic Divide at Ernie Pass and then follows Ernie Creek to its confluence with the North Fork Koyukuk. A base camp is set up from which trips are made into the surrounding area on skis, snowshoes and dogsleds to destinations such as the Gates of the Arctic, Hanging Glacier Mountain and Mt. Doonerak, the highest peak in the central Brooks Range. Wildlife in the area includes caribou, moose, foxes and wolves. Temperatures can get down to -25°F, so participants should be in good physical condition for the trip. There is a maximum of 2 clients for each guide and dog team. Sledders return to Bettles by ski plane. **Cost:** $995 includes roundtrip transportation from Bettles, food, equipment, guide. **When:** March. **Contact:** Sourdough Outfitters, Bettles, AK 99726, USA; phone (907)692-5252. *(M)*

Minnesota

Winter Weekend Trip: A weekend trip in the Nemadji State Forest offers cross-country skiing, dogsledding and winter camping. The 3-day trip explores a wild and isolated section of the state about 150 miles north of the Twin Cities, a region of mixed hardwoods and pines. Many trails and old logging roads provide excellent dogsledding and cross-country skiing. A cabin is used for base camp, and heated arctic trail tents are provided for camping. Winter wildlife is plentiful in this beautiful and undisturbed environment. Members of the group are limited to 10 people, and should have basic cross-country skiing experience. **Cost:** $90. **When:** February. **Contact:** Lynx Track Winter Travel, 5375 Eureka Rd., Excelsior, MN 55331, USA; phone (612)474-5190. *(M)*

RESOURCES
Clubs and Associations

International Sled Dog
Racing Association
Box 144
Ontario, NY 14519, USA

North Star Dog Sled Club
750 Stillwater St.
White Bear Lake, MN 55110, USA

Northern Pacific Sports
and Recreation
P.O. Box 2317
Renton, WA 98055, USA

Scott Polar Research Institute
Cambridge CB2 1ER, Great Britain

TREKKING

Toiling up the steep path high in the Himalayas, you gasp for breath at the 12,000-foot altitude. Every step takes conscious effort, and you marvel at the stamina of the porters, who carry 80 pounds on their backs with a tumpline passing over their foreheads. Just when you begin to doubt yourself, longing for the security of your favorite easy chair, a bend in the trail reveals a vista more incredible than any cinematic Shangri La: Everest, the world's highest peak, looming like a crystalline god over the rugged, convoluted chaos of the Khumbu Icefall. The hardship seems a small price to pay for such a vision.

Few forms of adventure travel offer the physical involvement, close encounters with native populations and wildlife, or scenic wonders that trekking does. Treks differ from backpacking in that porters or animals carry the bulk of your load; consequently, you can travel farther, over longer periods of time, and reach destinations only the hardiest explorers could ever reach otherwise. Some treks last a week; others a month or longer. Whether you cover the 50 miles on Peru's Inca Trail or 200 miles around the Annapurna massif in Nepal, the trek is the most immediate travel experience you can have. Consequently, most trekkers have to be in good physical condition, although people from 7 to 70 have made these trips. Group size also varies, from half a dozen to over 30, depending on the number of people who can safely travel through certain types of terrain.

The two most popular areas for trekking are the Himalayan region of Nepal, with its famous Everest Base Camp route, and the Inca Trail in Peru, which stretches to the ancient capital of Machupicchu. But even though over 5,000 people go trekking in Nepal every year, and at least that many trek to Machupicchu, several other trekking destinations are equally worthwhile. Ladakh, on the Tibetan Plateau in the northeast corner of India, features in its arid heights some of the few remaining Tibetan Buddhist monasteries in the world. Traveling on foot and by camel, trekkers can cross the southern Sahara in Niger. Elsewhere in Africa, Mt. Kilimanjaro can be climbed to its Uhuru Peak, at 19,340 feet the highest point on the continent. And in the Middle East, you can explore the Sinai Peninsula and its desert oases, Bedouin nomads and rocky canyons while your gear is packed along by camel and donkey.

Trekking may not be for everyone, but those who are willing to face the hardship of overland travel by foot, the rigors of weeks of camping, and the rarefied atmosphere of high altitudes will be amply rewarded. With its multiplicity of cultures and beautiful vistas of wilderness, trekking can bring the traveler closer to his or her environment than any other form of travel. ☐

Setting up camp in Peru's high country, trekkers view spectacular alpine scenery. (Keith Gunnar)

TREKKING

AFRICA

Algeria

Sahara Camel Expedition: Contrary to fiction and film the Sahara is not a desolate expanse of sand, and expedition members guided by desert nomads, the Tuaregs, discover the variety of landscapes: rock-ribbed plateaus, sandstone canyons, the volcanic Hoggar Mountains and the golden washes filled with tamarisks, oleanders, thorn trees and date palms. Traveling by camel and on foot, the 2-week trek begins in Tamanrasset, a seldom-traveled area that holds a wealth of possibilities for discovery. The journey circles the central Atakor pillar, a geological remnant from the pre-Cambrian era, where rock carvings, paintings, archaeological remains, unclimbed domes, basalt gorges and volcanic spires are visible. Once on the summit of the Assekrem Plateau, home of the hermitage of Father Charles de Foucald, participants may climb one or more of the famous Hoggar peaks. Hiking is moderate, with an average of 6 to 10 miles traveled a day. **Cost:** $1,550 from Tamanrasset includes guides, accommodations, meals, camel train, transportation. **When:** February. **Contact:** Mountain Travel Inc., 1398 Solano Ave.,

Trekkers cross the desert "moonscape" of the Sahara's Hoggar Mountains on a two-week camel trek offered by Mountain Travel. (Alla Schmitz)

Albany, CA 94706, USA; phone (415)527-8100. *(M)*

Kenya

Up African Mountains: A high-altitude expedition spends 4 days on Mt. Kenya and 5 days on Tanzania's Mt. Kilimanjaro, with an optional extension to view wildlife in national parks. The trip begins with a night in Nairobi and then a drive to Naro Moru River Lodge, a base camp for the climb of Mt. Kenya. After returning from the climb and taking an overnight rest at the lodge, the group flies to Tanzania and the Marangu Hotel where the trek up Mt. Kilimanjaro begins and ends. With porters to carry gear, the 2 climbs provide challenging hikes through moorlands, cedar forests, alpine deserts, glacial tarns and icefields to Point Lenana at 16,355 feet on Mt. Kenya and to Uhuru Peak at 19,340 feet, the highest point in Africa. A variety of environments gives ample opportunity to photograph and observe unusual plants and animals. **Cost:** $1,450 includes meals, transportation, lodging, guides, porters, most equipment. **When:** September. **Contact:** Adventures International, 4421 Albert St., Oakland, CA 94619, USA; phone (415)531-6564. *(M)*

Morocco

Atlas Mountain Trek: Group members hike to over 12,000 feet in the High Atlas Mountains during a trekking expedition of 14 days. After flying from London to Marrakech, participants travel to the Atlas foothills to begin a short warm-up trek to Asni from Imlil. Trekkers then set off into the remote areas of the High Atlas, following gorges or mountain crests on the desert edge of the range. Whenever possible, mules carry the gear, but travelers should be prepared to carry the equipment at times. The group camps out or spends the night in mountain huts or villages. Having experienced some rugged terrain and conditions, trekkers return to Imlil. Base camp is set up at 9,000 feet before the group climbs Toubkal, the highest mountain in Morocco. The itinerary is flexible and the group may climb other mountains if time permits before returning to Marrakech and London. **Cost:** $543 includes transportation from London, food, mules, accommodations, guide. **When:** March to June, August to October. **Contact:** WEXAS International Inc., Suite 354 Graybar Bldg., 420 Lexington Ave., New York, NY 10017, USA. *(M)*

Senegal

Trekking with the Tuaregs: Timbuktu, at the southern edge of the Sahara, is the starting point of many caravans, some of them consisting of several hundred camels bound for the great salt mines of Taoudenni. The central activity during a 15-day journey to Mali involves 6 days of caravanning with Tuareg guides in the southern Sahara region. Travelers depart from New York, fly to Dakar, Bamako, then Timbuktu, an old stronghold and center for Islam that was founded around 1100 A.D. Two days are spent in Timbuktu preparing for the caravan and becoming aquainted with traditions of the area as well as the techniques of travel on camelback; participants learn how to quickly raise a tent made of camel hides, how to arrange a sleeping place, and how to speak a few basic words and phrases in Tamachek, the language of the Tuaregs. On caravan, group members travel northwest to Lake Faguibine, then turn south toward Goundam, passing through country inhabited by jackals, warthogs, gazelles and ostriches. After about 200 miles on camelback, participants leave the caravan and fly from Goundam back to Bamako and Dakar, then depart for New York. **Cost:** $2,950 from New York includes transportation, most meals, accommodations, camping equipment, guides, camels. **When:** Year-round. **Contact:** East African Travel Consultants Inc., 33 Bloor St. E., Suite 206, Toronto, ON Canada M4W 3H1; phone (416)967-0067. *(M)*

ASIA

Bhutan

Darjeeling Sojourn: A 28-day journey combines an 8-day trek in the hills of northeastern India with a visit to Sikkim and an 8-day visit to Bhutan. Tenzing Norgay, the Sherpa who made the first ascent of Mt. Everest with Sir Edmund Hillary, guides the trip. The average altitude of the trek is 8,500 feet, and a leisurely pace is kept while hiking through the forests, rice terraces and winding ravines of alpine vegetation. Mountain vistas en route include Kangchenjunga at 28,208 feet, the third-highest mountain in the world, and Sandakphu at 12,000 feet, the highest point of the trek; Everest, Makalu and Lhotse can also be seen. After a drive into Sikkim, a land known for its sizable glaciers, trekkers spend the night in Gangtok, the capital village. If permits do not come through, the group travels on to the Jaldapara Game Sanctuary of northern Bengal. Once there, participants are transported by elephants to view native animals such as the one-horned rhinoceros. Finally the adventurers drive by Land Rover over a spectacular winding road to mountainous Bhutan, "the Land of Dragons," a country opened to visitors in 1974. Buddhist shrines and small temples dot the hillsides explored throughout the trek. **Cost:** $2,795 includes transportation from India, guides, meals, accommodations. **When:** April, October. **Contact:** Mountain Travel Inc., 1398 Solano Ave., Albany, CA 94706, USA; phone (415)527-8100. *(M)*

India

Kashmir Climbing and Trekking: On a hike through Himalayan valleys, travelers of all levels of experience explore peaks and hidden settlements. Depending on the location, duration and difficulty of the trip, group members may embark on journeys lasting anywhere from 6 to 30 days or more. In the lush, green Kashmir and barren Ladakh regions of India, there are several expeditionary climbs available to peaks reaching 23,000 feet. While departure points and durations vary according to group goals, treks in Kashmir Province include climbs to Kolhoi, Hormuch, Bobang and Parcha Kangri. Many of the routes provide travelers with the opportunity to meet local ani-

A trek in Nepal offers lush meadows and misty valleys like these, as well as the mountain scenery for which the country is famous. (Keith Gunnar)

mal herders or pass near rural villages of the Gujar nomads. Travelers explore and study the Hindu monasteries of Leh, the capital of Ladakh. Climbs are also made to the Kishtwar Himalayas, typified by fluted ice ridges and steep rock faces. A trip to the site of the Hindu sacristy of Nanda Devi at 25,645 feet in the Gharwal Himalayas is also possible. In winter, skiing trips may also be arranged. **Cost:** $135 to $190 a day by arrangement. **When:** By arrangement; climbing from June to September. **Contact:** Adventure Tours, Hotel Shaheen, 4-Gupkar Rd., Srinagar 190001, Kashmir, India; phone 5248.   *(M)*

Trekking to Ladakh: Travelers cross the mountains and valleys of Kashmir on the way to Ladakh. The 22-day trip begins in Delhi and includes sightseeing there and in Srinagar, where participants stay in houseboats on Dal Lake. Departing from Srinagar, the trek passes in succession through maple and wal-

nut, coniferous and stunted birch forests into open alpine meadow. After 3 days the group reaches the source of the River Lider at 11,200 feet. During the next 4 days the expedition hikes to Lake Tarsar and crosses the Yemnher Pass at 13,500 feet on the way down to Kulan. Cars then take the expedition to Sonamarg, where a 5-day jeep trip in Ladakh begins. In Leh, Ladakh's capital city, participants visit Tibetan Buddhist monasteries including Himis Gompa; ibex, goats, deer and yaks may be seen in the surrounding Himalayas. From Leh the expedition drives to Srinagar for a 2-day stopover and flies on to Delhi. Participants should be in good physical shape, as they camp above 7,000 feet for about 2 weeks. **Cost:** $3,104 includes roundtrip airfare from New York, gear, meals, accommodations. **When:** June, September. **Contact:** Hanns Ebensten Travel, Inc., 55 W. 42nd St., New York, NY 10036, USA; phone (212)354-6634.

Into the Indus Valley: A 35-day trip consisting of 3 segments takes participants to explore the Kashmir Valley and Ladakh. Traveling by shikara, a skiff-like boat, or by doonga, a native houseboat, the group traverses the heart of the Kashmir Valley on rivers, lakes and canals. Four days are spent living among the valley people, camping next to ancient villages and lotus-covered lakes. The boats provide a leisurely means of moving among rice farmers, fishermen and artisans. On the Ladakh section, travel is by jeep over the rugged terrain. A 1-week trek takes participants over the crest of the Himalayas through the pass of Zojila. Descending into the Indus Valley, the group visits Lamayuru Gompa. Four mountain treks explore remote and unusual places which require strenuous hiking. Among the areas visited are Sonamarg, the Sarbal Valley northeast of Srinagar, across Nichinai Pass to Kishen Sar Lake. After a hike up to elevations of 15,000 feet, participants return to Srinagar to shop and relax. **Cost:** $1,185 from San Francisco, $936 from New York includes equipment, cooking utensils, meals. **When:** June to September. **Contact:** Himalaya, 3023 Franklin St., San Francisco, CA 94123, USA; phone (415)441-2933. *(M)*

Trans-Himalaya Trek: In the lush Vale of Kashmir, adventurers begin a 30-day journey of strenuous climbing across 3 high mountain passes, the highest being about 17,000 feet, and 3 major mountain chains. Rural Kashmir villages and Gujar nomads are found in the Warwan Valley after a crossing of the Pir Panjal Range. The Bhatkal Pass through the Great Himalayan Range leads into the drier but still fertile Suru Valley, peopled by the Baltis, Muslims of the Shia sect. Nunkun Base Camp is reached and with it views of 23,410-foot Nunkun, highest peak in the Himalayas between Nanda Devi and Nanga Parbat. The first Buddhist gompa is reached in Ladakh, often called "Little Tibet." The final range, Zaskar, is crossed by the 17,000-foot Kanji La Pass. There the trekking ends and participants continue by jeep to Leh, the capital of Ladakh, where many Buddhist gompas are seen. The trip ends with a return to Kashmir by road and a rest of 2 days in houseboats on Dal Lake.

Cost: $1,775 includes accommodations, meals, guides, transportation from Kashmir. **When:** August, September. **Contact:** Mountain Travel Inc., 1398 Solano Ave., Albany, CA 94706, USA; phone (415)527-8100. *(M)*

Trekking in Lahul: Travelers on a 26-day trip climb 4 mountain passes as they circumscribe the region of Lahul, an arid and remote valley near the Tibetan border. Flights leaving from New York take group members to New Delhi, then on to Kulu, a small Hindu village. From Kulu the expedition motors through the Beas River Gorge to Manali and over the 13,500-foot Rohtang Pass on a road that has changed little since the days when it was a major Tibetan trade route. The trek enters Lahul where the landscape becomes more barren as travelers proceed by car to the trailhead near Patseo. Taking to the trail, trekkers quickly approach the highest point along the route, 16,000-foot Baralacha Pass, then descend to the Chandra River and the lake at Chandratal. After hiking through Batal and reaching 14,000-foot Hamta Pass, participants make a short trek back to Manali in the Kulu region, where the trip began. With the actual trek behind them, trip members make side trips to Chandigarh, the Sariska Game Sanctuary south of New Delhi, and the Bharatpur Ghana Bird Sanctuary. The trip ends in New Delhi, where travelers catch a plane back to New York. **Cost:** $2,109 from New York includes airfare, all meals, accommodations, guides. **When:** August. **Contact:** REI Adventure Travel, 1525 11th Ave., Seattle, WA 98122, USA; phone (206)322-7800. *(M)*

Walking in the Himalayas: Hikers walk along good forest paths at altitudes of up to 11,000 feet on treks in the lower ranges of the Himalayas. Walking in easy stages of 7 to 10 miles a day, participants pass through terraced valleys and picturesque villages in the area southeast of Kulu. Nights are spent in simple forest resthouses or in tents. The group determines its own itinerary and the duration of the trek. **Cost:** On request. **When:** April, May, October, November. **Contact:** West Himalayan Holidays, 49 Conduit St., London W1R 9FB, Great Britain; phone 01-439-4448.

From Srinagar to Sonamarg: After flying to Delhi from London, participants meet an English-speaking guide who accompanies them through India and Kashmir for 23 days. The group catches a train for Jaipur and spends a day there visiting markets and Hindu temples. Before returning to Delhi, trip members travel to Agra to visit the Taj Mahal. Another train takes participants to Jammu, from where the group rides on winding roads up Himalayan foothills to houseboat accommodations in Srinagar. For the next 8 days a trek is made from Srinagar to Sonamarg and Kargil, with participants walking over poor trails and camping out or occasionally staying at a bungalow. Trekkers return to the houseboats in Srinagar to spend the next 3 days exploring waterways in shikaras, boats similar to gondolas. Participants travel by bus and train to

Three trekkers take a moment to rest on their walking sticks and enjoy a view of the Himalayas. (Keith Gunnar)

Delhi for 2 more days of exploring before taking the return flight to London. **Cost:** $1,549 to $1,595 from London includes transportation, accommodations, most meals, guide. **When:** April, May, August to October. **Contact:** WEXAS International Inc., Suite 354, Graybar Bldg., 420 Lexington Ave., New York, NY 10027, USA. *(M)*

Nepal

Himalayan Holiday: Adventurous hikers are given the opportunity to spend 8, 28 or 41 days exploring the Solu Khumbu area near Mt. Everest. The 8-day trek begins with a flight from Kathmandu to Lukla, where participants start hiking at an elevation of 9,200 feet. Heading toward Everest, trekkers pass from Lukla to Namche Bazar, a local trading center, then on to Thyangboche monastery and Dingboche which, at an altitude of 14,000 feet, is the highest point in the journey. Participants return to Kathmandu

Sherpanis carry trekkers' supplies through a foggy forest near Arughat, Nepal. (Keith Gunnar)

via Lukla. Those who elect the 28- or 41-day journeys drive from Kathmandu to Lamosangu, where they begin walking over 5 different mountain ranges before reaching the Dudh Kosi River Valley. After passing through Namche Bazar and the Thyangboche monastery, travelers arrive at Lobujya, where the more acclimatized may press on to Everest Base Camp. Hikers then return to Lukla, and those who have signed on for 28 days head back to Kathmandu. The rest of the group continues east through Rai villages and deep jungle before arriving on the flatlands of the Terai. After a stay in Dharan hikers return to Kathmandu by air. The treks are strenuous and hikers must be in good condition. **Cost:** $344 for 8 days, $1,222 for 28 days, $1,703 for 41 days includes transportation from Kathmandu, guides, equipment, food. **When:** Year-round. **Contact:** Adventure Center, 5540 College Ave., Oakland, CA 94618,

USA; phone (415)654-1879. *(M)*

Spring Trek in Langtang/Gatlang: Participants on a 20-day journey traverse Nepalese landscapes in the high region around Langtang, near the Tibetan border. Departures by plane can be made from a number of Australian and New Zealand cities; group members arrive in Kathmandu for a short stay during which they may visit the city's bazaars and temples before beginning the overland trek. Following ancient footpaths, some of which lead toward the greatest concentration of high mountains in the world, trekkers hike through the lower mountainous terrain along routes where no technical climbing is required. Meals are prepared by the local people at tent campsites. Group members have the opportunity to spot a variety of bird species in the valleys and along the hillsides which bloom with rhododendrons. **Cost:** $2,169 to $2,527 from Australia or New Zealand includes roundtrip transportation, hotel accommodations, camping gear, most meals. **When:** March to April. **Contact:** Ausventure, P.O. Box 54, Mosman, N.S.W. 2088, Australia; phone 960-1677. *(M)*

Hiking the Himalayas: Four different treks involving long, strenuous hiking are offered in the Himalayas of Nepal. The first trek of the season is a 24-day hike which circles the Annapurna massif. On another late fall trek beginning in Lamosangu, trekkers wind through terraced hillside fields and cross several intermediate passes before climbing through Namche Bazar, the principal Sherpa village to the famous Thyangboche monastery at 12,700 feet. After acclimatizing, the travelers continue to 18,000-foot Kala Patar near the Everest Base Camp. The shortest trek, lasting 14 days, begins in Kathmandu and treks to Pokhara, where the group returns by jeep. A 25-day hike to Langtang Valley reaches a maximum elevation of 13,000 feet. Trekkers camp near villages and have opportunities for unhurried contact with the Nepalese people. **Cost:** $1,275 to $1,610 depending on the trek includes land transportation, meals, accommodations, guide, camping equipment, sightseeing, entrance fees. **When:** October to February. **Contact:** Himalaya, 3023 Franklin St., San Francisco, CA 94123, USA; phone (415)441-2933. *(M)*

High Mountain Hiking: Treks in the Himalayas take the classic route to the Everest Base Camp in 32 days or venture onto a less traveled path along the Annapurna Range for 35 days. Both routes pass through terraced hillside villages and afford spectacular views of snow-capped peaks. Sherpa porters carry most of the load, prepare camp and do the cooking. Departing from Kathmandu, the Everest trek crosses the Dudh Kosi Valley to Namche Bazar and then the monastery of Thyangboche. Trekkers walk on to the Everest Base Camp and a view there of the Khumbu Icefall. The trek returns by the same trail back to Lukla, from where participants may fly back to Kathmandu to catch a flight home or hike for 13 more days to Dharan. The Annapurna trek begins in the lowland ricegrowing country of the Marsyangdi Valley before climbing through pine and fir forests to the village of Manang, a trading center. Crossing the 17,700-foot pass of Thorong La, the trek continues through cypress forests, another high pass and rhododendron forests abounding with birds. In the final days the group has views from the Annapurnas and Machapuchare to Manaslu and Himalchuli. **Cost:** $1,225 for Everest trek, $1,425 with Dharan extension, $1,325 for Annapurna trek includes accommodations, meals, guides, equipment. **When:** March, April, October, November. **Contact:** REI Adventure Travel, 1525 11th Ave., Seattle, WA 98122, USA; phone (206)322-7800. *(M)*

Trekking around Everest: A variety of treks in the vicinity of Mt. Everest, the world's tallest mountain, is offered out of Kathmandu. Trekkers with only a week may fly to and from Lukla, trekking through the Khumbu district and visiting Sherpa villages and Thyangboche monastery. Those with another week's time can continue on the same route to Everest Base Camp. Treks in the Solu Khumbu region begin with a flight from Kathmandu to Paphlu airfield and after 2 weeks return by air from Lukla. A 25-day version of the same trip begins in Kathmandu and finds trekkers hiking all the way to the Khumbu region and Everest Base Camp, returning by air from either Lukla or Syangboche, located above Namche Bazar at 12,400 feet. Also offered are other treks in all accessible regions of Nepal. **Cost:** On request. **When:** September to June. **Contact:** The Sherpa Cooperative, GPO Box 1338, Kamal Pokhari, Kathmandu, Nepal; phone 13887; or Exodus Expeditions, 167 Earls Court Rd., London SW5 9RF, Great Britain; phone 01-373-7895; or Adventure Center, 5540 College Ave., Oakland, CA 94618, USA; phone (415)654-1879. *(M)*

Tibetan Trek: A 15-day trek to the popular Everest Base Camp visits religious shrines and Sherpas' homes. Flying from Kathmandu to a tiny airstrip at Lukla, participants trek to the Sherpa villages of Solu Khumbu and the Tibetan Buddhist monastery at Thyangboche. The trek passes through summer yak pastures at Pheriche and Lobujya, arriving at the foot of the great Khumbu Icefall, where the base camp is located. Opportunities are provided en route to meet villagers and the lamas of Thyangboche and Pangboche. **Cost:** $1,378 includes roundtrip airfare from London, food, camping equipment, transportation, porters. **When:** October, November, March, April. **Contact:** Sherpa Expeditions, 3 Bedford Rd., Chiswick, London W4, Great Britain; phone 01-994-7668; or Durbar Marg, P.O. Box 1519, Kathmandu, Nepal; phone 12422. *(M)*

Mixed Bag of Treks: A variety of treks in the Himalayas, ranging in length from 8 to 40 days, gives participants the opportunity to explore Nepal. The shortest trek begins with a flight from Kathmandu to Lukla airstrip at 9,200 feet and then travels on foot through temples and villages to Dingboche at 14,000 feet. Visits are made en route to Namche Bazar, Thyangboche monastery at 12,715 feet and Jorsale. Trekkers then return to Kathmandu by air. Other treks visit the Langtang Valley for 12 days and circle 26,545-foot Annapurna peak in 22 days. The longest trek travels to the Everest Base Camp; in covering about 350 miles the route gains over 7,000 feet in elevation, so participants need to be in good physical condition. Trekkers camp out during treks, and accommodations are available in Kathmandu either before or after a trek. **Cost:** From $280 for 8-day trek to $1,300 for 40-day trek includes food, equipment, camping accommodations, guide; additional accommodations from $15 a day. **When:** October to May. **Contact:** Treasure Treks, Ltd., Third Floor, Panton House, 25 Haymarket, London

SW1Y 4EN, Great Britain; phone 01-839-4267; or Adventure Center, 5540 College Ave., Oakland, CA 94618, USA; phone (415)654-1879; or Trek Adventures, 3 E. 54th St., New York, NY 10022, USA; phone (212)751-3250. *(M)*

Hiking to Everest Base Camp: Travelers spend 25 days touring the towns and backcountry of the Nepalese highlands. Starting in New York City, the group flies to Kathmandu for 2 days to view the city and acclimatize to the high altitude. The group then flies to Lukla to begin a 15-day trek to Everest Base Camp and back. From Lukla the group descends to the valley of the Dudh Kosi and after 2 days of easy hiking arrives at Namche Bazar. From there participants proceed to the Thyangboche monastery before hiking on to Pangboche at 13,000 feet and the yak pastures of Pheriche. Another day is spent acclimatizing before the group heads up the Khumbu Glacier to a campsite at Lobujya. During the next 3 days trekkers explore the area around Everest Base Camp, and ascend Kala Patar for a view of the entire area. The group then retraces its steps to Kathmandu and spends 4 days in the Royal Chitawan National Park for an elephant-back tour. On the way home to New York, the group stops in Agra for a visit to the Taj Mahal. **Cost:** $2,107 from New York includes airfare, accommodations, meals, guides, porters. **When:** October to April. **Contact:** WEXAS International Inc., Suite 354, Graybar Bldg., 420 Lexington Ave., New York, NY 10017, USA. *(M)*

Pakistan

Baltoro Glacier Trek: Trekkers hike a fairly arduous route to one of the world's most spectacular mountain amphitheaters on a 39-day trip. Setting out from Skardu with 100 porters, participants trek through Chakpo, Chango and Askole and then into the wilderness. The trek proceeds to Paiyu Camp at the base of Baltoro Glacier and continues into Concordia, the conjunction of the Baltoro and Godwin-Austen glaciers. Here within a 12-mile radius are 6 peaks over 26,000 feet, including K-2 at 28,741 feet. The trek involves rough glacier travel, difficult river crossings and hanging rope bridges. The vagaries of air travel in the mountains may result in delays of up to 2 weeks. **Cost:**

$3,380 from Skardu covers food, camping equipment, cooks, porters, guides, transportation. **When:** June. **Contact:** Mountain Travel Inc., 1398 Solano Ave., Albany, CA 94706, USA; phone (415)527-8100.
(M)

Thailand

Highlands Hike: Nine days of trekking in the tribal highlands along the Burmese border highlight a 22-day trip. Flying from London, participants arrive in Bangkok for 3 days of sightseeing, including visits to its floating market and Buddhist temples. The group then buses through massive teak forests to the northern city of Chiang Mai for more sightseeing. The expedition continues by minibus and boat to the village from where 9 days of walking begins. The trek passes through rain forests and fields of opium poppies, with overnight stays made in resthouses in the villages of several different tribes. After reaching Mai Sai, the country's northernmost town, trekkers bus to Chiang Saen, capital of the ancient Lanna Thai kingdom and situated on the Mekong River at the Laotian border. Return is made by plane to Bangkok from Chiang Mai before participants spend 2 days at the beach resort of Pattaya. Group members then return to Bangkok to catch a flight back to London. **Cost:** $600 from Bangkok includes transportation, hotel and camping accommodations, food. **When:** November to April. **Contact:** Exodus Expeditions, 167 Earls Court Rd., London SW5, Great Britain; phone 01-373-7895; or Adventure Center, 5540 College Ave., Oakland, CA

94618, USA; phone (415)654-1879
(M)

AUSTRALASIA

Australia

Through the Outback on Camelback: Participants travel by camel on a 10-day journey from Mt. Serle to Lake Eyre. Group members are driven from Adelaide to Mt. Serle Station, once a government camel-breeding station, to begin the camel safari. The route follows the bed of Frome Creek through the Northern Flinders Range and semi-desert country to Muloorina Station, where the normally dry creek bed is filled with water; bird life here is varied and dingoes may be seen. The expedition continues to Lake Clayton and along the coastline to reach Lake Eyre. A truck meets the party here and takes participants back to Mt. Serle. The trip ends in Adelaide. During the journey the group camps out in the open in "swags" rather than tents. **Cost:** $500 includes meals, camel, guide. **When:** April to October. **Contact:** Transcontinental Safaris, Douglas Scrub, McLaren Flat, South Australia; phone Adelaide 3830230.*(M)*

MIDDLE EAST

Israel

Sinai Peninsula Exploration: A 10-day hiking and climbing trip with a diving finale is offered in the Sinai to rugged explorers. Departing from Elat, the group flies to St. Katherine Monastery and begins 7 days of trekking by climbing Mt. Sinai. From there, the group hikes to desert oases, Bedouin settlements, narrow canyons and rock climbing sites. Gear is packed in by donkey and camel. The group is kept to a maximum of 20 people, and the guides offer helpful insights into the Sinai's geomorphology, archaeology and wildlife. At the end of the trip, 1 day is spent diving the coral reef in the Gulf of Elat. **Cost:** $270 includes food, overland transportation. **When:** Year-round. **Contact:** Haron—Sinai Tours Division, c/o Neot Hakikar, 28 King David St., Jerusalem, Israel; phone (02)221624. *(M)*

Sinai Sojourn: Groups of up to 12 spend 16 or 27 days traveling

A woman of Thailand's E-Kan tribe peers over her fence, smoking a pipe and scrutinizing passing foreigners. (REI Adventure Travel)

through the southern Sinai Peninsula. After an overnight stay in Tel Aviv, a flight is made to Elat, where the group boards jeeps for a drive into the desert. Staying in a modern hostel near the 11th-century monastery of St. Katherine, participants make several loop trips from the base of Mt. Sinai into the surrounding region, cooking traditional local dishes and camping. Bedouin settlements are visited as the group explores the area on foot. After an ascent of Mt. Sinai, the group heads to the shores of the Gulf of Aqaba, where participants camp away from tourist areas and spend time swimming, snorkeling and exploring. The trip ends in Tel Aviv. **Cost:** $985 for 16 days, $1,575 for 27 days includes meals, accommodations, flight from Tel Aviv. **When:** October, May. **Contact:** REI Adventure Travel, 1525 11th Ave., Seattle, WA 98122, USA; phone (206)322-7800. *(M)*

Jordan

Desert Bus Trek: Travelers and an experienced guide choose the campsites on a 14-day journey through Jordan. After a flight from London to Amman, the group boards specially equipped desert buses and drives north to Jerash to explore its Greco-Roman ruins. In the next week the route leads south to Madaba and Mt. Nebo, and through the mountains of central Jordan to the fortress of El Karak. Next, participants may explore the rock-cut city of Petra on foot or horseback while camping there for 2 days. At Aqaba on the Red Sea, the group spends 2 days on the beach swimming, snorkeling and diving among the coral reefs. Driving across the desert, trekkers reach the oasis of Wadi Rum; from a nearby Bedouin encampment participants may take a camel trek into the desert. The trek proceeds to Khan el Zebib, the desert palaces at Meshatta and Kharameh, and Azraq before returning to Amman for the return flight to London. **Cost:** $683 to $783 includes transportation from London, camping equipment, guide; $82 for food kitty. **When:** June to August. **Contact:** WEXAS International Inc., Suite 354, Graybar Bldg., 420 Lexington Ave., New York, NY 10017, USA. *(M)*

SOUTH AMERICA

Bolivia

Along the Andes and Altiplano: Trekking excursions of 7 to 15 days extend from lowland river basins to Andean passes in the western part of Bolivia. On the week-long trek participants depart from La Paz, hike to the base of Mt. Illimani, traverse a 16,000-foot mountain pass and visit both subtropical and altiplano villages before returning to the city. Starting near the town of Palca on the Altiplano, the 8-day journey follows the old Inca Road to Coroico in the Valley of the Yungas; members visit Tomonoco and canoe down the Beni River. On a 10-day trip that visits a largely unexplored archaeological zone, participants trek to the ancient Inca fortress of Iskanwaya. Group members on the 15-day trek leave from the altiplano town of Ancoma, the site of an abandoned Spanish colonial gold mine. On foot and by canoe the group descends the eastern slopes of the Andes to Rurrenabaque, then continues downriver for a visit to the Lake of the Caimanes. **Cost:** $280 for 7 days, $320 for 8 days, $400 for 10 days, $600 for 15 days. **When:** On request. **Contact:** Safari Travels, Edificio Libertad, Pasaje Peatonal No. 8, La Paz, Bolivia. *(M)*

Peru

Six Inca Walks: A selection of hikes through Peru's Inca country lasts from 3 to 20 days. The departure points vary; many trips leave from Cuzco, others from smaller towns. Most Inca ruins are connected by a network of trails, including the famous and partly paved Inca Trail, and it is along these that the trips are routed. Two 5- to 8-day trips departing from Chillka or Cuzco visit Machupicchu; another to the Vilcabamba highlands may last anywhere from 5 to 20 days and involves some mountain hiking; a hike among the glaciers and lakes of 20,000-foot Cordillera Vilcanota departs Cuzco and lasts from 5 to 7 days. Two other hikes set out for the mountain ruins of Waxra Pucara and Chinchero. Porters carry

most gear on the longer hikes. **Cost:** On request. **When:** On request. **Contact:** Explorandes, Nicoles de Pierola 672, Of. 205, Lima, Peru; phone 23-6992. *(M)*

Remote Andes Trek: Participants completely encircle the Cordillera Huayhuash, a compact range of mountains located on the Andean Cordillera, during a month-long journey. The Huayhuash rise abruptly from the surrounding highlands to heights well above 20,000 feet. In an area seldom traveled by westerners, participants meet Peruvians from tiny farming villages living in traditional ways. Although burros carry the bulk of the gear, hiking is fairly strenuous and at an average altitude of 13,000 feet. For climbers there are challenging rock faces and snowy peaks along the route. Qualified climbers can participate in a 10-day extension after the trek to climb either a major peak in the Huayhuash or 22,210-foot Nevado Huascaran, the highest peak in Peru. Trekkers explore a variety of terrain, from semi-desert canyons to rolling grasslands and high ice-bordered passes. **Cost:** $2,211 from Miami includes guides, meals, accommo-

dations, transportation. **When:** June. **Contact:** Mountain Travel Inc., 1398 Solano Ave., Albany, CA 94706, USA; phone (415)527-1800. *(M)*

Trekking with the Incas: Two trips that visit remote Inca ruins also feature trekking high in the Andes: a 28-day trip treks through the Cordillera Blanca, and a 25-day budget trip walks the Cordillera Vilcabamba. The first trip begins with a flight from Miami to Huaraz, for acclimatization and visits to local ruins. Then begins a 12-day trek from Quebrada Honda to Quebrada Santa Cruz that crosses 2 passes over 15,000 feet and affords views of Peru's highest peaks. Gear is carried by burros, but the walk is fairly strenuous. Finally a week is spent exploring the Urubamba Valley, including the Inca city of Machupicchu. The second trip convenes in Cuzco for acclimatization, organizing the sharing of equipment and visiting local ruins. The party then moves to Lucma to begin the 10-day trek to Santa Tereza, near Machupicchu, which encounters many spectacular alpine views. Participants should be strong hikers who can provide their

own gear, as this low-cost trip involves sharing equipment and chores; 20 pounds per person are carried by burros. Visits are made to several ruins, including Vitcos, the last Incan capital. **Cost:** $1,995 for 28-day trip includes transportation, food, equipment, pack animals, guide; cost for 25-day trip on request. **When:** June. **Contact:** South American Wilderness Adventures, 1760 Solano Ave., Berkeley, CA 94707, USA; phone (415)524-5111. *(M)*

Trek in the Cordillera Blanca: Starting in Huaraz, trekkers spend 15 days hiking to the town of Caraz on an 18-day journey in the Cordillera Blanca region. After a day of acclimatization, short hikes and visits to archaeological sites, the group buses to Yurakcorral where pack animals and staff are waiting to begin the trek. The route takes hikers up switchbacks, over plateaus, onto glaciers, down into canyons and valleys and through agricultural terraces, with visits to Inca and pre-Inca ruins along the way. Camps are established at scenic sites near lakes, mineral baths or caves. The trek crosses many peaks and passes, with a descent into the Quebrada Santa Cruz highlighting its final days. From the town of Caraz the group returns by bus to Huaraz. A day in Lima concludes the trip. Many other treks are also offered, and specialized treks can be arranged.**Cost:** $324 includes guides, accommodations, transportation from Lima, meals at camp, group camping equipment. **When:** May to September. **Contact:** Trekking Percy Tapia, P.O. Box 3074, Lima 100, Peru.*(M)*

RESOURCES

Clubs and Associations

National Campers and Hikers Assn.
7172 Transit Rd.
Buffalo, NY 14221, USA
Phone (716)634-5433

National Geographic Society
17th and M Sts. NW
Washington, DC 20036, USA
Phone (202)857-7000

National Hiking & Ski Touring Assn.
P.O. Box 7421
Colorado Springs, CO 80933, USA

The Sherpa Cooperative
GPO Box 1338
Kamal Pokhari, Kathmandu, Nepal
Phone 13887

Sierra Club
1050 Mills Tower, 220 Bush St.
San Francisco, CA 94104, USA
Phone (415)981-8634

South American Explorer's Club
Casilla 3714
Lima 1, Peru

Wilderness Society
1901 Pennsylvania Ave. NW
Washington, DC 20006, USA
Phone (202)293-2732

WILDLIFE SAFARIS

In the swaying expanse of elephant grass which stretches almost to the horizon, a lion might be stalking your party. Above you, peering down through the foliage of a nearby tree, a group of vervet monkeys watches as you pass. And at the river bank where you pause in the breath of a cool breeze, an 18-foot crocodile slides silently into the murky water.

Anthropologists tell us that *Homo sapiens* evolved in this environment. Our visual acuity, manual dexterity, upright posture and ability to reason developed as adaptations for survival in such a world, and although our species inhabits the far corners of the earth—the windswept tundras, the frigid arctic, the humid tropical islands and crowded urban centers—there is something like a homecoming in a wildlife safari to East Africa. Until recently such safaris were the exclusive province of men armed with rifles who wanted to bag a trophy for the mantle or a skin for trade. But thanks to the pressures applied by wildlife conservationists the camera has largely replaced the gun. Today, safaris are more popular than ever before.

The parks of Africa—Luangwa Valley, Samburu Game Reserve, Serengeti National Park and over 80 others—may conjure up the most exotic animal images, but other parks all over the world provide sanctuary for equally fascinating species of wildlife. In Nepal, the Bengal tiger is frequently sighted at Chitawan National Park; in Australia, a visit to Kuring-gai Chase National Park will reward you with kangaroo, koala and kiwi encounters; in British Columbia, moose, grizzly bears, timber wolves, gyrfalcons and many other indigenous species can be found within Mt. Edziza Park; and in Idaho, cougars, bighorn sheep and mountain goats all roam near the Salmon River in the southeastern part of the state.

Wildlife safaris are available to everyone in nearly every part of the world. While the more adventurous require that you be in good physical condition, just about any type of trip can be arranged. You might take a walking camera safari through parks in Zambia, or a 3-week trip by truck, train, boat and elephantback throughout parks in India and Bhutan. But whether you choose a rugged wilderness experience or a luxury excursion, on a good safari the boundaries between ourselves and our animal past become blurred. To watch the social organization of a pride of lions, the solitary foraging of a grizzly bear, or the highly structured grooming among a chimpanzee group, is to perceive our own behavior in a larger context, and to become aware of our place in the natural world. □

An African elephant coolly observes the photographer. Prized for their ivory and endangered by hunters, elephants are coming under increasing protection through the efforts of conservationists. (Bob Citron)

WILDLIFE SAFARIS

AFRICA

Camel Caravan: A major part of a 2-week visit to West Africa is a 200-mile caravan trek through Mali by camel. Meeting in Dakar in Senegal, the group flies to Bamako in Mali, where final preparations for the caravan are made. Participants then fly to Timbuktu where they learn the techniques, routines and traditions of travel by camel, including how to talk to camels. Instruction is given in setting up camp, and basic information is provided about the local culture and language. The camel caravan leaves Timbuktu, traveling in the morning and late afternoon with midday stops for lunch and siestas. The trip offers a chance to see the beauty of the desert and experience nomadic life. Nights are spent in tents and hotels. **Cost:** $2,095 includes double-occupancy accommodations, transportation, equipment, some meals. **When:** Year-round. **Contact:** East African Travel Consultants Inc., 33 Bloor St. E., Suite 206, Toronto, ON Canada M4W 3H1; phone (416)967-0067. *(M)*

Botswana

Botswana Safaris: From Johannesburg, participants fly north to view wildlife near the Savuti Channel on 5- and 7-day safaris in the African bush. In Chobe National Park safari members view prides of lions, families of hyenas and herds of roan antelope and buffalo that come to the Savuti marshland for water. An established tent camp provides safari groups with hot showers, beds, elaborate meals and morning and afternoon game drives. The safari moves on to San-Ta-Wani Lodge, a cluster of grass-thatched huts on the fringes of Okavango Swamp.

The zebra, an endangered equine species, may be observed on a seven-day safari offered by Afro Ventures for $195. (Bob Citron)

Canoes and guides from the local Batawana tribe take participants through narrow channels in the dense reeds to clearings where pygmy geese and great white herons may be seen. Traveling in jeeps, participants have the freedom to track through the bush to observe a herd of breeding elephants, wild dogs and cheetahs while visiting Moremi, the largest private game park in the world. Foot safaris are also offered during the trip. The safari ends with a return flight to Johannesburg. Personalized safaris from 1 to 30 days can also be arranged for individuals or special-interest groups. **Cost:** $139 for 5 days, $195 for 7 days from Johannesburg includes transportation, guides, accommodations, meals, entrance fees. **When:** April to November. **Contact:** Afro Ventures, P.O. Box 10848, Johannesburg 2000, South Africa. *(M)*

Kenya

Photographic Safaris in National Parks: Kenya's national parks and game reserves provide subjects for photographers during a variety of safaris. Nairobi National Park is the home of most big game including lions and rhinos; Tsavo National Park is the sanctuary of Kenya's largest concentration of elephants, and Masai Mara Game Reserve contains herds of plains animals including African buffalo, zebras and antelope. In addition, the Kenya coastline near Mombasa provides shark-free waters, coral reefs and big game fish. Self-driven and chauffeur-driven 4-wheel drive vehicles are used for photographic expeditions. Also available are special safaris for participants with

The orangutan, or "man of the forest," inhabits the tropical lowland rain forests of Borneo and Sumatra. (Bob Citron)

interests in geology, history, ornithology and sports. **Cost:** $10 to $425 depending on length of safari and transportation. **When:** Year-round. **Contact:** Across Africa Safaris Ltd., P.O. Box 49420, Nairobi, Kenya; phone 21593.

East African Wildlife Safari: A 21-day opportunity to observe and photograph a wide variety of African wild animals and birds is offered to a group of 10 to 18 persons. Members visit 8 major national parks and game-viewing areas including Masi Mara, Amboseli, Aberdare National Forest, Tsavo East and Tsavo West, Lake Nakuru National Park, the Samburu-Isiolo area and Kenya's Marine National Park. Other major points of interest are visits to Masai manyattas and tribal dancing, Lake Naivasha, Mzima Springs, Treetops Lodge, historic Mombasa and coral reefs in

the Indian Ocean. Mt. Kenya is circled and the group stays at the foot of Mt. Kilimanjaro. Nights are spent in game lodges and under canvas in camps with standard beds and showers. Minibuses with photographic hatches and some 4-wheel drive vehicles are used for transportation. **Cost:** $2,010 includes land cost from Nairobi, meals, lodging, guides, equipment, expedition leader. **When:** July. **Contact:** Adventures International, 4421 Albert St., Oakland, CA 94619, USA; phone (415)531-6564.

(M)

Weekends in the Northern Frontier: Camels, horses and horse-zebra hybrids called zebroids are the means of transportation on a weekend safari into the Kenyan veldt. Beginning in Nanyuki, participants ride along the Uaso Nyiro River, where wildlife is abundant.

Camping in the Anderobo Reserve provides participants with opportunities to meet members of the Anderobo tribe. Individual trips may also be arranged. **Cost:** $32 to $52 a day per person depending on the size of the group includes guides, equipment, food. **When:** Year-round. **Contact:** Amber May Safaris, P.O. Box 2, Nanyuki, Kenya; phone Nanyuki 2193.

Wildlife Camping: Two weeks of backpacking from the Mt. Kenya highlands to the coastal lands of the Indian Ocean offer hikers a variety of flora and fauna to observe. An optional excursion is a drive up Mt. Kenya to an altitude of 10,000 feet for hikes through the forests and moorlands of the Teleki Valley. During the next few days, trip members visit Thomson's Falls and Lake Nakuru National Park before proceeding south to camp for several days at Masai Mara Game Reserve. Hikers also camp at Lake Naivasha, known for its abundant bird life and hippo populations which can best be seen during an optional 2-hour cruise along the banks. Visits to Masai Amboseli Game Reserve and Tsavo National Park are scheduled before a few days' stay at Mombasa and Malindi on the coast. **Cost:** $457 to $998 depending on the size of the group includes transportation from Nairobi, park entrance fees, meals, camping accommodations. **When:** Year-round. **Contact:** Bestway Tours and Safaris Ltd., Woolworths Bldg., Box 44325, Nairobi, Kenya; phone 331261, 331262, 22297. *(M)*

Personalized East African Safaris: Parties of up to 4 people design their own itinerary and are driven by an experienced naturalist guide to game parks and other points of interest in Kenya. Accommodations are at lodges in the national parks, and generally 3 or 4 days are spent in each location. Between parks, travelers stay in a house overlooking Lake Naivasha for bird watching, fishing and boating. **Cost:** $65 to $158 a day includes food, transportation, accommodations, guide. **When:** Year-round. **Contact:** Fisherman's Camp, P.O. Box 79, Naivasha, Kenya; phone 542.

From Nairobi to Ngorongoro: Major wildlife habitats in Kenya and Tanzania are the destination of a 23-day overland journey. After flying to Nairobi participants drive to the highlands of central Kenya.

En route to Naro Moru River Lodge at the base of Mt. Kenya, the group stops at Mukuruwe wa Gathanaga, the traditional "garden of Eden" in the homeland of the Kikuyu. A day at the Samburu Game Lodge on the Uaso River allows wildlife enthusiasts to see species unique to the desert country of the Northern Frontier District such as the oryx, gerenuk, Grevy zebra and reticulated giraffe. In the forests of the Aberdare Range overnight game viewing may reveal elephants, waterbucks, leopards and bongo antelope. Once in Tanzania, overlanders visit Serengeti National Park, Ngorongoro Crater with its vast herds of game, Lake Manyara National Park and Arusha National Park near Mt. Meru. Africa's highest mountain, 19,940-foot Mt. Kilimanjaro, looms in the background during an outing to one last reserve, Amboseli, before partici-

A camel camp is set up in Wamba, Kenya. Mountain Travel uses the camels as pack animals on a 23-day hike through Kenya's Northern Frontier District. (Alla Schmitz)

pants return to Nairobi. **Cost:** $1,380 includes accommodations, some meals, land transportation, guide. **When:** February, April, June, August, October, December. **Contact:** Forum Travel International, 2437 Durant, No. 208, Berkeley, CA 94704, USA; phone (415)843-8294. *(M)*

East African Camping: A 3-week safari requires members to help out with chores such as setting up tents and building campfires, and is designed to give a broad experience of African camping. Participants may choose to visit Nairobi, Mt. Kenya, Samburu Game Reserve, the Rift Valley and Lake Nakuru National Park, or they may take an excursion to the ruined city of Gedi. Another overland journey, offering 2 weeks of travel from Johannesburg to Nairobi, consists of rugged driving and extensive wildlife observation near Victoria Falls and in the Masai Amboseli Game Reserve. **Cost:** $480 for 2 weeks; $580 for 3 weeks. **When:** Year-round. **Contact:** Kobe Safaris, 167 Earls Court Rd., London SW5, Great Britain; or Adventure Center, 5540 College Ave., Oakland, CA 94618, USA; phone (415)654-1879. *(M)*

Camel Safari: A safari on foot with a camel support caravan travels for 23 days through a land sparsely inhabited by the nomadic Samburu tribe. The reticulated giraffe, Grevy's zebra, Beisa oryx and the fragile gerenuk gazelle are found in the vast and unspoiled Northern Frontier District. Heading north from Nairobi by land cruiser, participants explore Meru National Park and go on to the Samburu

Game Reserve. Later at Serolevi Lugger the 9-day, 100-mile hike begins as trekkers rendezvous with the camel train. Hiking along the 8,000-foot Matthews Range with the weather warm and dry, campers sleep under the stars. Participants encounter the unusual game species of the area and perhaps some tribespeople herding their livestock. After the trek, safari members drive south to Mt. Kenya, Teleki Valley and Aberdare National Park to view wildlife, possibly seeing the elusive leopard, the bongo and the giant forest hog. The trip ends in Nairobi after a drive through the coffee and pineapple plantations of Thika. **Cost:** $2,045 includes accommodations, guides, meals, transportation from Nairobi. **When:** March. **Contact:** Mountain Travel Inc., 1398 Solano Ave., Albany, CA 94706, USA; phone (415)527-8100. *(M)*

Samburu Safaris: Wildlife observation trips out of Nairobi, from 1 day to several days long, are provided into various areas of Kenya. Day trips can be made to the Bomas of Kenya, Nairobi National Park, the Rift Valley or Lake Nakuru National Park. Other trips, ranging from 1 to 4 nights in length, are offered to the Aberdare Range, Masai Amboseli Game Reserve, Tsavo National Park, Samburu, Mt. Kenya and Nanyuki. Wildlife is plentiful on all trips, with the Samburu visit offering a chance to see rare reticulated giraffes, Grevy zebras and gerenuks. Overnight accommodations are provided at jungle lodges. **Cost:** $7 to $300 depending on length of trip includes food, transportation, guide, accommodations. **When:** Year-round. **Contact:** Nakutravel Ltd., Kearline Tours, Town House, Corner of Kaundra/Wavers Sts., P.O. Box 41564, Nairobi, Kenya; phone 332299 or 20363.

East African Natural History: Professional naturalists and other scientists guide adventurers on camping expeditions of 17 and 24 days through Kenya's parks, wildlife reserves and wilderness areas. Participants have the opportunity to study the natural and human history of Kenya and observe a variety of game animals. On the 17-day trips participants travel by 4-wheel drive vehicles and on foot to observe and photograph the wildlife and environments found in Meru and Tsavo national parks and Masai Amboseli Game Reserve, the Rift Valley lakes, Wamba and the Masai Mara Game Reserve. The 24-day trip in July emphasizes the northern frontier. A professional wildlife photographer accompanies the group in January. Travelers who would like to do more hiking can join a mountain walking safari of 24 days, beginning with a 4-day trek and game viewing in the Chyulu Range. **Cost:** $1,790 for 17 days, $1,690 for 24 days includes guides, meals, equipment, ground transportation. **When:** January, June, August, September. **Contact:** Nature Expeditions International, 599 College Ave., Palo Alto, CA 94306, USA; phone (415)328-6572.   *(M)*

Kenya Excursions: A variety of short trips is offered for an exploration of the African countryside. One is a 2-day trip to the Amboseli, Serengeti, and Ngorongoro areas.

Mt. Kilimanjaro is visible during the flight to Masai Amboseli Game Reserve. Members of the group then leave from Lake Manyara, proceeding to the Ndutu Tent Camp in Serengeti National Park, famous for its large zebra, gnu and antelope herds. The first stop thereafter is the Olduvai Gorge, where anthropological discoveries have included a 1.75-million-year-old skeleton. The group then drives to the 102-square-mile Ngorongoro Crater, the second largest crater in the world. An abundance of native African wildlife is visible throughout the trip. **Cost:** On request. **When:** Year-round. **Contact:** Pollman's Tours and Safaris Ltd., Kimathi St., P.O. Box 45895, Nairobi, Kenya; phone 27250.

Wildlife Safari by Canoe: Participants traveling overland and by canoe spend 26 days in the game parks and wildlife reserves of Kenya and Botswana. In Kenya the group travels through the Masai Mara Game Reserve, home of the nomadic herdsmen of east Africa, then on to the undisturbed Loita Plains area, the Aberdare Range, Lake Naivasha and the Samburu Game Reserve. Traveling to Botswana, participants visit the Chobe National Park, where great herds of African beasts reside. Okavango Swamp is the next stop; this area is almost uninhabited and teeming with wildlife. Canoeing is the means of travel through the swamp. At the conclusion of the journey an optional 6-day walking tour of Zambia's Luangwa Valley National Park is offered. **Cost:** $2,170. **When:** August. **Contact:** Sierra Club Outing Dept., 530 Bush

St., San Francisco, CA 94108, USA; phone (415)981-8634.

Rwanda

In Search of the Mountain Gorilla: After flying from New York to Kigali travelers begin 18 days journeying through Rwanda and Zaire. Driving to the gentle hills of Kagera National Park, participants explore grassy plains, marshlands and lake regions that provide habitats for an enormous variety of animals and birds including black-maned lions, large herds of zebras, sacred and hadada ibises, crested cranes and eagles. Heading north, travelers make an excursion along the Loya River in dugout canoes, visit a Balese village and trek into the tropical forests of Mt. Hoya. Hidden in the dense forests are a ring of 30 or more grottoes that conceal a maze of galleries with remarkable stalactite and stalagmite formations, ancient wall inscriptions and animal paintings. In order to catch a Lake Kivu steamer to Bakavu, participants head south to Goma. From there a short drive brings the group to Kahuzi-Biega National Park, one of the few remaining homelands of the mountain gorilla. On foot, pygmy trackers lead the way into the forest, following almost invisible tracks until the sound of a gorilla thumping its chest can be heard. Photographs can be taken, mutual curiosity pursued and a great deal of time spent with the animals by following the symbolic nonaggressive behavior that the pygmies demonstrate. After a return to Kigali, trip members board a plane for the return flight to New York. **Cost:** $2,600 to $2,800 depending on departure date includes transportation from Kigali, meals, accommodations, guide. **When:** June to March. **Contact:** Lindblad Travel Inc., Lindblad Travel Bldg., 133 E. 55th St., New York, NY 10022, USA; phone (212)751-2300 or tollfree (800)223-9700.

Zaire

Gorilla Safari: An exploratory trip through Rwanda and Zaire features 18 days of wildlife viewing in unusual, seldom-visited settings. In the Virunga Mountains a search begins for the rare mountain gorilla. The group, limited to 6 persons, follows local guides through Volcanoes National Park and Zaire's Ituri Forest on Mt. Hoyo, and finally to the gorilla sanctuary of Kahuzi-Biega to observe and photograph gorillas at relatively close range. During the trip, participants visit remote villages, hike in lush mountain forests, and float through the rain forest in dugout canoes. In the grasslands and scattered forest of Rwanda's Kagera National Park, explorers can see and photograph lions, leopards, topi, elands, impalas and the rare roan antelope. **Cost:** $1,400 includes transportation, meals, lodging, guides. **When:** July. **Contact:** Adventures International, 4421 Albert St., Oakland, CA 94619, USA; phone (415)531-6564. *(M)*

Zambia

Game Viewing in Africa: Central and East Africa provide the setting for 29 days of watching wildlife in their natural habitats. After arriving in Lusaka group members fly to Livingstone and then spend several days at Chunga Camp in Kafue National Park. Game viewing by Land Rover and on foot is spectacularly successful here as well as at Ntemwa/Moshi Camp, the next stopover in Kafue. The final game viewing in Zambia takes place in Luangwa Valley National Park. Here guides lead small groups through the bush over 6 to 8 miles of trails between campsites. The trails are not strenuous but are geared for people of all ages. The safari next travels to Kenya, where participants spend a night at the Ark watching animals visit the nightly lit water hole. Then the group departs for 9 days into the interior to camp and view more animals. Accommodations throughout the trip are in hotels, lodges and tents. Participants may join the trip for either the Zambia or Kenya portions if they so desire. **Cost:** $2,695 includes roundtrip airfare from London, transportation in Africa, accommodations, most meals, guides. **When:** June to November. **Contact:** Semjon Lass Associates, Action Tours, Box 1000, Lowell, MA 01854, USA; phone (617)459-2104; or Talisman Travel Service, 3440 Geary Blvd., San Francisco, CA 94118, USA; phone (415)668-2956. *(M)*

Wildlife Walking Tour: Participants visit areas in which wildlife is plentiful during a 6-day walking tour of the Luangwa Valley National Park, along the Zambia-Mozambique border. With 6 to 8 members in each group, participants trek from campsite to campsite, generally arriving in late morning. Game can be found close

Lions pause for a moment in a clearing in the Luangwa Valley. Zambia Airways sponsors game-viewing safaris on foot or in overland vehicles from Lusaka. (Zambia Airways)

to each camp for photography enthusiasts. Experienced guides lead each group. The camps have complete facilities, including refrigerators to preserve fresh produce for meals. **Cost:** $335 includes ground transportation, camp accommodations, guide, meals. **When:** June to October. **Contact:** Wilderness Trails Ltd., Cairo Rd., P.O. Box 3876, Lusaka, Zambia; phone 73027; or Zambia Airways, 1 Rockefeller Plaza, New York, NY 10020, USA; phone (212)582-6637. *(M)*

Game Viewing: Six-day vehicle treks begin with flights from Lusaka, Zambia's capital, to South Luangwa National Park. Itineraries are flexible to suit special interests. Emphasis is placed on educational aspects of the areas visited, so slide or film presentations and informal lectures are included. The Land Rovers used allow either roof viewing through hatches or open viewing. Six-day walking treks from Chibembe Safari Camp are also available; they are led by a trail guide and an armed guard. Between 5 and 7 miles are covered in the morning before a midday arrival at a bush camp for lunch and siesta. The walking safaris provide excellent opportunities for close-up photography of wildlife. **Cost:** $351 for vehicle safari, $448 for walking safari. **When:** June to October. **Contact:** Zambia Airways, 1 Rockefeller Plaza, New York, NY 10020, USA; phone (212)582-6637. *(M)*

ASIA

Tiger Haven Trek: Travelers ride elephants in Kaziranga National Park in India, stay on a tea plantation in Assam and visit Manas Wildlife Sanctuary in Bhutan on a 24-day safari to view game animals.

The trip starts in Delhi and ends in Bombay, with travel by truck, train, boat and plane. After visiting Calcutta, participants reach Royal Chitawan National Park and Tiger Tops Jungle Lodge in Nepal via the rapids of the Trisuli River. The safari crosses back into India for a 3-day stay at Dudwa National Park and the adjoining Tiger Haven, where members can wait in high tree lookouts to see Bengal tigers. Finally, adventurers hike and ride elephants in Kanha National Park in the sal forests of central India. Among the animals seen are Indian rhinos, golden langurs, wild buffalo, gaurs, barking deer, hyenas, samburs and leopards. Along the way travelers combine stays in hotels and lodges with camping in 2-person tents. **Cost:** $1,995 includes transportation from Delhi, food, accommodations. **When:** January to April, November. **Contact:** Mountain Travel Inc., 1398 Solano Ave., Albany, CA 94706, USA; phone (415)527-8100. *(M)*

Nepal

Wandering in Nepal: Participants fly from New York to Delhi, then on to Kathmandu to begin a 23-day adventure through landscapes ranging from jungle river valleys to Himalayan slopes. The first leg of travel in Nepal is by raft as group members float down the Trisuli River through the Muglin Gorge and into the jungle lowlands of the Terai. Camping each night is along the river. Dug-out canoes are then used to travel to the Tiger Tops camp in Royal Chitawan National Park, where group members spend 2 days exploring the jungle and viewing wildlife such as the rare one-horned Indian rhino, wild deer, crocodiles and over 300 species of birds. At Deorali Camp participants have good views not only of the Annapurna Range but also the Dhaulagiri Range; on this part of the journey, participants are accompanied by Sherpa guides and porters. The trip concludes with a flight back to Kathmandu, where group members may spend a day exploring before flying back to Delhi, then to New York. **Cost:** $2,361 to $2,507 depending on the season includes transportation from New York, most meals, guides and Sherpas, camping equipment and accommodations in hotels. **When:** October, November and April. **Contact:** WEXAS International Inc., Suite 354, Graybar Bldg., 420 Lexington Ave., New York, NY 10017, USA. *(M)*

A leopard stalks prey in a game sanctuary in Sri Lanka. The leopard is one of more than 200 species found in the country's many parks and reserves. (Ceylon Tourist Board)

Sri Lanka

Wildlife Trek: Sri Lanka offers travelers an intriguing exploration of wildlife and anthropology. Starting at the capital city of Colombo, participants take daily photography and bird watching trips by jeep, visiting the Yala Game Reserve, Hikkaduwa, Wirawila, Ratnapura, Wilpattu National Park and the ruined city at Anuradhapura. Kalamatiya, Bundala, Wirawila, and Deberawewa are bird sanctuaries on the southern coast of Sri Lanka where participants spend 3 days and 2 nights. From here a trip to the Yala Game Reserve is recommended. On another trip to Mahiyangana, travelers see the Veddha tribe, a native people of Sri Lanka whose way of life dates from the Stone Age. **Cost:** $54 to $112. **When:** Year-round. **Contact:** D.D.N. Selvadurai, 28 Kassapa Rd., Colombo 5, Sri Lanka; phone 82069.

AUSTRALASIA

Australia

Wilderness Trip Down Under: Traveling by coach to points of interest in Darwin, a 1-day trip takes travelers into the bush for wildlife observation. Wilderness areas visited include the magnetic anthills of McMinns Lagoon, the Marakai Plains, western Arnhem Land and the huge Cathedral Anthills. Frequently sighted wildlife include wallabies, wild pigs, buffalo, a wide variety of birds, and occasionally dingoes, donkeys and goannas. A barbecue lunch is served at midday, and some instruction in native culture is offered. **Cost:** $20 ($10 for children under 15) includes transportation, food, guides. **When:** Daily year-round. **Contact:** Marakai Safari Tours, P.O. Box 38956, Winnellie, NT 5789, Australia; phone Darwin 88 1177.

CANADA
British Columbia

Camping in Remote Canada: A 12-day trip visits Mt. Edziza Park, an area penetrated by only a few hunters and prospectors. Participants fly from Eddontenajon Lake into the park and stay at a base camp there, making expeditions of varying lengths into the surrounding area. The trip is especially tailored for photographers and naturalists. Wildlife is abundant on both the mountain and in the surrounding alpine plateau. Hikers may see grizzly bears, timber wolves, moose, caribou, Stone and Dall sheep, mountain goats, nesting gyrfalcons and many small animals. **Cost:** $840 includes transportation to and from Smithers' airport, hotel accommodation at Eddontenajon, camping equipment, food, guide. **When:** July, August. **Contact:** Black Tusk Touring and Guide Service Ltd., 3064 St. Kildas Ave., North Vancouver, BC Canada V7L 2A9; phone (604)985-9223. *(M)*

UNITED STATES

Idaho

Camera Safaris: Personalized trips for viewing wild animals in their natural habitat are available in the Idaho Primitive Area in the state's southeastern area. Accessible only by boat, the Salmon River Lodge is located in a mountainous gorge on the Salmon River; it is home base for photographic trips of any duration. Photographers may take once-in-a-lifetime photographs of elk, bears, deer, mountain goats, bighorn sheep and cougars. The animals roam free in the area, where there are no roads or cars and the nearest town is 47 miles away. Individually planned trips include float trips, jetboat rides and horseback trips for exploring the wilderness area. All equipment except sleeping bags is provided for nights spent away from the lodge. **Cost:** $40 a day from Salmon includes meals, lodging, guide services, horses, equipment. **When:** By arrangement from February to December. **Contact:** Salmon River Lodge, P.O. Box 58, Salmon, ID 83467, USA; phone (208)756-2646.

RESOURCES
Clubs and Associations

India Tourist Office
30 Rockefeller Plaza
New York, NY 10020, USA
Phone (212) 586-4901

Outward Bound Trust
34 Broadway
London SW1H 0BQ, Great Britain

Rover Company Public Relations Dept.
The Rover Company, Solihill
Worcestershire, Great Britain

WEXAS
45 Brompton Rd.
Knightsbridge, London SW3 1DE
Great Britain

Zambia National Tourist Bureau
150 E. 58th St.
New York, NY 10022, USA
Phone (212)758-9450

Vehicle Rental

Highways, Ltd.
Kilidini Rd., P.O. Box 84787
Mombassa, Kenya

NATURE TRIPS

During the round-the-world voyage of the H.M.S. *Beagle* from 1831 to 1836, Charles Darwin kept a journal of his observations of wildlife on the Galapagos, the geology of Patagonia, and the natives of the Pacific. When he returned to England, he was able to formulate a new theory of evolution. When John Wesley Powell conquered the Grand Canyon on the Colorado River in 1869, he collected geographical, ethnological and botanical notes to advance all three disciplines. Alexander Humboldt spent five years in South America at the beginning of the nineteenth century, and his extensive experimentation and records laid the modern foundations of physical geography, geophysics, meteorology and botany.

Exploration and curiosity go hand in hand to produce knowledge; science is as much a product of adventure as it is of research. And today, nature trips afford outlets for curiosity—that very human attribute—to flower. Accompanied by naturalists trained in species identification, history and natural phenomena, organized trips set out in all seasons of the year for journeys of discovery in Asia, Africa, the Americas and Europe.

Spring is the best time of year to watch for birds in Asia, and a 24-day expedition from Kathmandu explores the Trisuli Gorge and high pastures of India's Gatlang Valley searching for mynahs, bulbuls and spotted munias. In summer, an expedition to Alaska's Glacier Bay studies the fascinating geology and remote wildlife of the sub-arctic under its midnight sun. Come fall, the Mediterranean provides the scenic background for taking in the fall foliage, watching for eagles and visiting historical excavations at Mycenae, Argos and Mistra in Greece. And when the cold of winter sets in, you might wish to head south for a month-long tour of four South American wildlife areas—the Falkland and Galapagos islands, Tierra del Fuego and the highlands of Ecuador.

Gaining an understanding of the natural world, and coming to terms with its limited wilderness areas, its fragile ecologies and its endangered species is the first step toward protecting these resources. On a nature trip, it can be made exciting as well as rewarding. □

Whether walking through a forest or on mountain slopes, participants on nature trips discover the rich diversity of still unspoiled regions. (Nat'l. Publicity Studios—New Zealand)

NATURE TRIPS

AFRICA

Kenya

Nature and Wildlife: Guided by a zoologist and a biologist, group members study the flora and fauna of Kenya for 18 days. Participants depart from either Los Angeles or New York and fly to Nairobi via Europe. From Nairobi, overland travel is in minibuses with open roofs for wildlife observation and photography; overnight stops are made at hotels and lodges. Group members journey through the Rift Valley to Lake Naivasha for a boat exploration of some of the lake's islands. On Crescent Island participants observe over 300 species of birds. The group explores the gorge of Hell's Gate, following a footpath that leads down to hot springs and steam jets. From Lake Nakuru participants travel to Lake Baringo, stopping to observe the numerous species of waterfowl, waders and shorebirds in the region. In the heart of Kenya's tea-growing country the group studies the abundant avifauna of the Kakamega Forest. The route continues north into the Samburu region and Meru National Park, an area of particular interest to bird watchers. After spending a day observing the wildlife in the reserve, participants visit the Tana River bank, the acacia forests and a an area where dome palms are grown. **Cost:** $2,177 from Los Angeles, $1,955 from New York includes air and land transportation, guide, accommodations, meals.

When: June. **Contact:** Aventura Natural History Tours and Travel, 508 N. Sierra Dr., Beverly Hills, CA 90210, USA; phone (213)276-6081.

ASIA

Indonesia

Indonesian Wildlife and Flora Study: An experienced naturalist guides small groups of adventurers on a 24-day journey through Sumatra, Java and Bali. Flying from Los Angeles, participants stop in Hong Kong for one night, then proceed to Singapore and the Kranji Reserve. In northern Sumatra, Lake Toba and the islands of Samosir and Tau are explored. Returning to the coast, the group flies to Jakarta for a 2-day stay and a trip to the botanical gardens at Bogor before journeying to Krakatau. From a base on Peucang Island, participants make field trips into Udung Kulon National Park, home of many rare mammals including the Javan rhinoceros. In central Java, participants examine Brobudar, the world's largest Buddhist temple, then journey to Denpaser on the island of Bali. In the Baluran Game Reserve in the western part of Java, group members have an excellent opportunity to observe the wild ox and the wild water buffalo. Adventurers spend a final 2 days in Bali before flying to Los Angeles via Manila. **Cost:** $3,414 includes transportation from Los Angeles, meals, accommodations, guide. **When:** April, July, September. **Contact:** Questers Tours and Travel, Inc., 257 Park Ave. S., New York, NY 10010, USA; phone (212)673-3120.
(M)

Malaysia

Malaysian Mixed Tours: On any of 13 trips ranging in length from a half day to 3 days travelers visit cities, countryside and wilderness areas in Sabah, a Malaysian state in the north of Borneo. Trips depart year-round from the state capital, Kota Kinabalu. While most traveling is done by motorcoach, visitors also take to the sea or walk for activities such as exploration of a coral island or a 2-day climb to the summit of 13,455-foot Mt. Kinabalu. Participants traveling inland find the landscape of Sabah characterized by rubber plantations and rice paddies in inhabited regions, and tropical jungles and small villages in the more remote areas. On the coast, group members visit a Maja fishing village and a Dyak village where houses on stilts jut out into the sea. Special arrangements can be made to visit places of interest that aren't included in the package tours. **Cost:** On request. **When:** Year-round. **Contact:** Discovery Tours (Sabah) Sdn. Bhd., No. 5, Jalan Pantai, P.O. Box 1355, Kota Kinabalu, Sabah, E. Malaysia; phone 53721 or 55425; or Malaysia Tourist Information Ctr., Transamerica Pyramid, 600 Montgomery St., San Francisco, CA 94111, USA; phone (415)788-3344.

Sri Lanka

Indian Ocean Birding: An 8-day trip takes bird watchers to an area where there are over 380 species of indigenous birds and other migrant varieties. Within the 25,000 square miles of Sri Lanka, many bird sanctuaries are located, especially in the Dry Zone, an area less populated than the north. The trip begins with a tour of Colombo before heading south for the Kalametiya Bird Sanctuary, which features flamingos, spoonbills, painted storks and garganeys. The Yala National Game Sanctuary is the next stop, the home of elephants, samburs, jungle fowl and leopards. En route to Lahugala to see the Ceylon swamp elephant, bird watchers may spot kingfishers, mynahs, bee eaters and parrots. The best bird sanctuary is located in Kumana, where viewing is excellent in March, June and July, with opportunities to see spotted-bill pelicans, black-necked storks and plovers. The last 2 days are spent on a coast-to-coast drive through the central hills back to Colombo, where an afternoon can be spent at the zoological gardens and walk-in aviary. **Cost:** $220 includes transportation from Colombo, meals, lodging. **When:** Year-round. **Contact:** Walkers Tours and Travels Ltd., P.O. Box 1048, Colombo, Sri Lanka; phone 28575.

AUSTRALASIA

Australia

Wildflower Study Trips: Three different coach trips, each lasting 6 days, venture from Perth into the countryside where spectacular wildflowers are in bloom. The relatively unchanging habitat of Western Australia has resulted in the survival of many unusual species. Accompanied by a botanist, participants taking the northern route visit New Norcia, the Gunyidi and Coorow sand plains, the Greenough flats, Chapman Valley, the Eradu Plain and Moora. A second trip visits numerous ghost towns in the Menzies area as well as Jeedamya, Walleroo Rock and Coolgardie. The southern trip visits Bubury, Yoongarillup, Pemberton, Walpole Inlet, Albany, Stirling Range and Hectare national parks and Dryandra. All 3 trips begin and end in Perth. **Cost:** $175 for ghost town trip, $205 for northern or southern trip includes transportation, motel accommodations, meals, guide, entertainment. **When:** August to October. **Contact:** Railway Travel Centres, 772 Hay St. and City Arcade, Perth, West Australia.

New Zealand

South Pacific Nature Study: Participants on a 30-day trip study New Zealand's natural history and wildlife. Under the leadership of a professor of biology familiar with the region, trip members travel by 4-wheel drive vehicle and on foot to areas varying in climate, topology and natural history. Visits are made to Auckland, the Hauraki Gulf, Little Barrier Island, Rotorua, Tongariro National Park, Christchurch, Mt. Cook and Westland national parks, and Milford Sound via the Milford Track. **Cost:** $1,890 includes food, accommodations, land transportation, guide. **When:** March. **Contact:** Nature Expeditions International, 599 College Ave., Palo Alto, CA 94306, USA; phone (415)328-6572. *(M)*

CANADA

Far Northern Nature Trip: A 15-day trip provides wide-ranging opportunities for study of zoological, geological and historical rarities in Canada. The trip begins in Edmonton, Alberta with 2 days of field trips to Elk Island National Park with its elk and rare prairie bison. Participants then fly to Whitehorse in the Yukon to see Miles Canyon's high basalt cliffs. Then several days are spent at Dawson City in the Klondike for a look at gold rush territory—Bonanza Creek where gold was first discovered, Midnight Dome and the Dempster Highway. Next is a flight over the Arctic Circle and the Mackenzie Mountains to Inuvik on the Mackenzie River delta for a visit to the Eskimo community and trading center, followed by a flight across the Beaufort Sea to Herschel Island. This is a prime spot for viewing arctic wildflowers, as well as peregrine falcons and gyrfalcons. After a visit to Alexander Falls at Hay River, travelers fly to Fort Smith for 3 nights. The days here are spent in field trips to Wood Buffalo National Park, which is the world's second-largest national park, the home of the last remaining herds of wood bison and the only known nesting ground for whooping cranes. The trip returns to Edmonton for the last night. **Cost:** $1,942 includes food, double-occupancy accommodations, transportation from Edmonton, guide. **When:** June to August. **Contact:** Questers Tours and Travel, Inc., 257 Park Ave. S., New York, NY 10010, USA; phone (212)673-3120. *(M)*

Alberta

Helicoptering and Overlanding in the Cariboos: Three days of riding in helicopters through spectacular mountain terrain are featured on a 9-day trip. The trip begins in Calgary, Alberta with a motorcoach ride to Banff for a 2-night stopover.

QUESTERS WORLD OF NATURE TOURS

"Nature tour" has a special meaning when you travel with Questers. We are the *only* professional travel company specializing exclusively in nature tours. Our approach in planning Worldwide Nature Tours is to provide you with the broadest possible opportunity of experiencing for yourself the natural history and culture of each area we explore. With the leadership of an accompanying naturalist, we search out the plants and animals, birds and flowers ... rain forests, mountains, and tundra ... seashores, lakes, and swamps of the regions we visit. We also study the architecture, archaeology, museum collections, temples, and customs of the people.

Varying in length from 9 to 36 days, Questers Worldwide Nature Tours travel to virtually every part of the world. Groups are small, and early reservations are therefore suggested. Listed below is a sampling of the 33 destinations offered in 1979:

WORLDWIDE NATURE TOURS 1979 DEPARTURES
(Partial listing)

THE AMERICAS

EVERGLADES: 11 days, March 29 & November 8 • BAJA WHALE WATCH: 9 days, February 1 • HAWAII: 15 days, February 11, April 8, July 15, October 7 & December 23 • ALASKA: 17 days, June 9, 23 & 30, July 7 & 21, & August 11 • GUATEMALA: 19 days, January 27, February 17, March 17, November 3 & December 22 • ECUADOR & GALAPAGOS: 15 days, February 1 & 22, April 26, July 19 & October 11 • THE AMAZON: 14 days, February 8, April 12, July 5 & October 25 • PERU: 23 days, April 7, June 9, July 21 & November 3.

EUROPE

ICELAND: 16 days, June 8 & 29, July 20 & August 10 • ISLANDS & HIGHLANDS OF SCOTLAND: 23 days, May 25, June 15, July 13 & August 24 • SWITZERLAND: 17 days, June 15, July 20 & August 17 • GREECE: 22 days, April 6 & September 7.

ASIA AND AFRICA

KASHMIR & LADAKH: 23 days, July 6, August 3 & September 7 • NORTHERN INDIA & NEPAL: 36 days, February 23 & October 5 • SRI LANKA: 18 days, February 9 & November 23 • TANZANIA: 23 days, January 26, April 13, July 27 & October 26 • ZAIRE GORILLA WATCH: 23 days, May 4, July 7 & August 17.

OCEANIA AND AUSTRALASIA

THE COMPLETE AUSTRALIA: 35 days, August 31 • AUSTRALIA & NEW ZEALAND: 30 days, February 3 & September 22 • NEW ZEALAND'S MILFORD TRACK AND TAHITI: 23 days, February 23 & November 16.

Detailed itineraries for each tour listed above, and the latest Directory of Worldwide Nature Tours outlining the entire program, are available upon request from your travel agent or Questers. Call or write today!

Exploratory expeditions and special tours are announced from time to time in our newsletter Nature Tour Notes, *sent free to all on our mailing list. Copies of the most recent issue available upon request.*

Questers Tours and Travel, Inc.

DEPT. ITG, 257 PARK AVENUE SOUTH
NEW YORK, N.Y. 10010 • (212) 673-3120

Rafting the Bow River, hiking, photographing and golfing are available at the resort. Participants then continue along the Banff-Jasper Highway to Jasper National Park Lodge where they pare down their luggage to one small bag. The next day they board a helicopter for a lodge in the Cariboos, the base for 3 days of flying. A full day is spent exploring the territory and touching down for short walks or views through the largely untouched Cariboos. After a flight back to Jasper, travelers stop for a night at Lake Louise on the way back to Calgary for the trip's conclusion. **Cost:** $799 includes transportation, double-occupancy accommodations, food, guides. **When:** June to September. **Contact:** Tauck Tours, 11 Wilton Rd., Westport, CT 06880, USA; phone (203)226-6911.

Manitoba

Churchill Birding: The grain port of Churchill is the setting for 10 days of bird watching and wildlife observation. Trip members start in Winnipeg with some exploration of the surrounding plains and marshes, seeking out yellow-headed blackbirds, avocets, western grebes, Wilson's pharalopes and other prairie birds. The party then proceeds to Churchill's arctic environment, where the sun sets at 11:30 p.m. Here bird enthusiasts look for Hudsonian godwits, golden plovers, Smith's longspurs and other birds, as well as white beluga whales which travel the Churchill River spouting in unison. On the tenth day the trip returns to Winnipeg. **Cost:** $925 includes transportation from Winnipeg, accommodations, lunches in the field, guide.

When: June. **Contact:** Massachusetts Audubon Society, Lincoln, MA 01773, USA.

Northwest Territories

Visiting the Inuit of Pond Inlet: High above the Arctic Circle on Baffin Island, the Inuit Eskimos live in a community of 550 people on Pond Inlet. Until 15 years ago a nomadic people, they still live largely by hunting and fishing in their old style, although many now have town jobs. Six-day trips to their region leave from Montreal or Hamilton, Canada to visit the village's igloo-shaped cathedral, museum, and arts and crafts center. From lodgings in town, participants take day trips to neighboring Bylot Island, a bird sanctuary sheltering birds such as fulmars, snow geese, jaegars, king eiders, Lapland longspurs and snow buntings. Other side trips offer opportunities to observe and photograph seals and narwhals as well as ancient stone houses, arctic flowers and tundra. Warm clothing and waterproof boots are advised. **Cost:** $1,075 roundtrip from Montreal, $1,145 from Hamilton. **When:** August. **Contact:** Consolidated Tours Ltd., 550 Sherbrooke St. W., #480, Montreal, PQ Canada H3A 1B9; phone (514)849-1259. *(M)*

CARIBBEAN
Trinidad and Tobago

Field Trips in Trinidad: A variety of day trips in the countryside of Trinidad may be made from a nature center and lodge located in the north-central part of the country.

A downed Bermuda cedar is examined by a group interested in the ecology of Caribbean islands. Wonder Bird Tours offers trips to Trinidad and Tobago for $30 a day. (Martin Ray)

Available are an all-day trip through montane forest, secondary forest and cocoa to the village of Blanchisseuse on the island's north coast for swimming and observing forest wildlife; a day trip to Trinidad's east coast with stops at an agricultural station; an all-day trip to the Aripo Savannah and Area Forest with numerous stops at old roads along the way; a hiking trip up the Aripo Valley to the eastern summit of the Northern Range to observe high-altitude birds; and an evening trip to Caroni Swamp, home of a wide variety of bird life including egrets and scarlet ibis. A typical visit yields sightings of around 150 of the 400 species of birds in Trinidad. **Cost:** $30 a day includes food, accommodations; field trips vary in cost. **When:** Year-round. **Contact:** Wonder Bird Tours, 500 Fifth Ave., New York, NY 10036, USA; phone (212)279-7301.

CENTRAL AMERICA

Guatemala, Honduras and Belize: A flight from Miami to Guatemala City begins a 19-day trip in Central America. Participants drive to Chichicastenango, visit the open-air marketplace and observe the religious ceremonies performed by the local inhabitants. Once in Honduras, a 2-night stay at Copan allows a full-day field trip to the Mayan ceremonial center as well as observation of lowland tropical birds. Participants proceed to Quirigua, a site that contains the tallest monolithic structure in the Mayan world. After a return to Guatemala City for an overnight stay, the group flies to Tikal where they explore the jungle and more Mayan ruins. Tikal also has a rich bird life, including toucans, trogons, hummingbirds and macaws, the species sacred to the Mayas. The trip continues to San Ignacio in Belize, visiting en route Xunantunich, an eastern outpost of the group of Mayan centers that flourished in this district from the fourth to the ninth centuries. Three nights are spent in Belize City overlooking the Caribbean Sea; during the days one of two field trips is by boat to an early logwood town, Crooked Tree Village. The other field trip is to the world's second largest barrier reef, which lies 10 to 14 miles off the Belize coast. The next day participants depart for Miami. **Cost:** $1,430 or $1,678 includes roundtrip transportation from Miami. **When:** January to March, November, December. **Contact:** Questers Tours and Travels, Inc., 257 Park Ave. S., New York, NY 10010, USA; phone (212)673-3120. *(M)*

Belize

Island Exploring: A resort in Belize's Ambergris Cay is the base for a variety of island experiences including shell collecting on nearby beaches, observing tropical birds in the jungle and searching for lobsters in season among rocks along the shore. With the use of snorkeling gear, non-divers may explore an ocean reef by boat to observe many species of tropical fish in the clear waters. For those interested in botany, a large variety of exotic plants and trees is evident in the jungle. **Cost:** On request. **When:** Year-round. **Contact:** Casa Solana, Rt. 1, Box 40, Palacios, TX 77465, USA; phone (512)972-3314. *(M)*

Panama

Canal Zone Wildlife: Participants on a 15-day nature trip observe Panama's diverse bird and animal life. In the lush tropical zone, trip members walk on roads and trails through the jungle watching keel-billed toucans, tree-climbing sloths and the spectacular trogon. In the cooler volcanic mountain region, the varied countryside and rushing streams host motmots, chlorophonias and the resplendent quetzal. In all, about 400 species of birds and mammals are likely to be sighted. The trip doesn't involve standard sightseeing and the accommodations are not luxurious. Several early-morning outings are scheduled for dawn sightings. The trip leader is an expert on Panama's wildlife. **Cost:** $1,830 includes transportation from Miami, food, hotel accommodations, activities, guide. **When:** March. **Contact:** Massachusetts Audubon Society, Lincoln, MA 01773, USA.

EUROPE

England

Stoke Bruerne Walking Tour: Those who prefer quiet countryside can enjoy self-guided walking tours of Great Britain's historical canal system. Hikers start in the Northampton town of Wolverton and walk 8 miles along the Stoke Bruerne canal towpath. Along the way they pass 15 bridges, 1 tunnel and many aqueducts; the first is the Great Ouse Aqueduct, a cast-iron trough set on stone pillars. Just beyond lie the Cosgrove Locks and the old Stratford and Buckingham Branch Canal. Walkers pass these and other sights as well as farms, inns and, in the town of Stoke Bruerne itself, the Waterway Museum. The museum is housed in an old stone mill. Boat rides along the canal are available in Stoke Bruerne. **Cost:** Free. **When:** Year-round. **Contact:** Great Trips, Box 5199, Grand Central Sta., New York, NY 10017, USA.

Greece

Botanical Studies: A 6-week program is designed to familiarize college and advanced high school students with the landscape and

If a tripod isn't available on the trail, a steady shoulder can be called into use for photographing birds and wildlife on nature trips. (Christian Kallen)

summer flora of Greece, as well as many of the country's archaeological sites. A group of 8 students and 2 expedition leaders climbs 4 major mountains—Parnassos, Olympus, Dirfis on the island of Euboea, and Aroania in Arcadia. During the summer months the alpine areas display a wide variety of flora, including many species peculiar to the eastern Mediterranean. In addition to present-day botanical observation, the group studies modern herbal remedies, historical botany and the use of plants by ancient peoples. **Cost:** $650 to $700; partial scholarships are available. **When:** By arrangement. **Contact:** Expedi-

tion Training Institute, Inc., P.O. Box 171, Prudential Ctr. Sta., Boston, MA 02199, USA; phone (617)922-0577. *(M)*

Portugal

Penedageres Birding: Portugal hosts many of Europe's most interesting birds, and the relatively low prices and friendly people there make it an attractive place for bird enthusiasts. A 2-week trip explores a number of different areas of the country. After beginning in Lisbon with a brief look at that city, trip members proceed north to Penedageres National Park for several days of birding, and then drive to

Elvas on the Spanish border to look for great and little bustards and black-shouldered kites. The party then encounters an extremely wide array of bird life as it works its way south through olive groves and cork oak forests, eventually arriving at the Algarve. The trip is led by a professional naturalist. **Cost:** $1,650 includes transportation from Boston, food, accommodations, activities, guide. **When:** June. **Contact:** Massachusetts Audubon Society, Lincoln, MA 01773, USA.

Scotland

Shetland Nature Walk: Hikes of 2 weeks in the Shetland Islands provide participants with opportunities to explore a variety of cultural and natural interests. After arriving at Lerwick, capital of the Shetlands, the group drives to Sumburgh Head and Jarlshof, scene of human habitation from the second millenium B.C. Crossing to the island of Mousal brings the group to a defensive tower built by the Picts over 2,000 years ago. The third day of the trip is spent walking the sheep-cropped sward (there are no roads) on the island of Noss, where striking cliffs are home to colonies of guillemots, razorbills, shags, kittiwakes, gulls and gannets. From Inverness, Land Rovers embark to the Isle of Skye where participants can explore Loch Ness, Urquart Castle and the imposing mountain scenery of Glen Clunie and Glen Shiel. Further sights on the trip include Kyle, Ardvasar, Broadford, Elgol and the Inner Hebrides. **Cost:** $167 a week. **When:** March to October. **Contact:** Aigas Field Centre, Highland Wildlife Enterprises, Aigas House, Beauly, Inverness-shire 1V4 7AD, Great Britain; phone (046371)2443. **(M)**

Highland and Island Trip: A 20-day trip provides an introduction to the natural history and landscape of Scotland. Visits are made to the Highlands, the Shetlands and the Inner Hebrides. Under the guidance of professional naturalists, participants study huge colonies of breeding seabirds, abundant marine life and highland wildlife in regions that include Loch Ness, Inverness and Edinburgh. Travel is on foot and by 4-wheel drive vehicle. **Cost:** $1,490 includes food, accommodations, land transportation, guide. **When:** June, July. **Contact:** Nature Expeditions International, 599 College Ave., Palo Alto, CA 94306, USA; phone (415)328-6572. **(M)**

INDIAN OCEAN

Seychelles

Seychelles Seashores: At the start of a 5-day journey, travelers depart from Nairobi on a 3-hour flight that lands in Mahe, the largest island of the Seychelles archipelago. After relaxing, participants fly to Praslin Island. There they visit the Vallee de Mai, home of the strange coco-de-mer palm which produces double nuts on trees which sometimes reach heights of 100 feet. Interesting birds are also seen, such as elusive bulbuls, fruit pigeons and Praslin black parrots. A boat trip to Cousin Island is of special interest to ornithologists, for among the species encountered are Seychelles turtle doves, wedge-tailed shearwaters and fairy terns. Activities during the next 3 days include cycling around the island of La Digue, snorkeling among colorful tropical fish and visiting Bird Island, known for its 1 million sooty terns. **Cost:** $780 to $1,100 from Nairobi depending on the size of group includes meals, transportation, hotel accommodations, guides. **When:** On request. **Contact:** Abercrombie & Kent International, Inc., 1000 Oak Brook Rd., Oak Brook, IL 60521, USA; phone (312)654-2211.

MEXICO

Catemaco-Palenque Bird Watching: Amateur and professional ornithologists spend 14 days observing birds in 2 eastern Mexican regions where more than 300 species are found. Beginning in Vera Cruz, participants drive south to the Catemaco coastal area for bird watching in lagoons and fields. In the Catemaco area, participants have an excellent possibility of spotting a cotinga, considered one of the world's most beautiful birds. The group then travels south 275 miles to the historic forest region of Palenque, one of Mexico's richest birding grounds, where exotic species such as the white-bellied emerald hummingbird, salty-tailed trogon, keel-billed toucan and rufous mourner can be seen. The Palenque ruins are known for their beautiful temples, and are the most extensive Mayan ruins left. Two experienced ornithologists lead the trip. **Cost:** $495 includes transportation from Vera Cruz, guides, accommodations. **When:** December. **Contact:** Victor Emanuel Nature Tours, 1603 W. Clay, Houston, TX 77019, USA; phone (713)528-3725.

(M)

Baja California

Along the Sea of Cortez: Participants traveling in Land Rovers cover 150 to 250 miles a day on a camping trip to the Baja Peninsula and the west coast of the Mexican

A salt marsh is an impromptu classroom for a group studying tidal environments. Nature Expeditions International offers a 10-day trip on the west coast of the Mexican mainland. (David Roderick)

mainland along the Sea of Cortez. The trip takes place during the whaling season and lasts 3 to 4 weeks; possible side trips include a cruise across the Sea of Cortez aboard the Mazatlan ferry and an overland trip on the Chihuahua al Pacifico Railroad. Whenever practical, participants stay in villages or towns where they can enjoy the local food and people. **Cost:** $20 a day includes overland transportation. **When:** February, March. **Contact:** AMTREK Overland Expeditions, P.O. Box 206, Santa Clara, CA 95052, USA.   *(M)*

Discovering the Sea Life of Baja: A week-long natural history voyage to the islands and lagoons off Baja California offers participants a rare chance to see killer and grey whales, elephant seals, sea lions and other aquatic life in their natural habitats. Members of the expedition, led by several noted scientists, meet in San Diego and live on board the *Qualifier 150.* Desert flora, tide pools, shelling beaches and hikes of varying degrees of difficulty are highlights of the trip. Meals are served on board the boat. **Cost:** $695 includes a $50 tax-deductible contribution to the Museum of Comparative Zoology, which makes participants members of the Friends of the MCZ. **When:** January, February. **Contact:** Museum of Comparative Zoology, The Agassiz Museum, Harvard University, Cambridge, MA 02138, USA; phone (617)495-2463.   *(M)*

Sinaloa

West Coast Nature Trip: Ten days in the area of Mazatlan, on Mexico's west coast, provide opportuni-

ties for study of the area's tropical birds and flora. After an initial night in Mazatlan, the trip moves to a mountain lodge which serves as a base for exploring the unusual ecology of the area: the alpine realm, characterized by pines and oaks, and the tropical zone, characterized by magnolias, arboreal orchids and numerous tropical birds. The next few days are spent in and around San Blas, which lies at the southern edge of the mangrove swamps at the northwestern edge of a volcanic cordillera, and at the northern edge of tropical palm jungles. Boat trips are then taken into the mangrove swamps for further exploration before returning to Mazatlan. **Cost:** $590 includes accommodations, land transportation, most meals, guide. **When:** March, April. **Contact:** Nature Expeditions International, 599 College Ave., Palo Alto, CA 94306, USA; phone (415)328-6572.   (M)

MIDDLE EAST

Israel

Natural History Study Trip: A comprehensive journey explores the natural history, habitats and cultures of Israel during a 2-week stay. Participants travel through a variety of landscapes from snow-capped mountains in the north to vast deserts and the tropical coral reefs of the Gulf of Elat and the Red Sea. Trip members learn about Israel's rich heritage at a number of biblical and archaeological sites, and visit cities such as Jerusalem, Bethlehem and Galilee. Transportation is by chartered bus, with accommodations at the Society for the Protection of Nature in Israel

(SPNI) field study centers. An orientation session is given at UCLA in March several weeks before the trip begins. College credit is available. **Cost:** $675 plus airfare includes accommodations, meals, instruction. **When:** April. **Contact:** UCLA Extension, P.O. Box 24901, Los Angeles, CA 90024, USA; phone (213)825-7093.

Turkey

Watching the Fall Migration: Bird watchers see a wide variety of European species on a 16-day trip to Turkey, Denmark and Sweden. Participants observe early migratory flights in southern Europe as the birds journey to Africa, then catch the peak of the fall migration in northern Europe. The trip begins in Turkey, where participants may see thousands of birds of prey crossing the Bosporus. Also visited are Manyas and Apolyont lakes, where trip members observe both water and land birds, including such Turkish species as Kruper's nuthatch and the red-fronted serin. Travelers then fly north to Scandinavia to see wood pigeons, hooded crows, redwings and bramblings. Accommodations during the trip are in hotels. **Cost:** $2,800 includes roundtrip airfare from Boston. **When:** September. **Contact:** Massachusetts Audubon Society, Lincoln, MA 01773, USA.

Birding the Bosporus: Istanbul is visited on a 10-day bird watching trip that features that city's noted population of eagles. These raptors hover over the Bosporus, a 20-mile-long strait connecting the Sea of Marmara with the Black Sea. Standard trip accommodations at a hotel in Taksim Square offer a base from which to visit the shops and landmarks of Istanbul itself, while supplemental accommodations at a higher elevation offer an eye-level view of the eagles. Daily transport is provided to Camlica Hills where participants can view the movements of raptors. Excursions to other sites such as Lake Apolyont are optional. **Cost:** $400 includes transportation from London. **When:** September. **Contact:** Peregrine Holidays, Town and Gown Travel, 40/41 S. Parade, Summertown, Oxford OX2 7JP, Great Britain; phone 511341.

PACIFIC

South Sea Island Study: After flying from Los Angeles to Noumea, 15 travelers are led by a biology professor on a tour through New Caledonia, New Hebrides and the Solomon Islands for 22 days. While in New Caledonia, group members boat out to the barrier reef, visit offshore islands and drive to Boulouparis for a day in the field searching for insects, plants and birds, especially the cagou and fruit bat. In the New Hebrides, visits are made to Mele Village and to the botanical gardens, aquarium and aviary in the forests of Mt. Lama. In the Solomon Islands, participants explore the tropical jungles and highlands of Honiara and visit traditional Melanesian villages where they may watch shell money being made on Laulase and ride in villagers' war canoes. The chief conservationist for the trust territory joins group members as they

Participants on a nature trip in the South Pacific prepare to set sail in a crude catamaran. Offshore islands and barrier reefs are among the locations visited on a 35-day Goodtravel Tours trip. (Goodtravel Tours)

visit the floating garden islands in Koror, investigate caves and hike along jungle trails to waterfalls. A day in Guam allows time to observe the influence of Spanish, American and Chamorros cultures. **Cost:** $2,997 includes roundtrip transportation from Los Angeles, guide, hotel accommodations, meals. **When:** August. **Contact:** Aventura Natural History Tours and Travel, 508 N. Sierra Dr., Beverly Hills, CA 90210, USA; phone (213)276-6081.

Hawaii

Island Photo Safari: Participants on a 1-day photographic outing on Hawaii make an early morning departure from a resort hotel in 4-wheel drive air-conditioned station wagons. Coastal and inland locations are visited. In the Waipio Valley, group members hike between wooded slopes to a sandy beach; traveling the Saddle Road, participants visit the Parker Ranch backcountry which is inhabited by wild boar and bighorn sheep; trips are made to both active and extinct volcanoes, 2 of which are over 13,000 feet. Soft drinks and snacks are provided at picnic sites along the route. **Cost:** $45 includes food, transportation. **When:** Year-round. **Contact:** Big Island Adventures, P.O. Box 2639, Kailua-Kona, HI 96740, USA; phone (808)329-2676.

(M)

Volcanoes of the Pacific: The island of Hawaii provides enthusiasts with an opportunity to observe and learn about active volcanoes on a week-long visit to Hawaii Volcanoes National Park and Ka Lae. Four days are spent on the rim of Kilauea Crater exploring the fire pit of Halemaumau, Thurston Lava Tube, Devastation Trail and Chain of Craters. The expedition then proceeds part of the way up Mauna Loa and into Bird Park before arriving at the historic City of Refuge. From the Kona Coast, the expedition travels to the 227,000-acre Parker Ranch, isolated Waipio Valley and the Kohala Mountains for further study of human and natural history of the island. College credit is available. **Cost:** $859. **When:** December. **Contact:** Wilderness Walks, 2301 W. Raye St., Seattle, WA 98199, USA; phone (206)282-2301.

SOUTH AMERICA

Wildlife Observation: A 30-day trip to several areas of South America begins with a 10-day visit to the Falkland Islands where participants observe colonies of rockhopper, Magellanic, gentoo, macaroni and king penguins in the most extensive penguin rookeries outside of Antarctica. Group members then fly to Tierra del Fuego, the southernmost tip of the continent in Argentina, for several days of hiking and bird watching at Lapataia National Park. After a few days in the highlands of Ecuador, participants fly to the Galapagos Islands. The last week is spent cruising from island to island while observing and photographing animal and bird life. Local naturalists accompany the group during the journey. **Cost:** $2,800 includes roundtrip airfare

from Miami. **When:** January. **Contact:** South American Wilderness Adventures, 1760 Solano Ave., Berkeley, CA 94707, USA; phone (415)524-5111. *(M)*

Argentina

South American Nature Hikes: After a flight from Miami or Los Angeles participants spend 28 days hiking, camping and taking nature walks in the Lakes District of Chile and a similar area in Argentina. A day of sightseeing in Santiago precedes a flight to Valdivia and the actual beginning of the hiking and camping. Forests, lakes, rivers and glacier-covered volcanoes are explored during several days in the Lakes District. At the end of the trail hikers board a ferry and cross montane lakes into Argentina. Ascents of the volcanoes and granite spires near San Carlos de Bariloche provide options for group members hiking through countryside that is very much like the Chilean lake region. Buenos Aires is the departure point for return flights to the United States. Those who have additional time can extend the journey for 1 week to hike and camp on Easter Island. **Cost:** On request. **When:** November. **Contact:** Andean Outfitters, P.O. Box 4547, Aspen, CO 81611, USA; phone (303)925-3371. *(M)*

Ecuador

Galapagos Island Voyage: Passengers board the Ecuadorian vessel *Neptuno* for 4-, 5- and 8-day trips to the Galapagos Islands. Giant turtles weighing over 500 pounds can be seen along with land and marine iguanas, penguins, cormorants, sea lions, frigate birds, flamingoes and

The world's only marine iguana population is found in the Galapagos, where Ecuadorian Tours offers 4- to 8-day trips for studying the island's tropical life forms. (Galapagos Tourist Corp.)

blue-footed boobies. Passengers make wildlife visits to Bartolome Island, Buccaneer Bay and Charles Darwin Station, an active scientific research center. Opportunities are also available to visit the mainland, including the port city of Guayaquil, where cocoa beans are dried in the middle of the street and stevedores load bananas and balsa wood cargoes. Trips to the cities of Quito, Ibarra, Cuenca and Banos, the jungle gateway, give participants a varied view of Ecuadorian life. **Cost:** $5 to $670 depending on destination, length, and number of people. **When:** Year-round. **Contact:** Ecuadorian Tours, Amazonas 339, P.O. Box 2605, Quito, Ecuador; phone 520-777 or 528-177.

Surinam

Guianan Rain Forest Birding: A trip into the forests of Surinam (formerly Dutch Guiana) is designed for the serious bird watcher. Portions of the journey are rugged, with a great deal of difficult trail walking and an overnight stay in a jungle camp at the base of Voltzberg Mountain. In the past, groups have also encountered heavy rains. Participants should make every effort to search out the rare species indigenous to the area. Some of the birds encountered may be capped herons, white bellbirds, cayenne jays and over 25 species of raptors. Three days are spent at the Brownsburg Nature Park and 5 days at the Raleigh Falls-Voltzberg Nature Reserve. Several open savanna forests and coastal marsh areas are visited but the majority of the time is spent in undisturbed rain forest. **Cost:** $1,351 includes roundtrip airfare from New York. **When:** March. **Contact:** Wonder Bird Tours, 500 Fifth Ave., New York, NY 10036, USA; phone (212)279-7301.

Venezuela

Birds of Latin America: An 18-day

exploration of the natural history of Venezuela focuses on the numerous species of birds which can be seen. From Caracas the expedition travels by bus to wildlife areas such as Guatopo National Park, where participants explore evergreen rain forests and view some of the 400 species of birds living there. The trip continues through river valleys, deserts and farm country. At the Chichiriviche salt flats vast numbers of herons, egrets, ibis and other shore birds can be seen. After crossing a 13,000-foot pass high in the Andes, the group travels to La Azulita Road and University Forest areas to search for quetzals, toucans, woodcreepers, warblers and tanagers. The expedition continues to Henri Pittier National Park which contains 500 species of birds. In the lowlands at Camaguan participants view raptors, tree ducks and storks, as well as wildlife such as spectacled alligators. The trip is led by an associate professor of biology. **Cost:** $1,454 includes transportation from New York, guide, hotel accommodations, meals. **When:** January. **Contact:** Aventura Natural History Tours and Travel, 508 N. Sierra Dr., Beverly Hills, CA 90210, USA; phone (213)276-6081.

UNITED STATES

North American Environmental Study: Participants travel through a wide range of landscapes during an expedition that surveys the natural history, ecology and conservation of 51 distinct environments in the United States. Some of the environments studied include a northern hardwood forest, the North Atlantic intertidal zone, a coral reef, the Sonoran Desert, a Pacific Northwest rain forest, a Caribbean pinewood hammock and the White Cedar Swamp. Students and instructors participate in discussion groups, field trips, collecting trips, research and reading. The focus of the course is on ecological balance. **Cost:** On request. **When:** On request. **Contact:** Trailside Country School, Killington, VT 05751, USA; phone (802)422-3532.

Alaska

Mt. McKinley Adventures: A camping facility near Mt. McKinley National Park offers activities such as hiking, fishing, panning for gold and observing wildlife. Among the 35 kinds of mammals in central Alaska are caribous, grizzly bears, moose, mountain sheep, wolves, foxes, beavers and martens. Trips to and from Mt. McKinley National Park are made each Monday, Thursday and Saturday, and excursions of 3 to 4 days offer opportunities to canoe and photograph wildlife. Also offered are wilderness workshops with field discussions and evening seminars around a campfire. The camp is located 2 miles from Wonder Lake and includes 55 acres of tundra and spruce woods above Moose Creek. Facilities include cabins for 2 to 7 persons with wood stoves and cold running water; there is no central heating or modern plumbing, and electricity is available only for a few hours a day. Family-style meals are served. Vacation packages of 2 to 8 days are available. **Cost:** $30 for transportation to and from Mt. McKinley National Park; $504 for

2-week workshop; $472 for 8 days includes cabin facilities, food, guided trips; $80 a day for sourdough vacations or wilderness workshops includes transportation. **When:** June to September. **Contact:** Camp Denali, McKinley Park, AK 99755, USA; phone (907)683-2290, winter (907)683-2302. *(M)*

Arctic Birding: A 14-day expedition offers bird watchers an opportunity to observe several unusual arctic species during their prime migration season. Group members spend at least 3 days on Gambell Island at the southern end of the Bering Strait; Mongolian plovers, dotterels, bramblings, white wagtails and McKay's buntings may be seen from the island as the birds migrate from Siberia. Bird watching groups are limited to no more than 12. **Cost:** On request. **When:** May. **Contact:** Merlin Birding Tours, P.O. Box 19687, Houston, TX 77024, USA; phone (713)461-2589.

Arizona

Sonoran Desert Studies: Up to 60 participants and 6 qualified scientists and educators meet for 5 days of field studies in the Sonoran Desert. The institute, located 25 miles north of Tucson at the foot of the Catalina Mountains, is the base for daily sessions which include 3 field trips; afternoon study periods with optional workshops in environmental education, nature photography and water conservation; and a variety of evening programs. The course seeks to clarify the relationships between the plants, animals and physical characteristics of the desert, with an emphasis on how earth and life forms relate

rather than on classification or identification. Participants are required to furnish their own camping gear, though all food is provided by an experienced chef. **Cost:** $145 includes instruction, meals, services, workshops, registration. **When:** May. **Contact:** Audubon Institute of Desert Ecology, 1642 N. Westridge Ave., Tucson, AZ 85705, USA; phone (602)743-7862.

California

Mountain Field Studies: Participants on a 6-week backpacking field biology course in the Sierra Nevadas hike through mountainous terrain to the region's lakes and meadows. Hikers study wildlife communities and gain a better understanding of the wilderness during 3 interrelated courses taught by experienced naturalists; all of the courses stress self-reliance and learning by doing. Participants must be capable of hiking with backpacks for extended periods. **Cost:** $445 includes tuition, application fee, meals. **When:** April to June. **Contact:** Wilderness Studies, University of California Extension, Santa Cruz, CA 95064, USA; phone (408)429-2822.

Glacier Study: Students interested in the way glaciers form, grow and deteriorate spend 5 days on the McClure Glacier in the Tuolumne area of Yosemite Park. Most of the time group members are at altitudes above 10,000 feet and must do quite a bit of rock and ice scrambling on and around the glacier. A base camp at Mt. Lyell is used for most of the 5-day period, with students making forays onto the ice to study glacial structure

Seen close up, through binoculars or a telephoto lens, the colorful plummage and graceful form of the great blue heron is a rewarding sight on a birding expedition. (Henry Lloyd Bunker IV)

and motion. More general topics are also covered, including glacial types, distribution, structure and landforms. Participants can either pack their own gear or arrange for pack mules to carry it. **Cost:** $50 includes course tuition. **When:** August. **Contact:** Yosemite Natural History Association, P.O. Box 545, Yosemite National Pk., CA 95389, USA; phone (209)372-4532.

Florida

Kissimmee Wildlife Trek: Accompanying wildlife biologists on daylong research trips, participants observe over 30 varieties of birds and animals in their natural habitat. The major part of the 50-mile trip is in a 125,000-acre wilderness area of Glades County. It is the only unspoiled part that remains of the lower valley of the Kissimmee River. Participants see scrub jays which are found nowhere else in the world and endangered species such as red-cockaded woodpeckers and bald eagles. In the treeless prairies, dwarf palmetto palms, burrowing owls, gopher tortoises and indigo snakes are found. Evergreen swamps are the home of short-tailed hawks, wild turkeys and wild boars. At Lake Okeechobee participants view otters, alligators and a dozen species of large water birds. Wild oranges, grapefruit, lemons and limes are abundant in the unlogged cypress swamps. Photography and observation blinds are available on request. Groups are limited to 4 persons during the sunrise-to-sunset trip. **Cost:** $75 from Lake Placid includes meals, transportation, guide. **When:** Year-round. **Contact:** Florida Wilderness Wildlife Tours, 4005 S. Main St., Gainesville, FL 32601, USA; phone (904)376-6481.

Swampland Wildlife Study: For 11 days participants explore the terrain and inhabitants of the Everglades of southwest Florida under the guidance of a professional naturalist. Following a visit to refuges containing the last vestiges of the tropical hardwood forest that once covered Miami, participants walk through Paradise Key on the Anhinga and Gumbo Limbo trails in Everglades National Park to watch waterfowl, wading birds, alligators, herons, egrets and ibises. A day and a half at John Pennekamp Coral Reef State Park allows adventurers to explore a mangrove swamp and hardwood and mahogany hammocks, as well as to cruise over the reef in a glass-bottomed boat. Crossing the Tamiami Trail, trip members look for the rare Everglades kite and slog through the swamp waters of the Fakahat-

A child studies a deadly Amanita during a field lesson in mushroom identification. Conservation Summit offers special young people's nature study programs in the Great Smoky Mountains. (Joyce Murlless)

chee Strand in search of ghost orchids. Participants are apt to see roseate spoonbills, reddish egrets and great white herons on trips to J.N. (Ding) Darling National Wildlife Refuge. A boat trip through part of the Ten Thousand Islands, a day at the National Audubon Society's Corkscrew Swamp Sanctuary, and visits to Captiva, Marco and Sanibel islands are part of the itinerary. Participants return to Miami at the end of the trip. **Cost:** $695 in March, $655 in November includes meals, accommodations, guide, transportation from Miami. **When:** March, November. **Contact:** Questers Tours and Travel, Inc., 257 Park Ave. S., New York, NY 10010, USA; phone (212)673-3120. *(M)*

Georgia

Sea Islands Photography Workshop: The teeming flora and fauna of several islands off the coast of Georgia are subjects for a 1-week nature photography course. The course emphasizes environmental color photography, macro work, specialized equipment and wet-weather shooting. The group camps on an isolated private island, venturing out by boat to several other islands. Aside from a wide variety of marine life, participants may photograph the inhabitants of freshwater ponds, tidal creeks and mudflats, which include deer, alligators, shore birds and nesting osprey. Advanced photographic skills are not required, but participants must bring their own equipment and film. Swimming ability is also required, and camping experience is helpful. **Cost:** $305 includes camping equipment, food, boat transportation. **When:** June. Con-

tact: Wilderness Southeast, Rt. 3, Box 619 AA, Savannah, GA 31406, USA; phone (912)355-8008. *(M)*

Kentucky

Southern Winter Studies: Participants join in a variety of nature-related activities in the Kentucky countryside at a nature center staffed by ornithologists, wildlife biologists and naturalists. The 1- to 3-day winter programs include a study of the history of the area's rivers at Paris Landing State Park, bird migration studies, eagle searches and nature walks. A high point of the winter season is a weekend trek through the Land Between the Lakes during which participants study the golden eagle. Slides and lectures are usually combined with the outdoor activities. **Cost:** On request. **When:** November to March. **Contact:** TVA-Land Between the Lakes, Golden Pond, KY 42231, USA; phone (502)924-5602.

Maine

Photography off the Maine Coast: On a 7-day expedition to an island off the coast of Maine, nature photographers are given technical and artistic instruction to improve their skills. After meeting in Rockport, participants sail in a 22-foot dory to an island in Penobscot Bay to begin their photographic studies, which center mostly on the 10-acre is-

land's environment. A naturalist/photographer leads, critiques and discusses techniques for shooting in the field. In the afternoons there are nature walks and ample time for taking pictures. Most of the work is done with color film, but black-and-white photography is also encouraged. The program is designed for serious photographers who are interested in the wilderness. Participants should bring their own camera equipment, film, sleeping bag, tent and rain gear. Basic survival and wilderness living training is also provided. The program ends in Rockport with group and individual critiques of the week's photographs. **Cost:** $195 includes meals on the island. **When:** July, August. **Contact:** Island/Wilderness Expeditions, Ltd., Rockport, ME 04856, USA; phone (207)236-4788.

Minnesota

Nature Trips: An extremely wide variety of short courses, walks and participatory activities is offered out of 3 nature centers in Minnesota's Hennepin County Park Reserve District. The Whitney H. Eastman Nature Center is located in Elm Creek Park Reserve, the Lowry Center is in Carver Park and the Richardson Nature Center is in Hyland Lake Park Reserve. All feature spring and summer courtship and nesting grounds for great blue herons, boardwalks that span marshes and swamps, and large numbers of prairie wildflowers. The scheduled activities all last several hours and include searching out and identifying autumn wild edibles; examining animal architecture; walking in meadows with an interpreter; building log cabins; using plants decoratively; tracking at night using fluorescent powder; and many other classes, hikes and activities. Reservations are needed for some programs. **Cost:** Free. **When:** Year-round. **Contact:** Hennepin County Park Reserve District, Rt. 1, Box 32, Maple Plain, MN 55359, USA; phone (612)473-4693.

New York

Camping in the Adirondacks: During 1-week camping trips in upstate New York, families and individuals explore the natural environment through a variety of classes and special programs, as well as through independent studies. On the 1,300 acres of Silver Bay, participants study the homes and habits of nearby birds, mammals and insects; instruction is also given in using solar energy, cooking in camp and teaching creatively about the environment. Group members may take side trips to historic Fort Ticonderoga, Fort Mt. Hope and the Adirondack Museum. Swimming, boating and crafts activities are also included in the itinerary. **Cost:** $195 to $277 includes lodging, meals, guide. **When:** July. **Contact:** Conservation Summit, National Wildlife Federation, 1412 16th St. NW, Washington, DC 20036, USA; phone (202)797-6800.

North Carolina

Blue Ridge Ecology: Participants on a 6-day camping and study trip in the Blue Ridge Mountains study the plants, geology and wildlife of the region. The trip begins near Asheville and participants can choose from a number of field trips, evening and afternoon programs, and independent study trips to complete the itinerary. Group members study freshwater biology, natural art, camp cooking and identification of edible and medicinal plants. In addition, participants may swim, hike and take part in a variety of team sports as well as more traditional social activities such as clog dancing and ballad singing. Children's programs are also available. **Cost:** $200 to $270 includes lodging, meals, use of recreational facilities. **When:** June. **Contact:** Conservation Summit, National Wildlife Federation, 1412 16th St. NW, Washington, DC 20036, USA; phone (202)797-6800.

Tennessee

Wildflower Photography: Amateur photographers make 6 excursions from Gatlinburg on a 3-day exploration of the Great Smoky Mountains during the late spring wildflower season. A guide instructs participants on the basics of camera equipment as well as techniques and aesthetics of color transparency flower photography. Before turning the photographers loose to take pictures of flowers, the guide locates and describes some of the more than 250 kinds of plants blooming in the area. All the nature walks are roundtrip, except for one on the Appalachian Trail where special transportation arrangements are made. Participants should arrange their own transportation to Gatlinburg and supply their own camera equipment. Lodging is available at a number of nearby motels. **Cost:** $60 includes guide. **When:** May. **Contact:** Wilderness Adventure, 904 Mt. Hol-

yoke Pl., Swarthmore, PA 19081, USA; phone (215)543-4639.

Texas

Padre Island Beachcombing: The south end of Padre Island, a long, slender formation off the east coast of Texas, is the site of day-long beachcombing and history trips. The island's written history stretches back 100 years before the Pilgrims landed at Plymouth Rock and informal instruction is presented on such topics as the cannibalistic Karankawa Indians. About 60 miles are traveled by 4-wheel drive vehicle, and participants number about 4. The deserted beaches offer collectors driftwood, ropes, shells and other flotsam and jetsam, and bags are provided for collecting. Several stops are made, including one at the Lost Cities area before the principal stop at the Mansfield jetties. Participants bring their own food. **Cost:** $25 for adults, $5 for youths age 15 and under includes transportation to and from Port Isabel, drinking water, ice chest, collecting bags, guide. **When:** By arrangement. **Contact:** Don and Judy Veach, P.O. Box 663, Port Isabel, TX 78578, USA; phone (512)943-2270.

Utah

Desert Canyon Tours: Departing from Moab, participants explore desert landscapes carved out by the Green and Colorado rivers in Canyonlands and Arches national parks. Activities in Canyonlands include 1-day journeys across the White Rim, Walking Rocks and Grand View Point areas, as well as visits to Washerwoman Arch, Monument Basin and the Green River

A gray jay eyes a bird feeder in Washington. Nature hikes up Washington's Mt. Rainier are offered by Wilderness Walks of Seattle. (Christian Kallen)

and Lavender canyons. Half-day trips are also available; included are a trek through Arches National Park and hikes to the Gemini Bridges, Hurrah Pass, Porcupine Rim and Dead Horse Point State Park. Backpacking tours of 1 to 8 days are offered and activities include learning to identify the region's wild foods. Raft tours down the Colorado and Green rivers are also available. **Cost:** $20 for full day, $12 for half day includes lunch, transportation. **When:** May to September. **Contact:** Lin Ottinger Tours, 137 N. Main, Moab, UT 84532, USA; phone (801)259-7312.

Washington

Exploring Mt. Rainier: Participants learn about the human and natural history of Mt. Rainier National Park through a series of daily hikes, interpretive nature programs and supplemental readings. For 6 days, hikers explore the forests and flowering meadows of the park when wildflowers are at their peak and the weather at its best. Some of the destinations may include Sunrise, Chinook Pass, Mazama Ridge, Indian Henry's Campground and Emerald Ridge, where mountain goats are often sighted. In addition to the natural history provided by the trip leaders, evening programs are offered at the lodge and campgrounds. Participants may choose between accommodations at Cougar Rock Campground or Paradise Inn. A scenic flight over the mountain is also available at extra cost. College credit is available. **Cost:** $90 includes guides. **When:** August. **Contact:** Wilderness Walks, 2301 W. Raye St., Seattle, WA 98199, USA; phone (206)282-2301.

Wyoming

Nature Camp: A walking trip emphasizing ecological relationships provides participants with a well-rounded view of the plant and animal life in the Wind River Range and the Whiskey Basin Game Sanctuary. During 12-day sessions, groups of up to 14 people and a leader engage in carefully planned field trips. The trips are not intended to stress distance or hiking but rather the observation and interpretation of nature. The camp accommodations consist of log cabins outfitted with electric lights, electric heat and modern bath facilities. **Cost:** $300 includes accommodations, meals, field trips, instruction. **When:** June to August. **Contact:** Audubon Camp in the West, P.O. Box 3232, Boulder, CO 80307, USA; phone (303)499-0219; or in summer, Trail Lake Ranch, Dubois, WY 83513, USA; phone (307)455-2457.

RESOURCES

Clubs and Associations

Aigas Field Centre
Aigas House
Inverness-shire 1V4 7AD, Great Britain
Phone (0463 71)2443

American Forestry Association
1319 18th St. NW
Washington, DC 20036, USA
Phone (202)467-5810

Appalachian Trail Conference
Box 236
Harpers Ferry, WV 25425, USA
Phone (304)535-6331

Assn. Experiment in International Living
Otesage, Upper Wyche
Malvern, Worcestershire WR14 4EN
Great Britain

Brathay Exploration Group
Brathay Hall, Ambleside
Westmoreland, Great Britain

Camping Club of Great Britain
and Ireland
11 Lower Grosvenor Pl.
London SW1, Great Britain

Ducks Unlimited
National Headquarters, Box 66300
Chicago, IL 60666, USA

Environmental Action
1346 Connecticut Ave. NW
Washington, DC 20036, USA
Phone (202)659-9682

Federation of Western Outdoor Clubs
3340 Mayfield Ave.
San Bernardino, CA 92405, USA

Field Studies Council
9 Devereux Ct.
Strand, London WC2, Great Britain

Hebergement a la Ferme
Federation des Agricotours du Quebec
515 ave. Viger, 2e etage
Montreal, PQ Canada

National Audubon Society
950 3rd Ave.
New York, NY 19022, USA
Phone (212)832-3200

Nature Conservancy
Attingham Park, Shrewsbury
Shropshire, Great Britain

Rocky Mountain Nature Association
Estes Park, CO 80517, USA

Sierra Club
1050 Mills Tower, 220 Bush St.
San Francisco, CA 94104, USA
Phone (415)981-8634

Wilderness Society
1901 Pennsylvania Ave. NW
Washington, DC 20006, USA
Phone (202)293-2732

CARAVANNING

Summer is arriving on the Great Plains, and in the clear light of morning the draft horses and mules are hitched up to the wagons. Dressed in traditional pioneer clothing—a bonnet and a long dress, or a buckskin shirt—you climb into your wagon and grab the reins. A new day is beginning, but instead of contemplating the long and tortuous route from Missouri to Oregon, you are looking forward to a week-long taste of the 19th century. It took the pioneers months of hard traveling to reach America's Pacific seaboard, but today you can spend a week on a wagon train in the Dakotas, follow old rutted routes through Kansas or cross the border from Nevada to California over the pass made notorious by the ill-fated Donner party.

The frontier-seeking spirit of the people who migrated westward across the continent in search of a new life must be entrenched in all of us. As wagons jolt along 100-year-old tracks, that spirit comes to the fore, giving you a rush of excitement and a first-hand experience of our pioneering heritage. The landscape is framed in the arch of the wagon's canvas cover as wooden-spoked wheels roll unevenly down the trail. At day's end, just as it must have happened over a century ago, the wagon master calls his transient community to a halt. The wagons circle up for the night, and a hearty dinner is cooked and eaten in the declining light of the long summer dusk.

Wagon travel is almost synonymous with the Westward Movement in the American mythos, but wagons carrying families in search of a home crossed other continents as well. For the gypsies traveling through Europe and Asia in previous centuries, their houses were their wagons and their real estate was the spot of ground they camped on for the night. If this lifestyle is appealing, you might consider traveling in a gypsy wagon through the West Funen countryside in Denmark; or in a caravan or on your own through the Provence region of southern France.

Whether in North America or Europe, Denmark or Dakota, wagon travel provides a means of reliving an era now past. You learn to appreciate the hardships—and rewards—of traveling in search of a homeland, carrying all you own with you. Some of these trips provide the clothes of the homesteaders or gypsies to authenticate your experience; some of them visit abandoned ghost towns or re-create a nighttime outlaw raid. And the pioneer spirit prevailing over most of these latter-day migrations lets the imagination wander freely as a breeze crossing the rolling grassland. □

Modern-day citizens don pioneer garb to relive the days of America's westward migration on a Dakota wagon train trip. (South Dakota Tourism)

CARAVANNING

EUROPE

Denmark

Wagon Trek: Travelers spend time getting to know the countryside during a 1-week trip in a covered wagon. Participants drive the horse, harness and unharness it, make camp and put the horse out to feed. The journey runs through the West Funen countryside along the coasts and through woods and villages, where one can stock up on provisions and visit the churches, manor houses, castles and inns. The wagon is equipped with 2 berths, sleeping bags, kitchen equipment, crockery and cutlery, cool-box and two gas rings. At the start of the journey instructions are given in taking care of the horse as well as wagon handling and map reading. **Cost:** $300 June to August, $163 September to May. **When:** Year-round. **Contact:** Danish National Tourist Office, 75 Rockefeller Plaza, New York, NY 10019, USA; phone (212)582-2802.

France

Gypsy Caravan in Provence: Riding in a horse-drawn gypsy wagon through the Provence region of southern France gives travelers a week-long break from modern life. The vehicle is an authentic gypsy wagon restored in the style of the 1920s, with corner closets, dressers, wall cupboards and a full bed inside. Each wagon can sleep four comfortably. Leaving from the village of Entraigues-sur-Sorgue 9 miles north of Avignon, the caravan takes one of several routes: either through the plain of Carpentras to the vineyards of Cotes-du-Rhone at the foot of the mountains, or through the valley of Le Luberon toward the Mediterranean. Travel can be either by individual wagon or by group caravan, and food is purchased in villages along the way. **Cost:** $250 to $1,400 depending on duration and season. **When:** Year-round. **Contact:** Joel and Christine Moyne, Domaine de Saint-Sauveur, 84320 Entraigues-sur-Sorgue, France; phone (90)83-16-26.

UNITED STATES

Kansas

Pioneer Caravan: Traveling by wagon train along the grass-covered ruts of the Smoky Hill Trail, participants re-create pioneer days on a 3-day trip in western Kansas. Eight to 12 covered wagons are pulled by teams of horses and mules on the 55-mile trip, and passengers may choose to walk or ride a saddle horse alongside the caravan. Evenings are spent around the campfire listening to music provided by trip members and stories of drivers and local farmers. In an attempt to make the journey as authentic as possible, wagons circle up at night, traditional meals are served and pioneer dress is available. Luggage is transported by modern means to campsites each evening and participants' vehicles are moved to the end of the trail by the operator. **Cost:** $329 includes meals, sleeping gear. **When:** June to August. **Contact:** Wagons Ho, P.O. Box 1879, Quinter, KS 67752, USA; phone (913)754-3347. *(M)*

Travelers come to know their horses well on a week-long journey by gypsy wagon through the French countryside of Provence. (Joel Moyne)

South Dakota

Great Plains Wagon Trains: Traveling in covered wagons, group members traverse forested river bottoms and rolling prairies during a 4-day journey along the Grand River. The trip aims to recapture the feeling of America's westward migrations of pioneers. **Cost:** $175 special trip for South Dakotans, $278 for others includes meals, tents, transportation to and from Pierre. **When:** June. **Contact:** Dakota Wagon Train, Box 303, Eagle Butte, SD 57625, USA; phone (605)964-7971.

Wyoming

Wagon Train Trip: The Teton National Forest is the setting for a re-creation of pioneer wagon trains, with trips ranging in length from 2 to 6 days. The trips begin and end in Jackson and travel through the surrounding area. Besides riding in the wagon train, activities include hiking into forested areas, making horseback trips into the high country, observing and photographing wildlife, and studying flora and fauna. Evening activities are geared to the creation of a pioneer atmosphere, with singing, storytelling and group campfire cooking. **Cost:** $100 to $250 depending on length of trip includes meals, camping equipment, car shuttle. **When:** May to September. **Contact:** L.D. Frome, Outfitter, RFD, Afton, WY 83110, USA; phone (307)886-5240. *(M)*

HORSEPACKING

Picking its way down the steep trail, your horse maneuvers around the narrow switchbacks with surprising ease and agility. Rocking back and forth in the saddle with each step of your mount, you lean back to help take the weight off the horse's shoulders and forelegs during the descent. Your eyes take in more than the surrounding scenery—they watch the other horses ahead in line and check the sides of the trail for hazards the horses might not see. Your body is relaxed in the saddle, yet ready in case the horse should suddenly spook or stumble. Moving together as a team, you work to reach camp safely.

Horsepacking is more than a lazy man's way of seeing the backcountry. At its best it is an adventure where the understanding and cooperation between human and horse are essential to the success of the journey. It is a chance to live and work with animals while at the same time enjoying the wilderness, visiting areas often too difficult to reach on foot or by overland vehicle.

Horses and humans have been working together for centuries, and trips are available in a wide variety of areas—from dude ranches in Arizona to trails in the Alaskan wilds, from the Vosges of France and the high passes of the Hindu Kush to the slopes of Mt. Kenya. In all these places, people can experience the excitement of rides ranging from day and weekend outings to month-long expeditions.

In addition to the variety of trips and places, the animals vary too. Horsepacking is really a misnomer, for it covers trips on mules, donkeys and zebroids, as well as travel with a variety of horse breeds, from Arabians to Andalucians.

Horse trips are available to nearly anyone. Some are designed for those with little riding experience. These usually consist of short day and overnight trips along clear trails. Riders don't have to worry about caring for the horse's needs or packing the camp gear on these trips because the guides do all the work. On other trips designed for the more experienced rider, trip members participate directly with the daily chores of saddling, bridling, grooming, feeding and watering the horses. The mount you ride becomes your responsibility for the duration of the trip. Here your horse may not be the typical stable variety but wilder and harder to handle.

Horsepacking trips are unique. There are few adventures in which so much depends on your willingness and ability to handle, understand and cope with a large animal on a daily basis. The excitement of the scenery, the wildlife and the people met en route are made richer by facing the challenges of exploring the world with an equine companion. □

Horsepackers ford a stream in the Spanish hill country. WEXAS offers horsepacking trips to Andalucia from May to October. (Diane Hucks)

HORSEPACKING

AFRICA

Morocco
Moroccan High Country by Mule:
A group of 6 to 12 trip members
with native Moroccan and French
guides explores the Moroccan high
country during a 15-day journey.
After leaving Marrakech, participants walk and ride through the
valleys and bush west of Lakhdar.
The native guides provide useful
insights for participants as they
lead the group through local villages into mountainous areas. Traversing the red earth at Tichki and
the Valley of Tessaout, participants
learn to care for their pack and
transportation animals. Campsites
are chosen as the trip progresses,
with tents providing cover. **Cost:**
$800 includes food, equipment,
guide. **When:** June to September.
Contact: Explorator, 16 place de le
Madeleine, 75008, Paris, France;
phone 266-66-24.

ASIA

Afghanistan
**Horsepacking into the Hindu
Kush:** A month-long horseback trip
starts in Kabul and travels through
northern Afghanistan by bus or
jeep during the first week, visiting
Mazar-i-Sharif, a pilgrimage spot
for Moslems, and Tashkargan.
After returning to Kabul the horsepacking begins by crossing 4 passes between 14,000 and 8,000 feet in
the Hindu Kush. The exact route of
the expedition depends on the condition of the passes, but should
include Bamiyan Valley, with its
colossal Buddhas and cave cities
devastated by Genghis Khan, and
the 7 lakes of Band-i-Amir, as well
as an ancient Buddhist monastery
at Dokhtar Nirshirvan. The expedition spends the nights within the
protection of friendly villages, and
meals reflect the diet of the local
people. Participants should be ac-
customed to long hours in the
saddle. **Cost:** $2,500 from New
York includes all costs. **When:** May.
Contact: Wind Over Mountain, Box
1380, Telluride, CO 81435, USA;
phone (303)728-3651.

AUSTRALASIA

New Zealand
Horsepacking on North Island: A
trek to the Maori territory of the
Tuhoe tribe takes hikers around
North Island's Urewera country,
including 5 days in Urewera National Park. Accompanied by
packstock, the group begins the
trip at Mataatua Marae in Ruata-
huna between Rotorua and Wairoa,
following the Whakatane River
through native forest abounding in
wildlife and bird life. Following a
circular route along the valley floor,
hikers camp at Hanamahihi after
crossing the river at Tarakena Rapids. The group may proceed to
Ohaua Marae near an old Maori
meetinghouse, Marumaru and
Waikarewhenua, depending on the
length of the trip. The history and
natural beauty of the area lend
themselves to activities such as
photography, fishing, swimming,
nature study or horse trekking.
Weekend, 3- and 7-day variations
are also available. Hikers need only
provide and carry their personal

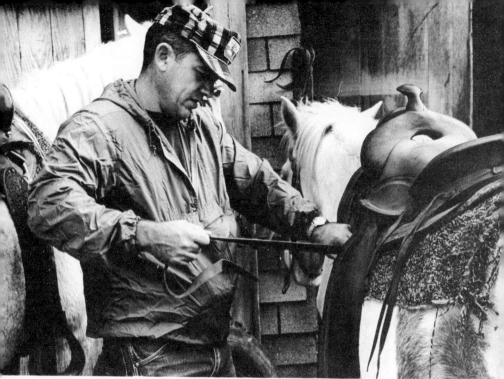

A rider cinches up a saddle in the hills of West Virginia. Horsepacking trips are offered throughout the United States. (West Virginia Dept. of Commerce)

effects. **Cost:** $39 to $145, with children's rates. **When:** November to April. **Contact:** Te Rehuwai Safaris Ltd., P.O. Box 2111, Rotorua, New Zealand; phone 89-063.

CANADA

Alberta

Willmore Wilderness Ride: A 15-day horseback trip takes participants into Willmore Wilderness Park accompanied by pack stock and a covered wagon. The trip begins with a flight from Grand Prairie to a base camp for the first night's stay before departing with a covered wagon to Dead Horse Meadows. The next 11 days are spent moving from camp to camp accompanied by pack stock, occasionally making a 2-night stopover for an unencumbered day trip. The Continental Divide is crossed several times as the route winds through alpine meadows and mountain scenery in the Sheep Creek and Intersection Mountain area. On some days participants may do as they please in or out of camp, canoeing, mountaineering, swimming, photographing or fishing. The area is full of wildlife including bighorn sheep, Rocky Mountain goats, elk, moose, deer, caribou and varied bird life. After the route makes a circle and returns to base camp with the covered wagon, participants fly back to Grand Prairie. **Cost:** $600 includes transportation from Grand Prairie, horses, equipment, food, guide. **When:** July, August. **Contact:** Rocky Mountain Trail Rides, Box 1212, Grand Prairie, AB Canada T8V 4B6; phone (403)567-2253.

Trail Riders of the Canadian Rockies sponsors $325 horsepacking trips near Mt. Assiniboine in Banff National Park. (Canadian Gov't. Travel Bureau)

Rockies Trail Ride: Participants choose between 5- and 10-day horsepacking trips traveling the Rocky Mountain wilderness areas of Jasper National Park, Willmore Wilderness Park or the Amethyst Lakes area in the Tonquin Valley. The wilderness trips cover over 100 miles of remote high mountain country, providing views of wildlife and spectacular scenery. A trail cook prepares meals, and accommodations are in tents or cabins. Horseback riding experience is not necessary as trail horses are gentle and reliable rather than speedy. **Cost:** $325 for 5 days, $650 for 10 days. **When:** July to September. **Contact:** Jim Simpson, Box 1175, Jasper, AB Canada T0E 1E0; phone (403)852-3909.

Hoofing the Skyline Trail: The alpine flowers and abundant wildlife of the Jasper National Park region are of interest to horsepacking visitors as they ride the Skyline Trail. Jaunts of 2, 3 and 6 days beginning at Maligne Lake or the Sunwapta River travel through the high mountain country by way of the Litt and Big Shovel passes. Overnight stops are made at wilderness cabins or tent houses. Previous riding experience is not required. **Cost:** $90 to $450 includes guide, horse, equipment, accommodation. **When:** July to August. **Contact:** Skyline Trail Rides Ltd., Box 207, Jasper, AB Canada T0E 1E0.

Tonquin Valley on Horseback: Tucked in the Canadian Rockies is the Tonquin Valley, an area of dark pine grasses and black jagged peaks. The valley may be reached on 3-day horsepacking trips departing from Viewpoint. Trip members ride saddle horses and are accompanied by pack animals and guides. Near the valley's southern end riders reach Amethyst Lakes, formed by a cascading sheet of water 3 miles long and a mile wide. Here participants stay at a camp which provides dining, sleeping and cooking facilities. **Cost:** $100 includes guide, meals, accommodations in cabin. **When:** June to September. **Contact:** Tonquin Valley Trail Trips, Brule, AB Canada T0E 0C0; phone (403)866-3946; summer, P.O. Box 508, Jasper, AB Canada T0E 1E0; phone (403)866-3980.

New Trails, Old Passes: Participants spend 5 days riding through the Canadian Rockies wilderness near Banff. After setting up a base camp near the Upper Spray River, riders set out each day to explore new trails and old passes through uninhabited valleys and craggy peaks. Travelers stay in traditional tepees and eat meals prepared by the camp chef. Cowboy guides attend to the horses. Riding experience is not essential, and participants are matched with animals to suit their own skill and temperament. **Cost:** $325 includes round-trip bus transportation from Banff, horse and saddle, meals, accommodations, membership fee. **When:** July, August. **Contact:** Trail Riders of the Canadian Rockies, P.O. Box 6742, Sta. D, Calgary, AB Canada T2P 2E6; phone (403)287-1746.

Riding in the Rockies: Participants mount well-mannered horses to ride for 6 days in the Alberta foothills or in the Cascade Valley and Lower Flints Park area of Banff National Park. Meals are prepared by camp cooks, and the small group sleeps in tents at camps along the trail. On the spring trip a small group drives from Banff to Lake Minnewanka to board a sightseeing boat for Devil's Gap at the end of the lake. There participants meet guides and horses for a 9-mile ride to Devil's Head Ranch located east of the Devil's Head and Aylmer mountains. Camping in tents at the ranch riders make forays during the day on horse. In summer, riders use 2 main camps in Banff National Park as bases for 6 days of riding. On these trips riders are transported by bus to the trail head corral at Mt. Norquay. From here the group heads out in a northerly direction across Elk Lake Pass to the first camp at Stoney Creek. In the Cascade River Valley the trip members have a chance to ford the river and see bighorn sheep, mountain goats, elk and moose. After a ride to Dormer Pass, riders move on to the Flints Park Camp and a day ride to Sawback Lake. Returning to Stoney Creek Camp, the group leisurely makes its way back to the trailhead corral. **Cost:** $275 to $330 depending on date of departure includes transportation from Banff, guides, meals, equipment, horses. **When:** April to September. **Contact:** Warner and MacKenzie Guiding and Outfitting, Box 448, Banff, AB Canada T0L 0C0; phone (403)762-4255.

British Columbia

Riding through Moose Valley: Packhorse expeditions from Moose Valley to Eaglenest Creek or vice versa cover 200 miles and last 17 days. A plane with supplies flies to the half-way point, making 8½-day trips possible. Through low river valleys and high mountain plateaus 12 riders and 5 crew members journey in the mountains of the Cassiar District, riding through the wilderness headwaters of the Skeena, Stikine and Finaly-Peace rivers. For many of the miles riders follow the old packing routes of the early 1900s. Several rivers are crossed during the trip, and rafts are used to transport riders and gear while the horses swim. Six hours of traveling time lie between each camp, and every fourth day is free for fishing, relaxing or hiking. All travelers participate in regular camp chores including setting up lean-to tents for sleeping. **Cost:** $1,640 for 17 days, $960 for 8½ days includes transportation from Smithers, meals, accommodations, horses, camping equipment. **When:** On request. **Contact:** Alpine Outfitters, Germansen Landing, BC Canada V0J 1T0; winter, Box 717, Fort St. James, BC Canada V0J 1P0.

Remote Trail Riding: One- and 2-week horsepacking trips cross the virgin forests of British Columbia, moving between established forest camps. The trips begin and end at a ranch at Chilko Lake, about 180 miles north of Vancouver, an area accessible only by air or 4-wheel drive vehicle. After a day acquainting themselves with the horses participants strike out onto trails through remote and wild mountain terrain, staking temporary camps as they go. The route runs through heavily timbered country, over mountain streams, and past snowfields and glaciers. Every 4 days a permanent tent camp, offering showers and amenities, is made home base for a few days of day hiking, fishing, photography or relaxing. Finally, the last night of the trip is spent back at Chilko Lake. **Cost:** $350 for 7 days; $700 for 14 days includes food, accommodations, horses, equipment, guide. **When:** June to September. **Contact:** Chilko Lake Wilderness Ranch Ltd., P.O. Box 4750, Williams Lake, BC Canada V2G 2V7; phone (604)-Chilko Lake Wilderness Ranch.

Wilderness Adventure on Lake Atlin: Meeting at Whitehorse or Atlin in the Yukon, participants begin a wilderness experience of 8 days with a ride to Bennett on the narrow-gauge Whitepass and Yukon Railway. After investigating the gold rush town and observing remnants of the Klondike era, participants return to Carcross to board a boat or van for a ride to Atlin, a tiny town on the shores of Lake Atlin. From there a 20-foot freighter canoe crosses British Columbia's largest natural lake, then shoots down the rapids of Atlin River to camp on Tagish Lake. Glacier-spawned streams from the Coast Range feed the lakes, which are suitable for fishing and swimming. Horsepacking trips into the mountains lead photographers or naturalists above the timberline to observe moose, caribou, Dall sheep, mountain goats, and grizzly or black bears. Transportation is provided back to Whitehorse. **Cost:** $475 from Whitehorse includes accommodations, camping equipment, meals, guides, horses. **When:** June to August. **Contact:** Taku Outfitters, Ltd., Box 30, Klahanie Dr., RR 2, Powell River, BC Canada V8A 4Z3; phone (604)483-9238. *(M)*

The Andalucian horse, known for its surefootedness and strength, takes riders into the Sierra Nevada near Grenada, Spain. (Diane Hucks)

EUROPE

France

Vosges Retreat: The mountainous Vosges region of Alsace-Lorraine provides participants with a relaxing experience on horseback for 3, 6 or 10 days. Groups of 4 riders travel through the lush, variegated countryside of eastern France, stopping at hostelries and restaurants for meals and accommodations. All trips are guided by experienced horsemen, and no day includes more than 20 miles of travel. The area traversed is rural and quiet. **Cost:** $290 for 10 days, $97 for 3 days includes meals, accommodations. **When:** July to September. **Contact:** Societe Hippique d'Epinal, Ravin d'Olima, 8800 Chantraine Epinal, France.

Spain

Horseback through the Spanish Nevadas: Andalucian horses, known for sure-footedness, strength, courage and kind temperament, are ridden through the Sierra Nevada on a 15-day trip. While on the trek riders are responsible for looking after the horses, including tasks such as feeding, watering, grooming and tacking up. The group departs London for Malaga by plane, then drives to Orgiva to meet the horses and guides. The trip begins with a morning briefing and an afternoon ride along the Guadelfeo River. Then participants head out to ride from village to village, stopping each night in local inns known as posadas, where they dine on Andalucian home cooking. In the summer months riders climb gradually from the Mediterranean lowlands, eventually crossing the snowline at over 10,000 feet and reaching the highest peaks of the Sierra Nevada. In spring and autumn, when the highest mountains are deep in snow, mounted travelers follow the Valle de Lecrin on a route which explores a lower and warmer area. Both trips include 2 rest days in which members of the group can make excursions to Gra-

nada and the coast. **Cost:** $875 and $913 from London includes transportation, accommodations, meals, guide. **When:** March to October. **Contact:** WEXAS International Inc., Suite 354, Graybar Bldg., 420 Lexington Ave., New York, NY 10017, USA. *(M)*

Switzerland

Valais Canton by Mule: The countryside and mule paths of the Can-

The forested mountainland of Valais on the Swiss-Italian border creates an idyllic atmosphere for horsepackers. (Swiss Nat'l. Tourist Office)

ton of Valais serve as unpaved highways for a week-long journey through mountainous terrain. Originally used to keep villages in touch with each other, the mule trails provide travelers an opportunity to meet residents of remote areas. Departing from Haute Nendaz or Grimentz, riders proceed over hilly country through meadows and larch forests to Beysonnaz for lunch and on to a view of the Rhone Valley at the day's end. The trip continues to the Pyramides of Euseigne, a rock formation caused by wind erosion; Rechy Valley with its abundant wildlife; and the mountain village of Vercorin. Participants generally walk 5 to 8 hours each day, with 2 people sharing each mule; luggage is transported by jeep. Accommodations are at local inns. **Cost:** $165 includes roundtrip rail transportation from Sion, meals, accommodations. **When:** May to October. **Contact:** Welcome Swiss Tours, 7 Ave. Benjamin-Constant, 1003 Lausanne, Switzerland; phone (021) 20 68 21.

Wales

Equestrian Experiences: Sixty riding centers throughout the Welsh countryside provide travelers with the opportunity to enjoy a variety of riding and trekking experiences. Some rides lead high into the hills while others follow easier routes. Most centers offer casual riding by the hour, half-day and day as well as week-long holidays that include accommodations. Riders at all levels of skill are equally welcome: experts can improve their competence and beginners can learn basic techniques. Specialized clothing is not required, though a list of recommended items is available. **Cost:** On request. **When:** Year-round. **Contact:** Wales Tourist Board, Llandaff, Cardiff CF5 2YZ, Great Britain; phone 022-27281.

Welsh Pony Trek: A week-long riding trip takes place in a remote area of Wales and is based at a youth hostel. Participants are met at the Abergavenny train station and transported to Capel-y-ffin hostel, a modernized farmhouse in the isolated Llathony Valley. After a day of getting acquainted with the horses and making a short ride, members spend the week on progressively longer rides into the ridges and valleys of the area; participants return to the hostel each night. One day off in the middle of the week lets the horses rest while trip members travel by car for a night's stay at a nearby hostel. Participants must be 16 or older and weigh under 200 pounds. The week is suitable both for novices wishing to receive basic riding instruction, and for experienced riders wishing to have some free time for exploring. **Cost:** $110 includes transportation during the trip, accommodations, food, horses, instructor/guide. **When:** April to October. **Contact:** YHA Adventure Holiday, Trevelyen House, St. Albans, Herts., Great Britain; phone St. Albans 55215.

MEXICO
Chihuahua

Adventure on the Border: An international horsepack trip takes riders from Lajitas, Texas to the arid re-

Burros are used for travel in the remote Sierra Madre of Mexico because of their intelligence and toughness. (Keith Gunnar)

gions of northern Mexico for 4 days. On the first day, participants ride to Nuevo Lajitas, a Mexican community on Arroyo San Carlos, where camp is set up in a cottonwood grove. On the second day, the group visits the Presidio Viejo and rides on to the village of San Carlos, an oasis in the desert. The route continues up San Carlos Canyon on the third day and ends with a ride back to Texas, stopping at a Mexican ranch for lunch. Riders must be at least 15 years old. **Cost:** $200 includes equipment, accommodations, food, guide. **When:** October to April. **Contact:** Lajitas Trading Post, P.O. Box 48, Terlingua, TX 79852, USA; phone (915)364-2234.

SOUTH AMERICA
Argentina

Circling Aconcagua: Adventurers can experience the grandeur of the highest peak in the western hemisphere by joining an expedition of 16 days that circles the base of 22,834-foot Aconcagua. Participants begin the adventure to the Andes from Mendoza. A cemetery for the many mountaineers who have been killed while climbing the peak is passed on the trail of the relatively safe and easy 11-day hike around Aconcagua's summit base. Horses carry the gear as well as participants who prefer riding to walking. In order to acclimatize comfortably to maximum elevations of 17,330 feet, the group of adventurers and guides travels approximately 3 miles each day. After the hiking and horsepacking, the trip is completed by a ride on the trans-Andean railway to Santiago, Chile. **Cost:** $1,035 for ground transportation, meals, accommodations, guides. **When:** February,

March. **Contact:** Sobek Expeditions, Inc., P.O. Box 67, Angels Camp, CA 95222, USA; phone (209)736-2924. *(M)*

UNITED STATES

Alaska

Nenana Horsepacking Trips: Central Alaska is the area where a guide service takes families and individuals through wilderness high country. The week-long trip follows a route from Brushkana Creek on the Denali Highway to Nenana Glacier at the headwaters of the Nenana River, and back. After one day at a remote lodge on Brushkana Creek, the group sets off for 5 days of packing in the vicinity of Mt. McKinley National Park. Dall sheep, moose, caribou and grizzly bears are common, and there are opportunities for fishing en route. **Cost:** $595 includes meals, lodging, camping equipment, guide. **When:** July, August. **Contact:** Alaskan Adventure, P.O. Box 18, Hope, AK 99605, USA. *(M)*

Central Range on Horseback: Relatively unstructured horsepacking trips into the central Alaska Range last at least 7 days but longer trips can be arranged. After being flown or driven to Central or Fielding Lake, participants explore open tundra and aspen, birch and spruce forests. Participants need not be experienced riders, but should be in good shape. **Cost:** $1,050 includes tack, equipment, food, guides. **When:** June to September. **Contact:** Lee R. Spears, Outfitter, Goldstream Rd., SR Box 20237, Fairbanks, AK 99701, USA; phone (907)479-3351.

Arizona

Ups and Downs of the Santa Catalinas: Riders travel on horseback through landscapes ranging from deserts to southwestern mountains on a 5-day pack trip leaving from a ranch near Tucson and heading toward the Santa Catalinas, the southernmost portion of the Rocky Mountains. As group members ride, they travel through several distinct ecosystems: the lower Sonoran life zone where the trip begins, and the Montane and Canadia ecosystems at the higher elevations. The country is much as it was in Arizona's pioneer days, and riders are likely to see remnants of earlier inhabitants. One part of the trail intercepts the old stagecoach line into Tucson, and the group follows it up to about 6,000 feet and through the Carleau Gap. Most of the country the group traverses is in the Coronado National Forest and is part of the Canada Del Oro watershed. The trip is meant to strike a balance between comfort and the appeal of traveling in pioneer fashion through characteristically Western landscapes; daily stints on horseback are limited to 3 or 4 hours. **Cost:** $1,000 includes horses, equipment, meals, lodging on the nights before and after the trip. **When:** September. **Contact:** American Wilderness Alliance, 4260 E. Evans, Denver, CO 80222, USA; phone (303)758-5018.

Horsepacking in the Superstitions: A 6-day horsepacking and camping trip explores many of the remains of the mixture of Spanish and Indian culture in the Superstition Mountains. Beginning in Apache

Junction, the group spends the first day riding to Reevis Camp at about 5,000 feet, which serves as base camp for the next day's ride to the Spanish walled ruins. The trip continues with a descent through Rogers Canyon into the desert to camp near the little-known Salado Indian cliff dwellings, which date from the 13th century. After a layover day here, participants ride past ancient Indian pictographs to White Rock Springs to spend a day in sight of Weaver's Needle. A side trip is made to Peralta Camp, site of an Indian massacre of Spaniards, and on the last day the trip returns to Apache Junction. The trip is also available as a hiking trip with packstock. **Cost:** $50 a day includes food, horses, equipment, guide. **When:** March, April. **Contact:** American Wilderness Experience, 753 Paragon Dr., Boulder, CO 80303, USA; phone (303)499-5703 or 499-0050. *(M)*

Horsepacking from Arizona Ranch: A family-run ranch in Douglas offers 5-day horsepacking trips in the Price Canyon area. Participants may stay at the ranch or use it as take-off point for the pack trips. At the ranch, bunk-

A mule team descends into the Grand Canyon of Arizona. Balance is vital on the narrow, winding trail. (Craig Sternagel)

house accommodations are provided, and there are opportunities for hiking, ranch work, swimming and fishing. **Cost:** $175 for pack trip includes food, equipment, guide; $33 to $45 a day for ranch stay includes food, accommodations, activities. **When:** June to October. **Contact:** Price Canyon Ranch, P.O. Box 1065, Douglas, AZ 85607, USA; phone (602)558-2383. *(M)*

California

Horsemanship and Packing School: An intensive field program in the John Muir and Minarets wilderness areas offers instruction in the handling and use of horses and mules on pack trips. Participants spend 7 days with experienced packers, using equipment from a working pack station. Those who wish to use their own horses may do so with a reduction in fee. The emphasis is on the enjoyment of horsepacking with minimal environmental impact and on the ethics of multi-use wilderness areas. Basic horse management subjects are taught, such as care and grooming, common ailments and cures, selection of saddle and bridle, horseshoeing, and safety and common sense in working with horses. Packing techniques include care and maintenance of pack equipment, making up a pack load, care of livestock in the wilderness and feeding procedures and practices. University credit is available through the University of California at Berkeley. **Cost:** $200 includes animals, instruction, food, equipment except bedroll. **When:** July. **Contact:** Red's Meadow Pack Stations, P.O. Box 395, Mammoth Lakes, CA 93546, USA; phone (714)934-2345 or 873-3928.

Sierra Nevadas Pack Trip: Participants may choose from among a wide variety of horsepacking trips into the Sierra Nevadas leaving from Bishop. A pack train takes travelers to one of 5 wilderness areas and returns later to pack them back out; the length of stay is up to trip members and does not affect packing costs. Or loads may be carried in to a specified area while parties hike or ride in to meet it. Another option is an extended pack trip on which the packer, stock and possibly a cook accompany participants throughout the trip. Day rides on saddle horses are also available. **Cost:** $50 to $140, depending on size of party and destination, for pack train trip; $102 a day for extended pack trip packer, stock, cook; $12 a day for saddle horses. **When:** Year-round except winter. **Contact:** Rock Creek Pack Station, Box 248, Bishop, CA 93514, USA; phone (714)935-4493, winter (714)872-8331.

Horsepacking for Youths: Separate week-long trips for boys and girls ages 12 and older are available in the Trinity Alps Wilderness. The trips include 5 days of horsepacking with supervision in horse handling and wilderness living. Other activities include fishing, swimming, hiking and photography. The Trinity Alps area contains high, snow-capped peaks surrounded by lush meadows and alpine lakes. Groups are limited to 15 members. **Cost:** $200 includes meals, accommodations, guides, camping equipment. **When:** June to

September. **Contact:** Trinity Pack Trains, P.O. Box 277, Trinity, CA 96091, USA; phone (916)266-3305.

Colorado

Crossing the Divide: The San Juan Mountains with their 14,000-foot peaks are the site of an 11-day horsepacking trip starting at Pine River Campground and twice crossing the Continental Divide. One of these crossings is at Sawtooth Pass. Camps are pitched at Ribbon Falls and Johnson Creek, and when the rivers and creeks are full, alpine river running is included in scheduled activities. A glacial basin called Columbine Pass also affords spelunkers and rockhounds an opportunity for exploration. **Cost:** About $550 includes food, equipment. **When:** June to August. **Contact:** American Wilderness Experience, 753 Paragon Dr., Boulder, CO 80303, USA; phone (303)499-5703 or 499-0050.   *(M)*

Grand Junction Horsepacking: The mountains of western Colorado provide the backdrop for horseback riding lessons, tent camping and horsepacking. From the departure point at Grand Junction, both experienced and inexperienced riders can participate in trips of 3 or 5 days that include fishing, swimming, wildlife observation and photography. Deer, elk, eagles, beavers and many smaller animals as well as wildflowers are often seen en route. Participants are based in remote tent camps high in a 12,000-foot mountain range. From these camps daily trail rides to different mountain areas are possible. Some trips involve horsepacking to establish a new camp almost

nightly. **Cost:** $175 for 3 days, $250 for 5 days at base camp, $330 for 5-day trail ride includes transportation from Grand Junction, meals, accommodations, guides, horses. **When:** July to September. **Contact:** Dick Pennington Guide Service, 2371 'H' Rd., Grand Junction, CO 81501, USA; phone (303)242-6318.

High Country Hiking: A 10-day hiking trip with packstock in Colorado's high country is open to teenagers 13 to 17. Departing from Eagle, the group hikes from Slim Jim Gulch to Tellurium Lake, where a base camp is established. Hikes to new campsites are made every other day with ample opportunities for exploring and relaxation. Hikers carry day packs, and horses pack in camping gear, food and personal equipment. Meals are prepared by the guides. **Cost:** $350. **When:** July. **Contact:** K.E. Schultz Guide and Outfitting Service, 0010 Ponderosa Dr., Glenwood Springs, CO 81601, USA.   *(M)*

West Elk by Horse: Gunnison National Forest and West Elk Wilderness provide the setting for a 6-day horsepacking trip into remote mountain terrain. In an area once frequented by Indians, mountain men and miners, participants make use of 2 mountain camps located a day's ride apart and accessible only by horseback. Several nights are spent at each camp, from where day trips into the surrounding country are made. Activities available to participants include wildlife observation, hiking, photography and fishing. The trips leave every Monday from Paonia. **Cost:** $180 ($160 for persons under 18) in-

Wilderness Adventures, Inc. provides food and mess gear on trips to the Weminuchi Wilderness and Sangre de Cristo Range. (Wilderness Adventures, Inc.)

cludes food, camping accommodations, horses and equipment, guide. **When:** May to September. **Contact:** Sid Simpson Guide Service, Paonia, CO 81428, USA; phone (303)527-3486.

Rio Grande Horsepacking: Participants can either ride or hike and pack their gear on horses during week-long trips in Colorado's Rio Grande National Forest and surrounding wilderness areas. Trips

are tailored to individualized interests. **Cost:** $35 or $40 a day. **When:** By arrangement. **Contact:** Wilderness Adventures, Inc., P.O. Box 82, South Fork, CO 81154, USA; phone (303)873-5331.

Idaho

Horsepacking and Ranching in the Panhandle: A family-run working ranch in Idaho's panhandle accepts guests for horsepacking trips, ranch work, swimming, photogra-

phy and other outdoor activities. The schedule is open and no activities are mandatory. Trips for overnight or longer into the surrounding high country can be arranged, with guests riding horseback and accompanied by pack mules. Rodeos and hay rides are also available. Most work on the ranch is still done with teams of Belgian horses. **Cost:** $185 a week, $125 for children under 12, includes food, accommodations, activities, transportation from Coeur d'Alene or Spokane. **When:** May to October. **Contact:** BAR-BQ Ranch, P.O. Box 173, Harrison, ID 83833, USA; phone (208)689-3528.   *(M)*

Horsepacking and Rafting along the Salmon: A 7-day adventure in the Chamberlain Basin area offers a range of wilderness activities for individuals and families. The week begins with a 1-hour flight from Boise over Salmon Breaks Canyon, the nation's second deepest, to the basin where participants are transported to the Stonebraker Ranch. After fishing, relaxing and getting acquainted with their trail horses, the group heads toward the Salmon River on horseback. The ride continues downstream along Chamberlain Creek for about 4 hours to a campsite at Jenkins Crossing. At noon on the third day, the group boards rafts for a float down the Salmon River, through Salmon Falls and past Barth Hot Springs to the mouth of Bargamin Creek. Two more days of rafting follow before arrival at the Mackay Bar lodge, where the variety of activities available includes trail rides, backpacking, jet-boating, swimming and kayaking. The return to Boise

is by charter aircraft. **Cost:** $600 includes meals, transportation, camping equipment except sleeping bag. **When:** July to September. **Contact:** Mackay Bar, Business Office Drawer F, Rm. 1010, 1 Capital Ctr., Boise, ID 83702, USA; phone (208)344-1881.   *(M)*

Montana

Riding in the Mountain's Shadow: Riders spend either 3 or 7 days horsepacking in the shadow of Granite Peak near the Stillwater River Basin. Starting at the Beartooth Ranch Lodge, the trip passes over rocky slopes, mountain trails, rivers teeming with trout and deep forest. Glacier-filled lakes serve as watering holes for elk, deer, moose, bears, beavers and bighorn sheep. Experienced guides provide horsepackers with their knowledge of the area's wilderness. The ranch itself provides activities ranging from square dancing and swimming to horse shows and cookouts. **Cost:** $255 for 3 days, $318 for 7 days. **When:** June to September. **Contact:** Beartooth Ranch, Nye, MT 59061, USA; phone (406)327-4353 or 327-4304.

Yellowstone Horsepacking: The wilderness areas of the Absaroka and Gallatin mountain ranges in south-central Montana and Yellowstone National Park are the setting for 5- and 10-day horsepacking trips. Horses follow trails through wooded mountain valleys to willow meadows frequented by moose and up to high ridges and rugged peaks above timberline where mountain goats are often sighted. A 16-mile horsepack ride over Wallace Pass takes riders to Grizzly Creek Camp, a semipermanent tent camp in the heart of the Absaroka Mountains, where fishing, rockhounding, artifact hunting and searching for wildflowers are possible options during day rides. Ten-day trips are conducted into the Absaroka Range. A variety of horses is available to meet the requirements of all levels of riding ability. **Cost:** $250 for 6 days; $462 for 10 days includes horses, meals, guides. **When:** July through August. **Contact:** Black Otter Guide Service, P.O. Box 93, Pray, MT 59065, USA; phone (406)333-4362. *(M)*

Riding in the Bitterroot Backcountry: Surrounded by the peaks of the Bitterroot Mountains, which straddle the borders of Montana and Idaho, a group of 6 riders makes a trail through the colorful high country. The 6-day trip provides time for guided trail riding, camping, fishing, photographing and other activities, chosen by the group. The trip originates at a ranch located in the Bitterroot Valley on the edge of the Selway-Bitterroot Wilderness, the largest designated wilderness area in the nation. **Cost:** $375 includes equipment, food, transportation. **When:** June to August. **Contact:** Bob Crick High Country Outfitters, Rt. 1, Box 99A, Victor, MT 59875, USA; phone (406)642-3233. *(M)*

Hiking and Horsepacking: Seven-day walking trips and 10-day horsepacking trips are offered in the western Montana wilderness. A wide variety of trail rides and backpacking and walking trips with packstock is available. To minimize the environmental impact the number of participants is limited to 8 on horseback and 10 on hiking trips. Wildlife observation is done along the way amid spectacular natural scenery. The outings attempt to recreate the methods of early pioneer travel, combining traditional horsepacking techniques with campfire cookouts. All participants must be in good physical condition. **Cost:** $380 for 7-day hikes, $750 for 10-day horseback trips. **When:** July, August. **Contact:** Wildlife Outfitters, Rt. 1, Box 99B, Victor, MT 59875, USA; phone (406)642-3262. *(M)*

New Mexico

Pecos Horsepacking: Two horsepacking options are offered, one with only light riding in the Pecos, and one with more strenuous riding in Yellowstone. The trip to New Mexico's Pecos Wilderness lasts 6 days, with an average of 7 miles of riding each day. The trip to Yellowstone National Park in Wyoming covers about 15 miles a day for 7 days. Both trips offer ample opportunities for the amateur photographer, naturalist and fisher to observe wildlife. The ride through Yellowstone, the nation's oldest national park, traverses grassy meadowlands and mountain trails, some as high as 10,000 feet. Riding mainly through mountains and valleys, the Pecos trip is an appropriate trip for inexperienced riders. **Cost:** $280 for Pecos trip; $360 for Yellowstone trip, includes food, camping equipment, horses, guide. **When:** June to October. **Contact:** Dode Hershey, Box 275, Pecos, NM 87552, USA; phone (505)757-6574.

New York

Adirondack Trail Rides: The Adirondacks of northern New York become the home of travelers during 3- to 5-day trail rides departing from near the town of Coreys. Participants travel the Cold River region of the mountains, from where the Santanoni and Seward mountains are also visible. Up to 12 riders join the trips from a ranch located between Tupper and Sara-

nac lakes. Trail rides are divided into groups as necessary to accommodate all levels of riding ability. Trout fishing and wilderness photography are featured activities on the trip. **Cost:** $155 to $250 includes food, horse, equipment. **When:** June to September. **Contact:** Cold River Trail Rides, Inc., Cold River Ranch, Rt. 3, Coreys, Tupper Lake, NY 12986, USA; phone (914)476-5386; summer, (518)359-9822.

North Carolina

Smoky Mountain Trails: A large ranch located at 5,000 feet in the Great Smoky Mountains provides a variety of horsepacking trips from a half day to 10 days. Fifteen hundred acres in size, the ranch borders the Great Smoky Mountains National Park, so a wide selection of isolated terrain is within easy riding distance. The network of

Skill and balance are needed to cross a fastwater river on horseback. The scene here is Wyoming, site of many horsepacking trips. (Wyoming Travel Commission)

trails through the ranch and the park is lined with wildflowers, and the elevation offers moderately warm, bright days and clear, cool nights. Other activities available to ranch guests include swimming, hiking, tennis and fishing. Trips lasting a week to 10 days may be arranged in advance. **Cost:** On request. **When:** By arrangement. **Contact:** Cataloochee Ranch, Rt. 1, Box 500, Maggie Valley, NC 28751, USA; phone (704)926-1401.

Oregon

Ambling along in Eagle Cap: Trail-wise horses take trip members through the Eagle Cap Wilderness in the northeastern corner of Oregon. Riders may fish, photograph or explore as they travel through the meadows, lakes and snow-filled glens of the rugged Wallowa Mountains on the breaks of Snake River's Hells Canyon. The historic ghost town of Cornucopia may also be explored. The guide can give instruction in how to separate flakes of gold from gravel to those wanting to pan for gold. At the trip's end participants return to Cornucopia Wilderness Pack Station near Halfway. The horsepacking party may travel fully outfitted or with just saddles and horses, and a cook is available to accompany the trip. **Cost:** $50 a day for guided trips with food, equipment; $80 for packing food, gear in and out. **When:** On request. **Contact:** Cornucopia Wilderness Pack Station Inc., Rt. 1, P.O. Box 177, Halfway, OR 97834, USA; phone (503)742-5687.

Riding and Rafting: A series of trips combines travel by horseback with whitewater river running. On one such trip, participants drive from Enterprise to a meeting point in the Imnaha River canyon where they pick out horses and pack string. The first day of the 8-day trip is spent riding out of the canyon to Freeze-out Saddle at over 7,000 feet, with a spectacular view of Hells Canyon and the Snake River. The group then winds its way down through a wild area along the rugged contours of Saddle Creek, camping only a short distance from the Snake River. The next day's 12-mile stretch takes riders along scenic trails, with grades alternately running along the river, then climbs over rugged cliffs, with more views of the gorge. River guides are met at Wild Sheep Creek that evening, and participants embark the next day for a 6-day float trip on the Snake. **Cost:** On request. **When:** On request. **Contact:** Lute Jerstad Adventures, P.O. Box 19527, Portland, OR 97219, USA; phone (503)244-4364.
(M)

Utah

High Uintas Pack Trips: Leaving from Vernal, 8-person groups plus guides travel north to the Ashley National Forest on a 6-day trip. From there, participants venture by horseback into the High Uintas, a land historically occupied by Ute Indians, French trappers and Mormon pioneers. An abundance of lakes and streams is seen, as well as deer, elk and occasionally moose. Supplies are carried by packhorses, and meals are cooked in dutch ovens over an open fire. The group rides only a few miles a day between camps, which gives members plenty of time for exploring and relaxing. **Cost:** $330 includes food, equipment, transportation, guide. **When:** July, August. **Contact:** Gypsy Wind Expeditions, 16601 Estralita Dr., Sonora, CA 95370, USA.

High Plateau Horsepacking: Each season, 2 horsepacking trips are run into the high desert country of the San Rafael Swell and the Maze and Grand Gulch of Canyonlands National Park. In the San Rafael Swell, a 5-day trip ventures to the area on the north end of the Swell along the San Rafael River. Another 5-day trip heads south into the area surrounding Muddy Creek. Other trips take horsepackers to the Maze, west of the confluence of the Green and Colorado rivers, one of the most austere regions of the Colorado Plateau. Participants may also choose to visit the Grand Gulch Primitive Area, a northern drainage of the San Juan River, which features one of the most extensive sites of the Anasazi culture outside Mesa Verde National Park. **Cost:** On request. **When:** By arrangement. **Contact:** Hondoo Rivers and Trails, P.O. Box 377, Ferron, UT 84523, USA; phone (801)384-2961. *(M)*

Canyonlands Packing: Canyonlands National Park is the site of a variety of 6- and 7-day horsepack trips to explore Indian ruins, eroded rock formations and abandoned camps of the Old West. The 7-day trips take participants through the park, past such natural wonders as Wedding Ring Arch, Fish Eye and Angel Arch. The 6-day journeys pass through the

Maze and the Butch Cassidy/Sundance Kid area. All supplies are packed by mule. Walking trips with packstock are also available. **Cost:** $300 to $420 includes meals, equipment, guide. **When:** June to August. **Contact:** Horsehead Pack Trips, P.O. Box 68, Monticello, UT 84535, USA; phone (801)587-2929. *(M)*

Outlaw Trail Ride: Far away from the noise and pollution of jeep roads, trail horses take riders on a 6-day trip to areas of Canyonlands National Park that are accessible only by horseback. After arrival in Hanksville, horses and riders set out on the trail, which stretches from Utah to Mexico and was once used by outlaws. Covering only a few miles each day, participants encounter such places as Robbers Roost Canyon, Dirty Devil River and Horseshoe Canyon. Continuing across the Spur to Big Spring country and into Horsethief Canyon, trip members ride down to the Green River, where they may join up with a 4-day raft trip if they wish. **Cost:** $375, $620 with raft trip. **When:** May, August, September. **Contact:** Outlaw Trails Inc., P.O. Box 336, Green River, UT 84525, USA; phone (801)564-3477. *(M)*

Washington

Northern Washington Horsepacking School: Instruction in mountain travel on horseback teaches participants how to ride safely and comfortably in an alpine environment. Group members learn the basics of horsepacking and guiding during the 2-week session, which qualifies them to lead a group on their own. Many of the skills learned apply particularly to horse travel in the North Cascades, since this is the site of the school, but the techniques are applicable to all similar locations. Instruction begins with tracking, finding and catching range horses. Students then learn how to halter, lead, shoe, saddle, pack and ride their mounts. Basic camping skills, such as cooking, building fires, and splitting wood are also included. Two trips through the mountains are planned for the session so that participants may practice and develop their skills. Anyone over 18 with good health and sufficient interest is eligible. **Cost:** $500 includes food, equipment, transportation to and from Chelan, Washington. **When:** Early summer. **Contact:** Cascade Corrals, Stehekin, WA 98852, USA; phone (509)663-1822.   *(M)*

Riding into Indian Heaven: Groups of 2 to 6 arrange their own programs and schedules on horsepacking trips into Mt. Adams Wilderness, Indian Heaven and the Goat Rocks. In this area of the South Cascades, riders enjoy views of Mt. Rainier as well as Mt. Adams, many alpine lakes, and excellent huckleberry fields in the fall. The Goat Rocks Wilderness offers some of the most rugged trails in the Cascades. **Cost:** $40 a day includes food, equipment, cook, horse. **When:** July to September. **Contact:** Spencer L. Frey, Box 43, Trout Lake, WA 98650, USA; phone (509)395-2021.

Horsepacking out of Indian Creek: A ranch located on the east side of the South Cascade Mountains is the base for horsepacking trips lasting from 1 to 7 or more days. Riders gather at Indian Creek where the ranch is located and ride with a pack string into high alpine meadows, glaciers and snowfields. A typical trip, lasting 7 days, visits the Goat Rocks Wilderness and provides 3 layover days for exploring the surrounding area's peaks and valleys, making short rides without packstock, observing wildlife (including the frequently sighted mountain goat) or fishing. At one point the route makes a pass right over the top of a peak called Old Snowy. Sites visited on other trips include Strawberry Meadows, the Rattlesnake River, Blankenship Meadows, the Cascade Crest Trail and countless small alpine lakes. Accommodations are available within a short distance of Indian Creek. **Cost:** $30 to $35 a day depending on length of trip includes horses, food, camping equipment, guide. **When:** Summer months. **Contact:** Indian Creek Corral, Star Rt., Box 218, Naches, WA 98937, USA.

Entering the Olympics: A variety of horsepacking trips into the Olympic Mountains is offered, from day rides in the high country to 10 days or longer deep into the wilderness. Participants leave from a ranch at Sequim and either ride or hike the Deer Ridge Trail, with its spectacular views of the Olympic Range on one side and the Strait of Juan de Fuca on the other, turning at the top of Blue Mountain to head toward Greywolf River, Cedar Lake, Greywolf Pass, Sunnybrook Meadows and Royal Basin. Sites visited

The Goat Rocks Wilderness of Washington is a favorite area for horsepacking. Other parts of the Cascades are explored by Indian Creek Corrals outfitters. (Jim Wilcox)

on other trips include the Dungeness Trail, Hayden Pass, Lake Quinalt and Dose Meadows. The pace is leisurely on all these trips with ample time allowed for side trips, individual exploration, swimming, wildlife observation and fishing. Seven different prescheduled trips are offered, as well as custom trip outfitting and hourly or daily riding. **Cost:** $55 a day for riders, $35 a day for hikers, includes packhorses, packer/guide, food, equipment; day rides from $5 per hour. **When:** Summer months. **Contact:** Lost Mountain Ranch, Rt. 6, Box 920, Sequim, WA 98382, USA; phone (206)683-4331.

West Virginia

Cacapon Riding: Participants engage in a 6-day horsepacking trek through the mountains of northern West Virginia. From the starting point at Berkeley Springs they ride out along the rim of the Cacapon Mountains to Bear Wallows and Seldom Seen Valley. Although the altitudes are never excessive the trail is sometimes rugged, and from time to time the horses must be led on foot. Participants ride along the historic C & O Canal to the Upper Potomac and Balance Rock. Midway through the excursion participants may take a 1-day raft trip down the Cacapon River. An experienced outfitter directs the trip, and each trip is limited to 20 riders. **Cost:** $295 includes food, equipment, guide. **When:** March to July. **Contact:** AFA Trail Riders of the Wilderness, 1319 18th St. NW, Washington, DC 20036, USA; phone (202)467-5810.

Seldom Seen Ride: Riders combine horsepacking with a short float trip to cover 80 miles of West Virginia, from Cold Run Valley to the Potomac River, in a week-long trip. The route passes along the Cacapon Ridge, past Bear Den Rocks and into a portion of the Seldom Seen

Valley near the Virginia border. The group then fords the Cacapon River and travels along Sideling Hill Mountain, camping at the Ingleside Farm. Riders then transfer to rafts for a day of floating on the Cacapon and relaxing at camp. The final leg of the trip begins with a ride down the old railroad bed to Paw Paw on the way to Greenridge Mountain. **Cost:** $290 includes food, horses, equipment, guide. **When:** June to August. **Contact:** Coolfont Re + Creation, Inc., Berkeley Springs, WV 25411, USA.

Wyoming

Youth Horsepacking near the Continental Divide: Wyoming's Bridger and Teton national forests provide the setting for a 10-day pack trip available to a group of 8 to 10 young people. In a wilderness area featuring some 3,000 lakes, participants receive instruction in western horsemanship, wood lore and orienteering as part of the trip activities. The parties are led by a wrangler, guides and host, with most of the outdoor activity centered in the Wind River Mountains. **Cost:** $400 includes transportation from Pinedale, horses, meals, camping equipment. **When:** July, August. **Contact:** Bridger Wilderness Outfitters, P.O. Box 951, Pinedale, WY 82941, USA; phone (307)367-2747.

Teton Wilderness Horsepacking: A horsepack trip into the Teton Wilderness area takes riders through Two Ocean Pass where a stream splits and part of the water goes into the Atlantic and part into the Pacific. The trip proceeds alongside the headwaters of the Yellowstone River over the Continental Divide, into the Crater Lake area and down the Soda Fork of the Buffalo River. The trip provides many opportunities to observe wildlife, flowers and the scenery. **Cost:** $50 a day includes food, equipment, guide. **When:** July, August. **Contact:** J Box Dot Guest Ranch, Box 616, Afton, WY 83110, USA; phone (307)886-5565. *(M)*

Summer Pack Trips: A trip geared to appeal to backpackers and riders alike takes horsepackers into the Teton Wilderness for 7 days. The trip includes layovers of 1 or more days at each campsite so everyone has plenty of time to enjoy the wilderness and engage in individual activities. The outfitter can also plan a route and itinerary to suit any group's particular interests and riding ability. Destinations of custom-designed trips include the Washakie Wilderness, Yellowstone National Park and the Gros Ventre Wilderness. Gentle mountain horses are assigned to each guest, and enough packstock accompanies the trip to insure fresh meats and vegetables rather than dehydrated foods. **Cost:** $50 a day for riders; $40 a day for hikers. **When:** July for scheduled trip; summer trips by arrangement. **Contact:** L.D. Frome, Outfitter, RFD, Afton, WY 83110, USA; phone (307)886-5240. *(M)*

From Corrals to Camps: Groups of 4 to 6 riders take week-long horsepacking trips along either of 2 routes in national lands of Wyoming. Following the northern route, trip members leave forest service corrals and head up the north fork of the Shoshone River,

Complete outfitting insures successful horsepacking expeditions to such remote areas as the Teton Wilderness in Wyoming. The J Bar Dot Ranch organizes trips into the region for $50 a day. (Wyoming Travel Commission)

making the first camp near the timberline at Stoney Lake. From the camp participants continue into the backcountry of northern Yellowstone Park. At the headwaters of the Lamar River, trip members observe wildlife including elk, deer and wild buffalo. A side trip to Saddle Mountain provides an overview of the area. The second trip, by the southern route, leaves the corrals at Eagle Creek, stopping for lunch beside the falls before continuing onto a wide meadow for the first camp. From here participants may explore a deserted gold mine before rejoining the trail, which climbs a pass into Yellowstone Park's Mountain Creek area. Camp is made on the upper Yellowstone River before a side trip takes participants into the Teton Forest and Bridger Lake. Here participants may board rubber rafts for fishing. Special trips lasting up to 3 weeks can be arranged for larger groups. **Cost:** $27 to $39 a day includes

meals, guide, cabin, horse. **When:** June to August. **Contact:** Rimrock Ranch, Cody, WY 82414, USA; phone (307)587-3970.

Young People's Riding Camp: People 10 to 15 years old spend a month learning and practicing the skills of wilderness horsepacking. Located under the towering Absaroka Range near Cody, a ranch offers complete training and outfitting for young riders of all levels of skill. Participants are matched with horses to suit their temperament and experience, and all pack trips are guided by experienced staff members. When not out on the trail, participants engage in such activities as hayrides, steak fries, volleyball, square dances and campfire sings. A craft shop and photography lab are also available. **Cost:** $975 for one month includes food, accommodations, instruction, equipment. **When:** July. **Contact:** Valley Ranch, South Fork Star Rt.,

Cody, WY 82414, USA; phone (307)587-4461.

Past Hot and Cold Running Waters: Travelers spend 10 to 12 days on a horsepacking trip through the wilderness of northwestern Wyoming. From camps at Golden Meadows, Beaver Creek and Basin Creek, groups ride along Heart Lake, up Mt. Sheridan and across other area highlands. The summer fishing is good, with 5 rivers containing rainbow, cutthroat, mackinaw, brown and brook trout. In addition, the trip visits 5 thermal areas, with their naturally warm water and geysers. Fourteen waterfalls are passed, several over 100 feet in height, including Silver Scarf and Rainbow Falls. Participants help with camp chores. **Cost:** $500 for 10 days, $600 for 12 days includes guides, horses, equipment. **When:** July to September. **Contact:** Wilderness Trails, P.O. Box 1113, Jackson, WY 83001, USA; phone (307)733-3526.

RESOURCES

Clubs and Associations

American Guides Association
Box B
Woodland, CA 95695, USA
Phone (916)662-6824

American Horse Council
1700 K St. NW
Washington, DC 20006, USA
Phone (202)296-4031

The Chalet Club
135 E. 35th St.

New York, NY 10022, USA
Phone (212)490-0126

Colorado Dude and Guest Ranch Assn.
Box 6440, Cherry Creek Sta.
Denver, CO 80206, USA
Phone (303)674-4906

Colorado Mountain Club
1723 E. 16th Ave.
Denver, CO 80218, USA
Phone (303)922-8315

Eastern Professional Outfitters Assn.
P.O. Box 252
Hot Springs, NC 28743, USA

Equestrian Trails, Inc.
10723 Riverside Dr.
N. Hollywood, CA 91602, USA

Federation of Western Outdoor Clubs
943 Mills Tower
San Francisco, CA 94104, USA

High Sierra Backpackers Association
Box 147
Bishop, CA 93514, USA

Idaho Outfitters and Guides Assn.
P.O. Box 95
Boise, ID 83701, USA
Phone (208)376-5680

National Trails Council
P.O. Box 29
Braddock Heights, MD 21714, USA

North American Trail Conference
1995 Day Rd.
Gilroy, CA 95020, USA

Ontario Trail Riders Association
2240 Kingston Rd.
Scarborough, ON Canada M1N 1T9

Trail Riders of the Canadian Rockies
P.O. Box 6742, Sta. D
Calgary, AB Canada T2P 2E6

The Wilderness Society
1901 Pennsylvania Ave. NW
Washington, DC 20036, USA
Phone (202)467-5810

Wyoming Outfitters Association
Box A1
Jackson, WY 83001, USA

CATTLE DRIVING

The sunburnt wrangler raises his hat, silhouetted against the clear, cloudless sky. Slowly at first, then with a rising rhythm, a thousand head of cattle move off toward the east, driven by the cowhands surrounding the herd. Clouds of dry dust fill the air; the earth quakes as the weight of the herd's hooves imprints their tracks on the soil; a stray calf is rounded up by a gruff but understanding cowboy. Miraculously, you ride along with it all, visions of a hundred Western movies suddenly paling in comparison to the real thing.

If you've always wanted to participate in a cattle drive, a roundup or even a rodeo but feared that you were born too late, don't worry. In the western United States and Canada, you can join up with teams of real cowboys, either at working ranches or out on the trail. These are not just "dude ranches." On the high plains, far from your city worries, you actually help with the daily chores of ranch life—brushing down mounts, herding cattle, feeding livestock and mending fences, the roundups and branding. At night, you can practice your rusty square dance steps at the hoedown, or perhaps tell a tall tale or two around the campfire. It is a unique opportunity to take an active part in a great American tradition.

Many of these ranches are in areas that allow for exploration of abandoned Indian settlements, as in Colorado, or of long-forgotten cabins in Idaho that once housed miners. Dinosaur bones and fossilized ferns might turn up in the mountains of Montana. Overnight pack trips in Wyoming cross over mountain ridges to offer you magnificent panoramas of distant ranges and plains. And winter visits to a stock farm in Alberta give you the chance to go ice skating on a frozen lake beneath a heavy gray sky.

Since these ranches are usually located in remote areas, far from the lights and sounds of civilization, the air is fresh and fragrant. At night, as you sit around the coals of the dinner fire, the stars above look like a million distant campfires ranged across the landscape of heaven. Whether your visit to a working ranch lasts just a summer week or turns into a new lifestyle for you, it's an adventure you won't soon forget. ☐

Branding is just part of the cowhand's spring chores. At this time of year, herds are also dehorned, weaned and turned out to summer ranges. (Jim Wilcox)

CATTLE DRIVING

CANADA

Alberta

Stock Farm Stay: A working stock farm in east-central Alberta invites vacationers for stays either to participate in the daily chores or to travel in the area. The farm is located about 160 miles east of Edmonton in the middle of an extensive and well-established farming area; participants may drive cattle, ride horses, help tend grain, visit other farms in the area or make a trip to nearby Dilberry Provincial Park. Winter visits provide opportunities for cross-country skiing and ice skating. Family activities on the farm are also open to guests. **Cost:** $15 a day for adults, half-price for children under 6 includes room and board in the main house or a furnished guest house; $2 a day for camping privileges. **When:** Year-round. **Contact:** Poplar Bluff Stock Farm, RR 1, Chauvin, AB Canada T0B 0V0.

British Columbia

Open Ranching: Participants gather at a historic cattle ranch in the Clinton Valley about 2½ miles northeast of the town of Clinton. At the working ranch, participants join in several outdoor activities including horseback riding, swimming and hiking. Guests are provided with a horse and tack suited to their ability and experience. A new trail ride occurs daily, led by experienced wranglers through meadows and open cattle ranges.

Horseback games such as gymkhana barrel racing and boot racing are among the activities scheduled. **Cost:** $75 to $140 depending on length of stay includes meals, accommodations, guides, horses, equipment. **When:** May to June, September to November. **Contact:** Three Bar J Ranch, P.O. Box 189, Clinton, BC Canada V0K 1K0; phone (604)459-2254.

Summer Roundup: Families can enjoy summer stays at a 5,000-acre working ranch on the eastern slopes of the Canadian Rockies near Dawson Creek. Visitors not arriving by car can take a bus to the town of Chetwynd, where they are met by ranch hands. There are more than 100 head of horses, and participants are encouraged to help with roundups and various ranch chores. Accommodation is provided in log cabins, with home-cooked meals served in a nearby lodge building. The ranch sponsors a special program for boys between 10 and 16 years of age; for 10 days during the summer they stay at the ranch and learn riding skills, packing, camping, wilderness survival and general wilderness lore. **Cost:** $200 for boys camp includes accommodations in house-tents, all meals; $250 a person for family cabins includes accommodations and meals for 1 week. **When:** Summer months. **Contact:** Pruckl Ranch, Box 88, Chetwynd, BC Canada V0C 1J0.

UNITED STATES

California

Horse Drive and Trail Ride: For 4 days participants help herd mules

Several working ranches in the western United States and Canada welcome help from tenderfoot wranglers. Participants can take a turn brushing down mounts, herding cattle or mending fences. Or they can use the ranch as a base for horseback trips into the wilderness. (Jim Wilcox)

and horses from a winter range in Owens Valley to summer headquarters at Rock Creek Pack Station in the High Sierras north of Bishop. Those joining the drive do not have to be expert riders, but should have had some time in the saddle. The group begins early in the morning, rides during the cooler part of the day and makes camp in the early afternoon. A cook and camp crew travels ahead of the group to set up camp. Tents are provided but participants may sleep in the open if they choose. Riders are given a horse to match their riding abilities and various mounts are available. **Cost:** $145.

When: June. **Contact:** Rock Creek Pack Station, Box 248, Bishop, CA 93514, USA; phone (714)935-4493, summer 872-8331.

Colorado

Roundup Welcome: Tenderfoot wranglers are invited to spend time at the Canyon Ranch at the mouth of Dry Creek Canyon. The canyon, long used by the Ute Indians as a wintering area, is replete with abandoned settlements, arrowheads, tools and crockery, not to mention dinosaur bones and old mines. At the ranch there is plenty of horseback riding, and participants may assist in the cattle driving as ranch hands move the livestock from pasture to pasture. Accommodations include a bunkhouse and a log guest house, both heated for the chilly summer nights, and meals are served in the dining hall. **Cost:** $125 a week includes horseback rides, accommodations, jeep trips, meals. **When:** On request. **Contact:** Canyon Ranch, Rt. 1, P.O. Box 61A, Olathe, CO 81425, USA; phone (303)323-5288.

Working Vacation: Travelers interested in the ways of a working ranch are invited to stay at the S Bar S Ranch near Steamboat Springs. On a daily or weekly basis participants stay in private cabins, in an old homestead log cabin or in a community bunkhouse. Each cabin has electricity, gas heat, a cooking range, utensils and hot water. Activities at the ranch include fishing and floating on the Elk River, hay rides, camping trips, pack trips and cook outs. Winter brings sleigh rides, skiing and snowmobiling. Because the ranch is a working one, guests may involve themselves in such chores as branding, mending fences, feeding livestock, haying, throwing dogies and driving cattle. **Cost:** From $70 a week, from $4 to $8 a day. **When:** Year-round. **Contact:** S Bar S Ranch, Steamboat Springs, CO 80477, USA; phone (303)879-0788.

Idaho

Ranching in Challis National Forest: A working cattle ranch nestled in a valley of the Salmon River Mountains, part of the Challis National Forest, provides all ranching experiences as well as goldpanning in local streams. Visitors use cabins while at the ranch, once the prime stop for the mule teams bringing supplies and equipment to the Lost Packer Mine. Guests may visit the local sawmill or climb to Pinyon Peak to view the Montana and Wyoming landscapes in the distance. **Cost:** $240 to $550 depending on party size, accommodations, length of stay. **When:** June to September. **Contact:** Diamond D Ranch, Inc., Clayton, ID 83227, USA; phone (208)879-2372; winter, P.O. Box 36005, Grosse Pointe Woods, MI 48236, USA; phone (313)821-4975.

Montana

Dude's Delight: Would-be ranchers stay at a working ranch in the heart of Montana's cattle country. Because the ranch is an operating concern, participants help, if they wish, in the chores which include branding, roundups, animal husbandry and more. Accommodations are provided in 2-, 3- and 4-room cabins; meals are provided in the central dining lodge. A new recreation building with ping pong and a pool serves as a family gathering place. Other activities include swimming, pack riding, excursions into the mountains and fishing. Everyone may go horseback riding, and horses and saddles are included. **Cost:** $190 to $235 a week. **When:** March to October. **Contact:** Sixty-three Ranch, Livingstone, MT 59047, USA; phone (406)222-0570.

Oregon

Ranching on the Rogue: Nestled in the Rogue River Valley in southern

Oregon is a working ranch where guests can participate in the functioning of the ranch or relax and be lazy. On 300 acres of meadows and timber, participants find good riding trails, excellent horses, nature paths, a stocked pond, photography opportunities, hay rides, hoedowns and pony races. During the week many different activities are planned such as a cattle roundup, a 5-hour ride to Jump-Off-Joe Creek with fishing and swimming on the way, and a raft trip down the Rogue to Indian Mary Campground. Dudes stay in a cottage or bunkhouse, and children's activities are supervised. During the snow ski season, transportation to the slopes is provided. **Cost:** $26 to $32 a day; $170 to $192 for 6 days depending on age and season includes transportation from Grants Pass, meals, accommodations, horses, river trips. **When:** Year-round. **Contact:** Paradise Guest Ranch, 7000 Monument Dr., Grants Pass, OR 97526, USA; phone (503)479-4333.

Wyoming

Cattle Ranch Visit: A working cattle ranch in Wyoming's Sweetwater Valley provides week-long visits for adventurers. Participants travel from Casper to the ranch at the base of the Ferris Mountains and start right in helping the cowhands with chores. Overnight pack trips are made into the surrounding high country and float trips, either on quiet water or rapids, are run down the Platte River. Swimming in Alcova Lake, riding and hiking are only a few of the possibilities open during the week of unscheduled activities. **Cost:** $350 includes food, accommodations, transportation to and from Casper, activities, most equipment. **When:** May to September. **Contact:** Special InteresTours, P.O. Box 37, Medina, WA 98039, USA; phone (206)455-1960. *(M)*

Working a Cattle Ranch: Participants may join in the operation and stay as long as they like at a cattle ranch located in Wyoming and Montana. At the ranch home guests are lodged in a trailer house or camper, but most of the time they stay at one of the cow camps, tending the herds. Sleeping in tents and cooking over campfires, participants join ranch hands in chores that vary according to the time of year: spring branding, summer fence mending, fall gathering from the summer pastures. Riders are followed by a 4-wheel drive pickup, and saddle-sore riders may take a break, although they may ride every day if they wish. The ranch is near the Pryor Mountain Wild Horse Range, and riders may have a chance to see the wild horses running. **Cost:** $200 a week. **When:** April through October. **Contact:** TX Ranch, P.O. Box 453, Lovell, WY 82431, USA; phone (406)484-2583. *(M)*

BACKPACKING

You take a deep breath and catch the scents of wildflowers, of sun-baked earth, and a cool breeze coming off a glacier. A jay squawks in the fir trees behind you, but your eyes are on the jagged line of peaks against the distant sky. You feel a harmony of the senses you rarely feel in the city, a well-being and self-awareness that comes from walking hard all day to arrive in the heart of a free and untrammeled wilderness. It might be in the Rockies, the Sierras, the Alleghenies or the Tetons. Or you may be hiking abroad, among the Swiss Alps, the Indian Himalayas or Peruvian Andes. Wherever it is, and however different the terrain, climate and wildlife, backpacking offers you the chance to rediscover your place in the natural world.

Backpacking is, by definition, the activity in which you carry all your needs on your back. It could be only a sleeping bag, a light stove, some "gorp" or hiker's mix, and a map; or it could be 50 pounds of gear in a tall, external-frame rucksack. Sturdy, lightweight equipment now fills the market, as backpacking has become one of the world's most popular adventure activities. Part of its popularity lies in the fact that almost anyone can take off alone or with a group of friends and hike on trails often no more than an hour's drive from metropolitan centers. But increasingly, people are taking advantage of the expertise, convenience and wide possibilities offered by professional backpacking groups.

Outfitters on almost every continent can supply the equipment and guidance needed to take you to the worlds' most exotic and remote regions on trips lasting from a weekend to a month. In the Middle East, for example, you can spend 10 days hiking and climbing in the Sinai Peninsula, learning about the environment and the lifestyle of the local Bedouin nomads. On the Canary Islands, you can take a two-week excursion which includes an ascent of a 12,200-foot peak and visits to Atlantic coast fishing villages. In Europe, backpacking trips range from two weeks in Norway's mountains to countryside walks near Lake Orta in northern Italy, as well as many excursions in the Austrian, French, Swiss and Yugoslavian Alps.

Whether you are looking for a cirque lake in the shadow of a glacier-carved peak in the Cascades, gazelle tracks in the game reserves of Zambia, a photograph of an eagle in the Brooks Range, or the end of a newly blazed trail, backpacking is the way to find it. In the process, you'll discover a warm pride in knowing you can find your own way in the wild parts of the world. □

Hikers in northwestern Washington can follow trails that lead into the mountainous backcountry of the Olympic National Park. (Keith Gunnar)

BACKPACKING

AFRICA

Mt. Kenya Expedition: During this 31-day expedition to East Africa, participants travel extensively in Kenya from the equatorial summit of Mt. Kenya to the Indian Ocean. Two weeks are spent on the Mt. Kenya massif, trekking through the dense, tropical rain forest to the high alpine regions. The expedition also spends time in the Aberdare Range and in the wild Samburu country to the north which extends into Somalia and Ethiopia. The last few days of the expedition are spent south of Mombasa on the Indian Ocean. Each participant is involved in a service project, usually with the National Forest. The project may include clearing forest trails or building a bridge across a high mountain stream. A major emphasis of the expedition is a consideration for the quality and preservation of the wilderness. There are opportunities to receive academic credit through colleges and secondary schools. **Cost:** $1,300 covers tuition. **When:** January. **Contact:** Challenge/Discovery, The Wilderness Center, Box 229, Crested Butte, CO 81224, USA; phone (303)349-5432; winter, Antioch College, Yellow Springs, OH 45387, USA; phone (513)767-7331.
(M)

Lesotho

Hiking the Malotis: Trip members stay in a base lodge near the Madibamotso River during a 17-day visit in the now independent kingdom formerly known as Basutoland. Located deep in the Maloti Mountains, the lodge provides easy access to varied walks through valleys, over rolling hills, along ridges and up to summits. Participants may descend to the river's banks for swimming, and a wide variety of bird life may be observed. Accommodations are in 2-bed chalets, with a comfortable lounge and dining room nearby. **Cost:** $999 includes roundtrip transportation from London, accommodations, some meals. **When:** March, October. **Contact:** Waymark Holidays, 295 Lillie Rd., London SW6 7LL, Great Britain; phone 01-385-5015.

Tanzania

Climbing Kilimanjaro: An 18-day trip to Africa combines visits to several game parks with a climb of Mt. Kilimanjaro, the continent's highest peak. The trip departs from New York with a flight to Tanzania via London, where 1 night is spent. After a night in Arusha, the party travels to the new Tarangire National Park for a night under canvas amidst the extremely dense wildlife population. Over the next 4 days, the group visits Ngorongoro Crater, Serengeti National Park and Lake Manyara National Park for wildlife observation and some conditioning hikes. On the trip's ninth day, participants reach the Marangu Hotel, the base for the climb to Kilimanjaro since the 1890s. The climb is made over the next 5 days, culminating in a spectacular sunrise view from the summit. The ascent is basically a strenuous high-altitude walk and does not require mountaineering techniques. The descent takes only 2 days, after which group members return by air to New York, again with a London stopover. **Cost:** $4,054 to $5,375 depending on type of flight and accommodations includes round-trip transportation from New York, equipment, food, fees, guide. **When:** February. **Contact:** Hanns Ebensten Travel Inc., 55 W. 42nd St., New York, NY 10036, USA; phone (212)354-6634.

ASIA

Japan

Fall Hiking in Japan: The only trip operator given permission to make this trek, Mountain Travel takes hikers to climb over and through areas of the Japanese North Alps too steep for habitation. The trails are rugged and narrow, making this a strenuous trek. Trekkers live Japanese style, eating native food and staying overnight in mountain huts. The trip is made in the autumn when the slopes of the mountains are wreathed in color. Time is also spent in Kyoto, Nara and Tokyo to visit temples, gardens and palaces. The coniferous and broad-leafed forests are the home of bears, deer, mountain goats, raccoons, and badgers. **Cost:** $2,456 includes airfare from San Francisco, meals, accommodations. **When:** September. **Contact:** Mountain Travel Inc., 1398 Solano Ave., Albany, CA 94706, USA; phone (415)527-8100. *(M)*

Hiking in remote areas of the lower Himalayas requires good physical stamina but no technical climbing ability. Himalayan Trekking Service offers a 32-day trip in Nepal. (Keith Gunnar)

Nepal

Himalayan Backpacking: After sightseeing in Kathmandu, a city of gilded Buddist temples and royal palaces, a flight to Jiri begins a rugged hiking trek in which participants walk uphill an accumulated distance of nearly 50,000 feet over 32 days. No technical mountaineering ability is needed, but members should have good physical stamina and some hiking experience. Applicants are subject to the approval of the group leader, who has previously led 2 successful Himalayan treks. Hikers spend 23 days enjoying views of the world's highest peaks. Along the way visits are made to centuries-old Sherpa villages, the famous Tibetan Buddhist monastery of Thyangboche and the outpost of Namche Bazar at the foot of Mt. Everest. The trip requires the services of a licensed physician, surgeon or general practioner, with a substantial reduction in cost offered in exchange for services. **Cost:** $2,300. **When:** October. **Contact:** Himalayan Trekking Service, 5730 Rising Sun Ave., Philadelphia, PA 19120, USA; phone (215)342-8394.

Sri Lanka

Highlands of Sri Lanka: Hikers explore Sri Lanka on a 7-day trek in higher elevations where temperatures range from 60° to 70°F. Participants stay overnight at guest houses, and the hiking sites are reached by car journeys of 30 to 100 miles. Expedition members climb 8,820-foot Mt. Pidurutalagala, neither a strenuous nor a hazardous climb, though the mountain is Sri Lanka's highest. At the summit of 7,353-foot Adam's Peak, or Sripada ("holy footprint"), participants may speculate concerning somewhat contradictory explanations for a footprintlike impression, and see a spectacular sunrise. On Horton Plains, a 7,000-foot plateau covered with pale green grass, dark forests, rhododendrons, orchids and clear pools, expedition members visit World's End, a precipitous drop-off of 2,000 feet. **Cost:** $220 from Colombo. **When:** Year-round. **Contact:** Walker's Tours & Travels Ltd., P.O. Box 1048, 11 York St., Colombo 1, Sri Lanka; phone 22553. *(M)*

Thailand

Trekking through the Golden Triangle: Members of a 22-day journey across Thailand travel over a wide variety of terrain by various modes of transportation. After a flight from Paris to Bangkok, a visit is made to its floating food market and principal temples. Trip members then travel by bus or taxi through Chinese villages and the central plains area. Participation in local singing, dances and cuisine is the highlight of a climb to the village at the Pass of the Three Pagodas. By the eleventh day participants begin the first ascent into the mountains by bus and then proceed in canoe to the village of Shan, where accommodations are provided by local residents. Travelers move on from Lissu through the deeper parts of the jungle, heading toward the frontiers of the world's largest poppy fields. After a rest for the night and a visit with the chief at the tribal village of Akha, participants hike 5 hours and then drive to other villages in the Valley Ikko. Trip members spend the journey's

Toward the end of a day in Iceland, backpackers pitch their tent at a campsite near Tungnafellsjokull. Iceland's landscapes include volcanic fissures, glacial rivers and lush meadows. (Kristin Tregillus)

final days at the beaches of Pattaya, with opportunities for swimming, sunbathing and water skiing. From Bangkok, participants board the plane for the return to Paris. **Cost:** $1,200 includes roundtrip transportation from Paris, hotels, some meals. **When:** June to December. **Contact:** Terres d'Aventure, 5, rue St. Victor, 75505, Paris, France; phone 033 63 51.

ATLANTIC

Greenland

Over Glacier and Fjord: Adventurers in good physical condition embark on a 15-day hiking trip with 7 to 10 hours of walking a day. After arriving in Greenland, group members go to Narssarssuaq where they camp. They then travel by boat up the Qoroq Fjord to begin the walk through mountain scenery toward

Jespersen Glacier. Crossing the glacier commences the next day, and the group camps at nearby Ulvesoen. Another boat is taken to Qagdumiut before participants hike toward Tasiluk. From here the route continues along the Igaliko Fjord, past Eqaluit and Qanisartut, and ends in Igaliko for camping. A return is made to Narssarssuaq by boat before a flight to Copenhagen. A detailed list of necessary equipment is supplied. **Cost:** $640 to $675 includes return flight to Copenhagen, local transportation, tents, meals, leader. **When:** July, August. **Contact:** DVL Rejser, Kultorvet 7,1, 1175 Kobenhavn K, Denmark; phone (01)132727.

Iceland

On Foot in Iceland: Groups of 10 to 15 hike past Reykjavik through farmlands and past fjords into the harsh terrain of mountains, deserts and icecaps. Accommodations are provided in huts or tents and vary according to the length of each trip. Trip members take part in carrying loads sometimes up to 44 pounds, cooking meals and helping with other camp chores. Treks hours or weeks long can be made, some in the Torfajokull region where hikers visit Eldgja, reputedly the largest volcanic fissure in the world, or Fljotsdalur with its icecaps, glacial rivers and views of Markarfljot gorge. Parties walk day after day, occasionally the entire length of the trip, without meeting any other human beings. Mountain buses are used to carry hikers to remote starting areas. Full motor safaris are also offered. **Cost:** $133 to $705. **When:** June to September. **Contact:** Dick Phillips, Whitehall House, Nenthead, Alston, Cumbria CA9 3PS, Great Britain.

Hiking Expedition: A variety of geologic features is explored during a 13-day backpacking trip across the Icelandic landscape. Participants hike through volcanic deposits ranging in size from granular to massive, over lush meadows and across icy streams. Group members sleep in tents and have layover days that may be spent at leisure. There is some bus travel to geysers, waterfalls and a museum. Children accompanied by parents are welcome, though all members are subject to leader approval. Members may want to read up beforehand on the geology and history of the terrain to better enjoy the trip. Sierra Club membership is required. **Cost:** $600. **When:** July. **Contact:** Sierra Club Outing Dept.,

530 Bush St., San Francisco, CA 94108, USA; phone (415)981-8634.

AUSTRALASIA

New Zealand

Hiking the Milford Track: With stops in Fiji and Tahiti, travelers journey on a 3-week trip from Boston to Christchurch, New Zealand. The university city of Dunedin and the Otago Peninsula are explored, as well as the flora and fauna of Stewart and Ulva islands across the Foveaux Strait. After viewing Mt. Cook from the Hermitage, travelers reach the trip's climax: the Milford Track from Te Anau to Milford Sound on the Tasman Sea. Passing over these 33 miles through the Southern Alps in Fiordland National Park has been compared to walking through the Alps down to a Norwegian fjord at easily hiked elevations. Hikers set out in small groups of 2 or 3, with each day's plans prearranged and directed by a local guide. Food and bedding are furnished at huts which have electricity and hot showers. **Cost:** $2,500 includes roundtrip airfare from Boston, overnights in Fiji and Tahiti. **When:** November. **Contact:** Appalachian Mountain Club, 5 Joy St., Boston, MA 02108, USA; phone (617)523-0636.

Hiking the Southern Alps: Participants hike along a trail discovered over 80 years ago as an overland route to New Zealand's Milford Sound. Both 6- and 7-day trips are offered, enabling hikers to explore the varied and rugged terrain. Huts along the way are staffed to provide good meals and bunkroom accom-

modations. During the trip, participants can see the towering rock walls of Clinton Canyon—often covered with waterfalls flowing from above—and Sutherland Falls, one of the highest falls in the area. A multitude of wildlife is seen, including many species of birds that inhabit the valley and glades. Although the trail's larger streams are bridged, some of the path is rocky and there is a mountain pass to traverse. Participants should be reasonably fit. **Cost:** $121 for adults and $81 for children on the 6-day trip, $141 for adults and $93 for children on the 7-day trip. **When:** November to March. **Contact:** Fiordland National Park, Chief Ranger, P.O. Box 29, Te Anau, New Zealand, phone 819.

Hiking in the Southern Alps: A 25-mile hike along the Routeburn Track on the South Island takes travelers through spectacular Fiordland and Mt. Aspiring national parks. The 4-day guided trip departs from Queenstown and explores the lakes, gorges and forests of this untouched region. Nights are spent in small mountain lodges. **Cost:** $110. **When:** November to April. **Contact:** Routeburn Walk Ltd., P.O. Box 271, Queenstown, New Zealand; phone 100.

Wanganui River Walk: The Wanganui River, on the North Island, flows from the slopes of Tongariro Volcano to the ocean in a sweeping arc through lowland bush country. A 5-day walking trip follows close

On a 4-day hike along the Routeburn Track in New Zealand, hikers admire the view of Hollyford Vally 3,000 feet below. The Darran Mountains rise in the distance. (Routeburn Walk Ltd.)

to the river for 25 miles and then returns by boat, providing participants the opportunity to see a variety of New Zealand scenery. The trip starts with a drive from the town of Taumarunui to Whakahora, on the river, where the walk commences. The amount of hiking increases from 3 hours the first day to 5 by the third, as the hikers pass through river gorges, cool forests and open grassy flats. The area is sprinkled with ruined homesteads and overgrown horse-paths, remnants of the region's early settlers, while small streams and waterfalls highlight the natural landscape. On the fifth day the walking route meets the river again, and participants climb aboard a jet boat for an hour's ride to their starting point of Whakahora, returning from there to Taumarunui by car. **Cost:** On request. **When:** On request. **Contact:** Venturetreks Ltd., P.O. Box 3839, Auckland, New Zealand; phone 379 847.

CANADA

Alberta

Backpacking in the Canadian Rockies: The trails of Banff, Kootenay, Yoho and Jasper national parks provide an alpine environment for backpackers on a 32-day trip in Alberta and British Columbia. Amid glacier-capped peaks, alpine meadows and cold, clear streams and lakes, participants learn the techniques of self-sufficiency in the wilderness for extended periods without damage to ecology. A week-long seminar with a certified Canadian Mountain Guide provides basic mountaineering instruction in snow, ice and rock skills with an emphasis on safety. The trip begins and ends in Calgary and offers challenging wilderness hiking. Physical fitness and conditioning are recommended for participants. **Cost:** $568 plus $30 emergency fund. **When:** July. **Contact:** American Youth Hostels, National Campus, Delaplane, VA 22025, USA; phone (703)592-3271.

Backpacking in Banff National Park: Beginning at the western boundary of the park, a 44-mile hike follows the Continental Divide through the forests and alpine meadows of the Canadian Rockies. Hikers travel 4 to 8 miles a day with professional guides who discuss the flora and fauna as well as cook, set up and break camp. A stay at 11,870-foot Mt. Assiniboine, the glacier-capped "Matterhorn of the Rockies," is planned. Opportunities are provided to see and photograph wildlife such as deer, elk, moose, bears, mountain goats, and small animals and birds. The hike is limited to 12 backpackers and lasts 7 days, starting and ending at Sunshine Lodge in the park. **Cost:** $235, all-inclusive. **When:** July. **Contact:** Aurora Borealis Expeditions, P.O. Box 9266, Missoula, MT 59807, USA. *(M)*

Backpacking and Canoeing the Kootenay: Beginning and ending in Banff, a 2-week hiking and canoeing trip can be taken either by adults or youths 12 to 17. Hikers plot their route, then find their way on trails not always well-marked; some are trap lines 60 to 80 years old. From Sunshine, 14 miles west of Banff, hikers travel some 70 miles to the Kootenay River via

Hikers turn their gazes and cameras toward the Canadian Rockies which rise on the other side of a valley in Alberta. (Tauk Tours)

Simpson Pass, down the Simpson River to Surprise Creek, over Ferro Pass and down the Mitchell River. Participants then cross over an 8,000-foot pass and travel down Daer Creek to the Kootenay River. Fishing is excellent along the way. At the Kootenay, participants are supplied with canoes and paddle 80 miles downstream to Canal Flats, where a bus takes them back to Banff. **Cost:** $350, all-inclusive. **When:** July, August. **Contact:** Canadian Mountain Holidays Ltd., P.O. Box 1660, Banff, AB Canada T0L 0C0; phone (403)762-4531.

Baker Creek Backpack: A series of 6-day hikes originating at Baker Creek trailhead introduces travelers to the many aspects of the Rockies.

Participants head from Baker Creek, about 30 miles west of Banff, along a trail which follows the flow of Baker Creek for 8 miles through a forest of lodgepole pine and spruce. Passing many mountain peaks and lakes, participants view 9,140-foot Protection Mountain to the east of the trail and Lipalian Mountain which rises up on the west. Trip members select a campsite on a flower-filled avalanche slope at the base of towering Redoubt Mountain, 9,520 feet high. Wildflower Lake, located high on Mt. Avens, and "Unnamed Lake" are found beside the mountain trails to Pulsatilla Pass. Hiking itineraries are flexible, depending on weather, ability or mood. Hikers camp in 4-person tents. **Cost:** $165 includes membership to Skyline Hikers, tent equipment, meals. **When:** July, August. **Contact:** The Skyline Hikers of the Canadian Rockies, P.O. Box 3514, Sta. B, Calgary, AB Canada T2M 4M2.

British Columbia

Camping North of Vancouver: On a week-long trip, participants camp at Lake Kowaskey north of Vancouver, with opportunities for a variety of activities. Travel from Vancouver is by vehicle as far as a logging road, then proceeds with a fairly easy hike to the lake, which is glacier-fed by Kwoiek Creek. It is a generally untraveled area, save for a few prospectors and anglers. From base camp adventurers may enjoy boating on the lake, fishing, hiking in the surrounding area, picking alpine flowers and blueberries, and watching and photographing wildlife. Animals in the area include black bears, deer, grizzly bears and mountain goats. Participants return to Vancouver by the same route. **Cost:** $210 includes transportation, camping equipment, food, guide. **When:** July, August. **Contact:** Black Tusk Touring and Guide Service Ltd., 3064 St. Kildas Ave., North Vancouver, BC Canada V7L 2A9; phone (604)985-9223. *(M)*

Hiking from Chilko Lake: Backpackers may hike for 7 or 14 days in the Coastal Mountains, from the base ranch at Chilko Lake about 180 miles north of Vancouver. For the first few days, hikers travel through the timbered country around the lake, then spend several days above timberline at 6,000 feet, the habitat of mule deer and mountain goats. Wildlife and views of peaks, snowfields and glaciers provide excellent photographic opportunities. Several permanent camps, situated about 4 days apart, are stocked with extra food for longer trips so that backpackers need not carry heavy packs. The maximum number of participants for each trip is 10. **Cost:** $260 to $520. **When:** June to August. **Contact:** Chilko Lake Wilderness Ranch Ltd., P.O. Box 4750, Williams Lake, BC Canada V2G 2V7; phone (604)Chilko Lake Wilderness Ranch.

Custom Alpine Hiking: Guide service is available for summer hiking and backpacking trips in the Canadian Rockies. Hiking is over a wide variety of terrain, from well-groomed park trails to rugged cross-country trips through remote wild areas. Wildlife is plentiful in the area and trips may focus on photography, mine exploration, wildflower gathering or other activities. **Cost:** $85 to $125 a week. **When:** June to October. **Contact:** Northern Lights Alpine Recreation, Box 399, Invermere, BC Canada V0A 1K0; phone (604)342-6042. *(M)*

Environmental Journeys: The rugged Inside Passage between mainland British Columbia and Vancouver Island provides an unequaled environment for a 2-week land and sea wilderness course. With a ratio of 1 instructor for every 5 students, the course is designed to impart basic techniques for safe enjoyment and preservation of the wilderness. Travel is by inflatable boat and on foot. A total of 200 miles is covered in 14 days, with camping on the beach at night and shore excursions during the day. Hiking routes wind through giant evergreen forests, across islands, up the slopes of Mt. Waddington and cross-country from inlet to inlet. **Cost:** $400 includes instruction, meals, group equipment, transportation. **When:** January, June to August. **Contact:** Pacific Northwest Sea Trails, Inc., 13062 Caminito del Rocio, Del Mar, CA 92014, USA; phone (714)481-9540. *(M)*

Cape Scott Hike: Participants spend about 4 days of an 8-day trip exploring the northwest end of Vancouver Island. Cape Scott lies on the westernmost tip, part of a provincial park area containing 40 miles of ocean front and 14 miles of beaches. Access to the park is by a muddy logging road 30 miles from Port Hardy on the east coast of the island. Camping is done on the beaches where participants observe the native wildlife and investigate the natural terrain. Some signs of humans are seen, including the remains of 19th-century log dwellings constructed by Danish settlers. Traveling eastward along the isolated coast, trip members explore sea caves and glaciated rock shelves. Bears, raccoons, deer, seals, sea lions and other animals are abundant. As the group leaves the ocean front, they pass through dense underbrush to the Nahwitti Plateau, a land of miniature trees, muddy bogs and Roosevelt elk. A logging road is used for the return to Port Hardy. **Cost:** $215. **When:** August, September. **Contact:** Western Outdoor Adventures Ltd., 16115 32nd Ave., White Rock, BC Canada V4B 4Z5; phone (604)531-3969. *(M)*

Parent-Child Camping: Participants fly by float plane from Vancouver across Howe Sound, up the Sunshine Coast, over Skookumchuck Rapids and up Jervis Inlet to camp for 7 days at Vancouver Bay. Guides are available for hikes in the Jervis Inlet area, but everyone is encouraged to explore individually. The inlet area has an average width of 1½ miles over a 50-mile length, forming a good photographic base for the 5,000- to 8,000-foot mountains in the distance. At Vancouver Bay, participants may swim in freshwater or saltwater, as well as fish for prawns, clams, ling cod and red snapper. Three days are allowed for individual exploration before further hikes are planned. Participants may hike to alpine lakes or secluded bays and inlets. Canoes are available. The emphasis is on individual planning and exploration. **Cost:** $250 for parents, $150 for children. **When:** June to September. **Contact:** Western Outdoor Adventures Ltd., 16115 32nd Ave., White Rock, BC Canada V4B 4Z5; phone (604)531-3969. *(M)*

Northwest Territories

Arctic Exploration: The first few days of this 15-day trip are spent in the Eskimo hunting and trapping community of Grise Fiord. Traveling by canoe to the adjacent Starnes Fiord, hikers set up a base camp, from which day hikes and easy climbs to local peaks are undertaken. Among the challenges of an arctic summer, participants are warned that terrain is rocky and rough, river crossings may be difficult and delays of up to 1 week may be expected for flights between Grise Fiord and Resolute Bay.

Though vegetation is sparse, indigenous wildlife includes caribou, musk oxen, wolves, polar bears and seals. **Cost:** $850. **When:** August. **Contact:** Canatrek Mountain Expeditions, P.O. Box 1138, Banff, AB Canada T0L 0C0; phone (403)762-3143. **(M)**

Nova Scotia

Maritime Backpacking Adventures: Weekends or weeks can be spent exploring the mixture of French and Scottish culture in the rolling hills and rugged Atlantic coastline of the Maritime Provinces. Organized and led by volunteers, trips may consist of hiking, canoeing or camping to meet the desires of each group. Among the trips offered are a whitewater canoe clinic, an 80-mile canoe trip and a hiking tour of Cape Breton. Tents, canoes, cooking gear and food are provided. **Cost:** $20 for clinic, $120 for canoe trip, $80 for hiking trip. **When:** June to August. **Contact:** Canadian Hostelling Association, P.O. Box 3010 S., Halifax, NS Canada B3J 3G6; phone (902)425-5450.

Ontario

Along the Bruce Trail: Backpackers hike for a week on parts of the Bruce Trail, which extends 430 miles along the Niagara escarpment and provides an unusual opportunity to explore the Ontario of yesteryear. Participants view scenic gorges, hidden waterfalls and panoramic views over Georgian Bay. The journey begins at Dunks Bay near

The rugged coastline of northern Vancouver Island provides an isolated campsite for a family of backpackers. Western Outdoor Adventures Ltd. offers an 8-day trip to the island for $215. (Keith Gunnar)

the tip of the Bruce Peninsula along Georgian Bay, and moves up toward Cape Croker. **Cost:** $195. **When:** July. **Contact:** Wilderness Experts Inc., 26747 Lake Vue Dr., #10, Perrysburg, OH 43551, USA; phone (419)874-8223.

CARIBBEAN

West Indies

Backpacking among Craters and Falls: St. Vincent, a mountainous island in the West Indies, offers outdoor enthusiasts opportunities to experience a variety of terrain and backpacking environments. The island, 11 miles wide and 18 miles long, rises to 3,900 feet in the central ridge; only half of the land is inhabited. Backpackers day-hike to the site of a silent volcano and from its rim look down to the crater lake, to the east at the Atlantic, and to the west at the Caribbean. Descending a path leading to the lake, hikers encounter a mile-wide echo chamber and may swim over to an island that first appeared in 1971. Pathfinders travel north of the volcano, where the slope is steeply inclined, and along the sea where roads are nonexistent. At the Falls of Baleine, most of the watershed funnels through one gap at the coast; at this location the stream plunges into an emerald green gorge, where backpackers make camp. Though the temperature stays between 70° and 75°F year-round, evenings are mild though wet with rainfall. **Cost:** $20 to $23 a day includes food, transportation, guide/porter. **When:** Year-round. **Contact:** Sugar Mill Inn, P.O. Box 119, St. Vincent, West Indies; phone 84216.

Hikers in the Virgin Islands National Park approach the remains of a sugar mill on a plantation built by Danish settlers. (Carol Baker)

CENTRAL AMERICA
Guatemala

Backpacking in Central America: Participants use the local means of transportation, bus and foot, to explore Guatemala on a 9-day backpacking trip from Guatemala City. The flexible itinerary includes a visit to Antigua and passes through Quezaltenango and Huehuetenango. Hikers spend 5 to 6 days in rural Guatemala, visiting markets, shops, churches and homes. A high point of the trip is a hike to the summit of Volcan de Tajumulco (13,845 feet), an 8-hour climb which requires no special equipment. Along the way backpackers both stay in hotels and camp outdoors. The trip is scheduled to allow interested parties to join a 3-day climb of Popocatepetl in Mexico a week later. **Cost:** $365 includes bus fares, guides, food in camp. **When:** February. **Contact:** Johann Mountain Guides, P.O. Box 19171, Portland, OR 97219, USA; phone (503)244-7672 or 288-1413. *(M)*

Backpacking through Jungles and Ruins: A group of backpackers explores Guatemala's lush jungles, towering volcanoes and ancient Indian ruins. The 24-day trip passes through much backcountry, allowing participants the opportunity to camp at summit areas of volcanoes such as Acatenango and Tacana. Backpackers walk for 2 days through remote, roadless Indian villages and hike to the tops of 5 volcanoes. The climbs are steep but non-technical and challenging for most. Each member of the trip carries a full pack weighing up to 35 pounds; optional activities are available for those who prefer to stay in local villages instead of making rigorous climbs. When participants are not on foot, transportation is provided by a minibus. Time is devoted to exploration of Mayan ruins at Tikal, the largest of all Mayan ceremonial centers, and at Copan and Quirigua, famous for intricately carved stelae. Other places included on the itinerary are Lake Atitlan, which is surrounded by volcanoes; Antigua, the ancient colonial capital; and Catamaran Island in the jungle environment of the Dulce River. **Cost:** $2,050 includes roundtrip transportation from Los Angeles. **When:** October to November. **Contact:** Mountain Travel Inc., 1398 Solano Ave., Albany, CA 94706, USA; phone (415)527-8100. *(M)*

Cultural Expedition: An 18-day trip concentrates on an active discovery of Guatemala by living close to the land and people. Beginning in Guatemala City, the group sets out on a drive toward the Caribbean coast, passing through the tropics region and stopping overnight at the shores of Lake Izabel. Dugout canoes transport participants down the Rio Dulce to a campsite at La Sirena, a working farm. Trip members continue down the river to Livingston to spend a night in thatched-roof cottages overlooking the water. The next few days are spent in the mountains, hiking into the tropical cloud forest of moss, orchids and tree ferns. An optional 10-day trip begins when the group returns to Guatemala City for a day of rest. A flight leaves early the next day to the tropical jungle of the Peten and the ruins at Tikal. An accompanying artist/archaeologist helps explain some of the history and secrets of the Mayan civilization. Among the other features of the trip are an optional hike up an active volcano and a visit to the market in Chichicastenango. **Cost:** $1,000 for 18 days, $850 for 10 days includes transportation from Guatemala City, accommodations, meals, camping equipment. **When:** February. **Contact:** Wilderness Southeast, Inc., Rt. 3, Box 619, Savannah, GA 31406, USA; phone (912)355-8008. *(M)*

EUROPE

Alpine Backpacking: A moderately paced hiking and camping trip for youths 15 to 18 explores the Alps of France and Switzerland. Time is divided among the Bernese Oberland, the Mont Blanc area and the Oisans in France's Dauphine Alps. Hikers encounter some snow and steep ascents on glaciers and mountain meadows, and spectacular views can be seen from the trip's highlight—a cable car ride across Mont Blanc. **Cost:** $1,150 includes roundtrip transportation from New York. **When:** July. **Contact:** American Youth Hostels, Metropolitan New York Council, 132 Spring St., New York, NY 10012, USA; phone (212)431-7100.

International Hiking: A month-long summer program takes young people ages 13 to 17 to a variety of countries for outdoor and cultural experiences. Trips are offered to Ireland, Scotland, Switzerland and possibly other countries, depending on interest. No exact itinerary is followed. Generally participants travel and camp together to explore the culture and landscape of the host country, with occasional stays in private homes, on farms and in other situations affording contact with local people. On the Switzerland trip some technical climbing instruction is given by a member of a Swiss Alpine rescue team. **Cost:** $1,250 includes airfare from New York, transportation, accommodations, equipment, instruction, guide. **When:** June to August. **Contact:** Odyssey, P.O. Box 128, Homer, NY 13077, USA; phone (607)749-3348.

Czechoslovakia

Hiking in the Tatry Mountains: Glacial lakes, wildlife and wide vistas await backpackers traveling in the high alpine country of the Tatry Mountains during a 2-week outdoor experience in Eastern Europe. Having traveled from Paris to Prague by plane, trip members board a train for Poprad and a 7-hour tramway ride heading for Stary Smokovec. An introductory lecture describing the terrain is scheduled at the Tatry park information center, in preparation for the next day of hiking among the massive limestone and granite cliffs at Lomnicki Stit. The trip itinerary, which changes somewhat from summer to fall, provides backpackers with a close-up view of several mountain peaks. In autumn, camp is made in the heart of a pine forest at Malepku. Backpackers ascend to heights of nearly 8,000 feet and view the Polish frontiers spread below before descending once more to the valley of Bieloudska. The trip ends with a train ride back to Prague and a plane trip to Paris. **Cost:** $708 in-

cludes all expenses from Paris.
When: July to September. **Contact:**
Terres d'Aventure, 5, rue St. Victor, 75005 Paris, France; phone 033
63 51.

England

Hiking the South West Way: A
2-week backpacking trip takes participants through a 100-mile section
of coastal scenery. The trek covers
the area from the fishing village of
St. Ives to the yachting harbor of St.
Mawes in the Fal estuary, all part of
the walking trail known as the
South West Way. A variety of terrain is traversed, some of it challenging, though no more than 10
miles are covered in any one day.
During the season of the trip, the
cliffs are empty and the beaches
nearly deserted. The cliffs and
sands are rich in flora as well as
wildlife that has been driven from
the inland pastures by intensive
modern agriculture. The villages
along the route provide travelers
with an understanding of local tradition, and in the evening participants may visit the local pubs and
meet some of the village inhabitants. Hikers carry only day packs;
other gear is transported by Land
Rover to the night's stopping place.
Accommodations are usually in
lodges, pubs, hotels or cottages.
Cost: $575. **When:** May. **Contact:**
Backpack Man, 11 Church St.,
Moulton, Northampton NN1 5DQ,
Great Britain; phone 0604 48559.

Walking through Britain: Three-week trips are offered to those

Terres d'Aventure offers a 2-week back-packing trip in the Tatry Mountains.
(Polish Information Bureau)

interested in exploring English, Scottish and Welsh culture and history. Numerous sites are visited, including historic castles, small villages and rural landscapes. England's Lake District provides a stopover, and the Isle of Skye in Scotland gives participants a chance to see coastal wildlife. Animal preservation is one of the topics discussed along the route, and a visit to one of the wildlife refuges of the area provides an introduction to preservation techniques. Variable weather can be expected, as well as simple accommodations and hiking of up to 12 miles a day. **Cost:** $1,150 plus airfare. **When:** June. **Contact:** Sierra Club Outing Dept., 530 Bush St., San Francisco, CA 94108, USA; phone (415)981-8634.

France

Backpacking a Balmy Island: The 3,369-square-mile island of Corsica is the site of 2-week hiking trips. Members meet at Calvi, in the northwestern corner of the island, and travel on a diagonal trail to Calenzana and Mt. Cinto. Backpackers ramble along the trail following the mountain peaks that provide vistas of the valleys and clear Mediterranean waters below. Along the trail, participants bathe in cascading waterfalls and camp under the stars. Climbing among 9 mountain peaks, backpackers reach altitudes higher than 6,000 feet, negotiating passageways cut through steep cliffs. Weary travelers often take time to swim in mountain lakes that lace the alpine terrain. About 5 to 8 hours of hiking are scheduled each day. **Cost:** $270 includes food, accommodations from Calvi. **When:** July to Septem-

ber. **Contact:** Terres d'Aventure, 5, rue St. Victor, 75005, Paris, France; phone 033 63 51.

Hiking in the Pyrenees: A 2-week trip follows the main ridge of the Pyrenees on high mountain paths across the French-Spanish frontier. A number of huts recently built make it possible to stay high in the mountains almost the whole time, with hiking generally at the 1,500-foot level. The starting point is Urdos in the Aspe Valley and the route continues steadily eastward to the Monte Perdido. Various summits are reached along the way, offering beautiful views of the rugged countryside. The route is rich with lakes and caves, some of these being well known from the work of Norbert Casteret and other speleologists. Snow fields and small glaciers are crossed en route. **Cost:** $400 includes roundtrip transportation from London. **When:** July to September. **Contact:** Waymark Holidays, 295 Lillie Rd., London SW6 7LL, Great Britain; phone 01-385-5015.

Germany

Southern Hiking Trip: German village life is experienced during a 2-week trip. Participants stay in small hotels and private guest houses and have many opportunities to meet town residents. The group is actively afoot much of the time, traversing ancient woods with their vestiges of Roman or Celtic civilizations and climbing old carriage roads to castle-topped viewpoints. In the picturesque Mosel valley, participants walk the byways through famous vineyards. Along the Rhine, trip members can see the constant traffic of steamers and barges. A boat ride takes hikers across Lake Constance, and individuals may explore a 1,000-year-old castle on their own. Various side hikes are available among the peaks and valleys of the German Alps. **Cost:** $1,300 includes airfare from Seattle, accommodations, some meals. **When:** June or September. **Contact:** Signpost, 16812 36th Ave. W., Lynnwood, WA 98036, USA; phone (206)743-3947.

Walking Andros and Euboea: Participants convene in London for the flight to Athens where a steamer and a bus transport them to Euboea, the second-largest Greek island, to begin a 14-day walking exploration. Hikers stay in Karystos, a rural market town and busy small port. After walking 5 hours each day on rocky tracks and sometimes the trackless mountainside, the group uses public transport to reach the highest village on 4,592-foot Mt. Okha, where they have a view of miles of the coast. On Andros, participants settle in at the little town of Batsi. From Batsi a path leads up to the steep western scarp of Mt. Petalos, and hikers may choose to continue to the summit at 3,280 feet or head down to the eastern coast of the island. Some in the group may decide to follow tracks leading to isolated mountain villages or remote monasteries. Free time is allotted for swimming and exploring. **Cost:** $392 to $418 depending on departure date includes accommodations, transportation from London, some meals. **When:** May to October. **Contact:** Waymark Holidays,

295 Lillie Rd., London SW6 7LL, Great Britain; phone 01-385-5015.

Ireland

Gouganebarra Walking Trip: Hikers embark from a walking center south of Killarney to explore a myriad of paths and trails. From the Lake Gouganebarra shoreline,

Ireland

Land of Youth-Land of Learning

The least expensive airfare to Europe lands you in Ireland. Low cost connections to the continent. Ireland offers excellent value for your dollars. The Irish have a way of making you feel welcome. Enjoy the Irish countryside. Cruise down the Shannon River on a barge. Or indulge in special adventure activities: pony tracking, horse drawn caravanning, cycling, pot-holing, or many other varied activities. You can always attend one of the many festivals throughout the year. Need some more reasons to come to Ireland? We'll send you lots of them in a special free adventure travel packet of information and ideas.

 Irish Tourist Board
Youth Travel Program
Box 1200/Dept.—OC—91
Long Island City, NY 11101

the slopes rise a thousand feet to a complex pattern of ridges with magnificent views of Macgillicuddy's Reeks or the waters of Bantry Bay. There are no restrictions on walkers except the natural ones of bogs and cliffs. Hikers may go north to Carran summit, or south to Conigar or the twin cones of Douce Mountain. Farther west is Knockboy, a day's journey away. There are easy walks around the lake area or through the valley of the Lee, and a minibus can be used to visit Killarney or Glengariff. Accommodations are provided at a family-owned hotel featuring home-grown produce. **Cost:** $244 includes roundtrip transportation from London, accommodations, meals. **When:** June to September. **Contact:** Waymark Holidays, 295 Lillie Rd., London SW6 7LL, Great Britain; phone 01-385-5015.

Italy

Appreciating the Appenines: Participants on a 14-day visit to the Appenines stay in the little hill town of San Marcello which features narrow stone streets winding between old houses. From this town situated just north of the valley where the Arno River cuts deep into the mountains, participants may head north to one of the Italian Alpine Club's long-distance paths, which follows a long section of the backbone of the Appenines and traverses a dozen summits in the range. Trip members walk up valleys thick with chestnut forests, and from the open ridges and summits glean a panorama of the mountains and the lands of Tuscany. On a walk west to Popiglio, the footpath crosses the deep Lima Valley by means of a suspension bridge. Participants may also take day trips to sightsee in Pisa and Florence. Participants stay in a hotel during the trip. **Cost:** $350 to $384 includes roundtrip transportation from London, accommodations, some meals. **When:** April to October. **Contact:** Waymark Holidays, 295 Lillie Rd., London SW6 7LL, Great Britain; phone 01-385-5015.

Norway

Heading out to Hardangerfjord: From a home base in a chalet 100 miles from the sea, at the edge of the great glacier of the Hardangerjokul, participants join an experienced leader in walking for 10 to 14 days through fruit-growing valleys to uplands above the tree line dotted with tarns. Hiking 4 to 6 hours daily, walkers encounter varying terrain from rolling hills and farmlands to sterner slopes leading to the snow-capped summits of Skardfjell and Onen. Hikers can follow an old abandoned coach road to Granvin or take a bus to gain 1,000 feet and set off to Tyssedal and the snows north of Skardfjell. Good hiking can be found further afield by taking a ferry across the fjord. Long summer evenings are spent on the veranda and lawn under the stars or around a fire in the chalet. Participants eat dinner in the nearby village of Ulvik and may decide to spend more time there after the meal. There is also access to a rowboat and plenty of time to pursue individual interests. **Cost:** $312 to $376 includes roundtrip transportation from London to Bergen, guide, breakfast. **When:** June to September. **Contact:** Waymark

The Royal Trail provides a route through the mountains of Lapland; over most of its length, backpackers follow an old nomad path marked with piles of stones. (Swedish Nat'l. Tourist Office)

Holidays, 295 Lillie Rd., London SW6 7LL, Great Britain; phone 01-385-5015.

Scotland

Highland Fling: A group of 10 hikes the north of Scotland and nearby isles. The 22-day trip begins in the Scottish Highlands where group members visit small villages and Ben Nevis, at 4,406 feet Britain's highest peak. Accommodations are provided by guest houses and small hotels along the route, and minibuses carry both participants and equipment. On the islands of Harris and Lewis in the Outer Hebrides, group members climb Clisham and hike through boulder-strewn moorlands; here seals and birdlife may be seen in rocky inlets. Next visitors explore part of the 60-island Orkney chain, only a third of which is inhabited.

A visit to historic Edinburgh, complete with a traditional Jacobean banquet, brings the trip to its end. **Cost:** $1,860 includes land costs; $752 airfare from New York. **When:** May, June. **Contact:** Mountain Travel Inc., 1398 Solano Ave., Albany, CA 94706, USA; phone (415)527-8100. *(M)*

Sweden

Trekking the Royal Trail: A 16-day journey starts at Abisko in northern Lapland and participants hike south as far as Lake Ladtjolaure. While at Abisko, a guided walk up Mt. Njuolia provides a splendid array of plant life to observe. Once trekkers leave this area, a number of huts provide shelter and cooking facilities. Hikers may have some ice and snow to contend with at Marmotstugan Pass before the descent

Well-kept footpaths afford opportunities to explore the lower slopes of the Alps. Hikers pause for a view across an alpine valley with the Todi in the distance and the Orstock to the right. (Swiss Nat'l. Tourist Office)

to Vistasstugan. Spectacular scenery is the rule along the way and the trip occurs at the height of the Lapland summer. Although the Lapps themselves are moving into communities now, many of them still herd reindeer and can be seen en route. After an overnight at Kebnekaise mountain center, trip members ascend Kebnekaise, the highest mountain in Sweden. The trek continues to Lake Ladtjolaure where participants take a spectacular flight by small sea plane over the entire route of the trek back to Abisko. Hikers carry packs of 25 to 35 pounds and should be in good condition. **Cost:** $670 includes roundtrip airfare from London. **When:** July. **Contact:** Thomas Cook Ltd., P.O. Box 36, Peterborough PE3 6SB, Great Britain; phone Peterborough (0733)632000.

Switzerland
Swiss Hiking: For a circuit of the Grindelwald and Lauterbrunnen areas of Switzerland, participants join an experienced guide for a 16-day trip. Hikers proceed at a leisurely pace using huts and mountain inns for overnight stays. From Kandersteg, a chairlift is used to transport hikers to the Oschinen See, the town of Murren and high alpine meadows for 2 days of peaceful walking. Then a cablecar ride to the summit of Schilthorn at 9,757 feet provides views of the Eiger, Monch and the Jungfrau. Following a descent of the Aletsch Glacier during the second week, the trip ends with a visit to the Loetschental. **Cost:** $850 includes meals, accommodations, guide, transportation from Bern. **When:** September. **Contact:** Canatrek

Mountain Expeditions, P.O. Box 1138, Banff, AB Canada T0L 0C0; phone (403)762-3143.   (M)

Alp Trip: A 16-day hiking trip begins with a flight from New York to Geneva. Trip members proceed to the town of Chamonix to explore the area near Mont Blanc, where massive glaciers descend almost to the town boundaries. Traveling to Zermatt by motorcoach, participants hike in the mountain valleys of the Matterhorn, with meadows and walnut trees at the lower elevations and imposing peaks at higher elevations. On the trip's tenth day hikers travel by bus to reach Grindelwald and the nearby vistas which include the peaks of Eiger and Jungfrau. The trip continues to Zurich for shopping and sightseeing and ends with a return flight to New York. Accommodations during the trip are in hotels. **Cost:** $1,050 from New York includes accommodations, breakfasts, guides. **When:** September, October. **Contact:** Holubar Adventures, P.O. Box 7, Boulder, CO 80306, USA; phone (303)442-7656.   (M)

Wales

Walking the Countryside: In walking adventures lasting 1 or 2 weeks participants hike with loaded rucksacks for 10 to 12 miles daily in the countryside of Wales. Leaving from St. Dogmaels near Cardigan, hikers take 2 weeks to walk 167 miles south along the Pembrokeshire Coastal Footpath to Amroth, alternately crossing rugged cliffs, secluded bays and sandy coves. A week-long trek begins at the Shrewsbury Youth Hostel in the heart of the border country between England and Wales; en route to the medieval town of Ludlow participants walk on the moorland of Long Mynd and in the Clun Forest. Those ready for more strenuous hiking can spend a week in North Wales at the Snowdonia National Park, climbing any number of peaks, including Snowdon. Another week of strenuous hiking begins on the coast at Llandber and heads eastward through Gynedd to Lake Bala and the Berwyns before moving on to Cynwyd and Llangollen where the journey ends. Most meals are taken in the youth hostels where the group spends the night. **Cost:** $90 for 1 week, $159 for 2 weeks includes accommodations, meals, guides. **When:** July, August. **Contact:** YHA Adventure Holiday, Trevelyen House, St. Albans, Herts., Great Britain; phone St. Albans 55215.

Yugoslavia

Hiking Slavic Slopes: Outdoor enthusiasts travel to the rugged limestone mountains of the Julian and Kamnik alps during 14-day journeys to the area just south of the Austrian frontier. Backpackers climb the network of mountain trails ranging from footpaths to lines of waymarks up rock faces lined with iron-pegged handholds. Backpackers carry about 4 to 5 pounds of food during the journeys, with miles traveled on daily jaunts varying. Triglav, the highest summit in the Julian Alps, as well as Prisojnik and Jalovec peaks, are scheduled points of interest during the trips. In addition, participants journey the immense ridge-walk on the mountains south of Bohinj Lake, viewing the Valley of the

Seven Lakes on the way. East of the Julian Alps, the less-visited Kamnik Alps provide walkers with many avenues of exploration to summits that include Kocna, Ojstrica and Skuta, all linked by high-level paths. Accommodations are in huts of the Slovenian Alpine Club during the trips. **Cost:** $303 includes roundtrip transportation, accommodations, some meals. **When:** July to September. **Contact:** Waymark Holidays, 295 Lillie Rd., London SW6 7LL, Great Britain; phone 01-385-5015.

MEXICO

Chiapas

Jungle Journey to Mayan Ruins: On a 10-day trip in the Lacandon Jungle, participants trek to ancient Mayan ruins. A bush plane takes group members from San Cristobal de las Casas, Chiapas to a trailhead at the ruins of Bonampak. In local villages, trekkers visit with Lacandon Indians, the last direct descendants of the Mayans. The sculpture and art at the ruins of Palenque are also viewed. Participants hike along rivers through the tropical forests of mahogany, red cedar, chicle and breadnut trees where bands of spider and howler monkeys feed. The bird life of the area includes parrots, toucans, scarlet macaws and the rare quetzal. Opportunities for photography, swimming and fishing are plentiful. **Cost:** $360 includes accommodations, meals, guides, local transportation. **When:** March. **Contact:** Sacred Monkey Expeditions, Box 363, Jerome, AZ 86331, USA; phone (602)634-5711. *(M)*

Mule trails in the Sierra Madre Occidental provide routes for backpackers on a 10-day Mountain Recreation trip through Mexico. (Keith Gunnar)

Chihuahua

Mule Trail Trek in the Sierra Madre: After meeting in El Paso, a group backpacks along mule trails in the Sierra Madre Occidental for 10 days between Chihuahua and the western coast of Mexico. At the end of a railway line in the town of Creel, participants begin a trek that takes the group through the Barranca del Cobre, an area with topography equivalent to the Grand Canyon. Hiking on to La Bufa and Batopilas, trip members cross the ridge between the Batopilas and Urique rivers to the silver-mining capital of Urique. The trail leads on to Bahuichrivi where backpackers meet the railway again for the trip out. Depending on the interests of the group, participants may venture down the west coast south of Puerta Vallarta to spend some time near the ocean and sand. The university offers other trips and activities including river rafting, ski touring and rock climbing. **Cost:** $150 includes equipment, guides. **When:** December, January. **Contact:** Mountain Recreation, University of Colorado, Boulder, CO 80302, USA; phone (303)492-6051.

PACIFIC

French Polynesia

Island Hiking: A 16-day trip includes a 3-day traverse of the island of Tahiti, explorations along ancient trails on the islands of Moorea, Huahine and Raiatea, and 2 days of snorkeling in the clear waters of Bora-Bora. On inland walks participants encounter ancient ceremonial platforms and archaeological ruins of Tahitian and Polynesian cultures. Tropical fruits abound on coastal and inland trails. The island people are generally warm and hospitable, particularly in the out-of-the-way villages where participants stay when not camping out. Opportunities to participate in evenings of informal singing and Tahitian dancing are available. The emphasis is on cultural experience. **Cost:** On request. **When:** May, June, August to October. **Contact:** Walkabout International, 386 60th St., Oakland, CA 94618, USA; phone (415)652-7825.

Hawaii

Wilderness Exploration for Youths: A variety of different programs, from 6 to 24 days, is offered for teenagers 12 to 15. Exploring Hawaii's oceans and mountains, participants also face the inner challenges of the mind as they learn to function completely alone or with the group. Every feature of the Big Island is explored, from 13,000-foot Mauna Loa to tropical rain forests and the powerful Pacific. Backpacking on lava, navigating an outrigger canoe, and discovering Hawaii's heritage, participants learn by doing. Following a few days of physical conditioning, expert instruction is provided on topics such as first aid, search and rescue techniques, route-finding, and environmental awareness. Food and equipment are furnished. Limited scholarships are available. **Cost:** $160 to $650. **When:** March to August. **Contact:** Hawaii Bound, 825 Keeaumoku St., Rm. 220, Honolulu, HI 96814, USA; phone (808)946-6502.

Backpacking Volcanic Areas: Departing from Hilo, members of a 5-day hike visit the ocean beaches, black lava cliffs and coconut groves that comprise much of the Big Island. Participants make camp near the edge of Halemaumau, an active crater where legend says the volcano goddess Pele makes her home. Lava formations, deep steaming earth cracks and banks of sulphur deposits line the route as hikers proceed across Kilauea Crater. At Halape participants spend some time exploring caves and snorkeling, before hiking down the coast to Keauhou Point, site of an ancient Hawaiian fishing village. Another trip into the Waipio Valley passes lush foliage and dramatic waterfalls en route to a black sand beach. At Volcano National Park hikers witness more interesting geological formations such as a 450-foot lava tube hidden in an exotic fern forest. Throughout the trip participants stay in cabins or camp outside. **Cost:** $150 includes meals, ground transportation, shelter, equipment. **When:** April to August. **Contact:** Hawaii Trails, 25 Akepa St., Hilo, HI 96720, USA.

Island Hiking and Camping: Members of a 2-week trip hike and explore the unspoiled regions of Maui and Hawaii. Day-hike routes wind past volcano craters, the warm Pacific Ocean and an old whaling village. Trip members generally camp at grassy parks, delving into less accessible areas on two exploratory overnight hikes. Except on the overnight hikes, a bus provides transportation and a means for equipment storage and shuttling. A visit to Mauna Loa and Kilauea Crater, the only currently active volcanoes in the islands, and a stop at the black sand beach of Kalapana are scheduled. On Maui the group hikes to Haleakala National Park, from where the giant Haleakala Crater can be viewed. An optional 3-day extension for hiking and exploration on Kauai is also possible. **Cost:** $1,159 includes airfare from San Francisco. **When:** May, October. **Contact:** Mountain Travel Inc., 1398 Solano Ave., Albany, CA 94706, USA; phone (415)527-8100. *(M)*

SOUTH AMERICA
Argentina
Exploring Patagonia: A 25-day trip to the southernmost end of South America begins in Tierra del Fuego with 3 days of hiking in and around Ushuaia and Lapataia National Park. Participants then fly north across the Strait of Magellan to Glacier National Park, site of the Fitz-Roy and La Torre massifs, where a week is spent backpacking in this region of glacier-encrusted peaks and thick forests. Visits are made to Lake Argentina and a boat is taken to view fjords and glaciers at the western end of the lake. Group members spend the final week hiking in Chile's Paine Towers National Park. **Cost:** $2,500 includes airfare from Miami. **When:** February. **Contact:** South American Wilderness Adventures, 1760 Solano Ave., Berkeley, CA 94707, USA; phone (415)524-5111. *(M)*

Bolivia
Hiking and Climbing Inca Regions: The salty inland sea of Lake Titicaca, the bleak Altiplano and the summit of Nevado Huayna Potosi at 19,924 feet highlight 1- to 3-week hiking trips to Inca lands.

Transportation on each trek is by boat, by bus and on foot. The pre-Inca ruins and colonial town of Tiwanacu afford trip members the opportunity of viewing the gateway, shattered terraces and roofless walls of a vanished civilization. Participants visit the Island of the Sun, legendary birthplace of the Incas, before embarking on a trek to the Nevado Huayna Potosi base camp at the foot of Andean glaciers. With porters and guides available, climbers ascend to high camp and then continue to the summit the next day. Another hike brings group members to the Camino de Oro, a road built by Incas to carry gold from mines at Tipuani. On this hike participants descend from passes nearly 14,000 feet high through zones of high mountains to hill forest and eventually arrive in tropical jungle. The road is still used for gold smuggling, and travel is done in groups for safety. Due to the rigor of some of the activities, climbers are expected to be experienced and self-reliant. Trips begin and end in La Paz. **Cost:** $390 to $880 includes transportation from La Paz, some meals, gear. **When:** May, June. **Contact:** Andean Outfitters, P.O. Box 4547, Aspen, CO 81611, USA; phone (303)925-3371. *(M)*

Ecuador

Equatorial Expedition: From Quito, the capital of Ecuador, participants travel to Guayaquil, a modern metropolis, and to Ingapirca, a major Inca ruin. Travelers can see the Andean highlands while traveling from Cuenca to Ibarra and tropical western lowlands from Esmeraldas to Guayaquil. Transportation is by a combination of plane, autocarril and bus, with accommodations varying from modest hotels to camping out. The group may spend a night at a wildlife sanctuary and do some hiking at Cotopaxi and Imbabura. The trip may be combined with one beforehand to the Galapagos and/or one afterward to Colombia. The trip is suitable for anyone in good condition. Participants must be Sierra Club members. **Cost:** On request. **When:** June. **Contact:** Sierra Club Outing Dept., 530 Bush St., San Francisco, CA 94108, USA; phone (415)981-8634.

Peru

Andes Mountains Hiking: A flight from Lima to Cuzco begins a 22-day hiking and sightseeing trip in the vicinity of Machupicchu and Huaraz. The first 3 days allow for exploration of the ancient Inca capital and for acclimatization to altitude. Participants establish camp in a jungle near Machupicchu to explore local ruins and ascend Andean peaks for spectacular views. Flying to Huaraz from Lima, the group proceeds to the base of 22,300-foot Nevado de Huascaran for a hike up to the lake and glacier area. Crossing the 15,000-foot pass of Portochuelo de Llanganuco, hikers spend a week returning to Huaraz along Inca trails. **Cost:** $1,145 covers food, accommodations, transportation from Lima, guides. **When:** May. **Contact:** Canatrek Mountain Expeditions, P.O. Box 1138, Banff, AB Canada T0L 0C0; phone (403)762-3143. *(M)*

Hiking in the Andes: Participants on a 15-day expedition may choose

On a 22-day trip in Peru offered by Canatrek, hikers traverse Inca trails around Huaraz and climb to the ruins at Machupicchu. (John Amatt)

between high-altitude climbing, backcountry treks and visits to Lima and Cuzco. Sightseeing includes rural areas of Peru and the backcountry of the Andes as well as museums and Inca ruins, including Machupicchu. Those who would like to climb should be in good condition as heights of 20,000 feet may be attained if the weather permits. The expedition departs from and returns to Tuxedo, North Carolina; participants may also depart from Miami or join at cities en route. **Cost:** $1,000 from Tuxedo includes all expenses. **When:** August. **Contact:** Globe Treks, 410 Fifth Ave., Suite 10, Hendersonville, NC 28739, USA; phone (704)692-4294. *(M)*

Venezuela

Exploring the Gran Sabana: Sandstone deposits in the eastern part of Venezuela have been uplifted and eroded until all that remains is a series of flat-topped mountains called by their Arekuna Indian name of tepuy. On a 2-week backpacking trip, participants visit the 8,500-foot Tepuy Roraima, located in the geological region referred to as the Gran Sabana and noted for its stark, other-worldly appearance. Departing from Caracas, group members set out in overland vehicles along the coastline to the Orinoco River. After a night at a hotel in Ciudad Guyana, participants travel on to El Dorado, former site of an infamous jungle prison, and to the Gran Sabana where the expedition takes to foot. Eight days are spent backpacking to the remote region of Roraima, with 2 days set aside for exploring the caves, chasms and waterfalls on the slopes and top of the mountain. The descent from Roraima is a leisurely journey allowing time for birding, photography and river swimming. Participants spend the final night in a Caracas hotel. Travelers wishing to spend more time in Venezuela can make arrangements for scuba diving in the Caribbean, jungle touring and birdwatching along the coast or in rain forests. **Cost:** $1,275 includes transportation from Caracas, lodging in Caracas and Ciudad Guyana, meals, guide. **When:** February, March. **Contact:** Ven-Turs, P.O. Box 15631, Seattle, WA 98115, USA; phone (206)568-9873.

UNITED STATES

America by Hostel: Bicycle touring, cross-country skiing, backpacking and hiking are among the opportunities available to both inexperienced beginners and seasoned experts. Local trips range from 1 day to a week, and longer expeditions of 1 to 4 weeks are available to more distant areas in the United States and Europe. Most short trips take place on weekends and include such activities as bike tours of Old Philadelphia, cross-country skiing in Vermont and hiking on the Appalachian Trail. Typical longer trips involve skiing in Sun Valley, Idaho, hiking on the Horseshoe Trail in central Pennsylvania and cruising 120 miles in the Grenadine Islands off Puerto Rico. Instruction is offered in all activities requiring special skills: canoeing, bicycling, sailing, horseback riding and skiing. Accommodations on all trips are in inexpensive hostels where travelers can prepare and eat their meals and enjoy the company of young people from all over the world. **Cost:** $2 to $550 for domestic trips; $800 and up for foreign trips. **When:** Year-round. **Contact:** American Youth Hostels, Delaware Valley Council, 4714 Old York Rd., Philadelphia, PA 19141, USA; phone (215)457-5700.

Backpacking along the Appalachian Trail: Self-organized trips are possible anywhere along the 2,000-mile Appalachian Trail. Extending from Mt. Katahdin in northern Maine to the end of the Blue Ridge Mountains in Springer Mountain, Georgia, the trail is the longest continuous marked trail in the world designed for foot travel only. Fourteen states share the trail, which winds through 8 national forests, 3 national parks and 1 national recreation area. Closed and open shelters are located about 8 miles apart along most of the trail and are available to hikers on a first come, first served basis. Exploration of side trails, photography or close observation of flora or geology is possible for the more leisurely hiker. **Cost:** Free. **When:** Year-round. **Contact:** The Appalachian Trail Conference Inc., P.O. Box 236, Harpers Ferry, WV 25425, USA; phone (304)535-6331.

Far-Ranging Backpacking: Students on 39- and 46-day outdoor trips to the western United States and Canada experience a wide variety of terrain and adventure sport. Trips originate in Poughkeepsie and take participants to the Great Sand Dunes National Monument which lies in the shadow of the Sangre de Cristo Mountains in Colorado. Trip members then backpack into the San Juan Range during a loop trip that passes through alpine meadows, across snow fields and into open pine forests. From the 14,000-foot peaks of the San Juan Mountains, the route continues to the Grand Canyon, where participants hike the Bright Angel Trail to the bottom of the canyon. Participants travel the Colorado River by raft, shooting rapids, swimming and exploring along the way. At Bryce Canyon National Park, hikers pass through a maze of rust-colored pinnacles and at Grand Teton National Park find valleys filled with blooming wildflowers. Depending on time available and weather conditions, students may ascend some of the Teton glaciers and alpine lakes. Participants continue northward to Boundary Waters Canoe Area in Minnesota and Ontario to embark on a canoe trip in a network of lakes and rivers. The trip ends back in Poughkeepsie. **Cost:** $1,595 includes transportation, accommodations, meals. **When:** June to August. **Contact:** Wilderness Bound, Ltd., RD 1, Box 365, Highland, NY 12528, USA; phone (914)691-2377.

Alaska

Trekking from Rainy Pass: Departing by float plane from Lake Hood in Anchorage, hikers fly 150 miles to Rainy Pass Lake to begin a trek along the 1,000-mile-long Iditarod Trail, which was used in the late 1800s for the mail run to Nome and is used today for the world's longest dogsled race. The trip provides a challenging 6-day hike over areas of the Alaska Range south of Mt. McKinley National Park and over forks of the Kuskokwim River. Trekkers are flown back to Anchorage from the other side of Rainy Pass. **Cost:** $400 includes meals, equipment, guide. **When:** July. **Contact:** Alaska Wilderness Treks, Inc., P.O. Box C, Eagle River, AK 99577, USA; phone (907)694-9400.

Arctic Hiking: A 12-day hike in the Brooks Range demands reasonably good physical condition. Anyone who can carry a 40- to 50-pound pack for 4 to 8 miles a day may join this trek into the unspoiled regions of central Alaska. The trip begins with a flight across the Yukon River, the Arctic Circle and the tundra to the Eskimo village of Kaktovik on Barter Island in the Arctic Ocean. The principal activities in this village of 150 are hunting, fishing and trapping. From Barter Island, a bush plane flies hikers 60 to 80 miles further into the untouched wilderness of the Brooks Range for hiking amid massive peaks such as Mt. Isto and Mt. Chamberlain. Attractions on the hike, which is in the heart of the Arctic National Wildlife Range, include a variety of wildlife, tundra vegetation, wildflowers, icefalls and hot springs. **Cost:** $585. **When:** August. **Contact:** Alaska Wilderness Unlimited, Drawer M, Anchorage, AK 99509, USA; phone (907)277-0197. *(M)*

Brooks Range Adventures: A variety of wilderness activities is offered by established camps on private property in the Brooks Range. The camps provide river boats, canoes and Zodiac rafts for participants to arrange their own float trips. Other trips that may be arranged include hikes, photo safaris and spring skiing. Access to the camps is via float-equipped aircraft during the summer and ski-equipped aircraft in winter and spring. Accommodations range from lodges to tents. **Cost:** On request. **When:** Year-round. **Contact:** Alatna Guide Service, P.O. Box 80424, Fairbanks, AK 99708, USA; phone (907)479-6354. *(M)*

Klondike Backpacking: A program of learning experiences for young people in climbing, wilderness survival, campfire cooking, river navigation, ecology and photography is set in the wilds of Alaska. The 26-day trip takes hikers 36 miles over the Chilkoot Trail from Skagway to Lake Bennett, 3,500 feet above sea level. The trip continues to the Yukon River to float 700 miles past Dawson to the trip end at Eagle. Stops on the river are made to visit abandoned settlements, old trappers' cabins and derelict paddleboats which once cruised the entire length of the river. The midnight sun is enjoyed until August, from which time the displays of the northern lights can frequently be seen. **Cost:** $974 includes lodging in Skagway, meals, transportation, camping equipment, guides. **When:** June,

August. **Contact:** Klondike Safaris, P.O. Box 1898, Skagway, AK 99840, USA. *(M)*

Brooks Range Backpacking: Two different backpacking trips, each lasting 8 days, are offered out of Bettles into Alaska's remote Brooks Range. Members on the first trip are flown to Walker Lake to hike through the highest peaks in the central and western mountains including 8,510-foot Mt. Igikpak. Frequently sighted wildlife includes peregrine falcons, eagles, caribou, Dall sheep, grizzly bears, wolverines and wolves. The trip ends in the Noatak drainage, where participants may arrange to join the Noatak River raft trip. The second trip begins with a flight to a lake near the Alatna River and the mouth of Arrigetch Creek for hiking in the Arrigetch Peaks area. A base camp may be set up for day hikes in the mountains; this trip may be combined with a float trip down the Alatna River. **Cost:** $500 for Noatak trip, $550 for Arrigetch trip, includes transportation to and from Bettles, food, equipment, guide. **When:** July, August. **Contact:** Sourdough Outfitters, Bettles, AK 99726, USA; phone (907)692-5252. *(M)*

The Chilkoot Trail provides access to rugged northern wilderness in Alaska and the Yukon Territory. The trail is an old route once used by gold seekers during the '98 Klondike Gold Rush. (Yukon Dept. of Tourism)

The Rivers and Streams of Brooks: Backpackers with considerable experience can join a 14-day trip in the largely unexplored Brooks Range. The entire journey is made without the benefit of trails, and many river and stream crossings are necessary along the way. The route crosses several passes, taking the group into the Arrigetch Peaks and the Mt. Igikpak area. The Brooks Range is one of the world's largest refuges for grizzly bears, Dall sheep, wolves and moose. Herds of caribou migrate through the valleys and passes, and the trip takes place when the arctic tundra is bursting with summer wildflowers. Due to the nature of the country, variations in route and schedule should be anticipated. **Cost:** $800 from Fairbanks includes charter float plane for drop-off, resupply and pickup. **When:** July. **Con**tact: The Wilderness Institute, 333 Fairfax, Denver, CO 80220, USA; phone (303)393-0400.   **(M)**

Glacier Exploration: A 2-day hiking and flying trip is offered to view the Matanuska Glacier and the Chugach Mountains. On the first day participants hike onto the terminal lobe of the 29-mile glacier, exploring deep crevasses, glacier tables and streams that meander through deep, winding ice gorges. The streams may eventually disappear into glacial mills called moulins and sometimes reemerge in fountains bursting upward from beneath the ice. The second day features a 3-hour flight over icefields, glaciers, cirques, glacial lakes and calving glaciers in the fjords of Prince William Sound. Meals are available at a mountain lodge or participants may camp and cook their own meals.

One-day trips on Matanuska Glacier are also available. **Cost:** $90 for 2 days; $20 for 1 day. **When:** Year-round. **Contact:** Wildernorth, Inc., Mile 102, Glenn Hwy., SRC Box 92E, Palmer, AK 99645, USA. *(M)*

Sailing and Hiking near Blackstone Bay: Sailors meet at the coastal town of Whittier on Prince William Sound to sail down Passage Canal en route to the glacial fjord of Blackstone Bay for a camping and hiking adventure of 7 days. During the boat trip, participants see harbor seals resting on floating icebergs and waterfalls that cascade down steep walls into the deep waters of the fjord. Group members continue up to the head of the fjord where they make camp near the termini of the Blackstone and Beloit glaciers. For several days participants hike in the vicinity of the camp and up onto the huge ice fields of Northland Glacier. In an inflatable boat equipped with a motor, the expedition travels to and explores Willard Island, a small piece of land, half glacially carved and half forested, that sits in the middle of the fjord. Blackstone and Beloit glaciers are still actively calving and participants can watch the continual drop of huge icebergs into the fjord. The group can also see kittiwakes, pigeon guillemots and glaucous-winged gulls nesting on the north side of Blackstone Glacier. **Cost:** $340 includes guide, food, glacier walking equipment, group camping and cooking equipment. **When:** July. **Contact:** Wildernorth, Inc., Mile 102, Glenn Hwy., SRC Box 92E, Palmer, AK 99645, USA. *(M)*

Wrangell Backpacking: Three different hiking trips follow routes through the Wrangell Mountains high country. One trip goes between the Nizina Glacier and the White River, another passes through the Chitistone Mountain high country and a third proceeds for 15 days from the Nizina Glacier to the old mining town of McCarthy. Emphasis is placed on nature interpretation and observation of plants, wildlife, geologic formations and human impact on the environment. Each trip is limited to a group of 5 with 2 guides. Access is by light aircraft only. **Cost:** $75 a day includes food, cooking gear. **When:** June to August. **Contact:** Wrangell Mt. St. Elias Outfitters, Dan Creek, via Glenallen, AK 99588, USA. *(M)*

Arizona

Backpacking Havasu Canyon: A group of 14 travelers explores the depths of the Grand Canyon during a 10-day hike. The journey, which covers about 40 miles, begins with a 10-mile hike to the Havasupai Indian Reservation for a visit

A hiker heads toward a rock spire in the Castle Crags State Park of California on a self-guided day-hike. (Christian Kallen)

with the inhabitants and a swim in the blue green pools which have given the canyon its name. The 7½-mile descent to Havasu Canyon, which is west of the main section of the Grand Canyon, is by way of the South Kaibab Trail, which leads to the Colorado River. After exploring the inner depths of the canyon, backpackers begin the ascent along the Bright Angel Trail, stopping midway at Indian Gardens before continuing to the rim the following day. The trip is designed for beginning and intermediate backpackers; the trails are long and steep but well maintained. **Cost:** $495 includes camping gear, food, transportation. **When:** September, October. **Contact:** Avalanche, 1794 N. Highland Rd., Pittsburgh, PA 15241, USA; phone (412)833-7800.

Grand Canyon Guided Hikes: Two 5-day trips for experienced hikers in good condition take participants along the Bass Trail and the Thunder River Trail. The Bass Trail hike begins at the North Rim of the canyon and proceeds over 30 miles of rugged terrain to Shinumo and the Colorado River. The trek involves some difficult hiking at the Redwall limestone stratum. The Thunder River Trail is a hike of medium difficulty running for 26 miles from the North Rim to Thunder Falls, where water gushes out of a cave to form Thunder River. Unlike the Bass Trail route, there is no water along the way. Both hikes require a minimum of 2 participants; the maximum group size is 7. **Cost:** $200 to $350, depending on the number of participants, includes transportation to and from Flagstaff, guide, food, equipment rental. **When:** June to September. **Contact:** Canyoneers, Inc., P.O. Box 2997, Flagstaff, AZ 86003, USA; phone (602)526-0924.   *(M)*

Thunder River-Havasu Hike: Leaders from the Flagstaff School District take hikers on a trek through the Grand Canyon for 8 days. Leaving Flagstaff, the first portion of the hike leads to Thunder River, a spring flowing from deep caverns in the lower wall of the Grand Canyon. The party then continues down Surprise Valley to Deer Creek Falls, where members board a raft for a 21-mile ride to the mouth of Havasu Creek. From here the hike continues up Havasu Canyon, which features many waterfalls and opportunities for swimming. The Havasupai Indians have lived in this area for hundreds of years; a visit to their community concludes the week before the return to Flagstaff. The expedition is geared for all ages, from children 7 or 8 years old to adults. **Cost:** $285 covers transportation from Flagstaff, food, equipment. **When:** June to August. **Contact:** Grand Canyon Youth Expeditions, RR 4, Box 755, Flagstaff, AZ 86001, USA; phone (602)774-8176.

California

Hiking in the San Francisco Bay Area: The Golden Gate Council of American Youth Hostels sponsors 1- to 2-day hikes on weekends. Point Reyes National Seashore is the site for several excursions, during which hikers may fish, beachcomb or view shore birds and other wildlife. Some steep hikes, such as the 10-mile Marathon Hike from Muir Woods to Stinson Beach and back, challenge the experienced hiker. A leisurely hike along Miwok Trail to Muir Beach offers less energetic hikers a chance to relax on the sand or stroll through the Elizabeth Terwilliger Grove to see monarch butterflies. The council also sponsors many expeditions in the Mt. Tamalpais area, where the average hike length is about 8 miles. There are also cycling trips of 15 to 20 miles which usually last no longer than 1 day and pass through state parks, historic sites and beaches. Other sites in the Bay area are visited as well. **Cost:** $2 to $4. **When:** Year-round. **Contact:** American Youth Hostels, Golden Gate Council, 625 Polk St., San Francisco, CA 94102, USA; phone (415)771-4646.

Boys Desert Camp: Trips in the mountain deserts of the Sierra Nevadas introduce boys ages 10 to 14 to remote camping. Areas visited vary from year to year and can include the ghost town of Cerro

Gordo and the ancient bristlecone pines of the White Mountains. Group activities include training in camping techniques, wilderness survival and swimming and special hikes to ghost towns and mountain peaks for photography. Each camper assists in daily chores, ranging from firewood duty and KP to maintenance of camp trucks and trailers. Sessions last from 10 days to 2 weeks; group size is limited, with the ratio of boys to adults no greater than 7 to 1. Transportation is by 4-wheel drive truck. **Cost:** $195 covers equipment, meals, transportation from Palm Springs or San Bernardino. **When:** July. **Contact:** Desert Expeditions, Inc., P.O. Box 1404, Palm Desert, CA 92260, USA; phone (714)346-6927. *(M)*

Mountain Skills Week: An isolated trailhead in the Sierra Nevadas is the point of origin for a 7-day wilderness skills trip. The first day is devoted to orientation as groups become familiar with equipment and itinerary. A few days are then spent learning camp craft, outdoor cooking, map reading, navigation, first aid and survival techniques. The group stays off trails whenever possible in order to learn to negotiate fallen timber, boulder fields and snow. Skills are tested as the exposure to tough hiking and problem solving increases with each day. On the last day, participants are introduced to rock climbing to round out the trip. **Cost:** $125 includes food, group equipment, transportation to and from the trailhead. **When:** June to September. **Contact:** Mountain People School, 157 Oak Spring Dr., San Anselmo,

CA 94960, USA; phone (415)457-3664. *(M)*

Colorado

Southwest Colorado Wilderness Exploration: An experienced guide native to the area takes groups on a variety of 6-day trips to the wilderness regions of southwest Colorado. Itineraries include the San Juan Mountains, the rugged Sangre de Cristo Mountains, or the mountain-lined terrain of the Great Sand Dunes. The guide provides instruction in outdoor and survival skills such as making a fire without matches, improvising shelters, trapping and preparing and cooking edible plants. Each journey is conducted according to the abilities of the group. Shorter and longer trips can be arranged, and discounts on equipment or food are available if participants provide their own. **Cost:** $35 to $40 a day. **When:** June through September. **Contact:** American Wilderness Experience, 753 Paragon Dr., Boulder, CO 80303, USA; phone (303)499-5703 or 499-0050. *(M)*

Easy Upland Climbing: Three-week trips into the Colorado Rockies depart from Denver, taking participants by car from the city to the trailhead. The first day in the mountains is primarily for warm-up, with daily hikes increasing in length as the trip progresses. Hikers cover 6 to 14 miles a day and make elevation gains of between 2,000 and 5,000 feet. There is no technical climbing during the daily hikes, but group members may attempt scrambling up some of the region's more challenging peaks, which rise to 14,000 feet and higher. Most of the hiking is in the vicinity of Rocky Mountain National Park, Leadville, Buena Vista, Fairplay and Aspen. All cooking and most camping equipment is provided. **Cost:** $575 includes group equipment, transportation, guides; $100 food kitty. **When:** July, August. **Contact:** Colorado Rocky Mountain Hiking, Box 376, North Conway, NH 03860, USA; phone (603)356-3594. *(M)*

Instruction at Estes: A 3-week trip departing from Estes Park combines high country hiking with instruction. The first week consists of moderate walking along the Cache La Poudre River, learning camping skills, fording, fishing, map and compass use and cooking. After returning to Estes Park for supplies, participants are transported to Green River Lake in the Bridger Wilderness of Wyoming for canoeing instruction. Topics covered include paddle strokes, portaging, rescue techniques and water navigation. After canoeing to La Barge, participants are transported back to Estes Park before a week of mountaineering in the Wind River Range near Mammoth Glacier. Gannet Peak, the highest point in the range, is the setting for instruction in remote, mountainous travel and camping. **Cost:** $950 includes food, transportation, equipment, guide. **When:** June to August. **Contact:** Rocky Mountain Ski Tours and Backpack Adventures, Box 413, Estes Park, CO 80517, USA; phone (303)586-3553.

Mines in the Mountains Hike: Part of a 7-day trip is spent underground exploring abandoned mine

shafts below Colorado ghost towns. The Wilson Mountains were an active mining center in days past, and much evidence of mining activity remains for the curious traveler. The area is also a true wilderness environment with 3 peaks over 14,000 feet and high alpine passes leading to grassy plateaus, dropping into steep canyons. Participants may observe high cataracts, home to the water ouzel (a cousin of the thrush) which builds nests of lichen and moss next to the cold spray of mountain streams. The group stops at abandoned mining camps to watch deer and elk graze in the many flowered meadows. The trip is designed for the history buff and wilderness traveler alike. **Cost:** $210 includes equipment. **When:** June. **Contact:** Three Eagles Expeditions, Inc., P.O. Box 2606, Jackson, WY 83001, USA; phone (307)733-4673.

Georgia

Appalachian Adventure: A 7-day camping trip combines backpacking in the southern Appalachian Mountains and rafting on the Chattooga River. Starting in Clayton, Georgia, hikers begin the trip with a warm-up hike to Ellicot's Rock Wilderness. Moving camp each night, the hikers proceed to Three Forks Gorge, a more difficult hike. Participants may spend their free time taking exploratory hikes. Programs in ecology, survival, first aid and orienteering emphasize responsible camping. After some whitewater rafting instruction, participants spend 2 days on the Chattooga River. Groups of 6 people per raft run numerous rapids requiring arm strength, stamina and good teamwork. Camping is primitive, with no facilities other than a spring or stream. **Cost:** $190 includes all meals, equipment. **When:** June. **Contact:** Wilderness Southeast, Rt. 3, Box 619, Savannah, GA 31406, USA; phone (912)355-8008.

(M)

Appalachian Leadership Program: Several opportunities are available for seasoned backpackers to learn outdoor leadership skills, covering safety, emotional and interpersonal growth, human relations and communications. Participants spend from 5 to 14 days traveling through the southern Appalachian Mountains in groups of no more than 10 people. A leadership course for outdoor instructors is also available, providing an opportunity to refine outdoor and instructional skills. Backpackers in the winter leadership seminar spend 5 days in extreme weather conditions at altitudes above 6,000 feet in the Mt. Mitchell area. A 2-day seminar in medical aid is also offered. Academic credit is available for some of the courses. **Cost:** $60 to $300 includes food, accommodations, equipment, transportation. **When:** November, December, May, July,

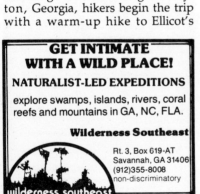

August. **Contact:** Wolfcreek Wilderness, P.O. Box 596, Blairsville, GA 30512, USA; phone (404)745-6460.

Idaho

Big Horn Backpacking: A 10-day backpacking trip explores the Big Horn Crags area of Idaho. The trip departs from a base camp at Panther Creek, following a steep ridge crest high over the Main Salmon River. From there participants travel on maintained trails through the wilderness, observing wildlife, stopping at alpine lakes for swimming and fishing, and viewing the spectacular geological formations in the area, part of the glacier-carved Idaho Batholith. On the fifth day an air drop supplies fresh fruit and other food. For the remaining 5 days, the hike's route is selected by participants according to their particular desires and interests; usual activities include swimming in the Middle Fork of the Salmon, a visit to a natural hot spring and a day spent learning and practicing mountaineering techniques. The return route descends steep-walled canyons to the river, returning to Panther Creek after a total walk of about 50 miles. **Cost:** $350 includes transportation from Pocatello, food, equipment, instruction, guide. **When:** June to August. **Contact:** Horizons Unlimited, P.O. Box 147, Pocatello, ID 83201, USA; phone (208)233-9428. *(M)*

Nights on Baldy Mountain: After landing at Thomas Creek on the Middle Fork of the Salmon River, participants travel upriver to Marble Creek on the start of a 15-day hike. The first 5 days of the trip are spent traveling up the creek's drainage to its head, a wide cirque valley surrounded by the jagged mountains of the Red Ridge. Crossing the ridge, the group enters the Baldy Mountain country. The remainder of the trip is spent traversing and traveling the ridge, winding up on the Middle Fork of the Salmon. There are a few days hiking on snow, but the group avoids sleeping in snow-covered areas, and the weather is usually warm at this time of year. The trip totals 80 miles and the elevation change is 8,500 feet. **Cost:** $450 for adults, $300 for children under 12, $1,600 for a family of 4. **When:** May. **Contact:** Wilderness Trails, P.O. Box 9252, Moscow, ID 83843, USA; phone (208)882-1955.

Montana

Northern Rockies Backpacking: The route on a 6-day expedition is a gradual and relaxed trail traversing the Lakes Plateau. Within the 230,000 acres of the primitive area, a land of deep canyons, glaciers and high mountains, the plateau is dotted with hundreds of mountain

Jagged peaks, year-round snow and alpine flora surround hikers as they pause to rest in the North Cascades Wilderness Area. (Keith Gunnar)

lakes and streams abundant with cutthroat, rainbow and brook trout. Setting up camp early and breaking camp late, guides prepare a full-course meal while hikers explore, photograph, fish or relax. The trip is as demanding as the group dictates, is for hikers of all abilities and is limited to 12 participants. **Cost:** $240 includes equipment, meals, guides, lodging at the rendezvous point. **When:** July. **Contact:** Aurora Borealis Expeditions, P.O. Box 20685, Bloomington, MN 55420, USA. *(M)*

Backpacking the Big Sky Country: Licensed guides lead small groups of 12 or less on wilderness backpacking trips into the Montana Rockies. Generally lasting about a week, the outings take backpackers into such areas as Yellowstone National Park, Beartooth Primitive Area, and Selway-Bitterroot and Bob Marshall wildernesses. Five or 6 miles are covered each day, and individual pack loads run 25 to 35 pounds. Private outings on foot, skis or snowshoes can also be arranged in appropriate seasons. Families are welcome, though children must be at least 8 years old. A full range of camping equipment is provided. **Cost:** On request. **When:** Summer. **Contact:** High Country Adventures, P.O. Box 176, Helena, MT 59601, USA; phone (406)443-2842. *(M)*

New Hampshire

Appalachian Backpacking: An entire system of mountain huts is available for overnight stays for hikers on self-guided trips through the White Mountains of New Hampshire. The huts are spaced at approximately a day's hike apart, connected by many miles of scenic trails for every kind of hiker. They are maintained by young people who pack up food and supplies and prepare family-style meals for guests. Blankets and pillows are provided in the bunkrooms. Most of the huts can be reached easily from the network of trails, but some are also accessible via cog railway or by descent from an aerial tramway. Discounts are available for Appalachian Mountain Club members. **Cost:** $10 to $14 for lodging, depending on meal plan. **When:** Year-round; varies with each hut. **Contact:** Appalachian Mountain Club, 5 Joy St., Boston, MA 02108, USA; phone (617)523-0636.

New Mexico

Black Range Backpack: Hikers led by a naturalist and environmental educator wander on foot for a week through the proposed Aldo Leopold Wilderness of the Black Range in southwestern New Mexico. Starting from Silver City, group members trek gradually upwards, studying the ecology of the Sonoran, Montane and Canadian life zones as they gain the higher elevations. Emphasis is placed on understanding a broad range of environmental issues connected with the region's past and future: the field ecology and natural history of the area, wilderness ethics, the role of federal agencies in public land management and the role of wilderness preservation in environmental education. Hikers are also introduced to the Indian folklore and gold rush history for which the area is famous. Backpacking equipment should be supplied by participants. **Cost:** $260 includes guide. **When:** September. **Contact:** American Wilderness Alliance, 4260 E. Evans, Denver, CO 80222, USA; phone (303)758-5018.

Gila Wilderness Investigation: The Gila Wilderness Area was America's first designated wilderness, and it incorporates an unusually wide variety of assets: mountains, hills, canyons, mesas, rivers, creeks, meadows, marshes, cottonwood bosques and varied wildlife including deer and elk. A 5-day backpacking trip explores the area and the proposed Aldo Leopold Wilderness at a leisurely pace, covering around 20 miles altogether, to allow a closer examination of the flora and fauna. These trips are suitable for novice backpackers or experts who want to stay in an area rather than just move through it. The trip leader is a naturalist guide who can provide instruction in natural history and wilderness techniques, with an emphasis on low-impact camping. **Cost:** $160 includes food, camping and cooking equipment, guide. **When:** September. **Contact:** University of the Wilderness, 29952 Dorothy Rd., Evergreen, CO 80439, USA; phone (303)674-4695. *(M)*

North Carolina
Wilderness Photography Trip: A 4-day backpacking trip into the Smoky Mountains is specifically designed to serve the needs of the wilderness photographer. Traveling between 1 and 5 miles a day on trails at low elevations, participants have ample time to concentrate on the natural beauty of the forest while improving their photographic skills. The speed and length of each day's travel varies with the availability of subject matter and the wishes of the group. In the evening, time is set aside for open discussions on various photographic techniques. **Cost:** $150. **When:** May. **Contact:** Globe Treks, 410 Fifth Ave. W., Suite 10, Hendersonville, NC 28739, USA; phone (704)692-4294. *(M)*

Southeastern Trail Tours: Informal weekend backpacking clinics geared for the novice hiker emphasize the basics of backpacking. Hikers gather on Friday night for an orientation meeting and camp that night at an area of their choice. On Saturday morning the group hikes to either Joyce Kilmer Memorial Forest, the Great Smoky Mountains National Park, the Shining Rock Wilderness or the Slickrock Wilderness. Hikers camp at a spot suited to the season and return on Sunday afternoon. **Cost:** $50 includes food, equipment, transportation, guide. **When:** May, October. **Contact:** Nantahala Outdoor Center, Star Rt., Box 68, Bryson City, NC 28713, USA; phone (704)488-6407. *(M)*

Texas
Chihuahua Desert Exploration: From a base in Texas, groups cross the Mexican border on trips lasting 2 to 4 weeks. Activities include caving, rafting, climbing and strenuous hiking through the limestone formations and canyons in the Chihuahua Desert and Rio Grande country. The "expedition for the spirit" offers participants a chance to discover something about the beautiful desert wilderness and about themselves. The groups, led by 2 guides, are limited to 5 men and 5 women. The minimum age is 22 and no experience is required. Equipment and a selection of natural foods are provided. **Cost:** $460 and $720. **When:** April to October. **Contact:** Desert Dance, Box 77, Terlingua, TX 79852, USA; phone (915)371-2211. *(M)*

Big Bend Backpacking: A 5-day hiking trip explores the contrasting terrain of the mountains and desert of Big Bend National Park. Backpackers hike mostly in the Chisos Mountains but also spend time on the floor of the Chihuahua Desert below. Participants encounter pine

With ice ax and pack, a hiker prepares for the trail in the Monte Cristo area of the North Cascades, where routes accommodate backpackers of any level of experience. (Carol Baker)

forests, flowered meadows, beautiful peaks and canyons carved by the Rio Grande River. The region presents a mixture of Indian, Spanish and Anglo-American history; hikers may come across Comanche trails, old presidios and quicksilver mines. The hiking is moderately strenuous, so participants should be in good shape. **Cost:** $160. **When:** April, November. **Contact:** University of the Wilderness, 29952 Dorothy Rd., Evergreen, CO 80439, USA; phone (303)674-4695. *(M)*

Utah

Grand Gulch Backpacking: Within the seemingly unbroken expanse of the Cedar Mesa Plateau in southeastern Utah, a group of backpackers explores the Grand Gulch Primitive Area for 7 days. Accompanied by an archaeologist, a naturalist and a wilderness photographer, participants hike 35 miles carrying packs of 25 to 35 pounds. From Bluff, hikers descend less than 1,000 feet into the mouth of the gulch and proceed along the canyon floor. The shallow gradient of the floor gives backpackers access to ancient Basketmaker and Cliff Dweller ruins. Participants have the opportunity to learn about the people who inhabited the region from 200 to 1260 A.D. The group follows carefully chosen routes; although the plateau is a unit with respect to topography and vegetation, it is virtually impassable without knowledge of the obscure paths that lead through the canyons. Group size is limited to 20 persons. **Cost:** $450 for Grand Gulch, $350 for Rainbow Bridge includes guides, meals, camping equipment, transportation. **When:** May. **Contact:** Wild & Scenic Inc., P.O. Box 2123A, Marble Canyon, AZ 86036, USA; phone (602)355-2222.

(M)

Wilderness Hiking: Groups of 5 may go on backpacking and river

Outfitted for a major backpacking trip, hikers file through a flower-filled meadow on the Teton Crest Trail in Wyoming. (Infinite Odyssey)

floating trips in the Utah wilderness. Possible routes are varied and may change with every trip. In the San Rafael Swell or Wasatch Range, backpackers may travel to Zcmi Mine, Burro Spring, No Man's Mountain, Devil's Monument, Ghost Rock and the Fathers, twin pinnacles named for priests who followed the Old Spanish Trail. Other possible trips go along a narrow slickrock trail between 2 canyons called Devil's Racetrack, or to Indian Cave, high on the sheer wall of Coal Wash. The itinerary is determined by the interests and abilities of the guide and participants. Activities vary according to individual tastes and backpackers may spend time rock collecting, photographing, sketching or searching for hidden desert springs, Indian ruins and remnants of outlaw hideouts. Charter trips for groups of 10 to 20 can also be arranged. **Cost:** $275 for 5 days, $365 for 7 days, $495 for 10 days includes guide, camping equipment, meals. **When:** May to October. **Contact:** Tu-Kay Renegades, 49 N. Main, Clawson, UT 84516, USA; phone (801)384-2608.

Vermont

Green Mountain Montage: Travelers with a limited amount of time but a desire to experience many outdoor activities may find a special 1- to 2-week trip to be a good solution to their dilemma. Hiking, horseback riding, bicycling and canoeing are means of travel through the countryside of the Green Mountain State. The hiking sections of the first week's journey traverse trails in the Chittenden and Lincoln areas while the horseback segment in the Stowe region includes lessons as desired, picnic rides and a possible overnight campout. A bicycle trip out of Woodstock starts the second week, followed by hiking near Lincoln. Various rivers in central Vermont (the exact selection depends on water conditions) are explored by canoe. Country inns provide participants with comfortable lodging, excellent meals and swimming opportunities as preparation and reward for each day's events. **Cost:** $293 for 1 week, $526 for 2 weeks includes meals, lodging, guides. **When:** July, August. **Contact:** Hike-Skitour Vermont, RFD 1, Chester, VT 05143, USA; phone (802)875-3631 or 875-3613. *(M)*

Washington

Glacier Peak Wilderness Trip: Located on the western side of Lake Chelan, the remote Glacier Peak Wilderness is dominated by massive glaciated peaks rising out of dense forests of fir, spruce, larch and whitebark pine. On an 11-day trip participants experience flowered valley floors and alpine meadows, craggy peaks and rock spires that cradle fields of blue-green ice. Glaciers radiate in all directions from the summit of Glacier Peak, the highest point in the region. Trip members may see huge blocks of ice break and tumble down icefalls. There are numerous lakes throughout the region, the most famous being Image Lake, mirroring Glacier Peak. Participants explore the richly foliated valley floors, climb up to the timberline and over several passes, cross snowfields, examine many of the ice formations at close range, and camp next to cascading streams and chilly alpine lakes. The hiking is fairly difficult, and trip members should be in good physical condition. **Cost:** $330 includes equipment, food, guides. **When:** August. **Contact:** The Wilderness Institute, 333 Fairfax, Denver, CO 80220, USA; phone (303)393-0400. *(M)*

Wyoming

Custom Hikes: A variety of backpacking trips, with pack animals carrying the bulk of the gear, is offered in the wilderness areas of Wyoming and Utah. Custom trips are available: planned trips departing from Las Vegas include 6 nights in the remote lower Grand Canyon and 6 nights in the southern Utah Red Rock Canyons. Trips departing from Jackson include 7 nights in the Gros Ventre Wilderness, 4 nights in the Teton Range, 7 nights in Yellowstone National Park, 9 nights exploring wilderness areas in Wyoming and 9 nights in the Washakie Wilderness. The hikes range in difficulty from easy to rigorous and take place in areas ranging from fairly accessible to very remote. **Cost:** $175 to $350 depending on length of trip, or $35 a day for custom trips, includes transportation to and from point of departure, all gear, food, guide. **When:** April

FREE INFORMATION ON REQUEST
The *Worldwide Adventure TravelGuide* has made it easy for you to obtain free information from our advertisers with our Reader Service program. To participate, turn to page 576, fill out the enclosed postcard, and drop it in the mail.

to August. **Contact:** L.D. Frome, Outfitter, RFD, Afton, WY 83110, USA; phone (307)886-5240.   *(M)*

Exploring the Mountains of Yellowstone: The backcountry of the north-central Rockies in Montana and Wyoming is the site of 1- and 2-week backpacking adventures for teenagers between 13 and 18. While in and around Yellowstone National Park participants learn orienteering, non-technical climbing, fishing, outdoor cooking and exploration. Traveling in all weather conditions, supervised groups hike over a variety of terrain. Young explorers learn the distinction between adapting to and intruding into the wilderness. The meeting point for the trip is Billings. **Cost:** $225 to $450 includes ground transportation, equipment, food, maps. **When:** June to August. **Contact:** Yellowstone Wilderness Guides, Box 446, Red Lodge, MT 59068, USA.   *(M)*

RESOURCES

Clubs and Associations

African Travel Association
1024 S. Robertson
Los Angeles, CA 90035, USA
Phone (213)659-7155

American Camping Association
Bradford Woods
Martinsville, IN 46151, USA
Phone (317)342-8456

American Forestry Association
1319 18th St. NW
Washington, DC 20036, USA
Phone (202)467-5810

American Indian Travel Commission
10403 W. Colfax Ave., Suite 550
Lakewood, CO 80215, USA
Phone (303)234-1707

Appalachian Mountain Club
5 Joy St.
Boston, MA 02108, USA
Phone (617)523-0636

Association of the Experiment
in International Living
Otesage, Upper Wyche
Malvern, Worcestershire WR14 4EN, Great Britain

Australian Youth Hostels Association
383 George St.
Sydney, N.S.W. 2000
Australia

Bruce Trail
33 Hardale Crescent
Hamilton, ON Canada L8T 1X7

Camping Club of Great Britain
and Ireland
11 Lower Grosvenor Pl.
London SW1W OEY, Great Britain

Canyon Explorer's Club
1223 Frances Ave.
Fullerton, CA 92631, USA

The Chalet Club
P.O. Box 3849, Grand Central Sta.
New York, NY 10017, USA
Phone (212)490-0126

Environmental Action
1346 Connecticut Ave. NW #731
Washington, DC 20036, USA
Phone (202)659-9682

Federation of Western Outdoor Clubs
943 Mills Tower
San Francisco, CA 94104, USA

Florida Trail Association, Inc.
4410 NW 18th Pl.
Gainesville, FL 32605, USA
Phone (904)378-8823

Forest Campers Association

79 Hill Farm Wy.
Southwick, Sussex, Great Britain

Friends of the Earth
529 Commercial St.
San Francisco, CA 94111, USA
Phone (415)495-4770

Hong Kong Youth Hostels Association
12-B Watson's Estate
North Point, Hong Kong

Icelandic Youth Hostels Association
Laufasvegi 41
Reykjavik, Iceland
Phone 2 49 50

International Backpackers Association
P.O. Box 85
Lincoln Center, ME 04558, USA
Phone (207)794-6062

Kenya Mountain Club
P.O. Box 45741
Nairobi, Kenya
Phone Nairobi 27747

Matterhorn Sports Club
3 W. 57th St., Dept. A
New York, NY 10019, USA
Phone (212)486-0505

Mountain Club of East Africa
P.O. Box 66
Moshi, Tanzania

Mulanje Mountain Club
P.O. Box 240
Blantyre, Malawi

National Campers and Hikers Assn.
7172 Transit Rd.
Buffalo, NY 14221, USA
Phone (716)634-5433

National Hiking and Ski Touring Assn.
P.O. Box 7421
Colorado Springs, CO 80907, USA

National Parks and Conservation Assn.
1701 18th St. NW
Washington, DC 20009, USA
Phone (202)265-2717

National Wildlife Federation
1412 16th St. NW
Washington, DC 20036, USA
Phone (202)797-6800

New England Trail Conference
33 Knollwood Dr.
East Longmeadow, MA 01028, USA

New York-New Jersey Trail Conference
15 E. 40th St.
New York, NY 10016, USA
Phone (212)697-8017

North American Family Campers Assn.
P.O. Box 552
Newburyport, MA 01950, USA
Phone (617)462-9541

Potomac Appalachian Trail Club
1718 N St. NW
Washington, DC 20036, USA
Phone (202)638-5306

Royal Scottish Geographic Society
10 Randolph Crescent
Edinburgh EH3 7TU, Great Britain

Servas
11 John St., Rm 406
New York, NY 10038, USA
Phone (212)267-0252

South African Mountain Club
P.O. Box 164
Cape Town, South Africa

South American Explorers Club
Casilla 3714
Lima 1, Peru

West Virginia Scenic Trails Assn.
P.O. Box 4042
Charleston, WV 25304, USA

WEXAS International Office
Suite 354, Graybar Bldg.
420 Lexington Ave.
New York, NY 10017, USA
Phone (212)697-6126

Wilderness Society
1901 Pennsylvania Ave. NW
Washington, DC 20006, USA
Phone (202)293-2732

Women in the Wilderness
13 Columbus Ave.
San Francisco, CA 94111, USA
Phone (415)982-4588

Youth Hostels Association
Trevelyan House, St. Albans
Herts. AL1 2DY, Great Britain

CAVING

While some of the jungles of New Guinea or the slopes of the Antarctic ranges never have felt the touch of human feet, beneath the earth's surface lies an even greater unexplored frontier. It is this world that lures cavers into the depths of our planet.

Whether on a guided tour through Carlsbad Caverns or crawling through a narrow passageway in the muck and mire of an underground stream, cave exploration is an exciting and enlightening trip to another world. From unique subterranean life forms, such as blind fish and bats, to unusual formations of stalactites and stalagmites, cavers are confronted with a world unlike any above ground. The speleological environment can provide vital information about the earth as a whole. From cave paintings and the remains of early cave dwellers we learn about our past; from the records left by geological activity we learn about the earth's crust; and from the observation and study of cave species we can form a better picture of the evolutionary laws of adaptation and survival.

There are many opportunities for exploring the underground wilderness. However, because caves are sensitive to outside disturbance, speleologists are wary of promoting travel in them. Yet it can be done safely and with little impact on the cave's ecology through clubs and trip operators who run supervised expeditions. The choices are wide: you can view the geological wonders of caverns in Peru, explore ice caves in the Austrian Alps, practice vertical and horizontal caving techniques in Wyoming's La Caverna de Tres Charros, or admire the crystals in South Dakota's Jewel Cave. Trips are usually limited to one day, but expeditions may be longer. The physical demands vary but usually require someone in good overall condition, with no aversion to small spaces or getting dirty.

Some caving trips offer tough physical challenges, such as wading through near-freezing cave pools, descending into deep pits on ropes or squeezing through tight crawlways. Special equipment, usually supplied, ranges from helmets and lamps to climbing gear. On some trips, participants may explore the depths of cave pools, requiring cold-water diving gear.

There are many kinds of caves to be explored, from the great limestone caverns of the American Southwest to the gypsum caves of the central states; from lava tubes, old mines and ice caves to sinkholes and sea caves. Each offers a unique view into a little-known part of our world. □

Steam from a crater produces surrealistic effects in a cave at the 14,200-foot summit of Washington's Mt. Rainier. (Keith Gunnar)

CAVING

EUROPE

Austria

Ice Cave Exploration: Eisriesenwelt in the Austrian Alps is an enormous system of caverns and ice caves just south of Salzburg. Participants on a 1-day excursion start out from the village of Werfen and either hike or take a minibus to a cable car base station. The car ascends 1,500 feet to a mountain lodge, and after another 15-minute hike participants arrive at the cave's entrance. Carbide lamps and magnesium flares light the way as the group climbs within the mountain to a huge ice wall that runs across the entire width of the cave. Beyond the ice wall a long, narrow corridor leads to chambers having fantastic ice formations, and finally to the Ice Palace, a half mile from the entrance and as far into the cave as regular tours run. For those who want to explore deeper reaches of the 30-mile-long cave system, private tours can be arranged in advance. Photography is officially forbidden within the ice caves, but the scenery on the way to the entrance makes a camera worthwhile. Overnight accommodations are available in a lodge at the base of the cable car. **Cost:** On request. **When:** May to October. **Contact:** Great Trips, Box 5199, Grand Central Sta., New York, NY 10017, USA.

SOUTH AMERICA

Peru

The Depths of Palcamayo Valley: After meeting in Lima, spelunkers journey by train to Palcamayo Valley, a region of Peru well known for its more than 60 caves and deep caverns with depths of up to 1,384 feet. On the 5- to 7-day trip, 1 day is spent in Tarma before the group sets up base camp near Huagapo's Cave at an elevation of 10,518 feet. Once inside spelunkers see a great number of stalactites and stalagmites, walk in large vaults and see an underground river. Participants should be prepared to walk through water, crawl in low galleries and use ropes and ladders in climbing different portions of the cave. Moving out into the light, the group visits the weaving town of San Pedro de Cajas before spending the final day on the train en route to Lima. **Cost:** $25 a day includes transportation from Lima, accommodations, meals while in camp, guides, caving equipment. **When:** May to September. **Contact:** Trekking Percy Tapia, P.O. Box 3074, Lima 100, Peru. **(M)**

UNITED STATES

Indiana

Underneath the Hoosier State: Caves in southwestern Indiana are explored on a variety of 2-day trips. The caves stay at a constant 55°F, and explorers should dress appropriately. Groups depart from Indianapolis by 12-passenger van, and all equipment for cave exploration is provided. The guide for the trip has 15 years of caving experience in the Indiana, Kentucky and Missouri area. Each trip explores 2 caves. **Cost:** $39 includes roundtrip

Cavers have to squeeze through tight crawlways in the underground passages of La Caverna de Tres Charros. (National Outdoor Leadership School)

transportation from Indianapolis. **When:** April, May, October, November. **Contact:** Eco-Expeditions, 726 E. 65th St., Indianapolis, IN 46220, USA; phone (317)255-3319.

South Dakota

Cave Exploring at Hells Canyon: A 4-hour trip introduces groups of up to 10 people to caving in the fifth largest cave in the world. Participants receive an orientation to Jewel Cave National Monument in the Hells Canyon area of the Black Hills prior to exploring about 3,000 feet of passageway. Since part of the trip is made on hands and knees or on stomachs through tight crawlways, it is limited to those in good physical condition. Each person is required to pass through an 8½-inch by 2-foot handspan squeeze before entering the cave. Participants should dress warmly and bring ankle-high boots with rubber soles. The cave is noted for its spectacular rock and crystal formations. **Cost:** $2. **When:** June to August. **Contact:** National Park Service, Jewel Cave National Monument, Custer, SD 57730, USA; phone (605)673-2288.

Wyoming

Wilderness Survival and Speleology Course: The first 20 days of a 35-day course in caving are spent above ground learning camping, conservation and wilderness skills before participants enter the subterranean passages of La Caverna de Tres Charros in the Big Horn Range. Moving through crawlways, group members observe natural features and practice vertical and horizontal caving techniques. Participants learn about equipment selection and maintenance. Also on the itinerary is instruction in photography, biology, geology and subsurface hydrology. Responsible exploration of these remarkable underground environments requires a thorough knowledge of minimum-impact techniques. **Cost:** $815 includes equipment, meals, local transportation. **When:** July. **Contact:** National Outdoor Leadership School, Box AA, Lander, WY 82520, USA; phone (307)332-4381.

ARCHAEOLOGY— ANTHROPOLOGY

Leaving your home for a distant land means leaving the security of your own culture behind. It means meeting new people, trying strange foods, learning to communicate in a foreign language, participating in celebrations, and experiencing cross-cultural hospitality that restates the unity of all people. The anthropologist makes a science of these encounters, learning what characterizes each culture, and what makes it a part of the global configuration of humanity. The archaeologist investigates temples, tools, burial sites and stone inscriptions—traces of civilizations long past.

Evolution proceeds by diversity; the multiplicity of wildflowers makes up for their relative simplicity and small size, while the toughness and longevity of tortoises balance their few numbers. In human beings, "diversity" is not only in physical types, but in cultural modes as well. Often, the adventure in travel itself is the opportunity to experience this diversity. From a New Guinea "Sing-Sing" to the highland games of Scotland; from the rituals and customs of the Bedouin nomads, the Lacandon Maya of Guatemala, to those of the cliff-dwelling Dogon of Mali and the Bushmen of the Kalahari—all of these societies can be visited on trips ranging from one week to a full month.

Human diversity stretches far and wide across the face of the earth, and across the breadth of time as well. Archaeologists and physical anthropologists are still pushing back the date that *Homo sapiens* emerged from its simian ancestry, and the uncovering of ancient buildings, firepits and stone tools all shed light on the mystery of our beginning. Cliff dwellings at the edge of the Gila Wilderness in New Mexico, the prehistoric houses of the Pueblo Indians 2,000 years ago, can be visited year-round today. Farther from home, journeys of two or three weeks explore the archaeological monuments of the Inca civilization in Peru, at its peak when Spanish conquistadores invaded the area just 400 years ago. And back to the beginning of Western civilization, 15-day expeditions to Egypt visit the ancient sites of the Temple of Amun at Karnak, the Sphinx of Giza and the Great Pyramid of Khufu. The mysteries of Stonehenge, the glory of the Acropolis and the beautiful petroglyphs of the southwestern United States all await your investigation—discover for yourself the roots of civilization both lost and enduring. ☐

Pacific islanders show an anthropologist the intricate art of basket-weaving. The anthropologist's work involves perseverance and an appreciation for different lives and cultures. (Goodtravel Tours)

ARCHAEOLOGY–ANTHROPOLOGY

AFRICA

Trans-Africa Medicine Trip: Participants traverse the continent from Senegal to Kenya during a 23-day tour that includes meetings with African herbalists, priests and healers who explain and demonstrate traditional medical practices. The trip begins with a flight from New York to Dakar in Senegal, a country of mixed religious backgrounds including Muslims, Christians and animists who deal with medical problems in differing ways. From there group members fly southeast to the Ivory Coast, where 3 days are spent touring by coach through coffee and cocoa plantations, visiting a witch doctor's school and talking with a doctor about the work done in a leper hospital in Zaranou. In Togo trips are made to the lake dwellers' village of Ganvie, entirely built on stilts over the water of Lake Nocoue, and to a market where traditional doctors purchase herbs, animal skeletons and other talismans and ingredients needed for their work. Participants stop for 2 days in Ghana, then fly to Nairobi, Kenya; from Nairobi a side trip is made to the Masai Mara Game Reserve for views of black-maned lions, buffalo, elephants, and blue-shanked topi. The final days of the trip are spent in Kisumu near Lake Victoria, where group members are introduced to local tribal doctors before returning to Nairobi, for flights to New York via London. **Cost:** $3,000 includes roundtrip airfare from New York, hotel accommodations, some meals, all transportation in Africa, guides. **When:** Year-round. **Contact:** East African Travel Consultants Inc., 33 Bloor St. E., Suite 206, Toronto, ON Canada M4W 3H1; phone (416)967-0067. *(M)*

Egypt

Egyptian Adventures: A trained Egyptologist accompanies travelers across a variety of historically and culturally rich terrain. Four days of the 15-day journey are spent in Cairo, where trip members visit the Cairo Museum, repository for the finest and most complete collection of pharaonic antiquities in the world. Vast expanses of wadis, dunes and rock-strewn desert are viewed from the air while flying to Luxor. Exploring the 60-acre ruins of Karnak, travelers may pass through the gateway and walk down the Avenue of Sphinxes. A crossing of the Nile amidst early-morning river traffic brings passengers to the "City of the Dead"—the necropolis of Thebes and the temple of Queen Hatshepsut. From the Valley of the Kings, the group proceeds across the plain to the Ramesseum and the Colossi of Memnon. Other stops include Aswan, Alexandria and sites that house more Egyptian treasures and monuments. **Cost:** $848 includes transportation, food, guides, accommodations. **When:** January, March, April, May, July, September, November, December. **Contact:** Forum Travel International, 2437 Durant, No. 208, Berkeley, CA 94704, USA; phone (415)843-8294. *(M)*

A remnant of the Avenue of Sphinxes stands in Karnak. Forum Travel International offers a 15-day trip through Egypt for $848. (Connie Balint)

Ghana

Begho Excavation: Drawing and surveying skills or previous field experience are assets to participants excavating the medieval town of Begho in the savanna region of northwest Ghana. Working for 3 to 4 weeks with a UCLA history professor, members of the project assist in all aspects of the excavation including field surveying, pottery analysis and drawing. The archaeological team can expect daily temperatures of 75° to 90°F. Begho prospered during the 14th century along the gold and kola nut trade routes between the ancient empire of Mali and the forests of the west coast of Africa. Recent excavations indicate that the town was divided into separate quarters for artisans, merchants and people of different tribal origin. A quarter which is thought to have been occupied by Muslim gold traders from Mali is the focus of the current study. Since the area has become one of the richest contemporary pottery sites in Ghana, participants also collect crafted ceramics and artifacts for the UCLA Museum of Cultural History. **Cost:** $925 tax-deductible contribution includes ground transportation, guides, instruction, meals, accommodations. **When:** January, February. **Contact:** University Research Expeditions Program, University of California, Berkeley, CA 94720, USA; phone (415)642-6586.   *(M)*

Kenya

Northern Frontier Safari: A 19-day trip takes members 1,200 miles through the Rift Valley and Northern Frontier District of Kenya. Along the way participants arrive at Lake Turkana, a 180-mile-long lake that is home for the El Molo tribe, a people who subsist on the lake's animal life. Their diet consists partly of Nile perch sometimes weighing over 200 pounds, crocodiles and hippos which are still hunted with traditional ceremony. Three days are spent on the Tana River, first explored from beginning to end in 1976. A variety of wildlife can be observed from tandem dugout canoes. Campsites along the river provide overnight accommodations. Other portions of the safari include drives through the Samburu Game Reserve, Meru National Park via the Nyambeni Hills and a little-used road via Benane, with camping near the village of Garissa. The Korokoro people are visited, and safari members witness an evening of traditional dancing. Persons wishing to participate only in the Lake Turkana and Samburu Game Reserve portion of the trip can leave on the eleventh day at Isiolo and travel by public transport to Nairobi, the safari's last stop. **Cost:** On request. **When:** August to January. **Contact:** Afrotrek Ltd., P.O. Box 40248, Nairobi, Kenya; phone 23186 or 334574.

ASIA

Journey to Central Asia: Landlocked and isolated with a society that has resisted modernization, central Asia has in places remained unchanged for centuries. A 24-day trip takes travelers to this region, through both Afghanistan and Soviet Central Asia. The emphasis is on architecture, art, culture, history, language and religion as participants visit Kabul, Bamiyan, Mazar-i-Sharif, Tashkent, Samarkand, Bukhara and remote Nuristan. The expedition leader is a professor of anthropology familiar with the region. **Cost:** $1,490 includes land transportation, accommodations, food, guide. **When:** May, August, October. **Contact:** Nature Expeditions International, 599 College Ave., Palo Alto, CA 94306, USA; phone (415)328-6572.

(M)

Mongolia

Culture of Central Asia: On an unusual 22-day trip participants visit remote areas of central Asia and Mongolia, live in yurt camps (tent-type dwellings) much of the time and explore sites of cultural and archaeological interest. Participants fly to Moscow via Copenhagen, spending a day in Moscow before proceeding by air to Samarkand in Soviet Central Asia. After viewing remnants from Tamerlane's empire, the group travels by coach to the Tajik Republic and the archaeological site at Pendjiket. A visit to the museum city of Bukhara precedes a flight to Tashkent and Khiva where time is allotted for sightseeing. Next is the flight to Irkutsk, in the heart of Siberia and an investigation of the unusual animal life at Lake Baikal. The explorers move to Mongolia for visits to a horse farm, Karakorum, the center of Ghengis Khan's empire and Ulan Bator. Three days are spent in the Gobi Desert observing wildlife, studying vegetation and watching Mongolian horsemen. Finally, a visit is made to Terelj before returning home. **Cost:** $2,340 includes airfare within Mongolia and the USSR, land transportation, accommodations, food, guide. **When:** June to August. **Contact:** Society Expeditions, P.O. Box 5564, University Sta., Seattle, WA 98105, USA; phone (206)324-9400. **(M)**

Sri Lanka

Silk and Gem Trip: Participants drive from Colombo to Ratnapura on a 1-day trip during which a number of Sri Lanka's cultural resources are seen. Rubber tree estates are passed along the route, and visitors may witness the process of turning the raw material into a finished product. Visiting Hanwella, 26 miles from Colombo and the center of silk production, participants watch silk worm rearing and weaving of finished thread. They visit the Halgashena Training Center, managed by the Nuns of the Good Shepherd, and may quench their thirst with a drink of thambili (king coconut) or taste the passion fruit grown on local farms. Ratnapura is renowned for precious stones such as sapphires, rubies, topaz and catseye, some of which adorn the British crown jewels; participants explore the gem pits and museums and may watch the process of cutting, polishing and setting. **Cost:** $20. **When:** Year-round. **Contact:** Tallman Tours, Ltd., 430 Galle Rd., Colombo 3, Sri Lanka; phone 33783.

Culture and Ceremonies: The island country of Sri Lanka has a rich cultural history dating from the fifth century B.C. Travelers investigate the remnants of this past on two 8-day trips focusing on the culture and ceremonies of the predominantly Buddhist nation. On the cultural tour participants visit a

Bactrian camels in the Gobi Desert are prized for their soft hair. Society Expeditions sponsors a 22-day trip to the Gobi. (Society Expeditions)

244 / LAND ADVENTURES

museum in the capital city of Colombo, sightsee in the sacred city of Anuradhapura, see the Dutch fortress of Galle and explore the Temple of the Sacred Tooth Relic of the Buddha in Kandy, a cultural sanctuary where age-old customs and arts are preserved. The ceremonies and rituals tour takes travelers to observe an exorcism ceremony at Colombo, to watch firewalking and propitiation rites at the festival at Kataragama, and to see masked dancing in Hikkaduwa. A trip is made to Kandy to see the perahera, a procession of 70 gaily adorned elephants, drummers, dancers and chiefs in full regalia. Both trips begin and end at Colombo, with transportation by motorcoach on the cultural tour and by car on the ceremonies tour. Accommodations are in hotels. **Cost:** $220. **When:** Year-round. **Contact:** Walkers Tours & Travels Ltd., P.O. Box 1048, 11 York St., Colombo 1, Sri Lanka; phone 22553. *(M)*

ATLANTIC

Greenland

Ice and Eskimo Explorations: The landscape and culture of the world's largest island are explored on a variety of trips departing from Reykjavik. Based in a hotel in Narssarssuaq, travelers may make a series of day-long excursions: a boat trip to visit Viking ruins and the ancient Eskimo winter quarters at Kagssiarssuq; a trip by boat and foot to the sheep-rearing village of Igaliko; a walk to the Greenland glacier; a trip by boat to see old fishing boats at Narssaq; and a boat trip to the mouth of Qoroq Fjord featuring close-up views of icebergs floating near the glacier. A day trip to Kulusuk Island enables participants to visit the primitive Eskimo village at Cape Dan. From Kulusuk travelers may continue by helicopter or boat to the seal-hunting and fishing village of Angmagssalik. On 4- and 5-day trips based at a hotel here participants may examine arctic flora and fauna and gain insight into the culture of people living in a remote area. **Cost:** $154 to $690 depending on length of trip includes airfare from Reykjavik, accommodations, excursions. **When:** June to August. **Contact:** Icelandic Airlines, 630 Fifth Ave., New York, NY 10020, USA; phone (212)757-8585. *(M)*

North Pole

Caviar at the North Pole: A 10-day journey by air takes travelers to lunch at the North Pole. Departing from Edmonton, 9 travelers accompanied by a world explorer fly to Resolute on Cornwallis Island and then on to Eureka on Ellesmere Island. Here participants change to an amphibious plane for a 1-hour flight to Lake Hazen where the polar base camp is established. The next morning the group flies 500 miles over the Polar Ice Cap to the North Pole. After landing, group members walk around a bit before celebrating with a champagne and caviar lunch. Returning through Hazen and Eureka, the expedition continues to the Fosheim Peninsula to explore the Grise Fjord, a valley containing such wildlife as musk oxen, caribou, foxes and arctic hares. The community of Grise Fjord hosts the group with kayak rides and an evening party. Another day in Resolute allows participants to visit an Inuit Eskimo village before taking a short flight to the Magnetic Pole for a picnic lunch. Travelers have a final free day in Resolute before flying back to Edmonton for the journey's end. **Cost:** $3,300 from Edmonton includes transportation, meals, accommodations, guide. **When:** March to June. **Contact:** Hefner Travel, 2975 Wilshire Blvd. Suite 608, Los Angeles, CA 90010, USA; phone (213)387-7225.

AUSTRALASIA
Papua New Guinea

Exploring the Sepik River: A 23-day expedition into New Guinea and the New Hebrides coincides with the national Sing-Sing in New Guinea, a yearly tribal celebration. During the trip, 4 days are spent on the Sepik River enabling participants to visit Baiyer River Wildlife Reserve and make forays on river launches to remote areas. Participants view the distinct cultural groups in New Guinea including lowlands people who continue a fairly unchanged way of life based on barter and collectivism. The Sepik area consists of small lakes, streams, and tributaries drained by the Sepik River and connected by man-made channels called barads. After exploring the river region, swimming, snorkeling, and visiting wildlife reserves are on the itinerary as trip members visit Port Moresby, Minj and Port Vila. Before returning to San Francisco the group makes a brief stopover in Fiji. **Cost:** $3,832 from San Francisco includes transportation, guide, meals, accommodations. **When:** May to July. **Contact:** Explorer Tours, Suite 307, 640 Cathcart St., Montreal, PQ Canada, H3B 1M3; phone (514)861-6763 **(M)**

Entering Stone Age Villages: While traveling with an experienced natural history guide and lecturer for 18 to 23 days, participants view the great cultural contrasts within New Guinea and Australia. The trip begins with 2 days in Sydney, after which participants fly to Port Moresby where they visit the National Museum, the university and the art center to receive an introduction to the culture and 1,000 tribes of the country. Overland travel precedes a visit to the Haus Tamberan (Spirit Houses which are the center of village life) to see the ceremonies of various tribes including the Andagalimp dancers and the cultural re-enactments of the Chimbu and the Mud Men. Korogo, Mindimbit and Washkuk are some of the villages where participants moor while aboard a houseboat on the Sepik River. Inaccessible by land, the Sepik area gives naturalists the opportunity to experience cultures that resemble those of the Stone Age. After 4 days on the river, adventurers fly to the coastal town of Madang and the village of Bilbil to view tribal artists work. Adventurers drive in the morning sun across the desert to the Olga Range for a day's visit before departing to Sydney. **Cost:** $2,075 for 18 days, $2,575 for 23 days includes transportation from Sydney, meals, accommodations, guides. **When:** Year-round. **Contact:** Society Expeditions, P.O. Box 5564, University Sta., Seattle, WA 98105, USA; phone (206)324-9400.
(M)

CANADA

British Columbia

Klondike Travel: A 100-mile float plane flight over remote forest and lake wilderness begins a 7-day trip into the Alaskan frontier. On the day after the plane lands at Lake Atlin, participants may choose to take a freight canoe trip to a turn-of-the-century railroad station and sawmill and continue to an abandoned hard-rock gold rush town at Lake Tagish. During the rest of the stay, opportunities are available for hiking, fast-water canoeing and gold panning at Llewellyn Glacier. Members observe a multitude of wildflowers, visit a hidden emerald lake and investigate an abandoned trapper's cabin. Grizzly bears can sometimes be seen and photographed. **Cost:** $845. **When:** June to September. **Contact:** Special InteresTours, P.O. Box 37, Medina, WA 98039, USA; phone (206)455-1960. *(M)*

CARIBBEAN

West Indies

Treasure Hunting Expedition: An 8-day trip takes treasure hunters to Guadaloupe, "Treasure Island" of the French West Indies, where participants explore deserted beaches, remains of 16th-century forts and empty plantation fields. Using metal detectors, trip members search these well-known areas for valuable objects such as coins and jewelry. In the past, hunters on the island have uncovered such military artifacts as cannonballs, musket balls, swords, pistols, belt buckles and breastplates. In addition, gun batteries exist throughout the island, some in remote areas, and participants visit settlements that were built in the 1600s. Several wrecks are to be found on the island's beaches. **Cost:** $695 includes roundtrip airfare, accommodations, some ground transportation, guides. **When:** April to October. **Contact:** Adventurers International, 215 E. Horatio Ave., Maitland, FL 32751, USA; phone (305)645-1332. *(M)*

CENTRAL AMERICA

Belize

Rum Point Field Studies: An 8-day program of informal field studies covers social anthropology, ethnology and archaeology. While living at Rum Point at a local inn, participants learn about the 3 major cultures in the area: the Creole, the Garifuna and the Kekchi Maya. Other ethnic groups are visited on the Placencia Peninsula and visits are made to archaeological sites in the mountains of southern Belize. There are also opportunities for sport diving. **Cost:** $300. **When:** December to April, June, July. **Contact:** Oceanic Expeditions, 240 Ft. Mason, San Francisco, CA 94123, USA; phone (415)441-1106.

Guatemala

Mayan Ruins Expedition: Twelve days by bus, native canoe and on foot take explorers over ancient Mayan routes in the Peten rain forest of Guatemala and Mexico. The trip begins in Guatemala City with a lecture on local archaeology. Participants are then flown to Flores where, after a bus trip to Sayaxche, they travel by dugout canoe to the camp on Lake Petexpatun.

From Lake Petexpatun the expedition visits the unexcavated site of Aguateca, El Chimino, Dos Pilas, and the recently discovered sites of El Duende and Arroyo de Piedras. On the sixth day the expedition travels by dugout canoe down the La Pasion River to camp at the confluence of the Salinas and the Usumacinta rivers. There participants visit the Altar de los Sacrificios, discovered in 1883 and studied extensively but now abandoned and overgrown. The next day the expedition continues down the Usumacinta River to Yaxchilan, Guatemala where, after making camp, members cross to the Yaxchilan site in Mexico for a look at the Mayan ruins. On the 3-day upriver return trip, participants camp the first night on the Usumacinta and La Pasion rivers. Then from Sayaxche they motor to Flores for the night with the flight to Guatemala City on the final day. No experience is required; expedition personnel cook and set up camp. **Cost:** $880 includes transportation from Guatemala City, hotel accommodations in Guatemala City and Flores, meals on the river. **When:** July, August. **Contact:** Panamundo Guatemala Travel Service, 14 Calle 7-71, Zona 9, Guatemala.

EUROPE

Early Civilization: Some of the oldest remains of human habitation and art are visited in a 22-day trip through western Europe. Traveling by motorcoach and spending nights in local chateaux, country inns and castles, participants see ancient sites in England, Wales, France, Brittany and Spain. Visits

are made to Stonehenge, the still-mysterious temple/observatory; Stone and Bronze Age sites in Salisbury Plain, North Wales and Brittany; and various other prehistoric ruins. Travelers view the paintings, engravings and reliefs that line the caves of northern Spain and France's Perigord. A series of lectures is presented en route by experts and professors. **Cost:** $2,495 includes transportation from London, food, accommodations, guide. **When:** May to October. **Contact:** Society Expeditions, P.O. Box 5564, University Sta., Seattle, WA 98105, USA; phone (206)324-9400. *(M)*

Yugoslavia

Skirting East/West Frontiers: Following an overnight flight from Canada to Venice, members of a 17-day trip to explore Rome, Greece and Slavic countries begin at Porec in Yugoslavia, the location of a 6th-century basilica. Participants continue the journey with a short drive to Pula, site of a Roman arena that could seat 23,000 spectators, and then proceed along narrow, winding roads to Plitvice Lakes National Park. Diocletian's Palace at Split provides a glimpse into the history of a town that houses thousands of artifacts from the Renaissance and Gothic eras to the present. Dubrovnik on the Adriatic offers vantage points for viewing the city's bone-tinted stone buildings and pavement, and visitors stroll through its narrow cobblestone streets where vehicles are banned. An overnight cruise brings participants to the island of Corfu for a brief visit before returning to the mainland. Visits to the monasteries of Meteora and the ruins of

the Acropolis in Athens bring the trip to a close. **Cost:** $1,210 plus airfare includes hotel, meals. **When:** April, October. **Contact:** Azalai Explorers Inc., Suite 1006, 75 The Donway W., Don Mills, ON Canada M3C 2E9; phone (416)449-8044.

MEXICO

Chihuahua

Camping in Barranca Del Cobre: The wilderness, history and peoples of Mexico are explored for 13 days by travelers first meeting in El Paso to cross the border via public transportation to Chihuahua. The next day, after hiking to the train station, explorers ride to a ranch near La Mesa for 2 days of visiting unexcavated archaeological sites. Descending into the Barranca del Cobre, participants camp for 5 days in the rarely explored canyon. The first night's camp is made at Urique River after which as much time as possible is spent hiking and exploring the tropical wilderness including hot springs and beaches. Travelers hike out via a new route to the rim, then take a train to Chihuahua, the ranch center for northern Mexico, to spend a day shopping. A farewell dinner is part of the trip's final night in El Paso. **Cost:** $295 from El Paso includes meals, transportation, equipment. **When:** October to April. **Contact:** Outdoor Leadership Training Seminars, 2220 Birch St., Denver, CO 80207, USA; phone (303)333-7831. *(M)*

Oaxaca

Archaeological Study of Oaxaca: For 10 days a professor of anthropology guides an expedition studying the ancient and modern culture of central Mexico, with a focus on the archaeological ruins and villages in and around Mexico City and Oaxaca. After a visit to the National Museum of Anthropology, the group visits Teotihuacan, constructed between the third and first centuries B.C. Participants travel north to Tula, once the capital city of the Toltecs, where they see the earliest known ball court, 10th-century frescoes and the step pyramid of Quetzalcoatl. After more explorations in Mexico City, including the National Palace, National Cathedral, Chapultepec Castle and the Museum of National History, participants fly to Oaxaca. Explorations are conducted through more than 200 ancient cities and towns of archaeological significance in the area starting with Monte Alban. A morning visit is made to the archaeological treasures in the Regional Museum of Oaxaca before journeying to Mitla and Yagul. Visits to several Indian markets near Oaxaca and the weaving center of Teotitlan del Valle introduce participants to some aspects of the cultural history of central Mexico. Villages and towns known for leatherwork, sculpture and pottery are visited before travelers board a plane for the flight to Mexico City and on home. **Cost:** $590 includes ground transportation, meals, accommodations, guide; airfare extra. **When:** January, April, July. **Contact:** Nature Expeditions International, 599 College Ave., Palo Alto, CA 94306, USA; phone (415)328-6572.   *(M)*

PACIFIC

Easter Island

Easter Island Archaeology: Easter Island is the most remote of the inhabited islands on earth, and its

Archaeologists study easily overlooked objects—such as these pottery sherds from Tamaulipas, Mexico—to uncover the past. (Carol Baker)

The moai, *or giant statues of Easter Island, are part of an ancient culture studied on a $790 trip by Society Expeditions.* (Society Expeditions)

cultural development in isolation is of special interest. A 15-day trip takes travelers there under the guidance of an expert for visits to anthropological and archaeological sites. After 3 days in Santiago, participants fly to Easter Island for a full week of activities. Visits are made to Ahu Tahai with its stone statues, Akahanga burial site, the ceremonial village of Orongo with its birdman petroglyphs, Vinapu Temple, Topknot Quarry, the abandoned statues of Rano Raraku and the restored temple of Ahu Akivi. Extensive archaeological and anthropological instruction is given. The trip may be extended with a week in the Galapagos for investigation of the archipelago's unique wildlife. **Cost:** $1,390 for Easter Island, $790 for Galapagos extension includes land transporta-

tion, accommodations, food, guide. **When:** Year-round. **Contact:** Society Expeditions, P.O. Box 5564, University Sta., Seattle, WA 98105, USA; phone (206)324-9400. **(M)**

SOUTH AMERICA

Bolivia

Amazon Jungle Expedition: Participants embark from La Paz on a 7-day journey by bus, boat and plane through a portion of the Amazon drainage basin. Crossing La Cumbre Pass from La Paz at the eastern edge of the Andes, groups descend by bus to the coffee and coca leaf region around Coroico. One day is spent traveling downriver to the Lake of the Caimanes which abounds with alligators and piranha. An outdoor barbeque with entertainment by local musicians highlights another day. Return to La Paz from the jungle is by commercial airline. Accommodations are provided in hotels along the route. **Cost:** $240 to $280 includes transportation from La Paz, accommodations, meals, guides. **When:** On request. **Contact:** Safari Travels, Edificio Libertad, Pasaje Peatonal No. 8, La Paz, Bolivia. *(M)*

Colombia

South American Natural History: Two slightly different trips provide opportunities to study the people, archaeology and natural history of South America. The first trip lasts 21 days and covers Colombia and Ecuador, with an emphasis on the Andes and Upper Amazon. Visits are made to Bogota, the Neiva-San Agustin area, Quito, the Napo River region, mountain villages and a variety of Andean vegetation zones, with a focus on Mt. Cotopaxi. On the second trip, which lasts 23 days, participants journey through Ecuador, Peru and Bolivia. Many Inca ruins and Indian markets are explored, with major stopovers made at Quito, Cuenca, Lima, Cuzco, Machupicchu, Lake Titicaca and La Paz. Both trips are led by professionals or scholars familiar with the area. **Cost:** $1,290 for either trip includes land transportation, accommodations, food, guide. **When:** January, April, July, August. **Contact:** Nature Expeditions International, 599 College Ave., Palo Alto, CA 94306, USA; phone (415)328-6572. *(M)*

Peru

Amazon Exploration: Fourteen days exploring the Amazon jungle begin with a riverboat journey down the Amazon from Iquitos. During 5 days at a jungle lodge 50 miles from Iquitos, participants have considerable contact with Yagua Indians. There are opportunities to observe a variety of Amazon wildlife, tour a sugar cane mill and fish for piranha. Further ventures from the lodge include an overnight safari and a night trip to see alligators. A mini-safari of 7 days is also available. **Cost:** $1,299 for the full trip includes roundtrip transportation from Miami, accommodations, most meals; $799 for the mini-safari. **When:** July, August, and by arrangement. **Contact:** Amazon Safari Club, Inc., RR 1, P.O. Box 2, Elverson, PA 19520, USA; phone (215)286-9041. *(M)*

UNITED STATES

Arizona

Exploring Southwest Indian Cultures: Leaving from Flagstaff, travelers study the culture and history of the Hopi, Navajo and Anasazi Indians with a professor of anthropology. For 15 days participants camp, hike and explore by van the Navajo National Monument, Monument Valley, Canyon de Chelly and the Navajo and Hopi reservations. Studies of the Indian cultures are enhanced by seeing Indian artisans at work and the ceremonial kachina dances. **Cost:** $690 from Flagstaff includes meals, accommodations, transportation, guide. **When:** May, June. **Contact:** Nature Expeditions International, 599 College Ave., Palo Alto, CA 94306, USA; phone (415)328-6572. *(M)*

OVERLANDING

If you have always wanted to see the canals of Venice, the ruins of Troy and the Taj Mahal but couldn't decide which one you could afford, why not go to all three on the same trip? The London-to-Kathmandu route taken by overland travelers each year visits all of these places, as well as the islands of Greece, the beerhalls of Bavaria, the Khyber Pass in Afghanistan and the gompas of Nepal—at a cost as little as $15 a day, including food, lodging, and *all* transportation.

Overland adventures are one of the fastest-growing, and most appealing, forms of adventure travel. From a handful of pioneering trip operators in the United States and Great Britain who started these expeditions in the 1960s, overlanding has become a major part of the travel industry. Over 100 firms take thousands of people across some of the most exciting areas in the world each year. You can travel down the length of Africa or South America, across Scandinavia or North America, through the Holy Land, as well as across Asia and Europe. All the marvelous diversity of these lands and their peoples can be experienced on a single trip.

All of the good long-distance overland operators use dependable, four-wheel drive vehicles, designed to cross the toughest desert, jungle and mountain areas on any continent. Group sizes range from 6 to 30, with 20 being about the average. While most participants are in their 20s and 30s, age is no limit. You'll find that the camaraderie which evolves on a long-distance trip breaks down the barriers of age and social background. Most overland trips last from one to four months, although shorter ones visit specific areas such as Iceland, Spain or Thailand. Camping is the most common way to spend the night on these trips, and participants often help with tenting, food preparation and moving the vehicle out of mud, sand, rivers and swamps along some of the more difficult routes. But there is no faster way to immerse yourself in a large number of cultures and landscapes than by participating in a transcontinental overland trip. If you have the time, are prepared to rough it and help with logistics—and if you have a pressing curiosity about the great diversity of the people who live on this planet—then it can be just the kind of adventure you're looking for. □

A sturdy, specially designed vehicle is often the only practical means of overland travel in remote areas such as Afghanistan. It serves as transportation, bunkhouse and mess hall on the road. (Encounter Overland)

OVERLANDING

AFRICA

Exploring Africa: A 3-month expedition departs from Kenya via 4-wheel drive truck and covers nearly 10,000 dusty, rugged miles through the African continent. Participants explore such well-known monuments as snow-capped Mt. Kilimanjaro, Tsavo National Park, home of giraffes and elephants, Lake Victoria, the volcanoes of Rwanda and the Ituri Rain Forest, home of the Pygmies. The flexible itinerary includes visits to Mombasa, Douala, Bangui and Mamfe. Trip members also visit Benin City, the capital of the old Ibo kingdom of Onitsha, on the banks of the Niger. Due to the rough conditions of many of the roads, party members may find themselves building bridges where old ones are washed out or levering the truck out of thick mud. The trip also includes explorations of Kano, the Sahara, Morocco and Fez before concluding in Europe. A Nepal/India extension is available. **Cost:** On request. **When:** December. **Contact:** Aardvark Expeditions, 14 Coleridge Rd., London N8, Great Britain; phone 01-340-7598. *(M)*

Overland Journey to Nairobi: An 18-week overland expedition between Southampton, England and Nairobi, Kenya crosses France and Spain on the way to the Algeciras-Ceuta ferry to Africa. From there the expedition passes through Morocco, Algeria, Niger, Nigeria, Cameroon, the Central African Empire, Zaire, Tanzania and Kenya. Highlights include a climb of Mt. Kahuzi in Zaire to search for the mountain gorilla, and a visit to Ngorongoro Crater in Tanzania. While in Tanzania participants may elect to climb Mt. Kilimanjaro. Throughout the trip, expedition members share in the daily camp work and should be in good physical condition. A trip from Nairobi to Southampton reverses the itinerary. **Cost:** $1,518 includes transportation from Southampton or Nairobi, accommodations, personnel, equipment; $10 a week for food kitty. **When:** July from Southampton, December and February from Nairobi. **Contact:** Adventure Africa, Stablings, 34b High St., Ramsbury, Marlborough, Wiltshire, Great Britain; phone (06722)569. *(M)*

Along the Nile: On a 30-day overland camping trip, participants follow the course of the Nile from Cairo to Nairobi in expedition trucks. From Cairo the group travels to Giza to view the pyramids, continuing south to Thebes. Once at Aswan, participants may visit the Temple of Ramses or venture into the surrounding desert. The itinerary follows the river through Luxor, Dongola and across the Nubian Desert to Karima. After camping in the Bayuda Desert and observing its wildlife, the group travels to Khartoum, where participants may visit the Ethnographic Museum or the Sudanese History Museum. Traveling to Sennar, Juba and Eliye Springs, the group eventually heads down the Rift Valley into Nairobi. Participants share

An oasis in the Sahara gives welcome relief to travelers in a Land Rover. Often considered a wasteland, the Sahara actually harbors a surprising variety of life. (WEXAS)

cooking, cleaning and camping duties. The trip may be taken in either direction. **Cost:** $470 includes transportation from Cairo, camping equipment, game park fees. **When:** Southbound in September, November, February; northbound in October, January, March. **Contact:** Africanus, 15 Central Chambers, Cooks Alley, Stratford-on-Avon, Warwickshire, Great Britain; phone (0789)5033. *(M)*

Trans-African Truck Safari: Transported by expedition trucks, travelers embark on a 17-week journey from London to Johannesburg or reverse. Participants camp during most of the trip and share in food shopping, cooking and camp chores. Algeria and the bordering Sahara are the first of 3 distinct types of African terrain that demarcate the journey. The desert portion of the trip covers nearly 2,000 miles and includes the Hoggar Mountains, the ancient walled city of Kano, Tamanrasset and encounters with Tuareg traders, the fabled "blue men of the desert." As northern Cameroon is reached, savanna, red dust tracks and simple hillside farms indicate a transition into forest. With permission of the village chief, overlanders camp on the edges of villages along the way. In this phase the group explores lush equatorial vegetation, capitals that have rivers as their main thoroughfares, the Ituri forests that are the home of the Pygmies, the active volcano of Nyiragongo and the Ruwenzori Mountains. Unfarmed scrub and the plains of northwest Tanzania mark entry into the final section of the trip. A challenging but not technically difficult ascent of 19,340-foot Mt. Kilimanjaro is possible at this point. The central region of the Masai Steppes abounds with wildlife and during the trip, group members choose 3 wildlife reserves to visit. Victoria Falls and the coast of the Indian Ocean are some of the final stops. Vagaries of the political climate, weather and the interests of the group may change the itinerary. **Cost:** $1,850 to $1,975 from London to Johannesburg; $1,790 Johannesburg to London; $1,575 to $1,737 from London to Nairobi includes transportation, accommodations, meals, equipment, guide. **When:** January to November. **Contact:** Encounter Overland, 369 Pine St.,

One of the more vigorous aspects of an overlanding journey to Zaire involves pushing one's truck out of what used to be a road. (John Carson)

Suite 516, San Francisco, CA 94104, USA; phone (415)421-7199.   **(M)**

French West Africa Expedition: Travelers spend 28 days in West Africa exploring 4 countries via train, plane, river and road transportation. Flying from New York, the group spends 3 days in Dakar before heading into the interior by way of a 30-hour train trip to Mali's tree-lined capital city of Bamako. Two days later, trip members follow the Niger River as it passes through Segou and Djenné, traveling in a fully equipped truck to reach Mopti. A 4-day river cruise in a large motorized piroque familiarizes participants with the people, animals and ways of the Niger River. Members then fly back to Mopti for a road trek to Ouagadougou, the capital of Upper Volta.

From there overlanders travel farther south to the cities of Tamale, Kumasi, Takoradi and Accra, from where they return to New York. The group camps under the stars in Mali and stays at hotels in Dakar, Bamako, Ouagadougou and the Ghanaian cities. **Cost:** $3,388 includes airfare from New York, meals, accommodations, local transportation. **When:** January. **Contact:** Exploration Africa, 17 Inkerman St., Toronto, ON Canada M4Y 1M5.

Africa from the Bottom Up: A trip by expedition truck takes participants from Johannesburg to London over the course of 16 weeks. Visits are made to most of Africa's major game parks, and there are many opportunities for side trips.

The first leg of the journey visits South Africa, Botswana and Zambia, with camping on the edge of the Okavango Swamps, where a dugout may be hired to track hippos and buffalo. Stops are made at Gaborone, Maun, Chobe National Park and Victoria Falls. In Tanzania and Kenya travelers visit Mikumi National Park, Dar es Salaam, Kilimanjaro, Nairobi, Mombasa, Ngorongoro Crater and Serengeti National Park. Through the dense jungles of Central Africa, participants travel in Rwanda, Zaire and the Central African Empire, with a visit included to the active volcano of Nyiragongo. Camping on the Atlantic coast of Cameroon follows during the excursion through West Africa. Finally the trip crosses the Sahara to visit Niger, Algeria and Morocco before crossing the Strait of Gibraltar to traverse France and Spain to London. Nights are spent camping (with occasional exceptions), and participants share cooking, cleaning and some road-clearing chores. **Cost:** $1,270 includes food, transportation, equipment, guide. **When:** February to November. **Contact:** Tracks, 165 Kensington High St., London W8 6SH, Great Britain; phone 01-937-5964.   *(M)*

Botswana

Bush Country Safaris: Participants view wild animals in their natural settings on a journey through the parks and riverlands of eastern Botswana. Starting in Johannesburg, travelers spend 14 days camping, hiking and driving through the southern African bush. Stops include a base camp at Okavango Swamp, where animals roam through grasslands and lagoon country; Chobe National Park, filled with elephants, antelope and a great variety of bird life; and famous Victoria Falls at the heart of the Zambezi River. Adventurers return to Johannesburg through the Transvaal high veldt. Dugout canoes are available for exploration of the river shallows, where hippos and buffalo may still be found. **Cost:** $515 from Johannesburg includes transportation, camping accommodations. **When:** April to November. **Contact:** Adventure Center, 5540 College Ave., Oakland, CA 94618, USA; phone (415)654-1879. *(M)*

Egypt

Viewing Ancient and Modern Egypt: Travelers voyage throughout the Nile Valley and points east on a 28-day tour. Starting in New York City, voyagers fly to London and then Cairo, where headquarters are established at the Nile Hilton. After visits to the pyramids of Giza and Memphis and a trip to the Sphinx, participants spend a day at the home of an Egyptian family, then fly to Luxor to see the Valley of the Kings and the religious center of Karnak. Day 7 opens with a flight to Aswan, home of a Sixth Dynasty temple; the next day is taken up viewing the 3,000-year-old temple of Abu Simbel, now relocated above Lake Nasser. Then it's back to Cairo via Alexandria for a few days of entertainment and bazaar-browsing. Khartoum in the Sudan is reached on day 12; travelers wander through this ancient city, having the chance to get acquainted with a Sudanese family. During the next few days voyagers travel to southern Sudan, with its great variety of wildlife and colorful Latuka and Bara tribes. After 4 days with the tribespeople, participants fly to Dar es Salaam, Tanzania where they then visit Selous Safari Camp in a 21,000-square-mile game reserve. Two days of camping precede the flight to the Indian Ocean enclave of Maritius. Participants travel to India for a 3-day stay in Bombay before the return to New York. **Cost:** $4,695 includes airfare from New York. **When:** October. **Contact:** Capers 400 Club, 960 N. Larrabee St., Los Angeles, CA 90069, USA; phone (213)657-0916.

Mali

Trekking in Southwest Africa: A 15-day trek begins in Mopti, where members set out on foot for a 5-day exploration of the Bandiagara Plateau. Nights are spent in Dogon villages, built into the cliff face like miniature fortresses. Dogon tribal life is dominated by ancient forms of worship symbolized in spectacular masked dances. During the next few days participants journey by dugout canoe on the Niger River, visiting some of the Bozo and Peulh villages in the delta. Along the river banks animals and birds are abundant. **Cost:** $1,376 includes round-trip airfare from London, transportation, meals, accommodations. **When:** February, April. **Contact:** Explore Beyond Ltd., 1 Ludgate Circus Bldgs., London EC4M 7LQ, Great Britain; phone 01-248-9082 or 01-236-4395; or Adventure Center, 5540 College Ave., Oakland, CA 94618, USA; phone (415)654-1879. *(M)*

Morocco

Mapping the Atlas: Travelers explore Morocco, home of the Moors and Berbers, in a 3-week motorized expedition starting in Malaga, Spain. After crossing the Strait of Gibraltar to Ceuta, the expedition travels to Fez, a city of many artisans, visiting along the way the ruins of Volubilis, a second-century Roman capital. From Fez the route climbs into the cedar forests of the Middle Atlas Mountains before twisting down into the Sahara. The expedition forges ahead through the desert for several days before turning toward the Atlantic Ocean. After crossing the High Atlas Mountains, trip members stop at the oasis city of Marrakech and then continue to the Atlantic at Rabat. On the way back to Ceuta and the crossing to Europe, the route passes along the coast through Asilah. Expedition members are fully involved in the operation of the trip, from pushing the Bedford trucks through soft sand to buying camping provisions. **Cost:** $370 from Malaga. **When:** June to September. **Contact:** Encounter Overland, 369 Pine St., Suite 516, San Francisco, CA 94104, USA; phone (415)421-7199. *(M)*

Overland to the Berbers: Driving overland in expedition trucks, a small group explores the deserts and mountains of the gateway to Africa ' ia France and Spain. The month-long, roundtrip journey begins in England and avoids the major modern cities of Morocco but includes Fez, the seat of Moroccan culture and religion: Marrakech, the fabled red city; and the coastal capital of Rabat. Eleven days are spent taking an unplanned route to M'Hamid and Ft. Taouz, on the northern edge of the Sahara. While en route overlanders camp under the stars sharing cooking and other chores. The Moorish and Roman ruins visited show part of a trade center that has known pilgrims, traders, invaders and adventurers of every nationality. Participants encounter the indigenous Berbers while in the mountain valleys. The return journey to England takes 5 days and ends with a night ferry crossing to Dover. **Cost:** $318 includes guide, camping equipment, transportation, accommodations, camping fees. **When:** January. **Contact:** Mistral Safari, 1A Whip Ma Whop Ma Gate, York, Yorkshire, Great Britain; phone York (0904)36775. *(M)*

ASIA

East-West Overland: Participants travel by bus on a 2½-month expedition across Asia and Europe. Travelers descend from Kathmandu, Nepal to the plains of northern India, stopping at the holy city of Benares. After visiting the temples of Khajraho and the Taj Mahal, participants spend 3 days each in Delhi and the Happy Valley of Kashmir. After stopping at Lahore in Pakistan, the expedition winds its way up the Kabul Gorge in Afghanistan. Travelers continue to Iran, entering the Great Sand Desert before visiting the ancient Persian cities of Bam and Persepolis. After 12 days in Iran, travelers proceed to Lake Van, 8,205-foot Nemrut Dagi, ancient Goreme, Roman Ephesus and Istanbul in Turkey. Delphi and Athens are explored in Greece before the group moves on to Venice, Florence and Pisa in Italy. Heading north, the expedition pitches camp in the Rhone Valley near Lyon, then continues to Paris. The group reaches the trip's end in London on the 80th day. Most overnights are spent in tents, away from campsites. A shorter trip of 60 days is also available. **Cost:** $500 includes transportation from Kathmandu,

Evening camp in Mali. Adventure Center sponsors an overland journey through Mali that includes a hike on the Bandiagara Plateau and a canoe trip down the Niger River. (Adventure Center)

accommodations, most meals. **When:** March, April, July, August, September. **Contact:** Asian Greyhound Ltd., 15 Kings Rd., Windsor, Berkshire, Great Britain; phone Windsor 69122.

Kathmandu to London via the Middle East: Two different routes are available for travelers who commence their transcontinental journeys in eastern Asia. The shorter trip is 80 days; the longer trip, 90 days. Traveling by motorcoach from the capital city of Nepal, both groups explore the Hindu and Buddhist cultures of Nepal and India, enter Pakistan via the historic Khyber Pass, cross Afghanistan and Iran, and travel up the Tigris River to Babylon and Baghdad. Those on the longer trip spend several days in Syria and Jordan visiting Damascus, King Hussein's palace and the Red Sea at Aqaba before crossing Turkey to Istanbul and Athens. The shorter European route crosses Yugoslavia, Austria and West Germany on its way to Belgium, where a Hovercraft takes the party to Ramsgate in England. **Cost:** $1,045 for 90 days; $785 for 80 days. **When:** February to November. **Contact:** Capricorn Travel and Tours Ltd., 21 Ebury Bridge Rd., London SW1W 8QX, Great Britain; phone 01-730-0657; or Adventure Center, 5540 College Ave., Oakland, CA 94618, USA; phone (415)654-1879. *(M)*

Trans-Asian Expedition: On a flexible itinerary of 11 or 12 weeks, an expedition-equipped truck transports participants from London to Kathmandu, where they may continue to Sydney over another 5 weeks. Accommodations are at campsites in Europe and Asia. Europe is crossed at a fairly brisk pace before the first major stopovers in Istanbul and Turkey's southern coast. Explorations are made of mosques, ruins and other places of interest. These explorations continue as the trip visits Goreme, eastern Anatolia, Lake Van, the Kurdistan region of Iran, Esfahan, Shiraz, Persepolis and Meshed, with a choice between the Tehran route or the cross-desert route. Afghanistan is visited with a stopover in Kabul, and then India with stops in Amritsar, Kashmir and Corbett National Park. After following the Ganges to the pilgrim city of Benares, the trip takes one of several routes up the mountains to Kathmandu. An opportunity to trek to Helmu is offered. Those continuing to Sydney

fly to Bangkok and take a 3-week trip through Thailand and Malaysia, traveling by train and bus with local guides. Next is a flight from Singapore to Perth and a 2-week overland journey through the remote outback to Sydney. Any or all of this trip may be made in reverse. **Cost:** $1,200 to $1,320 London to Kathmandu, $2,930 to $3,020 London to Sydney includes transportation, accommodations, camping equipment, most meals, guide. **When:** February to October. **Contact:** Exodus Expeditions, 167 Earls Court Rd., London SW5, Great Britain; phone 01-373-7895; or Adventure Center, 5540 College Ave., Oakland, CA 94618, USA; phone (415)654-1879.   (M)

England to Nepal Overland: Overlanders cross the English Channel at the start of an 80-day camping trek by motorcoach from London to Kathmandu. Arriving in Belgium, participants drive to Luxembourg, visit Germany and cross the Austrian border to Salzburg. The group pauses to explore the Austrian Tyrol, with its pine forests and streams, and the city of Graz. Then the group heads for Greece where the first stop is Kavalla, a quiet fishing village on the northern coast. After camping near the sea, participants drive on to Turkey, entering Istanbul in the evening for a stopover of 3 days. The trip continues through the Middle East, with the route depending on political conditions. Participants head into Afghanistan where they visit the mosques, shops and central bazaar of Esfahan. The trip continues to Pakistan, encountering ox-

Old and young in Afghanistan, a nation long known as a crossroads of East and West. For centuries, life has changed very little in this feudal society. (Treasure Treks)

ADVENTURE CENTER
THE ADVENTURE TRAVEL SPECIALISTS

Break out of your routine!
Make new friends!
Have the time of your life!

We have: many low-cost worldwide adventures, Himalayan trekking; journeys to Mainland China, Sikkim/Bhutan, Kashmir/Ladakh, Gilgit/Hunza; overland expeditions in Africa, Asia, South America; safaris in Kenya, Botswana, Australia, New Zealand; camping in Europe, Russia, Morocco; skiing in Australia and Switzerland. Hiking in Peru, rafting in New Guinea; Trans-Siberian Express and more.

WE'RE LIKE ALL THE OTHER ADVENTURE TRAVEL ORGANIZATIONS COMBINED

Contact us today for your free 40-page catalog.

5540AA College Avenue, Oakland, California 94618,

Phone (415) 654-1879

carts, tongas, bicycles and water buffalo in the roads of Peshawar. The trip concludes by passing through India and Kashmir to reach Kathmandu in Nepal. **Cost:** $375 from London. **When:** August. **Contact:** Tour East, 84 Oakleigh Park N., London N20, Great Britain; phone 01-445-8608.

Eurasian Hinterland: Overlanders spend 56 or 65 days exploring central Eurasia on a motorcoach expedition between London and Kathmandu. The 56-day trip begins with a transfer from London to the Continent; after stops in Cologne and Munich the group travels down the Dalmatian Coast of Yugoslavia, staying at campsites in Zadar and Dubrovnik. The historical regions of Macedonia and Greece are then explored, with visits made to Mt. Olympus, Athens, the sacred city of Delphi and the battle plain of Thermopylae. After touring Istanbul, the group follows the Turkish coast before turning north to the Turkish hinterland. The expedition loops around the mountains of Iran before swinging north again for a crossing of Afghanistan's Hindu Kush and Khyber Pass. Rawalpindi and Lahore are the jump-off points for a traverse of the Pakistan frontier before the expedition continues to the lush valley of the Ganges in India. After stops in Delhi and Agra, the group crosses into Nepal for the conclusion of the journey in Kathmandu. The 65-day trip follows much the same route, but starts in Kathmandu and ends in London. **Cost:** $1,033 to $1,233 depending on direction of trip includes transportation, camping and hotel accommodations, food kitty.

When: September to March. **Contact:** Transit Travel Ltd., 43 Kensington High St., London W8 5ED, Great Britain; phone 01-937-6662; or USSTS, 801 Second Ave., New York, NY 10017, USA; phone (212)867-8770.

Afghanistan

Afghanistan Expedition: After a flight to the capital city of Kabul, travelers begin a 3-week trip west into the mountains toward Bamiyan, once a great Buddhist center. The group visits Band-i-Amir and has the opportunity to take a swim in one of its 5 lakes. Four-wheel drive vehicles transport the group to the Minaret of Djam, excavated in 1957 and standing in a remote valley. The historic sights straddling the ancient Silk Route linking China to Europe are explored at Herat, Bost and Kandahar, followed by a crossing of the famous Khyber Pass. The finale includes an excursion into the tribal territory around Darrah, a gun-making and opium-producing village. **Cost:** $799 to $1,135 depending on departure date includes roundtrip airfare from London, all land arrangements; $92 for food kitty. **When:** May to October. **Contact:** Explore Beyond Ltd., 1 Ludgate Circus Bldgs., London EC4M 7LQ, Great Britain; phone 01-248-9082 or 01-236-4395; or Adventure Center, 5540 College Ave., Oakland, CA 94618, USA; phone (415)654-1879.
(M)

India

Kashmir Exploration: Travelers begin a 24-day trip to Kashmir with a morning in New Delhi, followed

Trans-Asian overlanders in Nepal are greeted with the sight of such mountains as Ama Dablam, shown here towering over the Buddhist monastery of Thyangboche. Both are on the route to Mt. Everest Base Camp. (Keith Gunnar)

by a midday flight to Srinagar. From here trip members go on a variety of trips, with opportunities to explore Nishat, the Moghul Gardens of Shalimar, Aru in the Himalayas and the mountain trails to the Kolahoi Glacier. Travel is often by horseback and houseboats are used as accommodations for several days. After returning to Shikara for a day, the group sets off by motor caravan for Ladakh. Once there, sites to be visited include an old fort and several abandoned gompas (monasteries). Overnight camping is done further along the route, and the trip eventually comes back to New Delhi. **Cost:** $1,617. **When:** On request. **Contact:** Azalai Explorers Inc., Suite 1006, 75 The Donway W., Don Mills, ON Canada M3C 2E9; phone (416)449-8044.

Himalayan Empire Expedition: A maximum of 8 people visit Bombay on the first stop of a 35-day trip. From there participants fly to Colombo, Sri Lanka, where they take part in a search by Land Rover for leopards. In Jaipur the group stays at the former residence of a maharaja, visits the Amber Forest by elephantback and then drives to Agra for a visit to the Taj Mahal and a nearby fort. Participants should dress for mild Himalayan mountain weather for the trip to Dharmsala in the Kulu Valley. The group proceeds by jeep to Marhi at 10,938 feet and the Rohtang Pass at 13,050 feet where excellent views of Mt. Shakarbeh, Hanuman Tibba and Mukerbher are available. Srinagar in Kashmir is reached by air, and the group stays here for 2 nights on a houseboat on Dal Lake. On the trip's 26th day participants travel by jeep along an old silk route to the foot of Mt. Rakaposhi in Hunza, where visits are made with the Hunzukuts in their homes. The trip continues to the Khyber Pass, the ruins at Udegram and Taxila, a site of an ancient city. Delhi is the last stop before a homeward flight to New York. **Cost:** $4,400 includes roundtrip airfare from New York, food, accommodations, supplies, guides. **When:** April. **Contact:** Capers 400 Club, 960 N. Larrabee St., Los Angeles, CA 90069, USA; phone (213)657-0916.

Kashmir Excursion: An expedition of 3 weeks begins with a brief stay in Delhi where participants may take sightseeing outings. From there group members are flown to Srinagar, where hikes or horseback trips are made into the surrounding hills. Accommodations are furnished on a houseboat in Srinagar. After a week in Srinagar, the expedition sets out by jeep and on foot for Ladakh by way of Dras. Members stay for 3 days in Leh, the capital of Ladakh, during which time they visit local monasteries, villages and bazaars. The expedition returns and stays 2 nights in Srinagar before flying to Delhi. **Cost:** $970 includes guides, food, accommodations, transportation from Delhi. **When:** June to August. **Contact:** Exodus Expeditions, 167 Earls Court Rd., London SW5, Great Britain; phone 01-373-7895; or

Adventure Center, 5540 College Ave., Oakland, CA 94618, USA; phone (415)654-1879. *(M)*

Overlanding the Hindu Interior: A 1- to 2-month expedition through the interior of India by Bedford bus commences at Kathmandu and includes an itinerary that leads to Delhi, Jaipur, Bombay, Goa and Ajanta. The roads are rugged on the way to Bombay, where participants visit Baba Muktananda's Ashram, observing Kundalini yoga in action. During the trip, group members share cooking responsibilities. In addition, visitors stay sometimes at Indian-style hotels and eat at local restaurants. On the return leg of the trip, participants explore Elora Caves and visit the cities of Agra and Gorakhpur before ending the trip. **Cost:** $150 one way; $250 roundtrip includes camping gear, cooking equipment. **When:** December to February. **Contact:** Hann Overland, 17 Stanthorpe Rd., London SW16, Great Britain; phone 01-769-6659. *(M)*

Asian Overland: A converted railway car provides both transportation and sleeping accommodations on a 32-day trip through India. Departing from Delhi, the trip begins with an overnight journey to Agra and the Taj Mahal, then to Jhansi, Manmad, and the caves of Elora and Ajanta. After a stopover in Bombay the journey continues to Madras on the east coast. From Madras side trips are possible to Kanchipuram, Pondicherry and Sri Lanka. A period of unscheduled time in Cochin enables travelers to visit the southern tip of India via bus and inland canal boat. In the fourth week, the group heads north again through Madras, Kazipet, Nagpur, Benares, Lucknow and Haridwar to the trip's end point at Delhi. **Cost:** $171 includes accommodations on the rail car, transportation, guides; $35 for optional side trips; $18 for food. **When:** August, November, February. **Contact:** Trailfinders, 46/48 Earls Court Rd., London W8 6EJ, Great Britain; phone 01-937-9631.

Indonesia

Across the Forgotten Archipelago: A combination of guided adventures and free days is offered to participants on a 3-week journey through Thailand, Malaysia, Singapore and Indonesia. The one-way trip from Bangkok to Bali or reverse includes an overnight on the Inter-national Express to Penang for a 2-day sojourn followed by a trip to the Cameron Highlands. Participants can visit a Chinese Taoist temple and take mapped jungle walks before continuing to Batu Caves and Kuala Lumpur. Before spending 2 days in Singapore, travelers stay in the ancient trading town of Malacca. The group visits the morning market in Jakarta, the botanical gardens in Bogor and the hot springs and volcano in Bandung. After 2 open days in Jogyakarta visits are made to see ancient temples, batik work, and silverware bazaars of Borobudar and Pambanan. Bali is the southern terminus of the trip and participants can spend time at Kuta Beach or travel in the cool mountains, teak forests, and terraced garden

fields of the volcano-encircled land. **Cost:** $940 from Bangkok or Bali includes accommodations, guide, transportation; $6 a day food kitty. **When:** November, February. **Contact:** Penn Overland Tours Ltd., 122 Knightsbridge, London SW1, Great Britain; phone 01-589-0016; or 330 Sutter St., San Francisco, CA 94108, USA; phone (415)391-5728.   *(M)*

Malaysia

Borneo Jungle Walk: After flying from London to Singapore, hikers travel for 3 weeks in Borneo, East Malaysia and Brunei. Participants spend 2 days in Singapore, then fly to Kuching, Borneo to examine tribal records in the Sarawak Museum and visit Ft. Margarita and Kuching Mosque. Members travel upriver by launch, then canoe to an Iban longhouse to stay for 3 days in the village on stilts. While there participants forge through the jun-

gle and may encounter former headhunters. During a 2-day stay in Bander Seri Begawan the group visits Omar Ali Saifuddin Mosque. Participants walk and climb through the rain forest in Kota Kinabalu National Park, reaching a summit of 13,533 feet, then trek down to Tanjong Aru beach for a final swim before returning to Singapore. **Cost:** $1,899 from London includes accommodations, guide, transportation. Meals extra. **When:** July, August, December, January. **Contact:** Penn Overland Tours Ltd., 122 Knightsbridge, London SW 1, Great Britain; phone 01-589-0016; or 330 Sutter St., San Francisco, CA 94108, USA; phone (415)391-5728.   *(M)*

Sri Lanka

Rail Adventure: Train trips of 1 to 6 days are available for travelers interested in exploring the historic and cultural fascinations of Sri

Remote Malaysian villages are seen by overlanders on a Penn Overland Tours expedition in the jungles of Sarawak on Borneo. (TDC Malaysia)

Lanka. A 1-day trip that winds its way up the mountains amidst lush greenery and terraced rice fields to the hill capital of Kandy offers participants a view of the Temple of the Tooth, the Tea Garden and factory, the Botanical Gardens and Elephant Bath. On another trip, Sri Lanka's ruined cities are seen— Buddhist temples, shrines and palaces of the great Sinhala civilization which flourished between the third century B.C. and the tenth century A.D. Other trips include Wilpattu, the second largest animal reserve in the northwest area, and the ruined city of Anuradhapura. **Cost:** On request. **When:** Year-round. **Contact:** Railtours, Bentota Rail Sta., Colombo Fort, Sri Lanka; phone 35838.

Thailand

Trans-Asian Expedition: A 3-week trip by bus and train offers glimpses of both rural and city life in Thailand and Malaysia. The journey begins with sightseeing in Bangkok, followed by a minibus trip to Chiang Mai and other towns in northern Thailand. After the return trip by road to Bangkok, several days are spent at the beach resort of Patthaya before taking a train to Malaysia. The train heads for Singapore, stopping for visits in Penang, a tropical town on the northwest coast of Malaysia, and to Kuala Lumpur, the nation's capital. A flexible schedule allows for an opportunity to explore villages and sights along the way. The trip is available separately or as part of a

A windy campsite near Tungnafellsjokull. The stark beauty of Iceland is explored on a 13-day overland journey sponsored by Arena Tours. (Kristin Tregillus)

trans-Asian expedition. **Cost:** $300 includes transportation, guide; plus $170 for food and accommodation kitty. **When:** December, January. **Contact:** Exodus Expeditions, 167 Earls Court Rd., London SW5, Great Britain; phone 01-373-7895; or Adventure Center, 5540 College Ave., Oakland, CA 94618, USA; phone (415)654-1879.   *(M)*

ATLANTIC

Iceland

High Country Camping Expedition: Participants depart from Reykjavik on a 13-day trip designed to explore a variety of Icelandic landscapes and culture. An overland bus is used for transportation across the rugged terrain. The first overnight is spent in Thjorsardalur, an area nearly destroyed by volcanic eruptions from nearby Mt. Hekla. The group heads northward into the highlands west of Veidivotn and then to the glacier at Tungnafellsjokull where camp is set up in Jokuldalur, the valley of glaciers. Spectacular mountain scenery dots the Sprengisandur trail, which eventually descends and leads members into Bardardalur. A day's excursion to the caldera at Askja and its surrounding craters provides a view of one of Iceland's volcanic, lunarlike landscapes, and in Namaskard members witness active hot springs and sulfur pits. The principal town of the north coast, Akureyri, is visited before the journey into the highlands of Hveravellir, a thermal area between two large glaciers. On the last day, participants travel to Gullfoss (Golden Falls) and the Great Geyser area, proceeding to Thingvellir, the ancient cliff-rimmed site where the Viking parliament was founded in 930 A.D. The group then returns to Reykjavik. **Cost:** $452 includes local transportation, food, tent accommodations, guides. **When:** June to August. **Contact:** Arena Tours, Hvasseleiti 26, Reykjavik, Iceland; or Adventure Center, 5540 College Ave., Oakland, CA 94618, USA; phone (415)654-1879. *(M)*

Geothermal Journey: A 5-day overland exploration of some of Iceland's geothermal phenomena starts off across lava fields at Krysuvik, location of boiling mud pools and steamjets. Traveling east along the south coast, members of the group proceed toward the glacier of Eyjafjalla for the first day's end at a waterfall named Skogafoss. After a morning given to studies of birdlife and sea-rock formations at Dyrholaey, participants continue further east across the vast Eldhraun lavafield to Kirkjubaejarklaustur, site of a former Benedictine nunnery. Participants then explore Skaftafell National Park, located at the foot of Europe's largest icecap, Vatnajokull. Party members return along the coast past Skogar and then north up the wasteland valley of Thjorsardalur where the volcano Hekla has created a miniature Pompeii. The seething area of erupting hot springs at Geysir hosts travelers before they move on to Laugarvatn. Here visitors may swim, hike, pony trek and partake of natural steam sauna baths. Beginning and ending in Reykjavik, the group travels by bus and stays at hotels. **Cost:** $265 includes transportation, accommodations, meals. **When:** June to August. **Contact:** Icelandic Airlines, 630 Fifth Ave., New York, NY 10020, USA; phone (212)757-8585. *(M)*

AUSTRALASIA
Australia
Arnhem Land and Katherine Gorge Trip: Participants on a 7-day overland expedition travel from Darwin into outlying wild areas, observing wildlife and visiting ancient archaeological remains. First traveling by motorcoach to the town of Katherine, with stops at historic and scenic sites, the group boats up the Katherine Gorge. Wildlife observation, photography and swimming are possible in the wilderness of the Jim Jim area. At Iberi Rock participants can relax in the natural amphitheater and see Nourlangie Rock and the aboriginal cave paintings. Buffalo, pigs, wallabies, dingoes, monitor lizards, wallaroos and a large variety of birds

predominate in this environment. The final 3 days are spent camping and fishing for barramundi and saratoga. **Cost:** $295 includes roundtrip transportation from Darwin, meals, camping and fishing equipment, motel accommodations, guide. **When:** May to December. **Contact:** Boothy's Safariland Tours, P.O. Box 40058, Casuarina N.T., Australia; phone 85-3023.*(M)*

Coongie Lakes—Birdsville Safari: A trek of 14 days designed primarily for those interested in ornitholo-

gy and wildlife photography travels cross-country over Sturt Desert to the Coongie Lakes complex where a base camp is made. The Coongie Lake area, set in rugged sandhill country, is the largest permanent body of water in Australia. The region gives ample opportunities for bird study, photography and general relaxation, with thousands of species of wildlife to observe. After spending 2 or 3 days at the camp, participants visit other remote lakes and water holes. A rarely used private track is taken

An overlander relaxes at the crest of a cliff on the Milford Track. The deep valleys and soaring peaks of New Zealand earn the region the name of the "Southern Alps." (National Publicity Studios)

into Mt. Serle through country not often visited. Besides wildlife observation, other interests include aboriginal rock carvings and paintings and an overnight stay in the historic Birdsville Pub. Covering a total of 3 states, the trip offers a complete outback experience. **Cost:** On request. **When:** By arrangement. **Contact:** Transcontinental Safaris, Douglas Scrub, McLaren Flat, South Australia, Australia; phone Adelaide 3830230.

Alice Springs Overland: Led by an experienced bushman, groups of 5 to 10 people spend 10 days exploring the outback between Alice Springs and Perth. The one-way camping trip includes Ayers Rock, the Olgas, the Petermann Ranges, Docker Creek and aboriginal settlements. Participants camp under the stars along the Gun Barrel Highway and the gold fields of Kalgoorlie. Outback conditions and climate can be harsh, so participants must be reasonably healthy and willing to tolerate primitive conditions. Special packages including airfare within Australia, and accommodations and guides in Alice and Perth are available. Expert photographic assistance is provided on the trip. **Cost:** $359 includes meals, equipment; $570 to $850 for special packages. **When:** March through October. **Contact:** Visitours Tour Service, Box 388, Alice Springs, NT 5750, Australia; phone 522350.

New Zealand

Home Stays with New Zealanders: Travelers wanting a personalized view of New Zealand can join an experienced guide in focusing on the country's culture and geography for 23 days. Participants begin the trip with a flight from Los Angeles to Tahiti to spend a few days swimming and sunning before flying on to New Zealand. Here group members stay with farm families in different locales on the North Island and at sheep stations in remote areas of the South Island. Participants visit volcanic craters, glaciers, mountain valleys and fjords on "flightseeing" adventures in small planes. On one such trip, the group flies over Mt. Cook, then for a different perspective lands to explore a glacier. The trip continues with a jeep ride up Mt. Tarawera, a bus ride to Cape Reinga on the hard sand of Ninety-Mile Beach and an excursion underground to see the Glow-Worm Grotto at Waitomo. There is time for swimming, sunbathing and improvisation as the trip allows for a great deal of personal freedom, with guide service available. **Cost:** $1,795 includes air and ground transportation, meals, accommodations, guides. **When:** February. **Contact:** Goodtravel Tours, 5332 College Ave., Oakland, CA 94618, USA; phone (415)658-2060.

Papua New Guinea

Coast and Highland Expedition: Participants of a 16-day trip to Papua New Guinea explore its rugged, mountainous countryside by foot, river raft and plane. Travelers are provided with a perspective into the varied cultures of the island where over 700 distinct languages are spoken. The journey begins with an overnight visit to the Wau Ecology Institute where participants learn about the flora and fauna of the area. Then trip members board inflatable rafts and float down the Watut River past gold-mining country and through Watut Gorge with over 100 major rapids. From the coastal town of Lae, participants fly into the highlands to Mt. Hagen. There local people are seen wearing elaborate feather headdresses as they walk pigs, which are considered signs of wealth. After a moderate climb to Mt. Giluwe, at 14,330 feet the second-highest peak in the country, participants descend to Baiyer River and Wildlife Sanctuary whose inhabitants include birds of paradise and the cassowary, which looks like a cross between an ostrich and a peacock and is indigenous only to New Guinea. After a night at Chimbu, nestled in pine groves, participants fly to Keglsugl (7,000 feet), a base camp for 14,793-foot Mt. Wilhelm. By hiking to an overnight hut on the shores of alpine Lake Pindaunde, just over 12,000 feet, a sweeping view is gained of New Guinea and the islands beyond. The trip concludes at Port Moresby. **Cost:** $1,286 to $2,795 depending on departure location, includes meals, camping equipment, guides, flights. **When:** June to October. **Contact:** Adventure Center, 5540 College Ave., Oakland, CA 94618, USA; phone (415)654-1879.   *(M)*

CANADA

Camping and Hiking out West: A 6-week trip designed for teenagers includes a wide variety of outdoor and urban activities in the Canadian and American Rockies and national parks in the West. Participants embark on a cross-Canada leg of the trip from Toronto, head-

Canadians had their own west to win. Goway Travel Ltd. uses the durable minibus—rather than the covered wagon—to travel all over the world's second largest nation. (Goway Travel Ltd.)

ing toward Banff and Jasper national parks. While camping at Lake of the Woods, students engage in horseback riding, rowing, canoeing and swimming activities. In Red Deer Valley participants look for fossils and petrified wood and climb the Hoodoos badlands. Trips are made to Calgary for the Stampede; Vancouver's Gastown, a restored section of the city; and Grand Beach at Winnipeg. Potlatch and lumbermill tours as well as man-made islands in Lake Ontario are also included in the itinerary. Full-day hikes into the rugged glaciers and icefields of British Columbia are among the activities arranged in the outdoor segments of the trip. Other national parks visited are Mt. Rainier, Yellowstone, Grand Teton and the Black Hills of South Dakota. **Cost:** $1,295 includes transportation from Toronto, meals. **When:** June, July. **Contact:** American Trails West, 92 Middle Neck Rd., Great Neck, NY 11021, USA; phone (516)487-2802. *(M)*

Camping in Western Provincial Parks: A selection of 1-, 2- or 3-week camping trips in the Rocky Mountains provides trip members with a wide variety of outdoor experiences. Mt. Robson Provincial Park, Glacier National Park, and Banff and Jasper national parks highlight most of the trips, which all begin in Vancouver, British Columbia. On the Columbia Icefield, participants walk on ice before taking a dip in Lake Louise. Opportunities for fishing, horseback riding and hiking are ample throughout most of the trips. In addition to the wilderness areas visited, histor-

ic areas are also explored, such as the deserted town of Tulameen near Osoyoos Lake, a once-famous gold mining area. Another old mining town, Barkerville, provides the opportunity for visitors to try gold panning themselves. The 21-day trip covers 2,700 miles and also includes a visit at Dawson Creek, the starting point of the Alaska Highway. **Cost:** $245 to $735 includes camping gear, transportation, food, gold pans. **When:** By arrangement from June to September. **Contact:** Black Tusk Touring and Guide Service Ltd., 3064 St. Kildas Ave., North Vancouver, BC Canada V7L 2A9; phone (604)985-9223. *(M)*

Maritimes Overland: Specially modified minibuses travel east from Toronto to the Canadian Maritimes on a 19-day trip. The route follows the Atlantic coast from Bangor, Maine to Cape Breton Island and Halifax, where interested participants may go deep-sea fishing. From here the buses travel north to Gaspe, where a cruise around Bonaventure Island Bird Sanctuary is scheduled, and then south through Quebec City and Montreal on the way to Toronto. Travelers may note the contrast between French and English cultures as they mingle with fishermen and lumberjacks. One of the geographical peculiarities of the area is the tidal bore at Moncton. Participants occasionally camp overnight along the route. **Cost:** $500 includes food, camping accommodations. **When:** June, July. **Contact:** Goway Travel Ltd., 53 Yonge St., Second Floor, Toronto, ON Canada M5E 1J3; phone (416)863-0799; or Adventure Center, 5540 College Ave., Oakland, CA 94618, USA; phone (415)654-1879. *(M)*

CENTRAL AMERICA

Overland South of the Border: A variety of individualized overlanding trips is available to the Panama Canal Zone, Belize and Guatemala. Generally a 2-month, full-circle trip is planned from Brownsville or Laredo, Texas through all Central America via Yucatan. After reaching the Panama Canal Zone, return is via Oaxaca and Veracruz to the U.S. border. A 1-month roundtrip journey from Guatemala to the Panama Canal Zone, and a 2-week one-way trip from Guatemala to the Panama Canal Zone are also available. Travelers interested in experiencing the rest of the southern hemisphere may take a 1-month roundtrip journey from Guatemala through El Salvador, Honduras, Belize and Yucatan. All trips use 4-wheel drive vehicles and provide participants with a great degree of freedom in determining the itinerary. **Cost:** $18 to $20 a day plus $10 a day for shared expenses. **When:** By arrangement. **Contact:** AMTREK-

Overlanders gaze out over a river valley in Guatemala. AMTREK Overland Expeditions runs 2-month, full-circle journeys that travel through Central America from Texas to the Panama Canal Zone, using 4-wheel drive minibuses. (Keith Gunnar)

Overland Expeditions, P.O. Box 206, Santa Clara, CA 95052, USA.

(M)

EUROPE

Overlanding in Search of Prehistoric Art: A 19-day journey weaves a path leading to many of Europe's outstanding examples of prehistoric art. Participants visit 14,000-year-old caves in southern France and Spain, including the caves at Altamira, known for the quality of their paleolithic murals. In addition, group members visit the famous structure of Stonehenge in England. Participants are housed in country inns, castles and chateaux throughout the journey. **Cost:** $2,708 includes all land costs; airfare extra. **When:** October. **Contact:** Adventure Tours and Travel Unlimited, Suite 414, Airport Plaza Bldg., 19415 Pacific Hwy. S., Seattle, WA 98188, USA; phone (206)824-2192. *(M)*

Southeast European Overland: Three variations are offered of a trip to Greece and Turkey by minibus. On the first days of the basic 2-week trip, the group travels by motorcoach through France, Belgium, Germany and Austria. Once through Yugoslavia and into Greece, the pace slows down, and trip members may visit archaeological sites, relax on beaches and enjoy tavernas and local activities on the island of Thasos. A 3-week trip option includes a stay on Thasos and a visit to Athens, stopping on the way to see Thessaloniki and Mt. Olympus. A third trip returns to England via a different route through Italy, southern France and

Switzerland, with stopovers in Venice, Chamonix and Paris. On all trips, an extra visit to Istanbul for 2 nights is available. **Cost:** $146 to $246 includes transportation, camping equipment; $20 for Istanbul trip; $18 for optional food kitty. **When:** May to August. **Contact:** Centaur Overland Travel Ltd., 146 Halfway St., Sidcup, Kent DA15 8DF, Great Britain; phone 01-302-5959. *(M)*

Overland Camping from London to Istanbul: Traveling by Bedford truck, overlanders spend 9 weeks camping through Europe. Departing from London, participants motor through central Europe and down the Mediterranean coast through Greece to Istanbul. Three days are spent exploring Corfu, a tiny island off the Greek mainland coast where trip members may take a yacht cruise or swim in the Ionian Sea. Participants then cross the Bosporus to spend 4 days in Istanbul before the return leg of the trip, which goes through the Yugoslavian Alps, Vienna and Cologne. Wherever possible, campers eat at local restaurants or prepare their own meals. A food kitty arrangement pays for some restaurant as well as campfire meals. Rural settings, such as the grounds of a French chateau or the olive groves in Sorrento typify the campgrounds used on the trip. **Cost:** $1,006 includes transportation from London, camping equipment, food kitty. **When:** April to September. **Contact:** Continental Coach Tours Ltd., 139 Earls Court Rd., London SW5 9RH, Great Britain; phone 01-370-1305 or 01-370-1044.

Trans-European Travel: In a group of 25 to 37 people, adventurers travel through 16 countries during a 9-week grand tour. Participants travel in coaches equipped with a P.A. system for informational commentary from the guide. The responsibilities of shopping and preparing meals are shared by all. From London, the group proceeds to Paris, Limoges, Barcelona, Antibes, Venice, Florence, Rome and Capri. Each stop includes visits to museums, markets, historical landmarks and cathedrals, as well as opportunities to experience the local nightlife. From Capri, adventurers take a ferry across the Adriatic Sea to the archaeological sites and secluded beaches of Corfu. Participants spend 2 weeks in Greece, including a week-long cruise off the coast of the Greek islands. Returning to the mainland at Istanbul, the group begins the return journey to London, using a different route that includes Turkey, Bulgaria, Yugoslavia and Hungary. Participants then travel through Vienna and Salzburg to Lucerne, then on to Munich, Heidelberg, Cologne, Amsterdam and Brugge. The August and September trips proceed in the opposite direction. **Cost:** $804 to $840 depending on departure date includes transportation from London, guide, camping fees; $156 for food kitty. **When:** April to November. **Contact:** Tracks, 165 Kensington High St., London W8 6SH, Great Britain; phone 01-937-5964. *(M)*

Overland through Europe: Nine weeks of travel by bus enables participants to see much of Europe. The trip begins in London and sweeps through 15 countries before ending back in London. Local guides assist in the sightseeing at all major cities. Travelers also visit Lourdes Grotto, the medieval city of Carcassonne, the ruins of Pompeii and the prehistoric caverns of Postojna, as well as take a cruise down the Bosporus and a ferry trip from Poros to Athens. Among the highlights of the journey are 5 days spent on Greek islands and 10 days on beaches of the Mediterranean, Adriatic and Aegean seas. Throughout the trip time is allotted for individual exploration. Overlanders camp out en route, sharing cooking and cleaning chores. **Cost:** $799 to $854 includes transportation, camping accommodations, equipment, guide; $158 for food kitty. **When:** March to September. **Contact:** Transit Travel Ltd., 43 Kensington High St., London W8 5ED, Great Britain; phone 01-937-6662; or USSTS, 801 Second Ave., New York, NY 10017, USA; phone (212)867-8770.

Denmark

Scandinavian Encounter: A month-long program for high-school students departs from Copenhagen, Denmark and offers insight into the people, land and history of Denmark and Norway. Family stays, farm visits, folk schools, beaches and museums are foremost on the itinerary. While in Denmark students often travel on rented bicycles. On the Norway segment of the program, group members hike in the mountains, cross glaciers and view fjords. Villagers, schoolteachers and fishing families host students along the route. In Oslo students explore the

Kon Tiki, the Munch Museum and Vigeland Park with its hundreds of statues depicting human history. The trip ends in Bergen, Norway. **Cost:** $1,375 includes transportation from Copenhagen, meals, accommodations. **When:** July. **Contact:** Crossroads International, Hillsboro, NH 03244, USA; phone (603)478-5251. *(M)*

England

British Cultural Trip: A 45-day camping trip by minibus begins in London with visits to plays, museums, parks and pubs along the Thames. The group of about 12 high-school students then visits with a local family for a week in a small coal mining town in Wales. Hikes and pony treks are scheduled in the area. Next, 4 days are spent learning to steer narrow boats and work the locks on the Midland canals. Hikes are scheduled in the Lake District, Scottish Highlands and the remote Isle of Skye. Cornwall Beach provides more hikes and discoveries of ancient castles. Edinburgh is the final stop on the itinerary, where group members attend celebrations of drama, music and art. **Cost:** $1,175 includes transportation, camping accommodations, meals. **When:** July, August.

"Those weary of London are weary of the world." The towering figure of Big Ben looks out over Parliament and the rest of this cosmopolitan city. Theaters, museums, parks and pubs make London a must on any overland trip to Great Britain. (Pan Am World Airways)

Contact: Crossroads International, Hillsboro, NH 03244, USA; phone (603)478-5251. *(M)*

Country Walks: Striking a balance between sightseeing and hiking is the basic aim of a 23-day trip to unusual places in rural England. Led by a British author, mountaineer and explorer, participants visit prehistoric stones on Dartmoor, centuries-old Cotswold Hill villages, mountains and castles in Wales, the walled medieval city of York, and Hadrian's Wall. Traveling by microbuses, participants journey from Cornwall to Scotland. A maximum of 10 participants is allowed, and inns or guesthouses provide lodging. **Cost:** $1,470 for lodging, meals, guides, local transportation. **When:** April, September. **Contact:** Mountain Travel Inc., 1398 Solano Ave., Albany, CA 94706, USA; phone (415)527-8100. *(M)*

France

Mediterranean Island Camping: After flying from London adventurers land in Ajaccio for 2 weeks of camping on Sardinia and Corsica. Participants travel south with a guide to Bonifacio where a ferry transports them across the straits to Sardinia. Traveling overland participants reach the towers and ramparts of medieval Alghero, then cross the rocky interior of Monti de Gennargentu to swim and dive at Lotzorai beach. Campers complete the last section of the triangular route by passing through mountains and ending in Palau and riding a ferry to Corsica. Before ascending to Restonica Gorges and River participants stay at the beach town of Porto-Vecchio. Participants climb to the mountain villages surrounded by holm oak, juniper, giant ferns, rosemary and lavender. From the citadel at Calvi, participants journey through the Porto Valley to the Gulf of Ajaccio and Napoleon's house. Once in Ajaccio again, participants board the plane for the return flight to London. **Cost:** $389 to $429 depending on time of year includes transportation, guide, camping equipment; $73 food kitty. **When:** June to September. **Contact:** Penn Overland Tours Ltd., 122 Knightsbridge, London SW1, Great Britain; phone 01-589-0016; or 330 Sutter St., San Francisco, CA 94108, USA; phone (415)391-5728. *(M)*

Greece

Overlanding in Historic Terrain: Participants on a 15-day journey to the countryside and mountains of Crete travel by boat, minibus and foot to view the sites of the historic island's legends. Flying from Paris, participants arrive in Iraklion, a city on the northern side of the island. Once on the island, trip members walk for about 4 hours a day, accompanied by pack mules carrying the camping gear. Participants view the towering peaks at Knossos before heading by minibus to Rethymnon, a village which reflects Turkish architecture and taste. Overlanders visit Chania on foot to see the ancient capital of Crete. The last 7 days of the trip are negotiated by foot on rocky roads. The majority of the time is spent along the Mediterranean side of the island, with campsites made in remote locations. The conclusion of the trip comes with a climb to the plateau at Lassithi in the mountains of Dikti.

Cost: $900 includes transportation from Paris, accommodations, meals. **When:** March to September. **Contact:** Explorator, 16, place de la Madeleine, 75008, Paris, France; phone 266-66-24.

Overlanding to Asia Minor: Travelers board an overland coach in London for a 28-day roundtrip journey to Greece and Turkey. The route to Istanbul passes through Cologne, Munich, Vienna, Budapest, Belgrade and Sofia. While spending 3 days in Istanbul, overlanders visit the Blue Mosque, Topkapi and the 90-block Grand Bazaar. Those who wish may take day trips to the Black Sea or down to the Sea of Marmara. Traveling via Tekirdag through the border town of Ferral, travelers head on to the fishing town of Kavalla in Greece. After a day or so in Kavalla, the trip continues to Platamon. The more adventurous can climb Mt. Olympus before traveling via Delphi to Athens. For 3 days participants choose from a number of options including excursions to other Greek islands or a stay in Athens to explore sites of classical history and architecture, and experience contemporary culture in tavernas. The return route begins with a ferry ride to Corfu where travelers can spend the day on a catamaran or hire a scooter to investigate the island beaches. From Corfu, the expedition boards a ship for Bari, then drives along the Rimini coast to Venice. Over the Brenner Pass the group reaches the heart of the Austrian Tyrol at Innsbruck before passing through Cologne again en route to London. Along the way participants camp in tents and take

turns preparing meals. **Cost:** $418 from London includes transportation, camping fees and equipment, guides; $66 food kitty. **When:** May to August. **Contact:** NAT Eurotours Ltd., 38 Poland St., London W1, Great Britain; phone 01-734-1087; or Trek Adventures, 3 E. 54th St., New York, NY 10022, USA; phone (212)751-3250.   *(M)*

Mediterranean Island Adventure: Overlanders travel from England across Western Europe by minibus to start a 22-day camping trip to Greece and Crete. Trip members reach Greece on the sixth day, spending 2 days visiting Athens and nearby Aegean islands. The trip's highlight is a 7-day stay on the island of Crete. Based here on a sandy beach at Hersonissos, participants camp within easy reach of the island's largest town of Iraklion and the fishing village of Ayios Nicholaos. An excursion is made over twisting mountain roads to the Lassithi Plateau, which provides a view of the island's thousands of windmills. Participants return to Athens before setting off westward on the return trip across Europe. Highlighting the return trip are stops at Venice and Innsbruck in the Austrian Alps. **Cost:** $326 includes land transportation from London, guide. **When:** July to October. **Contact:** Tentrek Expeditions, Ltd., Tentrek House, Sta. Approach, Chislehurst, Kent BR7 5NW, Great Britain; phone 01-467-3473.

Ireland

Emerald Island Trip: Lakeland scenery, ancient churches, provincial villages and hillside castles are

Ruins of a temple at Sounlon, near Athens, are an example of the archaeological wonders seen by travelers on a 28-day overlanding expedition to Asia Minor by NAT Eurotours. (Carol Baker)

seen on an 8-day motorcoach trip through Ireland. Travelers visit Wexford, Cork and Killarney counties. Opportunities are available for pony trekking, bicycling or shopping. Lunch is given on the Atlantic coast at the Cliffs of Moher, and Galway is the location for a medieval banquet. The group proceeds to Dublin, home of the Abbey Theater, colorful local pubs and many historic landmarks and buildings. Blarney Castle and the Blarney Stone are visited, and participants journey around the Ring of Kerry woodlands. **Cost:** $124 plus $18 food kitty includes transportation

from London, meals, accommodations. **When:** June to September. **Contact:** Contiki Travel Ltd., 7 Rathborne Pl., London W1P 1DE, Great Britain; phone 01-637-2121; or Adventure Center, 5540 College Ave., Oakland, CA 94618, USA; phone (415)654-1879. *(M)*

Netherlands

Individualized Camping Trips: Seven-day camping trips starting out in Amsterdam are offered to those who wish to explore the cultural and historical features of Holland. The emphasis is on flexibility. A Volkswagen camper with unlimited mileage is supplied, as well as tents, sleeping bags, pots and pans, ice buckets, cutlery, tables and chairs. A transfer from the Amsterdam airport is provided to the campgrounds 10 miles away, where participants can pick up their camper and set off on an independent journey. **Cost:** $231 a week. **When:** Year-round. **Contact:** Continental Campers, Inc., 1194 Walnut St., P.O. Box 306, Newton, MA 02161, USA; phone (617)964-5090.

Norway
Overland through Lapland: A 4-week trip travels through Scandinavia by minibus, with participants camping out along the way. Travelers ferry from England to Amsterdam and proceed to Copenhagen, Oslo and Trondheim. From here they drive up the Arctic Highway through the land of the nomadic Lapps and camp out under the midnight sun. Visits are made to Lyngen Glacier and the North Cape, a black granite cliff rising from the Arctic Ocean. The trip crosses into Finnish Lapland and continues down the coast of Sweden. Stops are made at Copenhagen and Amsterdam before the return ferry ride to England. **Cost:** $286 to $305 from London includes land transportation. **When:** June to August. **Contact:** Tentrek Expeditions, Ltd., Tentrek House, Sta. Approach, Chislehurst, Kent BR7 5NW, Great Britain; phone 01-467-3473.

Scotland
Caledonia Overland: In 4 days travelers explore the Scottish capital city of Edinburgh and the Lake District. An English breakfast begins the first day on which participants are guided through the Edinburgh Castle and the streets of Edinburgh, lying on the Firth of Forth in the county of Lothian. After a 1-day trip to the scenic Trossachs, visitors travel south into the Lake District, where there are opportunities to photograph the lovely Scottish hillsides and beautiful lake scenery. At the end of the fourth day, participants are transported back to London. **Cost:** $59 from Edinburgh. **When:** May, July, August, September, October, December. **Contact:** Tracks, 165 Kensington High St., London W8 6SH, Great Britain; phone 01-937-5964.
(M)

Spain
Iberian Camping: A glimpse into the people and lifestyles of Spain and northern Africa is captured on a 3-week trip by motorcoach. After passing quickly from London through France the group visits swordmakers and steelworkers in Toledo before heading on to Seville. A day in the capital of Andalucia is followed by a short ferry crossing to the Spanish port of Ceuta. The Tanger border is only a short distance away and participants soon head toward the Sahara via Casablanca and Marrakech. While camping near the river bed, there is time for exploration of Todra Gorge, which changes color with the time of day. During the next few days, participants ride camels in the desert to the oasis of Meski. Trip members stop in the markets of Fez and at Ceuta once more and then cross the Strait of Gibraltar to spend a day on the

beaches of Fuengirola. The route back to London is highlighted by the scenery through the Sierra Nevada, the Moorish stronghold of Alhambra and flamenco dancing in Barcelona. **Cost:** $450 includes camping equipment, meals, guides. **When:** May, June, October, November. **Contact:** Tracks, 165 Kensington High St., London W8 6SH, Great Britain; phone 01-937-3028. *(M)*

Yugoslavia

Slavic Sojourn: Participants spend 15 days in Yugoslavia or 27 days touring the greater Balkan area. Beginning in Croatia's city of Zagreb, travelers on the Yugoslavia trip journey by motor to Plitvice Lakes, Postojna Caves in Slovenia and Opatija in Istria. After 6 days on the Dalmatian Coast visiting such cities as Zadar, Split and Dubrovnik, participants continue to the Montenegran regions of Kotor Bay, Budva and Sveti Stefan Island. Travelers proceed to Bosnia and finally to Belgrade in Serbia. Those who elect to travel throughout the Balkan region spend 27 days viewing the sights and sounds of Yugoslavia, Bulgaria, Romania and Hungary. The trip starts in Zagreb and includes country towns, coastal resorts and the capital cities of the 4 countries. Accommodations are in hotels. **Cost:** $960 for 15 days, $1,745 for 27 days includes transportation from Zagreb. **When:** By arrangement. **Contact:** Maupintour, P.O. Box 807, Lawrence, KS 66044, USA; phone (913)843-1211.

Basking in the Balkans: Participants explore the capital cities of Belgrade, Sofia, Istanbul and Athens as well as wilderness areas and beaches on a camping journey of 3 weeks through Yugoslavia, Bulgaria, Turkey and Greece. Group members rendezvous in London for a flight to Belgrade where a specially equipped minibus takes them to Sofia. Visits are planned to Rila Monastery and Edirne's Great Mosque before 2 days in Istanbul seeing the Sultan's palace and the Grand Bazaar. On the Grecian coast at Kavalla Bay there are opportuni-

Camping in a Balkan meadow is part of a 27-day overland offered by Penn Overland Tours. A minibus takes travelers to Greece, Yugoslavia, Bulgaria and Turkey. (Polish National Tourist Office)

ties to swim, sunbathe and watch the fishing boats in addition to spending time in local tavernas. Travelers find refuge in Daphni and the sanctuary of the Eleusinian mysteries before a busy 2 days in Athens visiting the Acropolis, Parthenon and various museums. A boat crossing of Corinth Straits precedes the group's visit to Mt. Parnassus and Delphi, the site of Apollo's sacred oracle. Participants see cliff-hanging monasteries at Meteora, then head north through Macedonia and Skopje to Belgrade where the return flight to London concludes the trip. **Cost:** $579 from London includes transportation, guide, camping equipment; $100 kitty covers most meals, camping fees. **When:** June to August. **Contact:** Penn Overland Tours Ltd., 122 Knightsbridge, London SW 1, Great Britain; phone 01-589-0016; or 330 Sutter St., San Francisco, CA 94108, USA; phone (415)391-5728.
(M)

MEXICO

Mayan Overland: Participants help plan the itinerary of a 23-day journey via minibus through Guatemala and Mexico. Overlanders rendezvous with an experienced guide in Mexico City and camp or stay in inexpensive hotels during the trip, buying food and sharing meals as a group when possible. After visiting the pyramids at Teotihuacan, the group drives to the city of Taxco, known for its silver. Participants go to a local market in Oaxaca and also visit Monte Alban, an ancient complex of pyramids, palaces and observatories. Entering Guatemala, the expedition spends several days

at Lake Atitlan, surrounded by volcanoes, and travels to the Indian town of Chichicastenango. En route to Guatemala City overlanders walk to the edge of Agua Volcano and visit the ancient capital of Antigua. Once in Mexico again, the group visits the Mayan ruins at Palenque, then travels eastward to camp on deserted Caribbean beaches. The journey concludes with stops at Chichen Itza, a Toltec city, the Mayan ruins at Uxmal, and Merida, the largest city in the Yucatan. **Cost:** $310 from Mexico City includes ground transportation, guide, camping equipment; $10 a day covers food, fees. **When:** November to April. **Contact:** Trekamerica, Inc., 62 Kenway Rd., Earls Court, London SW5 0RD, Great Britain; phone 01-370-4013; or Adventure Center, 5540 College Ave., Oakland, CA 94618, USA; phone (415)654-1879.
(M)

Baja California

Overlanding Baja's Back Roads: One-way trips of 10 or 14 days in the Baja peninsula depart from Phoenix, Arizona or La Paz, Mexico. Participants proceed at a leisurely pace in 4-wheel drive vehicles, sticking to side roads and deciding the itinerary along the way. Whether on the coast or in desert backcountry, overlanders travel whenever possible on roads that avoid the new trans-peninsular highway. Sometimes the group camps under the stars on a Pacific Ocean beach or next to the Sea of Cortez, and sometimes in the interior among the cardon cacti or the boojum trees. At certain times of the year, gray whales can be seen with their new calves surfacing close to shore. Participants on the one 14-day trip reverse directions and slowly wind back to Phoenix, with a visit to Cuevas Pintadas, the painted caves of Baja, included on the itinerary. All other trips end in La Paz. **Cost:** $385 to $500 includes meals, camping equipment, ground transportation, accommodations, guide. **When:** January to April. **Contact:** Canyoneers, Inc., P.O. Box 2997, Flagstaff, AZ 86003, USA; phone (602)526-0924. *(M)*

Exploring the Peninsula: From San Diego, 4-wheel drive vans start out to explore the natural and historical features of Baja for 12 days. On the Pacific side are the breeding grounds of the California gray whale, where travelers can witness hundreds of these beautiful mammals in their natural habitat. Concepcion Bay near Mulege on the Sea of Cortez makes an interesting stop for rock hounds and shell collectors. Several side-hikes are made to an array of historical points of interest, including hot springs, old mines, and the ruins of Russian and English settlements. At the time of the trip, upper meadows are covered with wildflowers and elephant trees. An isolated area of Indian pictographs drawn on rock walls is included in the trip. Trip members camp out under the stars. **Cost:** $575 includes meals. **When:** November to January. **Contact:** Wilderness World, 1342 Jewell Ave., Pacific Grove, CA 93950, USA; phone (408)373-5882. *(M)*

Yucatan

Mayan Cultural Overland Trip: A trip of 15 days in the Yucatan of southeast Mexico features visits to Mayan ruins. After flying from San Francisco to Merida, participants spend a day there sightseeing and visiting the nearby ruins at Dzibilchaltun. En route to Palenque where several days are spent, stops are made at Uxmal and Kabah for viewing more ruins, including the pyramid at Edzna. Participants travel next to the Caribbean coast via Xpujil, Becan and Kohunlich. Then during 2 days in Akumal they visit the 600-foot-deep well of Cenote Azul. A 2-day stay at undeveloped Isla Mujeres is followed by a stop at Valladolid. One of the last ruins visited is the famous site of Chichen Itza. **Cost:** $698 includes transportation, food, accommodations, guide. **When:** February to December. **Contact:** Forum Travel International, 2437 Durant, No. 208, Berkeley, CA 94704, USA; phone (415)843-8294. *(M)*

MIDDLE EAST
Overland in the Cradle of Civilization: Members of a 3-week expedition travel by small coach through Jordan, Iraq and Syria, visiting sites of historical and archaeological interest. Leaving from Amman, the expedition passes through the ancient city of Petra, discovered in 1812, on the way to Aqaba and Wadi Rum. After returning to Amman, the expedition crosses into Iraq, traveling over the black basalt desert to Baghdad; from Baghdad a visit is made to Babylon. On the way to the Syrian city of Aleppo, participants stay overnight at Al Rosafa, an Arab/Byzantine city in the Euphrates Valley. From Aleppo to Amman the route includes Palmyra, Damascus and Jer-

ash. Expedition members share the work of making camp along the route. **Cost:** $500 from Amman includes transportation, food, equipment; $230 extra for roundtrip airfare from London. **When:** April through September. **Contact:** Treasure Treks Ltd., Third Floor, Panton House, 25 Haymarket, London SW1Y 4EN, Great Britain; phone 01-839-4267; or Adventure Center, 5540 College Ave., Oakland, CA 94618, USA; phone (415)654-1879; or Trek Adventures, 3 E. 54th St., New York, NY 10022, USA; phone (212)751-3250.   **(M)**

Iran

Persian Exploration: A trip of 3 weeks to the wilderness areas of Iran includes a 3-day walk in the Alamut Valley and explorations of the plains and gorges around Firuzabad, the traditional camping grounds of the Qashqa'i nomads. A camp near Karaj is the base for a series of walking expeditions to the ruined Assassin Castles of Alamut and Lammassar. Participants explore the Sassanian remains at Bishahpur before penetrating the rugged winter homeland of the Qashqa'i tribe, one of the last great migratory tribes of Central Asia. Stops at Persepolis and Esfahan are made en route back to Tehran. **Cost:** $1,558 includes roundtrip airfare from London, all land arrangements. **When:** May, June, August, September. **Contact:** Explore Beyond Ltd., 1 Ludgate Circus Bldgs., London EC4M 7LQ, Great Britain;

Qashqa'i nomads may be seen on a 3-week Explore Beyond expedition to Iran which includes a drive through the plains and gorges around Firuzabad, the traditional camping grounds of the Qashqa'i. (Explore Beyond Ltd.)

phone 01-248-9082 or 01-236-4395; or Adventure Center, 5540 College Ave., Oakland, CA 94618, USA; phone (415)654-1879.   *(M)*

Israel

Camelback Desert Exploration: An ascent of 7,540-foot Mt. Sinai is featured in 2- and 3-day tours of the Sinai Peninsula. Side trips take participants to Bedouin villages and the Monastery of St. Katharina, and the tours may be extended to include a climb of Mt. Katharina (8,072 feet) and visits to local points of interest. Transportation is partly by camel, with Bedouin guides available to lead individual explorations. Accommodations are provided in the Tzoukal David Field Study Center, located north of Sharm-el-Sheikh. **Cost:** $138 to $164 includes roundtrip airfare from Tel Aviv, accommodations. **When:** Year-round. **Contact:** Arkia Israel Inland Airlines Ltd., 100 E. 59th St., New York, NY 10022, USA; phone (212)421-5547.

Arab-Israeli Cultural Trip: Students share a 6-week cultural experience based primarily at Alonie-Aba, a community of 50 families. Participants may choose to work among the residents, helping to restore a house or sharing in such farm work as caring for animals or picking crops. Students can compare different lifestyles by also living in a kibbutz, a moshav and a Bedouin settlement. Students travel to visit Nazareth, a city populated by Arabs, Christians and recent immigrants, and to Beth Shemeth and Karliel. A week in Jerusalem provides a look into the area's ancient religious and historical traditions. In addition, students hike, camp and swim at Mediterranean beaches and participate in field schools in the desert. Guides offer instruction in wildlife identification, ecology and conversational Hebrew. **Cost:** $1,175 includes accommodations, food. **When:** July, August. **Contact:** Crossroads International, Hillsboro, NH 03244, USA; phone (603)478-5251.   *(M)*

Jordan

West Jordan Overland: The rock-hewn cliffs of Petra serve as the setting for a 2-week trip that includes visits to Jerash, Mt. Nebo, Herod's castle at Macheronte and the spectacular landscape around Karak. Participants may swim in the Red Sea, take a camel trek in Wadi Rum and explore Lawrence of Arabia's wartime headquarters in the wilds of Azraq. The Cairo Museum, Tutankhamun's treasure, the pyramids and the Sphinx are visited before an overnight train is taken to Luxor where participants may see the city from horsedrawn carriages. A donkey trek to the Valley of the Kings precedes the final 7 days of sailing to Aswan and the temples of Edfu and Kom Ombo. **Cost:** $490 to $530 includes roundtrip airfare from London, all land costs. **When:** May to August. **Contact:** Explore Beyond Ltd., 1 Ludgate Circus Bldgs., London EC4M 7LQ, Great Britain; phone 01-248-9082 or 01-236-4395; or Adventure Center, 5540 College Ave., Oakland, CA 94618, USA; phone (415)654-1879.   *(M)*

Turkey

Ottoman Empire Overland: Travelers gather in Geneva and fly to

Overlanders pause for a view of the traditional Turkish transit system. Land Rover expeditions to Turkey are organized by Jerrycan Expedition and last 3 weeks. (Explorado)

Istanbul to begin an overland adventure of 3 weeks. Traveling by Land Rover or minibus, overlanders take little-known routes through villages and deserted countryside to the suburbs of Ankara. After the high plateaus of central Anatolia and the Cappadocians, the route continues to Goreme and Nevsehir. In the Taurus Mountains participants meet gypsies and nomadic shepherds. A variety of animals can be seen here including wolves, bears and wild sheep. After driving through some rugged terrain, adventurers reach the coast and the national park of Olympus to visit Greco-Roman historical sites. Participants have plenty of time to explore deserted beaches and for 2 days venture by boat to investigate some small islands. En route to Istanbul, adventurers stop in Antalya, Aydin, Izmir and Bursa before the return flight to Geneva. The group camps in tents throughout the journey. **Cost:** $400 includes airfare, transportation, guide, camping equipment. **When:** May to September. **Contact:** Jerrycan Expedition, Ave. Legrand 86, 1050 Brussels, Belgium; phone (02)648-22-69. *(M)*

Mediterranean Overlanding: Groups of up to 12 people travel by minibus from London to spend 20 days camping in Turkey. Camping sites are well off the highway and campers use a minimum amount of equipment. Turkey has a history going back 7,000 years, and trip members investigate a multitude of cultural and historical curiosities. Of geologic interest is central Anatolia, a dusty gray and brown desert of volcanic origin, known in ancient times as Cappadocia. During the seventh century, the Christian inhabitants hollowed out underground churches here, decorated with crosses and illustrations of biblical scenes which can still be seen. Along the Mediterranean Sea trip members may take advantage of opportunities to swim and enjoy the sun, and individuals may leave the group to pursue their own activities. **Cost:** $325 includes transportation from London, equipment. **When:** July. **Contact:** Topkapi Safari, 99 Elmshurst Crescent, London, N2 0LW Great Britain; phone 01-883-0915.

Yemen

Arabia Felix: With the Red Sea and Africa to the west and the Arabian desert to the east, trekkers begin a 17-day journey through Yemen. Following a flight from New York to the capital city of San'a, with its old mosques and modern skyscrapers, trekkers set out for Mareb, an irrigation center known for its pre-Islamic Marel Dam. The next stop is the Tihama Plain, a coastal lowland, from which the Sabeans of old controlled much of the east-west spice trade. The group then returns to San'a to prepare for the rugged journey to the mountain town of Chahare, once a part of the kingdom of Sheba. On day 15, following the return to San'a, participants relax for 2 days, then fly back to New York via Cairo. **Cost:** $1,580 from San'a. **When:** March, October, December, February. **Contact:** Explorer Tours, Suite 307, 640 Cathcart St., Montreal, Canada H3B 1M3; phone (514)861-6763.

PACIFIC

Island Hopping in the South Pacific: A flexible 23-day trip takes travelers to American Samoa, Western Samoa, Fiji and Tahiti by air and local buses. Three different accommodation plans are offered for differing budgets. The trip begins with a flight from Los Angeles to Pago Pago for a night, and then continues at Lalomalava on the relatively unwesternized island of Savaii. Three nights' accommodation in the midst of a functioning, traditional Samoan village provide time for exploration and sightseeing plus side trips to plantations and the massive, truncated pyramid of Pulemelei. Next is a flight to Lefaga for 2 nights, with opportunities for fishing, snorkeling and outrigger exploring. The next 2 nights are spent at Apia, one of Samoa's more cosmopolitan towns, before a flight to Suva, Fiji, for a stay of 6 nights. Besides sightseeing and exploring the town, participants take a trip to Orchid Island with its rare Fijian parrots, sea turtles and mongooses. Then 3 nights of sightseeing in Nadi precede a flight to Papeete, Tahiti, the final stop on the trip; most of the 5 days here are spent exploring the area at leisure. The return to Los Angeles is by air. **Cost:** $1,099 to $1,404, depending on type of accommodations and date, includes transportation from Los Angeles,

A bus is often used to cover the great distances along the Andes in Chile. Treasure Treks uses a motorcoach to travel up the spine of the Andes on a 74-day overlanding journey from Rio de Janeiro, Brazil to Bogota, Colombia. (Treasure Treks)

food, accommodations, excursions, guide. **When:** May to December. **Contact:** Goodtravel Tours, 5332 College Ave., Oakland, CA 94618, USA; phone (415)658-2060.

SOUTH AMERICA

Pan-American Overland: A 6-month trip covers 28,000 miles from New York to Rio de Janeiro by way of Alaska. Overlanders travel in two 4-wheel drive vehicles, each with 3 or 4 passengers and a guide. The trip begins by crossing the United States and Canada to reach Fairbanks, where participants take a boat trip south through Alaska's Inside Passage. Highlighting the trip's South American section is a week-long sailing trip in the Galapagos Islands off Ecuador. The itinerary is very flexible, and river rafting, canoeing and mountaineering may all be undertaken. The expedition usually camps, but hotels are also used about once a week. The guides speak Spanish and Portuguese and are familiar with archaeology, anthropology and various outdoor activities. **Cost:** $5,600 covers all costs, including airfare from Rio de Janeiro to New York. **When:** October. **Contact:** Americas Expedition, 40 Sturgis Rd., Bronxville, NY 10708, USA.

Spanish-American Sojourn: An 82-day voyage through Brazil and up the spine of the Andes begins at Rio de Janeiro and travels to Sao Paulo—two modern cities bordering the vast Brazilian hinterland. A passage across the great Iguazu Falls takes sojourners to the city of Buenos Aires. After passing through Mar del Plata, travelers move into the Argentine heartland, where they may explore the Andean foothills of San Martin. Bariloche, the next stop, is a ski resort known for its alpine vistas and Santiago is the Chilean stopover before the mountains of Bolivia. It is here that travelers reach La Paz, at 12,500 feet the highest capital in the world. Crossing the mountains again, participants arrive in Cuzco and visit native villages on Lake Titicaca. Several more days are spent in Peru before heading north to Quito. In Bogota participants may view the Spanish architecture or attend a bullfight, still a national sport. Conditions vary throughout the trip, facilities may be crude and the voyaging rough. **Cost:** $1,100 to $1,280 depending on departure date includes transportation, guides, excursions. **When:** May to October. **Contact:** Goway Travel Ltd., 53 Yonge St., Second Floor, Toronto, ON Canada M5E 1J3;

phone (416)863-0799; or Adventure Center, 5540 College Ave., Oakland, CA 94618, USA; phone (415)654-1879. *(M)*

On the Road to Rio: Overlanders may choose a full 74-day trip from Rio de Janeiro to Bogota or divide the trip up into two 36-day journeys which can be joined at Bogota, Santiago or Rio. Transported by specially built motorcoach over rugged terrain, participants may travel in either direction. In a group of about 22 people accompanied by an experienced expedition leader, travelers stay in campsites and budget hotels in 8 South American countries. The itinerary is quite full and participants do not stop in any one place for more than 2 days. Some of the highlights are Rio de Janeiro, Iguazu Falls and Gran Chaco, the cattle country of Paraguay. After traveling south through the pampa of Patagonia, members see seals, sea lions and penguin colonies at the reserves around Valdez Peninsula. Through rugged San Carlos de Bariloche, participants approach Chile and drive across the Atacama Desert, then ascend to the Peruvian Altiplano before reaching Bolivia and the highest capital in the world, La Paz. Traveling through the Andes, the group reaches Machupicchu and Cuzco. Arriving at the coast of Ecuador at Machala, the journey continues to Quito. Participants have the opportunity to observe the blending of Spanish and Indian cultures mixed with Inca traditions before concluding the trip in Bogota. **Cost:** $1,660 for 74 days, $790 to $910 for 36 days includes transportation, guide, camping and cooking equipment; $10 to $12 a day for food and accommodations. **When:** Year-round. **Contact:** Treasure Treks Ltd., Third Floor, Panton House, 25 Haymarket, London SW1Y 4EN, Great Britain; phone 01-839-4267; or Adventure Center, 5540 College Ave., Oakland, CA 94618, USA; phone (415)654-1879; or Trek Adventures, 3 E. 54th St., New York, NY 10022, USA; phone (212)751-3250.   *(M)*

Ecuador

Equatorial Overland: Participants begin a 7-day overland trip by exploring the art and architecture of Quito. From here the expedition drives past volcanoes and visits a highland Indian marketplace on the way to the upper Amazon. On a boat trip down the Apo River visits are made to Indian camps, pre-Columbian rock carvings and the Jumandi caves. Returning to the highlands participants board a train to travel down to the coast, crossing Urbina Pass near Chimborazo, Ecuador's highest volcano, and then descending into the tropical lowlands where the trip concludes. Travelers stay in hotels and eat in restaurants. **Cost:** $394 from Quito includes all costs; airfare extra. **When:** On request. **Contact:** Forum Travel International, 2437 Durant, No. 208, Berkeley, CA 94704, USA; phone (415)843-8294.   *(M)*

Peru

Minibus to Peru and Bolivia: The Andes Mountains are the location of a 1-month overland minibus trip. The group leaves Zurich by plane and arrives in Lima, Peru for the commencement of the camping trip. There is no rigid itinerary and participants share in planning the trip, as well as helping with chores along the way. Generally the trip includes stops at Machupicchu, Ayacucho, Huancayo and Cuzco. The emphasis of the trip rests in exploring and experiencing the South American terrain and cultures, and efforts are made to taste local foods and meet area residents. The trip is led by French-speaking guides. **Cost:** $706 includes round-trip airfare from Zurich, breakfasts, camping equipment. **When:** June to August. **Contact:** Jerrycan Expedition, Ave. Legrand 86, 1050 Brussels, Belgium; phone (02)648-22-69.   *(M)*

UNITED STATES

Southwest Indian Country Expedition: A 3-week safari takes small groups by van, foot, horseback and river raft to the remote areas of northern Arizona and New Mexico, an area spanning 2,000 years of living history and 300 million years of geologic history. Leaving from San Francisco, the group follows an informal schedule which allows participants to meet the people who inhabit the region. Guides explain the rituals and philosophy of the Navajo, the Hopi and the Rio Grande Pueblo Indians, who consider this region to be a vibrational center of the universe. Trip members learn about the Indians' methods of survival in the desert, using plants and shrubs for food, clothing, shelter and medicinal cures. The itinerary includes overnight hikes and pack trips into remote areas, exploration of prehistoric Indian settlements, river rafting on the San Juan River and visits to

An explorer is dwarfed by the size of a natural bridge. American Trails West crosses the canyonlands of southern Utah on a 6-week overland trip that includes travel by both land and water. (American Trails West)

present-day Pueblo dwellings. Although the trip normally returns to San Francisco, arrangements may be made for those who wish to join the group in Flagstaff and end the trip in Albuquerque. **Cost:** $785 includes airfare, meals, guides. **When:** September, October. **Contact:** American Safari, 386 60th St., Oakland, CA 94618, USA; phone (415)652-7825. **(M)**

Western Adventures: A 6-week trip for teenagers provides a series of outdoor adventures in the American West. Following a flight from New York to Denver, the group embarks on a 10-day river trip down the Colorado and Green rivers of Utah. Riding in sportyaks encourages participants to learn whitewater skills at their own pace. A 2-day mountain climb to the top

of Grand Teton in Wyoming is preceded by basic climbing skills training in which the fundamentals of mountaineering are explained. Colorado is the location for a 5-day horseback ride in the Rocky Mountains, during which riders explore abandoned gold mines and trails. Both first-time riders and experienced equestrians can enjoy this leg of the trip. Gold pans are needed for travel along the Million Dollar Highway in southern Colorado, where stops are made in side canyons between Telluride, Ophir, Silverton, Ouray and Purgatory. Travel between areas is by van, but there is plenty of backpacking during each segment of the trip, on terrain ranging from mountain trails and boulder-strewn plateaus to frozen lakes and glacial areas. **Cost:** $1,650. **When:** June. **Contact:**

American Trails West, 92 Middle Neck Rd., Great Neck, NY 11021, USA; phone (516)487-2802. *(M)*

Western National Parks Exploration: For 42 days participants travel by van on a 6,000-mile trip to investigate some of America's national parks. Group members hike in the Grand Canyon and in southern Utah's Bryce and Zion canyons. A river rafting trip is taken down the Snake River in Grand Teton National Park. The Continental Divide is crossed in Glacier National Park, and participants swim in the waterfalls of Yosemite. Yellowstone National Park is visited, along with its many geologic features. The trip ends in San Francisco. Members should be in good physical condition, though the hiking is usually moderate. **Cost:** $678 from San Francisco includes accommodations food, guides, insurance. **When:** July. **Contact:** American Youth Hostels, National Campus, Delaplane, VA 22025, USA.

Travel in U.S. Communities: After gathering in Denver, Colorado teenagers plan their itinerary for a 6½-week journey across the United States. Under the supervision of adult leaders, the participants spend 1 week hiking in the Grand Tetons, the only pre-arranged activity of the trip. Activities chosen in the past include working at dairy farms in Colorado and Montana, helping a Makah Indian couple collect sea urchins on the Olympic Peninsula, and organic gardening at the United Farm Workers headquarters. Recreational and educational experiences are combined, and all the specifics are completely up to the participants as they travel by van. The program ends in Boston. Some scholarship help is available. **Cost:** $1,325 includes food, accommodations, group equipment, leaders, transportation. **When:** June. **Contact:** Crossroads International, Hillsboro, NH 03244, USA; phone (603)478-5251. *(M)*

North and Central America Overland: A 76-day overland trip starts in Anchorage, Alaska and travels south through Canada and the United States to Panama City. The route passes through Mt. McKinley National Park in Alaska and through the Yukon Territory, Alberta, British Columbia, Ontario and Quebec. From Quebec the group heads south through New York City and Washington, DC to Miami, and then along the Gulf of Mexico into Mexico. An alternative route starts in Los Angeles and reaches Mexico City by way of Las Vegas and Mazatlan, saving 40 days travel. From Mexico City both trips lead south through Central America, passing through Guatemala, El Salvador, Honduras, Nicaragua, Costa Rica and Panama. The trip ends in the Canal Zone. Participants travel in minibuses and camp outdoors some of the time. **Cost:** $1,450 Anchorage to Panama, $850 Los Angeles to Panama; $12 a day estimated cost for food and accommodations. **When:** March, May for Anchorage to Panama; August through February for Los Angeles to Panama. **Contact:** Treasure Treks Ltd., Third Floor, Panton House, 25 Haymarket, London SW1Y 4EN, Great Britain; phone 01-839-4267; or Adventure Center, 5540 College Ave., Oakland, CA 94618, USA;

Trek through this page for the best adventures of the year.

Start here for your sampling of our spectacular camping tours and overland expeditions.

First, our European Camping Tours. Exciting journeys by motorcoach lasting from 21 to 62 days. Featuring well-planned itineraries, guided sightseeing tours and the exhilarating experience of camping out. Examples: **Arctic Circle**—an exploration of Scandinavia's most breathtaking lands. **Western Europe**—an eight-country sweep of the historical and cultural centers of Europe...and everything in between. **Greece and Turkey**—an unusual in-depth excursion into two of Europe's most fascinating countries.

Then there's our Transcontinental Expeditions. More rugged, more challenging. Overland travel by expedition truck or motorcoach—from a 15-day mini-trek to a 3½ month journey. Including: **Africa**—an enlightening adventure into the heart of the Dark Continent. **Scandinavia, Russia & Japan**—a trek of intrigue and challenge as you travel overland by Trans-Siberian Express, Motorcoach and Steamship. **Europe, Asia and Australia**—119 days, 16,000 miles and 3 continents... a vast and incredible journey.

And there are others. Departures from Fall, 1978 through Winter, 1979. For complete details, write or call for a free brochure.

TREK ADVENTURES

A CORTELL GROUP COMPANY

3 E. 54th St., New York, N.Y. 10022 • (212) 751-3250

phone (415)654-1879; or Trek Adventures, 3 E. 54th St., New York, NY 10022, USA; phone (212)751-3250. *(M)*

Exploring the Eastern Seaboard: A 3-week camping expedition travels by minibus to explore historic sites from Boston to New Orleans. Leaving from New York City, participants travel south to Washington DC where they see the Smithsonian Institution and Capitol Hill. The group proceeds into Virginia and North Carolina to visit Kitty Hawk, scene of the first powered flight, and the Cape Hatteras National Seashore. Savannah, a town known for its beautiful squares is seen during the stay in Georgia. Heading south to Florida, the group camps out on the beach near St. Augustine before a visit to Cape Canaveral. Participants spend 2 days in Disney World, then move on to New Orleans, visiting Bourbon Street, the French Quarter, Preservation Hall and the many jazz clubs. Trip members may catch Norman Blake or Tut Taylor, famous pickers and singers, playing on their front stoops in Nashville. The expedition then travels north to New England where participants explore the historic city of Boston. **Cost:** $359 to $373 depending on departure date includes roundtrip transportation from New York, meals, accommodations. **When:** May to October. **Contact:** Trekamerica, Inc., 62 Kenway Rd., Earls Court, London SW5 ORD, Great Britain; phone 01-370-4013; or Adventure Center, 5540 College Ave., Oakland, CA 94618, USA; phone (415)654-1879. *(M)*

Alaska

Inland to McKinley: An 8-week camping trip for travelers ages 14 to 19 sweeps across eastern, central and western Canada before arriving at the final destination of the journey—Alaska. While on the Canadian segment of the trip, visits are scheduled to Banff and Jasper national parks in addition to cities such as Edmonton, Whitehorse, Ft. Nelson, Dawson City, Prince Rupert, Vancouver and Victoria. Along the route, students view massive glaciers and other geological remnants from a thousand years ago. Historic sites that participants visit are the fur factories, musk ox farms, Klondike gold fields and igloos of the region. In the United States, the fossil-filled Dinosaur Park, portions of the Rocky Mountains, Mt. McKinley and Mt. Rainier are visited. Participants may join or leave any of the tours anytime. **Cost:** $1,555 includes transportation, meals. **When:** July, August. **Contact:** North American Tour-A-Camp, Rockland County YMCA, P.O. Box 581, Nyack, NY 10960, USA; phone (914)358-0919.

California

Death Valley Days: A group of 10 passengers or less travels by 4-wheel drive vehicle through the rugged canyon and desert region of Death Valley. The week-long trip featuring ghost towns, old mining camps and desert wildlife provides a chance to camp in desert backcountry. The itinerary varies with weather and trail conditions, but always includes a day on the floor of Death Valley, with views of Zabriskie Point, Golden Canyon

Hikers take to the high country of Colorado. The American West includes an enormous variety of landscape, and overlanders may travel on foot, by boat or in Land Rovers. (American Trails West)

and Sand Dunes. A custom-built trailer serves as chuckwagon for preparing meals. **Cost:** $365 includes food, transportation, camping equipment. **When:** October to May. **Contact:** Desert Expeditions, Inc., P.O. Box 1404, Palm Desert, CA 92260, USA; phone (714)346-6927. *(M)*

Camping and fishing equipment is available for rent, and all other necessities are provided. Rates for groups are also available. **Cost:** $30 to $129 includes meals. **When:** Year-round. **Contact:** The Mountain Men, 11100 E. Dartmouth, No. 219, Denver, CO 80232, USA; phone (303)750-0090. *(M)*

Colorado

Across the Great Divide: Participants embark on journeys of a half day or longer from Denver into the mountains of the Continental Divide. Traveling by 4-wheel drive vehicles driven by experienced guides, groups wander over old pioneer trails normally inaccessible to travelers. Activities along the way include fishing, hiking and visiting such western favorites as ghost towns and old mining camps.

Scenic Jeep Trips: Experienced guides explain the history and lore of the Vail Valley in Colorado on morning or afternoon jeep trips. The trips range in length from 2 to 4 hours and include visits to ghost towns, abandoned mines, and game viewing areas. One of the popular trips is the Moniger excursion, which takes participants along the edge of the Eagles Nest Wilderness for 2 hours to view the alpine meadows. Included on the trip are 2 homesteads of the Piney River and the scenic country of the White River National Forest. A 3-hour trip winds through high meadows of Red and White Mountains for views into the Gore Range. Game is usually seen on this trip. On a 45-mile circular trip, participants visit the Gilman Mine on the way to Ptarmigan Mountain. The route descends along Wearyman Creek to Turkey Creek before another climb to Shrine Pass. **Cost:** $6.50 to $13 includes transportation. **When:** June to August. **Contact:** Vail Guides, Inc., P.O. Box 1474, Vail, CO 81657, USA; phone (303)476-5387. *(M)*

Nevada

Exploring the Great Basin: A series of expeditions brings campers to a diversity of desert habitats ranging from sharp-peaked mountains to alkali flats. Departing from Reno, participants spend 12 days driving and hiking in trips to Lander, Nye and Eureka counties or northwestern Nevada and Pyramid Lake. Guides trained in local geography, flora and fauna direct travelers through old mining towns, abandoned Pony Express stations, scrub desert and mountains. Plenty of time is provided for campers to pursue their own interests, such as botany, birdwatching or lazing in the sun. Participants help set up campsites along the way, with the area's arid climate making it necessary for individuals to haul their own water supply. Transportation is by van over dirt roads, with a modified bus serving as field kitchen. **Cost:** $750 includes motel in Reno, transportation, all meals. **When:** May to August. **Contact:** Holbrook Travel, Inc., 3520 NW 13th St., Gainesville, FL 32601, USA; phone (904)377-7111.

Texas

Family Camping at Big Bend: Travelers including families with children at least 9 years old join for a 7-day camping trip which explores the natural history of the Big Bend area. Exploring the Lower Chihuahuan desert environment of Big Bend National Park, the trip catches the reawakening of the desert at the start of spring. Participants learn basic wilderness camping techniques as well as desert wildlife identification. Itineraries are flexible, with some trips more strenuous than others. Groups of 15 to 25 people hike to campsites, averaging 8 to 10 miles of travel a day. Four-wheel drive vehicles accompany the entourage, carrying each participant's duffle bag in addition to all food and camping equipment. While meals are planned by staff members, trip members share cooking responsibilities. **Cost:** $300 includes meals, transportation. **When:** March. **Contact:** Sierra Club Outing Dept., 530 Bush St., San Francisco, CA 94108, USA; phone (415)981-8634.

Travelers journey on foot and by jeep to explore Arches National Monument in southeastern Utah. It took eons for the wind and rain to carve the delicate formations. (Keith Gunnar)

Utah

Canyonlands by Jeep: Participants can explore Canyonlands National Park on journeys of 6 to 10 days. Travel by 4-wheel drive vehicles and on foot provides choices among 7 different trips covering various regions of the park. Participants may investigate the Needles area on the east side of the Colorado River with visits to Angel Arch, Horse Canyon and Paul Bunyan's Potty. Robbers Roost, Land's End and Doll House can be seen on the Standing Rocks and Maze area venture. Participants see the old Gold Queen Mine, Hammond Canyon and Abajo Peak on the Blue Mountain trip, or Mexican Cry Mesa, Carrizo Mountains and Lukakachuka Mountains on the Four Corners journey. On one trip the group follows the route the Mormons used in the 1880s on their way to Bluff, Utah. The trip includes Comb Ridge, Natural Bridges National Monument and Shoot the Chute. Participants who take the Golden Circle trip start in Monticello and travel to the Valley of the Gods, the Navajo Reservation, the Grand Canyon, Standing Rocks and several other points of interest. Combination jeep, hiking, river float and packstock trips are available on request. One-day trips can be taken year-round with a minimum of 2 participants. **Cost:** $25 for 1 day; $43 a day for 6 to 10 days includes all camping equipment, transportation, meals, guides. **When:** April to November. **Contact:** Kent Frost Canyonland Tours, Inc., 180 S. Second E., Monticello, UT 84535, USA; phone (801)587-2929.

Southwest Camping Trips: Six-day camping trips through Arizona and southern Utah begin in Las Vegas, where participants are picked up and bused to remote campsites. The camps are located at or near such scenic sites as Zion National Park, Bryce Canyon, Lake Powell, the Grand Canyon, the Hopi and Navaho Indian reservations and Petrified Forest National Park. Campsites are normally chosen in remote areas, away from normal tourist haunts. Expedition personnel make camp and cook meals. The group usually stays at each campsite for 2 days to allow time for some exploration of the area. Longer trips of up to 12 days can be arranged. **Cost:** $275 from Las Vegas. **When:** April, May. **Contact:** L.D. Fromme, Outfitter, RFD, Afton, WY 83110, USA; phone (307)886-5240.   *(M)*

Overlanding from Moab: Participants in a 4-day trip to the remote areas of Canyonlands National Park travel by means of a 4-wheel drive vehicle departing from Moab. Passing through the town of Green River, travelers head south for a camp near Panorama Point and a wide vista of the Land of Standing Rocks country. Trip members descend into a maze of rock by means of the Flint Trail where masses of Wingate sandstone towering over a thousand feet high are visible. From there visits are made to a petrified forest, the Totem Pole and Tibbet Arch en route to the Doll House, a fantasy land of eroded rock. Heading southward, trip members pass Sunset Pass and Gunsite Butte, then go under the massive Orange Cliffs to the Sewing Machine. Camps provide participants with comfort and hot meals. Accompanied by a qualified guide, participants learn about the flora, fauna, geology and history of the area. **Cost:** $192 includes transportation, meals. **When:** May to September. **Contact:** Tag-A-Long Tours, 452 N. Main, Moab, UT 84532, USA; phone (801)259-6690 or tollfree (800)453-3292.

RESOURCES
Clubs and Associations

American Adventurers Association
444 NE Ravenna Blvd., Suite 301
Seattle, WA 98115, USA
Phone (206)523-2980

Calgary Explorers' Club
c/o Dept. of Geography
University of Calgary
2920 24th Ave. NW
Calgary, AB Canada T2N 1N4

The Chalet Club
P.O. Box 3849, Grand Central Sta.
New York, NY 10017, USA
Phone (212)490-0126

The Explorers Club
46 E. 70th St.
New York, NY 10021, USA
Phone (212)628-8383

Globetrotter's Club
BCM, Roving
London WC1 6XX, Great Britain

Guide Europeenne du Raid
15 quai de Conti
75006, Paris, France

Guildford Travel Club
MS. J.J. Tubbs
"Cliffe End," 9 Ridgemont
Guildford, Surrey, Great Britain

National 4 Wheel Drive Association
P.O. Box 386
Rosemead, CA 91770, USA

Overland Club
Third Floor, Queens Arcade
Auckland 1, New Zealand

Royal Automobile Club
RAC Touring Services
P.O. Box 92, RAC House
Lansdown Rd.
Croydon CR9 9DH, Great Britain

Special Travel
c/o Christopher Portway
Jasan, White Ash Green
Halstead, Essex, Great Britain

Trail Finders
48 Earls Court Rd.
London W8, Great Britain

Travel Wise Club
444 Robson St.
Vancouver, BC Canada

WEXAS
International Office
45 Brompton Rd.
Knightsbridge, London SW3
Great Britain

Expedition Consultants

Quest 4 Ltd.
Ashton Wold
Peterborough PE8 5LZ, Great Britain
Phone Oundle 2614

Vehicle Rental

Four by Four Ltd.
Twickenham Rd.
Feltham, Middlesex, Great Britain

Fram Expeditions Ltd.
c/o John Hamilton
69 Ledi Dr.
Bearsden, Glasgow G61 4JN
Great Britain

Guerba Expeditions Ltd.
Stokehill Farm, Erhlestoke
Devizes SN10 SUB, Great Britain

Land-Roving Ltd.
30 Sidbury
Worcester, Great Britain

Vantage Motor Co.
88 the Avenue
Highams Park
London E4, Great Britain

RESEARCH EXPEDITIONS

There is no greater adventure than one into the unknown. Every step brings the thrill of new knowledge and experience as you venture into unexplored regions, whether they are at the far ends of the continent or close to home. For the scientist, the unknown can be found in the daily life of remote societies, in the hidden codes of behavior of tropical animal life, or beneath the surface of a modern village, where fragile pottery shards reveal an ancient world.

Once the exclusive domain of academic institutions, museums and private foundations, scientific research is now open to the untrained enthusiast as well as the doctoral candidate. The value of outsiders—as volunteers, assistants and observers—has been recognized as an invaluable aid to research. It is a mutually beneficial arrangement: the novice becomes familiar with an endeavor he or she has always been interested in, and the project enjoys the enthusiasm, dedication and new perspective of the amateur. As a result, a number of organizations and universities now allow participation in some research projects, and the amateur and the professional scientist work side by side in nearly every corner of the world.

Research projects on land are as diverse as human inquiry. They seek to record and understand the ecological interactions of the plant and animal communities of the Great Basin Desert in Nevada; to excavate a pharoah's temple, built 3,000 years ago on the banks of the Nile; to study the colorful birds of the West Indies and the insect parasites which live off them; and to study the impact of European contact on the Eskimo societies of the Labrador coast. These are just a few of the projects which seek volunteer assistance.

Field conditions can be tough—these are indeed "working vacations," with few frills, long hours of often tedious work, and climactic conditions which range from the frigid temperatures of the Arctic to the humid confusion of tropical jungles. But nothing can dampen the reward of discovery. Whether you are uncovering a piece of bone, gaining a new insight from an old inscription, or sighting a species once thought to be extinct, the research expedition gives you a chance to expand your own boundaries of experience while working at the forefront of scientific inquiry. □

A researcher examines the impression of an ancient tree in the lava flows of the Craters of the Moon National Monument. The scorched tree toppled into molten lava during an eruption. (Idaho Div. of Tourism)

RESEARCH EXPEDITIONS

AFRICA

Egypt

Akhnaten Excavation: Joining a team of Egyptologists and archaeologists, participants act as site supervisors, planners and surveyors in the excavation of a temple built 30 centuries ago on the banks of the Nile in the city of Thebes. For 3 weeks team members stay in a small villa a short walk from the temple built in honor of the sun god, Aten, by command of Akhnaten. In addition to supervisory duties, volunteers sketch and photograph artifacts, mend pots, test soil samples and spend 1 day each week on field trips to nearby sites. Operating under a concession granted by the Egyptian government's Department of Antiquities, the project aims to unearth information on everyday life in ancient Thebes and Akhnaten's revolutionary art style and religion. Field conditions are rigorous and participants should be prepared for an abundance of insects and temperatures ranging from 105° to 125°F. **Cost:** $890 from Luxor includes transportation, accommodations, meals, instruction; scholarships are available. **When:** June, July. **Contact:** Earthwatch, P.O. Box 127 AG, Belmont, MA 02178, USA; phone (617)489-3030. *(M)*

Kenya

Documenting Prehistoric Art of Africa: An expedition of 19 days from the highlands of Kenya along the watercourses to the western provinces is being mounted as a joint United States-Kenya project to help preserve the latter's heritage. Participants join in the effort to trace, sketch and document already discovered petroglyphs and pictographs in caves and rock shelters then prospect for new sites. Searching for new sites involves hiking on foot through dense brush and rough terrain and interviewing local inhabitants, where conditions permit. African scientists direct the work of team members, and Kenyan students assist as interpreters for their American colleagues. Housing is provided in hotels, tents and in the homes of officials. **Cost:** $950 includes meals, accommodations, guides, equipment, transportation; scholarships are available. **When:** May through July. **Contact:** Earthwatch, P.O. Box 127 AG, Belmont, MA 02178, USA; phone (617)489-3030. *(M)*

AUSTRALASIA

Australia

Studying Sand Wasps in the Outback: On a 700-mile study near Perth, photographers, naturalists and observers join a University of Georgia professor in the discovery and naming of new sand wasp species. In the test area, which includes the dune areas warm, breezy Rottnest Island and the desert country of Kalgoorlie, as many as 10 different species have been found in a single sand dune. Teams work in the field between 9 to 4, when wasps are awake, and work in intervals of 2-week stints. In

Women are the house builders in Kenya. Here, research trips bring participants close to the bush and its inhabitants. (University Research Expeditions Program)

searching for new species, team members locate and excavate nests, observe and record behavior, examine parasites and nest architecture, prepare Maila Malaise traps and mount voucher specimens. Participants camp out and take side trips into the Yanchep Game Preserve for a look at Australia's animals, including kangaroos, koalas and kookaburras. Much recording is done photographically, through slides and movies. **Cost:** $875 includes food, shelter. **When:** January, February. **Contact:** Earthwatch, P.O. Box 127 AG, Belmont, MA 02178, USA; phone (617)489-3030. *(M)*

CANADA

Newfoundland

Eskimo Archaeology: Archaeolo-gists believe that the Inuit Eskimos who now inhabit the central Labrador coast descend from the Thule culture which spread from Alaska into the eastern Arctic between 900 and 1200 A.D. For 3 weeks interested persons may join a research team investigating sites on the small islands off the coast of Labrador near Nain, a small Eskimo village. The team is looking at the nature and time of Eskimo entry, the changes in subsistence and settlement patterns and the nature of Eskimo/European/American contact. The team surveys, maps and describes the environmental features of the sites, makes test excavations of some and keeps detailed records of any cultural material unearthed. Participants should be in good shape and be prepared to hike and camp. College credit is available. **Cost:** $950 from Nain includes food, equipment, transportation. **When:** June to August. **Contact:** University Research Expeditions Program, M19 Wheeler Hall, University of California, Berkeley, CA 94720, USA; phone (415)642-6586. *(M)*

CARIBBEAN

Trinidad and Tobago

Camouflage: A field project at Port of Spain involves participants in the study of predatory/prey relationships. Under the direction of a population biologist from Princeton, team members work in the mountain streams of Trinidad and Tobago, studying small tropical fish to see how they use camouflage. The team is housed at a biological station and members spend many hours by streams making detailed notes on the behavior of various predators. The data is used in understanding how genetic and environmental factors influence the coloration of animals which coexist with natural predators. Field instruction is provided and academic credit is available. **Cost:** $775 tax-deductible contribution includes food, accommodations, transportation from Port of Spain, instruction, equipment; scholarships are available. **When:** February to April. **Contact:** Earthwatch, P.O. Box 127 AG, Belmont, MA 02178, USA; phone (617)489-3030. *(M)*

CENTRAL AMERICA

Belize

Natural Science Research: Relative-ly little research has been conducted in Belize, a country that still offers diverse opportunities for study: untouched forest, deep jungle, abundant limestone caves, unpolluted water, uncharted species. Two-week expeditions under the supervision of experienced instructors are offered to high school or college students interested in archaeology, zoology, botany, marine biology, entomology, ornithology or limnology. There are 3 field stations for the project: one is in the extreme south of Belize, in the mountains of the primary rain forest; another in the central foothills, within reach of the principal limestone caverns and a tropical cenote; the third a marine biological station 14 miles off the coast and directly on the barrier reef. The study group has exclusive use of 2 small cays. Expeditions are arranged individually, depending on each person's or group's objectives. **Cost:** From $500 a person includes roundtrip airfare from the U.S., food, accommodations, equipment, instruction, transportation. **When:** Year-round. **Contact:** International Zoological Expeditions, 210 Washington St., Sherborn, MA 01770, USA; phone (617)655-1461.

Costa Rica

Volcano Expedition: A team of British scientists leads adventurers for 2 weeks in a study of andesite volcanoes. The purpose of the expedition is to climb to the boiling crater lake of the volcano Poas, measure the crater, and survey for unusual rock samples in order to assess the volcano's changing character. The team camps on the densely vegetated slopes of Poas,

Researchers photograph limestone cave formations in central Belize on a two-week trip offered by International Zoological Expeditions. (Int'l. Zoological Expeditions)

negotiating steep paths to work areas. After learning to identify the major structures and rock types of the volcano, participants measure the thicknesses of lava flows, identify and collect rocks, and record data. Topics such as plate tectonics and the geological history of Costa Rica are covered in informal evening discussions. Participants should be in good physical condition. Academic credit is available. **Cost:** $775 from San Jose covers meals, accommodations, transportation, equipment, guides; scholarships are available. **When:** January. **Contact:** Earthwatch, P.O. Box 127 AG, Belmont, MA 02178, USA; phone (617)489-3030. *(M)*

Guatemala

Volcano Research Expedition: Dur-ing a 4-week visit to several volcanoes in the Sierra Madre participants aid in geological research. At a small lake near the Pacoza Volcano participants make bathymetric maps and take temperature readings while learning research techniques. After climbing to the summit of Augo Volcano, which destroyed Antigua, the capital of Guatemala, in 1541, team members collect sediment samples from the remnants of the crater lake which may contain information concerning prehistoric eruptions from nearby volcanoes. The expedition ends with a rafting trip down the Dulce River. Some knowledge of the Spanish language is helpful. **Cost:** $550 plus airfare. **When:** June. **Contact:** Expedition Training Institute, Inc., P.O. Box 171, Prudential

Ctr. Sta., Boston, MA 02199, USA; phone (617)922-0577. *(M)*

EUROPE

Italy

Studying the Saracens: Although the Saracens are known to have invaded and occupied various areas of Italy during the 8th century, few archaeological remnants of their presence have been found. A 3-week research trip offers an opportunity to help excavate one of the few known sites which is yet uninvestigated. On the western Mediterranean coast near the medieval town of Minturno, participants learn techniques necessary for surveying, mapping and excavating the site, and drawing and photographing the materials uncovered. Some scuba diving may be necessary in an attempt to see whether any underwater evidence of the Saracen invasion remains. Accommodations are in small, comfortable hotels on the beach at Scauri, the nearest town to the research site. College credit is available. **Cost:** $925 from Minturno includes food, accommodations, instruction, activities. **When:** May. **Contact:** University Research Expeditions Program, M10 Wheeler Hall, University of California, Berkeley, CA 94720, USA; phone (415)642-6586. *(M)*

Scotland

Outer Hebrides Exploration: Previous experience in maneuvering small boats is an asset to campers who spend 24 days examining the environment of North Uist, Britain's most isolated inhabited island. Expedition members assemble at Brathay and travel by coach to Oban, then by boat to Lochboisdale. In consultation with the Nature Conservancy Council, the group works on a range of projects in the fields of ornithology, botany and biology. The environment of North Uist provides a wide range of

A researcher carefully inspects a remnant of a Viking settlement in York, once an important Norse town in England. (Carol Baker)

habitats for the many different types of wildfowl and waders that live in the area. Peat bogs, croft land, sand dunes, locks, islets and inter-tidal mudflats are explored. The expedition travels north to Harris for some portions of the project before returning to Ambleside at the conclusion of the trip. **Cost:** $225 from Ambleside includes transportation, food, camping equipment. **When:** July. **Contact:** Brathay Exploration Group, Brathay Hall, Ambleside, Cumbria, Great Britain; phone Ambleside (09663)2531.

Excavation on the Moor: In late summer work begins on Machrie Moor, where untouched Bronze Age stone circles lie beneath peat bogs. Volunteers are needed for 3 weeks to excavate the site on the Isle of Arran, examine possible astronomical alignments, and put a trench across what may be a Middle Bronze Age cremation cemetery. Team members are housed in 5-person cottages 3 miles from Machrie Moor and food is prepared by a staff cook. Work on the excavation is open to all, and any training necessary is provided. **Cost:** $700. **When:** August. **Contact:** Earthwatch, P.O. Box 127 AG, Belmont, MA 02178, USA; phone (617)489-3030. *(M)*

Spain

Archaeological Find in the Balearic Islands: A tiny village in the western corner of the Mediterranean is the setting for 16 to 20 days of archaeological research work. Classic excavation techniques are employed, and, in addition to field work, participants work in both the museum and laboratory identifying finds or doing ceramic reconstruction, bone classification, illustration and microphotography. The fossils and artifacts from the rock shelter of Son Matge and the cave of Son Muleta have origins in Europe and Mesopotamia, and have proven the presence of human life in Majorca as early as 6,000 years ago. The historical significance of the research is enhanced for participants by lectures and briefings from the staff. Apprentice archaeologists live in dormitories and have some free time to roam the countryside and beaches. **Cost:** $725 to $775 includes meals, accommodations, instruction, transportation, equipment; scholarships are available. **When:** June, August, September, December. **Contact:** Earthwatch, P.O. Box 127 AG, Belmont, MA 02178, USA; phone (617)489-3030. *(M)*

Sweden

Glacier Study: Glaciers along the Norwegian-Swedish border 100 miles south of the Arctic Circle are the focus of a 6-week study trip in Lapland. The aim of the expedition is to continue previous studies of the central Scandinavian mountain chain, particularly in the areas of glacial study, botany and geology. After assembling at Newcastle in England, participants travel by sea to Gothenburg in Sweden and then by train to the Narvik-Abisko region. From there 2 to 3 days of walking bring the group to base camp near Kebnekaise, Sweden's highest mountain. The group explores the country toward the Norwegian fjords and the Sarek mountains, one of the last wilderness areas in northern Europe. Previous expedition experience is required. **Cost:** $563 includes transportation from Newcastle, food, equipment. **When:** August, September. **Contact:** Brathay Exploration Group, Brathay Hall, Ambleside, Cumbria, Great Britain; phone Ambleside (09663)2531.

MIDDLE EAST

Israel

Nomads of the South Sinai: Herdspeople are observed, their campsites measured their seasonal movements plotted and subsistence methods examined in a 23-day study of the nomadic Bedouin. Team members join a prehistoric archaeology professor from Hebrew University in an expedition into the Sinai Desert to explore a timeless way of life through the excavation of the past and a people-to-people study of the present. The team compares the remains of recently discovered neolithic campsites near a 6th-century monastery in the foothills of the Gebel Mountains to the presently occupied camps of Gibalyeh Bedouin nearby. Resisting changes despite harsh conditions, the Bedouin wander the deserts in search of freshwater sources, tending their goats and cultivating small gardens where the land allows. Participants live in tents at the research site and share in all aspects of the field work. Academic credit is available. **Cost:** $850 from Jerusalem includes meals, accommodations, transportation, equipment, guides; scholarships are available. **When:** March. **Contact:** Earthwatch, P.O. Box 127 AG, Belmont, MA 02178, USA; phone (617)489-3030. *(M)*

PACIFIC

New Caledonia

Grande Terre Botanical Study: Members of a 20-day research expedition on Grande Terre Island, part of the French territory of New Caledonia, study two genera of the myrtle family. The genera *Cupheanthus* and *Piliocalyx* contain fleshy fruited plants with certain features of botanical interest including highly variable leaf size. Participants assist a botanist in amassing field data for the study of reproductive biology and structure by collecting, pressing and drying specimens, and by making observations on structure, habitat, pollination and seed dispersal. New Caledonia's terrain is mostly mountainous and the climate is mildly tropical. Team members may stay in field research stations but should be prepared to camp, work and hike in conditions that are often rugged. A knowledge of French and photography would be helpful. **Cost:** $1,075 from Noumea includes food, accommodations. **When:** July, August. **Contact:** University Research Expeditions Program, M19 Wheeler Hall, University of California, Berkeley, CA 94720, USA; phone (415)642-6586. *(M)*

SOUTH AMERICA

Chile

Observing the Guanaco of Patagonia: Where the Andean chain splinters into waterfalls and glacial lakes adventurers join a wildlife ecologist for 2 weeks to study the relationship between the camel-like guanaco and its environment and social

Investigators spend hours in waist-deep water to study the world's largest leech, found in French Guiana. (University Research Expeditions Program)

behavior. All-day treks over hilly shrubland alternate with days to rest and review data. Participants camp in the Paine Towers National Park just north of the Strait of Magellan where one of the few remaining herds of guanaco lives. Observation teams map the movements of the small, gentle animals, collecting and recording data on group size, habitat use, territorial defense, birth rate and newborn survival. Over-hunting and deterioration of their environment have endangered the animal, and participants are part of an effort to improve the guanaco's chance of survival. Academic credit is available. **Cost:** $775 from Punta Arenas includes food, accommodations, transportation, equipment, field gear, guide; scholarships are available. **When:** December. **Contact:** Earthwatch, P.O. Box 127 AG, Belmont, MA 02178, USA; phone (617)489-3030. *(M)*

Ecuador

Off to See the Lizard: The tropical rain forests of western Ecuador serve as a natural laboratory for a 2-week study of the ecological problems of frogs and lizards. Participants become members of a team headed by a biology professor, who, for the past 3 years, has been classifying newly found species of frogs. Team members help in several sampling procedures to determine the species present, the number of individuals, the available prey and potential predators. Observations are made of marked study populations of lizards as well. The team travels by car and, depending on the weather and road conditions, may survey the west slope of the Andes in addition to the Rio Palenque area. Academic credit is available. **Cost:** $775 from Quito includes meals, accommodations, transportation, equipment, guide. **When:** January. **Contact:** Earthwatch, P.O. Box 127 AG, Belmont, MA 02178, USA; phone (617)489-3030. *(M)*

UNITED STATES

Alaska

Bering Sea Research Institute: A 2-month interdisciplinary program of summer field courses and research projects is based in Dutch Harbor on Unalaska Island. It is open to faculty and students of various universities and others with a special interest in the Aleutian-Bering Sea region. The academic program includes courses in marine and terrestrial biology, ecology, geography, geology and meteorology, along with opportunities to conduct guided research projects in Russian-American history, education, undersea exploration and resource management. Fifteen-foot inflatable boats are used for transport between the islands. Some possible field studies include photographing archaeological sites of caves, graves and Aleut villages, studying flora and fauna of the islands, tracing the migration of sea birds and diving and exploring shipwrecks. An objective of the program is to develop new arctic and subarctic specialists to help plan the proper utilization of the resources of northern areas. **Cost:** $400 includes food, lodging, transportation at site, foul-weather gear.

When: July, August. **Contact:** American Institute for Exploration, 1809 Nichols Rd., Kalamazoo, MI 49007, USA; phone (616)381-8237. *(M)*

Kenai Ecosystems: A month-long expedition assists the Peninsula National Wildlife Refuge in its first year of a continuing study of the flora and fauna of the Kenai Peninsula. In one study to establish the relationship between wolves and moose, students record the range and feeding habits of the moose while measuring the wolf population. In another project, participants attempt to find ways to increase the population of the trumpeter swan by studying its habitat. Trip members may spend their spare time canoeing, hiking and exploring the fjord-like peninsula which contains both a glacier icefield and northern rain forest. No prior experience is necessary, but participants should have enthusiasm for the subject and a willingness to pitch in. **Cost:** $500 from Anchorage includes food, accommodations. **When:** July. **Contact:** Expedition Training Institute, Inc., P.O. Box 171, Prudential Ctr. Sta., Boston, MA 02199, USA; phone (617)922-0577. *(M)*

California

Bigfoot Expedition: Bigfoot, or sasquatch, is one of the 93 mammal species reported in southwestern Oregon and northwestern California, and it is in this region that expedition members search for this elusive being. Each team learns the basics of tracking and collects data such as hair samples and fecal matter, and also learns about the

Hikers investigate the cedars of Cumberland Island, Georgia with field microscopes supplied by Wilderness Southeast. (Wilderness Southeast)

local flora and fauna. The expeditions are led by scientists, naturalists or trackers, and members should have some backpacking experience. Participants select the expedition that matches their level of experience. **Cost:** On request. **When:** Year-round. **Contact:** Beamer Expeditions, P.O. Box 285, Canoga Park, CA 91305, USA; phone (213)883-3522. *(M)*

Florida

Marine Research at Crystal River: Participants study large bird rookeries, Indian mounds and tidal pools during an 8-day stay at the confluence of the Crystal and Salt rivers. The intensive program involves studies in both gulf and freshwater environments. Based at the Marine Science Station, students travel by boat to river headwaters to observe and collect specimens, then utilize well-equipped laboratories and holding tanks for the study and preservation of the specimens. All work is done in conjunction with a biologist/naturalist who coordinates the program. Program members have access to library, dormitory and dining hall facilities. An interest in marine sciences and membership in the Oceanic Society are requirements for participation. **Cost:** $210 from Crystal River includes accommodations, meals, equipment, transportation. **When:** July. **Contact:** Oceanic Expeditions, 240 Ft. Mason, San Francisco, CA 94123, USA; phone (415)441-1106.

Georgia

Sea Turtle Research: The Savannah Science Museum offers participants a chance to spend a week working on a research project at the Wassaw Island National Wildlife Refuge near Savannah. The object of the project is to learn more about the habits of the Atlantic loggerhead sea turtle *(Caretta caretta)*, an endangered species. The female loggerhead comes ashore during the summer to lay eggs in a nest buried in the sand, and participants spend the night patrolling the beaches in search of turtles to tag and measure. In addition to learning about the habits of the sea turtles and field research techniques, project members can explore the island and help with National Wildlife Refuge Management projects. Participants should be in good health and be prepared to endure some discomfort. **Cost:** $120 a week includes transportation to and from the island, food, housing. **When:** May to July. **Contact:** Wilderness Southeast, Rt. 3, Box 619 AA, Savannah, GA 31406, USA; phone (912)355-8008. *(M)*

Michigan

Great Lakes Gulls: Bird watchers with skills in photography, mapmaking or statistical analysis comprise the majority of team members on a 2-week study of Great Lakes gull populations near Rogers City. The group bands and tags birds, measures bird movements and collects mating data and other factors which affect ringbill populations during the current period of declining waters. Information gathered by the expedition is expected to be used in making decisions for gull management programs on the Sleeping Bear Dunes National Lakeshore and Manitou Island. About 800 acres of forest, trout streams and meadows provide the setting for the project. Volunteers should be prepared for cold weather and walks of long distances in loose sand and over hills. Travel to the islands is provided by boat or seaplane. **Cost:** $650 covers lodge accommodations, food. **When:** May, June. **Contact:** Earthwatch, P.O. Box 127 AG, Belmont, MA 02178, USA; phone (617)489-3030.
(M)

Oregon

Zeroing in on Life Zones: The plants and animals of Oregon's many life zones are the subject of a 2-week educational trip by motor coach. The emphasis of study is on the relationship between living organisms and their environments—how organisms have adapted and how habitats differ. Most of the major life zones in the state are visited. Basic field methods are utilized with the assistance of local resource people to help participants observe and sample the areas visited. Beginning and ending in Portland, the group camps out along the way while visiting Yaquina Head, McKenzie Pass, the Three Sisters area, Newberry Crater, Mt. Hood and Crooked River National Grassland. Nights are spent camping. **Cost:** $190 from Portland includes transportation, food, equipment, guide. **When:** August.

Contact: Oregon Museum of Science and Industry, 4015 SW Canyon Rd., Portland, OR 97221, USA; phone (503)248-5938.

Virginia

Archaeological Study in Front Royal: Secondary and college students spend 2, 4, or 8 weeks on 3 dig sites of the paleo-early archaic periods. Field study involves excavating Indian habitations, hunting and butchering stations, and pottery areas; a staff of geologists, pedologists and paleo-ecologists assists the group as they inspect the 12,000-year-old sites. Students spend their days in the field and evenings at lectures or in labs; weekends are free. College credit is available on the 4-week program. **Cost:** $150 to $800 depending on length of dig and credit requested; $50 a week for food and lodging. **When:** June to August. **Contact:** The Catholic University of America, Dept. of Anthropology, Washington, DC 20064, USA; phone (202)635-5080.

RESOURCES

Clubs and Associations

Archaeological Institute of America
260 W. Broadway, Dept. EX
New York, NY 10013, USA
Phone (212)925-7333

Archaeology Abroad Service
31/34 Gordon Sq.
London WC1, Great Britain

Arctic-Desert-Tropic
Information Center

Aerospace Studies Institute
USAF University
Maxwell AFB, AL 36112, USA

Egypt Exploration Society
2-3 Doughty Mews
London WC1, Great Britain

Expedition Research, Inc.
P.O. Box 467
Annapolis, MD 21404, USA
Phone (301)268-3222

Explorers Club
46 E. 70th St.
New York, NY 10021, USA
Phone (212)628-8383

Field Studies Council
9 Devereux Ct., Strand
London WC2, Great Britain

Iceland Information Unit
Losehill Hall
Peak National Study Center
Castleton via Sheffield S30 2WB
Great Britain

International Glaciological Society
Cambridge CB2 1ER, Great Britain

International Oceanographic
Foundation
3979 Rickenbacker Causeway
Virginia Key
Miami, FL 33149, USA

San Juan County Museum Association
Rt. 3, Box 169
Farmington, NM 87401, USA

Scientific Exploration Society
Home Farm, Mildenhall, Marlborough
Wiltshire, Great Britain

Scott Polar Research Institute
Cambridge CB2 1ER, Great Britain

Society for American Archaeology
c/o Culbert, Dept. of Anthropology
University of Arizona
Tucson, AZ 85721, USA

Society for the Preservation
of Archaeological Monuments
P.O. Box 5564, University Sta.
Seattle, WA 98105, USA
Phone (206)324-9406

BICYCLE TOURING

The last time you took a drive in the country, you might have been surprised to see a bicyclist toiling up a hill. It may seem like hard work, but if you took the trouble to dust off the two-wheeler in your basement and gave bicycle touring a try for yourself, you would rediscover a world of small, forgotten pleasures.

The smells of trees and wildflowers seem fresher, especially after a spring rain. A slight tailwind might speed your progress, but you still have time to notice the minutiae of plant life along the roadside and a crow which follows you, cawing, for a mile or two. The hill that lies ahead may seem insurmountable, but with patience, stamina—and low gears—you reach its crest soon enough. Then you gather speed and coast down into the valley beyond. And as the wind blows in your face, and the sun breaks through a bank of clouds to illuminate the countryside, you swear to yourself that there can be no better way to travel.

More than 100,000 Americans are realizing these joys by biking along the nationwide network of bicycle trails designated by federal, state or local agencies. You can bike all the way from Oregon to Virginia along the 4,422-mile TransAmerica Trail, inaugurated in 1976 by over 4,000 cyclists. Or you can follow scenic routes in Maine, Nova Scotia, Montana or Alberta, along the Mississippi or down the Continental Divide. For many of these long-distance bike tours, organizations offer guided trips of up to four months in length which include equipment, camping facilities and a "sag wagon" to pick up the weary.

Of course, bicycling in Europe has never gone out of fashion, and several groups take journeys throughout the capitals of the Old World. You can cross Western Europe in as little as three weeks and still have time for sightseeing; or take six weeks to cycle through Scandinavia into the Soviet Union and back again. In an even more exotic environment, a midsummer tour of the Hawaiian Islands is offered, and bikers can discover not only the wonders of surfing and canoeing in the warm coastal waters, but the lush forests and active volcanoes of the interior as well.

Bicycling appeals to so many people for several reasons—relatively inexpensive and ideal for family outings, it is also great for your health. By traveling across country, you get the chance to appreciate the landscapes you cross, to learn about the people and history of each region, and to improve your muscle tone, circulation and breathing with each passing mile. Indeed, what better way to travel is there? □

A nationwide network of bike trails traverses the U.S. Long-distance bike trips can pass through mountainous areas like Grand Teton National Park. (Wyoming Travel Commission)

BICYCLE TOURING

ASIA

India

Buddha Bike Hike: Cyclists spend 21 days exploring the region of the Ganges where Gautama Buddha was born and spent his life. Starting in Delhi participants take a short flight to Baranasi where the bicycling begins. The group goes on to Sarnath, where Buddha preached his first sermon over 2,500 years ago. From Sarnath bikers head north for a boat excursion up the Ganges, then continue to Lumbini, the Nepalese town where Buddha was born. Retracing their route, participants then go on to Kusinagar, the site of Buddha's death. Passing through Patna, Muzaffarpur and Rajgir, bikers arrive at Bodh Gaya, where the holy man sat under the pipal tree and attained enlightenment. The final leg of the journey returns bikers to Baranasi via Sasaram; from there participants may go on to Agra, site of the Taj Mahal, or back to Delhi. **Cost:** $1,110 from Delhi includes meals, accommodations, bicycles. **When:** November. **Contact:** REI Adventure Travel, Inc., 1525 11th Ave., Seattle, WA 98122, USA; phone (206)322-7800. *(M)*

AUSTRALASIA

New Zealand

Bike and Hike South Island: For 3 weeks during late spring, a small group of travelers bicycles 500 miles and hikes 50 miles in New Zealand. The longest distance is covered the first day out with a 100-mile ride across the flat and straight Canterbury Plain. Crossing Burke's Pass, the gateway to the high Mackenzie Plains, cyclists find spectacular views of the Southern Alps at Lake Tekapo. Riding days are interspersed with a few layovers in places including the alpine resort at Mt. Cook. Each night is spent in a hotel with access to a hot bath to ease the day's strain. Bicycles are left behind at Te Anau as the group ventures onto the Milford Track for a week of hiking over mountain passes and beside rivers, lakes, glades and fjords. Nights are spent in huts on the trail complete with showers and home-cooked meals. The end of the hike brings participants to the end of the journey with a return flight to Christchurch, Auckland and Los Angeles. **Cost:** $1,916 includes transportation from Los Angeles, guide, accommodations, most meals. **When:** November. **Contact:** Greenwood Travel Center, 5650 S. Syracuse Circle, Englewood, CO 80111, USA; phone (303)770-1113.

CANADA

Bicycling in Nova Scotia: A group travels by train to Montreal and Digby, then cycles up the rural Annapolis River Valley to Grand Pre, the last home of Acadian farmers and the setting for Longfellow's "Evangeline." Trip members can watch for the tidal bore as the world's highest tides surge into the Bay of Fundy. The group travels across the narrow peninsula to the eastern shore of Nova Scotia where

Bikes cross the Bay of Fundy by ferry on a cross-country trip through New England and Nova Scotia. (The Biking Expedition/Thomas Heavey)

coves and bays shelter small fishing villages. The group proceeds to Antigonish and Cape Breton Island, then travels the Cabot Trail before taking ferries to Prince Edward Island and Charlottetown. There are many opportunities for clam digging and swimming. The last stops are Quebec City and Montreal. Overnight camping is the norm along the way. **Cost:** $652 from New York includes meals, accommodations, guide; $50 emergency fund. **When:** June, July. **Contact:** American Youth Hostels, National Campus, Delaplane, VA 22025, USA; phone (703)592-3271.

Bicycling the Pacific Northwest: Participants on a 35-day bicycle trip

to the Northwest meet in Vancouver, British Columbia before boarding a ferry to the San Juan Islands for a few days of island hopping, clamming and swimming. Then, after a return visit to Vancouver, travelers continue by train through British Columbia's glaciers, streams, forests and icefields to the mountain city of Jasper. Time is allotted for hikes in the mountainous terrain along the extensive trail network of Jasper and Banff national parks. Along the trails, outdoor enthusiasts explore Bow Glacier Falls, Sundance Canyon, Sentinel Pass and Banff Hot Springs as well as Lake Louise. Biking involves gradual climbs on wide-shouldered roads. Participants camp and stay in hostels along the way. The trip ends in Calgary. **Cost:** $942 from Vancouver includes accommodations, gear. **When:** July, August. **Contact:** The Biking Expedition Inc., P.O. Box 547, Hall Ave., Henniker, NH 03242, USA; phone (603)428-7500; summer, Rt. 2, Hillsboro, NH 03244, USA; phone (603)478-5783.

Cross-Country Biking: Departing from Toronto participants on a 10-week trip bike across the prairie provinces of Manitoba, Saskatchewan and Alberta viewing wheat fields and oil rigs, before passing through British Columbia to end the journey at Victoria. In British Columbia bikers pedal past fruit groves, fjord country and towering mountains, continuing through to Canada's third largest city, Vancouver. Totem pole parks and mountains surround bikers proceeding farther west to the gardens, mansions, water views and European-style architecture of Victoria. During the trip all participants carry camping and repair equipment individually, and cyclists share in planning and preparing meals. **Cost:** $699 from Toronto includes cooking gear, meals, tents, camp fees. **When:** On request. **Contact:** Canadian Universities Travel Service, 173 Lidgar St., Ottawa, ON Canada K2P 0C3; phone (613)238-8222.

Alberta

Across the Prairies: A variety of outdoor activities awaits participants on a 35-day trip to the Canadian Rockies. Departing from Edmonton, trip members travel by train across the prairies before un-

loading the bikes and embarking on a 400-mile ride along the Jasper-Banff Highway. Bikers make day hikes in the surroundings of Jasper National Park and across the Columbia Icefield. Participants also undertake extended wilderness hikes, making good hiking boots a necessity. Scheduled on the itinerary are visits to Bow Glacier Falls, Banff Hot Springs, Sundance Canyon, Mt. Edith Cavell, Sentinel Pass and Emerald Lake. Pedallers wend their way through forests of spruce, pine and aspen and often spot bears, elk, bighorn sheep, golden eagles and mountain goats living in remote areas of the park. Accommodations are in hostels along the way. **Cost:** $872 includes accommodations; $30 emergency fund. **When:** June. **Contact:** American Youth Hostels, National Campus, Delaplane, VA 22025, USA; phone (703)592-3271.

British Columbia

Pacific Coastline Biking and Hiking: Young cyclists begin a 40-day trip in Rochester, Vermont, traveling across Canada by train to Vancouver where the bicycling part of the tour gets underway. Cycling and camping along the hilly Pacific coastline, participants explore Indian fishing villages, picnic near lagoons, swim in wooded coves and beachcomb along narrow fjords that jut into the coastal mountains. The group takes a ferry to offshore Canadian islands to hike, dig clams and scale mountains that afford views as far eastward as the Rockies. Crossing into Washington by ferry, participants cycle through lush farmland to the North Cascades where 7 days are spent backpacking, exploring glacial lakes and abandoned miners' cabins and hiking along ridges with views of the surrounding mountains and valleys. The trip ends at the airport in Seattle where cyclists board planes for home. The trip is designed for boys and girls ages 13 to 17. **Cost:** $1,055 includes bicycle touring equipment (excluding bicycle), transportation from Rochester to Vancouver, meals, guides, accommodations. **When:** June to August. **Contact:** Student Hosteling Program of New England, Inc., Maple Hill, Rochester, VT 05767, USA; phone (802)767-3297.

Nova Scotia

Biking along Canada's Atlantic Coast: A month-long trip for high school students from many different countries begins in Halifax and explores the east coast of Canada. Group members learn about the culture of the area by meeting farmers in the Northumberland Strait region, stopping at fishing villages on Prince Edward Island and participating in the Highland Games held annually at Antigonish. As the trip winds along the rocky Atlantic coast, many traditional town festivals are encountered. Group members can choose various destinations such as the huge inland lake of Bras d'Or, or the coal-mining town of Sydney on Cape Breton. Participants share responsibilities such as cooking, and should bring their own bicycles and be in good physical shape. **Cost:** $695 from Halifax includes meals, accommodations. **When:** July. **Contact:** Crossroads International, Hillsboro, NH 03244, USA; phone (603) 478-5251. *(M)*

Coastal Bicycling: Beginning cyclists are welcome on a 12-day trip which explores Nova Scotia. After meeting in Bar Harbor, participants are transported by ferry to Yarmouth, where the biking begins. The terrain consists of mildly rolling hills and long flat stretches of coastline. Emphasis is placed on meeting the people of the area, among them Acadian farmers and fishermen who familiarize cyclists with stories of Nova Scotia's history and culture. A visit is planned to the Bay of Fundy to see the highest tides in the world, and time is provided for informal explorations of deserted islands and rural fields. Included in the course is instruction in first aid, bicycle mechanics and minimum-impact camping. **Cost:**

Cyclists generally ride at their own pace but meet at prearranged places for meals and stopovers. (American Youth Hostels)

$375 from Bar Harbor includes transportation, meals, accommodations, guide. **When:** May. **Contact:** The Infinite Odyssey, 57 Grant St., Waltham, MA 02154, USA; phone (617)899-6050. *(M)*

Quebec

Weekend Land Cruises: Bicyclists on 2-day trips that extend from Montreal to the Maritimes start from the Montreal Youth Hostel and are transported to the area of their choice: the Adirondacks, the south of Quebec, the Laurentians, Mt. Washington, Toronto and Le Parc National de la Mauricie, to name a few of the possible destinations. The trips are available for individuals, couples, groups, families, etc. A discount is made for hostel members. **Cost:** $21 to $65 from Montreal includes transportation, accommodations, food, guide. **When:** May to October. **Contact:** Canadian Hostelling Association, Quebec Hostelling Federation, 1324 Sherbrooke St. W., Montreal, PQ

Canada H3G 1H9; phone (514)842-9048.

Pedaling the Maritime Provinces: Students aged 13 and older join in 2 separate age groups for a 27-day bicycling trip through the provinces of Quebec and New Brunswick. Meeting in Rochester, Vermont, participants bus to the U.S.-Canadian border and cycle through lush French-Canadian farmland, near wooded lakes and meandering brooks. A night train brings cyclists to New Brunswick and the next leg of the trip. Here, students cycle along a beautiful river valley surrounded by green, forested hills and fertile farmlands before heading back into Quebec for a final week of exploration. Students camp along the St. Lawrence River above Quebec City before embarking on the return leg of the trip. The trip ends at the Montreal airport. Accommodations are at campgrounds, and cycling is moderately easy throughout the trip. **Cost:** $725 from Vermont includes transportation, equipment, leader, food; $25 contingency fund. **When:** July to August. **Contact:** Student Hosteling Program of New England, Inc., Maple Hill, Rochester, VT 05767, USA; phone (802)767-3297.

EUROPE

Cycling Adriatic Lands: Participants on a 36-day journey to the Adriatic Sea countries of Italy, Yugoslavia and Greece begin from Rome and cycle through Florence and Venice. In Yugoslavia, they boat and cycle down the warm coast to Dubrovnik and proceed by boat to the Greek island of Corfu before returning to the mainland of Greece for a visit to the ancient cities of Corinth and Athens. A side trip is taken to one of the sun-drenched Greek isles, Mykonos, before the return to Athens and the flight home. The cycling is moderately difficult. **Cost:** $1,425 from New York includes transportation, accommodations, meals; $50 emergency fund. **When:** July. **Contact:** American Youth Hostels, National Campus, Delaplane, VA 22025, USA; phone (703)592-3271.

Bicycling through the Old World Heritage: Starting in London, members of a 22-day bicycle trip pedal to Dover and, after a cruise to Belgium, continue to Bruges, a 14th-century town restored to almost original condition. Cyclists ride along canals on Dutch bike paths to Amsterdam and the Hague. At Delft, home of the painter Vermeer, visitors view samples of the famous blue pottery made there. Group members encounter European cyclists who congregate in Holland every summer. The region provides a rural environment of ancient villages, old farmhouses and marketplaces alternating with woods, brooks and castles. The bicyclists proceed to Cologne and the Moselle Valley, location of famous wineries. The trip ends in England after 2 days in Paris. **Cost:** $1,119 to $1,259 from London includes transportation, accommodations, meals. **When:** June. **Contact:** Euro-Bike Tours, P.O. Box 40, DeKalb, IL 60115, USA; phone (815)758-8851.

The Northern Crescent: Students take 40 days to travel through Denmark, Sweden, the Soviet Union and Finland. Beginning with 4 days in the ancient sea coast capital of Copenhagen, the group takes a week-long bike jaunt through the fishing villages of the Jutland peninsula before passing by ship across the Kattegat to Gothenburg, Sweden, where each member spends a week with a Swedish family. From there the group goes by train to the capital city of Stockholm for a 4-day stay in the city of islands and bridges. Next, an overnight steamer transports the group to the Soviet Union; 11 days are spent in Leningrad and Moscow, and 6 days at a Soviet youth resort near Yalta on the Black Sea. These 17 days offer a combination of sightseeing, sports, parties and general travel in the world's largest country. The journey concludes with several days in the modern Finnish capital of Helsinki. **Cost:** $2,320 from New York includes transportation, food, accommodations, guide. **When:** June. **Contact:** Putney Student

Travel, Inc., Putney, VT 05346, USA; phone (802)387-5885.

Continental Wheeling: Participants on a month-long biking trip through England, France, Italy, Switzerland and Germany encounter a variety of experiences ranging from pedaling through rolling English countryside to crossing Mont Blanc by aerial tram. Accompanied by a sag van, bikers make intermittent use of train and ship transportation as they visit the old fortress town of St. Malo and the chateau of Mt. St. Michel for a look at medieval architecture and design. On the Cote d'Azur participants view resort areas and the port city of Nice. Five days are given to cycling in Britanny and the chateau country of the Loire Valley. Trip members also cycle from Lake Constance to the Rhine Falls, continuing along the northern shore of the Lake of Lucerne. Three days of exploration in Paris and 2 days in London bring the trip to an end. **Cost:** $1,162 from London includes transportation, accommodations, food, guide. **When:** June. **Contact:** Study Tours, P.O. Box 1119, Whittier, CA 90609, USA; phone (714)523-3414.

Austria
Austrian Steyermark Bicycling: A 14-day trip begins and ends in Graz. Most of the terrain along the trip is alpine and the hills may prove strenuous for neophyte bikers. Hotel accommodations are prearranged on the journey. Following the trip, a tour of the Salzkammergut follows for interested riders. **Cost:** On request. **When:** June. **Contact:** International Bicycle Touring Society, 2115 Paseo Dorado, La Jolla, CA 92037, USA.   *(M)*

Denmark
Cycling Jutland: Eighteen holiday trips through various Danish terrains provide cyclists with the opportunity to experience a cross section of Danish life. The trips, lasting 3 to 9 days, include visits to Fyn, called the Garden of Denmark, Odense, the home town of Hans Christian Andersen, the fishing hamlet of Lundeborg, Limfjorden with its diverse terrain and Grejs Valley and the fjord-side towns. Cyclists pedal through central Jutland on a trail along the Gudenaen, the longest stream in Denmark, and through a varied scenery that includes moorland plantations and hilly countryside. On another trip, participants may ride into the fields, forests and hills of Mols Bjerge and visit the castles of Clausholm and Rosenholm. On a trip to the southern border area, trip members learn some history of the country by visiting its castles and surrounding farmlands, then pedal along Flensborg Fjord to the marshland, containing large dikes and interesting old towns. The trips can accommodate cyclists with a varying degree of riding skills. **Cost:** $59 to $202 includes accommodations, meals. **When:** June to August. **Contact:** Danish National Tourist Office, 75 Rockefeller Plaza, New York, NY 10019, USA; phone (212)582-2802.

To Hamlet's Castle: A bicycle trip of 2 weeks on historic country roads enables participants to view Scandinavian dairy farms that produce internationally known chees-

On trips in Denmark, cyclists can visit Valdemar Castle, built by King Christian IV in the seventeenth century. (Danish Tourist Board/Eric Betting)

es and to pass through fishing hamlets and old sailors' towns. Cyclists walk and bike through a silent spruce forest where motorized travel is prohibited. Generally, cyclists pedal for 4 or 5 hours each day, with occasional stopovers for a day of individual activity and exploration. Participants also visit the setting of Shakespeare's *Hamlet,* Kronborg Castle, which presents a commanding view across the sound to Sweden 2 miles away. In addition, there are opportunities to view manor houses, monasteries, royal palaces, the changing of the guard and a prehistoric settlement reconstructed at Lejre. The wide beaches of Frederiksvaerk present cyclists with a close-up view of fjords and an opportunity to swim or sunbathe. The trip ends at Tivoli Gardens. **Cost:** $995 from New York includes meals. **When:** July. **Contact:** The Biking Expedition Inc., P.O. Box 547, Hall Ave., Henniker, NH 03242, USA; phone (603)428-7500; summer, Rt. 2, Hillsboro, NH 03244, USA; phone (603)478-5783.

England

Cornish Cycling: A 9-day trip is

based in the coastal town of St. Ives, Cornwall. An artist's colony at the tip of the Cornwall peninsula, St. Ives is less than a day's ride from Land's End. Each day a new tour is undertaken, including visits to the Scilly Isles, to Penzance and along the rocky and stormy coast. **Cost:** About $20 a day from St. Ives includes lodging, food. **When:** April. **Contact:** International Bicycle Touring Society, 2115 Paseo Dorado, La Jolla, CA 92037, USA. *(M)*

Cycling Seashores, Moors and Downs: Week-long trips are offered through various English landscapes, giving participants ages 11 to 15 a chance to explore areas as diverse as the southern coastline, the mountains of Wales and the university town of Oxford in the heart of England. In one trip beginning at the mouth of the Wye, cyclists move north to St. Briavel's Castle, an old Norman stronghold which has been renovated as a hostel for travelers. Leaving the Wye, the route winds into the Brecon Beacons and Black Mountains before returning to the river at Stauton-on-Wye where the trip ends. The North Downs and orchard areas of Kent offer fine cycling country on another trip beginning in Edenbridge Town. Trip members visit the historic city of Canterbury and finish the journey at Kemsing, a hostel situated along the ancient Pilgrims Way. In the north of England, participants can take part in a trip that combines the wide expanses of the North Yorkshire Moors National Park with the rugged cliffbound coastline. Starting from York, the route heads north and eastward to Malton, then crosses the Moors to Saltburn on the coast. Turning south along the coast, trip members cycle to Boggle Hole and Scarborough where they conclude the trip. Additional trips are available in the Yorkshire Dales National Park, the region of Suffolk and the South Downs. **Cost:** $77 includes accommodations, meals, sleeping bag, guide. **When:** July, August. **Contact:** YHA Adventure Holiday, Trevelyen House, St. Albans, Herts., Great Britain; phone St. Albans 55215.

France

Bicycling Le Paysage: The French countryside provides the backdrop for a 2- to 3-week cycling trip along 500 miles of rolling, winding roads. The ride is geared to any cyclist; fast riders may race while slower riders may enjoy the scenery at a more leisurely pace. The journey is scheduled to cover about 35 miles each day. Bicycling on lightly traveled roads through fields, forests, farms and vineyards, participants visit several of France's museums and cathedrals. The route passes through Chartres, Blois, Tours, Mont-Sur-Guesnes, Chateaudun and Versailles before a return to Paris. **Cost:** $1,185 from New York includes transportation, hotel accommodations, most meals. **When:** May. **Contact:** Bike Tour France, P.O. Box 1392, Charlotte, NC 28232, USA; phone (704)332-8265.

Germany

Teutonic Trails: Easy biking is found on the back roads of Germany and Austria on a 2-week trip from Heidelberg to Salzburg. The journey begins with transportation from Frankfurt Airport by the same bus which carries group gear along the way to Austria. Among the sights seen during the journey are the Neckar River, various vineyards and castles, and the sinuous Jagst River. Cyclists are encouraged to take individual side trips and are provided with detailed road maps for that purpose. Accommodations are in local hotels near Heidelberg, Rothenburg, Munich, Bad Wimpfen and Krautheim; meals are taken at local restaurants and village inns. Other highlights of the journey include visits to the Deutsches Museum, Alte Pinakothek and other local cultural centers. **Cost:** $495 from Frankfurt includes bus transportation, hotels, most meals. **When:** July. **Contact:** Gerhard's Bicycle Odysseys, 1137 SW Yamhill, Portland, OR 97205, USA; phone (503)223-5190. *(M)*

Ireland

Pedaling through Killarney: Bicyclists travel winding back roads through the green countryside from County Claire to Dublin on a 13-day trip. The terrain is gentle for most of the journey that takes participants from deep bays and rocky cliffs to wild moorlands and quiet inland towns of thatched roof cottages, interspersed with castles, monastic ruins and Stone Age remains. The group cycles through such towns as Limerick, Tralee, the fishing village of Dingle, Killarney and the seaport of Cork, and cyclists may even stop to kiss the Blarney Stone. Plenty of time is allowed for exploring historic sites among the villages and moors. Participants stay at farmhouses and inns and it is recommended that they bring their own bikes, though rentals are available. **Cost:** $300 from Shannon includes guide, accommodations, some meals. **When:** June. **Contact:** REI Adventure Travel, 1525 11th Ave., Seattle, WA 98122, USA; phone (206)322-7800.
(M)

Netherlands

Biking amid Windmills: The extensive system of cycle paths in the land of windmills, canals and tulips provides participants on a 16-day bicycle trip with quiet views of storybook countryside. The trip originates in Amsterdam and includes periodic free days which enable bikers to travel individually and follow personal pursuits along the way. Bikers pass dikes and

polders and pedal along dunes and fine beaches of the coastline in addition to traveling through inland forests. Towns visited include Delft, a 17th-century town, Alkmaar, famed for its cheese auctions, and Rotterdam, a thriving seaport. Cyclists pedal no more than 4 or 5 hours a day on the generally flat terrain. Participants have time to explore the castles, cathedrals and crafts stalls during much of the trip. **Cost:** $429 from Amsterdam includes meals, accommodations, guide. **When:** August to September. **Contact:** The Biking Expedition Inc., P.O. Box 547, Hall Ave., Henniker, NH 03242, USA; phone (603)428-7500; summer, Rt. 2, Hillsboro, NH 03244, USA; phone (603)478-5783.

Switzerland

Countryside Cycling: A 2-week bicycling trip through the market towns and historic villages of Switzerland and France begins on the Swiss side in Lausanne. After a brief orientation session, the cyclists head for France via Nyons and Geneva, passing through vineyards, orchards and forests. Despite the mountainous terrain, flat routes are followed wherever possible and the group never travels more than 31 miles a day. There is plenty of time for taking unplanned excursions and meeting the local people. Upon returning to Switzerland, the group spends a few days exploring the towns of Interlaken and Lucerne by bike and bus. Nights are spent in hotels. **Cost:** $495. **When:** May through October. **Contact:** Directions Unlimited, 344 Main St., Mt. Kisco, NY 10549, USA; phone (914)241-1700.

Bicycling through Wine Country: Equipped with bicycles, partici-

Cyclists travel back roads through small German towns en route to Rothenburg on a trip offered by Gerhard's Bicycle Odysseys. (Gerhard Meng)

pants pedal along country lanes through several vineyards, including Le Cote and Chablis, during a 5-day trip originating in Lausanne. Bikers round Lake Geneva, following a varied route visiting both Swiss and French cities including Geneva, Lausanne, Montreux and Evian-les-Bains. Participants cycle a grand total of 118 miles averaging about 20 miles each day. Visits are made to the Roman and medieval town of Nyons, Hermance, the medieval village of Yvoire where fresh lake fish is the specialty, Thonon-les-Bains, the fishing villages of Tourronde and Meillerie and St. Gingolph on the Swiss border. The final day of the trip covers 22 miles and includes a steep climb shortly after leaving Vevey. Accommodations are in hotels. **Cost:** $292 from Lausanne includes accommodations, bike rentals, guide, breakfast. **When:** May to October. **Contact:** Welcome Swiss Tours, 7 Ave. Benjamin-Constant, 1003 Lausanne, Switzerland; phone (021) 20 68 21.

PACIFIC

Hawaii

Biking around the Islands: Cyclists explore the islands of Oahu, Kauai, Maui and Hawaii during a 38-day trip to the Hawaiian islands. Participants fly from San Francisco and begin the journey in Oahu with enough time for swimming, surfing and canoeing in coastal waters. Amid the steep sands and silent craters, participants slide down the sands and shoot over Waipahee lava tube into a pool of cold water 18 feet below. In the interior areas, bikers discover dense jungles, sugar cane plantations, waterfalls and fern forests. Aboard a riverboat, trip members ride up the Wailua River to Fern Grotto and then travel by van through Haleakala National Park past the crater's peaks and cinder cone floor to Hana Bay. **Cost:** $950 from San Francisco includes accommodations, food, transportation; $50 emergency fund. **When:** June, July. **Contact:** American Youth Hostels, National Campus, Delaplane, VA 22025, USA; phone (703)592-3271.

Cycling around the Big Island: Bicyclists travel about 400 miles around the Big Island during a 2-week trip that includes visits to black sand beaches and colorful orchid fields. The route provides a variety of terrain, ranging from flat areas to moderate grades. Participants visit active volcanoes, Akaka Falls, Puna Lava Flows and Puukohola Heiau (Temple of Old Hawaii). Cyclists learn about the history of the island people and find time for visits with local residents. Accompanied by a sag wagon, participants carry minimal loads during the ride. Adequate repair parts, tools and mechanics are available throughout the trip. Seven nights are spent camping, with another 6 nights spent in hotels and cabins. Participants should supply their own bicycles and helmets, but bike rentals are available. **Cost:** $375 from Hilo includes accommodations, meals. **When:** Year-round. **Contact:** Bicycle Tours—Hawaii, c/o Pacific Sports Products, 110 Alae St., Hilo, HI 96720, USA; phone (808)961-6936.

SOUTH AMERICA
Peru

Pedaling Peru: While bicycling on paved mountain roads around Cajamarca and Huaraz, participants visit local villagers and Peruvian bikers. The 21-day trip begins with a flight to Peru from Miami or Los Angeles then continues with some cruising on the Peruvian coast to view pre-Incan ruins such as Chan Chan. Biking on quiet roads through the foothills of the Andes, participants climb to mountain villages by one of 2 routes. One loop reaches Cajamarca at approximately 9,000 feet before returning to the coast by another road. Another route passes through the Cordillera Blanca and reaches Huaraz at 10,140 feet. Along the route participants sleep in moderately priced hotels, private homes or school houses, or camp out. **Cost:** $890 from Peru includes guide, accommodations, food, camping equipment. **When:** July, August. **Contact:** Andean Outfitters, P.O. Box 4547, Aspen, CO 81611, USA; phone (303)925-3371.
(M)

UNITED STATES

Bicycling across the Border: A 35-day trip for young people over 14 begins in the town of Springfield, Massachusetts and ends in Boston. Cyclists travel through the Green Mountains of Vermont to the Canadian border. Along the way, a variety of activities is experienced including antique auctions and county fairs. Participants learn about local crafts. Once in Quebec, the group turns east through French-Canadian villages, heading toward Montreal; outdoor concerts and a French picnic on the Plains of Abraham in Quebec City are among the highlights. Cyclists then return to New England and the White Mountains of New Hampshire where they see a variety of waterfalls, gorges and panoramic landscapes. Before continuing down along the Atlantic coast, travelers pause to swim in Lake Winnipesaukee and pick wild blueberries in North Conway. Participants then visit historic houses at Strawberry Banke and the saltwater beaches of Gloucester and Newburyport. **Cost:** $500 from Springfield includes hostel accommodations, food, accident and health insurance, group leaders; $50 for emergency fund. **When:** June, July. **Contact:** American Youth Hostels, National Campus, Delaplane, VA 22025, USA; phone (703)592-3271.

Bluegrass Bicycling: Adventurers examine the history of the nation's capital before heading west along the Potomac for a cycling journey of 28 days. The group travels 40 to 55 miles a day, camping together and sharing food preparation and dishwashing. Cyclists explore the Chesapeake and Ohio Canal, Harpers Ferry, the caverns of the Shenandoah Valley and the hiking trails of Skyline Drive. As the group reaches the Appalachians, the land is characterized by steep hills, high ridges and narrow valleys. Participants learn about the customs and cultures of the Appalachian mountain people at roadside museums along the Blue Ridge Parkway and by viewing the people and lifestyles en route through the Cumberland Plateau in Virginia and Kentucky.

Cyclists can camp on the beach after riding along the coasts of Hawaii, the San Juan Islands or southern England. (American Youth Hostels)

In the Virginia Highlands, participants see a region of twisting back roads, footstomping banjo and fiddle music and mountain crafts. After traveling 821 miles with 5 rest days along the way, participants conclude the trip in the Bluegrass region of Kentucky. **Cost:** $320 includes food, leader, camping fees. **When:** June to August. **Contact:** Bikecentennial, P.O. Box 8308, Missoula, MT 59807, USA; phone (406)721-1776. *(M)*

Western Wheeling: After a few short practice runs in Wisconsin and South Dakota bikers embark on a 40-day tour of parks in the western United States. Yellowstone and Grand Teton national parks mark the beginning of the challenge as group members bike and camp their way west. Lake Tahoe or Yosemite Valley are next on the agenda—2 difficult areas which test a biker's skill and endurance. The trip is rounded off by sightseeing in San Francisco, Los Angeles and spots in Mexico, with bike tours into remote areas. The Grand Canyon, the Navajo Indian Reservation, Zion and Bryce Canyon national parks and the foothills of the Rockies complete the excursion. **Cost:** $1,347 includes use of bikes, camping equipment. **When:** July. **Contact:** North American Tour-a-Camp, Rockland County YMCA,

P.O. Box 581, Nyack, NY 10960, USA; phone (914)358-0919.

Alabama

Southern States Bike Trip: A 2-week bike trip rolls along from Montgomery to Mobile in the first week. The second week finds bikers taking a jaunt from Pensacola to Navarre; then the group heads back to Mobile. Accommodations are provided in hotels along the way, and some food is included. **Cost:** On request. **When:** March, April. **Contact:** International Bicycle Touring Society, 2115 Paseo Dorado, La Jolla, CA 92037, USA. *(M)*

Colorado

Cycling through the Mountains: A trip beginning and ending in Durango wanders for 7 days through mountainous terrain, stopping overnight in various mining towns and resort areas. Before the cycling gets underway, participants begin the excursion with a ride on the narrow-gauge train from Durango to Silverton. From there the route leads over alpine trails through the Uncompahgre and San Juan national forests, into Montezuma Valley and finally to Mesa Verde National Park where group members can explore the area's prehistoric cliff dwellings. Cyclists cover 25 to 30 miles a day, with 2 days of 50-mile rides; if the pace proves too much for some cyclists, a sag wagon is available for rest periods. Participants must provide their own 10-speed bikes. **Cost:** $250 includes accommodations, most meals, map book, guides. **When:** July. **Contact:** Bike Dream Tours,

Inc., P.O. Box 20653, Houston, TX 77025, USA; phone (713)771-1172. *(M)*

Indiana

Covered Bridge Bike Tours: Parke County offers maps and descriptions of bicycle routes through its covered bridge area. Routes are mapped out in 5-mile, 18-mile and 32-mile segments. Bikers may see many of the 36 covered bridges remaining in the area, as well as the restored turn-of-the-century town, old coal mining towns, chapels, old mills and the Little Raccoon and Wabash valleys. The bridges are built with Burr arches, and many have windows through which 19th-century travelers saw oncoming traffic. **Cost:** Free. **When:** Year-round. **Contact:** Parke County, Inc., P.O. Box 165, Rockville, IN 47872, USA; phone (317)569-5226.

Kentucky

Bluegrass Bicycle Run: Acres of rolling blue hills, thoroughbred horse farms and fields of aromatic tobacco comprise the setting for a 12-day trip on the 420-mile Kentucky loop. From Lexington, cyclists head west across the outer edge of the Bluegrass region, stopping at Knobs State Park and the Lincoln homestead in Bardstown. Journeying on through the countryside, travelers spend at least 1 full day seeing historical sites in Harrodsburg, founded in 1774 as the first English settlement west of the Allegheny Mountains. To add to an appreciation of the mountain culture and heritage, the trip pauses at Pleasant Hill, home of restored Shaker colony, and Berea, where a century-old college serves

Appalachian youth. The eastern side of the loop is formed by the scenic Daniel Boone National Forest. Here a side trip to the Natural Bridge State Park or a jaunt into the Red River Gorge's hiking trails and nature walks provides a change of pace. After the return to Lexington, a visit to the Kentucky State Horse Park, with descriptions of the history of the horse and its importance to the region, is recommended. **Cost:** $190 for camping, $270 for hotel/motel accommodations includes meals, maps, guides, transportation from Lexington. **When:** May to September. **Contact:** Bikecentennial, P.O. Box 8308, Missoula, MT 59807, USA; phone (406)721-1776. *(M)*

Clincher tires are recommended for touring because of their low cost, durability and ease of repair. (Northwest Bicycle Touring Society/Paul Boyer)

Maine
Cycling Camden and Castine:
Some of the villages in the Penobscot Bay region date back to the early 1600s when the French and English first arrived on the northern coastline. Cyclists explore the area during weekend and weeklong guided and unguided tours which include overnight accommodations at inns overlooking the bay. On one of the weekend trips, participants take a ferry from Rockland to Vinalhaven Island, the site of a fishing village 11 miles off the coast; both days are spent on the island, which is famous for its huge granite quarries. Other 2-day trips are based in Camden and Castine. On the latter trip, the Blue Hill Peninsula gives more seasoned cyclists a chance to experience difficult biking terrain. The week-long trip also begins in Castine; trip members explore the Castine Peninsula for a day, then cycle to Sargentville on

Long-distance tours can take their toll on bicycles. A tool kit is a necessity for repairs and quick adjustments. (Infinite Odyssey)

the Blue Hill Peninsula where a country inn serves as a base for day excursions over the 250 miles of roadway in the area. Routes vary in difficulty from novice to expert, and cyclists are given opportunities to explore on their own. **Cost:** $90 to $200 includes some meals, guides, maps, accommodations. **When:** On request. **Contact:** Overland Rolls, P.O. Box 4134, Sta. A, Portland, ME 04101. *(M)*

Sail and Cycle: Group members depart from Camden harbor early Monday morning aboard a sailboat equipped with gear, food and bicycles. The next week is spent in the Penobscot Bay area, where participants arrange their own relaxed itineraries; bikes can be taken ashore on either the islands or the coast for exploring excursions along the roadways of the Blue Hill Peninsula, Vinalhaven Island and Isle au Haut. All of the islands provide excellent hiking trails and participants can swim either from the islands or the sailboat. Camp is pitched ashore on some nights, with a special lobster bake arranged during one of the island layovers. Cyclists of all abilities may participate and groups are limited to no more than 10. **Cost:** $275 from Camden includes boat, crew, guide, accommodations on board, meals. **When:** On request. **Contact:** Overland Rolls, P.O. Box 4134, Sta. A, Portland, ME 04101, USA. *(M)*

Michigan

Bicycling around the Great Lakes: Participants 14 years and older spend 42 days on bicycle, horseback and in canoes as they visit points along Lake Huron and Lake Michigan. Departing from Detroit, bikers head out along northern Michigan's coastline where a few small towns are set in areas of undeveloped wilderness. A visit is made to Mackinac Island in Lake Huron as well as to forts used during the French and Indian Wars. Group members canoe lakes and spring-fed streams in northern Michigan's forests of Norway pines, then continue west via horseback on a trail ride while bicycles are transported by vehicle. After a ferry ride to Wisconsin, cyclists head down the coast of Lake Michigan, stopping for visits

to Green Bay's railroad museum and to the brewery cave and Clydesdale horse stables in Milwaukee. Some areas of Wisconsin are still rich in European traditions; members travel through both Norwegian and Swiss communities, then pedal eastward to Lake Geneva where they ride a riverboat. The trip ends in Chicago. The cycling pace includes a few 50-mile days and some rough terrain. Cyclists either camp or stay at hostels along the route. **Cost:** $530 includes hostel lodging, food, transportation during the trip, guides; $50 emergency fund. **When:** July, August. **Contact:** American Youth Hostels, National Campus, Delaplane, VA 22025, USA; phone (703)592-3271.

Mississippi

Natchez Trace Bicycle Tour: A 1-week trip takes cyclists to a variety of places in the general region of Jackson. The itinerary is left open to meet the wishes of the group. Cycling is moderate to strenuous in this countryside and the emphasis of the trip is on "Deep South" atmosphere. Visits are made to antebellum mansions, plantations and small villages. Participants spend the nights in campgrounds, hotels or hostels. **Cost:** About $25 to $35 a day covers food, accommodations. **When:** April. **Contact:** International Bicycle Touring Society, 2115 Paseo Dorado, La Jolla, CA 92037, USA. *(M)*

A month-long Biking Expedition trip combines cycling through New England villages with hiking on mountain trails. (Thomas Heavey)

Montana

Clearwater National Forest Bikepack Trip: Experienced cyclists can pedal a 350-mile route for 10 days through Montana and Idaho on roads that range from pavement to packed earth and gravel. Participants experience a combination of bicycle touring and backpacking, with everyone carrying the food supplies and equipment. Starting in Missoula, Montana, cyclists face some steep climbs as well as pine forests, clear streams and a variety of wildlife—regions that Lewis and Clark charted. Bikers camp in Clearwater National Forest in both Idaho and Montana and have 2 rest days to explore according to individual interests. The route is circular and participants return to Missoula to conclude the trip. **Cost:** $155 from Missoula includes food, camping fees, leader. **When:** August. **Contact:** Bikecentennial, P.O. Box 8308, Missoula, MT 59807, USA; phone (406)721-1776. *(M)*

New Hampshire

Exploring Backroads on a Bike: Cyclists explore New England by bicycle, canoe and on foot during a 31-day trip. Starting in New Hampshire, cyclists pedal many of the lightly traveled back roads that cut through the green valleys, quaint villages and small towns of the state. A visit to Lake Sunapee provides travelers with the opportunity to take a side trip to Vermont on the way to Hanover and Dartmouth colleges. Heading into the White Mountain National Forest, participants take a break from cycling and hike mountain trails to the top of Mt. Washington, the highest peak

in the northeast. Group members also visit the White Mountain Festival of Arts as part of the trip. Bikers continue to North Conway and take a 3-day canoe trip on the Saco River into Maine en route to Lake Winnipesaukee. Aboard the Mt. Washington ferry, cyclists cross the lake and continue the journey through rolling woods and farmlands of central New Hampshire. Bikers carry full-load packs and camp along the way. The trip terminates in Boston. **Cost:** $680. **When:** June to August. **Contact:** The Biking Expedition Inc., P.O. Box 547, Hall Ave., Henniker, NH 03242, USA; phone (603)428-7500; summer, Rt. 2, Hillsboro, NH 03244, USA; phone (603)478-5783.

Learning by Cycling: Bicycles provide the primary means of travel for participants in a 3-week outdoor course beginning and ending in Hanover, New Hampshire. Course activities include cycle maintenance and repair, physical conditioning, rock climbing, emergency care and rescue, outdoor living, natural history exploration and a final expedition planned and carried out by students. After leaving Hanover, the tour winds through northern New Hampshire and up into Quebec. Participants are expected to supply their own 10-speed bicycles and cycling helmets. **Cost:** $550 includes accommodations, meals. **When:** July, August. **Contact:** Dartmouth Outward Bound Center, Box 50, Hanover, NH 03755, USA.

New York

Wheeling through Wine Country: A group of 10 to 12 cyclists travels around several of the Finger Lakes

on a 6-day tour through New York's wine region beginning and ending in Watkins Glen. The basic routes average 25 to 40 miles a day but those wishing a more challenging ride can take longer routes of up to 55 miles a day. Shorter rides can be arranged with the sag wagon driver. Though terrain is relatively level along the lakeshore, the land between the lakes is very hilly and offers some real challenges. Accommodations and meals are found in lake resorts and wine producing towns. Additional time may be spent visiting points of interest such as the Glass Center in Corning where workers fashion Steuben crystal by hand, the wineries in Hammondsport and, at the beginning or end of the trip, the group visits underground grottos and 18 waterfalls in Watkins Glen. Sag wagon transfers are available to and from Elmira airport and the Watkins Glen bus station. Scouting of the routes has shown traffic to be minimal. **Cost:** $250 from Watkins Glen or Elmira includes transportation, accommodations, meals, guides, sag wagon. **When:** September. **Contact:** Bike Dream Tours, P.O. Box 20653, Houston, TX 77025, USA; phone (713)771-1172.
(M)

Oregon

Pedaling the West Coast: Starting and ending in Portland, Oregon, cyclists ride 168 miles in 8 days. Participants travel in groups of 8 formed according to accommodation preference. There are several accommodation and meal plans, ranging from camping and preparing meals to hotel and motel accommodations and eating meals in restaurants. All groups follow secondary roads across the Oregon Coast Range to Astoria and traverse some hilly terrain to the coast where they see Ft. Clatsop, the home of early fur traders, and Neahkahnie Mountain, where buried treasure still lies according to Indian lore. The pace is leisurely and with a rest day participants have plenty of time for exploring, swimming and hiking. Bicycling ends in Tillamook where participants catch a bus for the return trip to Portland. **Cost:** $130 to $275 from Portland depending on accommodations and meal plan includes leader, guidebook, maps, transportation, bike shuttle from Portland. **When:** July to September. **Contact:** Bikecentennial, P.O. Box 8308, Missoula, MT 59807, USA; phone (406)721-1776.
(M)

Tennessee

Tennessee Two-Wheeler: A week-long autumn tour through the backcountry of Tennessee offers cyclists the opportunity to see many rural handicrafts and arts close-up. Participants meet at Montgomery Bell State Park about 50 miles south of Nashville on a Saturday afternoon and return on Sunday a week later. The route follows back roads and trails resplendent with fall colors. Generally 45 to 65 miles a day are covered through hilly terrain; a transport vehicle accompanies the group for those wishing shorter rides. Visits are made to numerous small towns to watch quiltmakers, listen to local stories and sample the area's famous pies. There is little traffic in the area and accommodations are in small inns and hotels along the way. **Cost:** $250 from Montgomery Bell includes accommodations, most meals, map book, guide. **When:** October. **Contact:** Bike Dream Tours, Inc., P.O. Box 20653, Houston, TX 77025, USA; phone (713)771-1172. *(M)*

Texas

Two Texas Trips: Two bicycling trips through the hill country of Texas are offered: one through the wildflower area of central Texas and the other from San Antonio to the Mexican border. The first trip, lasting 4 days, originates and ends in La Grange, 85 miles west of Houston. Spring brings as many as 40 different wildflowers to this area dotted with Czech and German villages, historic sites and local fairs such as the Winedale Festival. Riders travel 40 to 45 miles a day for 3½ days, with optional routes ranging up to 60 miles over relatively easy terrain. The second trip is a week's tour through Alamo country, beginning and ending in San Antonio. The countryside has dramatic canyonlands laced with rivers, followed by the hilly Pecos region near the Mexican border. Flowering cactus, wildflowers and a wide variety of bird life are evident on the trip. Between 45 and 65 miles are covered each day through moderate to challenging terrain. Participants cross the Mexican border at Ciudad Acuna, then return to San Antonio and the United States by bus. Both trips are accompanied by a sag wagon to provide shorter riding days if desired. **Cost:** $150 for central Texas trip; $250 for southern trip includes accommodations, breakfasts and dinners, maps, sag wagon, guide. **When:**

March for central Texas, May for southern trip. **Contact:** Bike Dream Tours, Inc., P.O. Box 20653, Houston, TX 77025, USA; phone (713)771-1172. *(M)*

Vermont

Country Inns by Bicycle: Cyclists tour through Vermont's farmlands and gentle mountain country on self-guided trips of 2 days to 2 weeks and longer, spending nights in a number of the area's historic inns. The most popular trip covers 200 miles in 7 days, beginning at the Churchill House Inn on the western face of the Green Mountains, then following a route which circumscribes the southern half of Vermont. Stopping places include the Kedron Valley Inn in Woodstock, the 1811 House in Manchester and the Tulip Tree Inn, an early 19th-century country home in Chittenden. Cyclists can also tackle shorter tours, such as a weekend 100-miler that takes in Fort Ticonderoga and the Hubarton Battlefield, or a shorter run up through the Champlain Valley. Longer trips of 2 weeks or more can also be organized along variations of the 200-mile route, using the network of country inns for stop-over points along the way. Ten-speed bikes with bags and panniers can be rented for any of the tours. **Cost:** $160 for 7 days includes lodging, breakfast and dinner. **When:** Summer. **Contact:** Churchill House Inn, RFD #3, Rt. 73E, Brandon, VT 05733, USA; phone (802)247-3300. *(M)*

New England Cycling: A variety of bicycle trips, ranging in length from 5 to 28 days, tours rural areas of

Vermont. The 5-day trips visit such areas as the islands of Lake Champlain, maple tree country near the Canadian border, southern Vermont near the Green and Taconic mountains and the northeastern area along the Connecticut River. All these routes are suitable for beginning to intermediate cyclists, with 30 to 45 miles ridden a day during a 4- or 5-hour stretch. A more strenuous 5-day trip, covering 60 to 75 miles a day, is also offered. Longer trips, from 9 to 28 days, cover much of the same territory. On all the trips, each rider or group is given a map and directions and may ride at an individual pace to the next night's stop, generally an informally run country inn with swimming available. **Cost:** $190 to $212, depending on pre- and post-trip arrangements, includes most meals, accommodations, guide. **When:** May to October. **Contact:** Vermont Bicycle Touring, RR 2, Bristol, VT 05443, USA; phone (802)388-4263. *(M)*

Washington

Skagit Country Bicycling: A weekend bicycle tour for cyclists who enjoy flat to moderately rolling terrain begins in the town of La Conner, a small fishing village on the Skagit Flats. Group members gather Friday night to receive route information, then spend Saturday meandering through the flats, an area characterized by old Victorian houses as well as truck and dairy farms. Cyclists ride at their own pace, alone or in small groups.

After spending the night at an inn, participants head north on Sunday toward Bayview State Park on the shores of Padilla Bay, then return to La Conner. Additional routes of slightly greater mileage are available to more experienced riders. A limited number of 3-, 5- and 10-speed bicycles is available for rental. **Cost:** $75 includes lodging, breakfasts and dinners, tour guides. **When:** August. **Contact:** Bicycle Tours Northwest, 6850 48th Ave. NE, Seattle, WA 98115, USA.

Northwest Passage: Bike enthusiasts are invited to spend 1 to 9 days traveling the back roads and main routes of northwestern Washington. The single-day trip is a 50-mile loop in the Skagit and Samish flats area west and north of Mt. Vernon. Those who elect to take a 2-day excursion have a choice: either the 117-mile loop tour from Seattle to Port Townsend and Fort Worden, passing Winslow, Bainbridge Island, Agate Pass and the Olympic Peninsula; or the Mt. Rainier tour, passing from Enumclaw to Paradise, Stevens Canyon and Cayuse Pass. A 3-day excursion takes place on Orcas Island in the San Juan Islands. Participants who elect the 9-day trip bike 450 miles through Washington and British Columbia and visit such points as the Olympic Peninsula, Victoria, the San Juan Islands, Point Roberts, the Fraser River Valley, Whatcom County and Whidbey Island. Accommodations and meals vary for each trip. **Cost:** Upon request.

Cyclists pause for panoramic views of the Cascade Mountains on a cycling trip around Mt. Rainier. (Northwest Bicycle Touring Society/Paul Boyer)

When: May to September. **Contact:** Northwest Bicycle Touring Society, P.O. Box 724, Mercer Island, WA 98040, USA; phone (206)243-1880.

Wisconsin

North/South Biking: Guided bicycle tours designed for novices and intermediate cyclists spend anywhere from 2 days to 2 weeks exploring the roads and countryside in midwestern and southern states from Minnesota to Florida, depending on the season. One of the more unusual trips involves a cruise up the Mississippi River on the historic steamboat *Delta Queen.* Participants start out from La Crosse and disembark at St. Paul after 2 nights on the river, cycling back to La Crosse along riverside roads and spending nights in motels on the route. Other trips in the northern Midwest include a 10-day trip from La Crosse to Kenosha, a 2-day La Crosse historical ride complete with a paddle-wheel boat ride, and a bicycle brewery tour along the Elroy-Sparta Trail. **Cost:** $282 to $373 for *Delta Queen* tour, $58 to $349 for other midwestern trips includes motels, dinners, breakfasts, guides. **When:** May to October for midwest tours, November to March for southern tours. **Contact:** Bicycle Travel Tours, 1025 Green Bay St., La Crosse, WI 54601, USA; phone (608)782-6011.

The Wisconsin Bikeway: A weeklong trip covers the specially designed Elroy-Sparta Trail, which is entirely free of auto traffic and features tunnels and trestle bridges. Six days of mild to moderately challenging biking take riders through hilly countryside dotted with farms and pastures. Some non-biking activities are part of this trip, including a hike in Devil's Lake Park, a boat cruise on the Dells River and a tour of a cheese factory. Overnight stops are made in several old railroad towns and in the Dells resort region. The trip begins and ends in Baraboo, located 40 miles north of Madison, and returns there by bus at the ride's conclusion. Between 25 and 35 miles are covered each day, and shorter rides may be arranged with an accompanying sag wagon. **Cost:** $250 includes accommodation, breakfasts and dinners, maps, activities, sag wagon, guide. **When:** June. **Contact:** Bike Dream Tours, Inc., P.O. Box 20653, Houston, TX 77025, USA; phone (713)771-1172.

(M)

Bicycling the Badger State: Young people between the ages of 13 and 17 bicycle through Wisconsin for 31 days. The emphasis of the trip is on the group experience and participants prepare and plan all the meals as well as set up camp every day. The group meets in Madison and moves on to the rolling terrain of Green County, famed for its cheeses, Swiss architecture and Old World customs. Following the old railroad bed on the Sugar River Trail, cyclists pass patchwork farmland, outcroppings of rock and caves and a wildlife refuge. On the Wisconsin River, the group has opportunities for canoeing or hiking remote trails. The group bikes the Elroy-Sparta Trail, an abandoned rail line with 33 trestle bridges and 3 tunnels cut through wooded hills. After seeing the Mississippi

River cyclists circle back through Baraboo to the Wisconsin Dells and conclude the trip in Madison. **Cost:** $685 includes guides, meals, camping equipment, accommodations. **When:** June, July. **Contact:** The Biking Expedition Inc., P.O. Box 547, Hall Ave., Henniker, NH 03242, USA; phone (603)428-7500; summer: Rt. 2, Hillsboro, NH 03244, USA; phone (603)478-5783.

RESOURCES

Clubs and Associations

Alliance Sportive du Quebec
11652 Alfred Laliberte
Montreal, PQ Canada H3M 1Y3

Amateur Bicycle League of America
Box 669, Wall St. Sta.
New York, NY 10005, USA

American Youth Hostels
National Campus
Delaplane, VA 22025, USA
Phone (703)592-3271

The Association of Cycle
and Lightweight Campers
30 Napier Wy.
Wembley, Middlesex HA0 4UA
Great Britain

Bicycle Manufacturers Association
1101 15th St. NW
Washington, DC 20005, USA
Phone (202)452-1166

Bicycle Touring League
260 W. 260th St.
New York, NY 10471, USA

Canadian Cycling Association
333 River Rd.
Vanier City, ON Canada K1L 8B9
Phone (613)746-5753

Central Indiana Bicycling Club
5304 Crown
Indianapolis, IN 46208, USA

The Countrywide Holidays Assn.
Birch Heys, Cromwell Range
Manchester M14 6HW, Great Britain

The Cyclists Touring Club
69 Meadrow
Godalming, Surrey GU7 3HS
Great Britain

Elkhart Bicycles Club
301 S. Main
Elkhart, IN 46514, USA

Feder. Francaise de Cyclotourisme
8 rue Jean Marie Tego
75013 Paris, France

Friends of Bikeology
1035 E. De La Guerra St.
Santa Barbara, CA 93103, USA

Holiday Fellowship
142 Great North Way, Hendon
London NW4 1EG, Great Britain

International Bicycle Touring Society
2115 Paseo Dorado
La Jolla, CA 92037, USA

Northern Pacific Sports
and Recreation
P.O. Box 2317
Renton, WA 98055, USA

Northwest Bicycle Touring Society
6166 92nd Ave. SE
Mercer Island, WA 98040, USA
Phone (206)232-2694

U.S. Cycling Federation
P.O. Box 669, Wall St. Sta.
New York, NY 10005, USA
Phone (212)344-2808

WILDERNESS SURVIVAL

Many of us have at one time or another felt unable to rely on our own skills in the outdoors. The prospect of facing the unknowns of the wilderness may be enough to frighten many into never leaving their cars as they drive through Arches National Park, the Colorado Rockies or Death Valley. Even the fall of darkness on a weekend camping trip makes the effort to light a fire more hurried. Yet humans have not always been so dependent on the automobile and electric light. Our species' very adaptability is testimony to the survival skills we inherently possess. Those skills are not lost now that we call ourselves civilized. They are merely dormant. Wilderness survival schools attempt to reawaken these abilities, reestablishing our precious link with the natural world.

There are several different types of wilderness survival programs. At its most basic level, there is training of the "Stone Age" school—intense application of plant identification, fire starting and cooking, shelter construction, tool making and even solo wilderness experiences of one to three days. Another type of program concentrates on group behavior; leadership training is emphasized, with group members organizing and carrying out their own short expeditions at the end of month-long outdoor schools. And the third type of program is for the photographers and naturalists who want to journey from civilization and immerse themselves in the wilderness for intensive study of their art or interest.

Many wilderness survival courses offer training in a wide variety of adventure travel activities. You might learn canoeing in Minnesota, borrowing techniques from the Ojibway Indians who lived there for thousands of years; or skiing in Wyoming, learning how to identify avalanche hazards; or river rafting in Colorado, mountaineering in Idaho or horsepacking in Alberta. These courses differ from the ordinary adventure trip, however, in that the emphasis is on making your own decisions, relying on the skills that you have learned and drawing upon your inner resources to strengthen your self-reliance.

Nearly all such programs place the highest value on minimum impact camping, ecological awareness and integration with the environment. So whether you are learning to cope with the aridity and heat of the deserts of Utah, acclimatizing to the altitude and cold of the Arrigetch Peaks in Alaska, or orienteering and rock climbing in the mountains of Colorado, the wilderness survival experience will renew your primal contact with the world around you. You may begin such a course fragmented, uncertain, even fearful; but you will emerge amazed at your own abilities to learn, adapt, and survive. ☐

A student learns to ascend a fixed rope on an iceface. Mt. Baker Guide Service offers instruction in alpine survival skills. (Dunham Gooding/North Cascades Alpine School)

Wilderness Survival

CANADA

Alberta

Indian Wilderness Experience: Young people spend 12 days on the Stoney Indian Reserve located between Calgary and Banff. Here they learn traditional crafts including tepee construction and leather work. Horsemanship is emphasized, as well as self-reliance and wilderness survival techniques. Backpacking and horsepacking trips are made into the surrounding area, penetrating rugged terrain where participants may observe moose, deer, bighorn sheep, buffalo and wild horses. Special guides have been selected to instruct participants on Indian ways of coping with the wilderness, with an emphasis on minimum environmental impact. Campers learn how to identify edible and medicinal plants and how to recognize animal trails and weather indicators. **Cost:** $275 includes meals, accommodations,

The Yukon's Kluane National Park is the base for two weeks of wilderness travel offered by Canatrek for $530. (Yukon Dept. of Tourism)

equipment, transportation to and from Calgary. **When:** June to September. **Contact:** Stoney Wilderness Center, Box 204, Exshaw, AB Canada T0L 0C0; phone (403)881-3049.

Yukon Territory

St. Elias Wilderness Exploration: Kluane National Park is the base for 2 weeks of backpacking and mountaineering in the Canadian wilderness. Following a bus trip from Whitehorse in the Yukon Territory to Kluane Lake, participants set up base camp. No specific itinerary is followed for the remainder of the trip so that participants may take advantage of terrain and weather conditions to plan their own expeditions. Possible day and overnight outings for mountaineers include ascents of nearby Mt. Wallace, Outpost Mountain and Mt. Cairns. Backpackers may hike around Vulcan Mountain by following a route along the Slims River Valley to the foot of the Kaskawulsh Glacier, continuing east along the Kaskawulsh River, north to the Jarvis River and back. During the excursions, there are opportunities to observe and photograph wildlife which inhabit the park, such as moose, Dall sheep and lynx. **Cost:** $530 includes guides, food, accommodations, transportation. **When:** August. **Contact:** Canatrek Mountain Expeditions, P.O. Box 1138, AB Canada T0L 0C0; phone (403)762-3143. *(M)*

EUROPE

Sweden

Wilderness Training: During a 3-week wilderness training seminar, participants prepare for a survival test in which groups of 4 set out on a pre-planned route using their survival skills and eating only what nature provides. The rations during the training period, consisting of fish, plants and berries, are gradually cut back in preparation for the test. Equipment is provided for the test, and instructors wait on call in Kvikkjokk. At the high mountain camp instruction addresses the more difficult tasks of emergency bivouacking, first aid and self-reliance. Training is adapted to each participant's needs. **Cost:** On request. **When:** August. **Contact:** IWT Survival, Fjallstation Kvikkjokk, 96045 Kvikkjokk, Sweden.

Switzerland

Alpine Educational Expedition: A comprehensive educational program in the Swiss Alps is designed for high school students. The 22-day backpacking expedition begins in the village of Lauterbrunnen with several days of preparation and orientation. Conditioning sessions and the use and care of equipment are taught, as well as first aid, trail safety, and map reading. En route hikers sleep in tents and study the geology and biology of the Alps. Each day's study may vary from how to choose a campsite to how to identify local flora and fauna to when and how to build a snow cave. Alpine farming, ecology, wilderness ethics and the history of mountain climbing are also discussed. Toward the end of the trek, there is intensive training in knot and rope handling, mountain safety and rescue, rock climbing, belaying, rappelling and the use of

Muir Glacier juts out into Glacier Bay, Alaska. Many wilderness training courses are available in the 49th state. (Keith Gunnar)

ice ax and crampons. After returning to Lauterbrunnen Valley, students attempt a climb of the Breithorn, a 12,000-foot peak. Though the climb is not hazardous, it challenges the alpine skills learned during the trek. **Cost:** $1,095. **When:** July, August. **Contact:** Earth Journeys, 3400 Peachtree Rd., Atlanta, GA 30326, USA; phone (404)231-0073. *(M)*

UNITED STATES

Alaska

Camping on Alaskan Peaks: Participants spend 2 weeks in the Arrigetch Peaks of Alaska's Brooks Range. Campers fly in to an established base camp, with an open itinerary allowing for day hikes or extended trips into the surrounding area. Much of the Brooks Range is still unexplored and untouched, and wildlife abounds, including wolves, lemmings, grizzly bears, caribou and bird life. Fall colors are already out, and opportunities for photography are ample. Participants fly out at trip's end. **Cost:** $620 includes transportation, meals, equipment, guide. **When:** August. **Contact:** Aurora Borealis Expeditions, P.O. Box 9266, Missoula, MT 59807, USA. *(M)*

Alaska Wilderness Camping: Individual or group camping is provided in the remote areas of the Kenai Peninsula, an area first settled in the 1890s by homesteaders and now left to its first inhabitants—

black bears, moose, mountain goats, eagles and other wildlife. From Homer campers are flown into a lakeside lodge where guided and unguided hikes are planned. Depending upon the arrangements of each particular trip, members may pack in their own food and equipment or may be provided with all camping necessities. Trips are available into nearby ice caves and to mountain meadows above the timberline. **Cost:** $30 a day includes camp facilities; $50 includes guide service; food and camp gear provided upon arrangement. **When:** June to October. **Contact:** Kachemak Bay Wilderness Lodge, China Poot Bay, Homer, AK 99603, USA; phone (907)235-8910. *(M)*

Arctic Wildlife Camps: Wilderness youth camps are located on the southeastern slope of the Brooks Range, near the Arctic National Wildlife Range. This area is without human-made structures, roads, trails or vehicles. A base camp and 8 permanent outlying camps ranging in distance from 2 to 18 miles from the base are open to youths 9 years old and up for 10 days or more. Camp staff and leaders train and assist campers in wilderness travel and living, which may include plant and animal identification, pack dog handling, mountain navigation, arctic ecosystems and guiding techniques. An 85-mile canoe trip on an Alaskan river is available for more experienced campers. The region, which has never been permanently inhabited by people, is rich in wildlife. **Cost:** $70 a day includes all expenses upon arrival at base camp. **When:** June to September. **Contact:** Wilderness Wildlife Camps, c/o El Rancho Motel, SR 60338, Fairbanks, AK 99701, USA; phone (907)488-2983. *(M)*

California

Tahoe Wilderness Course: Over the course of 14 days in California, a small group undergoes intensive training in leading wilderness expeditions. In the Tahoe National Forest, part of the Sierra Nevada Range, an experienced climber and guide provides instruction in outdoor skills and arranges special situations for testing participants' abilities. Activities include climbing high peaks, finding routes and leading the group through the wilderness. Emphasis is placed on low

environmental impact. The minimum age is 14. **Cost:** $225 includes equipment, transportation, food, instruction. **When:** July, August. **Contact:** Mountain People School, 157 Oak Spring Dr., San Anselmo, CA 94960, USA; phone (415)457-3664. *(M)*

Colorado

Outdoor Skills Courses: Seven-day courses provide an intensive introduction to the techniques and practice of technical rock climbing, whitewater river rafting and high alpine mountaineering. Instruction in rock climbing encompasses all aspects from basic knot tying and belaying to steep face climbing and rappelling. Two-day rafting trips on the Arkansas River offer a rigorous introduction to paddling through fast, narrow rapids. The mountaineering expedition attempts to scale a 14,000-foot peak in the Crestone area of the Sangre de Cristo Mountains. Each course is based out of a primitive 800-acre working ranch located at 9,000 feet. Each member is asked to specify personal expectations and goals for the course; progress in meeting these goals is monitored by the instructors and shared with other participants. Whenever possible, responsibility for the planning and organization of activities is handled by a mutual decision-making process. **Cost:** $200 includes instruction, food, equipment. **When:** June to August. **Contact:** Outdoor Leadership Training Seminars, 2220 Birch St., Denver, CO 80207, USA; phone (303)333-7831. *(M)*

Wilderness Photography: Travelers develop skills in nature photography on trips of 5, 10 or 23 days in primitive areas. The journeys are designed to combine studies of the environment with backpacking, survival training and photography. Other possible experiences include whitewater rafting, caving, mountaineering and rock climbing. The 10-day expedition includes 2 days of organization and training at the beginning, then a few days of processing and printing at the end. All courses are geared to each participant's level of experience. All group equipment, including a darkroom setup, is provided; participants must supply their own photographic equipment and basic clothing. **Cost:** $150 for 5 days, $325 for 10 days, $625 for 23 days. **When:** By arrangement. **Contact:** Wilderness Encounter, 720 Grand Ave., Glenwood Springs, CO 81601, USA; phone (303)945-8365. *(M)*

Idaho

Mountain Survival Course: All aspects of mountaineering and outdoor survival are covered in a 21-day course in the Sawtooth Mountains. Skills included are snow and rock climbing, conservation, compass and map reading and search and rescue techniques. Students travel in remote, primitive country without their instructor, sometimes eating only what they can forage from the wilderness. Only average strength is required, but participants should be in good health. **Cost:** $600 includes transportation from Sun Valley, food, some equipment. **When:** June, July, August. **Contact:** EE-DA-HOW Mountaineering, P.O. Box 207, Ucon, ID 83454, USA; phone (208)523-9276. *(M)*

Wilderness Skills Courses in the Rockies: Ten- to 24-day mountaineering, backpacking and rock climbing courses are conducted within the Big Horn Crags portion of the Idaho Primitive Area, a region of high alpine lakes rimmed by precipitous cliffs, crags and spires.

Based at a camp on Panther Creek, students in the 10-day course become familiar with techniques of food preparation, equipment organization, mountain hiking, navigation, basic rock climbing and cross-country travel among the 9,000-foot summits of the primitive area. The 18-day course focuses more on climbing, allowing students to become familiar with the use of chocks, nuts and natural runners as a means of increasing their ability to use natural features in climbing situations; the course also covers expedition dynamics, tyrolean traverses and time control planning. Participants who enroll in the 24-day course study every aspect of backpacking and mountaineering, including the fundamentals of wilderness survival. In the final phase

A wilderness trainee applies nose protection in Alaska. Reflection of light off snow and ice makes such protection necessary. (Hondo Rast and Co.)

of the course, students split up into small groups which plan and execute their own expeditions. **Cost:** $350 for 10 days, $550 for 18 days, $700 for 24 days includes most wilderness gear, food, course tuition, transportation from Salmon to base camp. **When:** June to August. **Contact:** Horizons Unlimited, P.O. Box 147, Pocatello, ID 83201, USA; phone (208)233-9428. *(M)*

Maine

Carter-Mahoosuc Camping: Outdoor enthusiasts ages 16½ and up spend 10 days learning about and experiencing winter camping in the Carter-Mahoosuc Range. The course is divided into 3 sections. In the first, or training phase, participants learn first aid, map and compass work and methods of winter camping. Taking minimal equipment, each student then spends 2 days and nights on a solo outing in the wilderness, practicing newly acquired skills. The group reunites for a final expedition to one of the

highest peaks in the area. **Cost:** $400 includes meals, equipment, accommodations. **When:** January to March. **Contact:** Hurricane Island Outward Bound School, Box 429, Rockland, ME 04841, USA; phone (207)594-5548.

Minnesota

Log Cabin Building: Courses in basic log construction are offered in the Superior National Forest in northeastern Minnesota. During the 9-day session, participants construct a multi-room cabin on a remote lake. Skills taught include tree-felling; skidding; peeling; use of many specialized tools; saddle-notch, chinkless construction methods; and floor, window, door and roof building. Many of the logs are cut near the cabin site. Participants may stay in bunkhouses at Grindstone River Base Camp or at various campsites along the river. Courses in advanced log construction and fireplace construction are also offered. **Cost:** $80 includes tuition, lodging and the use of some tools. **When:** April, May, July. **Contact:** Minnesota Trailbound, Inc., 3544½ Grand Ave., Minneapolis, MN 55408, USA; phone (612)822-5955.

Montana

Winter Mountaineering in the Rockies: Acquisition of winter survival skills is the focus of a 15-day mountaineering course out of Hamilton, Montana. Instruction is given in ski mountaineering, camping, packing and control of body temperature before the expedition moves deeper into the mountains. After establishing camp above treeline, where participants live in snow caves, a summit attempt is made. Team members learn about avalanches, route finding with maps and compasses, winter shelter use, evacuation techniques and first aid. The expedition is rigorous and demanding. **Cost:** $330 roundtrip from Hamilton includes most equipment. **When:** December to March. **Contact:** Hondo Rast and Co., P.O. Box 231, Hamilton, MT 59840, USA; phone (406)363-3440.

(M)

Survival School: A variety of locations provides students of a wilderness survival and mountaineering program with 2 weeks of training and experience. With sites in Colorado, Montana and Wyoming, the school provides students with an insight into primitive areas such as Uncompahgre Primitive Area, Gros Ventre Wilderness, Beartooth Primitive Area, Absaroka Wilderness and Cabinet Mountains. The courses commence with instruction in the fundamentals of wilderness living: navigating by map and compass, selecting a camp, building a safe fire and preparing food. Then instruction is given in the use of climbing rope, climbing knots, belay procedures and techniques in rappelling. Students also learn the use of the ice ax and attempt climbs and belays on steep snow fields. Once the initial basic material is absorbed, students spend the remainder of the course on the move, carrying all their gear individually on the assaults of 14,000-foot peaks. Near the end of the course, students embark on solo survival jaunts without food, where time is available for meditation and exploration of the wildlife, flora and

geology of the area. The course ends with a final group expedition. **Cost:** $350 includes equipment, food. **When:** June to August. **Contact:** The Wilderness Institute, 33 Fairfax, Denver, CO 80220, USA; phone (303)393-0400. *(M)*

New Hampshire

Winter Wilderness Instruction: A 10-day course provides instruction in winter camping and travel, including equipment use, safety procedures, emergency care and rescue, expedition planning, map and compass reading and group interaction. The course emphasizes the development of self-confidence and personal growth. No previous experience is necessary, and instruction is given in all skill areas prior to expeditions. Activities include ski expeditioning, first aid instruction, a 2-day solo outing and a peak ascent. The course is open to anyone 18 and older in good health. **Cost:** On request. **When:** February. **Contact:** Dartmouth Outward Bound Center, Box 50, Hanover, NH 03755, USA.

New York

Wilderness Schooling: Adirondack Park is the site of a boarding school for grades 6 through 9. The physical education program includes instruction in a wide variety of outdoor sports, and the summer program consists largely of wilderness camping in the High Peaks Wilderness, 250,000 acres of wild mountain country in the Santanoni and Seward ranges. During the academic year classes of 1 to 6 students meet 5 days a week, and after students complete a course of study, the school helps to place them in higher academic situations suited to their needs and abilities. **Cost:** On request. **When:** Year-round. **Contact:** Adirondack Mountain School, Long Lake, NY 12847, USA; phone (518)624-3845 or 624-4581.

North Carolina

Challenging Winter Mountaineering: The Great Smoky Mountains and southern Appalachians are the setting for rigorous 3-week courses in winter camping, wilderness survival, climbing, canoeing and caving. Participants also perform some public service at educational and rehabilitative centers. Minimum age for the course is 16½, and a 2-week intensive course is offered for people 18 and older. **Cost:** $625 for 3 weeks, $475 for 2 weeks; some scholarship aid is available. **When:** January. **Contact:** North Carolina Outward Bound School, P.O. Box 817, Morgantown, NC 28655, USA; phone (704)437-6112.

Edible Plants Training: Based in the Cataloochee Cove area of the Smoky Mountains, a 4-day program of leisurely day hikes concentrates on the edible fruits, roots, flowers, leaves and mushrooms of the area. Instruction is provided in recognizing, gathering, preparing and using the foods and medications which grow wild. The ideal time for hunting nature's foods coincides with the end of the nesting season, so the time is good for bird watching as well. Moving from lower elevation forests to a high ridge top with Canadian zone forests of spruce and fir, participants may observe variations in flora and fauna. **Cost:** $60 includes meals, tents, camping fees. **When:** August. **Contact:** Wilderness Southeast, Rt. 3, Box 619 AA, Savannah, GA 31406, USA; phone (912)355-8008. *(M)*

Oregon

Northwest Mountain Trips: Guided ascents of Mt. Washington, Three Fingered Jack, the Three Sisters, Mt. Hood, Mt. St. Helens and Mt. Adams are among the alpine outings offered for both beginning and experienced climbers. Winter survival classes on Mt. Hood cover snowshoeing, igloo and snow cave construction and mountain rescue techniques. Backpacking trips featuring glacial travel and exploration are available into any of the region's wilderness areas. **Cost:** $25 a day for climbs; other costs on re-

quest. **When:** Year-round. **Contact:** Johann Mountain Guides, P.O. Box 19171, Portland, OR 97219, USA; phone (503)244-7672 or 288-1413. *(M)*

Winter Mountaineering in the Wallowas: Cross-country skiing and winter mountaineering are taught in a 20-day survival course in northeastern Oregon. The course begins at Catherine Creek in the Wallowa Mountains with instruction in cross-country skiing and snow camping. Students build igloos and snow caves and learn to use maps and compasses. Then using the skills they have acquired, group members climb one of the peaks in the range. Other features of the course are a solo— where the student is left alone with minimal food and basic shelter— and a day of local community service. The course concludes with a 3-day cross-country ski expedition with minimal instructor supervision. No experience is required. **Cost:** $610 from Pendleton, Oregon. **When:** January, February, March. **Contact:** The Northwest Outward Bound School, 0110 SW Bancroft, Portland, OR 97201, USA; phone (503)243-1993. *(M)*

Pennsylvania

Earth Sports Experiences: During weekends of a 10-month period an outdoor skills program is offered for participants 21 and over, and one annual expedition is made to Africa, Asia, Central or South America departing from base camp at Bear Rock in Acme, Pennsylvania. The program is centered around 14 "Earth Sports" and related affective experiential education, including rock and mountain climbing, winter camping, skiing, canoeing and kayaking, spelunking, parachuting and diving. **Cost:** $135 includes 16 weekends of field trips, skill sessions. **When:** September. **Contact:** Angeda Kimonhon, 205 Sheldon Ave., Pittsburgh, PA 15220, USA; phone (412)276-6953. *(M)*

Utah

Survival Training: One phase of a 24-day seminar emphasizes survival in the wilderness. Participants are placed in an area where they must cope with the tasks of physical survival. Basic skills acquired during the training include first aid, goal setting, meal planning and solo backpacking. Another phase of the program emphasizes personal success experiences: opening interpersonal communication, building self-esteem and decision making. **Cost:** On request. **When:** By arrangement. **Contact:** Outdoor Seminar Retreats, Box 1301, Salt Lake City, UT 84101, USA; phone (801)355-0110. *(M)*

Washington

North Cascades Leadership Course: Based at a high camp in the North Cascades, students learn skills which enable them to introduce others to the mountain environment. The 7-day course includes instruction in minimum impact backpacking, climbing ethics, leadership responsibilities, first aid and basic mountaineering skills

which make for safe mountain travel. Rock and snow climbing as well as an overnight hike are also included; all the activities are designed to show how to bring a group into the wilderness with as little environmental damage as possible. Groups meet in Mazama on the North Cascades Highway before heading into the mountains. **Cost:** $200 includes group equipment, meals, transportation from Mazama, instructors. **When:** June, July, September. **Contact:** Liberty Bell Alpine Tours, Mazama, WA 98833, USA; phone (509)996-2250.

North Cascades Mountain Course: An 8-day course teaches mountaineering in the area around Silver Star Mountain in the North Cascades. Designed for people over 21 who lack the time to take the longer "standard" course, the program is rigorous but physically less demanding than the standard course; lighter packs are used and less hiking is done. The course covers campcraft, backpacking, map and compass navigation, rock climbing, rappelling and snow travel. Participants make use of these skills on a 24-hour solo with minimal supplies and an ascent of a North Cascade peak. **Cost:** $300. **When:** June to August. **Contact:** The Northwest Outward Bound School, 0110 SW Bancroft, Portland, OR 97201, USA; phone (503)243-1993.   *(M)*

West Virginia

Monongahela Forest Trip: A group of 8 to 12 hikers explores wilderness areas in the Monongahela National Forest for 8 days. Each day involves strenuous cross-country hiking designed to challenge experienced backpackers. An expert instructor advises trip members on wilderness problem solving, including first aid, search and rescue, survival and the psychology of climbing. Minimum age for participants is 17. **Cost:** $154 includes transportation, food, gear, maps. **When:** July. **Contact:** Wilderness Trails, 728 Prospect Ave., Cleveland, OH 44115, USA; phone (216)696-5222.

Wyoming

Snowslide Studies: Participants are offered 5 different courses in avalanche research. The first of the 2- to 5-day courses is intended for professional avalanche researchers. Taking place in Jackson Hole, the course involves lectures on snow structure, mechanics, weather forecasting and explosives. Another course designed as an avalanche patrol refresher based in Snowbird, Utah covers metamorphism, post control releases and the use of artillery. A touring course is designed for backcountry travelers and covers topics such as slab recognition, route finding, backcountry rescue and stability evaluation. Advanced Snow Physics is the title of another course; field work consists of digging and plotting snow pits, observation of metamorphosis and snow crystal photography; studies are centered in the Silverton, Colorado region. The final course is a weekend touring expedition held in the Front and Wasatch mountain ranges. **Cost:** $70 to $180 includes course tuition and some technical equipment. **When:** January, February. **Contact:** American Avalanche Institute, Box 308, Wilson, WY 83014, USA; phone (307)733-3315.

Yellowstone Survival Course: Passing silently through forests shrouded in rising steam from underground fumaroles, cross-country skiers can well understand why Yellowstone was holy ground to the Indians. For 15 days participants in a winter travel and survival course explore the region and its natural features, which range from Rocky Mountain peaks to lowland geysers and thermal mud springs. Emphasizing long-distance cross-country skiing, the course provides instruction in technique, waxing, snow physics, cold-weather physiology and avalanche safety. Course topics also include igloo and snow cave construction, expedition planning and emergency procedures. All instruction stresses ecological awareness and minimal impact camping techniques. For the exceptionally hardy there is an extended 21-day version of the course. **Cost:** $425 includes instruction, guides, food, group equipment. **When:** December to March. **Contact:** National Outdoor Leadership School, Box AA, Lander, WY 82520, USA; phone (307)332-4381.

RESOURCES

Clubs and Associations

Canadian Orienteering Foundation
P.O. Box 6206, Terminal
Toronto 1, ON Canada

Larry Dean Olsen Survival Assn.
Box 1301
Salt Lake City, UT 84101, USA

New England Orienteering Club
c/o Bengtsson
Garrison House Ln.
Sudbury, MA 01776, USA

Orienteering Services USA
Box 547
La Porte, IN 46350, USA
Phone (219)326-7462

Rainbow Camp and
Wilderness Survival School
Anaconda, MT 59711, USA

Survival International
36 Craven St.
London WC2N 5NG, Great Britain

United States Orienteering Assn.
933 N. Kenmore St., Suite 317
Arlington, VA 22201, USA

United States Orienteering Federation
P.O. Box 500
Athens, OH 45701, USA

Air Adventures

AIR ADVENTURES

From the myth of Icarus to the footsteps of Neil Armstrong, much of our science and imagination has been possessed by the dream of flight. Now, all of us can feel the lift of the wind, sail over open fields and turn with the grace of a condor, experiencing the wide freedom of our dreams in waking life. All over the world, you can learn the skills of the aeronaut beneath a hang glider, ride thermal updrafts in a sailplane, free fall for a mile before opening your parachute or just float in a gondola beneath a colorful hot air balloon.

The variety of air adventures displays the creativity with which people have taken the leap into the atmosphere. Suspended beneath a nylon wing, hang gliders are lifted aloft on invisible air currents to heights over 1,000 feet above the earth. Gliders have even been launched from locations as elevated as Mont Blanc and Mt. McKinley, but you don't have to go that far—first-flight courses wherever wind conditions are right offer instruction in the theory and techniques of hang gliding.

If a more traditional form of flight appeals to you, many local small craft airports serve as soaring centers. Over 20,000 licensed soaring pilots will take you up in two-person sailplanes from Oahu or Utah to Colorado or Connecticut, as well as in England over the Welsh countryside or in France on the slopes of the Alps. Power plane trips take the curious over such regions as the Arctic and the South Pole, the Florida Everglades, the jungles of Sri Lanka, or along the course of total solar eclipses.

One of the most popular forms of flight is hot air ballooning. This colorful sport has provided thousands of people with a gentle, panoramic lift into the skies above the wine country of California, the lakes of Wisconsin or the farmlands of Virginia. Some operators even offer courses for novices to train for an FCC balloon pilot's license.

Most exciting of all is the adventure of parachuting—leaping from an airplane toward the distant, receptive earth, and reaching terminal velocity of over 120 miles an hour before pulling the ripcord and releasing the life-saving canopy. Instruction is available all across the continent for first-jump courses, and from there you are only a leap of faith away from relative work—combining with other free-fallers in giant geometric patterns hurtling toward the earth.

These opportunities, and many more like them, offer the adventurer the chance to realize the ancient dream of flight, to see the world from a new perspective and to expand the definitions of the possible. And who knows—the day may not be far off when ascents to space stations or even a moon base may extend adventure travel beyond the confines of Spaceship Earth. □

After taking off from a high ridge, a hang glider rides on shifting air currents down to a safe landing. (Keith Gunnar)

BALLOONING

AFRICA
Kenya

Balloon Safari: A safari led by a former zoological administrator of a wildlife park and an experienced African traveler combines a thorough visit to Kenya's major game reserves and cities with a unique opportunity to ride in a hot air balloon over the African plains. The safari lasts 22 days, beginning with 3 days at Meru National Park. The group then travels to the Aberdare Range, the habitat of many of Africa's rarest species. One day is devoted to hiking on the lower slopes of Mt. Kenya before proceeding to Masai Mara Game Reserve. During the stay in the game reserve, group members may ride in a hot air balloon, which gives an entirely new perspective of the land and animals. Lions, cheetahs, antelope, giraffes, wildebeests and zebras predominate in this environment. Leaving the plains, the group travels via steam train to Mombasa and Malindi on the Indian Ocean coast for several days of scuba diving, mini-sailing, water skiing, exploring coral reefs and swimming. After departing from Nairobi, the group spends 1½ days in Copenhagen before returning to Los Angeles. Accommodations throughout the trip are in lodges and tents. **Cost:** $2,695 includes roundtrip airfare from Los Angeles, meals, accommodations, guides. **When:**

Balloonists find rugged mountain scenery at eye level as they float close to snow-covered peaks in the Swiss Alps. (Multimatic A.G.)

July. **Contact:** Plaza Travel Centre, 1121 W. Orangethorpe Ave., Fullerton, CA 92633, USA; phone (714)879-6241.

Ballooning above the Masai Mara: A panorama of the plains in southwest Kenya is afforded during an hour-long balloon flight above the Masai Mara Game Reserve just to the east of the Tanzanian border. Often unaware of the balloon's presence, herds of giraffe, zebra, and wildebeeste can be seen grazing throughout the early morning flight. There are no modern obstructions such as buildings or telephone wires, which makes for a breathtaking view and wonderful photography. The 4-passenger balloon is followed by a ground crew in 2 vehicles. Participants can stay at the Keekorok Lodge on the Masai Mara Reserve. Following the flight, a champagne breakfast is given to the passengers. **Cost:** $125 a person. **When:** Year-round. **Contact:** Alan Root, P.O. Box 43747, Nairobi, Kenya; phone 27217.

EUROPE

France

Ballooning over the Wine Country: Participants travel by motorcoach and hot air balloon through the regions of Champagne, Burgundy and the Loire Valley for 2 weeks during the grape harvest. Balloons are launched from town centers, medieval castles and historic chateaux for 1-hour flights covering 2 to 15 miles. Group members alternate riding in 2-person, professionally piloted balloons with riding in chase vehicles to meet balloonists with champagne as they land; par-

ticipants may choose to remain on the ground throughout the trip. Members stay at hotels along the way. **Cost:** $2,689 includes round-trip transportation from New York, meals, accommodations. **When:** September, October. **Contact:** The Bombard Society, Suite 1823, 30 E. 42nd St., New York, NY 10017, USA; phone (212)697-6230 or toll-free (800)223-7733.

UNITED STATES

Arizona

Balloon Flights over Phoenix: Hot air balloon excursions scheduled to participants' own convenience fly passengers over the Arizona desert. Flights are limited to weekends throughout the winter season. Summer balloon flights in this area are impossible due to high temperatures which don't provide enough contrast to the balloon's hot air to permit it to ascend. For an hour and a half, 1 or 2 persons float over the Phoenix area, participating in flight maneuvers if they wish. **Cost:** $150 for 1½ hours. **When:** October through May. **Contact:** Cat Balloon, 2911 E. Sherran Ln., Phoenix, AZ 85016, USA; phone (602)956-8945.

California

Napa Valley Champagne Flight: Beginning at sunrise, participants help launch a hot air balloon for an hour flight over California's wine country. The aeronaut guides the balloon over vineyards and farmland using "wind sense" and adjusting altitude by changing the air temperature inside the balloon. After a gentle descent to a field or pasture, balloonists are joined by the ground crew for a champagne breakfast. Certified instruction is also offered. **Cost:** On request. **When:** Year-round. **Contact:** Aerostat Renaissance, 1644 Silverado Trail, Napa, CA 94558, USA; phone (707)255-6356 or 255-6863. *(M)*

Balloon Flights and Courses: A variety of balloon activities is provided, ranging from short introductory flights to full training programs. Participants ride in a balloon that, when fully inflated, stands as tall as a 6-story building. On a combined 10-hour ground course and 10-hour flight course aeronauts learn to alter directions and speeds and to accomplish landings. Passengers on a 30-minute flight over the Antelope Valley view wildflowers below and celebrate with champagne after landing. A ground chase crew follows flights in a pickup truck to return balloons and riders to the launch site. **Cost:** $35 for 30-minute flight to $995 for full course. **When:** Year-round. **Contact:** Golden Bear Enterprises, Raven's Roost Balloon Port, 60th St. W. and Ave. K, Quartz Hill, CA 93534, USA; phone (805)943-1313.

Bay Area Ballooning: Participants spend 2 to 3 hours floating above woods and cultivated fields in modern Montgolfier balloons. Navigated by an experienced aeronaut, the balloons take off from San Martin's Winery east of the San Francisco Bay area and, depending on winds and thermal conditions, rise to between 200 and 13,000 feet. Tradition calls for balloonists to carry a bottle of champagne which everyone shares at the end of the ride. **Cost:** $40 a person for a group of 6, $50 a person for 5 or less. **When:** Weekends. **Contact:** Hot Air Unlimited, 137 E. Hamilton Ave., Suite 208, Campbell, CA 95008, USA; phone (408)379-2122.

Colorado
Wilderness by Land and Air: Travelers spend 6 days hiking and ballooning through the La Garita Wilderness of south-central Colorado. After 2 nights at a ranch resort in Del Norte, participants journey deep into the wilderness by jeep and then by foot. Then 3 days are spent wandering through the wilderness area at a leisurely pace. The guides instruct hikers on various aspects of survival training as progress is made along the trail. The group is met on the fourth day by balloonists who take members out of the mountains and high over the San Luis Valley some 10 miles downwind. A chase team meets the balloons as they touch down, and the group drives back to Del Norte for a final afternoon and evening of relaxing at the resort. The ballooning takes place only in good weather, which occurs most of the season. **Cost:** $410 to $430 includes lodging, meals, gear, guides.

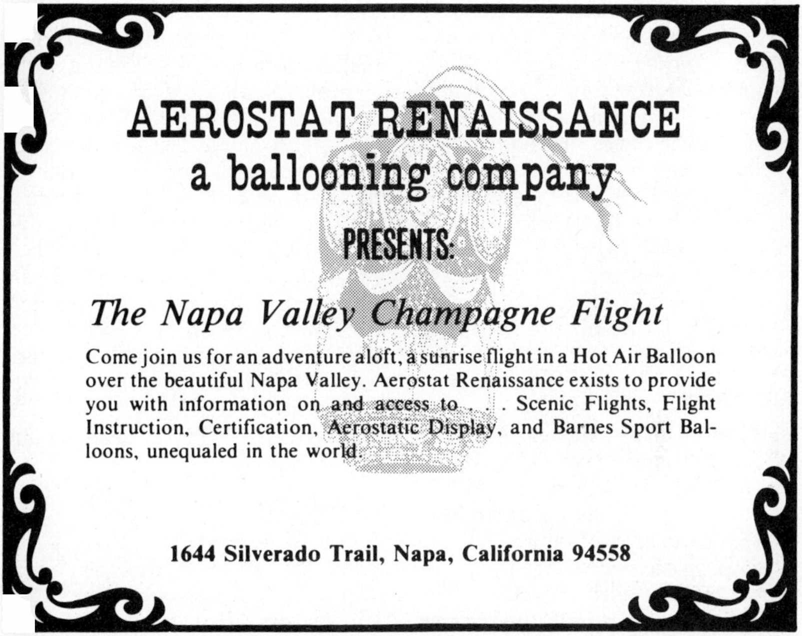

AEROSTAT RENAISSANCE
a ballooning company

PRESENTS:

The Napa Valley Champagne Flight

Come join us for an adventure aloft, a sunrise flight in a Hot Air Balloon over the beautiful Napa Valley. Aerostat Renaissance exists to provide you with information on and access to . . . . Scenic Flights, Flight Instruction, Certification, Aerostatic Display, and Barnes Sport Balloons, unequaled in the world.

1644 Silverado Trail, Napa, California 94558

When: June to September. **Contact:** American Wilderness Experience, 753 Paragon Dr., Boulder, CO 80303, USA; phone (303)499-0050 or 499-5703. *(M)*

San Luis Valley Balloon Ranch: A 140-acre ranch in southern Colorado combines hot air balloon trips and lessons with more conventional activities. Participants may enjoy excellent ballooning in the open spaces, and the dependable weather conditions of the area are well-suited for observation, chase and easy recovery. The ranch features a launch area, balloon school, training site and radio-equipped chase vehicles to facilitate hour-long flights. In summer, guests may also river raft, hike, ride horses, fish and play tennis; in winter, guests may ice skate, snowmobile and downhill and cross-country ski. The ranch also offers accommodations and meals. **Cost:** $45 for 1-hour flights, $85 for introductory course, $800 for complete certification course with 10 hours of flight time. **When:** May to February. **Contact:** The Balloon Ranch, Star Rt., Box 41, Del Norte, CO 81132, USA; phone (303)754-2533. *(M)*

Florida

Blimp Ride over Miami: A unique opportunity is available for a half-hour ascent in the 160-foot-long *Mayflower*, popularly known as the Goodyear Blimp. Ascents are available on a day-to-day basis from its winter home in Miami. Passengers ride in the small gondola, viewing the world from altitudes of 1,000 to

3,000 feet and cruising at 35 miles an hour. A maximum of 6 persons a flight is taken aloft, with reservations made the day of the flight. Trips may be temporarily suspended when the airship is required for special network television or other engagements. **Cost:** $8 adults, $5 children under 12. **When:** November to April. **Contact:** Goodyear Airship Operator, 950 MacArthur Causeway, Watson Island, Miami, FL 33123, USA; phone (305)358-7644.

Montana

Ballooning over Billings: An array of balloon activities is available throughout the year for beginning and advanced aeronauts alike. Pilot instruction and pleasure flights provide participants with the experience of quiet, airborne travel. The balloon is equipped with a triple burner system capable of producing heat at a rate of 8 to 10 million BTUs per hour. Aeronauts may fly for 3 to 4 hours without landing, depending on the wind. **Cost:** On request. **When:** Year-round. **Contact:** Euphoria, Tom Barrow, Aeronaut, 733 Highland Park Dr., Billings, MT 59102, USA; phone (406)259-1038.

North Carolina

Floating on Air: Two-person balloons take passengers for an hour's ride over the North Carolina countryside. Beginning from a ballooning center in Statesville, participants help with the carrying and launching of the craft and then float over the foothills of the Smokies. There is little sensation of movement as the craft hovers over rolling wooded hills, farmlands and pastures. The balloon rarely flies over 1,000 feet in elevation and makes close passes, allowing participants to grab a leaf off a treetop or follow the contour of a brook. The landing is usually made in a vacant lot or pasture where the balloon is deflated, folded and packed into a waiting vehicle for the return drive to Statesville. New and used balloon sales and other related services are also offered. **Cost:** $50 includes balloon and equipment, recovery vehicle, guide. **When:** Year-round. **Contact:** Balloon Ascensions, Ltd., Rt. 11, Box 279, Statesville, NC 28677, USA; phone (704)873-2266.

Oregon

Northwest Hot Air: Participants learn the art of ballooning from experienced instructors, both on the ground and in the air. Three basic types of courses are offered. The first is a series of earthbound classes held at Portland State University and an inn at Beaverton. The second option is in-the-air training done in either privately supplied or rented aircraft. The final course offering is in pre- and postflight instruction and involves practical instruction covering the material from both the ground school classes and in-the-air training classes. Participants may also serve as the ground crew for the flights of others. **Cost:** From $5 an hour to $150 an hour. **When:** April to July. **Contact:** Northwest Aviation, P.O. Box 468, Portland, OR 97207, USA; phone (503)228-0089.

Virginia

Ballooning over Farmlands: Demonstration balloon flights are available near historic Manassas, Virginia. Rides depart in early morning or early evening for 1 to 2 hours over scenic Virginia farmlands, ending with a champagne celebration. Flight training is also offered and consists of complete ground school and 10 hours of flight time. **Cost:** $75 for demonstration ride, $950 for training. **When:** By arrangement. **Contact:** Blue Ridge Balloon Port, 11010 Bristow Rd., Bristow, VA 22013, USA; phone (703)361-1690.

Wisconsin

Hot Air over Water: Participants may view the sunset while aloft in a 70-foot hot air balloon. One- and 2-hour flights glide along over Green Lake, Lake Puckaway, Little and Big Twin lakes, Puchyan River and Fox River. Flights of varying duration are also offered, including a morning champagne flight. Piloted by licensed commercial aeronauts, the flights include a guaranteed pickup at the point of landing. Lodging is provided in a Swiss-style chalet in the town of Green Lake. **Cost:** $85 includes return vehicle after balloon transportation. **When:** On request. **Contact:** Heidel House, P.O. Box 537, Green Valley, WI 54941, USA; phone (414)294-3344.

RESOURCES

Clubs and Associations

Balloon Association of New Zealand
P.O. Box 51-182
Auckland 6, New Zealand

Balloon Club of America
P.O. Box 114
Swarthmore, PA 19081, USA

Balloon Federation of America
2516 Hiawatha Dr. NE
Albuquerque, NM 87112, USA
Phone (505)298-5284

The Bombard Society
30 E. 42nd St., Suite 1823
New York, NY 10017, USA
Phone (212)697-6230
Or tollfree (800)223-7733

British Balloon and Airship Club
Kimberley House, Vaughn Way
Leicester, LEI 4SG, Great Britain

Club Aerostatique de France
28 rue Lauriston
Paris 18, France

Danish Balloon Club
Gyvelhoj, 3600 Frederickssund
Denmark

Dublin Balloon Club
Colrye, Kellystown, Leixlip
County Kildare, Ireland

Erster Deutscher
Montgolfieren Klub
4400 Munster/Westfalen
Horsterstrasse 7, West Germany

Les Femmes de l'Air
535 S. Crane
Independence, MO 63124, USA

Heisseluft Balloon Club
Kinderdorf, Kusnachterstrasse 59
8126 Zurich, Switzerland

International Society
of Balloonpost Specialists
Statenlaan 2a
The Hague, Netherlands

Japan Balloon League
Saruta Bldg., 1-4-10 Akasake Minato-ku
Tokyo 107, Japan

National Aeronautics Association
806 15th St. NW
Washington, DC 20005, USA
Phone (202)347-2808

National Association
of Balloon Corps Veterans
116 S. Main St.
Tekonsha, MI 49092, USA

370 / AIR ADVENTURES

SOARING

EUROPE

England

Catching the Updraft: A 6-day gliding course is offered to both youths and adults at the Lakes Gliding Club airfield. Flying is done in T49 Capstan 2-seaters, with launches made by aerotow or, in the event of high winds, by winches on the ground. Flights afford views of the countryside around Barrow in Furness, on the coast of the Irish Sea. Courses begin on Sunday evenings and end the following Saturday, allowing make-up time on Saturday for flying time lost due to bad weather during the week. **Cost:** $170 includes dormitory accommodations, meals, instructor, equipment. **When:** July, August. **Contact:** YHA Adventure Holiday, Trevelyen House, St. Albans, Herts., Great Britain; phone St. Albans 55215.

France

Soaring over the Alps: Chamonix in Upper Savoy marks the starting point of a 2-week training course in glider flying. Take-offs are from slopes such as Tignes, Meribel, La Plagne, La Clusaz and Alpes d'Huez. Flights range from Plan Praz to Plaine des Praz in 7 to 10 minutes, and from Grands Montets to Les Chosalets in 13 to 20 minutes. Half-day beginners' courses take place at Chamonix every afternoon, and complete training courses are also available. **Cost:** $24 for half-day course; $200 for complete training course; $495 for 2-week package includes room, board. **When:** Summer. **Contact:** Hobby Voyage, 8 rue de Milan, 75009 Paris, France.

PACIFIC

Hawaii

Soaring over Oahu's North Shore: The prevailing tradewinds on the northwest shore of Oahu create favorable soaring conditions for experienced and neophyte enthusiasts alike. A variety of instructional programs is available providing students use of 1- to 3-person gliders. A program geared toward earning a private pilot license includes: 7 hours of solo flight plus 20 solo flights using aero-tow; instruction on FAA written exam; and oral and flight test preparation for FAA flight examination. An average of 6 to 10 hours (20- to 30-minute lessons) is available for solo flight preparation. **Cost:** $10 an hour for instructional fee; $150 to $500 for license fees. **When:** Year-round. **Contact:** Honolulu Soaring Club, Inc., Box 626, Waialua, HI 96791, USA; phone (808)623-6711.

UNITED STATES

Arizona

Sierra Estrella Gliding: Scenic glider and sailplane flights and instruction are available in an area exceptionally suited to soaring. During spring and summer, thermal lifts rise from the desert daily, and during fall and winter, ridge and wave soaring are excellent due to the nearness of the Sierra Estrella. Passengers may enjoy scenic flights

A soaring pilot briefs his passenger just before a flight near Monroe, Washington. Many introductory flights are available for less than $25. (Elizabeth Watson)

over the mountains as well as aerobatic glider flights which include loops, rolls and inverted flight. Soaring and flying instruction, glider competition and glider aerobatic techniques are also organized by the gliderport. All models of Schweizer sailplanes are available for instruction, rental or sale. **Cost:** $18 for trainer flights, $50 for high performance flights, $30 for aerobatic flights. **When:** Daily year-round. **Contact:** Arizona Soaring, Inc., P.O. Box 27427, Tempe, AZ 85282, USA; phone (602)568-2318.

(M)

California

Sailplane Pilot Training: Soaring courses of varying length and pur-

pose provide students with a wide range of flight experience, from beginner to commercial ratings. For persons with little or no flight experience, a series of 36 instructional flights provides the basis for a solid piloting background. Students learn to prepare a sailplane for flight, tow behind an airplane, perform precision maneuvers, negotiate steep turns and find thermals. In addition, emphasis is placed on ability to perform accurate approaches and landings, and to function under emergency conditions. Ten hours of ground instruction concerning the theories of sailplaning are given before students start their 36 training flights. If qualified, students may solo by the

35th flight. **Cost:** $525 includes ground school, sailplane rental, tow cost. **When:** Weekends. **Contact:** Great Western Soaring School, P.O. Box 189, Pearblossom, CA 93553, USA; phone (805)944-4161.

Soaring Studies: Instruction is offered in the art of sailplaning at one of the busiest gliderports in the nation located between Oakland and San Jose. Prospective pilots learn about thermal lift, wave lift and slope soaring; they operate 2-33 Schweizer gliders, as well as 1-26 solo aircraft and 2-32 triple-seaters. Block rates are available for instruction, and 20-minute demonstration rides are also offered. **Cost:** $13 for ride, $22 for introductory lesson. **When:** Year-round. **Contact:** Sky Sailing Airport, 44999 Christy St., Fremont, CA 94538, USA; phone (415)656-9900.

Colorado

Rocky Mountain Soaring Instruction: A gliderport in Colorado's high plateau country surrounding Colorado Springs offers soaring instruction and sailplane rentals. Courses are flexible and students are given private instruction. Half-hour introductory flights are available, as is a mini-course; their fees may be credited toward a complete course if desired. Other courses cover preparation for solo which involves 30 flights of practice take-offs, landings and flight maneuvers. A solo license course requires 37 flights and 7 hours of solo time. A power pilot soaring course prepares the student to solo in 6 to 8 flights. **Cost:** $20 for introductory flight, $55 for mini-course, $395 to $675 for other courses. **When:** Daily

year-round. **Contact:** Black Forest Gliderport, 9990 Gliderport Rd., Colorado Springs, CO 80908, USA; phone (303)495-4144. *(M)*

Colorado Springs Youth Soaring Camp: Youths 14 to 18 may combine custom-designed soaring instruction in the front range of the Rocky Mountains with backpacking training at a camp near Pikes Peak. All soaring instructors are FAA licensed, and training is given in Schweizer sailplanes. Experienced pilots may receive advanced soaring instruction, and solo flying is available. Group members learn backpacking skills on a trip into the Sangre de Cristo Mountains in the San Isabel National Forest and in the Lost Creek area of the Pike National Forest. Skills taught include high altitude hiking, first aid, compass reading, ropes and knots, and wilderness survival. **Cost:** $870 includes equipment, meals, accommodations. **When:** June to August. **Contact:** Black Forest Gliderport, 9990 Gliderport Rd., Colorado Springs, CO 80908, USA; phone (303)495-4144. *(M)*

Connecticut

Soaring in New England Skies: A fleet of new Schweizer sailplanes is on call 7 days a week, from 9 a.m. to dusk. The Connecticut Soaring Center can fulfil soaring fantasies for novices and veterans alike. Sailplane rental with or without instruction, storage of privately owned sailplanes and towing and tie-down services are all available at the gliderport. Soaring enthusiasts can join the Connecticut Soaring Club whose members fly the newest and most up-to-date sailplanes at half the commercial rate. Gift certificates are available for all services and sailplanes may be rented at a daily rate for a half hour or more. The center also sells planes and insurance. **Cost:** $16 to $25 for 1-hour sailplane rental; $29 with flight instructor; $9 for aerotow. **When:** Year-round. **Contact:** Connecticut Soaring Center, Waterbury Gliderport, Plymouth, CT 06782, USA; phone (203)283-5474.

Illinois

Soaring over Chicago: Free introductory flights and demonstration rides are available west of Chicago. Once in the air, the pilot explains and demonstrates the techniques of soaring and even hands over the controls if the passenger is willing. Previous flight experience is not necessary to learn to fly a sailplane. Lessons can be arranged one at a time or as a complete course. A package beginner's course consists of 48 flights, all tows and sailplane use. A solo course for beginners involves 25 flights. Schweizer sailplanes may also be purchased. **Cost:** $12 for demonstration ride, $10 an hour for instruction, $355 and $630 for complete courses. **When:** April to November. **Contact:** Hinckley Soaring, Inc., Hinckley, IL 60520, USA; phone (815)286-7200.

Minnesota

Soaring over Minneapolis: A variety of instructional courses, rental arrangements and tow fees is available to soaring pilots. Though no package flight training is available, instruction is and charges are based on the pilot's ability and progress. Generally, students require about 25 lessons to become competent at solo flight. Each lesson lasts about 20 to 30 minutes, though schedules

Ground crews make last-minute preparations and safety checks as sailplanes wait to be towed aloft by a powered aircraft. (South Carolina Dept. of Parks)

A glider soars from one mountain ridge to another to catch upward-moving currents of air. In mountainous regions pilots need a thorough knowledge of atmospheric conditions. (Swiss Nat'l. Tourist Office)

are flexible. Requirements for a private glider pilot's license necessitate solo competence, 7 hours of solo flight including 20 solo glider flights launched by aerotow, and passage of the FAA flight test. Tows and rentals are available. **Cost:** $5 to $475 depending on course, rental or training. **When:** Year-round, weather permitting. **Contact:** White Bear Gliding, Benson's Airport, White Bear Lake, MN 55110, USA; phone (612)871-8036.

Montana

Soaring at Teton and Yellowstone: The mountains at the base of the Teton Range on the Idaho-Wyoming border at Driggs are the setting for a variety of year-round

soaring opportunities for beginning and licensed pilots alike. Beginners may enroll in an introductory mini-course which includes 2 flights, one 4,000-foot tow and one 1,000-foot tow, instructional book and logbook. Students may also enroll in a license course, solo course, or a more advanced power pilot transition course. Glider rentals, tows and rides are available as well. Winter ridge and wave soaring provide enthusiasts with ample opportunity in the sport or in sailplaning. While soaring in the brisk, silent sky, pilots often view the irregular patterns of skiers making their way down the powdery slopes below. In summer, soaring buffs may also partake in a variety of wildwater sports available in the national parks in addition to riding the air waves. **Cost:** $12 an hour to $1,052 depending on type of instruction includes equipment, instruction. **When:** Year-round. **Contact:** Red Baron Soaring, Box 247, Teton Peaks Airport, Driggs, ID 83422, USA; phone (208)354-8131.

Nevada

Sailing in the Sierra Nevada: Glider rentals, tows and instruction are available near Reno, Nevada. Facilities for aircraft care are available to those who fly in. An introductory flight offers the inexperienced an opportunity to soar over the arid countryside. **Cost:** $12 to $14 an hour for rental; $8 for tow; $12 an hour for instruction; $15 for introductory ride. **When:** Year-round.

Contact: Sierra-Nevada Soaring, P.O. Box 60036, 4895 Texas Ave., Reno, NV 89506, USA; phone (702)972-7757.

New Hampshire

Soaring near Salem: Gliders take off from a single 2,000-foot sod strip runway near Salem at an elevation of 130 feet. Over 20 private gliders are based at the gliderport; 3 tow planes and 8 Schweizer gliders are available for public use. Those interested in soaring can take gliding lessons or ease into the sport with a demonstration sailplane ride. Flight tests are given by an FAA examiner for both commercial and private sailplaning. Thermal activity with occasional wave and mini-ridge lift contributes to excellent soaring

conditions in the greater Salem area. **Cost:** $19 average for lessons; $14 to $16 for demonstration ride; $16 to $28 for 1-hour glider rental; $39 for beginner's special includes 2 lessons, text book and pilot's log. **When:** Weekends April to December; weekdays June to October. **Contact:** Northeastern Light Aircraft, Inc., Box 252, Lynn, MA 01903, USA; phone (603)898-7919.

New York

Soaring Instruction: Complete soaring courses are available near the famous Harris Hill in western New York. A division of a major sailplane manufacturer, the school has facilities for several types of training. An introductory program includes 3 dual soaring flights and a soaring manual. A complete soaring course leads students from initial instruction to a private glider certificate. Fifty flights are involved, one of which is a cross-country dual flight, and 12 hours of flying time are scheduled. Other services and courses offered are a commercial soaring course, an instructor's course, auto or winch tows, and cross-country retrieve. Flights for 1 or 2 passengers are also available. **Cost:** $60 for introductory program to $875 for complete private course; $15 to $25 for passenger flights. **When:** May to September. **Contact:** Schweizer Aircraft Corp., P.O. Box 147, Elmira, NY 14902, USA; phone (607)739-3821.

(M)

Ohio

Soaring the Midwest Thermals: Students learn soaring via sailplane rides in the thermals over farmland near Montpelier. On an introducto-ry flight, the instructor explains the basic techniques of soaring and lets the passenger take a turn at the controls. Afterwards the participant may choose to obtain a student license and learn the art of soaring. At least 25 additional flights with an instructor are required before the student may fly solo. A variety of courses has been designed to accommodate students ranging from complete beginners to those who have had power flying experience. The gliding center also offers assistance to enthusiasts who are building their own sailplanes. Participants staying for more than a day can camp near the airfield or sleep in bunks at the center. **Cost:** On request. **When:** Year-round. **Contact:** Elf Soaring Enterprises, RR 3, Airport Rd., Montpelier, OH 43543, USA; phone (419)485-3716.

Pennsylvania

Northern Appalachian Sailplane Soaring: Bald Eagle Ridge, stretching 500 miles from Pennsylvania through Maryland and West Virginia to Tennessee, is the setting for motorless sailplane courses. Several world endurance records have been set along this ridge, where wind lifts make soaring possible all year round. Individually tailored courses under the guidance of qualified soaring instructors teach the student to fly solo and attain a license. The average length of training covers from 20 to 25 lessons before solo flights are permitted. Introductory flights are also available, during which the rider may take the controls once the instructor has demonstrated the basic techniques. **Cost:** $15 for introductory flight, approximately $300 for training course. **When:** Year-round. **Contact:** Ridge Soaring, Inc., RD, Julian, PA 16844, USA; phone (814)355-1792.

Texas

Learning to Soar: Beginners' instruction in soaring is offered through a 5-phase course that can be completed in 5 days, or at a more leisurely pace. Each student is initially issued study materials. After reading these the course begins: phase 1 covers the fundamentals of flight, preflight inspection, function of the controls and some simple flying; the subsequent phases cover, in order, formation flight behind the tow plane, signals, take-off, landing; airport traffic patterns and air turbulence; steep turns, stalls, cross-wind landings, pattern planning, emergency procedures; and finally a solo flight. Upon completion of the course participants receive student solo pilot licenses. All tows are provided, and until the fifth phase students are accompanied by an instructor in the sailplane. What is learned in the course applies equally well to power airplanes. **Cost:** $395 includes equipment, about 20 tows, instructor. **When:** Year-round. **Contact:** Southwest Soaring, Inc., P.O. Box 460, Caddo Mills, TX 75005, USA; phone (214)527-3124.

Virginia

Gliding over Virginia: In a series of hourly lessons, participants learn to soar on the rising air currents above the Blue Ridge Mountains. Under the guidance of an instructor, students are taught how to take off and land, make gentle turns and find thermals. When the techniques of gliding have been mastered, students begin solo flights. **Cost:** $25 an hour plus tow includes rental, instruction. **When:** April to November. **Contact:** Warrenton Soaring Center, P.O. Box 185, Warrenton, VA 22186, USA; phone (703)347-0054.

RESOURCES

Clubs and Associations

Mid-Atlantic Soaring Association
Frederick Municipal Airport
Frederick MD 21701, USA
Phone (301)663-9753

Midwestern Soaring Association
6120 W. Cleveland
Gladstone, MO 64119, USA
Phone (816)537-6074

National Aeronautic Association
821 15th St. NW
Washington, DC 20005, USA

New England Soaring Association
Airport Dr.
Southbridge, MA 01550, USA

Northern Pacific Sports and Recreation
P.O. Box 2317
Renton, WA 98055, USA

Soaring Society of America
P.O. Box 66071
Los Angeles, CA 90066, USA

Soaring Symposia
408 Washington St.
Cumberland, MD 21502, USA

Southern California
Soaring Association
28612 Parthena St.
Canoga Park, CA 91306, USA

FLYING

ANTARCTICA

South Pole Flights: Leaving Auckland, New Zealand for a 13-hour flight over Antarctica, passengers view the surrounding area and 12,450-foot Mt. Erebus before flying west over the Magnetic South Pole. In good weather alternate routes include Cape Hallet and McMurdo Sound in Ross Sea. The flight is available only in conjunction with a roundtrip Air New Zealand flight from North America. **Cost:** $265. **When:** October, November. **Contact:** Air New Zealand, Suite 1000, 510 W. Sixth St., Los Angeles, CA 90014, USA; phone (213)629-5454.

ASIA

Sri Lanka

Hovering over Beaches and Jungles: Flying in 4-seat helicopters from hotel bases, adventurers take short trips over a variety of the natural sights of Sri Lanka. The island has many wildlife sanctuaries with elephants, bears, leopards, deer and jungle fowl, as well as numerous beaches for surfing, boating, water-skiing and swimming. The native Hindu peoples have a rich history, and several temples and festivals can be explored first-hand. **Cost:** On request. **When:** By arrangement. **Contact:** Helitours, Box 594, Colombo 2, Sri Lanka; phone 31584 or 33184.

AUSTRALAISA

Excursions to the South Pacific: A 17-, 22- or 29-day trip to the South Pacific provides travelers the opportunity to visit Australia, New Zealand, Fiji and Tahiti. All trips depart from Los Angeles and include overland trips to 3 of Australia's major cities: Sydney, Canberra and Melbourne. In New Zealand trip members climb Evans Pass to the Summit Road to view Lyttleton Harbor with its many bays and inlets. In addition, a 40-minute ski plane ride to the upper snowfields of the Tasman Glacier is scheduled. A flight to Rotorua brings visitors to the Whakarewarewa Maori Village, the heavily forested Mamaku Hills and Waitomo Caves. Also scheduled is a trip along the underground river into the Glow Worm Grotto. Visitors leave New Zealand after driving through rich farmlands to the city of Hamilton. The Tahiti portion of the trip includes a cruise across the Sea of Moon for a day on the fabled island of Moorea. **Cost:** $2,220 to $3,646 includes roundtrip airfare from Los Angeles, meals, accommodations. **When:** Monthly. **Contact:** Air New Zealand, Suite 1000, 510 W. Sixth St., Los Angeles, CA 90014, USA; phone (213)629-5454.

Australia

Northern Bush Country Flights: Three day-long flights are offered between Cairns, Cooktown and Lizard Island near Australia's Great Barrier Reef. One trip flies over the rugged north Queensland tropical coastline from Cairns to Cooktown, where participants visit the historic mining town before flying back over the Great Barrier Reef. Another trip flies participants from Cooktown to Lizard Island on the Great

Barrier Reef for an outing to the Blue Lagoon before returning to Cooktown. A third trip departs from Cairns, flying over the Atherton Plateau to Chillagoe Caves and then to Cooktown before the return flight to Cairns. **Cost:** $50 to $70 includes lunch. **When:** May to October. **Contact:** Bush Pilots Airways, 8b Shields St., Cairns, Australia; phone (070)2158.

Flights to the Olgas: Small aircraft flights are available to visit Ayers Rock and the Olgas in central Australia. Half-day and day trips depart from Alice Springs in the early morning for Ayers Rock, stop for a tour around its base, then continue 15 miles west to explore Mt. Olga before a return flight in the early afternoon or evening. Overnight, 2-day and 3-day trips spend more time in the vicinity of Ayers Rock and allow time for a climb of Mt. Olga. A flight to the aboriginal settlements of Docker River or Ernabella is added to the 3-day trip. Accommodations are at a motel near Ayers Rock. Other trips include weekly mail flights to remote cattle stations and flights over aboriginal settlements and geographical features. **Cost:** $25 to $140. **When:** Year-round. **Contact:** Connair, 51 Todd St., Alice Springs, NT 5750, Australia; phone 52-1755.

New Zealand

Glacier Flights: Glacier areas and rain forests may be viewed on a variety of 1-day flying trips departing from Lake Tekapo. Participants may choose flights over the ice fields of the Franz Joseph and Fox glaciers, Mt. Cook National Park and South Island, with opportuni-ties to stop and sightsee at midday. Much of the country seen by air is completely inaccessible by road. On the South Island route passengers arrive at Milford Sound for lunch, then set off again to view Sutherland Falls and Lake Te Anau. The route takes participants through glacier-carved valleys to Queenstown for a short stop, then north to Wanaka, Hawea, Lake Benmore and the Mackenzie country to Tekapo. **Cost:** $5 to $45. **When:** Year-round. **Contact:** Air Safaris, Box 21, Lake Tekapo, New Zealand; phone 880.

Helicopter Ski Lift Adventure: Plane or helicopter transport is offered to and from areas selected in the Tapapa, Wharetoto and Kaimanawa regions. The service begins with a flight to Taupo, where individuals can choose destinations into the backcountry. Activities into remote areas include horse trekking, whitewater rafting and fishing. The Tapapa area contains 18,000 acres of beech forests and tussock grassland. The Wharetoto region covers 5,800 acres and is bounded by the Repia, Otupua and Mohaka rivers. The Kaimanawa region consists of 18,000 acres situated near the headwaters of the Ngaroro River. Large areas of tussock land reach upward to the beech forests with sika and red deer among the trees. The rivers adjacent to this area have a large number of trout, and eels can be found downstream. Either hut or tent shelter is available in all the traveled areas. Guide service is also available. **Cost:** $50 from Taupo to airstrips, $130 a day for field guide service; helicopter transport prices

Pontoon planes are useful in getting to remote lakes which are either inaccessible or reached only by arduous hiking over rugged mountain terrain. (Canadian Gov't. Office of Tourism)

on request. **When:** By arrangement. **Contact:** Lakeland Aviation Ltd., P.O. Box 858, Taupo, New Zealand; phone 2364.

Papua New Guinea

Stone Age Air Safari: A 17-day expedition explores Papua New Guinea by twin-engine aircraft, focusing on its primitive native tribes. Members observe peoples who have retained much of their Stone Age culture due to their inaccessible location. The expedition visits the Biami people on the Nomad River and the people of the remote Oksapmin area. The group also spends several days exploring the culture of the Sepik River area and the Kuka Kuka of the Marawaka Valley. Participants also travel up the Bensbach River to see the area's wildlife, which includes wallabies and crocodiles as well as numerous species of birds. The expedition is composed of 7 members plus an experienced guide and pilot. **Cost:** $4,435 from Los Angeles includes transportation, accommodations, meals. **When:** March, May, July, October, November. **Contact:** Society Expeditions, P.O. Box 5088, University Sta., Seattle, WA 98105, USA; phone (206)324-9400.   *(M)*

CANADA

Eclipsing: The 1979 total solar eclipse will throw its shadow across northern Canada, and participants on a 4-day trip learn about eclipses while watching this one from a specially equipped 727 jet. The first day of the trip is spent in Chicago, where participants meet each other and the group leaders. The next day is spent attending lectures and audio-visual presentations by an astronomy professor. Then, early on the third day, the group boards the jet and heads northwest into the eclipse's central line, letting the shadow overtake the plane. When the plane is completely in shadow, it makes a shallow turn to the left to observe the shadow moving away. All the right-hand seats have been removed from the aircraft, allowing room for easy window access and use of observation equipment. The trip returns to Chicago in the early afternoon and ends with another night there. Since the windows in the jet are small, there are different rates for exclusive or shared use of a window. **Cost:** $485 for shared window, $700 for exclusive window includes double occupancy accommodations, most meals, presentations, transportation to and from airport; rates available for single room and for flight without accommodations. **When:** February. **Contact:** VIP Travel, P.O. Box 157, Sierra Madre, CA 91024, USA; phone (213)355-1438.

PACIFIC

Hawaii

Eight Island Plane Trip: The Hawaiian Islands are seen by air during a 1-day trip. Participants board twin-engine aircraft from which they see Hanalei Valley on Kauai, the 2,000-foot waterfalls of Molokai, the huge crater of Diamond Head on Oahu, the Haleakala Volcano of Maui and the barren wastelands of Kahoolawe. During several landings along the route, passengers are able to take side trips to nearby points of interest, dine on native food and see cultural and historic sites. **Cost:** $110 includes air and land transportation, meals, guides. **When:** Year-round. **Contact:** Hawaiian Air Tour Service, 2371 Kalakauu Ave., Honolulu, HI 96815, USA; phone (808)923-6577.

Helicopter to Milolii: Visitors to Kauai have the opportunity to get an overview of the island's spectacular scenery via helicopter. Flights vary in duration and provide access to remote areas of the island, including Milolii which is known for its rare shells; Nualolo Aina and Nualolo Kai, location of abandoned taro patch terraces and homesites; and other sites in the "Valley of the Lost Tribe," where traces of an early civilization still exist. The flight to Milolii begins with a trip to the Waimea Canyon where the variations of canyon coloration and frequent waterfalls are observed from 4,000 feet up. From this altitude, the waterfalls and archaeological sites along the Na Pali coast are also viewed. **Cost:** $80. **When:** Year-round. **Contact:** Papillon Helicopters, Princeville Airport, P.O. Box 608, Hanalei, Kauai, HI 96714, USA; phone (808)826-9180.

UNITED STATES

Southwest Natural History Trip: A trip focusing on the natural history of the American Southwest—New Mexico, Colorado, Utah and Arizona—uses a 6-passenger bush plane for transportation. This allows wide topological overviews, "classroom" time while in flight and the ability to cover large distances within a 6-day trip. The trip begins and ends in Santa Fe and visits numerous Indian ruins including Anasazi dwellings in Aztec, Salmon and Chaco canyons; Pueblo Bonito; the Mesa Verde cliff dwellings; Canyonlands in Utah; Navajo dwellings in Monument Valley; and Marble Canyon. The trip's fifth day is spent rafting the San Juan River, with its rapids and ruins, while studying first-hand the geological formations of the area. Most stops include jeep transportation to nearby points of interest, including one with a visit to and lunch at a traditional Navajo Indian hogan. Horseback riding can sometimes be incorporated, with advance notice. The pilot serves as instructor and guide. **Cost:** $699 includes food, camping accommodations, transportation, guide; discounts for larger groups available. **When:** April to October. **Contact:** Southwest Safaris, P.O. Box 945, Santa Fe, NM 87501, USA; phone (505)988-4246. *(M)*

Alaska

Flights over Fort Yukon: On the banks of the Yukon River just north of the Arctic Circle, Fort Yukon has operated as a fur-trading center since 1847. On a 5-hour trip participants fly from Metro Field in Fairbanks to a guided tour of the reconstructed Hudson's Bay Company Fort and other points of interest in the village, including fish wheels for drying salmon. After spending 2 hours on the ground, passengers take a return flight following the route of the trans-Alaska oil pipeline. **Cost:** $74. **When:** Daily year-round. **Contact:** Air North, P.O. Box 60054, Fairbanks, AK 99706, USA; phone (907)456-5555.

Flying above Mt. McKinley: Several flights, lasting between 1 and 2 hours, are available above Mt. McKinley National Park. Sights include the Denali earthquake fault, which runs 110 miles between Mt. McKinley and Mt. Deborah. These 2 peaks were once adjacent, and from the air it can easily be seen how they have moved apart. Dall sheep are visible along the higher ridges, and hundreds of caribou can be spotted during their summer migration. Moose are plentiful among the willow browse in the eastern part of the park. Glaciers streaked with lines of volcanic ash can also be seen from the plane. **Cost:** $30 to $40 a person. **When:** By arrangement. **Contact:** Denali Flying Service, P.O. Box 82, McKinley Park, AK 99755, USA; phone (907)683-2261.

Three Thousand Six Hundred Pontoon Miles: A charter air trek leaves from Juneau for a 2-week survey of Alaska's wilderness, parks and cities. By 6-seat pontoon plane, trip members cover a circuit that includes stops at Seward, Prince William Sound, Mt. McKinley National Park, Fairbanks, Fort Yukon, Nome, and Katmai National Monument as well as McNeil River Bear Sanctuary for the final touch-down in Anchorage. About 20 hours of flying time are logged on this trip, with many of the panoramic views being provided at altitudes as low as 100 feet above the mountainous landscape. Camps and lodges provide accommodations. **Cost:** $1,800; $2,046 includes roundtrip airfare from Seattle. **When:** June. **Contact:** Mountain Travel Inc., 1398 Solano Ave., Albany, CA 94706, USA; phone (415)527-8100.   *(M)*

Arctic Bush Flying: Opportunities are available to accompany working bush pilots on flights from Nome to remote areas on the tundra and the Bering Sea. Travelers can join mail carriers on a variety of flights and journey to secluded arctic settlements such as Little Diomede Island and the villages of Wales, Golovin, Shishmaref, Savoonga and Gambell.From Little Diomede located in the Bering Sea on the International Date Line, it is possible to see the Siberian coast just 22 miles away. At Wales and Shishmaref hunting and fishing continue to be the major means of support for the Eskimo population. A reindeer station established at Golovin in 1896 offers voyagers who disembark there a perfect view of the large herd. Gambell, on St. Lawrence Island, is of particular interest to bird watchers, naturalists and archaeologists. **Cost:** $37 to $73 depending on the chosen destination. **When:** Year-round. **Contact:** Munz Northern Airlines, Nome Airport, Nome, AK 99762, USA; phone (907)443-2215.

Arctic Adventures: Wilderness explorers, river runners, photographers and backpackers can determine their own expedition lengths and pick specific areas of exploration within Alaska's remote regions of the Noatak and Kobuk rivers. Bush plane service into the wilderness departs from Kotzebue, just north of the Arctic Circle. The inhabitants of the region are mainly Eskimos who live in small bush communities. The terrain varies from vast areas of tundra lakes to the Brooks and Baird mountain ranges. Expedition services offered to adventurers include reprovisioning, base site relocation, progress monitoring and planning consultation. The northern season is short and the rugged, remote terrain requires that participants be self-reliant and experienced outdoorspeople. Air transportation to Kotzebue can be arranged from the lower states through Seattle and Anchorage. **Cost:** $325 to $975 depending on the expedition base site, includes bush plane transportation, site relocation and reprovisioning. **When:** June to September. **Contact:** Northwest Arctic Alaska, P.O. Box 733, Seattle, WA 98111, USA; phone (206)324-4437.

Mt. McKinley Overview: For travelers who want to see McKinley without making a rugged overland trek, flights of slightly over 2 hours are offered for a minimum of 4 passengers which explore the mountain's major features and give members a view of the surrounding country. The flight leaves from Anchorage and travels north, up the Susitna River past the old railroad settlement of Talkeetna and into the Alaskan Range. Approaching the mountain, the plane climbs to 10,000 feet, then after a close look glides down over the sheer faces of the Ruth and Kahiltna glaciers. At the lower elevations, participants are likely to see moose, black bears or grizzly bears. The flight then returns to Anchorage. **Cost:** $95. **When:** By arrangement. **Contact:** Rust's Flying Service, Box 6325, Anchorage, AK 99502, USA; phone (907)243-1595.

Arizona

Grand Canyon Flying: A variety of narrated scenic air trips over the Grand Canyon provides visitors with the opportunity to view the expanse of the national park in a few hours. One- and 2-hour flights are available, and both originate on the South Rim of the park. Flights are available between the North and South rims of the canyon for access to meals, overnight accommodations and mule trips on the North Rim. Three-hour air explorations include views of Glen Canyon Dam, Lake Powell, Painted Desert, Marble Canyon and the Havasupai Indian village. The 3-hour trips cover about 350 miles of terrain. The 1-hour trip covers 130 miles and includes views of Snoopy Rock, Phantom Ranch, Mooney Falls and the Havasupai Indian village. **Cost:** $24 to $68; less for children. **When:** Year-round. **Contact:** Grand Canyon Airlines, P.O. Box 186, Grand Canyon, AZ 86023, USA; phone (602)638-2407.

Grand Overflight: Participants spend 1 day and a night visiting the Grand Canyon, from both the ground and the air. The trip begins with a flight from the South Rim that winds its way through the canyon, flying under the rim at certain intervals. The plane passes river rapids, waterfalls, extinct volcanoes and ancient Indian villages. At one point it soars through the narrow pass between Powell Plateau and the North Rim. Once the group arrives back at the airport, arrangements are made for participants to travel to the South Rim for a ground view of the region just viewed from the air. **Cost:** $142 includes 2 meals, accommodations. **When:** May to September. **Contact:**

Scenic Airlines, 241 E. Reno Ave., Las Vegas, NV 89119, USA; phone (702)739-1900.

Florida

Exploring the Everglades: On a 4-day journey through the Everglades by plane and boat, trip members examine the many biological zones in the area. After meeting in Miami, group members spend the first day flying in a private plane above the "River of Grass" to gain an overall picture of the swampy land and to survey routes. Stops are made for meals, photography and a closer look at the ecology of the area. During the next 3 days, participants travel through the Everglades by airboat learning about the various ecosystems, hammocks and heads while camping in remote parts of the interior. The sloughs and grass-filled prairies are explored, and participants have a chance to see many varieties of birds, native orchids and rare tree snails. Side trips to other Florida wilderness areas are also available. **Cost:** $345 includes transportation, meals, accommodations. **When:** Year-round. **Contact:** Wilderness Experiences, Rt. 1, Box 12, Thonotosassa, FL 33592, USA; phone (813)986-2963.   *(M)*

HANG GLIDING

CENTRAL AMERICA

Guatemala

Hang Gliding School: One-month courses cover the theory and prac-

tice of hang gliding. Classes in theory are held at night in Guatemala City and include films and a flight simulator; the practical aspects are taught in the field on Saturdays. Private lessons are also available on a daily or hourly basis. **Cost:** $100 includes equipment. **When:** Four times a year. **Contact:** Vuelo Libre, 20 Calle 3-50 Zona 10, Guatemala City, Guatemala; phone 32 42 52.

EUROPE

Norway

Scandinavian Sky Sailing: The steep mountains and narrow valleys of Norway are ideal for hang gliding, and instruction in the sport is offered at several sites. The Norwegian Hang Gliding School, based in Oslo, arranges courses throughout the country. A school at Vikersund offers special courses for beginners in an area that includes the giant "ski flying" hill which was the site for the 1977 world championship. Hang gliding is also available in northern Norway through clubs at Narvik and at Bodo, situated just above the Arctic Circle and reached by air or rail from Oslo. **Cost:** On request. **When:** On request. **Contact:** Norwegian and Swedish National Tourist Offices, 75 Rockefeller Plaza, New York, NY 10019, USA; phone (212)582-2802.

UNITED STATES

Colorado

Hanging above Aspen: Hang gliding provides spectacular views of the Rocky Mountains. Enthusiasts may take a half-day beginning course in the sport, using the best equipment available. The courses take place near Aspen, with Mt. Aspen the jump-off point. **Cost:** $20 includes equipment. **When:** April to August. **Contact:** Aspen Reservations, Inc., P.O. Box 4546, Aspen, CO 81611, USA; phone (303)925-4000.

Hang Gliding from Mt. Zion: Double surface airfoil hang gliders provide participants interested in instructional and recreational free flight with the means of achieving powerless, silent locomotion. Basic instruction commences with a ground school lecture and the use of a flight simulator before students learn the body positions used in flight. Instruction includes a total of 20 hours (4 hours each lesson) of actual practice in preflight techniques, ground handling, take-off and landing procedures, and directional and air speed control. Participants are encouraged to thoroughly understand the theory of flight, basic airfoil design and meteorology. The 20 hours of outdoor flight instruction are solid preparation for later flights of 10, 30 and even 75 miles. All equipment is available on a rental-for-purchase basis. **Cost:** $30 for single lesson of 4 hours; $90 for 5-lesson package. **When:** By arrangement. **Contact:** Golden Eagle Gliders, 501 Lookout Mt. Rd., Golden, CO 80401, USA; phone (303)277-1300.

Rocky Mountain Hang Gliding: Individual attention is the emphasis of classes in hang gliding west of Denver in the town of Golden. Courses, offered at all levels, are limited in number to insure that everyone receives thorough instruction in good flight techniques and safety. Course offerings include a basic course of instruction indoors and 4 outdoor lessons, a towing course, an advanced mountain course and a high-performance course for Hang III or IV pilots. Golden's proximity to the Rocky Mountains affords unlimited opportunities for high-altitude flying, and an array of new flying sites is nearby. Gliders are also available for purchase. **Cost:** From $50 for high-performance course to $90 for basic course. **When:** June to October. **Contact:** Golden Sky Sails, 572 Orchard St., Golden, CO 80401, USA; phone (303)278-9566.

Michigan

Riding the Midwest Wind: Daylong individual instruction in windsurfing and hang gliding takes place in the classroom and outdoors in New Buffalo. Aspects of aerodynamics, weight shift control, safety and construction of the glider are covered in blackboard instruction, illustrated by the use of a model. Students begin with flat-area runs to get the feel of the glider before harnessing in and taking off for short flights from a gentle hill. Warren Dunes State Park or 135-foot Mt. Baldy are used for repeated flights in which the student works on turning and banking. Certification programs up to the Hang 3 level are all tailored to the stamina and ability of the individual, though participants can expect to obtain their Hang 1 classification in one day. Windsurfing is also taught on an individualized basis using the windsurfer turntable, a

In courses offered by Free Spirit Hang Gliders in Oregon, participants sail near the Pacific coast in an area of high sand dunes and sea. (Val Hawes)

simulator that allows the student to go through the same corrective motions that are required on the 12-foot windsurfing board. After an hour on the simulator, and blackboard instruction for the non-sailor, the day is spent on either Lake Michigan or on the calmer waters of Lake Pine. Certified individuals may rent equipment without instruction. **Cost:** $45 for 5 to 8 hours includes instruction, equipment. **When:** Year-round. **Contact:** AA Flightsystems, Inc., 10 N. Barton St., New Buffalo, MI 49117, USA; phone (616)469-1643.

Minnesota

Hang Gliding Instruction: Fully certified by the United States Hang Gliding Association, a center located in St. Paul offers beginning, intermediate and advanced training programs to hang gliding enthusiasts. Participants spend the first 3 hours of the beginning course in a comprehensive ground school program, which covers all aspects of hang gliding technique and practice. Trainees view films, practice on a simulator and engage in discussions. The following day provides participants with actual hang gliding flights using a graduated height method. By the end of the training period, participants are proficient enough to earn a USHGA Beginners Certification Card. Beyond the initial training programs, students may pursue the sport on intermediate and advanced levels, preparing for effective take-offs, landings, aerial maneuvers and, most challenging of all, sustained flight. **Cost:** $60 includes instruction, use of glider. **When:** Summer. **Contact:** Northern Sun Hang Gliders, 628 W. Larpenteur Ave., St. Paul, MN 55113, USA; phone (614)489-8300.

Montana

Western Sky Gliding: Beginning hang gliding instruction is offered during 1-day courses near Billings. Most courses take place on Sunday, while weekday lessons can also be arranged for groups of 6 or more at locations up to 200 miles from Billings. During the lessons the *Guide to Rogallo Flight Basic* is used, and students are given various articles on hang gliding to read before their flight. Hang gliders can also be purchased at the school. **Cost:** $15 a lesson includes basic instruction. **When:** By arrangement. **Contact:** Beartooth Hang Gliders, 3010 Rimrock Rd.; Billings, MT 59102, USA; phone (406)656-5409.

Nebraska

Hang Gliding Instruction: Sand hills with vertical drops ranging from 30 to 100 feet provide a hang gliding training location in Sutherland. Due to the terrain in the midwestern area, there is little opportunity for free flight beyond initial training stages. However, the potential of thermal soaring may be explored with the aid of a tow winch and gliders. For more advanced flight, Scotts Bluff has good ridge soaring possibilities for enthusiasts. Students are trained in ground reference maneuvers, stall recognition and recovery techniques. **Cost:** $30 for 3 hours of training flight. **When:** As weather permits. **Contact:** Billy B. Beamway's Flying Machine Shoppe, Box 651, Sutherland, NE 69165, USA.

New Hampshire

New England Hang Gliding: Schools located at Attitash, Cranmore and Pleasant in the Mt. Washington Valley provide instruction to beginners wishing to experience the feeling of flight. A beginning plan is available to students and includes 3 hours of intensive instruction and introduction to the sport, with emphasis on safety and understanding of flight theory. All levels of instruction may be arranged on a group or individual basis as well. Following the ground instruction, neophytes practice glider handling and begin an instructor-assisted first take-off run on a gentle slope. After a few practice runs, students take to the air and land softly in the grassy tuft below. The Attitash school provides students with hills as high as 2,300 feet with a vertical drop of 1,525 feet and northern exposure. Cranmore, elevation 2,000 feet, provides a vertical drop of 1,500 feet and western exposure, while Pleasant, at Bridgton, Maine, provides a vertical drop of 1,400 feet. **Cost:** $10 to $25 depending on type of instruction. **When:** June to October. **Contact:** Sky People Hang

Gliding School, Box 898, North Conway, NH 03860, USA; phone (603)356-5872.

New Jersey

Hang It Up: Instruction and beginner's certification in hang gliding are offered at a New Jersey school. The course, which lasts 6½ hours, begins with 2½ hours of classroom instruction covering basic flight theory, winds, safety, kite types and flying site locations; demonstration films are shown and a flight simulator is used. Next is an hour's session of handling the kite on the ground, including preflight inspection, ground running with the glider and proper ground handling procedures. Finally, a 3-hour flying session allows supervised practice in smooth take-offs, straight, slow controlled flights and smooth landings. At the course's end participants receive a "Hang Rating 1," certifying that they have a beginner's competence. Repeats of the 3-hour flying portion are available if desired or needed. **Cost:** $45 includes instruction, equipment; $25 for repeat of flying session. **When:** Year-round. **Contact:**

A hang gliding enthusiast slung in a prone position maneuvers his sail by shifting his weight on the steering bar he is holding. (Judy Frostega)

New Jersey School of Hang Gliding, P.O. Box 240A, Oxford, NJ 07863, USA; phone (201)852-1116.

North Carolina

Gliding at Nag's Head: Courses for all levels of hang gliding, from the novice to mountain flying, are taught along the sand dunes on the Atlantic coast. Ground school and flying lessons are taught in 3 lessons, while special packages offer more intensive instruction for the serious students. In advanced classes pilots must provide their own equipment. Participants should wear long pants and tennis shoes. The final courses in the program offer opportunities for flight altitudes of 1,500 feet. **Cost:** $15 to $27 for individual classes, $57 to $122 for packages. **When:** Year-round. **Contact:** Kitty Hawk Kites, P.O. Box 386, Nag's Head, NC 27959, USA; phone (919)441-6247.

Ohio

Hang Gliding School: A series of courses enables students to develop flight skills and gain United States Hang Gliding Association ratings. A 3-hour ground school course, First Flights, includes lectures on basic hang gliding and aerodynamics, demonstration and practice of control movements, practical demonstration of assembly, disassembly and transportation, and exercise on ground handling, take-offs, controlled flight and landings. The second course is designed to qualify students for Hang I rating of the USHGA. It includes both First Flights and 3 additional days of instruction. There is some classroom work on advanced flying and micrometeo-

rology. Two further courses are offered for the advanced hang glider. **Cost:** $35 for First Flights; $95 for "Hang 1." **When:** On request. **Contact:** Metalhawk, 311 Miami St., Toledo, OH 43605, USA; phone (419)691-4377.

Oregon

Sandy Glides: Would-be and experienced hang gliders spend 2 days practicing the art on the sand dunes of northeastern Oregon. Groups of 5 to 8 travel to Cape Kiwanda where they receive instruction on V-shaped, 18-foot dacron kites. The teachers give special training on wind and weather variables and use of equipment during 8-hour day and evening classes. A full 40-second flight is the objective by the end of the second day. Participants may stay in nearby Pacific City or may camp out on the dunes. **Cost:** On request. **When:** April to November. **Contact:** Free Spirit Hang Gliders, 14615 NE 91st St., Redmond, WA 98052, USA; phone (206)827-0341.

Pennsylvania

Hang Gliding: A basic course in hang gliding is offered at locations in Pennsylvania, New Jersey and New York. The course includes a 2-hour indoor class designed to familiarize students with the history of hang gliding, the theory of hang gliding flight, and the common sense safety rules that must be observed. Control movements are practiced in the flight simulator. A 2-hour ground running session is next, in which students practice controlling the glider while on flat ground and learn preflight inspection. Then there is a 4-hour flying period in which participants practice take-offs, smooth flights and safe landings. After completion of the basic course, everyone is invited for a following day of instruction for 6 hours. **Cost:** $45 for basic course, $20 for follow-up. **When:** Year-round. **Contact:** Up-It, 1103 Cottman Ave., Philadelphia, PA 98111, USA; phone (215)722-8212.

RESOURCES

Clubs and Associations

Aerodelta Club
49 Blvd. Saint Michel
75005 Paris, France

AeroKlub CSSR
Opletalova 25
11631 Prague 2, Czechoslovakia

Aeroklub Polskiej
Rzeczypospolltej Ludowej
ul. Krakowskie Przedmelscle 55
00-71 Warsaw, Poland

The Australian Self-Soar Association
11/51 Noble St.
Allawah, NSW 2218, Ausfralia

Canadian West Coast
Hang Gliding Association
P.O. Box 77123, Sta. S
Vancouver, BC, Canada V7L 1N3

Canterbury Hang Gliding Club
P.O. Box 22-481
Christchurch, New Zealand

Dansk Dregeflyver Union
Bremensgade 11, 1 tv
2300 Copenhagen S., Denmark

Deutscher Hangeglieterclub
Hauptstrasse 16
881 Burghagel, Germany

Federation Francaise de Vol Libre
29 rue de Sevres
75006 Paris, France

International Hang Gliding Secretariat
WOK
6435 Kossen, Austria

Irish Hang Gliding Association
12-P Home Farm Park
Dublin 9, Ireland

Japan Hang Glider Association
5-12-18 Yafumo Meguru-ku
Tokyo 152, Japan

New Zealand Hang Gliding Assn.
P.O. Box 6680
Te Aro, Wellington, New Zealand

Scottish Sailwing Association
c/o W. Cowell, The Castle
Edinburgh, Great Britain

South Australian
Hang Gliding Association
P.O. Box 156
Parkholme, Adelaide, SA 5043
Australia

Swiss Hang Gliding Association
Badener Strasse 109 CH8004
Zurich, Switzerland

U.S. Hang Gliding Association
Box 66036
Los Angeles, CA 90066, USA
Phone (213)390-3065

PARACHUTING— PARASAILING

EUROPE

Parasailers' Overland Trip: An overland trip of 8 weeks through Europe and North Africa focuses on parasailing, as well as sailing and hang gliding. The trip originates and ends in England and visits France, Spain, Morocco, Algeria, Tunisia, Sicily, Italy and Switzerland. The party of about 18 stops at prime parasailing sites en route, including a mountain base north of Madrid for private parasailing, ballooning, hang gliding and parachuting. In North Africa a series of semipermanent base camps is established for side trips and activities, including bicycling, sand sailing and parasailing. The European portion of the flexible itinerary is primarily a travel tour; most leisure time is spent in Africa. **Cost:** $1,722 includes food, transportation, accommodations, equipment, guide. **When:** May, July, September. **Contact:** Skytrek Overland Expeditions, Hill End Farm, Tyttenhanger Green, Barley Mow Ln., St. Albans, Herts., Great Britain; phone St. Albans 56193.

PACIFIC

Hawaii

Parasailing on the Kona Coast: Participants may sail for 10 minutes over Kailua Bay on a kite-like para-

A parasailer is pulled around the bay at Acapulco by a heavy line attached to a motorboat below. Parasailing can also be done on trips to Hawaii and Europe. (Bob Citron)

chute towed behind a jet boat. Passengers are secured by a harness, which frees the hands for photography. A waterproof camera or camera casting is recommended. **Cost:** $20. **When:** Daily year-round. **Contact:** Big Island Adventures, P.O. Box 2639, Kailua-Kona, HI 96740, USA; phone (808)329-2676.
(M)

Pacific Parachute Jumping: A day-long jump course starts at Dillingham Airfield in Mokuleia every Saturday morning. A jump using automatically opening parachutes with radio-guided descent is made at the conclusion of the training period, weather permitting. After completing the first, a second course may be taken in which a minimum of 5 static line jumps (wherein the parachute is automatically opened) is required before participants advance to free-fall and autonomous rip cord pulling. Jump altitude is 2,800 feet for the first 5 jumps. As participants progress, higher altitudes are reached. A typical jump is made from 7,500 feet with a free fall of about 1 mile (30 seconds) before the parachute is opened at 2,500 feet. Life preservers are required since the drop zone is near the ocean. **Cost:** $85 for 1-day course includes equipment; $13 a jump in groups of 5 for advanced course. **When:** Year-round. **Contact:** Jump Hawaii, 206 Lagoon Dr., Honolulu, HI 96819, USA; phone (808)841-2427.

UNITED STATES
Michigan
Leaps and Landings: Beginning

parachutists are offered a complete first jump course on weekends at a drop zone near Tecumseh, Michigan. Classes begin at 10 a.m. on Saturday and Sunday, and participants who are anxious to jump may receive their ground instruction and make the first jump on the same day. Once the student has made the initial leap, 4 subsequent static line jumps are required before progressing into free-fall. Training in more advanced jumping techniques is also offered. Participants must be at least 16. **Cost:** $45 for first jump course includes all equipment, jumpmaster, aircraft. **When:** On request. **Contact:** Tecumseh Parachuting Service, Tecumseh, MI 49286, USA; phone (517)423-7720.

New Jersey
Sky Diving Course: Beginners can learn to parachute in a day during a course at the Burlington County Air Park near Lumberton, New Jersey. The course is held on Saturdays and Sundays. Automatic opening systems are installed on the main and reserve chutes, and ground-to-air radio systems are provided to help guide the student to the landing area. **Cost:** $70. **When:** Year-round. **Contact:** Ripcord Paracenter Inc., Burlington County Airport, Medford RD, NJ 08055, USA; phone (609)267-9897.

New York
Sky Diving over Johnstown: Reaching speeds of 120 miles an hour or more, sky divers experience the sensation of free-falling during jumps in Johnstown, New York. For beginners, a classroom training program outlines the basics of the sport, which include care and use

of equipment, safety procedures and parachute control methods. The course, lasting about half a day, prepares the student for the jump later that same day. Properly equipped, the jumper boards an aircraft and prepares for the premier free-fall. Once the airplane is in proper position above the landing site, the sky diver exits from the side of the aircraft and free-falls to about 2,500 feet before pulling the rip cord and floating to the ground. Soft, stand-up landings are often achieved even on the first jump. **Cost:** $45 includes training, equipment, jump. **When:** Summer. **Contact:** Drop Zone Parachute Club, Fulco Airport, Rt. 67, Johnstown, NY 12095, USA; phone (518)762-4900.

Ohio

Sky Diving in the Midwest: A sport parachuting center in Ohio instructs sky divers to jump safely from an altitude of 7,000 feet and drift freely toward the ground target. Instructors and jumpmasters are licensed professionals with over 2,000 jumps to their credit. Safety is stressed during all the phases of the course and on subsequent jumps. The jump course lasts for 4 hours and covers every aspect necessary to make the first jump. Included are familiarization with the parachute equipment, the aircraft and safety procedures; exits from the aircraft and body stability; possible malfunctions; emergency procedures; canopy manipulation; and parachute landings. The novice parachutist makes 5 static line jumps at 2,800 feet with automatic parachute opening. The free-fall jumps are then taken from 5 different altitudes between 3,600 and 7,200 feet. These jumps provide the opportunity for further coaching in stability, spotting, turns, loops and other maneuvers. Any person over 18 is eligible for training (16-year-olds are eligible with authorized permission). **Cost:** $45, or $35 for groups of 5 or more includes training program, equipment, first jump, advanced free-fall training. **When:** Year-round. **Contact:** The Greene County Sport Parachute Center, 113 S. Monroe Siding Rd., Xenia, OH 45385, USA; phone (513)376-9293.

Texas

Sky Diving over Dallas: Sky diving lessons, including 5 jumps, are available for beginners and experienced jumpers during classes held near Dallas. Beginners enroll in 5½-hour ground courses which include instruction in equipment handling and parachute theory. After the classroom session, which also includes a training film and lectures, students practice procedures at a drop zone while reviewing classroom discussions prior to making the actual jumps. For enthusiasts with more background in the sport, additional advanced training is available in parachute packing, free-fall maneuvers and competitive sky diving. **Cost:** $15 to $75. **When:** Daily year-round. **Contact:** Skydivers of Texas Inc., 5301 Parkland Ave., Dallas, TX 75235, USA; phone (214)824-3540.

Washington

Parachuting in Issaquah: Persons wishing to experience free-fall parachuting participate in day-long training sessions originating from

First-jump courses are offered by the Issaquah Parachute Center for anyone wishing to experience a few moments of free fall. Students are accompanied by a jumpmaster the first time out. (Bill Jeswine)

an airfield in Issaquah. The training includes classroom film and slide presentations introducing beginners to the basics of parachuting and equipment. This is followed by training on aircraft exit, canopy steering, emergency procedures and landings. Participants take a lunch break before boarding the airplane. Then, from an altitude of 2,800 feet and accompanied by a jumpmaster, individuals make their first jump. For trained jumpers, a variety of altitude drops is available. **Cost:** $12 to $50 includes equipment, training, aircraft. **When:** Year-round. **Contact:** Issaquah Parachute Center, Skyport Airfield, P.O. Box 765, Issaquah, WA 98027, USA; phone (206)392-2121.

Wisconsin

The Sky's the Limit: Interested

persons learn the art of parachute jumping from experienced professionals. On the ground and up in the skies over southern Wisconsin, participants develop skills in safe parachuting. Upon successful completion of the ground training classes, potential jumpers are sent up for their first static line (or automatic parachute opening) jump; as the student advances, higher jumps are made until the free-fall jump. Training includes basic orientation, observation of all phases of sport jumping, instruction in stable-fall procedures and familiarization with equipment. Opportunities are available for competitive jumping as well. Participants need to be 18 or over and in good health. **Cost:** $65 for first jump training, $120 for 6-jump package. **When:** May to October. **Contact:** Southern Wisconsin Skyhawks, Inc., Rt. 1, Box 453, Bristol, WI 53104, USA; phone (414)857-2007.

RESOURCES
Clubs and Associations

Aero Club
Lidorstrasse 5
6006 Lucerne, Switzerland

Aeroklub
Prinz Egen Strasse 12
Vienna, Austria

Australian Parachute Federation
P.O. Box 21
Doveton, Victoria 3177, Australia

Canadian Sport Parachuting Association
P.O. Box 848
Burlington, ON, Canada

Deutscher AeroClub
Lyoner Strasse 16
6000 Frankfurt/Main 71, West Germany

Federation Argentina de Paracaidismo
Anchorena 275
Buenos Aires, Argentina

Federation Francaise Parachutiste
35 rue St. Georges
Paris 9-E, France

Irish Parachute Association
15, Upper Pembroke St.
Dublin 2, Ireland

National Collegiate Parachute League
P.O. Box 104
Monterey, CA 93940, USA

Norges Luftsportforbund
Nedre Slottsgate 17
1, Oslo, Norway

Para Club Caracas
Apartado 80016
Caracas 108, Venezuela

U.S. Parachute Association
806 15th St. NW, Suite 444
Washington, DC 20005, USA

Water Adventures

RIVER RAFTING

Riding inflatable rafts of tough, rubberized nylon, a worldwide tribe of adventurers slides over the rocky floors of rivers from Alaska to New Zealand. They brave the turbulence of whitewater rapids, where the rivers are pushed into confusion and molded into waves frozen in space by submerged boulders. Each standing wave and threatening rock appears suspended in an eternity of danger—and a dozen such eternities add up, in most rapids, to less than a minute of real time.

You can feel the surge of the river and enjoy the spray of whitewater by joining any one of the several hundred river rafting trips which are offered all over the world. Each of the rivers is different, from the Noatak in Alaska with its spectacular scenery and wildlife to the intense whitewater of the short Youghiogheny run in Pennsylvania. Different, too, are the experiences you will have on each trip—one could easily spend a lifetime migrating from river to river and never weary of the sport.

Many people go for the excitement of the Class V or VI rapids on the Colorado in Arizona, California's Tuolumne or Idaho's Snake, but the scenic wonders of Canada's Tatshenshini, with its calving glaciers and grizzly bears, should not be overlooked. Neither should the Usumacinta, which flows between Guatemala and Mexico through the monkey-populated jungle of the Mayan heartland, or the exotic Watut in Papua New Guinea, flowing through a deep gorge filled with a kaleidoscope of tropical birds.

With the wide selection of rivers to run, the adventurer usually makes a decision based on location, time and money. Here, too, the choice is often great—one-day trips are possible in California, Washington, Pennsylvania, Georgia and New Mexico as well as in many other states. Longer trips, of four days to a week, can be charted in Idaho, Colorado, Oregon, Texas and overseas in Yugoslavia and New Zealand. And trips of two weeks or even longer float down the Marañon River in the Peruvian Andes, the Rio Grande de Santiago in Mexico, the Thula Beri in Nepal, and through the spectacular Grand Canyon of the Colorado.

Indeed, in no other activity of adventure travel is the choice so great. Whether you're 6 years old or 80, you can river raft; and whether you do it in Tennessee or Ethiopia, you'll never forget it.   □

Powering through Lava Falls on the Colorado River is a thrilling maneuver that requires an oarsman's skill to successfully execute. (Bart Henderson/Sobek Expeditions)

RIVER RAFTING

AFRICA

Ethiopia

Rapid Running on the Omo: Travelers in river rafts join about 1,600 hippos and 200 crocodiles on the remote Omo River in Ethiopa. Members work together during the expedition and should be in excellent physical condition to run a river that tumbles and spumes over scores of cataracts and rapids. As the Omo winds through dense jungle, dramatic savannas and 4,000-foot forested gorges, participants see a variety of African wildlife on shore as well as 400 species of tropical birds. Participants may also observe Nile perch which often weigh 200 pounds or more. On the lower shores of the river, rafters have the opportunity to interact with the Bodi tribe, a people who adorn themselves with decorative scars, ear or nose rings, and clay lip plates. The water of the Omo often changes, and rafters pass through or around countless waterfalls including the 1,000-foot Royal Falls. Waterslides, tributary swimming holes and hot springs are also encountered. **Cost:** $1,950 for 28 days, $2,040 for 32 days includes guide, ground transportation, meals, rafting equipment. **When:** September, October. **Contact:** Sobek Expeditions, P.O. Box 67, Angels Camp, CA 2924. *(M)*

ASIA

Nepal

Whitewater beneath the Himalayas: Participants spend 10 days of a 17-day trip rafting down the Thula Beri, the greatest western river of the Nepal Himalayas. Arriving in Kathmandu, group members spend a day sightseeing before traveling by plane to the starting point of the river run. On the days that follow, rafters depart downriver after breakfast, stop in the early afternoon to set up camp and spend the rest of the day bird watching, fishing, swimming, hiking to the local villages or learning about the local wildlife from the

In Ethiopia, rafters often see a yawning hippo between stretches of rapids. A 28-day Sobek Expeditions trip down the Omo River is available for $1,950. (Jim Slade)

expedition's guides. Leaving the river for 2 days, participants visit a safari camp in the Karnali Wildlife Reserve where tigers, leopards, wild boars, deer, antelope and a variety of birds may be observed. A fast 22-mile run to the last camp just north of the India/Nepal border concludes the river run. Group members fly to Kathmandu where the trip ends. **Cost:** $1,250 from Kathmandu includes camping gear, river equipment, meals, land and air transportation in Nepal, guides. **When:** January, February, March. **Contact:** REI Adventure Travel, 1525 11th Ave., Seattle, WA 98122, USA; phone (206)322-7800.   *(M)*

AUSTRALASIA

Australia

River Running in New South Wales: Up to 300 sets of rapids, depending on rainfall, are negotiated on a 5-day float trip down the Nymboida River. Beginning in Coff's Harbour, participants are shuttled to the put-in point near Dorrigo. Once on the river, rafters encounter perils ranging from staircase drops to 90-foot chutes while passing through dense rain forest. Trip members spend approximately 5 hours a day on the river and may be asked to assist in "roping" the rafts through shallows encountered in the early part of the trip. The wildness of the Nymboida River makes protective helmets and life jackets mandatory. Guides set up camp along the riverbank at night, and precautions are taken to avoid degrading the natural environment. Return transportation to Coff's Harbour is provided from the take-out point at Nymboida.

Cost: $211 to $247 includes guide, food, equipment. **When:** November to May. **Contact:** Australian Whitewater Expeditions, P.O. Box 3077, Sydney, N.S.W., 2001, Australia; phone 969-1457.

New Zealand

Alpine River Rafting: New Zealand's backcountry is explored on 1-day river rafting trips. Passengers and craft are transported 16 miles upstream from Woodstock into the high country reaches of the Waimakariri River. At this point, accompanied by an experienced guide, the raft sets off downstream in the alpine river waters. Along the way a number of stops are made including one for a picnic lunch. All raft parties should take clothing which can get wet, and a pair of soft shoes. Passengers should be in good physical condition. **Cost:** $17 for the trip only, $6 for road transportation. **When:** October to March. **Contact:** Canterbury and Alpine Travel Ltd., P.O. Box 8107, Christchurch, New Zealand; phone 65-022.

North Island Rafting: Groups of 5 or more fly from Taupo into the surrounding hills for raft trips through remote, untouched terrain, highly recommended for photographers and naturalists. Paddling inflatable rafts, participants spend 1 to 5 days or more rafting wild rivers and viewing sheer cliffs, waterfalls and virgin bush. The area is populated with a variety of wildlife including sika, goats, wild sheep and wild cattle. Discounts for large groups are available. **Cost:** $50 a day. **When:** Year-round (except in winter). **Contact:** Kaimanawa Tours

Their raft seemingly swallowed up by whitewater, a group of river runners makes the initial drop into the rapids on a river in Ontario. (Canadian Govt. Office of Tourism)

& Treks, P.O. Box 321, Taupo, New Zealand; phone 87902.

CANADA

Alberta

Rafting Afternoon: Two short raft trips lasting about 3 hours each are offered down the Bow and Athabaska rivers. The Bow trip departs from Banff by bus to the put-in point nearby, spending 2 to 2½ hours on the river. A large neoprene raft takes participants to Canmore, where a bus awaits to return them to Banff. The Athabasca trip is based in Jasper, and on this trip, too, a bus transports par-

ticipants to and from the river, where about 2½ hours are spent. Wildlife abounds in these areas, as do opportunities for photography. An overnight trip out of Banff down the Kootenay is also offered. **Cost:** $13 for adults, $7 for children under 12 on Bow and Athabasca trips includes transportation, equipment, guide; $120 on Kootenay trip includes food, camping equipment, transportation, guide. **When:** June to September. **Contact:** Rocky Mountain Raft Tours, Box 1771, Banff, AB Canada T0L 0C0; phone (403)762-3632.   *(M)*

British Columbia

Stikine River Photography Expedi-

tion: A 10-day raft trip down the Stikine River combined with a photography workshop provides participants with an opportunity to explore and record the Canadian wilderness. The trip begins in Wrangell with a bush plane flight to Telegraph Creek in British Columbia. The intensive field experience, offered in conjunction with the University of Alaska, emphasizes holistic perception of the environment and the refinement of photographic skills. The guides are always ready to share their knowledge of the land and the river, and evening campfires serve as a forum for lectures and discussions. Students must bring their own rain gear, tents, sleeping bags and camera equipment; the outfitter supplies film, waterproof camera bags and a floating reference library. **Cost:** $750 includes rafting equipment, meals, transportation from Wrangell. **When:** June. **Contact:** Alaska Wilderness Expeditions, Inc., P.O. Box 882, Wrangell, AK 99929, USA; phone (907)874-3784. *(M)*

Chilcotin-Fraser Whitewater: Members of a 10-day expedition through the Chilcotin-Fraser river area make their way using a variety of transportation. The trip commences in Vancouver and includes the Surge Narrows with its 9-knot tidal current; tidal rapids in Okisollo Channel; a 45-minute flight over the Homatko Icefields; and a campsite located at Chilko Lake. Whitewater experiences include runs in the Chilko River, the Chilcotin River, Moran Canyon, and the Bridge River Rapids. Expedition members are then transported to Lillooet where they board a train that travels back through the Coast Range. **Cost:** $835 includes meals, transportation. **When:** June to September. **Contact:** Canadian River Expeditions Ltd., 1005 Highland Dr., West Vancouver, BC Canada V7S 2G7; phone (604)926-4436. *(M)*

Thompson River Whitewater: Lytton is the meeting place for a 2-day whitewater experience on the Thompson River. A 1½-hour drive by bus brings participants to the put-in point just out of Ashcroft, and the gear is driven to the campsite downriver. In Black Canyon rafters view wildlife grazing on the river banks. Lunch is eaten on Asparagus Island where wild vegetables may be picked when in season. The remainder of the afternoon finds the raft floating in quiet water until camp is made near Spences Bridge. The second day of the trip provides a run down to Lytton through the Pitquah Canyon and 20 large whitewater rapids that include the Frog, the Cutting Board, Devil's Cauldron and the Jaws of Death. At mid-afternoon the bus transfers participants back to Lytton and the trip's end. **Cost:** $80 includes meals, some gear,

Wilderness Tours runs day-long trips on both the Petawawa and Ottawa rivers in Ontario. Both feature some difficult rapids matching those of the Colorado. (Wilderness Tours)

transportation from Lytton; tents and sleeping bags may be rented. **When:** May, June. **Contact:** Cascade River Holidays, P.O. Box 65, Yale, BC Canada V0K 2S0; phone (604)863-2332. *(M)*

Thompson and Fraser Rafting: A variety of whitewater experiences on the Thompson and Fraser rivers lasts from 2 to 7 days and covers various stretches of water. Trips begin in Lytton, where the Thompson and the Fraser converge, and run the rivers between Savona, Boston Bar, Ashcroft, Yale and Lytton. Wildlife is abundant in the area, including beavers, deer, bears, salmon, eagles, ospreys, hawks, kestrels, falcons and kingfishers. The rafts are 22 feet long and are powered by outboard motors. Whitewater instruction is available in the spring. **Cost:** $99 to $258, depending on duration and location, includes transportation to

and from Lytton, food, equipment, guide. **When:** May to September. **Contact:** Kumsheen Raft Adventures, Suite 116, 525 Seymour St., Vancouver, BC Canada V6B 3H7; phone (604)669-0415. *(M)*

Northwest Territories

River Running and Hiking: A 12-day float trip combines running the South Nahanni River with hiking to points of interest on shore. Meeting at Watson Lake in the Yukon, participants take a 1½-hour flight by float plane to the put-in point near the confluence of Glacier Creek and the South Nahanni. Rafting the Nahanni varies from floating a lake-like river in a broad glacial valley to running a swift-flowing current through a narrow canyon. Stops are made to hike to Rabbitkettle Hot Springs, to photograph Virginia Falls and to hike up the vertical-walled Dry Creek Canyon. Participants camp on an island

and hike through a canyon to reach Caverne Valerie, a large cave with stalagtites, an ice passage and a passage containing the bones of Dall sheep hundreds of years old. Rafters continue the float to a point beyond the boundaries of Nahanni National Park, where they are picked up by float plane. Group members assist in paddling, setting up camp and portaging, but the crew prepares meals. **Cost:** $1,500 from Watson Lake includes transportation, meals, guides. **When:** July. **Contact:** North-west Expeditions, Ltd., P.O. Box 1551, Edmonton, AB Canada T5J 2N7; phone (403)452-4433. *(M)*

Ontario

A Day of Rafting: Two day-long river rafting trips are offered in Ontario, one down the Petawawa and one down the Ottawa. The first, inside the Algonquin Provincial Park, offers an itinerary involving rapids of Classes III to V. In a 4-mile stretch the river drops about 400 feet. The second trip, on the Ottawa River, features large, heavy rapids similar to those found on the Colorado. Each trip may be run as a day excursion or a package, including accommodations before and after the trip, meals and other amenities. Both trips may also be taken together. **Cost:** On request. **When:** On request. **Contact:** Wilderness Tours, P.O. Box 661, Pembroke, ON Canada K8A 6X9; phone (613)238-2361.

Yukon Territory

Rafting the Gold Rush Trail: A 6-day raft trip down the Yukon River follows the Trail of '98 to Dawson and the Klondike. The put-in point is Pelly Crossing on the Pelly River, and the first day of the trip takes the rafts down the Pelly to the Yukon. On the following days participants float down the Yukon, looking for nesting peregrine falcons, moose and other wildlife, panning for gold and visiting historical sites. The trip ends in Dawson. **Cost:** $650 from Whitehorse. **When:** August, September. **Contact:** Special InteresTours, P.O. Box 37, Medina, WA 98039, USA; phone (206)455-1960. *(M)*

CENTRAL AMERICA

Guatemala

Mayan Waterways: Members of a 14-day rafting expedition explore the Usumacinta River located along the Mexico-Guatemala border. The river and jungle contain myriad species of tropical wildlife such as eagles, toucans, howler monkeys and scarlet macaws; epiphytic orchids are found in the tall forest trees as well. Participants also have time to explore the ancient Mayan jungle cities along the river, including Yaxchilan and Piedras Negras. From the starting point of the trip at San Cristobal de las Casas, participants are flown and then driven to

---

the put-in point near Lacanja, visiting the ruins of the Mayan city of Bonampak and modern Lacandones along the way. After running the river, where the rapids reach Class III, the rafts are taken out at Tenosique in Mexico. The trip ends in Palenque, which is reached by bus. **Cost:** $480 from San Cristobal de las Casas to Palenque. **When:** January to April. **Contact:** Sacred Monkey Expeditions, Box 363, Jerome, AZ 86331, USA; phone (602)634-5711. *(M)*

Rafting the Pathway of the Gods: Once known as the "pathway of the gods," the Usumacinta River may be explored along with the Mayan ruins on its shores on a 13-day rafting trip. Departing from Flores in Guatemala, participants help row on the calm stretches and moderate rapids of the Usumacinta as it passes through the jungle. Rafters stop to swim and explore the deep green pools at the waterfalls of Budsilja River. Participants also investigate the stone sculptures, carved stelae and polychrome ceramics at the Mayan sites of Yaxchilan and Piedras Negras. The take-out point is Palenque in Mexico, site of another Mayan ruin. **Cost:** $745 includes equipment, meals. **When:** March. **Contact:** Wilderness World, 1342 Jewell Ave., Pacific Grove, CA 93950, USA; phone (408)373-5882. *(M)*

EUROPE

Camping and Rafting through Europe: Participants meet in London to begin a camping and rafting adventure of 37 days through 9 European nations. For the land portions of the expedition, adventurers travel by coach, buying and preparing food together while camping out. The group is accompanied by experienced river runners, a driver and, while in Russia, an Intourist guide. A week is taken to descend the Lora and Sjola rivers in Norway. Participants also have the opportunity for wilderness camping in the mountains and fjords of Norway. Leaving the wilderness, travelers spend time in major cities, with a canal cruise in Amsterdam and a visit to the Tivoli Gardens in Copenhagen. Adventurers explore Hamburg's Reeperbahn, board Viking ships in Oslo, go below decks on the Wasa Galleon in Stockholm, view the Hermitage and the Czar's winter palace in Leningrad and attend the ballet or circus in Moscow. The return to London concludes the trip. Academic credit is available. **Cost:** $1,300 includes accommodations, meals, guides, rafting equipment, ground transportation. **When:** July. **Contact:** Whitewater Voyages/River Exploration Ltd., 1225 Liberty St., El Cerrito, CA 94530, USA; phone (415)236-7219.

Yugoslavia

Slavic River Run: Flowing through the spectacular Dinara Range, the waters of the River Tara are traveled by raft during a 10-day journey. Starting from the medieval town of Dubrovnik, travelers set out on traditional handcrafted log rafts to float past rugged mountains with steep cliffs rising from the riverbed to form a 3,400-foot canyon. The water is clear and clean

A raft that seems to be almost airborne momentarily dips its nose into a hole of churning whitewater. Rafters paddle to gather speed before the drop. (American River Touring Assn.)

with rushing rapids and stretches of whitewater. Rafters may go ashore to explore limestone caves and hike meandering trails to villages along the route. Guided by local woodsmen, participants have the opportunity to learn the region's history, folklore, ecology and culture. Pitching tents in the meadowlands along the shore and sharing campfire meals round out each day's activities. Upon returning to Dubrovnik, the old-world towns of Zabljak and Foca are visited during the International Music and Folk Dance Festivals in progress throughout the summer. **Cost:** $860 includes camping equipment, meals, lodging, guides. **When:** June to August. **Contact:** American River Touring Association, 1016 Jackson St., Oakland, CA 94607, USA; phone (415)465-9355.

MEXICO

Mexican Wilderness Whitewater: Some of the finest whitewater in Mexico and Central America is featured on a 15-day journey down remote sections of the Rio Grande de Santiago. Hundreds of rapids highlight the 200-mile trip through the canyons of Mexico's plateau. During the last part of the trip group members reach a small hot spring that shoots out of a rock wall into the river. Rafters who can communicate in Spanish have plenty of opportunity to talk with the local people along the river. **Cost:** $535 includes transportation from Guadalajara. **When:** March. **Contact:** Expeditions by Wayne Hussing, 11120 Raphel Rd., Upper Falls, MD 21156, USA; phone (301)592-7247.

On a 20-day Sobek Expeditions rafting trip in Turkey, river runners negotiate rapids on the Euphrates as it pours through large cataracts on the Adiyaman Plateau. (Richard Bangs)

Running the Rio Grande de Santiago: A guided 7-day river trip travels through the canyons of the southern Sierra Madre. Participants on the expedition encounter hidden gold and silver mines, villages of Huichole Indians, hot springs, geysers and stretches of Class IV whitewater on the Rio Grande de Santiago. Group members are met at the Guadalajara airport as they arrive from the United States; a day is spent shopping and sightseeing in the city before putting in the river at Presa Santa Rosa, about 30 miles away. For 3 days group members float the rapids and camp along the shore. Arriving at Presa Rosario, they join a Mexican guide, visit an isolated Mayan ruin and feast on barbequed goat. The next day, members move on to Pueblo Viejo, an early gold mine and surviving community of the Spanish colonial era, then embark on a jeep tour into the high mountains before returning to Guadalajara. A knowledge of Spanish is an advantage but not a requirement for trip members. **Cost:** $350 from Guadalajara includes all lodging, meals, guides, river equipment, pack stock, ground transportation. **When:** December to February. **Contact:** Far Flung Adventures, Box 31, Terlingua, TX 79852, USA; phone (915)371-2489.

MIDDLE EAST

Turkey

Turkish Tandem: A 20-day expedition includes 6 days rafting the Euphrates and Coruh rivers. Flying in from New York, travelers tour Istanbul before flying on to the old Roman town of Malatya. From here participants take a bus to the Euphrates to spend 3 days rafting through a series of large cataracts. When the river slows down upon breaking from the Adiyaman Plateau, rafters take out and travel by plane and bus to Isper. Here group members put in for a 3-day float on the challenging Coruh River, called "the Crazy River" by those living on its shores. The take-out point is Artvin near the Russian border, from where participants fly back to Ankara before the return flight to New York. During the trip visits are made to small Turkish villages, the Mausoleum of Antiochus I on Mt. Nemrut and an abandoned monastery on the shores of the Euphrates. Travelers stay in hotels while in cities and camp out in tents on the rafting portions of the trip. **Cost:** $1,495 from Istanbul includes land and air transportation, meals, hotels, rafting equipment, guides. **When:** May to July. **Contact:** Sobek Expeditions, Inc., P.O. Box 67, Angels Camp, CA 95222, USA; phone (209)736-2924. *(M)*

SOUTH AMERICA
Chile
The Bio-Bio by Raft: Rafters travel through heavy whitewater for 15 days on the Bio-Bio, the largest river in Chile, named by the Mapuche Indians after the song of a native bird. Participants follow the river down the steep western slope of the Andes, camping on the banks and stopping at hot springs along the way. The absence of snakes and mosquitoes in this region is a feature that many participants may appreciate. When not challenged by the river's powerful rapids, adventurers observe and photograph the scenery including a 9,700-foot-high smoking volcano. The Andes present snow-capped panoramic views and participants pass by alpine lakes, glaciers and many tributary waterfalls including one plunging 230 feet directly into the main river. **Cost:** $1,065 includes ground transportation, guides, rafting equipment, meals. **When:** January to March. **Contact:** Sobek Expeditions, Inc., P.O. Box 67, Angels Camp, CA 95222, USA; phone (209)736-2924. *(M)*

Peru
Running the Marañon River: A month-long expedition that runs the Marañon River also takes participants by foot and truck into mountain and jungle areas. The trip begins in Lima with a day of sightseeing, then proceeds by air to Trujillo for local touring and swimming. Traveling by truck, with hiking side trips, participants arrive in Imacita where the river trip begins. Twelve days are spent rafting through huge canyons and walking the desert valleys and Andes foothills. Considerable rapids are crossed on the way to the take-out point, where a difficult truck journey is made to Chachapoyas. From here participants trek for 5 days to Rioja, and from there fly back to Lima via Chiclayo. All aspects of the trip involve active participation, including probable digging and pushing of the truck. Shorter trips are also available. **Cost:** $1,500 to $1,575 from Lima, depending on length of advance notice, includes food, guides, all transportation, accommodations. **When:** June. **Contact:** Amazon Expeditions, 310 W. Grandview Blvd., Erie, PA 16508, USA; phone (814)866-0701.

The slow pace of the Alatna River in Alaska allows time for fishing and relaxing. The Northern Wilderness Co. offers a 10-day float trip on the Alatna. (Pete Karp)

Peruvian Adventure: Inca and earlier Chimu ruins, notably at Cuzco, Chan Chan and the Andean city of Machupicchu, make Peru an interesting country for archaeologists and travelers alike. Beginning at Cuzco, 5- to 8-day trips provide participants with opportunities to explore a variety of ancient landmarks and artifacts. Routes used are the Urumbamba River run and the Inca Trail to Machupicchu. Cuzco itself provides a variety of experiences among stone streets and colorful shops. Knowledgeable guides provide an introduction to Peruvian culture, both ancient and modern. **Cost:** $297 for 5 days, $250 for 6 days, $460 for 8 days. **When:** May to September. **Contact:** Explorandes, Nicolas de Pierola 672, Of. 205, Lima, Peru; phone 23-6992. *(M)*

UNITED STATES

Alaska

Rafting Alagnak River: More than 80 miles of western Alaska wilderness is explored on an 8-day river trip. After a flight from Anchorage, members are flown by float plane from Dillingham to the put-in point at Kukaklek Lake. Class III whitewater and a waterfall are highlights of the river experience. Several species of fish inhabit the Alagnak, including salmon, rainbow trout, arctic char, grayling and northern pike. Other wildlife in the area include moose, bears, caribou and wolves. **Cost:** $800. **When:** June. **Contact:** Alaska Raft Adventures, Box 73264, Fairbanks, AK 99707, USA; phone (907)452-1465. *(M)*

Self-Guided Trips: The Stikine River provides a moderately fast but not whitewater run for rafters or canoeists. Unguided raft and canoe trips may be arranged through package plans which enable travelers to view the snow-capped peaks lining the river's path. The package includes a fly-in for 2 persons for a 6-day trip by canoe or inflatable raft. The trips are for experienced boaters only. **Cost:** $475 includes fly-in trip, paddles, flotation vest. **When:** Summer. **Contact:** Alaska Wilderness Expeditions, Inc., P.O. Box 7814, Ketchikan, AK 99901, USA. *(M)*

Rafting the Yukon Headwaters: Lakes Bennett, Tagish and Atlin, located in the northwest corner of British Columbia, form the headwaters of the Yukon and are the setting for a week-long trip. Participants gather in Skagway, Alaska for sightseeing and an overnight stay, and then travel by rail to Carcross, British Columbia. Here the rafting begins through the lake system and onto the Yukon with visits to ghost towns and points of interest along the way. The final 2 days are spent in Atlin sightseeing and making a day trip to a hot mineral spring. **Cost:** $550 includes food, accommodations, equipment, sightseeing, guide. **When:** July, September. **Contact:** Klondike Safaris, P.O. Box 1898, Skagway, AK 99840, USA. *(M)*

Fingers of the Hand Float: A 10-day rafting and backpacking trip takes group members to the Alatna River and the Arrigetch Peaks of north-central Alaska. Starting from the outpost of Bettles, the group takes a float plane flight to a small lake near the Alatna River. From there the expedition floats through the Arrigetch Peaks area, so named by the Eskimos because the peaks resemble the "fingers of the hand extended." Long days and short nights give participants the chance to observe wildlife and plantlife, take photographs and explore the region. The group hikes to a few lakes not far from the Alatna. The journey ends with a flight back to Bettles from Help-Me-Jack Lake, 80 miles south of the put-in. Groups are limited to 4 members plus guides. **Cost:** $828 includes meals, equipment, guides, flight from and to Bettles. **When:** July. **Contact:** The Northern Wilderness Company, P.O. Box 25795, Seattle, WA 98125, USA; phone (206)633-3946.   *(M)*

Floating Glacial Waters: An 11-day trip down the Tatshenshini River and a 7-day trip down the Copper River provide rafters close-up views of Alaska's remote landscape. The Tatshenshini trip floats along a glacial river fed by bluish ice running through the towering St. Elias Mountains to Alaska's Dry Bay. Participants walk on one glacier and watch another as huge chunks of ice calve hundreds of feet into an adjacent river. Draining the southern flank of the Alaskan Range, the Copper River provides rafters with a close-up view of mountain peaks which often loom directly above. While approaching the ocean, participants watch glaciers spill into the river and often pass near seals sunning on the gravel bars. **Cost:** $930 for Tatshenshini trip, $530 for Copper trip includes meals and transportation. **When:** July, August. **Contact:** Out-

Canyoneers runs 7- to 12-day trips down the Colorado, offering unforgettable whitewater runs as well as red sandstone canyon scenery. (Arizona Office of Tourism)

door Adventures, 3109 Fillmore St., San Francisco, CA 94123, USA; phone (415)567-9938. *(M)*

Arizona

River Rafting through Marble Canyon: A series of 7-, 10- and 12-day pontoon and rowboat trips down the Colorado River includes shooting Grand Canyon rapids and cruising still waters. Adventurers put in at Lees Ferry, the beginning of Marble Canyon, and run the river for 280 miles. About 47 miles downstream, at Buck Farm Canyon, participants may hike through the smooth, twisting walls that spread only a few feet apart in places and open in other areas into clear spring water streams. Moving past Indian ruins at Nankoweep Rapids, trip members plunge onward to Havasu Creek before reaching Lava Falls, the largest rapids on the river. From there trip members continue to the take-out point at Pierce Ferry. Participants in each trip camp along the river wherever possible and may hike along side trails. **Cost:** $460 to $640 depending on length and type of trip, includes equipment, meals. **When:** May to September. **Contact:** Canyoneers, Inc., P.O. Box 2997, Flagstaff, AZ 86003, USA; phone (602)526-0924. *(M)*

Glen Canyon Float Trip: Surrounded by sandstone cliffs, participants spend 1 day leisurely riding through Glen Canyon in whitewater river rafts. After motoring from Page, Arizona through a 2-mile tunnel to the base of Glen Canyon Dam, a maximum of 12 participants boards each boat to join 2 guides who are well versed in the geology and history of the canyon. On the 15-mile run to Lees Ferry, participants stop for short hikes and for a midday lunch. Trip members have the opportunity to investigate Indian petroglyphs and pictographs along the shore. After taking out at Lees Ferry, the group returns by bus to Page. **Cost:** $25 for adults, $20 for children under 12 includes transportation from Page, lunch, guides, rafting equipment. **When:** On request. **Contact:** Fort Lee Company, P.O. Box 2103, Marble Canyon, AZ 86036, USA; phone (602)355-2212.

Grand Canyon River Rafting: The muddy, swirling waters of the Colorado River provide an exciting river rafting trip through the jagged rock walls of the Grand Canyon. A bus transports passengers from Las Vegas to the staging area at Lees Ferry for a 9-day float to Pierce Ferry. A shorter trip lasting 6 days ends at Whitmore, 188 miles downstream from Lees Ferry. Passengers may also board at Whitmore for a 4-day trip. Participants should bring sleeping bags weighing not more than 5 pounds. Rain gear is essential, as participants often get wet and the water is quite cold. The trip ends with a banquet in Las Vegas. **Cost:** $375 from Lees Ferry to Pierce Ferry, $250 for 6 days, $125 for 4 days. **When:** May to September. **Contact:** Georgie's Royal River Rats, Box 12489, Las Vegas, NV 89112, USA; phone (702)451-5588. *(M)*

Arkansas

Ozark River Travel: Two expeditions take travelers into the Ozarks of Arkansas and Missouri to learn the techniques of river travel and experience the outdoors. A 12-day expedition into the Boston Moun-

tains area in northwestern Arkansas offers backpacking, whitewater canoeing on the Buffalo River and instruction in outdoor and river skills. Some rock climbing with instruction is done at Hemmed-In Hollow, the highest free-falling waterfall between the southern Appalachians and the Rockies. The other trip, lasting a week, travels by canoe down the Eleven Point River, a clear, fast-flowing stream. Included is instruction in basic river skills as well as some caving and a day's solo in the Irish Wilderness. Enrollment in each expedition is limited to 16 people aged 16 and older. **Cost:** $174 for Buffalo River trip, $105 for Eleven Point River trip includes transportation, instruction, food. **When:** May, August. **Contact:** Touch of Nature Environmental Center, Southern Illinois University, Carbondale, IL 62901, USA.

California

River Rafting on the Tuolumne: Led by highly experienced guides, these 2- to 4-day trips down the wild Tuolumne River are not for everybody. Only those with whitewater experience should consider taking this roller-coaster ride on some of the most thrilling rapids that California has to offer. Less demanding trips are available on other rivers but this is the one with the explosive excitement that veteran river-riders demand. Children under 12 will not be accepted and only the guides will be allowed to handle the oars. **Cost:** $125 for 2 days, $155 for 3 days, $185 for 4 days includes food, gear, transportation back to point of origin. **When:** April to October. **Contact:**

Adventours—Wet & Wild, Inc., Box B, Woodland, CA 95695, USA; phone (916)662-6824.　　　*(M)*

Western Whitewater: In a fleet of 4 to 5 boats, rafters can join up to 30 other people in 2- to 4-day trips down the Klamath, Merced and Tuolumne rivers. During the journey, participants choose between joining a paddle crew to navigate a course down the river, paddling inflatable kayaks, or sitting back while guides handle the oars. The Klamath flows through the heavily forested coastal range and provides warm waters with plenty of rapids and swimming holes. Camping on sandbars or along shore, rafters who want excitement can run the Tuolumne as it plunges down 585 feet over 17 miles. The river is very swift the first 2 days out, offering almost continuous whitewater, then it slows down a bit, allowing participants to better observe the sheer canyon walls. **Cost:** $79 to $185 depending on the river, participant's age, day of the week, number of days out; includes equipment, meals, instruction, guides. **When:** April to October. **Contact:** ECHO: The Wilderness Company, Inc., 6505 Telegraph Ave., Oakland, CA 94609, USA; phone (415)658-5075.　　　*(M)*

Whitewater Workshops: California's second-largest river, the Klamath, serves as a whitewater classroom for 5 rafting workshops. The workshops vary in length from 3 to 6 days and include both oar and paddle instruction. A 67-mile run takes rafters from Horse Creek to Ti Bar on the upper Klamath, and those unable to attend the full workshop may join the 40-mile rarely run section of the river from Horse Creek to Happy Camp. A more challenging run is from Happy Camp to Ti Bar—30 river miles. The emphasis of the trips is on the theory and technique of whitewater boating, canoe strokes in paddle rafts, equipment purchase, maintenance, first aid, rescue activities and wilderness ecology. **Cost:** $115 to $200 includes meals, accommodations, instruction. **When:** April, July. **Contact:** James Henry River Journeys, 1078 Keith, Berkeley, CA 94708, USA; phone (415)527-4649.

California Rafting: River rafters can run any or all of 7 whitewater rivers in California, be it a short 1-day float down the popular Stanislaus or a longer 4-day excursion deep into the Siskiyous on northern California's Klamath River. The rivers each offer a different challenge and mood. The Tuolumne is the wildest run, pouring from Yosemite in one of the steepest navigable river gradients in the world. The middle fork of the Eel is the most remote, and rafters have a good chance to view wildlife such as deer, otters, turtles and bears

wilderness river trips

Idaho's
Salmon & Snake Rivers
Also trips in Alaska, California, Oregon.
ECHO: The Wilderness Co.
6505 A.T. Telegraph Ave.
Oakland, CA 94609
(415) 658-5075

along its shores. More experienced whitewater veterans may want to try the Merced, a steep 22-mile course with at least one portage and frequent stretches of rapids. Participants camp at night along the rivers. **Cost:** $35 to $180, depending on the trip, includes river equipment, meals, guides. **When:** March to September. **Contact:** OARS Inc., P.O. Box 67, Angels Camp, CA 95222, USA; phone (209)736-2924 or 736-2661. *(M)*

Rapid Rafting: Two-day trips are offered on the American and Stanislaus rivers. The American River trip begins with a few rapids widely spaced by gentle current. Further downstream, the canyon constricts into a gorge, the river gathers speed, and rafters race through several miles of continuous whitewater. The Stanislaus River offers the fastest water at the beginning of the trip, starting one minute after the put-in point and continuing for 5 miles. The canyon through which the river flows has high limestone cliffs and river-scoured rocks. New Melones Dam is nearing completion, and while it is not clear when the canyon will be flooded, there is not much time left to see the canyon unchanged. **Cost:** $75 to $85 depending on day of week; $45 for a 1-day trip. **When:** April to August for American River, April to September for Stanislaus River. **Contact:** Outdoor Adventures, 3109 Fillmore St., San Francisco, CA 94123, USA; phone (415)567-9938. *(M)*

The American Way: The American River runs through the heart of gold rush country, and a 2-day float trip takes participants into the state park at Coloma, site of the discovery of gold in 1849. From the put-in point at Chili Bar the river moves rapidly westward through a large cleft in the lower Sierra, producing challenging whitewater. On the first day the group runs a number of rapids, including Endurance, Sharon's Chute and Kiss Me Lightly, which are followed by a calm stretch leading into Coloma. After going ashore to explore there, participants pitch camp a short distance downriver. The next day's ride passes from calm water to the Gorge, with its long stretch of rapids leading to Folsom Lake, the take-out point. Wildlife likely to be seen en route includes mule deer, black bears, wild goats, beavers, otters, blue herons and chukars. Opportunities are provided for photography. **Cost:** $66 to $72 includes food, equipment, transportation to and from the river, guide. **When:** April to September. **Contact:** Outdoors Unlimited, 2500 Fifth Ave., Sacramento, CA 95818, USA; phone (916)452-1081. *(M)*

Golden State Water Run: Some of the lesser-known rivers in the western United States are available to participants on 2- and 4-day rafting expeditions. The first of the 2-day trips involves a run down the American River over such whitewater areas as the Meatgrinder, Old Scarey and the Troublemaker, past Sutter's Mill (site of the original California gold strike) and onto shore for the night. The next day participants rush through 5 miles of rapids before floating out to Folsom Lake near Sacramento. Another option is the Merced River, which

The guide yells instructions from the stern and steers a course through a section of rapids on one of California's popular rafting rivers. (Thomas Morse/Zephyr River Expeditions)

starts in the Yosemite Valley and winds its way 14 miles to Briceburg. On this journey a portage must be made past a 20-foot waterfall close to a 300-yard stretch of whitewater known as Quarter Mile Rapids. A somewhat calmer voyage takes rafters down the Stanislaus River, another 2-day excursion through a semi-wilderness area. Participants on this trip gain the skills needed for more advanced whitewater work. Finally, there is a 4-day expedition through the wilds of the Eel River, a remote and unusual geographic area. Deer, bears and coyotes surround this river system, one of the few in North America which flows northward out to sea. **Cost:** $75 for 2 days, $225 for 4 days. **When:** April to June. **Contact:** Wilderness Associates of North America, P.O. Box 1285, Monterey, CA 93940, USA; phone (408)649-4868. *(M)*

Floating Western Rivers: Several California rivers are used for a variety of whitewater river experiences lasting from 1 to 4 days. The Stanislaus River, originating in the High Sierras, combines whitewater with lush side canyons and explorable creeks, as well as numerous abandoned gold-mining sites. During segments of the trip, participants pass below limestone cliffs punctuated at their bases by outcroppings of pure marble. Indian petroglyphs and pestle holes, evidence of the Miwok Indian culture, are also visible. The American River provides a challenging 18-mile whitewater run where trip members negotiate such rapids as the Meatgrinder and Troublemaker. The Eel River is the only whitewater river in California without road access that offers a trip longer than 3 days. The river is a spring river, permitting a brief running season with 2- to 5-day trips. Other trip locations available to rafting enthusiasts are the Kern, Merced, Klamath and East Carson rivers. **Cost:** $32 to $180 depending on trip includes equipment, food. **When:** March to October. **Contact:** Zephyr River Expeditions, P.O. Box 529, Columbia, CA 95310, USA; phone (209)532-6249. *(M)*

Colorado

Thundering down the Colorado: Adventurers spend 2 days on a partially motorized, partially oar-powered journey that is tranquil at some points and roaring at others. Comparable in excitement and beauty to the Grand Canyon, the Westwater Canyon stretch of the Colorado has the advantage of being less traveled. On the first day after busing to the river from Grand Junction, rafters take neoprene pontoon rafts through Horsethief and Ruby canyons, leaving the rafts on shore to go camping and hiking. The second day takes the group into the more challenging part of the trip where the Colorado snakes through the narrow gorge of Westwater Canyon in a series of rapids. One-day trips through the canyon are offered for those with less time. **Cost:** $25 to $35 for 1 day, $80 to $90 for 2 days includes meals, guides, rafting equipment, transportation from Grand Junction. **When:** May to September. **Contact:** Adventure Bound, Inc., 6179 S. Adams Dr., Littleton, CO 80121, USA; phone (303)771-3752. *(M)*

Backcountry Boating: River trips lasting 1 to 6 days reach parts of Colorado accessible only by boat. Guided by experienced river runners, small groups travel by either oar-powered or paddle-powered rafts. Rafters experience whitewater on 3- and 6-day trips down the

Picking their way through boulders and rapids, rafters ride the wild water of the Colorado River in Colorado. (Snowmass Resort)

Dolores River, and both calm waters and challenging rapids are encountered on trips of 1, 2 or 3 days on the Colorado. Those with only a half-day available can have an introduction to whitewater paddling on the Poudre River, and the spectacular Glenwood Canyon may be seen on half- and 1-day trips. Boatmen interested in learning to guide a raft may enroll in a 9-day springtime course in river running. All trips allow plenty of time for hiking, swimming, cliff diving and fishing. Participants are involved in pitching camp, cooking and loading the rafts. **Cost:** $8 to $215 depending on length of trip includes food, guides, communal camping equipment, accommodations, instruction. **When:** May to September. **Contact:** International Aquatic Adventures Inc., 2047 Broadway, Boulder, CO 80302, USA; phone (303)444-5829 or tollfree (800)525-2545. *(M)*

Colorado River Trips: Professional guides take rafters on half-day, 1-day and overnight expeditions in the area of Vail. On the half-day trip, travelers stop at historical sites including the old stagecoach route and an abandoned mining town. The full-day journey includes a trip through the isolated Gore Canyon region with its old mining town and famous dinosaur tracks. Each trip includes a special shoreline picnic provided by boatmen, and plenty of time is allotted for swimming and hiking. Rain gear, if necessary, is provided. **Cost:** $18, $30 and $65. **When:** Summer. **Contact:** Vail Guides Inc., P.O. Box 1474, Vail, CO 81657, USA; phone (303)476-5387. *(M)*

Roaring Fork River Trips: Day trips leaving from Glenwood Springs are offered on the Roaring Fork and Colorado rivers. For those wishing a half-day trip, a route begins on the Roaring Fork and terminates at Riverside Park; those out for the day stay on the boat and continue through the confluence of the Roaring Fork and the Colorado floating down that river to take-out at South Canyon. The area is rich in striking geological formations, and fairly rugged rapids are encountered, including Shoshone, Horseshoe Bend and Cemetery. Lunch is served, but a "brown bag" arrangement can also be made. Rafters not desiring a guide can rent rafts and equipment for their own trips. **Cost:** $18 for half-day, $22 for full day ($14 and $18 without lunch) includes food, rafts, equipment, guide; $23 a day for raft rental. **When:** On request. **Contact:** Wilderness Encounter, 720 Grand Ave., Glenwood Springs, CO 81601, USA; phone (303)945-8365. *(M)*

Georgia

Rafting the Chattooga: A guide accompanies each raft on a day-long journey down the Chattooga River, famous for both its whitewater rapids and as the location of the film *Deliverance*. Rafters meet for the Chattooga trips in the morning at the Chattooga Outpost in Sumter National Forest. Participants have the opportunity to paddle the rafts on wild and scenic whitewater characterized by frequent ledges and falls of up to 6 feet. Paddlers find that the river drops a total of 275 feet in the final 6 miles. Lunch is provided on the trip and participants are transported back to the Outpost sometime around 5 p.m. Waterproof bags are supplied for cameras. **Cost:** $25 includes lunch, guides, transportation, equipment. **When:** Year-round. **Contact:** Nantahala Outdoor Center, Star Rt., Box 68, Bryson City, NC 28713, USA; phone (704)488-6407. *(M)*

Southeastern Rapids Trips: Rafters spend 1 or 2 days exploring the Chattooga or Chattahoochee rivers along the Georgia-South Carolina border. A full-day float down the Chattooga includes over 40 sets of rapids, waterfalls and wild southern scenery. A calmer section, with a dozen rapids and large mountain vistas, is also available. Adventurers may also spend 2 days on the river, with wilderness camping and a steak dinner at night; if participants wish, the second day may be given to hiking through mountain areas such as Chauga Gorge, Raubun Bald and the Bartram Trail. Smorgasbord lunches are available on all trips, and camping is allowed in the surrounding Sumter National Forest. **Cost:** $25 and $75 for Chattooga trip, $10 for Chattahoochee. **When:** April to October. **Con-**

Plowing through a small wave in a sportyak offers the same excitement as running heavy rapids in a larger river raft. (Pat Conley/American Wilderness Alliance)

tact: Southeastern Expeditions, Inc., Suite 330, 2220 Parkelake Dr. NE, Atlanta, GA 30345, USA; phone (404)491-9439.

Idaho

Rafting the Lower Salmon: A 6-day raft trip on the Lower Salmon covers miles of whitewater and scenic river lands. Participants row neoprene boats over 80 river miles, with instruction and guidance given all along the way. Each raft takes 3 to 5 people, and a large support boat is used to transport supplies. Camps are made on the shoreline, with plenty of time allowed for hikes and exploring. Rafters travel through one of the 3 deepest river canyons in North America and may explore geological formations and the surrounding Idaho Primitive Area that contains a variety of protected wildlife. **Cost:** $380 from Lewiston includes equipment, meals, guides, instruction. **When:** August. **Contact:** American Wilderness Experience, 753 Paragon Dr., Boulder, CO 80303, USA; phone (303)499-5703 or 499-0050.

(M)

Middle Fork Float Trip: A 6-day trip down the Salmon Middle Fork River starts at either Dagger Falls or, when the river is lower following mid-July, at Indian Creek 24 miles downstream. The Salmon Middle Fork was designated as a Wild and Scenic River in 1968, and concentrations of wildlife can be found along the river during spring when the winter snow prevents animals from entering the mountains. The trip ends at the confluence of the Middle Fork and Salmon rivers, where participants are

transported back to Boise. A minimum of 4 rafters is necessary to schedule a trip, and a maximum of 24 is allowed on each. **Cost:** $465 includes all transportation and equipment. **When:** April to September. **Contact:** Idaho Adventures, P.O. Box 834 AD, Salmon, ID 83467, USA; phone (208)756-2986.

(M)

Salmon River Float: An 80-mile trip by raft down the Salmon River starts at Corn Creek Campgrounds near the town of Salmon. Participants are flown in from Boise for the 6-day trip, which ends near Riggins. The Salmon is bordered on both sides by 2 vast primitive areas and passes through the second deepest gorge in North America. Among the rapids crossed are Devil's Teeth, Gun Barrel and Growler. Wildlife is abundant along the river in April, and in May the wildflowers are at their peak. Return transportation to Boise is provided. **Cost:** $435 includes roundtrip transportation from Boise, equipment. **When:** April to September. **Contact:** Idaho Adventures, P.O. Box 834 AD, Salmon, ID 83467, USA; phone (208)756-2986. *(M)*

Moving down the Middle Fork: Whitewater lovers spend 5 days and 4 nights floating down the Salmon Middle Fork River. Experienced boatmen guide rafts through the primitive area as participants view the scenery, fish or take a turn at the oars. After a charter flight from Boise to Indian Creek, travelers start down the river, which drops 22 feet a mile. Stops are made frequently along the way to inspect historical sights and geological curi-

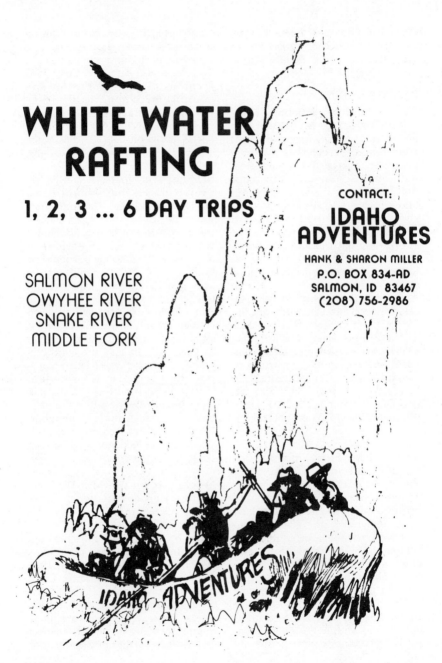

WHITE WATER RAFTING

1, 2, 3 ... 6 DAY TRIPS

SALMON RIVER
OWYHEE RIVER
SNAKE RIVER
MIDDLE FORK

CONTACT:

IDAHO ADVENTURES

HANK & SHARON MILLER
P.O. BOX 834-AD
SALMON, ID 83467
(208) 756-2986

osities. Each afternoon the rafts pull into a sandy beach where participants can do more fishing, hiking or just plain relaxing. Complete meals are served by boatmen. People of all ages above 8 are welcome. **Cost:** $475 includes meals, equipment, roundtrip transportation from Boise. **When:** July, August. **Contact:** Mackay Bar, Business Office Drawer F, Rm. 1010, 1 Capital Ctr., Boise, ID 83702, USA; phone (208)344-1881. *(M)*

To Hells Canyon and Back: Adventurers descend 1½ miles into a gorge separating the Wallowa Mountains and the Seven Devils to spend 6 days on a river running expedition. In the course of 85 miles participants plummet over furious rapids and float across the gentle straits of the Snake River in Hells Canyon. During the first 2 days rafters encounter a precipitous drop which has created some of the best cataracts in the deepest gorge in North America. The imprint of past inhabitants can be seen in Stone Age shelters, petroglyphs, weathered homesteads and worn corrals. As a natural sanctuary, the canyon gives rafters the opportunity to observe abundant mammals, birds and fish while hiking or rafting. Participants have ample time for exploring and photographing and are returned to Boise when the trip comes to a close. **Cost:** $370 for adults, $295 for youths includes accommodations, food, guides, roundtrip transportation from Boise. **When:** June, July. **Contact:** OARS Inc., P.O. Box 67, Angels Camp, CA 95222, USA; phone (209)736-2924 or 736-2661. *(M)*

Floating the Salmon Middle Fork: A variety of trips is offered down the Salmon Middle Fork River, ranging in length from 3 to 6 days. A 3-day fly-in trip traverses 80 river miles, while the 6-day trip covers 130 miles. The Middle Fork offers outstanding whitewater, remote terrain, abundant wildlife and clear mountain water filled with trout. Some trips are tailored for particular interests, such as family activities, photography or fishing. Also, certain trips run mostly whitewater while other trips catch the calmer stretches. The 6-day trip begins near the Sawtooth Mountains at the head of the Middle Fork and terminates 9 miles below the confluence of the Middle Fork and Salmon rivers. Other available trips travel down the Selway and Salmon rivers. **Cost:** $225 to $375, depending

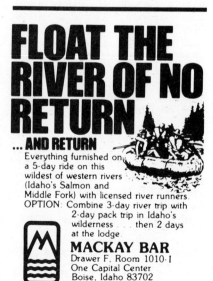

on date and type of trip, includes transportation, food, equipment, guide. **When:** April to September. **Contact:** Primitive Area Float Trips, Inc., P.O. Box 585, Salmon, ID 83467, USA; phone (208)756-2319.

(M)

Paradise Guard Put-In: Guided by river runners who have a background in natural history, participants journey for 4 days in small oar-powered rafts on the Selway River. Seventy percent of the 60-mile trip from Paradise Guard Station to the take-out at Selway Falls is on whitewater. Rafters can see a variety of wildlife on the wooded mountain slopes that rise up from the banks of the river. Meals are prepared by the guides at secluded campsites. The journey begins and ends at Hamilton, Montana, where a bus transports participants to and from the river. **Cost:** $400 from Hamilton includes transportation, meals, rafting equipment, guides. **When:** June. **Contact:** Western Rivers of Idaho, P.O. Box 7129, University Sta., Provo, UT 84602, USA; phone (801)377-9750 or tollfree (800)453-1482. *(M)*

Maine

Rapid Transit: Rafters experience whitewater amid the woods of northern Maine on day and overnight trips down the west branch of the Penobscot River. Both trips run a combination of calm water, fast water and rapids, and camping out on the river's banks is included on the overnight trip. Departing from near Millinocket, participants travel along the southern boundary of Baxter State Park, with Mt. Katahdin, the state's highest peak, visible throughout the trip. Deer, moose and bears may be seen along the riverbank. **Cost:** $35 for day trip, $90 for overnight includes transportation, meals, equipment. **When:** June to September. **Contact:** Penobscot Raft Adventures, 59 Lowell Rd., North Reading, MA 01864, USA; phone (617)664-2932.

Minnesota

Family Rafting: A 5-day trip in wooden rafts down the St. Croix and Namekagon rivers, national wild and scenic rivers punctuated by occasional rapids and whitewater, are provided for those interested in running rapids. During a moonlight float planned for 1 night of the trip, participants see deer, raccoons and great blue herons. The trip starts near Trego and ends at Snake River Ferry, 60 miles downriver. Families are easily accommodated and are encouraged to participate. **Cost:** $175 (20 percent off for children under 17). **When:** June. **Contact:** Spirit Waters, 5375 Eureka Rd., Excelsior, MN 55331, USA; phone (612)474-5190.

(M)

New Mexico

Floating through Bandelier: Participants explore the White Rock Canyon of the Rio Grande during a day-long float trip. Meeting at Santa Fe, group members launch their boats at historic Buckman. Often, trip members see the overgrown beds of the Chile Line narrow-gauge railroad that runs through the deserted settlements. Passing through basalt outcroppings that constrict the river into moderate rapids, fast riffles and quiet pools, participants may see eagles and hawks soaring overhead. Trip members then paddle through Bandelier National Park, location of early Pueblo kivas and cave dwellings, and the group may stop and hike to the remote ruins accessible only from the river. To end the trip, participants paddle to the calm Cochiti Lake, and after crossing its 6-mile expanse, take out at the Cochiti Pueblo. **Cost:** $35 includes lunch, guide, boat. **When:** By arrangement. **Contact:** Rio Bravo River Tours, P.O. Box 400, Santa Fe, NM 87501, USA; phone (505)982-8781.

North Carolina

Personalized Raft Trips: Small-group, instructional or recreational whitewater trips are offered on the rivers of western North Carolina. A regular schedule of trips is not offered; rather, arrangements are made on an individual basis. The area contains 5 mountain ranges and a variety of rivers, the main ones being the Nantahala and the Chattooga, and to the west is the rugged Nantahala National Forest. Arrangements may be made for self-guided trips by raft, canoe or kayak, guided trips with food and logistics handled by professionals, or instructional outings for special groups. A store offers rentals and sales of all necessary equipment. **Cost:** On request. **When:** June to August. **Contact:** Cullowhee Wilderness Outfitter, P.O. Box V, Cullowhee, NC 28723, USA.

Oregon

Hells Canyon Float Trips: Hells Canyon, bounded by the Payette and Nez Perce national forests on the Idaho side and by the Wallowa-Whitman National Forest on the Oregon side, is the site of an 85-mile adventure by raft. From Hells Canyon Dam to the confluence of the Snake and Grande Ronde rivers, trip members spend 5 days riding through thundering rapids, fishing, swimming and hiking in a relaxed camp atmosphere. Participants float the river in 15- to 17-foot oar-powered pontoon rafts. As the rafts pass through the deep-

On a trip down the Snake River through Hells Canyon, an experienced guide rows and maneuvers the raft. (Ray Wheeler/ECHO: The Wilderness Co.)

est canyon in the United States, all the life zones of North America come into view, from alpine tundra to desert environment. Participants may have their cars shuttled to the take-out point or fly back to Oxbow at the end of the trip. **Cost:** $295, plus $45 for flight, $75 for car shuttle. **When:** May to September. **Contact:** Hells Canyon Navigation Co., P.O. Box 145, Oxbow, OR 97840, USA; phone (503)785-3352.

(M)

Rogue River Whitewater: On 3-day trips groups of up to 10 people raft the Rogue River, which has been designated a Wild and Scenic River. The rafts are put in at Sizemor's Bar, just above the river's major whitewater. The schedule allows time for swimming and hiking as well as running such rapids as the Devil's Stairs and Tyee Rapids. At camp the meals are prepared by the guides. Also offered is a spring driftboat trip down the Owyhee River in eastern Oregon, where the high desert canyons provide excellent opportunities for photography and bird watching. **Cost:** $180 for

Rogue trip includes shuttle, Owyhee prices on request. **When:** May to August. **Contact:** Ken Robertson and Sons Guide Service, 3424 Amber Ln., Grants Pass, OR 97526, USA; phone (503)479-9554. *(M)*

Shooting Deschutes: In groups of 10 with 2 instructors, participants learn the skills necessary for running rivers in all types of watercraft: how to manage paddle rafts, "read" water, pick routes through the rapids and load and unload boats. Situated in north-central Oregon, the Deschutes flows north into the Columbia through a deep sandstone and basalt canyon, offering challenging whitewater during the 8-day course. Participants begin the expedition with instruction in the basic skills of food preparation, shelter construction and minimum impact travel. Students also stop along the banks of the river, journey to side canyons and engage in rock climbing, rappelling, hiking and exploring. In all courses participants spend 24 hours on a solo, a time spent camping alone with minimal but adequate food, gear and shelter. **Cost:** $300 includes equipment, meals, instruction, guides. College credit/scholarships available. **When:** June to August. **Contact:** The Northwest Outward Bound School, 0110 SW Bancroft, Portland, OR 97201, USA; phone (503)243-1993. *(M)*

From the Cascades to the Coast: Three-day rafting trips in southern Oregon float down 34 miles of the Rogue River, which originates in the Cascade Mountains and flows toward the Pacific Ocean. Put-in at Grave Creek begins the trip down the protected Wild and Scenic Rivers stretch, which includes rapids of up to Class IV difficulty. The foothills terrain includes tall stands of fir mixed with oak and madrone trees, as well as ferns and wild rhododendrons. Rafting parties can ride in an oar-powered raft or paddle a raft in groups of 6, and 2 inflatable kayaks are available for kayaking enthusiasts. Complete technical instruction by the guides is provided to those who wish to row the rafts or paddle the kayaks. **Cost:** $170 includes transportation from Grants Pass, food, equipment. **When:** May to September. **Contact:** Osprey River Trips, Inc., 11468 Redwood Hwy., Wilderville, OR 97543, USA; phone (503)479-4215. *(M)*

Rogue Wild River Expeditions: Boats are put in the Rogue River near the town of Almeda and are taken out 4 days later near Agness after taking river voyagers through some of Oregon's most scenic country. Floating in either rubber rafts or wooden drift boats, group members may fish and swim in

quiet spots as they drift through the whitewater of the renowned Rogue River. One of the most exciting stretches of water is Devil's Staircase, where the river drops 20 feet in 300 yards. In the evenings participants may watch for deer and black bears near the riverside lodges which provide accommodation. Shorter trips, including fishing expeditions, are offered during the fall and winter. **Cost:** $160 to $350, depending on length of trip, includes equipment, food, accommodations, guide. **When:** May to March. **Contact:** River Trips Unlimited, 900 Murphy Rd. W., Medford, OR 97501, USA; phone (503)779-3798. *(M)*

River Outfitting: During 1- to 5-day trips on several of Oregon's rivers,

participants may choose to paddle 1-person inflatable kayaks or ride in large rafts that are piloted by experienced river runners. For those wishing to use inflatable kayaks, outfitters provide trip itineraries as well as instruction. A support raft carries all personal gear and camping equipment. Groups may choose from the Rogue, Klamath, Umpqua and Deschutes rivers. The Rogue and Klamath offer steep black-walled canyons, abundant wildlife and waters that are safe even for the beginner. More skill in pad-

dling and maneuvering is required on the Umpqua and Deschutes trips. The Umpqua is the less traveled of the 2 rivers and has a number of campsites among the evergreens and deep foliage that border the river. Flowing through central Oregon into the Columbia River, the Deschutes lies in high desert country. On all trips stops are made for exploring trails along the river, photography, swimming and relaxing. **Cost:** $30 to $240 depending on location and length of trip includes transportation to

Seconds before a group of rafters enters a narrow chute, their guide shouts final positioning instructions. (Wilderness Voyageurs)

the put-in point, guides, meals, camping and rafting equipment, instruction. **When:** May to September. **Contact:** Sunrise Scenic Tours, P.O. Box 447, Klamath Falls, OR 97601, USA; phone (503)882-0033.

(M)

Pennsylvania

Youghiogheny River Rush: Participants take a 1-day trip on the Youghiogheny River in southwest Pennsylvania. Traveling through an 8-mile stretch of whitewater and calm pools, rafters start in Ohiopyle and finish in Stewarton. Along the way, they pass over such rapids as Entrance, Cucumber Chute, Railroad, the Dimples, Double Hydraulic and World's End. The expedition includes an experienced guide, all equipment and transportation to and from the river. Group tours and weekday package tours are available. **Cost:** On request. **When:** May to October. **Contact:** Laurel Highlands River Tours Inc., 1286 Washington St., Indiana, PA 15701, USA; phone (412)465-2987; summer, Box 107, Ohiopyle, PA 15470, USA; phone (412)455-3703.

Yough Rafting: Whitewater enthusiasts may participate in a day-long float down the Youghiogheny River. A mixture of rapids, calms and waterfalls, the Youghiogheny presents a challenge to any river rafter, expert or beginner. Bounded on both banks by the Ohiopyle State Park, the river is unspoiled by industrialization. Journeys down the river include the use of 4-person rubber rafts, all other necessary equipment and a sack lunch for the noon hour. People ages 12 and over are welcome. **Cost:** $25 a person on weekends, $20 on weekdays. **When:** May to October. **Contact:** White Water Adventurers, Box 31, Ohiopyle, PA 15470, USA; phone (412)329-8850.

South Carolina

Chattooga and Nolichucky Trips: Day trips are offered for both beginning and experienced rafters on the Chattooga and Nolichucky rivers. Participants run the Chattooga in groups of 4, paddling 12-foot rafts. The 7-hour trip is relatively easy and is open to people ages 12 and older. No previous rafting experience is necessary as guides provide instruction in proper techniques for running rapids. Rapids are larger and more frequent on the Nolichucky trip, as the river drops into a canyon 11 miles long. Larger rafts are used on the Nolichucky, and rafters must be at least 15 years old; previous river running experience is recommended. **Cost:** $15 to $25 includes equipment, food, guide. **When:** June to November. **Contact:** Wildwater Ltd., Long Creek, SC 29658, USA; phone (803)647-5336; winter, 400 West Rd., Portsmouth, VA 23707, USA; phone (804)397-6658.

Tennessee

Rafting in the Smokies: A day trip provides participants with the opportunity to spend 2 to 3 hours sailing down the little-known Ocoee River, near the borders of North Carolina, Georgia and Tennessee. The river has greatly increased in speed and volume of water ever since the TVA shut down one of its rerouting flumes upstream. The result is a fast stretch of whitewater 5 miles in length. All necessary equipment is provided, as is shuttle service from point of completion to point of departure. The minimum age for the trip is 14. **Cost:** $15. **When:** On request. **Contact:** Smoky Mountain River Expeditions, Inc., P.O. Box 398, Hot Springs, NC 28743, USA; phone (704)622-7260.

Texas

Float Trip on the Rio Grande: Several river float trips lasting from 1 to 2 days are available to outdoor enthusiasts who wish to experience the Rio Grande. Participants may visit Santa Elena Canyon, a 17-mile trip taking approximately 8 to 10 hours; Boquillas Canyon, 23 miles requiring 2 days; and Colorado Canyon, 7 miles long and taking

about 4 to 6 hours. The Santa Elena Canyon trip begins at the Lajitas Trading Post and is followed by a 10-mile hike through rugged country. Once inside the canyon, the river drops swiftly for the first mile. One mile inside the canyon participants view a giant rockslide on the Mexican side of the river, which occasionally requires trip members to disembark and portage over large boulders. Below the rockslide Santa Elena Canyon is narrow and sheer, gradually rising to heights of 1,500 feet above the river waters. Other trips also offer a wide variety of historic, ecological and geological highlights. **Cost:** $45 to $135 includes equipment, guide, meals. **When:** By arrangement. **Contact:** Villa de la Mina, P.O. Box 47, Terlingua, TX 79852, USA; phone (915)364-2446.

Utah

Row Your Own: Participants themselves handle the boats on 5-day trips down the Green River. Traveling in 10-person neoprene rubber boats, group members learn whitewater boat handling under the guidance of experienced rafters. A flight from the town of Green River to the river put-in point begins the trip. The rafts float by unusual rock formations and alluvial flats covered with pampas grass, rabbit brush and thickets of willow and tamarisk. Rafters set up camp on the banks of the river where they may explore the many canyons that the river passes through. A minimum group of 6 is required for the trip. **Cost:** $220 for adults, $190 for those under 18 includes instruction, guides, rafting equipment, 2 meals a day, transportation from

Green River. **When:** May, June, August. **Contact:** Adventure River Expeditions, 4211 Mars Wy., Salt Lake City, UT 84117, USA; phone (801)278-1867. *(M)*

Self-Guided Raft Float: Experienced rafters outfit and help participants put-in at the town of Green River where 2-, 6- and 10-day river journeys begin. Rafters on the shortest trip float past Old Crystal Geyser, Little Valley, Anvil Bottom, Dry Lakes and Dellenbaugh Butte, ending up at Ruby Ranch. Travelers on the 6-day journey glide into Labyrinth Canyon, past side canyons like Tin Alcove, Spring Canyon and Hell Roaring Canyon, stopping at Mineral Canyon. At the confluence of the Green and Colorado rivers, participants on the 10-day trip are met by the outfitters after having rafted 120 miles, and are returned to the starting point. **Cost:** $210 for 2 days, $575 for 6 days and $1,150 for 10 days includes all equipment, assistance with put-in, transportation from take-out to Green River. **When:** By arrangement. **Contact:** Outlaw Trails Inc., P.O. Box 336, Green River, UT 84525, USA; phone (801)564-3477. *(M)*

Desolation Row: Four-day rowing expeditions float participants through the Green River Wilderness in the Desolation Canyon and Grey Canyon regions. Professional guides lead groups along 97 miles of rushing water including such rapids as Coal Creek, Rattlesnake, Three Fords and more than 50 others. The itinerary begins in Grand Junction, where participants are met and bused to the airport for a charter flight into Sand Wash; here the journey downstream begins. It continues until the middle of the fourth day, when the group leaves the river for a bus ride back to Grand Junction. All meals and accommodations on the river are provided. **Cost:** $190 individual, $171 group or family. **When:** May to September. **Contact:** Western Adventure Safaris, Inc., P.O. Box 1732, Grand Junction, CO 81501, USA; phone (303)242-6621. *(M)*

Monument Valley Run: River rafters spend 6 to 8 days floating down the San Juan River. Although the San Juan is a little-known tributary of the Colorado, a vertical drop of 8 feet a mile makes it the fastest major stream in the United States. Each member of the group uses his or her own fully equipped Sportyak to row through red rock gorges 2,000 feet in depth, seeing ruins of ancient Indian civilizations and experiencing small but exciting rapids along the way. The 6-day journey starts from Mexican Hat and moves 56 miles downstream; the 8-day trip begins 28 miles farther upstream, near the town of Bluff. Plenty of time for off-road exploration is available; the group may hike along the Honaker Trail, Slickhorn Canyon and Grand Gulch. The minimum age for the trip is 14. **Cost:** $400 for 8 days, $300 for 6 days includes meals, equipment, guides. **When:** March to October. **Contact:** Wild & Scenic Inc., P.O. Box 2123A, Marble Canyon, AZ 86036, USA; phone (602)355-2222. *(M)*

Washington

Northwest River Run: Two or 5 days are spent rafting courses on several western Washington rivers. A 2-day course introduces novices to waterways on either the Wenatchee, Skykomish or Toutle rivers; 5-day trips are designed for intermediate paddlers along the same water courses. The instruction includes such essentials of rafting as navigation skills in oar- and paddle-powered craft; river etiquette; water safety; camping and campfire skills; and logistics in the wilderness. Groups are limited to 3 students for each instructor to insure complete individual instruction. Advanced wilderness trips are also available. **Cost:** $55 for 2 days, $130 for 5 days. **When:** By arrangement. **Contact:** The Northern Wilderness Company, P.O. Box 25795, Seattle, WA 98125, USA; phone (206)633-3946. *(M)*

Rafting in the Cascades: Float trips ranging from 1 to 5 days take participants down isolated rivers in Washington's Cascade Range. On the west slopes of the Cascades trips are scheduled down the Sauk and Suiattle rivers, the Skagit River, the Nooksack River and the Skykomish River. The Sauk and Suiattle rivers, in the Glacier Peak Wilderness, are run on day and overnight trips which negotiate over 30 major rapids; the Skagit River is run in a 3-day trip through the North Cascades National Park, where participants can see one of the nation's largest concentrations of bald eagles. The Skykomish River is especially demanding, owing to harsh rapids which increase in difficulty yearly because of rock erosion. On the east slope of the Cascades a 5-day trip runs the Methow, from Mazama through apple-growing country and Black Canyon to the Columbia River; and 1- to 3-day trips take participants down the Wenatchee River, where the whitewater is especially exciting in the summer months. **Cost:** $40 to $150 for adults includes transportation back to the starting point; youth fares 15 to 25 percent less. **When:** Year-round. **Contact:** Pacific Northwest Float Trips, 829 Waldron St., Sedro Woolley, WA 98284, USA; phone (206)855-0535 or 855-0417. *(M)*

Olympic Peninsula Rafting: The lush Olympic rain forest can be experienced on float trips down rivers fed by the snow-capped peaks of the Olympic Mountains. With 5 passengers to a boat, daily trips are offered on the Queets, Hoh and Quinault rivers in Olym-

The Northern Wilderness Co. runs the mild rapids of Washington's Skykomish River on two-day introductory courses. (Bob Citron)

pic National Park. Groups are encouraged to participate in all aspects of the river trip, keeping in mind the environmental ethics of rafting. The trips depart from Lake Quinault Lodge at 9 a.m. and return at 5 p.m. **Cost:** $25 for adults, $20 for children includes lunch, transportation to and from the river. **When:** June to September; winter weekends by reservation. **Contact:** Rivers Northwest, 141 Eagle St. NE, Winslow, WA 98110, USA; phone (206)842-5144. *(M)*

Weekend River Trips: Rafting the rivers of the Pacific Northwest offers a profusion of trip possibilites, all of which can be explored on weekend trips throughout the year.

Whitewater day trips running from April to October explore the Wenatchee, Sauk and Toutle rivers which flow westward from the flanks of the Cascade Mountains. From September through November, special interest trips concentrate on the abundance of mushroom species which flourish in the rainy climate of Puget Sound. Day trips are also offered all summer long on the Queets, a river which flows from the Olympic Mountains on the Olympic Peninsula west of Puget Sound, where elk and river otters can be seen along the riverbank. Whitewater overnight trips are available only on the Sauk and Methow rivers during spring and summer, with campsites selected in the open pine forests of the Sauk or in the sagebrush hills of the Methow. **Cost:** $30 day trips, $110 overnight trips includes meals only on overnight trips. **When:** Year-round. **Contact:** Zig Zag River Runners, REI Adventure Travel, 1525 11th Ave., Seattle, WA 98122, USA; phone (206)322-7800. **(M)**

West Virginia

New River Rafting: Paddling along in a large rubber raft, passengers enjoy the beauty of the Appalachian Mountains along the New River, which has carved a magnificent gorge. River experts guide the raft through quiet waters, until the current picks up and suddenly the raft is charging through the froth and turbulence of rapids. In midday, rafters pause to share lunch on the riverbank. The New River is one of the earth's oldest rivers and has been called the "Grand Canyon of the East." One- and 2-day trips leave Hico every day in the summer and every weekend in off-season to give guests the opportunity to experience this wild water. Transportation is provided to the put-in point and a tram takes rafters out of the canyon at Hawk's Nest State Park. **Cost:** $32 for day trips, $85 for

2 days includes equipment, meals, transportation to and from the river. **When:** April to October. **Contact:** Mountain River Tours Inc., Box 88, Sunday Rd., Hico, WV 24854, USA; phone (304)658-5817. *(M)*

Wildwater from Thurmond: Participants on a 1- and 2-day river trip experience the New River Canyon, sometimes called the Grand Canyon of the East. Nestled in the foothills of the Appalachian Mountains, the canyon provides turbulent whitewater passing beneath towering hills and rock formations. Participants camp overnight along the riverbanks on the 30-mile route. The year-round float trips include hot meals. Three trips are also made yearly down the Gauley River. **Cost:** $40 per day includes equipment, guide. **When:** Year-round. **Contact:** Wildwater Expeditions Unlimited Inc., P.O. Box 55, Thurmond, WV 25936, USA; phone (304)469-2551. *(M)*

Wyoming

Snake Rafting: Group participation is essential to the success of the expedition down the Snake River Canyon. Everyone paddles through the low waters of the river, so each person is responsible for his or her share of the work and pleasure. The journeys are a day long, cover 10 miles and leave 3 times each day. Professional guides help to steer the craft through whitewater. **Cost:** $15 for adults, $10 for youths under 18. **When:** May to September. **Contact:** Lewis and Clark Expeditions, P.O. Box 720, Jackson, WY 83001, USA; phone (307)733-4022 or 733-6858.

RESOURCES
Clubs and Associations

American River Touring Association
1016 Jackson St.
Oakland, CA 94607, USA
Phone (415)465-9355

American Rivers Conservation Council
317 Pennsylvania Ave. SE
Washington, DC 20003, USA
Phone (202)547-6900

American Whitewater Affiliation
P.O. Box 1584
San Bruno, CA 94066, USA

Appalachian Mountain Club
5 Joy St.
Boston, MA 02108, USA
Phone (617)523-0636

Colorado Whitewater Association
4260 E. Evans Ave.
Denver, CO 80222, USA

Eastern Professional River Outfitters Association
P.O. Box 252
Hot Springs, NC 28743, USA

Outdoor Education Association
11468 Redwood Hwy.
Wilderville, OR 97543, USA

Ozark Wilderness Waterways Club
P.O. Box 8165
Kansas City, MO 64012, USA

Professional River Outfitters Association
c/o Canyoneers
P.O. Box 2997
Flagstaff, AZ 86003, USA

West Virginia Wildwater Association
Rt. 1, Box 97
Ravenswood, WV 26164, USA

Western River Guides Association
994 Denver St.
Salt Lake City, UT 84101, USA

CANOEING

One of the most satisfying ways to experience the wilderness is to follow the flow of a river downstream, paddling with a friend in a canoe. You slip noiselessly along the quicksilver current, sliding close to the shore where waterfowl scurry into the dense undergrowth, wildflowers sweep down from the mountains to the very edge of the water, and deer, moose and bears forage for food. As you float in an eddy or on a broad, slow expanse, you pull out your fishing gear and cast for trout. The time could be in the cool morning or the heat of midday, during the warm summer, the riotous-colored autumn, the still whiteness of winter or the rebirth of spring.

The canoe is a native American craft, descended from the dugouts Columbus saw on his first voyage to the New World almost 500 years ago. For 200 years, the trappers and voyageurs of America and Canada paddled at the forefront of westward expansion, sharing with the Indians the waterways of a strange land for their solitary, often dangerous, trades. Today, thousands of people, young and old, find canoeing a rugged yet relaxing way to explore the backcountry. The New World can be rediscovered as you drift with the current, portage around falls, or sweep through rapids in the Canadian Rockies, the Boundary Waters Canoe Area or even the jungles of Peru.

Traveling some 600 miles down the Orinoco River in Peru and Ecuador, a spring expedition paddles canoes and kayaks through a remote region of unexplored rain forest. You can sign up for the full journey or partial segments through an outfitter in Canada. There are many trip opportunities in Canada itself, from the whitewater of the upper Albany River in Ontario to the arctic Indian village of Webique in the Northwest Territories. Trips of this nature can range from a few days to almost a month in duration, passing through many of the areas made famous by the French voyageurs.

But perhaps most famous of all canoe areas is the Boundary Waters Canoe Area in northern Minnesota, an impressive 15,000 square miles of interlacing lakes and streams which can be navigated into the Quetico Provincial Park in southern Ontario. Formerly known as the Superior-Quetico Wilderness, the region provides an ideal setting for canoeing most of the year in the former homeland of the now-extinct Ojibway Indians. Canoes are available for rental by the day or week, and guided trips lead adventurers deep into the wilderness for forest camping, wildlife observation, and some of the best canoeing in the world. □

Canoeists paddle the calm waters of Ross Lake in Washington's North Cascades. On canoe trips paddlers may drift with the current, portage around falls and sweep through rapids. (Keith Gunnar)

CANOEING

AFRICA

Kenya

The Tana by Dugout: A 4-day trip out of Nairobi takes participants down the Tana River to the home and work area of George Adamson, noted conservationist. The trip begins with a flight from Nairobi to Garissa on the Tana River, and after a short drive to Saka, is followed by a canoe trip navigated by the Kora Kora people. For 2 days participants canoe quietly down the river past sandbars, sunken trees and groups of hippos. Other wildlife along the banks includes monkeys, crocodiles and a wide variety of tropical birds. Stops are made at local villages to meet the residents and observe ceremonial dances. On the third day the party disembarks and follows a small train up the hinterland to George Adamson's home in the Kora Game Reserve. Participants spend the rest of the day with Adamson and his hand-raised lions, which he is retraining to survive in the wild. After camping by the river that night, participants return to Nairobi by air. **Cost:** $849 to $1,118, depending on size of party and type of plane, includes all transportation, meals, fees, equipment, guide. **When:** Year-round. **Contact:** Abercrombie & Kent International, Inc., 1000 Oak Brook Rd., Oak Brook, IL 60521, USA; phone (312)654-2211.

CANADA

Alberta

Wildhay and Athabasca Canoeing: Young people between the ages of 12 and 17 spend 2 weeks canoeing on the Wildhay and Athabasca rivers while learning the fundamentals of wilderness living. The strenuous and demanding trip covers more than 180 miles from the confluence of Rock Creek and the Wildhay to Whitecourt, where a bus takes participants back to

Paddlers glide through the early morning mist on the St. Croix River. (Sunrise County Canoe Expeditions/Marty Brown)

Banff. Before the canoeing begins, the group hikes north of Jasper over high mountain passes and across the Snaring and Indian rivers, camping along the way. Much of the hiking time is devoted to learning and using wilderness skills, including plotting and following routes, setting up camp and survival. **Cost:** $350 includes transportation from Banff, food, equipment, instruction. **When:** August. **Contact:** Canadian Mountain Holidays Ltd., P.O. Box 1660, Banff, AB Canada T0L 0C0; phone (403)762-4531.

British Columbia

Canoeing Tweedsmuir Provincial Park: A 7-day canoe trip in the Coast Mountains covers 22 miles of waterway with 6 connected lakes and several short river courses. A float plane transports participants from Williams or Chilko Lake to the trip's starting point in the Turner Lake chain. Since the access roads to the area are often washed out and impassable, development in the park is minimal. Mountain chains are often interrupted by high plateau regions and lower valleys where lakes and waterfalls often form. Munlen Falls, one such waterfall, is the second highest in Canada. The mountain lakes are surrounded by towering alpine peaks and heavily timbered shores. Moose, deer, bears, wolves and coyotes are often seen along the trip route. Trip members share in the work of the outing, including collecting firewood, setting up tents and cooking meals. **Cost:** $280. **When:** July, August. **Contact:** Chilko Lake Wilderness Ranch

Ltd., P.O. Box 4750, Williams Lake, BC Canada V2G 2V7; phone (604)Chilko Lake Wilderness Ranch.

Canoeing Discovery: Saltwater channels provide canoeing routes among the Discovery Islands between Vancouver Island and the west coast of British Columbia. Group members fly from Lake Union in Seattle to Quadra Island where the 7-day canoe trip begins. Most of the areas visited are accessible only by boat and contain an abundance of wildlife: whales, porpoises, seals, ospreys, herons, eagles and deer. Participants camp in 2-person tents at sites selected at the end of the day's paddle, and plenty of time is allowed for exploring the wilderness environments of the different islands. Basic canoeing instruction is offered to those who need it. **Cost:** $275 includes transportation from Seattle, canoes, tents, meals, guides. **When:** June to September. **Contact:** Discovery Islands Canoe Trips, P.O. Box 69, Quathiaski Cove, Quadra Island, BC Canada V0P 1N0; phone (604)285-3198.

Wilderness Canoe Trips: Seven- and 12-day guided trips into the Cariboo Mountains offer a chance to experience an area only trappers have frequented in the past. The trip offers excellent wildlife photography opportunities. Waters tend to be calm and clear. Small outboard motors are sometimes added to canoes for carrying freight. Campfires at night often feature dinners of freshly caught fish. Trips are limited to 5 people. **Cost:** $65 includes canoe rental, meals,

Canoeists use poles to maneuver their boats in shallow water on the Allagash River. (Maine Forestry Dept.)

guides. **When:** By arrangement. **Contact:** Lowry's Lodges Ltd., Box 40, Horsefly, BC Canada V0L 1L0.
(M)

Canoeing the Sea Islands: Canoe trips among the islands off the coast of British Columbia are offered in 2-week sessions. Trips depart from Gold River on a coastal freighter for passage up Nootka Sound to Esperanza. Then travelers paddle through the inlets in double cockpit canoes, camping on uninhabited islands and cooking their meals over driftwood fires. The area has lost very little of its primitive character, and canoeists have the chance to experience the life lived there for centuries by its native peoples. Ample time is allotted for beachcombing, canoe exploration and hikes in the forests. **Cost:** $185 includes canoe, equipment, guide; $18 for freighter passage. **When:** June to September. **Contact:**

Northwest Waters, P.O. Box 212, Portland, OR 97207, USA.

Vancouver Bay Voyages: Freedom to explore is the keynote of partially guided 7-day canoe trips on Jervis Inlet in Vancouver Bay. A float plane brings participants from Vancouver Harbor across Howe Sound and up the coast to base camp on Vancouver Bay. During the first 3 days trip members become acquainted with the area, practice canoeing techniques and get the feel of the daily wind and tidal patterns. While paddling through the 50-mile-long inlet past 8,000-foot mountains with cascading waterfalls, participants have the opportunity to explore the intertidal zones and hike in the surrounding forests along abandoned logging roads. Group members decide how far to canoe each day. The only scheduled stop is a rendezvous with a supply boat to replenish food stocks. At the end of the trip participants are flown by float plane back to Vancouver Harbor. Trip members should provide their own camping equipment. An extended trip to Porpoise Bay in Sechelt Inlet is also available. **Cost:** $150 includes equipped canoes, instruction, guide at base camp, food, cooking equipment; $75 for float plane fare. **When:** July to September. **Contact:** Western Outdoor Adventures Ltd., 16115 32nd Ave., White Rock, BC Canada V4B 4Z5; phone (604)531-3969.   *(M)*

North Woods Photography: The backcountry of the Cariboo Mountains is the setting for a 14-day canoeing and photography trip. Accompanied by a naturalist and nature photographer, participants learn effective camera techniques in both landscape and close-up nature photography using 35 mm film, color and black and white. Instruction features personal attention as canoeists paddle through 73 miles of remote wilderness lakes surrounded by quiet forests and magnificent mountain peaks. Enrollment is strictly limited. Group members should be good swimmers and capable of assisting in portages of moderate difficulty. **Cost:** $140 all-inclusive. **When:** August. **Contact:** Wilderness Studies, University of California Extension, Santa Cruz, CA 95064, USA; phone (408)429-2822.

Northwest Territories

Canoeing through Taiga and Tundra: Almost completely uninhabited, the 1,300,000 square miles of the Northwest Territories provide numerous wilderness canoeing op-

portunities. Parties of 6 can arrange trips lasting a minimum of 2 weeks in any part of the taiga and tundra. Guided by a biologist/ecologist, participants explore a land green with lichens, grasses, mosses, sedges and dwarf shrubbery, a land where water covers about 38 percent of the ground. Traveling in almost continuous daylight, all voyagers paddle and help set up camp along sandy beaches. Headnets are provided for the occasional times when insects are overwhelming. Wildlife including herds of caribou, musk oxen, arctic wolves, foxes and squirrels may easily be photographed. Birdlife is teeming and ornithologists can request canoe trips designed to maximize viewing of loons, horned larks, gyrfalcons, jaegers, ptarmigan, gold eagles and Lapland longspurs. There are routes to challenge the most avid whitewater canoeist as well as routes suitable for those with no previous canoeing experience. **Cost:** $735 to $1,090 includes guide, group equipment, food, canoes; $195 to $550 for air transportation while on trip from Yellowknife or Fort Smith. **When:** June to September. **Contact:** Canoe Arctic Inc., 9 John Beck Cresc., Brampton,

ON Canada L6W 2T2; phone (416)451-0290.

Ontario

Trans-Algonquin: A 12-day trip from the northwest corner of Algonquin Park to Lake Opeongo is designed for those seeking canoeing skills and experience for leading groups or on their own. During the 90-mile journey experienced staff members are on hand to provide expertise in navigation, route planning, outdoor cooking and canoe handling. Further skills acquired are those of survival, emergency procedures and fire making. The schedule allows 3 layover days. **Cost:** $285. **When:** August, September. **Contact:** Algonquin Waterways Wilderness Trips, 271 Danforth Ave., Toronto, ON Canada M4K 1N2; phone (416)469-1727.

Winisk River Expedition: Over 1,000 miles of bush flying are necessary to get a group in and out of the remote area of a 2-week river trip in the Arctic. The starting point of the trip, Webique, is an Indian village located 188 air miles north of Armstrong. No roads and very few people ever travel near there, and the community is the closest outpost to the remote Winisk River. After leaving Webique, participants are not likely to see another person on the 270 miles of arctic river ending at Hudson's Bay. Seven major sets of rapids are crossed, and once beyond the treeline in tundra country caribou and polar bears can be spotted. **Cost:** $500 includes equipment, guides; float plane transportation extra. **When:** July. **Contact:** Canoes North/Can-

oes South, Box 5656, Armstrong, ON Canada P0T 1A0; phone (807)583-2055. **(M)**

Summer Canoeing on Lake Huron: Six-day canoeing trips are run all summer long on the North Channel of Lake Huron and in neighboring areas. The region is ideal for scenic photography, and special emphasis is placed on the area's geology, particularly the contact between Precambrian and Paleozoic rock strata. Many historic and archaeological sites are visited in this sparsely populated area. Following the route of the voyageurs between Manitoulin Island and the north shore of Lake Huron, the trips can be taken in either freighter canoe under sail or by standard canoe, as determined by the preference of the group. Swimming and fishing are available along the route. **Cost:** About $100, depending on group size, includes food, equipment, guide. **When:** July, August. **Contact:** Geo Expeditions, Box 8, Gore Bay, ON Canada P0P 1H0.

Wilderness Study in Precambrian Shield Country: In 2 weeks participants experience wilderness living in the midst of the unspoiled lakes and watersheds of the Precambrian Shield country. Staged from a base camp on Lake Timagami, the course touches on every aspect of conducting an expedition, including the fundamentals of canoeing, planning and researching a trip, outdoor cooking, the selection and maintenance of equipment, campcraft, orienteering and safety. The first 2 or 3 days are spent in the base camp becoming familiar with equipment, canoe travel and basic wilderness skills. Each group of 8 to 10 participants and 2 guides then selects a canoe trip route that best suits the interests and physical abilities of its members. Choices for the 10-day trip are plentiful since the surrounding area offers a number of large lakes linked by short portages as well as falls and rapids on 2 lower branches of the Lady Evelyn River. Special programs are available for people 13 to 16. **Cost:** $345 from Timagami includes transportation, meals, guide, accommodations, camping equipment, canoes, backpacks, rain gear. **When:** July, August. **Contact:** Headwaters, P.O. Box 288, Timagami, ON Canada P0H 2H0.

Northern Canoeing: A 28-day trip offers canoeists with basic skills an opportunity to sharpen their skills by canoeing on the Missinaibi River in northern Ontario. The group meets in Sudbury and puts in at nearby Missinaibi Lake. In this area once traveled by Indians, traders and explorers, participants may spot otters, beavers, mink and muskrats. Canoeing is on both calm water and whitewater, and guides teach canoeing techniques such as portaging, lining and whitewater strokes. The take-out point is the town of Moosonee on James Bay, from where participants are transported back to Sudbury. **Cost:** $975 includes transportation from Sudbury, camping equipment, meals. **When:** June. **Contact:** The Infinite Odyssey, 57 Grant St., Waltham, MA 02154, USA; phone (617)899-6050. *(M)*

Boys' Camp on Lake Timagami:
One of North America's oldest boys' camps operates from Devil's Island on Lake Timagami. The lake is surrounded by a network of rivers, streams, lakes and islands in the wilderness area of the Timagami Reserve and was the original home of the Ojibway Indians. Devil's Island has facilities for tennis, baseball, soccer, swimming and other sports, and there is access to the surrounding wilderness for camping, canoeing, fishing and hiking. The camp is divided into 3 divisions for boys 10 to 19, with the older boys making increasingly difficult camping and canoeing trips. Wilderness skills and environmental awareness are emphasized. An adult facility on the north end of the island is open during the camping season so parents can share in their children's experience. **Cost:** $1,075 for 6 weeks, $24 a day for adult lodge. **When:** June to September. **Contact:** Keewaydin Camp and Ojibway of Keewaydin, 4242 Brookdale St., Jackson, MS 39206, USA; phone (601)353-6233; summer, Timagami, ON Canada P0H 2H0. *(M)*

Retracing the Hudson's Bay Company Water Route: Among several canoe trips available in the northern Canadian wilderness country is a 2-week journey which traces the Hudson's Bay Company route down the Albany River to Ft. Albany on James Bay. Departing from the train station at Cochrane, participants are transported to Hearst and the put-in point. The party moves at an unhurried pace, allowing time for full appreciation of river travel techniques. In addition, a weekend training trip near Lake Cathchacoma provides participants with an intensive introduction to canoeing and light whitewater skills. The Lady Evelyn River, a Provincial Wild River Park which lies northwest of Lake Timagami, is the site of an 8-day river trip which includes a flight by bush plane to the headwaters of the river. For canoeists with moderate experience, an 8-day trip on the Spanish River and a 14-day trip on Churchill River are also available. For strong, healthy canoeists with moderate experience, a 2-week journey on the Coppermine River in the Northwest Territories is planned. **Cost:** $65 to $1,700 includes food, canoes, tents, paddle, life jacket, other equipment, transportation. **When:** May to August. **Contact:** Wanapitei, 7 Engleburn Pl., Peterborough, ON Canada 9KH 1C4; phone (705)743-3774; summer, Camp Wanapitei, Timagami, ON Canada P0H 2H0; phone Timagami Island 1-R-13 (New Liskeard). *(M)*

Yukon Territories

Yukon Canoeing: Canoeists push off from Whitehorse and spend 10 days riding the Yukon River northwest through the heart of the Yukon Territory. The Yukon, North America's most recently discovered river, flows through remote wilderness environments visited by few people. Group members paddle as far as Dawson, viewing many animals along this stretch of the river. Travelers frequently spot geese as well as canvasback, wood and black ducks; in addition, bald eagles soar occasionally overhead, while moose, bears and wolves feed along the banks. Canoeists paddle

Canoeists travel to remote mountain lake areas of northern British Columbia to fish, swim and hike. (Canadian Wilderness Experience)

through Lake Laberge to the abandoned Indian villages of Hootalinqua and Minto. They also visit the old Hudson's Bay Company outpost at Fort Selkirk and finally arrive at the town of Dawson—the hub of the Klondike. Group members have a chance to explore this partially restored gold rush town before leaving the Yukon. **Cost:** $350 includes rail transportation from Skagway, Alaska to Whitehorse, plus canoe, camping and cooking equipment, food, guide. **When:** July. **Contact:** The Wilderness Institute, 333 Fairfax, Denver, CO 80220, USA; phone (303)393-0400. *(M)*

CENTRAL AMERICA

Guatemala

Ruins by River: Ten days of travel on the remote Usumacinta River and a week of land sightseeing explore Latin culture old and new. Traveling in small dugouts, participants investigate a number of archaeological sites along the river,

including Tikal, Palenque, Dos Pilas, Aguateca, Altar de Sacrificios, Yaxchilan and a recently discovered site near Playa del Caribe. Nights are spent at encampments and lodges along the river. The river portion of the trip ends at San Cristobal de las Casas as travelers shift to the Mexican countryside, nearby Indian villages, markets and museums, with nights spent in hotels. **Cost:** $998 includes accommodations, most food, equipment, transportation, sightseeing costs, guide. **When:** January to March. **Contact:** Forum Travel International, 2437 Durant, No. 208, Berkeley, CA 94704, USA; phone (415)843-8294.

SOUTH AMERICA

Remote River Expedition: A canoe expedition into the remote and unexplored jungle south of the Orinoco River is available to experienced canoeists. The total length of the trip is approximately 600 miles, which is traversed in 45 days. Openings exist for 2-, 4- and 6-week intervals, and groups are comprised of 8 or 10 members utilizing 2 kayaks and 3 canoes. The expedition intends to use satellite photographs provided by NASA to navigate. **Cost:** $1,159 includes food, equipment, guides, local transportation. **When:** March. **Contact:** Canoes North/Canoes South, Box 5656, Armstrong, ON Canada P0T 1A0; phone (807)583-2055. *(M)*

Ecuador

Riding the Agua Rico: During a 16-day trip to Ecuador, participants canoe down 100 miles of the Rio Agua Rico, a tributary of the Amazon. Exotic plants and wildlife typical of the Amazon Basin waterways include the hallucinogenic yaje vine, the wild boar, fruit-eating bats, the 30-foot long anaconda and 1,300 species of birds. Expert Ecuador explorers who guide the trip point out these and other natural wonders during the 6-day canoeing portion of the trip. Other places visited include the capital city of Quito with its colorful native markets and archeological museums, and the lakeside city of Otovalo in the Andean foothills. A day hike in the mountain air of Cotopaxi in the high, rugged Andes searches for the condor, a South American raptor whose wingspan often exceeds 12 feet. Participants are urged to help with camp chores and canoeing, and should anticipate warm summer weather with temperatures in the 80's throughout the trip. **Cost:** $1,375 from Quito includes accommodations, meals, field supplies. **When:** November to February. **Contact:** Zig Zag River Runners, REI Adventure Travel, 1525 11th Ave., Seattle, WA 98122, USA; phone (206)322-7800. *(M)*

Peru

Jungle Jaunts: Travelers spend 2, 3 or 4 days in the Peruvian wilderness, exploring the region of the Tambopata Natural Wildlife Preserve. The 2-day trips involve either settling in at the Turistas Amazon Hotel in Puerto Maldonado, then touring the city by bus and the Tambopata River by dugout canoe; or, touring the river up to the Explorer's Inn, deep in the wildlife preserve, and staying there for the night. Both trips conclude on the second day with breakfast at the Turistas Amazon and a return flight back to Lima or Cuzco. The 3-day journey includes a dugout canoe tour to the Explorer's Inn on the first day; on the way participants visit a Huarayo Indian community and a pristine jungle lagoon. The second day travelers explore the area around Cocococha Lagoon, with a return on the third day after a breakfast in Puerto Maldonado. The 4-day excursion is identical to the above, except the second night and third day are spent in a camp near the lagoon.

Cost: $94 to $135; group rates available. **When:** Year-round. **Contact:** Explorer's Inn, Garcilazo de la Vega 1334, P.O. Box 10088, Lima (1), Peru; phone 313047.

Surinam

Paddle and Foot: Both canoeing and walking, participants on a 3½-week trip explore remote areas of Surinam and Venezuela. Canoe expeditions, using native dugouts with inflatable rafts as a backup, are made down the Cuyuni, Chicanan and Carrao rivers through forests overflowing with rare orchids and exotic birds; altogether almost 200 river miles are traversed. Surinam's 2 major reserves are Raleigh-Voltzberg, where trip members boat, camp and hike in uninhabited tropical rain forest, and Wia Wia, with its nesting sea turtles and large variety of coastal sea birds. Ample time is allotted on the trip for freshwater swimming, individual exploration, photography, nature study and fishing. **Cost:** $1,745 from Venezuela includes land transportation, equipment, food, accommodations, guide. **When:** February. **Contact:** Sierra Club Outing Dept., 530 Bush St., San Francisco, CA 94108, USA; phone (415)981-8634.

UNITED STATES

Alaska

Alaska by Paddle and Pack: Adventurers combine canoeing and backpacking for 7 days on Admiralty Island, in southeast Alaska's Tongass National Forest. Wildlife is abundant, including bald eagles, Alaskan brown bears and Sitka blacktail deer. Opportunities are provided for photography. Novice canoeists receive instruction. **Cost:** $350 includes food, transportation to and from Juneau, canoes, camping equipment, guide. **When:** By arrangement. **Contact:** Alaska Discovery Enterprises, P.O. Box 337, Juneau, AK 99802, USA; phone (907)586-6245. *(M)*

Canoeing the Yukon Headwaters: In 6 days canoeists cross the lake system which forms the headwaters of the Yukon, continuing downriver to Whitehorse. The trip begins at Lake Bennett, an area rich in mining history. From Bennett travelers paddle through Tagish and Marsh lakes before entering the river, and the group pauses en route to investigate old settlements, mining sites and Indian villages. At Whitehorse participants may arrange to continue on the Whitehorse to Dawson trip. **Cost:** $325 includes rail transportation from Skagway, food, canoeing instruction, canoes, camping equipment, guide. **When:** By arrangement. **Contact:** Alaska Discovery Enterprises, P.O. Box 337, Juneau, AK 99802, USA; phone (907)586-6245. *(M)*

Wild River Canoeing: Completely outfitted canoeing trips of 6 to 8 days are offered to adventurers wanting to explore the central Brooks Range, former home of the Nunamiut Eskimos and Athabascan Indians. The trip is designed for people willing to take an active part in the wilderness; everyone helps with chores at the camps that are established along the river. Five-mile-long Wild Lake is the starting point of an 8-day voyage up meandering Wild River. Swift and shallow for part of the way, the river also has calm stretches where participants may see beavers swimming in the river or near their dams, eagles, molting Canada geese and bull moose. The North Fork of the Koyukuk River is relatively easy to canoe except for a 2-mile stretch of Class II rapids. As on the other canoe trip, there is ample time to hike and photograph. **Cost:** $450 for the Wild, $400 for the Koyukuk includes transportation to and from Bettles, food, equipment, guide. **When:** June for Wild River, August for Koyukuk. **Contact:** Sourdough Outfitters, Bettles, AK 99726, USA; phone (907)692-5252. *(M)*

Arkansas

Ozark River Trip: Participants are invited to spend a leisurely 6 days canoeing along the calm Buffalo River in northwest Arkansas. Start-ing near the foot of the Boston Mountains, clearwater enthusiasts pass through unsurpassed scenery and fine swimming areas. During the late spring, the weather in the Ozarks is usually warm during the day and cool at night. An experienced guide leads the expedition. The minimum age is 12 years and some canoeing experience is required. Rental canoes are available. **Cost:** $150 includes food, guides, group equipment. **When:** May. **Contact:** Sierra Club Outing Dept., 530 Bush St., San Francisco, CA 94108, USA; phone (415)981-8634.

Colorado

Canoes on the Colorado: On a quiet stretch of the Colorado River between Loma, Colorado and Westwater, Utah participants and guides canoe for a weekend. The river passes through a wilderness protected by 1,000-foot sheer canyon walls that make the area accessible only from the river. The trip's

Families paddle to shore for beachcombing on a canoe outing in West Virginia. (West Virginia Dept. of Commerce/Arnout Hyde, Jr.)

leisurely pace allows time for hiking into remote side canyons and discovering spectacular sandstone formations. Participants should have some canoeing experience. **Cost:** $60 includes equipment, food, guides. **When:** June to September. **Contact:** North Woods Canoe Trips, 2659E S. Xanadu Wy., Aurora, CO 80014, USA; phone (303)750-8438. *(M)*

Florida
Alafia Trips: The Alafia River winds through southwest Florida and flows into Tampa Bay. Short trips are offered along its course, highlighted by occasional whitewater shoals. The trips last either a half day, a full day or overnight. Participants float along the river's narrow bends under a natural canopy of oaks, cypresses and cabbage palms; opportunities abound for the photographer and naturalist. The trip departs from Valrico. **Cost:** On request. **When:** Year-round. **Contact:** Canoe Outpost, Rt. 1, Box 414-K, Valrico, FL 33594, USA; phone (813)681-2666.

Down upon the Suwannee: Loosely scheduled week-long canoe trips are offered down the Suwannee, Alapaha, St. Mary's and Ochlockonee rivers in Florida. Each of the trips leaves from a different location and participants must transport themselves to these spots. The logistics and equipment are all handled by professionals, but the daily pace, activities, particular goals and tone of the trip are left up to the participants. Except for the Ochlockonee trip, no experience is required; however, prospective canoeists are advised to be in good shape. Opportunities abound for photographers and fishermen and facilities are available for underwater exploration. Custom trips, in or out of Florida, may also be arranged. **Cost:** $190 to $210, depending on location, includes food, camping and canoeing equipment, guide. **When:** May to December. **Contact:** Nature Trek, Rt. 1, Box 1224, Palatka, FL 32077, USA.

Everglades Excursion: Participants are invited to spend 7 days exploring a famous though little-known area of the country, once the homeland of the Seminole Indians and now threatened by overuse, though conservation efforts have helped preserve much of the Everglades. The once-threatened fauna of the area is still extant, including alligators, bald eagles, pelicans and spoonbills. Participants explore the area by canoe, by houseboat and on foot, and experienced guides lead the expeditions. **Cost:** $240 includes meals, accommodations, equipment. **When:** December. **Contact:** Wilderness Southeast, Rt. 3, Box 619 AA, Savannah, GA 31406, USA; phone (912)355-8008. *(M)*

Georgia

Swamp Trail: Canoeing enthusiasts spend 3 days examining animal and plant life in and around Okefenokee Swamp in southeastern Georgia, along the Florida border. The swamp is an enormous primeval wilderness; its clear, dark waters encompass a large portion of the country's cypress trees, as well as alligators, sandhill cranes, owls and turtles. Many other birds and reptiles inhabit the waters of Okefenokee. Experienced guides lead canoeists through the waterways, around small prairies and through lakes. The group camps each night on dry land. **Cost:** $55 includes meals, accommodations, equipment. **When:** April, May, October. **Contact:** Wilderness Southeast, Rt. 3, Box 619 AA, Savannah, GA 31406, USA; phone (912)355-8008.
(M)

Maine

Allagash Canoeing: Camping and canoeing are taught on the shores and waterways of a 56,000-acre state park in the northern part of Maine. Stretching for 100 miles along the Allagash River and lake chain, Allagash Park offers canoeing, photography, hiking and fishing in a remote wilderness area. Depending on the speed at which participants like to travel, a journey of 100 miles usually takes between 6 and 8 days. The waterway begins at Telos Lake and ends with rapids before emptying into the St. John River. Handling a canoe and negotiating rapids adequately can be learned by most people in a few days. Those who would like an easier outing can lessen the difficul-

ty of the journey by taking along additional guides. **Cost:** $35 a day includes instruction, guide, meals, canoeing equipment; $35 for extra guide. **When:** On request. **Contact:** Allagash Canoe Trips, 6 Winchester St., Presque Isle, ME 04769, USA; phone (207)764-0494.

Paddling the Androscoggin: Kayakers and canoeists of all abilities learn whitewater skills on mild to moderately challenging stretches of the Androscoggin River during 1- to 5-day courses. Teaching starts with a dry-land discussion of basic kayaking and safety procedures, progresses to training in flat water, and eventually allows participants a chance to test their skills in fast currents where the techniques of balance, turning and bracing, and wet exiting are brought into play. Most students gain enough expertise to enjoy running Class III water, but there is also an advanced river running class for experienced boaters who want to try paddling on the area's more difficult rivers such as the Rapid and the Magaloway, both of which have Class IV stretches. The school has also set up a slalom course for participants who have mastered basic river running skills. For younger river paddlers there is a 7-day session that includes daily instruction in kayaking as well as evening supervision at a campground. Visitors to the Androscoggin can either camp or stay in a nearby motel. **Cost:** $10 to $95 includes course tuition for adult instruction; $185 includes boat, instruction, sleeping bag, tent and meals for 7-day teenage session. **When:** May to September. **Contact:** Saco Bound/Northern Wa-

A paddler uses strong strokes to propel a canoe through light whitewater on Maine's Machias River. (Sunrise County Canoe Expeditions/Marty Brown)

ters, Post Office, Fryeburg, ME 04037, USA; phone (603)447-2177.

Canoe Trips for Teens: A variety of wilderness trips for teenagers, ranging in length from 3 to 7 weeks, is offered in the St. John/Penobscot rivers area of Maine. The mode of travel on all these trips is canoeing, though simple mountaineering may also be involved. A 7-week trip to the St. John River visits a calm area soon to be lost to a hydroelectric project; another trip of the same length travels down the Penobscot to Allagash Lake. Each of these spends its last week descending the challenging Allagash Wilderness Waterway, also available as part of a 4-week trip. There are also 2- and 3-week trips offered in the same areas for children 11 and 12 years

old. All trips involve camping and some lodge use; no experience is necessary as instruction is provided in all aspects of outdoor living and travel. **Cost:** $425 for 3 weeks, $840 for 7 weeks includes food, equipment, accommodations, transportation. **When:** June to August. **Contact:** St. Croix Voyageurs, Box 197, China, ME 04926, USA; phone (207)968-2434.

Canoeing the St. John River: Trips of 9 to 11 days take participants down the wild St. John River. Beginning as a narrow woods stream, the river increases in size and difficulty to the heavy whitewater of the Big Rapids. The St. John, currently threatened by the proposed Dickey-Lincoln Dam Project, passes through remote wilderness. On the 9-day trip, which puts in at

Baker Lake, participants paddle 111 miles to Dickey, just below the Big Rapids; the 11-day trip, beginning at Fourth St. John Pond, covers 135 miles. Canoeing experience is not required as there is plenty of opportunity to acquire the necessary skills. Ample time is set aside for swimming and fishing. Participants should bring their own sleeping bags. **Cost:** $335 to $395 includes roundtrip transportation from Bangor, gear, canoes, meals. **When:** May, June. **Contact:** Sunrise County Canoe Expeditions, Inc., Cathance Lake, Grove Post Office, ME 04638, USA; phone (207)454-7708.
(M)

Minnesota

Boundary Waters: The Superior-Quetico wilderness area has several million acres of lakes and forests for campers who wish to explore waterways by canoe and light boats. Private trips in the region are available from an outfitter in Grand Marais who supplies canoes, equipment and food. Assistance is given in selection of route and general trip planning. All beginners may receive free instruction in paddling, packing of gear, portaging and tent pitching. Experienced guides and packers are also available to cook, portage and help establish camp. Equipment and food are selected for compactness and weight. Accommodations nearby are available for overnights before and after the trip. **Cost:** On request. **When:** May to October. **Contact:** Gunflint Northwoods Outfitters, Box 100-AD, Grand Marais, MN 55604, USA; phone (218)388-2296.
(M)

Canoe Outfitting: From an outfitting post in the Superior-Quetico Wilderness, canoeists may strike out in any direction along the long, narrow Moose Lake chain of lakes, navigable in all weather conditions. Large bodies of water such as Basswood Lake are also an option when starting out from Fall Lake. The outfitter helps clients choose their routes, pointing out such special areas of interest as the best campsites, fishing holes and Indian paintings. Gear and equipment are guaranteed to be lightweight. Canoe towing service is also available. **Cost:** $17, $18 and $19 a day, depending on length of trip. **When:** May to November. **Contact:** Moose Lake Wilderness Canoe Trips, Box 358, Ely, MN 55731, USA; phone (218)365-5837.
(M)

Portaging and Paddling: Experienced guides join participants in Ely, Minnesota to begin 7- and 10-day canoe trips through the Boundary Waters Canoe Area or through Quetico Provincial Park. Traveling with 9 other companions including the guides, participants are grouped according to interests and ability, with some trips designed for families, some for photographers and some for canoeists who want a challenge. Instruction in paddling, campcraft and portaging is given to beginners. Evening campfires with songs, stories and discussions of the human and natural history of the region are a part of the voyage. Paddling and portaging alternate with days at camp where participants may take side trips, hike, fish or relax. **Cost:** $250 for 7 days, $325 for 10 days from Ely includes guides, all equipment,

CANOEING / 453

food, transportation. **When:** June to August. **Contact:** North Woods Canoe Trips, 2659E S. Xanadu Wy., Aurora, CO 80014, USA; phone (303)750-8438. *(M)*

Wilderness for Special People: Canoeing trips of 5 to 8 days are offered to people who might not otherwise obtain a wilderness experience: the developmentally disabled, the physically handicapped, senior citizens and those who have had difficulty adjusting to society. Taking place in the pristine environment of the Boundary Waters Canoe Area, the trips focus on canoeing, camping and portaging. Other activities include nature walks, hiking, rock climbing, log rolling, swimming and lake navigation. Most staff members have experience in social work as well as a special interest in introducing the disadvantaged to wilderness life, and all believe that many culturally or self-imposed limitations can be overcome. Groups are limited to 6 members plus counselors. Adjustments can be made to suit specific groups and goals. **Cost:** Not to exceed $20 per day. **When:** May to October. **Contact:** Wild Places, Inc., Box 758, Ely, MN 55731, USA; phone (218)365-5884.

Montana

Canoeing Historic Waters: The Missouri River, once frequented by keelboats and steamboats when it was the principal pioneer route to the Northwest, is the waterway for guided and self-guided canoe trips of varying lengths. Canoeists put in at Ft. Benton, Montana, the beginning of the Mullan Trail, and can paddle as far as Kipp State Park, a 160-mile stretch of river which was once a major gold rush route. Along the banks, monuments and landmarks document the river's rich history. Pick-up service from Kipp State Park or upriver is available. **Cost:** $54 to $75 depending on trip length includes canoe, gear, pick-up. **When:** May to September. **Contact:** Missouri River Cruises, Inc., Box 1212, Ft. Benton, MT 59442, USA; phone (406)622-3295. *(M)*

Nebraska

Canoeing Midwest Rivers: From mid-March to mid-November experienced canoeists guide groups of 16 to 55 on explorations of Midwest rivers. All scheduled trips are of 2 days' duration although longer trips may be arranged. Most trips traverse 25 miles of river in 17-foot aluminum canoes. Scheduled getaways often focus on a cultural event or some aspect of wildlife or natural history. In March canoeists follow the sandhill crane migration down the Central Platte, Kearney and Wood rivers with a visit to Fort Kearny. Other trips involve learning about the edibles and the folklore of the Central Platte area, traveling to Nebraska's largest rodeo on the North Platte, going to the Brownville Pickin Festival via the Missouri River and enjoying a family trip on the Niobrara River. Participants camp in waterproof tents provided by the outfitters and are given plenty of unscheduled time to fish, swim, hike, photograph and observe wildlife or beachcomb on sandbars. Discounts are available for the midweek and the pre- and post-season trips. **Cost:** $50 to $90 from put-in point depending on trip and number in party includes guides, meals, camping and canoeing equipment. **When:** Mid-March to mid-November. **Contact:** Wilson Outfitters, 6211 Sunrise Rd., Lincoln, NE 68510, USA; phone (402)489-6241.

New York

Northeastern Canoe-Camping and River Running: Mild to challenging whitewater activities ranging from an easy guided run on the Housatonic River in Connecticut to a week-long canoeing excursion on Quebec's Rouge River begin in Ossining, New York, where participants gather for car trips to various rivers in the region. Canoeists who choose one of the 2- to 3-day camping trips help out with all aspects of the trip and usually spend 4 or 5 hours a day paddling, with camp sites selected each night on islands or along the river bank. Instruction in whitewater technique is also offered on stretches of whitewater ranging in difficulty to Class IV. Orientation meetings at the homes of the guides are offered during the spring, before the heavy whitewater season begins. **Cost:** $10 for 1-day river run; $260 for week-long camping trip includes canoes, camping gear, life jackets, guides, instruction, meals. **When:** May to August. **Contact:** Sport Rites Club, c/o LeClair, Brayton Pk., Ossining, NY 10562, USA; phone (914)762-5121.

North Carolina

Whitewater Canoe Clinics: The rivers and wilderness areas of the Appalachian Mountains are the setting for instruction in fast-water canoe techniques. For paddlers who are already familiar with flat-water paddling, instruction concentrates on whitewater skills and safety. By the second day of the 5-day clinic, canoeists put in on the Chattooga River to practice the theoretical skills acquired in the classroom. Clinics are offered for novice, intermediate and advanced canoeists, and participants must be good swimmers. Three-day courses are available for the solo intermediate paddler. **Cost:** $135 to $225 includes equipment, food, lodging, local transportation, instruction. **When:** March to August. **Contact:** Globe Treks, 410 Fifth Ave., Suite 10, Henderson, NC 28739, USA; phone (704)692-4294. *(M)*

Whitewater Instruction Program: The rivers of North Carolina are the site of whitewater canoe clinics and week-long camping trips for canoeists of all levels of ability. Weekend clinics begin with an orientation session on equipment and safety followed by 2 days on the Little Tennessee, the Nantahala or other rivers. A 5-day trip takes beginning canoeists on a gentle section of the French Broad River with the goal of becoming intermediate paddlers by the time they take out at Hot Springs 75 miles downstream. Class III and IV water is encountered as the river breaks through the Appalachian Mountains. For intermediates, a 5-day program provides instruction while running a variety of rivers in the Smoky Mountain area, such as the Oconaluftee, Tuckaseigee and Nolichucky. Advanced canoeists may learn decked boat racing or follow an instruction certification program. All courses may be taken on decked boats or open canoes. Private instruction and women's clinics are also available. **Cost:** $85 for weekend clinics to $190 for 5 to 6 days includes instruction, equipment, transportation, all meals and, depending on the trip, lodging. **When:** April to November. **Contact:** Nantahala Outdoor Center, Star Rt., Box 68, Bryson City, NC 28713, USA; phone (704)488-6407. *(M)*

Oklahoma

Canoeing the Illinois: The meandering waters of the Illinois River in northeastern Oklahoma are the scene of daily, year-round canoe trips covering from 6 to 70 miles and lasting from 1 to 5 days. Groups of varying sizes can choose their own itinerary from the put-in point just outside Tahlequah, the capital of the Cherokee Nation. A circuit through the scenic Sparrow Hawk Mountain Primitive Area is one of the highlights. **Cost:** $6 to $12 a day includes canoes, equipment, shuttle service. **When:** Year-round. **Contact:** Sparrow Hawk Camp, Tahlequah, OK 74464, USA; phone (918)456-8371.

Texas

Boquillas Canyon: A 7-day canoeing trip begins with a review of canoeing techniques at the town of Evergreen. Then the group sets off for the Boquillas Canyon in Big Bend National Park. There are many side canyons to explore, where people may see a variety of wildlife; the river attracts huge numbers of birds and bird watching is usually excellent during the trip. The river environment is the focus

of the trip and there are 2 layover days used specifically to investigate it. No canoeing experience is required as there are no rapids on this river, but some familiarity with river travel is helpful. **Cost:** $295 includes transportation from Evergreen, food, equipment, guide. **When:** April, October. **Contact:** University of the Wilderness, 29952 Dorothy Rd., Evergreen, CO 80439, USA; phone (303)674-4695. *(M)*

Virginia

Shenandoah River Canoe Trips: Commissioned guides knowledgeable about local wildlife lead canoeists down the legendary Shenandoah River on trips of variable lengths. Rugged cliffs rising from the banks of the river contain caves and caverns that participants may explore along the way, and white-

Splash into an Exciting Vacation Excursion

A canoe trip down the Shenandoah River cools a paddler off during the dog days of summer. (Shenandoah River Outfitters)

tailed deer, raccoons, and great blue herons populate the area. Canoeists glide through Class I and Class II rapids between Shenandoah National Park on the Blue Ridge and the George Washington National Forest on Massanutten Mountain. The water of the Shenandoah is clean and participants can swim in it as well as camp along its banks. If canoeists decide to make the journey without a guide, route planners give advice and help in matching the trip, route and equipment to individual abilities and interests. **Cost:** $80 for 3 days; $60 for 2 days includes guide, meals, canoeing and rafting equipment. **When:** Year-round. **Contact:** Shenandoah River Outfitters, Inc., RFD 3, Luray, VA 22835, USA; phone (703)743-4159. **(M)**

Washington

Pacific Northwest Canoeing: Three trips are designed to explore the waters of Washington State, in-

cluding the San Juan Islands, Lake Chelan and Ozette Lake. Island hopping in the San Juans, participants canoe to Cypress, Blakely and Decatur islands. Lake Chelan in eastern Washington has camp sites along the shore, accessible only by boat. Many short hikes from the lake are available, and the weather is generally warm and often hot. The Indian villages at Ozette Lake may be explored at archaeological sites, and easy hikes to Cape Alava, the Pacific Ocean and rain forests embellish the trip. **Cost:** $175 includes meals, equipment, guide; $10 for transportation from Seattle. **When:** August for San Juans and Chelan, September for Ozette. **Contact:** White Water Sports, 307 NE 71st St., Seattle, WA 98115, USA; phone (206)523-5150.

Wisconsin

Kickapoo Canoeing: Three of the Midwest's most scenic rivers are experienced on a 2-day trip combining canoeing in historic voyageur paddle canoes and regular canoes, as well as kayaks. The Kickapoo, Wisconsin and Mississippi rivers, flowing through southern Wisconsin's hill country provide an appropriate setting for an introduction to family canoeing and shore camping. Beginning on the Kickapoo River near Wauzeka, participants paddle and drift downstream until they join the Wisconsin River, where an overnight camp is set up on one of the many islands. After winding through sandbars and islands on the Wisconsin the next day, paddlers meet the Mississippi River, where downstream vistas encompass the broad Mississippi Valley and its towering limestone bluffs. The route continues on the backwaters of the Mississippi to the final destination at Wyalusing State Park. **Cost:** $52 includes meals, guides, canoe equipment. **When:** August, October. **Contact:** Spirit Waters, 5375 Eureka Rd., Excelsior, MN 55331, USA; phone (612)474-5190.   *(M)*

RESOURCES
Clubs and Associations

Alaska Pioneers Canoers Association
Box 931
Soldotna, AK 99669, USA

American Canoe Association
Box 9137
Chicago, IL 60690, USA

American Indian Center Canoe Club
115 N. Walnut
Boise, ID 83702, USA

American Rivers Conservation Council

317 Pennsylvania Ave. SE
Washington, DC 20003, USA

American Whitewater Affiliation
P.O. Box 1584
San Bruno, CA 94066, USA

Canadian Canoe Association
33 River Rd., Place Vanier
Vanier City, ON Canada K1L 8B9

Eastern Professional River
Outfitters Association
P.O. Box 2997
Flagstaff, AZ 86003, USA

Indooroopilly Club
P.O. Box 36
Indooroopilly, Queensland, Australia

International Canoe Federation
905 6th St. SW
Washington, DC 20024, USA

Irish Canoe Union
91, Kilfenora Rd., Kimmage
Dublin 12, Ireland

National Friends of the River
1964 Menalto Ave.
Menlo Park, CA 94025, USA

Professional River Outfitters Association
c/o Canyoneers
P.O. Box 2997
Flagstaff, AZ 86003, USA

Sierra Club Canoeists
625 W. Barry
Chicago, IL 60657, USA

Townsville Canoe Club
11 9th Ave.
Railway Estate, Queensland
Australia

United States Canoe Association
1818 Kensington Blvd.
Ft. Wayne, IN 46805, USA

Western River Guides Association
994 Denver St.
Salt Lake City, UT 84101, USA

Rentals

Rent-A-Canoe Directory
Grumman Boats
Marathon, NY 13803, USA

KAYAKING

Have you ever watched the movement of a kayaker through rapids? Back straight out of the water, paddle only rarely called into use, he floats through the raging waters at a pace all his own. The slight draft of the kayak makes it almost independent of the river's current as it bobs smoothly between standing waves, turns effortlessly in the midst of a thundering whirlpool, and catches an unseen eddy to float, miraculously, upstream to try the rapid one more time.

Kayaking is for someone who wants to become immersed in an extraordinary element. The rider sits in a narrow fiberglass craft, double-bladed paddle in hand, and slides through the water, running rapids, riding the ocean surf, or paddling the quiet waterways of an inland sound. Wherever you do it, you must learn the proper techniques—the many strokes, the skill of balancing in rough waters, and the life-saving Eskimo roll to right yourself when the river, inevitably, gains the upper hand.

The Eskimos, in fact, are credited with inventing the kayak, and the sub-arctic regions of Alaska and Canada offer some stimulating adventure travel opportunities. You can explore the fjords outside Juneau near the Hubbard Glacier or paddle up the tidewater estuaries of Tracy Arm during the summer months, watching glaciers calve and listening to thousands of birds whose rookeries are nearby; or you can study the land as well as the sea in the south of Alaska for over two months, learning outdoor survival skills and environmental awareness.

At the other end of the spectrum, you can journey by kayak along an isolated part of the Baja California coast, fishing for food, snorkeling, and watching a variety of sea life which includes whales, sea lions and dolphins. The two-week trips are offered in October and November, an excellent time of the year to visit this isolated part of North America.

While these exotic trips often do not require previous kayaking experience, many people prefer to take instruction closer to home. Outfitters from California to Colorado offer trips on scenic and wild rivers that teach participants the many skills of kayaking in beautiful surroundings—the rapids of the Rogue River in Oregon, the volcanic canyons of the Salmon and Snake in Idaho, the evergreen forests of Lake Wenatchee in Washington and the high-mountain region of the Crystal River in Colorado.

If you want to know your craft as only a builder can, a three-week course on Catalina Island off the California coast offers a chance to build a kayak, learn to use it, then circumnavigate the island. From then on, the kayak—and the skills—are yours to explore the rivers, lakes and coasts in style. □

Open-water kayaking along coastlines or on lakes is a popular means of exploration in areas from the Sea of Cortez to British Columbia's Inside Passage. (Galland)

KAYAKING

CANADA
British Columbia

Vancouver Island Kayak Programs: Beginning and intermediate whitewater kayaking courses are offered on Vancouver Island. The courses, which last 6 days, are held on the Campbell, Elk and Gold rivers. The beginning course starts on a lake, where paddling and maneuvering techniques can be learned, and progresses to easy whitewater in a series of day trips. The intermediate program is offered when the rivers are at their highest. All programs emphasize safety, and include instruction on how to read a river, navigation of rapids, eddy turns, Eskimo rolls and kayak rescue. Participants should be competent swimmers. **Cost:** $260. **When:** July. **Contact:** Strathcona Park Lodge, Outdoor Education Society, Box 2160, Campbell River, BC Canada V9W 5C9; phone Campbell River radiophone operator.

MEXICO
Baja California

Bahia de Conception Kayaking: Along the most rugged and isolated part of the Baja Coast, participants journey by kayak and folbot from Mulege to San Sebastian or Laredo. The San Sebastian trip takes 12 days and covers 35 miles while the Laredo trip takes 18 days and covers 85 miles. Kayaking, snorkeling and food gathering skills including pole and spear fishing are taught in Bahia de Conception. Food is carried on the journey but there is also a heavy reliance on catching red

In calm water near Vancouver, kayakers become skilled in the basics before progressing to whitewater runs. Many operators offer kayaking instruction as part of their trips. (Canadian Hostelling Assn.)

Alaska Discovery Enterprises offers a kayak trip that explores the glaciers, forests and tidewater estuaries in the Tracy Arm region of southeastern Alaska. (Alaska Discovery Enterprises)

snapper and other fish along the way. During the exploration, paddlers see whales, sea lions, dolphins and extensive bird life. The trip is strenuous and requires good health and endurance. **Cost:** $350 for 12 days, $480 for 18 days includes transportation from Mulege, guides, instruction, food, equipment. **When:** October, November. **Contact:** James Henry River Journeys, 1078 Keith, Berkeley, CA 94708, USA; phone (415)527-4649.

PACIFIC

Hawaii

Water Sports around Maui: Trip members spend 5 days kayaking, snorkeling and sailing around the remote islands near Maui. After meeting in Kahului, participants are transported by sailboat to a base on one of the islands where camp is set up. From here, group members can snorkel among the coral reefs, ride the surf in 2-person kayaks or pilot one of the sailboats. Rafts provide participants with the op-

portunity to investigate ancient Hawaiian villages, petroglyphs, shipwrecks and hidden caves, accessible only from the sea. Local foodstuffs are used in meals. The group size is limited to 20, and the minimum age is 8. **Cost:** $345 includes most camping equipment, transportation, meals. **When:** Year-round. **Contact:** International Aquatic Adventures, Inc., 2047 Broadway, Boulder, CO 80302, USA; phone (303)444-5829 or toll-free (800)525-2545.   *(M)*

UNITED STATES

Alaska

Kayaking Tracy Arm: Tracy Arm, first explored by John Muir, is surrounded by terrain that includes tidewater estuaries, rain forests, alpine meadows, high peaks and large glaciers. Participants fly from Juneau to arrive at a remote stream that meets the Arm, and spend the next several days exploring the area at their discretion. Generally, camp is pitched on a nearby plateau in the vicinity of Sawyer and South Sawyer glaciers. Wildlife in the area includes brown and black bears, deer, mountain goats, marmots, eagles, terns, gulls, murres and ptarmigans. The trip concludes at or near the Indian village of Sumdum, with the charter pilot making an overhead pass to signal pickup time. **Cost:** $350 covers transportation to and from Juneau, food, kayaks, equipment, guide. **When:** By arrangement. **Contact:** Alaska Discovery Enterprises, P.O. Box 337, Juneau, AK 99802, USA; phone (907)586-6245. *(M)*

California

Kayaking from the Ground Up: Students spend 3 weeks building and then using their own kayaks for a circumnavigation of Santa Catalina Island. The program is divided into 3 basic parts: construction of the kayaks, water work to acclimate the group to the use of kayaks and basic skills, and a series of lectures and field trips designed to introduce students to the environment of the island. During the trip, camping sites include Silver Canyon, Ben Weston Beach, Parson's Landing and Goat Harbor. Each day enough time is given to hiking and observation of the native flora and fauna so that students may have a practical nature experience. **Cost:** On request. **When:** Summer. **Contact:** Catalina Island School, Toyon Bay, P.O. Box 796, Avalon, CA 90704, USA; phone 611 (operator assistance required).

Colorado

Going with the Flow: Water lovers of all skill levels are introduced to or continue studies in the art of kayaking. Three courses are offered: the first is a beginner's class in which students learn the basics of sweep and power strokes as well as balance techniques. It is first held at a lake, then moves to a slow river current as students progress. The second opportunity is open to intermediate kayakers; faster, more exciting water is used as students work on high and low braces as well as learn to read the river. Surfing and ferrying are also introduced as the students work on the Blue, Little Snake and Colorado rivers. The third offering is an advanced class; here kayakers in small groups work on technique and gate running. The water boated is quite difficult. All classes are held weekly. **Cost:** $149. **When:** May to October. **Contact:** Aspen Kayak School, Inc., Box 1653, Keystone, CO 80435, USA; phone (303)468-2222.

Idaho

Salmon and Snake Special: Using inflatable kayaks, 15 river runners paddle through the narrow volcanic canyons of the Lower Salmon and Snake rivers for 4 days. Numerous rapids, huge waves and swells make this Class III voyage better suited to those with previous kayaking experience. Guides and paddlers in a ratio of 1 to 3 or 4 meet in Lewiston, then drive to Skookumchuck Park for orientation, instruction and drills in boat handling techniques and water safety procedures. Traveling in individual kayaks, participants average 18 miles a day and camp on beaches along the way. The course winds through Green and Blue canyons to a convergence with the

A line of sportyakers runs a section of rapids on the Rogue River in Oregon. Rougher parts of the Rogue challenge even experienced kayakers. (Orange Torpedo Trips)

Snake River and a final 22-mile run to the take-out point at Grande Ronde. From there the group travels by van to a celebration dinner at Lewiston. **Cost:** $275 from Lewiston includes transportation, guides, food, equipment. **When:** July, August. **Contact:** Orange Torpedo Trips, P.O. Box 1111, Grants Pass, OR 97526, USA; phone (503)479-5061.

Maine

Learning Whitewater Kayaking: A 2-week program for boys 14 and older stresses instructional skills in fundamental whitewater kayaking. Enrolled students learn basic skills such as rolling, river reading and kayak paddling, while experiencing the water of Maine's Pleasant Lake and the faster currents of the St. Croix River. The Mattawamkeag River provides challenging whitewater for students near the end of the course. Students are required to display excellent swimming ability

to join the program. The campsite is a short trip from Maine's highest peak, Mt. Katahdin in Baxter State Park. **Cost:** $310. **When:** Summer. **Contact:** Maine Wilderness Canoe Basin, 246 Neptune Dr., Groton, CT 06340, USA; phone (203)536-7980.

Oregon

Kayak School: The first 5 days of a 10-day kayaking course consist of day-long outings on different sections of the Rogue River, increasing in difficulty as the days pass. Skills taught include dry and wet exits, basic strokes, the Eskimo roll, surfing, safety and rescue techniques

After pushing the nose of his kayak into the current, a kayaker backs down the river. (Sundance Expeditions)

and kayak etiquette. In evening sessions, the group discusses the day's events, reviewing wilderness skills, first aid and expedition preparation, with supplemental slides and movies. Skills are put to the test for a day on the Klamath River, then on a 4-day trip down the lower Rogue. Traveling in traditional touring formation, kayakers encounter 40 miles of challenging whitewater and rapids. Crafts beach at Foster Bar on the last day and students are transported back to the riverhouse. The course may

also be taken in two 5-day segments. **Cost:** $425 for 10 days, $225 for each 5-day session includes meals, lodging, instruction. **When:** June to September. **Contact:** Sundance Expeditions, 14894 Galice Rd., Merlin, OR 97532, USA; phone (503)479-8508. *(M)*

Utah

Sportyak Workshops: Instruction in sportyak use, including pivoting, pulling and pushing, ferrying and righting, is available along quiet stretches of the Green River's Desolation Canyon. After the instruction, groups test their skills on rapids like Steer Ridge, Wire Fence and Rattlesnake. The trip lasts 8 days and includes time spent drifting quietly, studying canyon geology and rock formations, observing wildlife such as eagles, herons and hawks, and hiking up side canyons to visit cliff dwellings, petroglyph sites and old horse trails leading to abandoned ranches. **Cost:** $425 includes equipment, meals, transportation to and from the river, instruction, flight over Sand Wash. **When:** June to September. **Contact:** Wild and Scenic, Inc., P.O. Box 2123A, Marble Canyon, AZ 86036, USA; phone (602)355-2222. *(M)*

Washington

Cascades Paddling: Instruction is offered in 7-day segments for prospective or experienced kayakers. Taking place on Lake Wenatchee in the Cascade Mountain foothills, the course is designed for students of all ages and abilities, allowing participants to work and develop at an individual pace. The instructor-to-student ratio is 1 to 5, and all equipment is provided. In addition

With his kayak almost out of the water, a paddler surfs through a wave of whitewater on the Skykomish River in Washington. (Keith Gunnar)

to activity on the lake, instruction and practice take place on the White, Chiwawa, Nason and Wenatchee rivers. All participants must be able to swim 100 yards. Safety and rescue techniques, river reading, trip planning and flat water skills are also studied. Meals and lodging are provided at the Cougar Inn; bedding is included and the rooms are dormitory-style. **Cost:** $250 includes food, lodging, instruction and equipment. **When:** June, July. **Contact:** White Water Sports, 307 NE 71st St., Seattle, WA 98115, USA; phone (206)523-5150.

RESOURCES

Clubs and Associations

American Whitewater Affiliation
P.O. Box 1584
San Bruno, CA 94066, USA

Citrus County Kayak Club
c/o Rademaker, Rt. 1, Box 415
Floral City, FL 32636, USA

Hawaii Kayak Club
407-D Keariani St.
Kailea, HI 96734, USA

Kayak Hawaii
1328 Front St.
Lahaina, Maui, HI 96761, USA

Metropolitan Canoe and Kayak Club
c/o American Red Cross
150 Amsterdam Ave.
New York, NY 10023, USA

Montana Kayak Club
c/o Abelin, Box 2
Brady, MT 59416, USA

Oregon Kayak and Canoe Club
c/o Kiel, P.O. Box 692
Portland, OR 97207, USA

Vancouver Kayak and Canoe Club
4022 W. 27th
Vancouver, BC, Canada

Washington Kayak Club
c/o Aaker, Box 24264
Seattle, WA 98124, USA

Western Wyoming Kayak Club
Donald L. Hahn, Gen Del.
Wilson, WY 83014, USA

Whitewater-Northeast Kayak Club
Box 1081
Spokane, WA 99201, USA

SAILING

"The bow cut through the water as a 15-knot wind billowed the sails. On the command, 'Ready about! Helms alee!' we released the sheets on the starboard side and gathered them portside. The tack was quick and the trim was neat. As our bow passed through the wind, the boat heeled hard to port and we proceeded on a starboard tack."

Thus one landlubber described his first sailing trip, in terms as colorful and evocative as they are practical. The art of sailing has evolved over centuries of marine exploration, and the often obtuse technical language that goes with it is testimony to the antiquity of the activity. And the same wind which brought the European to the Americas and the Asian to Polynesia is still taking modern travelers to foreign lands.

The sailing trips which are offered in nearly all the waters of the world take place on single-masted or double-masted boats and ships varying in size from nimble Hobie Cats skimming over the waves off California to an 82-foot yawl which cruises the waters of the Aegean Sea. Sailing trips can range in duration from weekend instruction courses to two-month sailing trips from Seattle to Hawaii and back or even a 21-month circumnavigation of the world. Many of them offer more than just a sail—instruction in techniques, navigation by the stars, and helping with a host of shipboard chores make these trips as informative as they are exciting.

There are three basic types of sailing trips available—"bareboat," skippered and "cruise-and-learn" trips. The former is essentially a rental arrangement, in which the boat is chartered with all its gear, including binoculars, compass, life jackets, cooking gear and spare parts. A skippered cruise frees you from the responsibility of knowing how to sail and usually provides an informative trip under the guidance of a sailor familiar with the waters and their history. The "cruise-and-learn" option combines the best of both—under the expert eye of seasoned sailors you learn the techniques of sailing and the marine sciences in the laboratories and workshops of the natural world.

Over three-fourths of the earth's surface are covered by water—offering an almost unlimited world for the sailor to explore. You can relive the age of exploration and the era of pirates in the waters of the Caribbean; you can sail the Inside Passage off Canada's west coast and watch grey whales frolic; you can sail a Tall Ship along the coasts of England and France, cruise the Channel Islands off the California coast or investigate the Galapagos in the Pacific. But wherever you go—at no time does the world seem as boundless or freedom as great as from the decks of a sailing vessel.
□

Novice sailors take the wheel on trips ranging from weekend instruction courses to an 8-week sail across the Pacific or a 21-month circumnavigation of the world. (Steve Rees)

SAILING

AFRICA

Egypt

Felucca Trip on the Nile: Aboard an authentic felucca, a Mediterranean lateen-rigged vessel, 8 to 10 travelers sail down the Nile River. During the 14-day journey participants pass among some of Egypt's most renowned sights. The vessel sails quietly from Aswan before docking at the temples of Kom Ombo, Horus, Edfu, Karnak and the necropolis at Thebes. At these locations participants may disembark for individualized exploration of the sites. During the course of the trip, crew members visit the Sphinx and pyramids at Giza and a historic museum in Cairo. Participants bivouac along the riverbanks, though they stay occasionally in hotels. **Cost:** $1,150 includes meals, accommodations. **When:** July to August. **Contact:** Explorator, 16, place de la Madeleine, 75008 Paris, France; phone 266-66-24.

Nile Sail Trek: Participants fly from London to Cairo to begin a 16-day trip down the Nile River in boats known as feluccas. The felucca is a swift, low-riding sailboat with no motor, and sleeps 6 persons on deck under a canvas canopy. Sites visited include the Temple of Luxor, built in the age of Amenhotep III and famous for its lotus bud columns, and the temple of Karnak, largest of all Egyptian temples. If passengers desire, a side trip by donkey may be taken from the west bank of the river to the Necropolis and the Valley of Kings. From Luxor it takes 7 days to reach Aswan by boat, which gives everyone a chance to experience a bit of Egyptian culture during village stops where food is bought at local markets. Participants help sail the boat, cook the food, and plan each day's itinerary. **Cost:** $575 to $595 depending on departure date includes roundtrip airfare from London, local transportation, guide. **When:** Year-round. **Contact:** WEXAS International Inc., Suite 354, Graybar Bldg., 420 Lexington Ave., New York, NY 10017, USA.

(M)

T.F.A.I.

Red Sea Trimaran Trip: Waters of the southern Red Sea provide the sailing grounds for 8 to 14 people during a 2-week trip aboard a trimaran. Participants gather at Djibouti for the commencement of the activities scheduled by the French crew, including seafood cookouts and beach camping. Group members are free to partake in underwater exploration of the numerous coral reefs as well as share in the cooking and sailing chores while underway. At L'Ile du Diable, one of the scheduled stops, visitors may witness the "frozen" remains of the cascading lava flows that created the volcanic island. The sea's condition can range from calm and mirrorlike to turbulent. Beaches provide campsites that are generally chosen by participants. **Cost:** $1,218 from Paris, includes transportation, food. **When:** June to September; also fall and winter on request. **Contact:** Explorator, 16, place de la Madeleine, 75008 Paris, France; phone 266-66-24.

Dragon Class sloops tack during a race in the waters of Bermuda, where the sailing season is year-round. (Bermuda News Bureau)

ASIA

Sailing the Coral Islands: Departing from Phuket, Thailand, and sailing southward to Penang, Malaya, the 38-foot yacht *Gypsy* explores the coral islands off Sumatra in the Andaman Sea. Two weeks are spent relaxing and exploring the islands, many of which are uninhabited. Participants help sail the yacht and may take advantage of opportunities to snorkel and swim. **Cost:** $320. **When:** November to March, May to September.

Contact: Encounter Overland, 369 Pine St., Suite 516, San Francisco, CA 94104, USA; phone (415)421-7199. *(M)*

ATLANTIC

East and South Coast Cruising: Landlubbers and sailors alike journey from 4 to 14 days among the Bahamas or along the Atlantic coast of the United States. Groups of 4 to 8 sail 40- to 50-foot yachts in waters ranging from the remote areas of the Caribbean in the winter to the rugged coasts of Maine and Nova Scotia in the summer; in the spring, participants sail in Chesapeake Bay. Because of the small size of the crew, individual instruction in seamanship and celestial navigation is offered. Workshops during special cruises deal with marine biology, meteorology, scuba diving, medicine at sea and island ecology. Guest instructors join some of the voyages. It is recommended that participants be able to swim. **Cost:** From $220 includes meals, instruction, scuba gear, sailing dinghies. **When:** Year-round. **Contact:** Avalanche, 1794 N. Highland Rd., Pittsburgh, PA 15241, USA; phone (412)833-7800.

CANADA
British Columbia

Sailing the Inside Passage: A group of no more than 10 sails aboard a 55-foot ketch on a 300-mile, 8-day journey through the Straits of Georgia. Embarking from Vancouver, participants cruise among the high coastal mountains and jutting fjords in the sheltered waters along the Canadian shores. Participants may learn sailing skills while traveling, or they may simply relax and enjoy the rugged beauty of the Inside Passage. Participants who wish to sail on their own have access to a skiff. At Stuart Island, crew members go ashore to explore

Sailors take advantage of calm weather to mend the staysail on a trip through the fjords of Canada's Inside Passage. (Carol Baker)

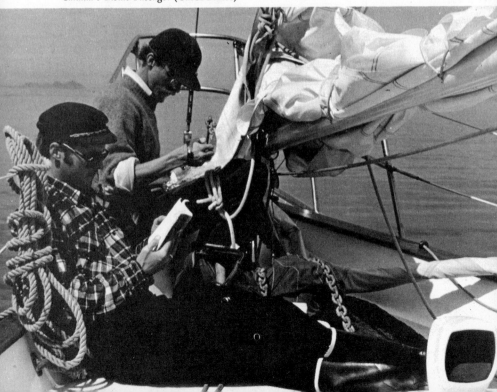

island wildlife on hiking trips and to camp on the beach. Sailing among the seascape of fjords and evergreen islands, members may sight whales spouting or hear porpoises calling. Motor power is used only when the craft is becalmed. **Cost:** $435 includes accommodations on the boat, meals, guide. **When:** June to August. **Contact:** American River Touring Association, 1016 Jackson St., Oakland, CA 94607, USA; phone (415)465-9355.

Strait Sailing: Group members spend 6 days sailing among the islands and fjords of the Georgia Strait on the coast of British Columbia. In skippered and outfitted boats 26 to 46 feet long, participants study sailing skills, navigation, weather, tide and currents, anchoring and marine ecology. The group also has a chance to learn about the preparation of fresh seafood. Small coves and estuaries are explored with canoes, and group members also travel inland to visit historical sites, wilderness lakes and waterfalls. The journeys begin at Heriot Bay, about 100 miles north of Vancouver. No previous sailing experience is necessary. **Cost:** $200 for 6 days includes food, boat, skipper. **When:** July to August. **Contact:** Sailing Explorations, Box 91436, West Vancouver, BC Canada V7V 3P1; phone (604)929-6364.

Canadian Coastal Cruise: Participants spend 4 or 8 days sailing along the British Columbia coast. On the 4-day cruise the group travels south through the Gulf Islands, exploring the waterways and camping on the beach or spending the night on board. On the 8-day

excursion, travelers sail past 12,000-foot peaks and enter glacier-fed fjords. From secluded anchorages group members hike to areas where Indian relics and rock paintings can be found; fishing throughout the area is rewarding. The region is inhabited by a great variety of wildlife, including whales, seals, porpoises, sea lions and many different bird species. On both voyages, passengers are welcome to lend a hand with the ship's chores; the crew is eager to teach sailing skills. Meals are prepared by the crew. **Cost:** $210 for 4 days, $435 for 8 days, includes meals, accommodations, crew. **When:** June to September. **Contact:** Whitewater Adventures Ltd., P.O. Box 46536, Vancouver, BC Canada V6R 4G8; phone (604)736-2135. *(M)*

CARIBBEAN

Bahamas

Sailing in the Bahamas: A 15-day cruise covers over 400 miles in the waters around the Bahamas and includes 2 open-water runs through rough ocean. Aboard a 39-foot sailing vessel, participants take part in the cooking, housekeeping and watch-standing during the ocean passage. The islands visited are relatively unsettled and have been slow to change, so visitors may explore almost untouched cays; 13-foot Boston whaler dinghies are available for shore excursions. Group members learn the basics of seamanship such as holding a course and taking bearings. Novice sailors may find some segments of the trip difficult. **Cost:** $795 to $1,493. **When:** September to October. **Contact:** Caribbean Sail-

ing Yachts, Ltd., Roadtown, Torto-
la, British Virgin Islands; or CSY,
Inc., Box 491, Tenafly, NJ 07670,
USA.

Cuba

Sailing to Reopened Waters: A
13-day sailing expedition heads to
the island of Cuba which until
recently was closed to many outsiders. Living onboard, the crew
members set sail from Port au
Prince, Haiti to Santiago, the first
capital of Cuba. The vessel travels
along Cuba's southern shores
which are lined with the Sierra
Maestra, and then on to the Manza-
nillo Cays on the eastern side
where participants can dive in waters rarely visited. The trip contin-

*Passengers may sail a dinghy to shore to explore Caribbean island beaches on Blue Water
Cruises trips.* (Virgin Island Yacht Charters)

ues to Grand Cayman in the British West Indies where the journey ends. The cruise to Cuba is a chance to visit waters unfrequented by yachts for nearly 2 decades. **Cost:** $935 includes meals, accommodations onboard. **When:** February. **Contact:** Oceanus, P.O. Box 431, Hohokus, NJ 07423, USA; phone (201)447-0393. *(M)*

Netherland Antilles

Caribbean Charters: Daily sails aboard the 61-foot *Maho* are scheduled from St. Maarten. The *Maho*, which has won the 800-mile St. Maarten Tradewinds Race the last 3 consecutive seasons, provides fast and comfortable yacht trips in the Caribbean waters. Among the trips available are 2-hour coastal sightseeing sails through the Bonaire Trench, whole and half-day picnic sails, private and group charters, and sunset cocktail sails which can take yachters to the Los Rogues Trench area. **Cost:** On request. **When:** Year-round. **Contact:** Courtwell N.V., P.O. Box 346, Philipsburg, St. Maarten, Netherlands Antilles; phone 2433.

West Indies

Sailing Instruction in the Virgin Islands: Group members can take sailing lessons for 2 or 5 days while visiting St. Thomas in the Virgin Islands. During the 2-day course, participants receive morning lectures on basic techniques, then board 24-foot Rainbows for sailing in the afternoons. The 5-day course follows a similar itinerary for the first 2 days, after which participants combine sailing practice with land exploration. Arrangements for 1-day sails on a larger vessel to St.

John's can be made. The longer course is designed for either beginners or more experienced sailors. In all courses group members sail fiberglass keel sloops. **Cost:** $110 to $395 for 2 days, $195 to $495 for 5 days, depending on the number of persons includes instruction, use of sailboats. **When:** Year-round. **Contact:** Annapolis Sailing School Headquarters, 601 Sixth St., P.O. Box 3334, Annapolis, MD 21403, USA; phone (301)267-7205 or toll-free (800)638-9192.

Sailing Camp in the Bahamas: A camp for young sailing enthusiasts is located on the island of Antigua, where a hotel provides accommodations reserved exclusively for program members. High school aged participants are offered all

levels of sailing instruction as well as the opportunity to study marine biology, underwater photography and dramatics during the 6-week course. Skin and scuba diving courses are also available to interested students. A variety of small and large craft is used by apprentice and journeyman sailors during the program. Students choose their own course of study on an elective basis and may participate in non-sailing activities. **Cost:** On request. **When:** June. **Contact:** Bahama Sailing Camp, 480 W. 246th St., New York, NY 10471, USA; phone (212)548-1184.   *(M)*

Antilles Cruising: Individualized yacht cruises of varying durations are available to the U.S. Virgin Islands, the Grenadines and Martinique. Cruises are geared toward group desires and can include fishing and diving in the Caribbean. Snorkeling gear, water skiing equipment and sailing dinghies are available onboard for group members. Cruising guests may share the onboard duties or simply relax as they choose. Meals are often prepared from seafood caught during the day's run. **Cost:** $50 to $70 a day includes meals, equipment. **When:** Year-round. **Contact:** Blue Water Cruises, Box 758-AX, St. Thomas, VI 00801, USA; phone (809)774-0650.   *(M)*

CENTRAL AMERICA

Guatemala

Dulce River Expedition: A journey of 11 days begins with a sail downwind from Coxen's Hole to Livingston, Guatemala, where travelers enter the Dulce River with its 300-foot gorges and lush greenery. From Lake Isabel at its head, the group takes a small plane over the dense jungles of Peten for an all-day visit to the Mayan ruins of Tikal, the New World's tallest buildings before the 20th century. There are opportunities for aerial photography on the way. Participants return to Lake Isabel and then set sail north for Belize along a barrier reef. **Cost:** $780. **When:** May. **Contact:** Oceanus, P.O. Box 431, Hohokus, NJ 07423, USA; phone (201)447-0393.   *(M)*

EUROPE

Sailing Britain and Brittany: Group members with previous sailing experience embark on 8- or 15-day journeys along the islands of Great Britain and the French coast. As active members of the crew, participants take a hand in all sailing duties aboard the gaff-rigged schooner *Hoshi*. The regions visited include Ireland, Scotland, the Hebrides, the Channel Islands and southwest Brittany. A highlight of the season is the "Old Gaffer's" race in the Solent, held each year in September. **Cost:** $300 for 8 days, $600 for 15 days includes accommodations onboard. **When:** May to September. **Contact:** Oceanic Expeditions, 240 Ft. Mason, San Francisco, CA 94123, USA; phone (415)441-1106.

Sailing the Cote d'Azur: For 2 weeks, participants on a cruise along the French Riviera sail 36-foot boats without the aid of a skipper or guide. Leaving from New York, group members fly to Paris, then to Nice where they begin the voyage aboard a fleet of sloops. Ports of call include St. Honorat, La Napoule, Pt. Grimaud, St. Tropez, Cavalaire and Porquerolles. Port Cros and Port Mans provide visitors with quiet harbor settings along the route. Dropping anchor at Cap Ferrat toward the end of the journey, participants view an unspoiled stretch of the Mediterranean coast. All members participate in sailing the boats; duties may include navigating the sloop during the temperate wind squalls, called mistrals, which often rise to 60 knots. Participants who lack seafaring experience may join if they are willing to learn. **Cost:** $1,340 includes round-trip airfare from New York, boat rental, some meals, berth, hotel accommodations. **When:** September. **Contact:** Offshore Sailing School, Ltd., 820 Second Ave., New York, NY 10017, USA; phone (212)986-4570 or tollfree (800)221-4326.

England

Tall Ship Training: Young people ages 16 to 24 work as a team during a 14-day voyage aboard either the *Sir Winston Churchill* or the *Malcolm Miller*. The schooners are designed to take on 39 trainees, in addition to permanent officers. Trip members spend the majority of the time sailing, but there are opportunities to go ashore as well. Students engage in most of the normal shipboard activities: care and maintenance of the ship, rigging, steering, galley work and standing watch. Each day's program is arranged to take advantage of the prevailing wind and weather conditions.

Trainees must provide their own transportation to and from Chichester, where the trip begins and ends. Ports visited range from Alderney to St. Helier. **Cost:** $300 includes insurance, berth, meals. **When:** February to December. **Contact:** The STA Schooners, Bosham, Chichester, Sussex, PO18 8HR, Great Britain.

Youth Sailing Holiday: Participants ages 11 to 15 spend 7 days sailing under the instruction of experienced professionals. Group members have the option of using 2 different areas: Lake Bala in North Wales or the River Dart in Devon. Young people electing the first area stay at the Plas Rhiwaedog Youth Hostel, and those who choose the River Dart stay at the Maypool Youth Hostel. Each area has a fleet of fiberglass dinghies, plus life jackets and waterproof parkas. **Cost:** $113 includes accommodations, meals, sleeping bag, instruction. **When:** July, August. **Contact:** YHA Adventure Holiday, Trevelyen House, St. Albans, Herts., Great Britain; phone St. Albans 55215.

Greece

Cruising the Cyclades Islands: Participants spend 2 weeks sailing bareboat in the waters surrounding the Greek islands. Departing from New York, group members fly to Athens, then board a small fleet of boats near the capital city. Depending on wind conditions, trips may follow a route through the Cyclades Islands or along the Peloponnese coast. Among the probable ports of call are Kithnos, an uninhabited area where group members can swim and explore deserted bays;

Aegina, where the Temple of Aphaia rises above the bay of Aghia Marina; Delos, another uninhabited island, once used as a religious center; and Spetse, a secluded harbor where donkeys and horse-drawn buggies provide the only transportation. A guide who knows the Mediterranean accompanies the cruise, but trip members sail the boats themselves and should have some sailing experience. Trip itinerary is flexible enough to allow for route variations. **Cost:** $1,375 includes roundtrip airfare from New York, cruising, hotels, some meals, accommodations on board. **When:** July. **Contact:** Offshore Sailing School, Ltd., 820 Second Ave., New York, NY 10017, USA; phone (212)986-4570 or tollfree (800)221-4326.

Cruising the Aegean: Participants plan the course of a 12-day sail among the Greek islands. Fifteen days total, the journey offers snorkeling, scuba diving, water skiing and swimming off of a skippered and outfitted 75-foot ketch, along with days on land at Athens and other island locations. Group members may take a pilgrimage to Delos, Apollo's birthplace, or journey to Crete to explore the remains of ancient Minoan cities and to view the Knossos Palace frescoes. Religious relics on Patmos, terraced vineyards and white villages on Naxos, or windmills and tavernas on Mykonos can be visited. Participants spend the final days of the journey in Athens visiting the Parthenon, the Flea Market or the Plaka, a section of Athens composed of narrow, winding alleyways filled with tavernas. **Cost:**

$935 from Greece includes meals, accommodations, guide. **When:** June. **Contact:** REI Adventure Travel Inc., 1525 11th Ave., Seattle, WA 98122, USA; phone (206)322-7800.
(M)

Netherlands

Low Country Sailing: Participants 10 years and older study the art of sailing in the Netherlands. Courses in both beginning and advanced sailing are given on a 1- and 2-week basis aboard 52-foot Frisian sailing scows. Other activities include rowing, fishing, swimming and small-ship sailing. Accommodations are in 1- to 4-person dormitory rooms. Groups are separated by age: 10 to 14, 15 to 22 and 22 to 60. Private and group lessons are available. **Cost:** $125 to $230 includes instruction, equipment, accommodations, meals. **When:** May to September. **Contact:** Zeilinstituut "De Bird," Egon B.P. Brenninkmeijer, Heeg (Friesland), Holland.

Scotland

Outdoor Activities for Businessmen: A week-long course in Scotland is offered specifically for businessmen ages 30 to 70. Base camp is a cedar lodge, where most nights are spent. Daytime activities include sailing around the Loch Laxford islands, rock climbing, canoeing, fishing and some mountaineering. Allowances are made for different degrees of physical fitness and no activity is compulsory. Visits are made to Handa Island bird reserve and Foinavon Mountain. A 2-day expedition is made to a remote bothy for overnighting. **Cost:** $194 includes meals, accommodations, equipment, transporta-

On a skippered sailing trip travelers enjoy the waters of the Aegean Sea while others take responsibility for maneuvering the boat. (WEXAS)

tion, instructor/guides. **When:** March to June. **Contact:** John Ridgway School of Adventure, Ardmore, Rhiconich, By Lairg, Sutherland IV27 4RB, Great Britain; phone Kinlochbervie 229.

Outdoor Training in the Scottish Highlands: A number of courses offer participants of all ages a chance to develop skills in sailing, hiking, rock climbing and canoeing. On one 12-day course designed for 16- to 20-year-olds, 5 students and an instructor sail 28-foot open ketches. Leaving Loch Eil, crews learn to sail and navigate their craft among the fjord-like sea lochs and may venture into the Inner Hebridean islands. During another course, students are trained in a full spectrum of activities including camping and canoeing in the wilderness, field studies and craftwork sessions. Evenings are used for films and lectures, though much free time is also available. **Cost:** $106 to $386. **When:** Year-round. **Contact:** Outward Bound Loch Eil, Achdalieu, Ft. William, Inverness-shire, Great Britain; phone Corpach 320.

MIDDLE EAST

Turkey

Cruising the Aegean Coast: One-and 2-week sailing trips on an 82-foot gaff-rigged yawl, the *Eblis*, visit many of the remote islands and coastal regions of the Aegean Sea off Turkey. Departing from Samos, the *Eblis* follows a flexible route between the Greek islands of Samos and Rhodes. Stops are made at the islands of Patmos, Lipso and Leros and the uninhabited Gulf of Kos on the Turkish coast, though each trip's route and daily schedule are determined by the weather and passengers' wishes. The area is rich in myths and history, and a number of archaeological sites are visited. **Cost:** $490 to $980 includes food, accommodations, activities, transportation. **When:** September, October. **Contact:** Oceanic Expeditions, 240 Ft. Mason, San Francisco, CA 94123, USA; phone (415)441-1106.

PACIFIC

Northern Pacific Passage: Students with all degrees of experience in seamanship take part in a roundtrip voyage between Seattle and Hawaii. Sailing for 2½ to 3 weeks from Seattle to the islands and taking slightly longer to return, participants live aboard 36- and 50-foot yachts rigged for cruising in the open ocean. Because the voyage is designed to give students experience in deep water sailing, all members serve as crew and take part in standing watch, steering, handling sails and preparing meals. After the first leg of the journey, group members lay over in Kauai for 36 hours, then begin the return trip. Students should provide wet weather gear and sleeping bags. **Cost:** $875 includes meals, instruction. **When:** June, September. **Contact:** Rawhide Harris Ocean Sailing School, 2401 N. Northlake Wy., Seattle, WA 98103, USA; phone (206)633-5135.

Hawaii

Ocean-Going Classroom: Students of all ages, backgrounds and nationalities board either the *Machias*, an 80-foot steel schooner, or the *Paragon*, a 38-foot ocean racing sloop, for classes in the Hawaiian Islands covering a variety of topics: geology, volcanology, marine biology, sailing, ethnobotany, oceanography, meteorology, seamanship and navigation. Classes last 4 to 18 days, and participants may receive college credit or simply take them for the sake of experience. On the *Paragon*, students become an integral part of the crew, and with a maximum enrollment of 6, instruction is individualized. During a 4-day course, group members study the marine life in Hawaii's reef communities; during 7-, 10- and 15-day expeditions to several islands, students learn techniques of sail handling and seamanship and study marine life environments. Aboard the *Machias*, participants take 4- to 18-day courses cosponsored by the University of Hawaii. Stopping at different islands, group members hike across volcanoes, investigate petroglyphs, walk through lava tubes, collect and prepare traditional Hawaiian foods, snorkel among reef formations and explore caves and waterfalls on isolated coastlines. **Cost:** $50 a day includes food, accommodations, instruction. **When:** February to November. **Contact:** Sea Trek Hawaii, Inc., 244 Dole St., Honolulu, HI 96825, USA; phone (808)948-8111.

Sandwich Island Sailing and Hiking: Travelers spend 10 days sailing around and trekking over the island of Hawaii. The journey begins with 6 days of sailing fast, nimble Hobie Cats along the island's coast; no prior experience in sailing is needed. As the group sails down the coast, anchorages are made at various spots where the snorkeling, spear fishing and surfing are good and where coastal parks and villages may be visited. The next part of the trip brings participants inland

to hike through the terrain of the island first explored by Captain Cook. Group members pass through rain forest, savanna and volcanic desert before reaching the rugged seacoast once again. Highlights along the route include a descent into Kilauea Volcano and a visit to the ruins of Wahaula Heian, the oldest temple in Hawaii. The journey ends in Hilo. **Cost:** $650 includes meals, guide, catamarans. **When:** April to October. **Contact:** Sobek Expeditions, Inc., P.O. Box 67, Angels Camp, CA 95222, USA; phone (209)736-2924. *(M)*

SOUTH AMERICA

Ecuador
Sailing the Islands of Discovery: While exploring the archipelago

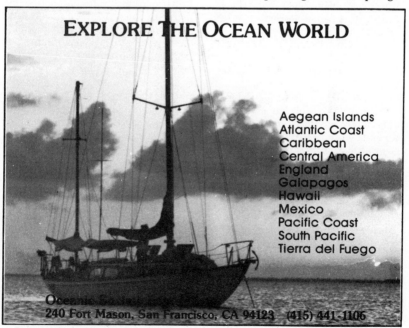

that engendered the ideas for Darwin's *The Origin of the Species*, 12 travelers may gain a deeper appreciation of the natural world. For 19 days participants join the naturalist leader and crew of a small sailing vessel on a cruise of the Galapagos Islands. Near the equator, 600 miles west of Ecuador, voyagers encounter iguanas and sea lions along the shores, giant tortoises roaming the cactus lands, and an array of birds ranging from Galapagos penguins and flightless cormorants to tiny flycatchers and Darwin finches. Most nights are spent on board the boat but with the emphasis on exploring the islands, several day hikes are planned. **Cost:** $1,405 from Baltra includes meals, equipment, accommodations, guide. **When:** November. **Contact:** Earth Journeys, 3400 Peachtree Rd., Atlanta, GA 30326, USA; phone (404)231-0073.

Galapagos Charters: The Galapagos archipelago, consisting of 15 principal islands, is an Ecuadorian national park, and the site of private yacht charters of 1 or more weeks. Five private yachts are available for hire. Each yacht is fully crewed and carries an English-speaking naturalist guide. The yachts, which accommodate 4 to 10 passengers, are simply furnished. Itineraries vary with the time of year and park regulations; a typical 1-week itinerary may include Plazas, Barrington, Hood, Floreana, Santa Cruz, Bartholome and Seymour. Most of the cruising is done at night to allow ample time for first-hand observation of the remarkable flora and fauna, which made a lasting impression on Charles Darwin during his visit in 1835. **Cost:** $1,900 to $5,800 a week, depending on number of passengers, includes all food and services. **When:** Year-round. **Contact:** Galapagos Yacht Charters, Casilla 9481, Guayaquil, Ecuador; phone Guayaquil 390933. *(M)*

UNITED STATES

Sailing along the Pacific Coast: A group of 10 people rides the wind and the current down the California coast from San Francisco in a 25-foot inflatable pontoon fitted with sails, motor and oars. In the company of a marine biologist participants row and sail to Big Sur, crashing through the surf and camping on the beaches for the night. In the morning all 10 participants are at an oar, pulling through the breakers until, once outside the surf, the group raises sail, coasting between ¼ and ½ mile from the coast until evening when they are ready to camp. The voyage includes observing sea otters at close quarters, visiting the permanent sea lion colony on the island of Anonuevo, investigating tide pools, skin diving, fishing and exploring caves and beaches inaccessible from the cliffs above. On the final day of the journey a van ride back to the launch point near San Francisco concludes the trip. **Cost:** $275 from San Francisco includes transportation, meals, guide, ocean-going pontoon. **When:** September. **Contact:** Whitewater Voyages/River Exploration Ltd., 1225 Liberty St., El Cerrito, CA 94530, USA; phone (415)236-7219.

A winch helps hoist the mainsail of the 60-foot Cibola, *which makes an 11-day voyage from Roatan to Belize City.* (Oceanus Expeditions)

Alaska

Cruising Prince William Sound: In a coastal wilderness region explored by Captains Cook and Vancouver nearly 200 years ago, participants may cruise for a week or 13 days aboard sailboats that leave from Whittier, 40 miles southeast of Anchorage. Trip members rent a 22-foot Tanzer sailboat which follows a larger guide boat through the sound and along scenic coastline offering secluded coves, tidewater glaciers and sculptured fjords. Guides provide sailing lessons until participants have acquired enough seamanship experience to skipper the boat on their own. Week-long cruises either sail north up Port Wells and around Esther Island or go south down Culross Passage to Port Nellie Juan. Longer trips sail to Columbia Glacier or further south through the Nellie Juan Wilderness Study Area to Icy Bay. For participants who wish to enjoy a skippered cruise, berths are available aboard the guide boat. In May, cross-country skiing can be combined with sailing, while hiking is best after mid-July when the snow disappears from the upper elevations. To reach Whittier, participants must travel by train either from Anchorage or Portage. **Cost:** $750 to $1,400 includes fully equipped sailboat, navigation equipment, charts, raft for trips ashore. **When:** May to September. **Contact:** Alaska Wilderness Sailing Safaris, Dan Riker, P.O. Box 4-275, Anchorage, AK 99509, USA; phone (907)277-0160.

California

San Diego Bay Sail Training: The basics of sailing are taught in a variety of courses lasting from 2 to 5 days. In a 2-day course offered on weekends, individuals with no previous sailing experience learn the fundamentals during 4 hours of classroom instruction and 8 hours on the water. A 5-day course includes basic training and supervised sailing, as students test their newly acquired skills. **Cost:** $98 to $195. **When:** Year-round. **Contact:** Annapolis Sailing School Branch at San Diego, 1715 Strand Wy., Coronado, CA 92118, USA; phone (714)435-6000.

San Francisco Windsurfing: During a couple of 3-hour lessons on the San Francisco Peninsula, participants learn how to windsurf. Students are taught the techniques of windsurfing on a dry-land training machine if the wind is more than 4 miles an hour. On the water the instructor demonstrates the necessary basics of windsurfing, and then travels along side until the student becomes comfortable with the board and sail and has learned how to catch the wind, make turns and maintain balance. In the second lesson, participants learn to tack, change sides of the board and sail upwind. No experience is necessary although participants should be able to swim. **Cost:** $40 to $60 for 2 lessons includes instruction, equipment. **When:** May to July. **Contact:** Bay Surf Windsurfers, Box 776, Menlo Park, CA 94025, USA; phone (415)323-7527.

Coastal Cruising: A 3- or 5-day jaunt 25 miles off the coast of Santa Barbara provides sailors with the chance to sharpen skills in day sailing or weekend gunkholing. Instruction in areas such as sail trimming and adjustment, helmsmanship, celestial navigation and use of a sextant are available for both the novice and seasoned sailor. Sailing conditions in the Santa Barbara Channel cover the range from mild to exhilarating. Summer in the channel is warm and delightful, while the fresh breezes of winter provide some of the year's best aquatic conditions. **Cost:** $230 to $335 includes boat equipment, instructors, meals, accommodations. **When:** Year-round except December. **Contact:** Coast Navigation School, 22 N. Milpas, Santa Barbara, CA 93102, USA; phone (805)963-7837.

Florida

Sailing in Mangrove Swamps: Students snorkel among coral reefs, explore the Everglades and sail in the Gulf of Mexico near the Florida Keys during a 2-week program. Climbing aboard a pulling boat at Big Pine Key, students sail south of the Keys into the crystal waters of the Florida reefs reaching into the Gulf Stream. Group members navigate north and east across the Florida Bay, penetrating the dense forests of mangroves in the Everglades

National Park. The outdoor experience concludes with a 3-day solo excursion within the park boundaries. During this period students identify and study the lowland birds such as roseate spoonbills, pelicans, ibises and the flamingos which are indigenous to the area. Following an exploration of the shallow creeks and bays of the Everglades, participants travel along the windward passage offshore, through the Gulf of Mexico and back to the Keys for the conclusion of the program. **Cost:** $525 includes meals, accommodations, equipment. **When:** November to March. **Contact:** Hurricane Island Outward Bound School, Box 429, Rockland, ME 04841, USA; phone (207)594-5548.

Maine

Sailing Maritime Coastlines: Aboard a 46-foot brigantine, group members embark from Baddeck, Cape Breton, on an individualized cruise of the waters northeast of New England. The specific location and duration of the voyage depends solely on the desires of the participants. Locations visited on former trips include the Newfoundland fjords, the French Islands of St. Pierre and Miquelon, the Bras d'Or Lakes, the St. Lawrence Islands and, farther north, the straits of Belle Isle and Southern Labrador. The trips may last from 6 days to 1 month. Possible itineraries also include explorations along the coast of Labrador and parts of Greenland or a trip from Nova Scotia to Maine at the season's end. Accommodations onboard provide facilities for charter groups of up to 4. Showers with hot and cold fresh-

water are available. **Cost:** $150 to $170 a day includes meals, crew, accommodations on board. **When:** Summer, by arrangement. **Contact:** Glad Tidings, Box 394, Oakland, ME 04963, USA. *(M)*

Sailing Penobscot Bay: Sailing in Penobscot Bay is one of several outdoor activities available to participants during a 5-week New England trip. Aboard an 88-foot schooner, the group learns from a naturalist what lives and grows in

Maine's waters, as well as the intracacies of sailing, knot tying and navigation. Other activities of the trip, which departs from Portland, include bicycling on backcountry roads and canoeing the length of the Allagash Wilderness Waterway. Two special projects of the trip are working with local farmers and climbing Maine's highest peak, Mt. Katahdin. The responsibilities of daily chores, bicycle maintenance, and first aid are shared by members of the group. **Cost:** $1,025 includes food, accommodations, transportation from Portland. **When:** June, July. **Contact:** The Infinite Odyssey, 57 Grant St., Waltham, MA 02154, USA; phone (617)899-6050. *(M)*

Cruising Classroom: Members of 7- and 10-day sailing trips along the coast of Maine receive instruction in history and natural sciences as well as boat and sail handling. College credit may be arranged for studies in meteorology, navigation, invertebrate biology, ornithology, nautical history and marine biology. The vessel, a 60-ton, 88-foot schooner built in 1920 and reputedly the strongest vessel ever built, sails out of Camden, Maine and cruises among the islands of Penobscot Bay and along the coast. **Cost:** 7 days $375, 10 days $535 includes instruction, berth, meals. **When:** June to September. **Contact:** Oceanic Expeditions, 240 Ft. Mason, San Francisco, CA 94123, USA; phone (415)441-1106.

Maryland

Sailing from Scratch: Three beginners' sailing courses at Annapolis in Maryland offer students basic classroom and on-the-water instruction on Chesapeake Bay. In a single-weekend course, participants receive an intensive dose of training; 4 hours are spent in the classroom and 8 hours in fiberglass sailboats. Basically the same instruction is offered on another schedule which lasts 4 weeks. Meeting 1 day a weekend, the course is designed for students with limited weekend free time. A longer 5-day course repeats the weekend program for the first 2 days, then allows 3 practice days for participants to solidify their new skills. Students may take family and friends sailing during the practice sessions. **Cost:** $98 to $195 depending on length of course. **When:** April to October. **Contact:** Annapolis Sailing School Headquarters, 601 Sixth St., P.O. Box 3334, Annapolis, MD 21403, USA; phone (301)267-7205 or tollfree (800)638-9192.

New York

Spring Sailing: Novices and those already trained in the basics of sailing take advanced courses during the month of April. Three days at 4 hours a day are spent in introductory and refresher courses on 27-foot Solings. Class size is between 3 and 4 students. Four courses are offered—a learn-to-cruise package; an advanced/refresher spinnaker class; a basic racing course which covers regular sailing as well; and a spinnaker workshop designed to teach students how to make a working sail out of the spinnaker. Half-season and full-season rates are available. All courses last 3 days with the exception of the spinnaker work-

Taking a fix on the sun by sextant enables sailing students to find their ship's location on nautical charts. (Oceanic Expeditions)

shop, which runs for 4 half-day sessions. **Cost:** $109 to $139 includes tuition, gear. **When:** April. **Contact:** The New York Sailing School, 340 Riverside Dr., New York, NY 10025, USA; phone (212)864-4472.

East Coast Cruising and Racing School: Intensive week-long sailing courses for participants interested in cruising and racing are available in New York, South Carolina, Martha's Vineyard, Florida and the British Virgin Islands. Participants learn the care and handling of 27-foot cruising boats and practice trimming the sails. Cruising classes commence year-round on Sundays and racing classes start on first and third Sundays, January to April; participants must be at least 12 years old for cruising courses, 14 for racing. Sailing is done without an instructor aboard by the final days of the course. **Cost:** $199 to $249 includes instruction. **When:** Year-round by arrangement. **Contact:** Offshore Sailing School, Ltd.,

820 Second Ave., New York, NY 10017, USA; phone (212)986-4570 or tollfree (800)221-4326.

South Carolina

Sailing Instruction at Sea Pines: Students can learn sailing skills during 6- and 7-day courses based at Sea Pines Plantation on Hilt Head Island, which is bordered by the protected waters of Calibogue Sound on one side and by the Atlantic Ocean on the other. Aboard 27-foot sailboats, group members study the basics of boat handling, navigation and reading of the water and weather. Instruction is also given in rigging, heeling, wind shift adjustment, emergency procedures, docking and knot and spinnaker techniques. By the end of the course, students are able to sail the boat without instructors aboard. **Cost:** $199 includes instruction. **When:** May to October. **Contact:** Offshore Sailing School, Ltd., 820 Second Ave., New York, NY 10017, USA; phone (212)986-4570 or tollfree (800)221-4326.

Washington

Sailing the Sound: The San Juan Islands and Cascade and Olympic mountains provide the backdrop for a 5-day instructional, live-aboard cruising expedition in Puget Sound. Instruction on all aspects of sailing is covered, from docking and anchoring to setting sails and using spinnaker gear. Both optical and electronic methods of navigation are demonstrated and used. Ports of call include Roche and Rosario harbors, where hotels converted from turn-of-the-century mansions provide swimming pools, saunas and showers. Weekend trips devoted to roaming the waters and visiting Puget Sound ports are also available out of Seattle. **Cost:** $300 for 5-day cruise includes sailing gear, instructors, breakfast, lunch; $69 for weekend cruise includes sailing gear, meals. **When:** On request. **Contact:** Cascade Sailing School, 2300 W. Ninth #35, Olympia, WA 98502, USA; phone (206)943-8085.

San Juan Sailing: A 5-day trip takes passengers among the San Juan Islands of the Pacific Northwest. While meandering from Anacortes to Fidalgo Island to San Juan and Orcas islands, group members may receive sailing instruction and help navigate the boat. Sail trim and reefing, helmsmanship, docking and anchoring, spinnaker handling and sailing safety are among the topics covered. When the boat docks at Friday Harbor, Roche Harbor and Rosario, passengers may disembark for horseback riding, hiking, tennis and swimming. One night is kept open for guests to pick the anchoring spot, which could be a town already visited or a deserted beach on one of the outer islands. The 50-foot boat sleeps up to 8 people and is equipped with private staterooms and 2 heads with hot showers. **Cost:** $300 includes

The captain keeps a watchful eye on a student taking the helm on a Seawind Sailing School trip in Puget Sound. (Elizabeth Watson)

lunch, snacks, instruction. **When:** May to October. **Contact:** Seawind Sailing School, 6535 Seaview Ave. NW, Seattle, WA 98117, USA; phone (206)246-7245. *(M)*

Sound Sailing: Advanced sailors learn to skipper their own craft during 2-day courses aboard Westsail 28- and 32-foot boats. Students study the fundamentals of performance sailing, navigation and general seamanship. Little time is spent in the classroom; most of the course takes place at sea where participants practice new techniques. Included in the first day's curriculum are subjects such as handling on all points, hull and air dynamics, navigation, weather and oceanography. Students who take the second day's course study mooring techniques, engine maintenance and repair, knots, reefing and jury rigging. As a prerequisite, students must have intermediate training from Wind Works or have completed 40 hours of sailing. **Cost:** $25 for 1 day, $50 for 2 days; 30 percent discount from October to April. **When:** Year-round. **Contact:** Wind Works, 7001 Seaview Ave. NW, Seattle, WA 98117, USA; phone (206)784-9386.

WORLD

Southern Equatorial Circumnavigation: Nassau in the Bahamas is the departure point for a 21-month global circumnavigation. The voyage takes place aboard a 55-foot aluminum light-displacement ocean racer and a 45-foot fiberglass cutter-yawl; the 2 boats cruise together, with 13 members plus the crew on board. The wind and weather as well as local political conditions partially determine the route, but a general plan calls for a southern equatorial course that includes stops at the Galapagos Islands, Tahiti, Australia, Bali, Singapore, Sri Lanka, Greece, Turkey, France, Spain and as many other locations as time permits. Participants have the opportunity to dive, fish, snorkel, watch birds and explore in ports of call. The boats have libraries, extensive cassette collections, a doctor and a sauna. **Cost:** $777 to $855 a month includes meals, accommodations, crew. **When:** February. **Contact:** Poseidon Circumnavigations, 107 15th Ave. SE, St. Petersburg, FL 33701, USA; phone (813)894-3914.

Around-the-World Cruise: A 21-month circumnavigation of the world is offered to sailing enthusiasts familiar with shipboard routine or to novices who are willing to learn and work. Participants travel and live aboard a well-equipped 55-foot sailing yacht with a professional crew that includes a captain, first mate and chef. The itinerary provides for visits to remote ports and reefs in areas such as the South Sea Islands, the Indian Ocean and the Mediterranean and Black seas. Optional instruction on board includes big boat seamanship, celestial navigation and scuba diving; a compressor is available on the boat. A marine science and diving expert accompanies the expedition. **Cost:** $1,000 a month includes all living provisions; 3-month minimum preferred. **When:** Departs in February or March. **Contact:** Voyage, 1009 Susan Rd., Philadelphia, PA 19115, USA.

WINDJAMMING

The image of a fully rigged windjammer cutting across the open sea is a powerful one; it stirs a longing for adventure even for those of us who have never been closer to the sea than a movie screen. The multi-masted windjammer represented the culmination of wind-driven ocean travel, and the Tall Ships served nobly throughout the 18th and 19th centuries as the world's main cargo and passenger vessels. The age of sailing the seven seas may have been eclipsed by the advent of the coal-burning steamship a century ago, but many people have recently returned to windjamming for the excitement and romance of that bygone era.

Learning the difference between one type of sailing ship and another is the first step in a nautical education. However, a windjammer can be any one of several types of boats. You might sail aboard a 90-foot brigantine—a two-masted ship with a square-rigged foremast—for over a week among the Virgin Islands of the Caribbean. Or you could take a week-long cruise aboard a narrow-beamed, square-rigged clipper to see the New England coast. Other New England windjammers include schooners from 81 feet to 132 feet long, which are either authentic survivors from the Tall Ships era or carefully constructed replicas.

Whether you choose to sail the Caribbean or explore the craggy coastline of Maine windjamming is an experience you won't soon forget. Standing at the bow as the saltwater spray blows across the deck, you watch the sea being split before you into twin wakes by the ship's prow. The powerful, slightly irregular cadence of the schooner's pitch becomes a part of your own physical rhythms, and your knees bend unconsciously to absorb the movement. At the skipper's call for volunteers, you might help hoist the mainsails to take full advantage of a wind rising from the east.

After a hearty meal, you can take a shift of the evening watch. Like Richard Henry Dana and Herman Melville before you, this is your time to experience the essence of windjamming: alone on deck beneath a panoply of stars, with the soothing hiss of the wind whispering through the rigging, and the plankton-rich waters of the endless sea incandescent under the silent moon. □

Two sailors stand in the toprigging. Climbing ratlines into the high sail—while the ship heaves from side to side—is a difficult and exciting part of windjamming. (Dirigo Cruises)

WINDJAMMING

CARIBBEAN

West Indies

Virgin Island Sailing: Sixteen passengers share the facilities of the 90-foot brigantine *Romance* on an 8-day trip. The ship has no set itinerary, but makes use of the trade winds to visit the largest number of islands and anchors in an island cove each afternoon. Passengers may explore coral gardens, view colorful tropical fish and make shore excursions. Aboard ship, cabins have double berths, large skylights, wash stands and ample luggage space. Fresh water showers are also available. The vessel is the world's only brigantine in regular passenger service, and was designed under the supervision of the Royal Danish Government for Greenland trade. **Cost:** On request. **When:** Year-round. **Contact:** Kimberly Cruises, Box 5086, St. Thomas, VI 00801, USA; phone (809)774-9003.

UNITED STATES

Semester at Sea: Students participate in a fully accredited educational experience for 8 weeks aboard the 100-foot schooner *Harvey Gamage*. The campus extends from Maine to the Bahamas, and 15 college credits are earned through courses in coastal oceanography, icthyology, navigation and seamanship, ornithology and maritime history. Ports of call to educational institutions, research laboratories, museums and historical sites complement the curriculum. Students have responsibility for operating and crewing the gaff-rigged schooner that carries 4,200 square feet of sail. Snorkeling gear, small boats and a mini-sailboat are available for instructional or recreational use. A maximum of 24 students participate each semester. **Cost:** $3,100 includes tuition, room, board, laboratory fees. **When:** September, March. **Contact:** Dirigo Cruises, Schooner *Harvey Gamage*, 39 Waterside Ln., Clinton, CT 06413, USA; phone (203)669-7068.
(M)

Maine

Down East Windjamming: Penobscot Bay is explored during a 6-day cruise out of Rockland on board the two-masted schooner, *J. & E. Riggin*. Participants explore deserted islands, quiet fishing villages and resort areas, and while under sail may choose to lend a hand with steering or trimming, assist in the galley or simply relax on deck. Penobscot Bay provides some of New England's best sailing conditions as well as spectacular scenery. Many varieties of marine life and wildlife can be observed along the coast including seals and whales. **Cost:** $200 to $225 includes accommodations, meals. **When:** July to September. **Contact:** Capt. Dave Allen, Schooner *J. & E. Riggin*, Box 571, Rockland, ME 04841, USA; phone (207)594-2923.

Summer Coastal Cruises: Cruises along the New England coast aboard the schooner *Harvey Gamage* leave from the city dock in Rockland at 10:00 a.m. on Mondays during the summer. A week of

A messline forms in the galley of the Harvey Gamage. *Dirigo Cruises offers 7-day voyages aboard the schooner for $250.* (Dirigo Cruises)

sailing follows, past pine-edged seascapes and rocky coastlines, stopping each evening at a different island. Wind and tide determine the exact itinerary, but passengers can expect to visit such ports as Camden, Stonington, Monhegan, Boothbay and Christmas Cove. The atmosphere is informal and trip members are welcome to participate in the operation of the ship. Swimming equipment, fins, masks and snorkels are provided for those hardy enough to brave the 60° New England waters. A sailboat is also carried aboard for those who wish to learn to sail or just sharpen their sailing skills. Passengers occupy staterooms with 2, 3 or 4 berths.

The small sacrifices of limited electricity and cold water are more than compensated for by the coastal scenery, fresh air and relaxation aboard ship. **Cost:** $250 includes meals. **When:** Mondays from June to September. **Contact:** Dirigo Cruises, Schooner *Harvey Gamage*, 39 Waterside Ln, Clinton, CT 06413, USA; phone (203)669-7068.

(M)

By the Schooner: A genuine 2-masted sailing vessel is used for 6-day trips in the Penobscot and Bluehill Bay area. The ship sails out of Rockland Harbor at 10 a.m. Monday morning and returns the next Saturday. Passengers visit remote harbors and secluded coves during the voyages, and there are opportunities for beachcombing, clamming and exploring. Along the way, each person may take a turn steering the ship, trimming the sails or engaging in various other shipboard tasks. Fresh running water is available in each cabin, as well as outside windows for good light and ventilation. Once during the week, everyone participates in a lobster bake on the beach. The number of passengers is limited to 18 with a crew of 4, and the itinerary is variable. **Cost:** $200 to $225 a person depending on month. **When:** June to September. **Contact:** David A. Johnson, Schooner *Richard Robbins, Sr.*, P.O. Box 951, Rockland, ME 04841, USA; phone (207)354-6865.

Sailing Penobscot Bay: Five-day windjammer cruises in the Penobscot Bay area enable passengers to enjoy the experience of being at sea without having the responsibility of handling a boat. Participants cruise aboard the *Mattie* or *Mercantile*, both old-time Yankee merchant vessels. Trips depart Monday mornings from Camden, and itineraries vary with wind and weather conditions. The ships are anchored at different harbors each night, with time allowed to swim or to go ashore to visit coastal towns. Passengers stay onboard in comfortable cabins, and New England family-style meals are cooked on the galley's wood stove. **Cost:** $205 to $225. **When:** June to September. **Contact:** Maine Windjammer Cruises, Inc., Les and Ann Bex, P.O. Box 617, Camden, ME 04843, USA; phone (207)236-2938.

Down East Cruise: The islands and the coast of Maine are the setting for a 7-day trip aboard the *Nathaniel Bowditch*. The 81-foot schooner sails the waters between Boothbay Harbor and Bar Harbor, stopping frequently for beachcombing and sightseeing. Passengers are welcome to assist in the daily routines of sailing, which may include hoisting sails or navigating along the rocky shorelines. When the ship is moored, participants may fish for mackerel, pollack, bluefish and other species. Accommodations on the ship are small, but cozy, and meals are served onboard. In the evening participants may go ashore or provide their own entertainment on deck. **Cost:** $225. **When:** June to September. **Contact:** Capt. Gilbert E. Philbrick, Schooner *Nathaniel Bowditch*, Harborside, ME 04642, USA; phone (207)326-4496; summer, 326-4440.

Maine Sail: With the first morning tide, participants set sail from Camden to travel along the coast of Maine on a course determined by the weather. In 6 days aboard the 112-foot *Rosemary* or the 121-foot *Adventure*, sailors take the helm, learn to navigate, help weigh anchor or haul up the sails if they wish. The schooner may sail in the shadow of the hills of Mt. Desert or cross Blue Hill Bay for an anchorage among the hundreds of rockbound

494 / WATER ADVENTURES

islands in Penobscot Bay. Evenings are spent ashore exploring small fishing villages or singing sea chanties around the fireplace and pump organ in the main cabin. There are opportunities to row ashore for hikes, and once each trip the whole group has a Down East lobster cookout on the beach. **Cost:** $225 from Camden includes transportation, accommodations, meals, instruction; reduced rates in June and September. **When:** June to September. **Contact:** Yankee Schooner Cruises, Box 696, Camden, ME 04843, USA; phone (207)236-4449.

Massachusetts

Yankee Windjamming: Aboard a square-rigged clipper, members of a 7-day cruise lift anchor from Vineyard Haven Harbor to follow a route largely determined by the wind and the tide. The vessel adheres closely to mid-19th-century construction, including varnished hatches and oiled pine decks, and provides visiting crew members with a glimpse into the bygone days of the great American clippers used by privateers and slavers. The ship is powered soley by wind, with no auxiliary motors other than those of a diesel-powered yawlboat carried on the stern davits. Passengers help with the work, all of which is done by hand, including pulling up anchor and hoisting the mainsail. Traveling easily at 12 knots or more, the vessel cruises from mid-morning to dinner time, finding ports of call in places like Nantucket, Pasque Island, New Bedford, Point Judith, Stonington and Mystic. Passengers may visit ports by means of yawlboat and whitehall pulling-boats while the

schooner is at anchor. **Cost:** $275 includes meals, accommodations aboard, access to yawlboat. **When:** June to September. **Contact:** Coastwise Packet Co., Inc., Vineyard Haven, MA 02568, USA; phone (617)693-1699.

Rhode Island

Jamming from Newport: Sailing enthusiasts spend 2, 3 or 7 days aboard the schooner *Bill of Rights*. Departing from Newport, the ship sails for New England harbors such as Mystic, Stonington, Point Judith and Block Island. Other possible ports of call include the Elizabeth Islands, Martha's Vinyard, Padanarum, Edgartown and Nantucket, once the world's greatest whaling port. Some voyages may reach as far as the Chesapeake Bay and Annapolis. The *Bill of Rights* is a 124-foot vessel with sails totaling 6,300 square feet. Participants choose from 16 private staterooms, each well-ventilated and roomy. Meals onboard occasionally include a starlight buffet. **Cost:** $100 for 2 days, $150 for 3 days, $305 for 7 days. **When:** May to October. **Contact:** Davis, Capt. Joseph M., Jr., Schooner *Bill of Rights*, Box 447, Newport, RI 02840, USA; phone (401)724-7612.

Washington

Puget Sound Sailing School: A 101-foot schooner is the classroom for 10-day sailing lessons offered to high school-age youths. The course begins at Shilshole Bay Marina in Seattle with some orientation and preliminary sailing. Then the schooner leaves to spend the following days in Puget Sound and the San Juan Islands, with the

The Mattie, *an old-time Yankee merchant schooner, hosts passengers on 5-day cruises through Penobscot Bay, Maine.* (Maine Dept. of Commerce and Industry)

trainees serving as crew. Students have galley and watch duties, and sail the schooner when the wind is favorable. There is free time for small boat sailing, rowing and exploring. **Cost:** On request. **When:** On request. **Contact:** Youth Adventure, Inc., P.O. Box 23, Mercer Island, WA 98040, USA; phone (206)232-4025.

CRUISING

If you are looking for the stimulation of exotic environments, the beauty of remote regions, and travel without rigors and stress, then cruising may be the adventure for you. Although it rarely requires strenuous activity, a cruise can be far from a luxury trip; rather, it is an excellent way to learn about a particular region of the world and explore its sights and traditions for yourself. Regions as diverse as the Amazon jungle, the Antarctic Peninsula, and the land of the pharaohs along the Nile can all be investigated on a cruise.

There are three types of cruise adventures. The first is the slow scenic tour through a region of great natural beauty or historic interest. One example of this type is a trip on the "Mother of Rivers" through the Amazon Basin. A month-long cruise leaves Iquitos, Peru for Belem, Brazil each year to explore the rituals, customs and wildlife of this remote jungle region. Month-long trips also visit Antarctica, sailing along its coast and exploring remote islands to learn about the geology and biology of this cold and beautiful continent.

Another type of cruise takes you through an area on a vessel traditional to that region, such as a fishing trawler off the coast of Greenland or a barge in France. The Greenland cruise makes frequent stops to visit small fishing villages, and passengers take day hikes up the deep, rugged fjords of the world's largest island. The barge voyage makes a point of sampling the culinary delights of the Burgundy countryside during a three-week cruise on the canals of southern France. Medieval villages and castles, historic battlefields and ancient forests provide a constantly changing backdrop on this enjoyable journey.

The third type of cruise is more exciting—jetboating. The flat-bottomed, motorized jetboats can actually run against the current, even over sizable rapids, to provide an unusually thrilling trip. If you want to travel up the Waimakariri River in New Zealand, down the Snake River in Idaho, or on Oregon's Rogue River, then jetboating is the cruise for you.

Nearly all these cruises are staffed by expert guides, and they make it a point to select the itinerary that will best exemplify the land you choose to visit. So as you watch the natives of the Amazon, sample the wines of France, or splash through Hells Canyon, your cruise becomes not only an adventure but an education. □

Cruising is the principal method of transportation in Venice. Shown here is the Grand Canal, which cuts an S-shaped pattern through the heart of the city. (Carol Baker)

CRUISING

AFRICA

Egypt

Boating up the Nile: A large number of Egyptian antiquities are explored for 21 days during a 600-mile boat trip from Cairo to Aswan. Travelers view museum artifacts, explore the mosques and bazaars of Cairo and then depart up the Nile toward Luxor. Shore excursions en route provide opportunities to investigate Memphis, the Pyramids, Giza, Abu Kerkas and the shrine of Osiris at Abydos with its beautiful murals. Further along, the Valley of the Kings contains the gigantic sculptured and painted tombs of the pharaohs and the funerary temples of western Thebes. Travelers roam through the Temple of Karnak before sailing for Esna, Edfu and Kom Ombo, which once commanded the caravan route to Nubia. The Aswan Dam and its nearby granite quarries are explored before the return to Cairo by air. **Cost:** $1,341 includes roundtrip airfare from London, accommodations, transportation, meals, guides. **When:** May, September to December. **Contact:** Bales Tours Ltd., 16-17 Coventry St., Picadilly, London W1V 8BL, Great Britain; phone 01-437-7992.

ANTARCTICA

Voyage to Antarctica: Travelers cruise to Antarctica aboard a 12,000-ton vessel on a 24-day nature trip. The expedition begins with a lecture series in Buenos Aires, after which participants fly to Tierra del Fuego where a motorcoach takes them to board the ship at Ushuaia. After seeing their first icebergs, group members stop at the Shetland Islands before proceeding to the Antarctic. The boat cruises through channels and straits, passing by high, ice-covered peaks and active volcanoes. Whales may be seen spouting water, and a visit is made to a colony of 40,000 penguins. The trip's naturalist is on hand to provide insights into the area's natural history and unusual flora and fauna. The cruise returns to Ushuaia, from where participants have the option of extending the trip with a 10-day journey in Patagonia. **Cost:** $2,575 to $4,075 depending on accommodations, includes transportation from Buenos Aires, accommodations, meals, guide. **When:** January. **Contact:** Society Expeditions, P.O. Box 5088, University Sta., Seattle, WA 98105, USA; phone (206)324-9400. **(M)**

ATLANTIC

Bermuda

Glass-Bottom Boat Cruise: A 4-hour trip leaves Somerset by glass-bottom boat for North West Perimeter Reef, 5 miles offshore, for snorkeling and viewing. Here the coral reef is fairly shallow and inexperienced snorkelers have no difficulty, though deeper areas are also available. Fish, coral and shipwrecks abound. The trips are dependent upon weather but normally leave twice daily. **Cost:** $15 includes transportation, instruction, snorkeling gear. **When:** May to November. **Contact:** Pittman's Boat Tours, Somerset 9-10, Bermuda.

In the thick jungles of the world's equatorial regions, river cruising is often the only practical means of travel. (Bob Citron)

Greenland

Coastal Cruising: Greenland's coastline is made up of rugged mountains cut both by glaciers flowing down from the ice cap and by the longest fjords in the world. Participants cruise along the coastline in a converted fishing vessel on a 24-day trip begun by a flight from New York. Frequent stops are made to hike up the fjords, into the hills and through tiny fishing villages. Photographers, botanists, bird watchers and anglers find ample outlet for their interests; visits are also made to many Norse ruins surviving from the area's Viking colonization. The trip ends with a flight back to New York. **Cost:** $2,541 includes roundtrip-transportation from New York, food, accommodations, guide.

When: July. **Contact:** Mountain Travel Inc., 1398 Solano Ave., Albany, CA 94706, USA; phone (415)527-8100. *(M)*

AUSTRALASIA

New Zealand

New Zealand Alpine River Jet Tours: Jetboats transport trip members through the turbulent rapids and shallow waters of the southern alpine region. Full-day and half-day tours are available for groups of 6 or more persons. All regularly scheduled tours depart from Woodstock Depot, though special stops to pick up others may be arranged along the route. Rest stops are planned and food is provided during each trip. Weather permitting, the full-day trip includes a ride upstream past the Hamilton Rapids to a view of the spectacular High Gorge area where cliffs loom 1,000 feet above the river. Transportation to Woodstock Depot may be arranged from Christchurch as well. **Cost:** On request. **When:** Daily; private tours by arrangement. **Contact:** Canterbury and Alpine Travel Ltd., P.O. Box 8107, Christchurch, New Zealand; phone 65-002.

Doubtful Cruises: The vessel *M. V. Waverley* affords participants the opportunity to sail deep into Doubtful Sound on the west coast of New Zealand. Two- and 3-day voyages start at Deep Cove and proceed to the head of Hall's Arm and Crooked Arm before anchoring for a night at First Cove. The cruise continues up Crooked Arm for a day of fishing, exploration onshore and off-vessel sailing. Evening finds the group moored at Blanket Bay. The final day of the voyage opens with a jaunt to Goal Passage for lobstering before the return to Blanket Bay and Deep Cove. Evenings are spent in entertainment or fishing; possible catches include grouper, blue cod and tuna. **Cost:** $74 on weekends, $126 on weekdays includes meals, accommodations. **When:** On request. **Contact:** Fiordland Cruises Ltd., P.O. Box Manapouri, New Zealand; phone Manapouri 609.

EUROPE

Cruising Western European Waterways: For 16 days participants travel aboard a large yacht along rivers, canals and saltwater channels important to the development of trade and culture in Western Europe. Trip members fly from New York to Lisbon where the trip begins with a short cruise down the Tagus River to the sea; other stops on the Spanish peninsula include Oporto, La Coruna, Santander and San Sebastian, where participants may visit a Basque fishing village or drive to small towns in the Pyrenees. In France the yacht sails up the Gironde and Garonne rivers to the Bordeaux region where 1½ days are spent exploring the countryside, museums and the city of Bordeaux, center of the world's largest fine wine district. Participants continue north to Brittany, visiting Nantes and Brest. After stops at St. Malo and Rouen, the boat sails across the English Channel to Southampton where the cruising portion of the trip ends. Museum scientists and other scholars with knowledge of the diverse environments and cultures accompany the trip. Participants fly from London to New York to end the journey. **Cost:** $2,560 to $3,675 includes roundtrip airfare from New York, accommodations on the yacht, cruise activities, meals. **When:** May. **Contact:** The American Museum of Natural History, Central Park West at 79th St., New York, NY 10024, USA.

England

Inland Waterways: Participants aboard canal boats, power cruisers or sailboats travel on a variety of British and Continental waterways. Traveling the Norfolk Broads, passengers explore a series of shallow lagoons connected by rivers and short canals, where several large

Sailors pilot gaff-rigged boats in Great Britain's Norfolk Broads. Bargain Boating offers summer cruises along the broads to Norwich. (Bargain Boating)

nature reserves, historic ruins and the cathedral city of Norwich may be visited. Canal travel is also possible in Holland, as well as in the Burgundy and Loire regions of France. In Scotland, the Caledonian Canal connects Inverness and Banavie Top Lock; participants sailing the canal can make side trips to Loch Ness and an assortment of old Highland castles and ruins. Boat travel is available on several English rivers including the Thames, the Avon and the Severn; on Ireland's River Shannon—the longest river in the British Isles—group members view scenery that ranges from mountains to flat marshland and vast loughs up to 20 miles long and 10 miles wide. Most trips require no previous boating experience. **Cost:** $130 to $550 a week includes boat, kitchen equipment, safety gear, bedding, mooring. **When:** May to September. **Contact:** Bargain Boating, 127 High St., Morgantown, WV 26505, USA; phone (304)292-8471.

France

Barge Trip in France: The delicious food of France's most famous culinary region can be sampled en route through the Burgundy countryside aboard the *Palinurus*. The food, wine and history of the area are experienced for 3 weeks along the Burgundy and Nivernais canals between Dijon and Baye, Montbard and Auxerre, or Auxerre and Baye depending on itinerary. Burgundy's past is evident from the barge as it floats past chateaux, medieval towns, churches and ancient forests. Each of the 3 trips visits different attractions, among them the Pouilly tunnel, the 12th-century castle of Chateauneuf and the battlefield of Alesia, where the Gauls fought Julius Caesar's troops in 52 B.C. Visits can be made to the medieval villages of Flavigny and Semur or to the fortified town of Beaune, the center of the wine trade where auctions are held in famous 15th-century hospices. **Cost:** $390 to $510 depending on occupancy and season. **When:** April to October. **Contact:** Continental Waterways Ltd., 22 Hans Pl., London SW1, Great Britain; phone 01-584-6773.

Soviet Union

Volga Boat Trip: A 10-day cruise down the Volga River on a 216-passenger Soviet cruise ship explores several ports between Kazan and Rostov-on-Don. The ship is boarded in Kazan, capital of the Tatar Republic and rich in historical relics and art, and after 2 days of sailing reaches its first port of call, Ulianovsk, the birthplace of Lenin. After some sightseeing, the trip proceeds to Zhiguli, one of the Volga's best-known recreation spots. After a stop at Maiden's Island for swimming and sunbathing, passengers arrive at Volgograd, where a sightseeing tour is taken. A stop at Green Port-on-Don precedes the trip's conclusion at Rostov-on-Don, where a Cossack museum is among the attractions. The cruise may be taken in conjunction with a roundtrip package from San Francisco which includes sightseeing in and around Moscow as well. **Cost:** $595 includes transportation from Kazan to Rostov-on-Don, food, double-occupancy accommodations, shore excursions. **When:** June. **Contact:** Siemer & Hand, Ltd., 465 California St., San Francisco, CA 94104, USA; phone (415)397-6737.

INDIAN OCEAN

Madagascar

Island-Hopping off Madagascar: A group of 6 to 12 persons camps, sails and hops from island to island in the Four Fathers Island chain, off the northwest shores of Madagascar. The 2-week sojourn includes 10 days of sailing and exploration of the sandy beaches of the archipelago. Participants embark from the town of Nosy Be after a flight from Tananarive. Some scuba diving equipment is available for participants who wish to explore the underwater life and the numerous coral reefs. Much of the trip brings group members in contact with remote, uninhabited areas. Among the animal and fish life prominent in the area off the Indian Ocean are tortoises, crabs, barracuda and a wide variety of colorful tropical fish. Sailings between islands generally take 2 to 3 hours. All group members play a part in the decision-making processes of the trip. **Cost:** $1,800 from Paris includes transportation, food. **When:** April to November. **Contact:** Explorator, 16, place de la Madeleine, 75008 Paris, France; phone 266-66-24.

Seychelles

Cruising Forgotten Islands: Aboard the yacht *Dwyn Wen* 10 guests cruise for 10 days among the Seychelles located in the Indian Ocean. Trip members make shore excursions and snorkeling trips during the course that passes Praslin, LaDigue, Cousin and Bird islands. Shore excursions made in landing craft are planned for all of these islands and atolls. The return trip is via Mahe. **Cost:** $775 to $1,075 includes food, cruise transportation. **When:** Year-round. **Contact:** Lindblad Travel, Inc., Lindblad Travel Bldg., 133 E. 55th St., New York, NY 10022, USA; phone (212)751-2300 or tollfree (800)223-9700.

SOUTH AMERICA

Ecuador

The Giant Tortoises: Transported by plane and boat, travelers spend 5 to 8 days in the islands named "Galapagos," the Spanish word for giant tortoises. All trips begin with 2 initial options: either a flight to Baltra Island or a cruise to Punta Suarez on Hood Island. Once in the archipelago participants cruise during the night on a 90-passenger ship and make shore excursions during the day. Participants either fly or cruise back to Guayaquil to conclude the trip. **Cost:** $456 for 5 days, $672 for 8 days includes transportation from Guayaquil, meals, guide, shore excursions, accommodations. **When:** Year-round. **Contact:** Galatour, P.O. Box 5284, Guayaquil, Ecuador; phone 512-229; or 888 7th Ave., New York, NY 10019, USA; phone (212)582-7373.

Galapagos Expedition: From Guayaquil, Ecuador's largest city, the cruise ship *Buccaneer* departs for 5- to 8-day trips to the Galapagos Islands, providing opportunities to visit Punta Espinosa on Fernandina Island, Academy Bay on Santa Cruz and Hood Island. Due to their volcanic origin and their isolation the Galapagos offer spectacular plant and animal life found nowhere else in the world. Giant tortoises, weighing over 500 pounds, land iguanas, marine iguanas, cormorants, penguins, large colonies of sea lions and thousands of exotic birds inhabit the environs. Travelers may find 40-foot cactus in dry coastal areas and creepers and ferns in dense rain forests only a few miles up in the mountains. Of the 13 major islands that constitute the archipelago, 5 are inhabited, and travelers have the opportunity to talk to residents along the way. **Cost:** $456 to $672. **When:** Year-round. **Contact:** Gordontours Cia. Ltd., P.O. Box 5284, Guayaquil, Ecuador; phone 5-19481.

UNITED STATES

Alaska

Glacier Bay Cruise: Voyagers board the *Chaik*, a new, fully equipped 50-foot boat, and journey into Alaska's Glacier Bay National Monument or Tracy Arm Glacier Wilderness. The tidewater glaciers of these wilderness areas can be seen in their full splendor from the sea. The group explores areas abounding with seals, whales, eagles, mountain goats, sea bird rookeries and many other unique flora and fauna. Certified for up to 30 passengers, the *Chaik* sleeps 10 in semi-private accommodations, and trip routes and duration vary. Glacier Guides also offers 6-day wilderness backpacking and glacier exploring trips via the *Chaik*. **Cost:** From $600 a day for chartering boat, $595 for backpacking trip. **When:** June to August. **Contact:** Glacier Guides, Inc., 205 S. 300 W., St. George, UT 84770, USA; phone (801)673-3697. *(M)*

Private Yacht Charter: A 6-day and a 3-day excursion take passengers to remote beaches and ice floes near the area of Juneau. The 58-foot vessel penetrates into waters not often visited, where passengers can observe whales, seals, eagles and other native wildlife up close. Dinner may consist of personal catches of crab, shrimp or salmon. During land stops a variety of activities includes exploration of isolated villages, native shops and historic sites. Participants ride the narrow gauge railroad over White Pass to Lake Bennett where the Sourdoughs built their rafts and flimsy boats for the trip down the Yukon. The track follows "The Trail of '98" past Tunnel Mountain and Dead Horse Gulch. Back aboard the yacht, passengers travel to Juneau, surrounded by ice-covered mountains; this city exhibits a full spectrum of Alaskan history and culture. **Cost:** $995 for 6-day cruise, $490 for 3-day cruise. **When:** May to September. **Contact:** Special InteresTours, P.O. Box 37, Medina, WA 98039, USA; phone (206)455-1960. *(M)*

Montana

Missouri River Cruising: Canopied riverboats carry groups down the Missouri River for 1 to 5 days. The 160-mile stretch of river from Ft. Benton to the headwaters of the Missouri in western Montana was a part of the Lewis and Clark Expedition in the early 1800s. The trips, which vary from 48 to 150 miles, depart from Coal Banks or Ft. Benton and can be scheduled according to the wishes of each group. Experienced guides well versed in history share their knowledge, as participants float down the river or take hikes to points of interest on the way. Low-water conditions during the late summer may require the use of smaller boats, and the trip may be terminated at Judith Landing. Canoe rentals, shuttle services and canoe trip outfitting are also available. **Cost:** $45 to $200 includes equipment except sleeping bag, meals. **When:** May to September.

Contact: Missouri River Cruises, P.O. Box 1212, Ft. Benton, MT 59442, USA; phone (406)622-3295.

Oregon

Whitewater Jetboat: Oregon's Rogue River is the scene of a 104-mile jetboat trip through pools, riffles, rapids and hidden channels. All roads cease above the town of Agness where the whitewater begins. The trip passes the 1,500-foot vertical rock walls known as Paradise Canyon. Boat pilots tailor each trip to the interests of those aboard, and the number of people per trip is kept to a minimum. Chances are offered to observe deer, otters, eagles, wildflowers and a variety of geological features. The full trip takes 2 days, beginning in coastal fog and coming into the sunshine a few miles upstream. Casual clothing is recommended. **Cost:** $62 for adults, $40 for children on the 2-day trip; $25 for adults, $15 for children on the 1-day trip. **When:** April to November. **Contact:** Court's White Water Trips, Box 1045, Gold Beach, OR 97444, USA; phone (503)247-6504.   *(M)*

Washington

Cruising Rush Creek: Wilderness habitats as well as sites associated with the history of the Hells Canyon region are the highlights of a single-day Snake River trip. Traveling about 182 miles roundtrip by diesel-powered boat from Clarkston, Washington, passengers visit Rush Creek, the site of an abandoned mine, historical spots, exposed lava flows and cattle and sheep ranches. Time is allowed for swimming, photography and viewing wildlife and petroglyphs. In addition, the trip itinerary includes Nez Perce Indian crossings at Cottonwood Creek and Dug Bar as well as the site of Rogersburg Trading Post at Limestone Mountain. **Cost:** $40 includes meals and snacks, guide, transportation. **When:** On request. **Contact:** Helds Canyon Tours, 118 Sycamore, Clarkston, WA 99403, USA; phone (509)758-3445.

RESOURCES
Clubs and Associations

Boat Owners Association of the U.S.
880 S. Pickett
Alexandria, VA 22304, USA
Phone (703)823-9550

Club Washington
411 N. Washington St., Suite 302
Alexandria, VA 23314, USA
Phone (703)836-2000

Cruising Club of America
100 William St.
New York, NY 10038, USA
Phone (212)285-2850

Freighter Travel Association
40-21 Bell Blvd.
Bayside, NY 11361, USA

Freighter Travel Club of America
P.O. Box 504
Newport, OR 97365, USA

Irish Yachting Association
2, Roby Pl. Dun Laoghaire
County Dublin, Ireland

Seven Seas Cruising Association
P.O. Box 38
Placida, FL 33946, USA

Rentals

Worldwide Yacht Charter Guide
456 Shelbourne
Grosse Point Farms, MI 48236, USA
Phone (313)881-5095

HOUSEBOATING

While the leisurely pace of life on a houseboat may not stimulate your adrenal glands, some of the most beautiful areas and culturally diverse regions of the world can be explored from the deck of a houseboat. From Kentucky to Kashmir, chartered houseboats can give you and your family a floating base camp to take off on adventures such as hiking or sailing.

Houseboats are easy to operate, and a crew of beginners needs only 30 minutes of instruction and practice to be ready to take the vessel out. Most houseboats come equipped with cooking utensils and furniture, as well as such extras as radios, barbecues and even hot showers. A small houseboat may be about 25 feet long and half that wide, but it can sleep up to six adults in bunks. A luxury houseboat includes private staterooms, sleeps 10, and can be up to 48 feet in length. Patio boats, not true houseboats at all since they can only serve for day use, are also available in many areas and are less expensive to rent.

But it's really *access* the boat provides that attracts many people to houseboating. 8ring along your hiking boots if you are floating on Lake Powell in southern Utah and Arizona, since what remains of the once-beautiful Glen Canyon region is still worth exploring. Take along fishing tackle for the bass, trout and crappie of Lake Cumberland in Kentucky. And be sure to have your camera and plenty of film for the scenic value and historic interest of a houseboating trip along the St. Lawrence River, Lake Ontario or the Eerie Canal. You might even think about bringing along a gold pan for mining the mineral-rich streams that feed into Lake Camanche in the Sierra Nevada foothills near Sacramento, California.

Houseboating is not just a domestic activity. One of the most beautiful areas of the world—the Valley of Kashmir in northern India—is an ancient center for houseboating. Dal Lake in the capital city of Srinagar has been termed an earthly paradise for centuries, and you can float its waters in the wake of kings all year round. With its cultural heritage, magnificent Himalayan surroundings and rich vegetation, Kashmir is a perfect vacation spot, and well located as a take-off point for adventures into Pakistan, central India and the Tibetan Plateau. With all those stimulating sights surrounding you, a few days of houseboating can be just the kind of relaxation any traveler would enjoy. □

A houseboat on Dal Lake in Srinagar offers gracious living with an adventurous bonus—the Himalayas in the background. (Stuart Williams)

HOUSEBOATING

ASIA

India

Srinagar Houseboating: Stays of any length can be booked aboard a variety of houseboats on Dal Lake, ranging from deluxe to simple, and priced accordingly. The boats may be rented for a relaxing stay in the lush surroundings of Kashmir or tied in with various activities, including camping on Himalayan peaks, jeep tours of Ladakh, shopping in the area's bazaars, sightseeing and fishing. Advance reservations are necessary and arrangements can be made for airport pickup in Srinagar. **Cost:** $4 to $26 a night includes food, accommodations, some services. **When:** Year-round. **Contact:** M.S. Baktoo & Sons, P.O. Box 32, Srinagar, Kashmir, India; phone 8698.

Dal Lake Floating: Houseboats situated on Kashmir's Dal Lake may be rented for almost any length of stay. With a spectacular view of the Himalayas, the floating houses offer access to a wide range of recreational activities including area sightseeing, hiking, photography, backpacking, trekking and river trips. The Dal Lake area was once the retreat of kings, when its lush foliage and striking alpine surroundings first earned it the name "earthly paradise." Some of the houseboats are large and deluxe and can accommodate large groups; others are smaller and more economical. **Cost:** On request. **When:** Year-round. **Contact:** Sabana Travel, Shabina No. 328, Dal Lake, Srinagar-190001, Kashmir, India.

UNITED STATES

Arizona

Wahweap Rentals: Houseboats and powerboats are available for rental on the shores of Lake Powell in southern Utah and Arizona. For periods of 3, 4 or 7 days groups may take vee- or pontoon-hull houseboats around the lake as well as on the surrounding waterways. Possible areas to visit include Wahweap Bay, Glen Canyon Dam and Bridge, Rainbow Bridge and Antelope Island. The houseboats vary from 28 to 50 feet; powerboats are 14 to 18 feet in length. The powerboats are rented for 1 hour, 4 hours, daily or weekly. The houseboats are fully equipped with fuel, water, utensils, range and oven, icebox and toilets. Water skis, dinghies, grills and bedding are also available for rental. **Cost:** $110 to $850 for houseboat, $6 to $400 for powerboat. **When:** Year-round. **Contact:** Wahweap Lodge and Marina, P.O. Box 1597, Page, AZ 86040, USA; phone (602)654-2433.

California

California Houseboating: A variety of houseboats, from 35 to 44 feet long, may be rented and operated on either Shasta Lake or Lake Camanche. Shasta, an artificial lake standing behind Shasta Dam about 250 miles north of San Francisco, offers a variety of islets and bays surrounded by pines and manzanitas growing down to the water's edge. The area contains some interesting geological formations for the fossil and mineral hunter; other available activities include swimming, hiking and fishing. Camanche is a recreational development lake situated just southeast of Sacramento in the Sierra foothills, in the middle of a 15,000-acre park. The area is rich in relics of local history, from Indian caves to gold mines, and there are opportunities for hiking, swimming, fishing and other activities. **Cost:** $36 to $79 a day, depending on season and type of boat includes houseboat, most equipment, maps. **When:** Year-round. **Contact:** Holiday Flotels, P.O. Box 8771, Stockton, CA 95208, USA; phone (209)478-6002.

Delta Cruising: The 1,000 miles of waterways that make up the San Joaquin-Sacramento Delta can be explored aboard 37- to 47-foot houseboats. After picking up the craft at a marina northwest of Stockton, houseboaters are fully instructed in piloting and operating the boat before taking off through White Slough and historic Disappointment Slough, so named for its deceptive resemblance to a bend in the main river channel. Detailed maps guide pilots through all the waterway's ins and outs, which offer remote, secluded channels and shoreside nightlife. The boats, which sleep anywhere from 6 to 10, have complete cooking and recreational facilities onboard. **Cost:** $46 to $130 a day, depending on season, size of boat and duration. **When:** Year-round. **Contact:** Paradise Houseboat Rentals, Paradise Point, 8095 N. Rio Blanco Rd., Stockton, CA 95209, USA; phone (209)368-1053.

Idaho

Coeur d'Alene Cruise: In a setting of forest-covered hills and mountains, houseboat cruises are available on Lake Coeur d'Alene and the shadowy St. Joe River. There are beds for 6 people on the houseboats but more can be accommodated in sleeping bags on the decks. The St. Joe and the Coeur d'Alene rivers and their tributaries are considered to be some of the best fly fishing areas in the northwest. Boaters can tie up at Popcorn Island in Killarney Lake or follow the winding St. Joe as it flows between several lakes and terminates in the south end of Lake Coeur d'Alene. Few extremes in the weather combined with the many small bays in Coeur d'Alene make rough water a rarity. Water temperatures in the summer are agreeable to swimmers. Top speed in the houseboats is 12 miles per hour and after a short trial run, renters can maneuver the boat quite capably on their own. **Cost:** On request. **When:** April to October. **Contact:** Aqua Villa, Sun-up Bay Resort, Lake Coeur d'Alene, Worley, ID 83876, USA; phone (208)664-6810.

Indiana

On the Brookville: Cruising the waters of Indiana's Brookville Reservoir may be done aboard rental houseboats ranging in length from 32 to 45 feet. The reservoir, 15 miles long, is rimmed by 62 miles of shoreline dotted with inlets and bays, all open to houseboats. The area offers opportunities for hiking, small boating, botanical study, fishing and relaxing. Beaches around the reservoir provide bases for swimming. The houseboats may be rented for a weekend, a 5-day week or a full week; the smallest boats can handle 6 persons, the larger ones 8. **Cost:** $200 to $350 for weekends, $400 to $575 for 7 days includes houseboat, equipment, maps. **When:** Year-round. **Contact:** Horn's Houseboats of Indiana Inc., Box 265, Columbus, IN 47201, USA; phone (812)342-4966.

Kentucky

Southern Cumberland Houseboating: Individuals have access to a number of retreat locations by use of houseboats or other craft available at a resort on Lake Cumberland. The 101-mile-long lake is formed by backup from the 240-foot-high Wolf Creek Dam. The river which flows into the lake comes from the deep valleys of the Cumberland Mountains, down through the Daniel Boone National Forest and over the Cumberland Falls, eventually arriving to form the 63,000-acre lake. Over 1,255 miles of shoreline are available for exploration. **Cost:** On request. **When:** Year-round. **Contact:** Conley Bottom Resort, Rt. 1, Box 124, Monticello, KY 42633, USA; phone (606)348-6351.

Cumberland Cruise: Thirty-four- to 46-foot houseboats are available for rent along the shores of Lake Cumberland. Renters choose between 1 day, 4 days or a week to cruise along the 1,255 miles of shoreline, bays and deep, clear lakewater. The region around Lake Cumberland is made up of the foothills of the Appalachians and is forested with various hardwood trees as well as being carpeted with Kentucky bluegrass. **Cost:** $55 to $500. **When:**

Year-round. **Contact:** Grider Hill Dock, Albany, KY 42602, USA; phone (606)387-5501.

Cruising Cumberland: The waters of Lake Cumberland may be plied in 40- or 50-foot houseboats for periods of 2 days to a week. The lake, which is 11 miles in length and an average of 90 feet deep, features over 1,200 miles of shoreline and a large population of crappie, bream, trout and 5 species of bass. The large number of small coves and inlets allows houseboaters to find secluded moorage for swimming, photography or relaxing. Rates are available for 2 days, 4 midweek days or a full week. **Cost:** $59 to $10 a day, depending on season, size of boat and duration. **When:** Year-round. **Contact:** Popplewell's Alligator Dock No. 1, RR 5, Box 261, Russell Springs, KY 42642, USA; phone (502)866-3634.

Maryland

Chesapeake Bay Houseboat Cruise: Up to 10 adults can be accommodated on 40-foot houseboats that are rented from Castle Marina near the eastern end of the Chesapeake Bay Bridge. As soon as reservations are made a complete cruise planning kit is sent to participants so that each group can set up an itinerary to fit their particular interests. After receiving instruction on operation of the boat, the group sets out for a minimum of 3 nights of exploration through the extensive waterways connected to Chesapeake Bay. About 40 rivers empty into the bay, each with countless creeks and coves. Houseboat cruisers can explore St. Michael's, Kent Island, Chester Town, Tilighman Island, the port of Georgetown-Sassafrass and other parts of the 6,000 miles of shoreline. A particularly recommended cruise takes passengers up the Chester River at the north end of Kent Island. Historical sites from the colonial period are to be seen on the cruise including Rock Hall and Queenstown. The quietly winding Wye River offers grassy or wooded banks along 2 arms that encircle 1,800-acre Wye Island. There is little evidence of civilization at Dun Cove on the Choptank to mar the scenery. Insurance is included in the cost of the rental. **Cost:** $375 to $750 depending on length of cruise. **When:** April to October. **Contact:** Holiday Houseboats, Inc., Suite 750, 5272 River Rd., Bethesda, MD 20016, USA; phone (301)656-2443.

Minnesota

The Leech Life: Leech Lake, located just east of Walker, is the second largest lake in Minnesota. Houseboats may be rented to cruise its waters and investigate its 640 miles of lakeshore. Sandbars, islands inlets and bays dot the lake, and there are many opportunities for hiking, swimming, skin diving and other activities. Leech is also noted for its duck population including blue bills and mallards and its fish such as walleyes and muskies. The houseboats come in several sizes, from 12 by 30 feet to 14 by 44. **Cost:** $155 to $245 for weekends, $275 to $495 for 7 days, includes houseboat, equipment, maps. **When:** Year-round. **Contact:** Fishers Houseboats, Box 488, Walker, MN 56484, USA; phone (218)547-1162.

Missouri

Huck Finn Houseboating: Floating homes are available for 2 days to 1 week of rental along the Mississippi River just north of St. Louis. Starting from Piasa Harbor renters may take houseboats up and down the region made famous as the boyhood home of Mark Twain. Each boat features a complete galley, marine lavatory and toilet, sundeck, and all Coast Guard required safety equipment. Linen, cookware and navigational charts are also included. No experience in houseboating is required; a demonstration run is given to each new customer. **Cost:** $140 to $450. **When:** April to November. **Contact:** House of Martin Sales Enterprises, P.O. Box 9111, St. Louis, MO 63117, USA; phone (31)725-6320.

New York

Erie Area: Out of a marina on Vermont's Lake Champlain, houseboats may be rented to travel the lake, the Richelieu River, the St. Lawrence River, Lake Ontario and the Erie Canal. This area, dotted with historical remains of an era when the Erie was a major commercial waterway, offers scenic natural areas, too. Using either a 34-foot or 40-foot houseboat, renters may choose from a wide variety of routes: to the 1,000 Islands area via the Richelieu; to Niagara and Taughannock Falls; into Lake Ontario to Rochester and Toronto; down the Champlain Canal from Troy to Whitehall; up the Richelieu to Montreal and Quebec; and others. Provided with each houseboat is a dinghy for more detailed explorations, docking and excursions.

TRIP EVALUATION FORM

The Association is in the process of setting standards and evaluating adventure travel organizations with regard to their experience, reliability and responsibility (both to their clients and to the environment). We are also evaluating adventure trips with regard to their cost, environmental impact and adventurous desirability.

The Association would be grateful to both members and non-members if they would fill out this Trip Evaluation Form in as much detail as possible and return it to us. Please be as candid as possible. Your honest evaluation will assist us in developing the information needed to improve the quality and minimize the environmental impact of adventure trips that will be taken by future adventurers. Additional forms may be obtained by writing to Trip Evaluation Service, American Adventurers Association, Suite 301, 444 NE Ravenna Blvd., Seattle, WA 98115, USA.

AMERICAN ADVENTURERS ASSOCIATION
SUITE 301, 444 NE RAVENNA BLVD.
SEATTLE, WASHINGTON 98115 USA
TELEPHONE: (206)527-1621
CABLE: ADVENTURE SEATTLE

TRIP EVALUATOR

NAME			ADDRESS		
CITY		STATE	ZIP	COUNTRY	
TELEPHONE		MEMBER OF THE ASSOCIATION? YES ☐ NO ☐			
AGE	OCCUPATION				

THE TRIP

NAME OF TRIP			
TRIP OPERATOR (NAME OF COMPANY)			
ADDRESS	CITY		STATE
ZIP	COUNTRY	TELEPHONE	
DATE OF TRIP			
LOCATION OF TRIP			
NUMBER OF PARTICIPANTS	NUMBER OF LEADERS		

RELATIVE SCALE RATING: CHECK ONE

	0 None	1 Poor	2 Fair	3 Good	4 Excellent	5 Out-standing

HOW DO YOU RATE YOUR TRIP OPERATOR?

	0	1	2	3	4	5
1. PRE-TRIP INSTRUCTIONS AND PLANNING MATERIALS						
2. PROFESSIONAL APPROACH TO ADVENTURE TRAVEL						
3. EXPERIENCE IN THIS TYPE OF TRIP						
4. CONCERN FOR ENVIRONMENTAL IMPACT OF THEIR ACTIVITIES						
5. EXPERIENCE IN THIS GEOGRAPHICAL AREA						
6. CONCERN FOR THE HEALTH & WELFARE OF THE PARTICIPANTS						
7. TRIP FOLLOW-UP PROCEDURES						
8. OVERALL RATING OF THE TRIP OPERATOR						

HOW DO YOU RATE YOUR TRIP LEADER(S)?

	0	1	2	3	4	5
1. PRE-TRIP ORIENTATION						
2. KNOWLEDGE & EXPERIENCE IN THIS TYPE OF TRIP						
3. ENTHUSIASM, PATIENCE & PROFESSIONAL APPROACH						
4. CONCERN FOR ENVIRONMENTAL IMPACT OF THE TRIP						
5. EXPERIENCE IN THIS GEOGRAPHICAL AREA						
6. KNOWLEDGE OF THE CULTURE & HISTORY OF THE AREA						
7. CONCERN FOR THE HEALTH & WELFARE OF THE PARTICIPANTS						
8. RELATIONSHIPS WITH THE LOCAL VENDORS & PEOPLE						
9. OVERALL RATING OF THE LEADER(S)						

HOW DO YOU RATE THE TRIP ITSELF?

	0	1	2	3	4	5
1. ADVENTUROUS DESIRABILITY						
2. CULTURAL AND/OR HISTORICAL EXPERIENCE						
3. ECOLOGICAL AND/OR ENVIRONMENTAL EXPERIENCE						
4. OPPORTUNITY FOR SELF-KNOWLEDGE						
5. OPPORTUNITY FOR INTERACTION WITH LOCAL PEOPLE						
6. OPPORTUNITY FOR INTERACTION WITH WILDLIFE						
7. ACCOMMODATIONS AND FOOD						
8. TRANSPORTATION PROVIDED BY TRIP (IF ANY)						
9. OVERALL RATING OF THE TRIP						

WAS THE COST OF THE TRIP: TOO HIGH? ☐ JUST RIGHT? ☐ LOW? ☐
WOULD YOU RECOMMEND THIS TRIP TO FRIENDS? ABSOLUTELY ☐ POSSIBLY ☐ NO ☐

COMMENTS:

American Adventures

ASSOCIATION

Cost: $350 to $450 for weekends, $525 to $735 for 7 days, depending on season and type of boat, includes houseboat, equipment, maps. **When:** May to October. **Contact:** Houseboat Vacations, Inc., Flat Rock Rd., Lake George, NY 12845, USA; phone (518)668-4644.

Tennessee

Dale Hollow Houseboat: Thirty-six- to 50-foot houseboats are available for rental on the shores of Dale Hollow Lake near the Tennessee/Kentucky border. For 3 days to 1 week participants may fish and swim in the waters of the lake, which is part of the Cumberland River system. Each houseboat is equipped with full galley, electricity, toilet facilities and complete safety gear; linen and dishware are also onboard. The weekly rate includes a small fishing boat. No special skills are required to drive the houseboat. **Cost:** $150 to $450. **When:** Year-round. **Contact:** Livingston Boat Dock, Rt. 1, Allons, TN 38541, USA; phone (615)823-6666.

Utah

Living on Lake Powell: Houseboats from 32 to 50 feet in length are available to those who want to cruise Lake Powell in the southeast corner of Utah. After a short but thorough shakedown cruise, participants can operate any of the houseboats. Every season has its special attractions at Lake Powell. Winters are relatively mild with sunny days and a placid surface on the lake. Swimming and water skiing are especially popular in the summer. Spring months bring winds and the best fishing season, and even when the winds are extreme, boaters can explore in one of the numerous narrow canyons that edge the lake. Photographers find the best conditions in the fall when the sun's southward position creates rays that bathe the region in pinks and lavenders, producing extraordinary sunsets. The canyon forests are changing color at this time, too. Boats 16 feet or under can be towed behind the houseboats. Houseboats must be rented a minimum of 3 days. **Cost:** $105 to $170 a day for rental. **When:** Year-round. **Contact:** Aqua-Cruz, Halls Crossing, Blanding, UT 84511, USA; phone (801)684-2264 or 684-2265.

Wisconsin

Cruising the Eagle Chain: The Eagle chain of lakes, a system made up of 8 lakes, can be explored aboard a 40-foot houseboat. Three-, 4- and 7-day trips are available from a marina in Lynx Lake, just north of where the Eagle River flows into Yellow Birch Lake. After complete instruction in the craft's operation, houseboaters may explore the chain at their leisure, swimming, cruising or just relaxing. **Cost:** $82 to $108 depending on duration of trip. **When:** Year-round. **Contact:** Holiday Harbor, Rt. 3, Eagle River, WI 54521, USA; phone (715)479-4250.

RESEARCH EXPEDITIONS

Have you ever heard a humpback whale sing? Or sighted a monk seal, a species which thrived in the West Indies at the time of Columbus? These are just two of the experiences possible on ocean research expeditions—trips which chart a scientific course across the world's seas. Whether participants help record the humpbacks' eerie vocalizations or spot a species of seal last seen in 1952, the opportunity to contribute to scientific research is a never-to-be-forgotten adventure.

The ocean has inspired the mythologies of every culture whose boundaries have touched an open expanse of saltwater. Research trips offer a chance to explore myths and expand our knowledge of the marine environment. Orcas, for instance, were once regarded as sea monsters. Today, on a research trip in the San Juan Islands of Puget Sound, you can assist in identifying and photographing these whales, a species whose image as a "killer" becomes softened as more is learned about its behavior. Exploratory voyages to the South Pacific sail and study in waters once crossed by the seafaring island cultures of Polynesia and the Bismark Archipelago. Straits, shorelines and coral atolls all become outdoor classrooms.

Adventures on the open sea are not the only kind of research trips. Shorelines provide valuable ecological insights and unique glimpses of lifeforms straddling the boundary between land and sea. A totally different kind of research is done off the coast of England where ships victimized by storms, tides and reefs lie in quiet graves. Here participants gather data on wrecks, with marine archaeologists contributing to their study of the sometimes violent relations between humans and the sea.

Covering almost three-fourths of the earth's surface, oceans appear vast and timeless. But as environmentalists keep warning us, they are becoming increasingly finite. It is important to gain a further understanding of the sea—by seeking to decode the songs of the whales, "communicate" with porpoises, and learn more about the role of plankton in the marine food chain. Whether you find yourself exploring the shores of the Galapagos, sailing alongside a pod of humpback whales in the Caribbean, or studying the tidal environments of California's Morro Bay, you can be assured of an experience that will prove both memorable and valuable. □

Members of a research expedition study tidal estuaries and marshes, using a fine-meshed net to scoop up small marine organisms to be examined in a field laboratory. (University Research Expeditions Program)

RESEARCH EXPEDITIONS

ATLANTIC

Falkland Islands

Sailing Ship Survey: Port Stanley, in the Falkland Islands, is the staging area for a project of about 20 days that aims to gather data and accurate measurements on old vessels. Project leaders are a marine historian and a marine archaeologist who seek ultimately to restore and preserve the ships. Ship lines, construction details and building materials are recorded on such vessels as an American clipper ship and a 19th-century packet boat. Volunteers also assist in excavating lower hulls, cataloging artifacts and preserving parts of the ships. Team members share rooms in Port Stanley, with overnight camping when working on outlying wrecks. Most of the work is on beaches or in port, with some wet suit diving for certified divers. **Cost:** $850 from Port Stanley. **When:** January, February. **Contact:** Earthwatch, P.O. Box 127 AG, Belmont, MA 02178, USA; phone (617)489-3030. *(M)*

CARIBBEAN

Search for the Caribbean Monk Seal: The Caribbean Monk seal, abundant in the West Indies when Columbus came to America, was decimated by hunters who found it unafraid of man and an easy prey; it was last sighted in 1952 off Jamaica and is now probably extinct. A month-long research cruise under the sponsorship of a Harvard University commission sails the western Caribbean Sea in an effort to locate any survivors of the species. Beginning in Miami, Florida and finishing in Panama City, the expedition visits Pedro Bank, Serranilla Bank (scene of the 1952 sighting), Serrana Bank and other reefs and islets in the area. Shipboard time not spent in observation is used for recreation and study of the species. Academic credit is available, and the expedition cost is a tax-deductible contribution. **Cost:** $2,000 includes food, accommodations, instruction, activities. **When:** June. **Contact:** The Ocean Research and Education Society, Inc., 51 Commercial Wharf 6, Boston, MA 02110, USA; phone (617)523-3455.

Dominican Republic

Listening to the Humpbacks: The song of the humpback whale, performed by lone males on the calving grounds in the winter months, lasts 30 minutes and is continually repeated in a precise and complicated format. A 14-day sailing program studies humpback singing and its relation to whale behavior in the Caribbean. The expedition sets sail in two 50-foot wooden sloops, *Snowshoe* and *Caribe*, for the winter breeding grounds of 800 whales, the largest known assembly of humpbacks. Its mission is to record songs and correlate them with photographs of the whales and their identifying characteristics. Whale behavior is observed with special attention to interactions between single animals, calling animals, pairs and trios. Everyone pitches in

In the Sea of Cortez, a boatload of observers approaches close enough to a finback whale to take detailed photographs as the whale surfaces. (Nature Expeditions International)

with the sailing and upkeep of the boats, and takes turn standing daylight watch. Experience with photographic or recording equipment, as well as sailing experience, is helpful. Patience, powers of observation and the ability to co-exist cheerfully in cramped quarters are most important. Two expeditions are planned, one out of South Caicos Island and the other out of Puerto Plata, Dominican Republic. **Cost:** $850 includes all costs while at sea. **When:** January, February. **Contact:** Earthwatch, P.O. Box 127 AG, Belmont, MA 02178, USA; phone (617)489-3030. *(M)*

West Indies

West Indies Marine Field Research: An intensive 3-week program provides practical experience in marine field research for members of the selected crews. Participants work with professional biologists on either a specific investigation or ongoing ecology projects. The site of the field investigations is on the island of Carriacou in the Grenadine Islands, West Indies. Participants are trained in relevant skills: data handling and statistics, sampling designs, navigation and

seamanship, scientific photography, identification of marine organisms, collection and processing of biological specimens, study of communities and populations and estimation of physical factors. Seminars and lectures are held on topics in chemistry, research planning, marine ecology, physiology and oceanography. Participants with a valid scuba certificate have opportunities to dive during the program. **Cost:** $600 includes room, board, instructional materials, use of all facilities. **When:** June to August. **Contact:** Environmental Research Projects, 105 Davenport Rd., Toronto, ON Canada M5R 1H6; phone (416)924-0185.

EUROPE

England

Plymouth Shipwrecks: At Penlee Point, near the entrance to Plymouth Sound, England, a 17th-century warship lies in 35 feet of gray water. Not far away, in the River Plym, is a wreck tentatively dated from the early 16th century, missing since the cannons of Sir Francis Drake sank the Spanish Armada. Volunteers are needed for 10-day periods to assist Cmdr. Alan

D. Bax, Royal Navy (ret.) in mapping and excavating these wrecks, as well as locating artifacts which have been spread about the ocean floor by centuries of tides and currents. Metal detectors and probes are used, and members of the team assist the staff in bringing artifacts to the surface and in photographing the sites. British waters tend to be cool, even in summer, so wet suits are necessary and scuba certification is required. Participants are comfortably housed at Fort Bovisand Underwater Center, a huge 19th-century castle overlooking the sea. **Cost:** $775. **When:** July, August. **Contact:** Earthwatch, P.O. Box 127 AG, Belmont, MA 02178, USA; phone (617)489-3030.   *(M)*

PACIFIC

French Polynesia

Shark Study in Polynesia: Expeditions lasting from 8 to 12 days are offered to assist in shark research in the magnificent reefs of Rangiroa Island. Working with a marine biologist, group members learn about shark feeding patterns and social behavior. By assisting in dives, participants hopefully overcome any exaggerated fears of sharks they may have. Groups sail aboard the 40-foot ketch, the *S.E.A. Quest*, which is used as a base to explore the 30-mile-wide lagoon. The small, low-lying atolls of the Tuamotus, which are visited on the longer trips, have some of the best underwater scenery in the South Pacific. Although no special training is required, participants should have an interest in research. Accommodations are in a small house on Rangi-

roa in the village of Avataru, and time is available for exploring the island. **Cost:** $480 to $680. **When:** Year-round. **Contact:** Oceanic Expeditions, 240 Ft. Mason, San Francisco, CA 94123, USA; phone (415)441-1106.

UNITED STATES
California

Marine Biology of Morro Bay: The biologically diverse Morro Bay region of southern California is the setting for an intensive 5-day course in marine biology. With a geodesic dome serving as a classroom and dining room, the course uses a meadow as base camp for daily field trips. Each day's trip focuses on a particular environment—rocky shore, mudflats, sandy beach, etc., and is followed by lectures, discussion and lab work back at the base. The Morro Bay region is host to a number of unusual creatures that come under study, including ghost shrimp, bent nose clams, fat innkeeper worms and sea rocket plants. The instruction, provided by 2 professors of life sciences and a professional naturalist, includes background information, lab exercises for all levels and handout sheets; the course is especially suitable for an instructor who wishes to teach a course in marine biology. Academic credit is available. **Cost:** $185 without credit, $195 with credit includes food, accommodations. **When:** June. **Contact:** UCSB Extension, Santa Barbara, CA 93106, USA; phone (805)961-3231.

Massachusetts
Maritime Study: An intensive 12-

week course offers the opportunity to learn about the sea through study and actual shipboard experience. Students spend the first 6 weeks at Woods Hole utilizing the resources of Woods Hole Oceanographic Institute, a marine biological laboratory, and other area museums and research centers. The course material is divided into marine science (oceanography, marine biology and geology, meteorology), the relationship of man and the sea (food extraction, ocean commerce, marine law and history) and nautical science (navigation, naval architecture, seamanship). About 55 hours a week are devoted to study; then, for the next 6 weeks, there are 2 options: either a seaman/research assistant apprenticeship aboard the research vessel *Westward*, or more advanced study at Woods Hole. Up to 22 student apprentices complement a regular staff of 8 on the ship, and they keep watches, collect and process oceanographic data, and maintain the operation of the ship. Those who choose the advanced shore class study intertidal ecology with emphasis on the Cape Cod area including current topics in marine policy, waste disposal, fisheries management, deep sea mining, etc.; and advanced marine science. Academic credit is available. **Cost:** $3,000 includes instruction, equipment, food and lodging on ship. **When:** March to October. **Contact:** Sea Education Association, Inc., P.O. Box 6, Church St., Woods Hole, MA 02543, USA; phone (617)540-3954.

Washington

Puget Sound Marine Biology Cruise: A comprehensive 1-day oceanographic expedition on Puget Sound provides participants with an opportunity to observe undersea life. Plankton is easily examined by use of a plankton trawl and the many varieties brought up are viewed and identified through the microscope. Students learn what a secchi disc is used for, how to perform a plankton tow as well as other technical testing procedures. Instruction and practical experience in navigation, weather observation and boat handling are also available. The trip offers a unique opportunity for studying many types of marine organisms not otherwise available for observation. **Cost:** On request. **When:** On request. **Contact:** Pacific Marine Institute, Inc., 11065 SE Lake Rd., Bellevue, WA 98004, USA; phone (206)454-8311.

NATURE TRIPS

A 40-ton gray whale breaches in an erupting cascade of water not 30 yards from your skiff during the annual breeding season in the Baja lagoons. Looking like dragons from an ancient Chinese painting, a large group of marine iguanas sunbathes and sneezes saltwater on black lava formations of the Galapagos Islands. Your canoe slides noiselessly over the reeds as a blue heron stands ready to strike, intently searching for food in the Florida Everglades. A stream of innocuous air bubbles marks the quiet descent of an alligator into the dark water below. In these locales and others, fascinating life forms depend on water for their livelihood as they have for millions of years. In addition to observing these wonders on your own, you can participate on a variety of trips that explore the far corners of the natural world.

You don't have to be a trained scientist to be curious about the plant and animal life that inhabits the oceans, rivers and swamplands. Under the guidance of experienced naturalists, you can paddle through the Everglades, sail around the Galapagos Islands or visit the whale breeding areas to learn more about the behavior, ecology and natural history of the world's aquatic residents.

Nature trips can last anywhere from 1 day walking the tideflats of the Netherlands to 9 days watching whales off Baja California. Longer trips are also available, such as a 52-day ornithology cruise around the perimeter of South America. Petrels, albatrosses, Magellan geese and cormorants are just a few of the birds that are sighted on this extensive journey. Other long trips include a three-week cruise down the Amazon River to observe tropical wildlife, and a three-week trip from Italy to southern Turkey that combines ornithology with archaeology and the study of classical civilizations.

The urge to explore the waters of the world may be as old as any of our instincts, inherited from our ancestors. Your interest may be bird watching, cetacean behavior or the tribal rituals of the Amazon Basin. But linking them all together is water, the "blood" of the earth. Nature trips offer you opportunities to study the diverse life forms that water supports.

Reacting instinctively to an intruder in its territory—perhaps the photographer—a mute swan begins to raise its wings, assuming a threat posture. (Henry Bunker, IV)

NATURE TRIPS

ATLANTIC

Falkland Islands

Cruising the Islas Malvinas: The Falkland Islands archipelago, a British colony northeast of Cape Horn with less than 2,000 inhabitants, provides visitors with an interesting mixture of wilderness and civilization. Participants on weekly circumnavigation cruises of the archipelago have the chance to see large colonies of seabirds including black-browed albatrosses, petrels, shearwaters, prions, skuas and 5 species of penguins. The islands are also well known for their colonies of sea lions, elephant seals and fur seals. Longer cruises with a wider variety of activities such as hiking, scuba diving and trout fishing are also available. Between 24 and 32 passengers are included on each cruise, and are accommodated in double and quadruple cabins aboard the boat. **Cost:** On request. **When:** On request. **Contact:** Julian Fitter, Drifts, Chinnor Hill, Oxford OX9 4BS, Great Britain. *(M)*

CANADA

Ontario

Whale Watching: A 10-day trip provides a chance to view dozens of whales on the lower St. Lawrence River. Participants fly from London to Montreal and travel by motorcoach to Riviere du Loup. Here 3 days are spent watching whales first from a boat, then from cliffs on shore. Species that may be seen include fin, sei, minke and even blue whales. The trip then continues to Montreal, Algonquin Park and Niagara before the return flight to London. An expert from the Fauna Preservation Society escorts travelers to provide an introduction to the birds, trees and wildflowers of eastern North America. Accommodations throughout the journey are in hotels. **Cost:** $1,500 includes round-trip airfare from London. **When:** August. **Contact:** Twickenham Travel Ltd., 2 Chester Row, London SW1W 9JH, Great Britain; phone 01-730-2297.

EUROPE

Netherlands

Walking the *Wad*: The *wad*, or tideflats, off the Dutch coast can be traversed on foot at low tide, providing a close-up view of the indigenous plant and animal life. A 5- to 10-mile *wadlopen* or hike begins daily from Pieterburen, with others departing from Uithuisen and Friesland. Six different walks are provided for hikers with varying abilities and desires, from 5-milers near Pieterburen to walks to the islands of Simonszand and Schiermonnikoog, with a return trip by boat. Guides steer participants across sandbars and away from drop-offs. In the morning the ground is mostly exposed, but by the hike's end the water may reach as high as waist level. Flora and fauna observed include sea lettuce, scholekster, wulp birds, mussels, jellyfish and seals. Participants must wear ankle-high tennis shoes and knee socks for protection from shells. **Cost:** $2 to $7 includes trans-

A seemingly desolate island and its offshore waters in the Sea of Cortez contain an abundance of wildlife including sea lions, finback whales, pelicans and boobies. (Nature Expeditions International)

portation, guide. **When:** On request. **Contact:** Wadloop Centrum, Hoofstraat 118, Pieterburen, Gronigen, The Netherlands; phone 05952-345.

MEXICO

Baja California

Sea of Cortez Nature Trip: An 8-day nature trip explores the area of the Gulf of California, formerly known as the Sea of Cortez. Participants travel by bus from San Diego to the fishing port of San Felipe, where boat travel begins. Traveling aboard a 75-foot sport-fishing vessel, trip members explore seldom-visited islands and may spend time fishing, snorkeling, photographing or watching birds. Wildlife that can be observed includes sea lions, pelicans, boobies, finback whales and dolphins. During breeding seasons Raza Island and other bird islands are visited. The group sleeps aboard ship during the trip, and the crew cooks all meals. Return to San Diego is made by air

Cruising the waters off the Galapagos Islands, participants gaze over the side of the vessel at the porpoises which swim alongside. (Nature Expeditions International)

from La Paz. **Cost:** $595 from San Diego includes food, transportation, equipment, guide. **When:** April, June. **Contact:** Adventures International, 4421 Albert St., Oakland, CA 94619, USA; phone (415)531-6564. *(M)*

Baja Panga Expedition: Pangas, 22-foot Mexican fishing boats, transport participants on an 8-day camping trip in southern Baja. Travelers take a bus from San Diego to Tijuana, from where a flight is made to La Paz to board the pangas. The group sails to the islands of Espiritu Santo and Partida, making camp on sandy beaches. Partici-

pants may choose to hike, swim, snorkel or fish. A wide assortment of vegetation may be seen, as well as sea lions and dolphins. A visit is made to La Paz for sightseeing and shopping, with a night spent there in a hotel before the return trip to San Diego. **Cost:** $475 includes roundtrip transportation rom San Diego, meals, camping equipment. **When:** March to June, October. **Contact:** Baja Expeditions Inc., Box 3725, San Diego, CA 92103, USA; phone (714)297-0506.

San Ignacio Whale Watching: Members travel by sea along the Pacific coast of Baja California to

San Ignacio Lagoon, winter quarters of the California gray whale. Embarking from San Diego, on the 7½-day trip, participants make stops en route at Todos Santos Island and at San Martin Island, where harbor seals can be seen. Visits are also made to the island of San Benitos, home of California sea lions and sea elephants, and to the abandoned silver mine on Cedros Island before arriving at San Ignacio. In the lagoon group members alternate whale watching from skiffs with beachcombing, dune and marsh exploration, and a paddle down mangrove channels inhabited by several species of birds. A professional naturalist and authority on the ecology and wildlife of Baja and the California gray whale accompanies the trip. **Cost:** $550 includes meals, trip passage. **When:** December to April. **Contact:** H & M Landing, 2803 Emerson St., San Diego, CA 92108, USA; phone (714)222-1144. *(M)*

SOUTH AMERICA

Ecuador

Tropical Wildlife Cruise: A 12-day expedition in tropical waters focuses on observing nature. Following a 3-day stay in the capital city of Quito, trip members depart Guayaquil and sail to the Galapagos Islands on a week-long cruise. Among the stops made is Academy Bay, site of the Charles Darwin Research Station and home of the giant tortoises. South Plaza Island, James Bay, Punta Espinosa and Punta Suarez are among other ports of call. A wide range of wildlife is seen on the cruise, including iguanas, sea lions, fur seals, cormorants and albatrosses. Experts in natural history lead daily island excursions as well as provide briefings and lectures. Accommodations are onboard a cruising ship which provides all basic comforts. **Cost:** $1,885 to $2,485 includes roundtrip transportation from New York, accommodations, meals, guides. **When:** April. **Contact:** American Museum of Natural History, Central Park West at 79th St., New York, NY 10024, USA.

Amazon Nature Trip: For 15 days participants take an extensive nature and cultural trip down the Amazon. The first 5 days are based in Quito, with full- or half-day excursions to areas of interest, including Mt. Cotopaxi, Indian burial mounds, the mountain country near Otavalo, Laguna Cuicocha and Chorlavi. For the next 5 days participants cruise the Napo River, a tributary of the Amazon, aboard a large floating hotel, observing wildlife and making frequent side trips by canoe and foot. Visits are made to a linguistics institute, Lake Tarcoa, Monkey Island and numerous native villages. The final 5 days are spent in Quito with free time and organized expeditions, including a visit to the huge Central Bank Museum with over 23,000 artifacts. The guides accompanying the trip are trained naturalists and anthropologists. **Cost:** $1,495 from Los Angeles includes transportation, food, accommodations, guide. **When:** June to August. **Contact:** Aventura Natural History Tours and Travel, 508 N. Sierra Dr., Beverly Hills, CA 90210, USA; phone (213)276-6081.

Photographers can get surprisingly close to the waved albatross on Hood Island. Marine iguanas, cormorants and penguins are among the other unusual species viewed on nature trips in the Galapagos. (Nature Expeditions International)

Galapagos Jaunt: Participants in a nature study trip travel 14 days in Ecuador and the Galapagos Islands. Journeying 2 days from New York to Quito, participants rest and explore the capital city and countryside of Ecuador for 3 days. After a passage from the Andean highlands to the coastal city of Guayaquil, a sea journey begins. Following about 3 days of open-water travel, the ship arrives at its first port, the island of San Cristobal, capital of the Galapagos archipelago. From there trip members sail to Espanola and Floreana, home of waved albatrosses, boobies and marine iguanas. Santa Cruz and South Plaza are the next stops. Upon leaving the site of the Charles Darwin Research Station on Santa Cruz, participants head to San Salvador for a day before reaching Fernandina and Isabela, where the steep cliffs carry the names of 200 years of visiting ships. The final

visits in the Galapagos are the islands of North Seymour and Baltra; from there a flight returns passengers to Guayaquil, then New York. **Cost:** $895 to $1,065 from Quito. **When:** May to October. **Contact:** Hanns Ebensten Travel Inc., 55 W. 42nd St., New York, NY 10036, USA; phone (212)354-6634.

South American Nature Trip: A yacht cruise in the Galapagos Islands and a canoe trip on the Amazon River introduce participants to the natural beauties of Ecuador. For 18 days trip members observe the exotic animals and birds which inhabit environments ranging from lowland rain forests to mountain regions and Pacific islands. Throughout the trip patient observers may spot tapirs, anacondas, monkeys, hummingbirds, flamingos, lava lizards and marine iguanas. After departure from Quito the group first heads for Baños, a small mountain village, for an early-morning bath in the hot springs of Tungurahua, an active volcano which last erupted in 1944. Cruising down the Napo River in motorized canoes, the group spends a few days in the jungle, followed by a flight to Baltra Island in the Galapagos to board a private yacht. On this leg of the trip there are opportunities to snorkel off Floreana, visit underground lava caves, and hike in search of giant tortoises. After returning to the mainland, the group heads for Cuzco for an early-morning train to Machupicchu. An overnight at the site provides plenty of time for individual exploration of the ruins. The group returns to Cuzco and proceeds to Pisac to attend the local market. After a morning in Pisac, participants return to Cuzco for the flight home. **Cost:** $2,057 includes airfare from Miami, meals, lodging. **When:** July. **Contact:** Holbrook Travel, Inc., 3520 NW 13th St., Gainesville, FL 32601, USA; phone (904)377-7111.

Peru

Amazon Ecology: Travelers learn about the natural history and ecology of tropical rain forests on a 3-week trip down the Amazon. Participants travel from Iquitos in Peru to Leticia in Colombia in a specially chartered double-deck riverboat, stopping at simple lodges along the river. Explorations are made by small boats and canoes as well as on foot. The tropical rain forest, with its rich variety of trees and epiphytes, houses exotic birds such as macaws and toucans in addition to many species of insects and amphibians. The instructors are University of California professors of botany and zoology. There are no prerequisites for the course which is open to all interested adults. Trip members should be prepared for some discomforts, as the climate is hot and humid and there is a lot of rain and mud. **Cost:** $1,615 includes roundtrip airfare from Los Angeles, food, accommodations, river transportation. **When:** June. **Contact:** UCLA Extension, P.O. Box 24901, Los Angeles, CA 90024, USA; phone (213)825-7093.

UNITED STATES

Alaska

Boreal Biology Expedition: A professional wildlife biologist leads an

18-day expedition exploring Glacier Bay and Katmai and Mt. McKinley parks. Participants study natural history and wildlife, including brown bears, birds, marine mammals, glaciers and physical geography. A special boat charter at Glacier Bay is included, and travelers have the option to extend the expedition to the Pribilof Islands. **Cost:** $1,390. **When:** June to August. **Contact:** Nature Expeditions International, 599 College Ave., Palo Alto, CA 94306, USA; phone (415)328-6572. *(M)*

California

Channel Islands Cruise: Participants on a 6½-day journey cruise among the Channel Islands off the coast of southern California, exploring free-form grottos, ancient Indian sites and weather-beaten shores. Accommodations are onboard the cruise boat, from which participants embark on excursions to the islands. Trip members may view sea lions, brown pelicans, gray whales and island foxes. A naturalist accompanies the trip. **Cost:** $470 includes accommodations, meals, guidance. **When:** December, May. **Contact:** H & M Landing, 2803 Emerson St., San Diego, CA 92108, USA; phone (714)222-1144. *(M)*

Florida

Photographing the Everglades: A photography seminar is the core of a 10-day canoeing and backpacking expedition in the swamplands of the Florida Everglades. The leaders of the course instruct students on the basic concepts of outdoor pho-

tography through lectures and field trips. Participants learn advanced techniques of shooting and processing color slides. While canoeing and hiking in the surrounding subtropical wilderness students photograph the varied flora and fauna which include many endangered species. Emphasis is also placed on wilderness skills and the ecology of the Everglades. College credit is available. **Cost:** $375 includes accommodations, meals, canoes, instruction. **When:** December, January. **Contact:** Wilderness Encounter, 720 Grand Ave., Glenwood Springs, CO 81601, USA; phone (303)945-8365. *(M)*

Massachusetts

East Coast Ocean Study Cruise: Participants can take courses in marine geology, natural history and first aid at sea while sailing the Elizabeth Islands to Cape Cod. Group members learn something of the unusual glacier formations and landscape evolution of the region while enrolled in the marine geology course. Under the direction of a New England Aquarium staff member, participants gather marine organisms and watch for birds and ocean mammals from the boat. The medical course offers instruction in first aid, C.P.R., setting fractures, treating wounds and burns and dealing with heatstroke, genito-urinary emergencies, seasickness and tropical diseases. Participants in both courses embark and disembark at Newport. **Cost:** $250 includes meals, accommodations, instruction. **When:** July. **Contact:** Oceanus, P.O. Box 431, Hohokus, NJ 07423, USA; phone (201)447-0393. *(M)*

Underwater
Adventures

UNDERWATER ADVENTURES

The urge to explore has led humans to climb the highest peaks, to cross the greatest continents, to brave the jungles and deserts—and to descend to the depths of the sea. Far from being a recent sport, diving has a history almost as old as civilization itself. Over 6,000 years ago, treasure hunters dove as deep as 100 feet on a lungful of air to search for mother-of-pearl and precious corals. Legends tell us that Alexander the Great was submerged in history's first diving bell in 332 B.C., and among Leonardo da Vinci's imaginative inventions was a diving outfit complete with fins. Today, scuba equipment has made diving a safe activity enjoyed by millions all over the world—an adventure as close to you as the nearest body of water.

Most dive trip operators and schools own their own equipment, so all you need to bring is your swimming skill and a bathing suit. You can learn the basics of snorkeling or scuba diving in a pool at dive schools from upstate New York to southern California, but not until you submerge yourself in the waters of the Florida Keys, the Bahamas, the Red Sea or the South Pacific can you really appreciate what diving is all about. You can search for long-lost pirate ships in the Caribbean or sunken warships in Truk Lagoon in Micronesia. You can explore the pillar coral off the coast of Roatan or the Great Barrier Reef running along the Australian continent. Or you can marvel at the abundance of life forms off Vancouver Island in Canada, scout for amphora on the Mediterranean floor or study the geology and biology of reefs off the Jamaican shore. You can even learn hard-hat diving, commercial dive techniques or underwater medicine at special schools for the advanced diver.

Diving is unlike any other form of adventure. Down in the depths, your body responds differently than it does on land. You are in another medium, and the bouancy of it lifts the burden of gravity from your movements. Sounds are distorted—some muffled, others crystal clear. The quality of light is different since the filtering effect of water cuts out first the red colors, then the oranges and yellows until you are swimming in an alien world of shadows. Whether you are making a brief snorkel dive on a single breath of air or exploring a convoluted coral reef for half an hour with a compressed air tank, diving is a visit to the world beneath the surface, a world all its own. □

Divers enter the clear waters of the Pacific near Fiji via ladders and a cutaway transom. (Scubahire *Ltd.*)

DIVING

AFRICA

Kenya

Scuba Divers' Safari: An 11-day safari in eastern Kenya combines wildlife viewing with diving in the Indian Ocean. Beginning in Nairobi, trip members proceed to the Masai Amboseli Game Reserve and Tsavo National Park near Mt. Kilimanjaro to view rhinos, elephants, buffalo, zebras, giraffes and cheetahs. On the fourth day, participants arrive at a rustic beach resort near the coastal city of Malindi for 5 days of diving. The site provides easy access to coral gardens, subterranean caves and barracuda groves. For the novice diver, a diploma course is available that includes a 2-day pool and 3-day open sea instruction program. **Cost:** $367 to $770 depending on group size and diving supplement includes meals, accommodations, guide, land transportation. **When:** On request. **Contact:** Bestway Tours and Safaris Ltd., Woolworth Bldg., Box 44325, Nairobi, Kenya; phone 331261, 331262, 22297.

Sudan

Red Sea Diving: The Red Sea off Port Sudan is the site of dive trips lasting 2 or 3 weeks. The waters in

---

ADVENTURE TRAVEL NEWSLETTER
For a free complimentary copy of the *Adventure Travel Newsletter*, see page 544. A lively, 16-page update with the latest news on adventure travel activities around the world, *Adventure Travel Newsletter* has become the most quoted source of adventure travel information anywhere.

---

this area are warm and clear. Throughout the trips, dive masters and marine biologists guide participants to Sanganeb Reef, Wingate Reef, Towartit Reef, Barrier Reef and the Umbria Wreck. Large quantities of tropical fish inhabit these areas, along with barracuda, sharks, dolphins, large turtles and mantas. An average of 2 dives a day is made in groups of 6 to 20. Divers can on occasion hand-feed the fish. **Cost:** $1,096 for 2 weeks, $1,303 for 3 weeks includes roundtrip airfare from London, all land arrangements. **When:** Year-round. **Contact:** Explore Beyond Ltd., 1 Ludgate Circus Bldgs., London EC4M 7LQ, Great Britain; phone 01-248-9082 or 01-236-4395; or Adventure Center, 5540 College Ave., Oakland, CA 94618, USA; phone (41⊃)654-1879. *(M)*

Red Sea Scuba Expedition: Trip members study marine life in the coral regions near Port Sudan. The 15-day itinerary remains flexible, allowing groups of no more than 12 to explore a variety of locations. Much of the time is spent diving from a reef platform situated on the edge of the Towarfit Reef, about 6 miles offshore. The platform has sleeping quarters, kitchen, dining and work areas. Boat trips are made from Port Sudan to other reef areas including Umbria, Wingate and Sanageb. Overnight camping is done on some of these excursions. The water often reaches 85°F, ideal for many hours of continued diving. **Cost:** $1,105 to $1,158 depending on departure date includes roundtrip airfare from London, meals, accommodations. **When:** Year-round. **Contact:** WEXAS Interna-

Divers off the coast of Port Sudan attempt to hand feed the less aggressive species of fish. Explore Beyond Ltd. offers diving trips of two or three weeks in the Red Sea. (Explore Beyond Ltd.)

tional Inc., Suite 354, Graybar Bldg., 420 Lexington Ave., New York, NY 10017, USA; **(M)**

ASIA

Philippines

Diving the Philippine Deep: Participants explore the clear waters and coral reefs of the Philippines during a 33-day trip that departs from San Francisco. Several days are spent in each of a handful of diving locations that include Dumaguete City, Bacong, Bais City and Amlan. Some sightseeing is involved, but group members devote most of their time to scuba diving expeditions on which they view hundreds of different species of fish: striped sweet lip, leopard-presser fish, emerald or neon reef perch, saddle-stain butterfly fish and snipe fish. During the last 3 days of the trip participants have an opportunity to relax, shop and sightsee in Hong Kong before the return flight to San Francisco. Transportation on the islands is by private motorcoach, and travelers spend nights in hotels. **Cost:** $1,575 from San Francisco includes airfare, accommodations, continental breakfasts, guides, land transporta-

Students may explore the reefs and wrecks near Bermuda during courses and trips offered year-round by Dave McLeod's Diving Adventures. (Gene Ray)

tion. **When:** June to July. **Contact:** Philippine Airlines, 212 Stockton St., San Francisco, CA 98101, USA.

Reef and Island Diving: A fully equipped, 102-foot dive cruiser takes participants to various diving areas in the Philippines on a 5-day trip. The trip begins on Thursday with a flight from Manila to Cebu, second largest city in the Philippines and the departure point for the sea trip. The boat then proceeds to selected diving spots in the Camotes Islands and Capitancillo Reefs. High visibility, dramatic coral walls and hundreds of varieties of tropical fish highlight the area. All equipment is supplied, and there is no limit to the number of dives a passenger may make; also on board is 110-volt electricity for photographic lighting equipment. On Monday morning the ship docks again at Cebu and participants return to Manila by air. More extended diving trips are also offered regularly. **Cost:** $242 from Manila includes all transportation,

use of boat and equipment, meals, diving, shipboard accommodations, guide. **When:** July to January. **Contact:** Seaquest Ventures, Inc., Philippine Village Hotel, Mia Ave., Pasay, Metro Manila, Philippines; phone 80-70-11; or Philippine Airlines, 212 Stockton St., San Francisco, CA 98101, USA.

Thailand

Hotel Dives: A 7-day diving vacation in Pattaya is offered year-round by a resort hotel. The dive package includes 5 days of diving at coral reefs, tropical fish feeding grounds and shipwreck sites. American dive instructors accompany each diving trip. Modern diving equipment and dive boats are provided. Arrangements include 6 nights, accommodations, breakfasts and lunches, diving equipment, guides and transportation to and from dive sites. **Cost:** $199 a person for double occupancy, $249 single accommodations. **When:** Year-round. **Contact:** Holiday Inn Sands Hotel Sales Office, Eighth

Floor, Kongboonma Bldg., Silom Rd., Bangkok, Thailand; phone 2330802; or Holiday Inn Sands, Pattaya, Thailand; phone 418755.

ATLANTIC

Bermuda

Mid-Atlantic Plunge: Beginning and new divers take day journeys out along the reefs of Bermuda. Starting with snorkels, divers learn the basics of diving and diving safety before graduating to scuba gear and more advanced diving. The classes start in shallow water and work their way down, eventually moving on to inspect old shipwrecks. The reefs are full of living and dead coral as well as sea fans and many different types of tropical fish. A highlight of the journey is a visit to the Arcade Walk, a coral formation that resembles an underwater mall. Two dive boats are available, each glass-bottomed and fully equipped. **Cost:** On request. **When:** Year-round. **Contact:** Dave McLeod's Diving Adventures, The Gables Guest House, Paget, Bermuda; phone 1-6207.

AUSTRALASIA

Australia

Diving Down Under: Scuba diving during a 17-day tour off the outer fringes of the Great Barrier Reef enables divers to view coral reefs and the indigenous marine life. Starting from either Los Angeles or San Francisco, the group flies to Sydney then sets sail on the dive boat *Coralita* for 11 days in the Coral Sea. The *Coralita* is a 79-foot boat with excellent accommodations and

diving facilities. The waters are unpolluted and contain nearly every species of coral and reef fish, as well as rays and sharks, turtles and sea snakes. Night dives are made throughout the cruise. **Cost:** $1,895 includes airfare, accommodations, meals, diving guide service, equipment. **When:** October. **Contact:** Atlantis Safaris, P.O. Box 530303, Miami Shore, FL 33153, USA; phone (305)754-7480.

Heron Island Diving: With 18 days in Australia, divers and non-divers can choose between spending the entire time on an island near the Queensland coast or spending 1 week there and the other week on an overland excursion through the mainland. From Sydney, the group journeys to Gladstone where a launch or helicopter transports participants to the white sand beaches and tropical fauna and flora on Heron. For the next 7 or 15 days divers come to know Heron as a marine sanctuary with more than 1,200 species of fish, giant manta rays, large turtles and coral in every shade. Non-divers find tennis, snorkeling, swimming and turtle watching among activities available. During the summer months giant sea turtles can be seen coming ashore at high tide, nesting in the sand to lay their eggs. With the overland option, participants receive an open bus ticket that allows each person to design an individualized itinerary while staying at any hotels owned by one company. The last stop on the 1-week overland journey is Sydney, where both groups meet for the return flight to the west coast of the United States. **Cost:** $645 to $760 for 2 weeks diving includes accommodations, meals, 10 days boat diving, boat guide, air, backpack, weights; $470 to $585 for non-divers includes accommodations, meals; $475 to $620 for diving/overland combination from Gladstone. **When:** Year-round. **Contact:** Bay Travel Diving Adventures, 2435 E. Coast Hwy., Corona del Mar, CA 92625, USA; phone (714)675-4321. *(M)*

Keppel Islands: Divers explore the Great Barrier Reef from Great Keppel Island, 30 miles east of Rockhampton. Dive spots are varied throughout the island group, featuring corals, bommies, caves and drop-offs. The dives use large inflatable sports boats as a platform, and a pickup boat with propeller guard is in attendance. Divers must be of certified competency and hold a current diver's medical certificate. Equipment is available for rental. **Cost:** $739 a week, depending on accommodations and time of year includes airfare from Brisbane. **When:** May to January. **Contact:** Safari Diving Services, P.O. Box 29, Clayfield, Brisbane, Queensland, Australia, phone 07-574321.

Great White Shark Search: Carefully selected participants under the supervision of Australia's leading white shark authority spend 7 days of a 14-day expedition off the coast of south Australia luring sharks within range of underwater cameras. Flights from Los Angeles bring divers to Sydney; local planes continue to Port Lincoln where 2 shark boats are harbored. During the first days in Port Lincoln group members view shark movies and spend time aboard one of the boats becoming acquainted with procedure, shark cages and safety precautions. The second boat lies offshore baiting the area where sharks normally appear. Until a great white is spotted, participants can make dives among the sea lions, reefs and plentiful fish populations of the region, away from the shark site. When a shark is spotted, divers with cameras descend alongside the boat in strong shark cages, letting the great white sharks, up to 16 feet long, gently nudge and test the bars. Preparation for the experience is essential; divers must be in good physical condition and have the ability to function well emotionally as well as physically when dealing with sharks. **Cost:** $4,400 includes hotels, boats, meals, daily diving, tanks, safety equipment, transportation within Australia. **When:** January, February. **Contact:** See and Sea Travel Services, Inc., 680 Beach St., Suite 340, Wharfside, San Francisco, CA 94109, USA; phone (415)771-0077. *(M)*

CANADA

British Columbia

Basic Skin and Scuba: Every 2 weeks a new course begins in skin and scuba diving for the beginner. Instruction is carried out in the classroom, pool and ocean and prepares students for the NAUI exam. Everything the beginning diver needs to know is taught: diving equipment, physics, water safety, physiology, the marine environment. After passing the 40-hour course students are ready to participate in some of the more advanced classes that are offered such as a NAUI sport diver program and a series of 5 open water ocean dives. In the sport diver course students dive near the Gulf Islands and the Sechelt Peninsula on night dives, current dives and wreck dives. **Cost:** On request. **When:** Year-round. **Contact:** Rowand's Reef, 2828 W. 4th Ave., Vancouver, BC Canada V6K 1R3; phone (604)732-1344.

Nova Scotia

Maritime Dive: Underwater enthusiasts spend 1 to 7 days exploring the wreck-filled reaches off Louisbourg, Nova Scotia. Since 1733 ships have foundered and sunk under the difficult tides and treacherous currents of the Cape Breton shelf; now participants may inspect such wrecks as the *Evelyn*, the *Montara*, the *Afgan Prince* and the *Langley Range*. The 1-day package allows divers 2 dives to the various wrecks; 2-, 3- and 5-day trips travel to between 4 and 10 wreck areas. The 7-day excursions, which require 10 to 24 dives, allow divers to either camp or stay at a motel in Sydney. Diving guides, lunch and a lobster dinner are included in each tour. Diver certification is required. **Cost:** $35 to $515. **When:** June to October. **Contact:** Dive Cape Breton Ltd., P.O. Box 130, Louisbourg, NS Canada B0A 1M0; phone (902)733-2877 or 733-2840.

CARIBBEAN

Bahamas

Diving the Bahamas: At least a dozen top diving spots are visited

on trips lasting from 5 to 10 days. A charter service is available to take participants on cruises which generally stop at such ports of call as Mimini, Freeport, Great Exuma and Nassau. Members of the cruise sleep and eat aboard the yacht, allowing maximum time for diving. Gear for scuba and skin diving, unlimited air refills, shark cage, photography and diving instruction, and fishing tackle are available while underway. **Cost:** $285 to $790 includes double-occupancy accommodations aboard the yacht, diving gear, meals. **When:** January to September. **Contact:** Adventure Cruises, Inc., P.O. Box 22284, Ft. Lauderdale, FL 33316, USA; phone (305)735-4045. **(M)**

Bahamas Treasure Diving: Two different trips allow qualified divers to assist in a licensed salvage operation, looking for treasure on ancient shipwrecks. The first trip, based in Nassau, requires certified divers who live either at guest houses or on a dive boat; the second trip is based in the Abacos, or Bahamas Out-Islands, and involves searches in areas containing known wrecks with underwater metal detectors. Certified divers are preferred, but the trip is also open to non-certified divers. On both trips there is some time for shell collecting, underwater photography and individual exploration of the area. **Cost:** About $350, varying with time of year, includes roundtrip airfare from Florida, accommodations, salvage license, guide. **When:** Nassau trip year-round, Abacos trip May to August. **Contact:** Adventurers International, 215 E. Horatio Ave.,

Maitland, FL 32751, USA; phone (305)645-1332. **(M)**

Underwater Medicine: Techniques for diving-related medicine and cardiac support are taught in a week-long session held in Freeport. Participants may finish the week by achieving Provider Level certification in Advanced Cardiac Life Support. Intended for physicians, nurses, dentists and paramedics who may be called upon to deliver emergency medical treatment to divers, the course requires a month of fairly intensive prior study at home. The week's program combines didactic and practical sessions covering decompression sickness, recompression procedures, physical examination of divers, airway management, dysrhythmia recognition, defibrillation, useful drugs and other topics. There is free time every day for recreational diving, including some night dives, with scheduled trips to nearby reefs. The Freeport area also offers opportunities for beachcombing, hiking and duty-free shopping. **Cost:** On request. **When:** May. **Contact:** Atlantis Safaris, P.O. Box 530303, Miami Shore, FL 33153, USA; phone (305)754-7480.

Divers Special in the Bahamas: Guided reef trips and diving trips are provided daily for both experienced and novice scuba divers and snorkelers. Instruction, including official certification classes, are available. Dive boats transport participants to tropical beaches, coral reefs and canyons. Half-day, full-day and night trips are available, as are special group rates and charters. **Cost:** $15 to $28 for half-day

Divers in the Caribbean can make dives and live aboard a yacht for 5 or 10 days during trips offered by Adventure Cruisers, Inc. (Carol Baker)

trips, $40 to $100 for extended trips. **When:** Year-round. **Contact:** Bahama Divers Co., P.O. Box 5004, Nassau, Bahamas; phone 28431; eves. 34463; overseas (809)322-8431.

Small Hope Dive: The island of Andros, the largest of the Bahama chain, sits on a tropical barrier reef that divers explore during 3- to 7-day stays at Small Hope Bay. Participants arrive by plane at Andros Town and are met at the airfield by a car that takes them to Small Hope, on the east coast of the island. Dives in the area explore locations such as Red Shoal, Love Hill Channel, Smuggler's Run, the Edge and Hole-in-the-Wall. One of the best dives involves swimming down the vertical face of the Andros Bank, into the Tongue of the Ocean. Diving instruction is available for the novice. Participants should be ready to spend a lot of time diving, since there is little else to do in Small Hope Bay, and virtually no place to spend money. **Cost:** $150 to $350 includes accommodations, meals, diving equip-

On a wreck 60 feet below the surface, a diver examines coral growth on the gussets at the base of the ship's steel mast. (Scubahire)

ment, transportation between the Andros airfield and Small Hope Bay. **When:** July, October. **Contact:** Underwater Safaris, P.O. Box 291, Back Bay Annex, Boston, MA 02117, USA; phone (617)283-4933.

Caymans

Grand Cayman Diving: A dive resort on Grand Cayman is the base for expeditions in the surrounding Caribbean waters. The regular package includes either a 4- or an 8-day stay with a half-day dive each day. There is a live coral reef offshore, and the Grand Cayman Wall, a sheer underwater drop-off of 50 to 600 feet, is nearby. Shipwrecks and a variety of marine life populate the area. Devoid of rivers and mountains, the Cayman Islands are free of runoff, mud flats and silty water, making for excellent diving. **Cost:** $105 to $126 for 4 days, $245 to $294 for 8 days depending on season includes food, accommodations, dive trips. **When:** Year-round. **Contact:** Bob Soto's

Lodge, P.O. Box 1050, Grand Cayman, British West Indies.

Diving the Cayman Islands: Divers can explore the waters surrounding the British West Indies island of Grand Cayman. For 4 days divers investigate any of 325 shipwrecks, huge coral heads (part of a live coral reef), underwater caves and deep or shallow reefs. Over 300 species of seashells exist in the Cayman waters including the queen conch, triton trumpet, purple dye shell and the chestnut Latirus, found only in Cayman. Visits can be made to the world's only green turtle farm, and 148 kinds of birds can be observed in the area. **Cost:** $114 to $135 for divers, $81 to $102 for non-divers, includes accommodations, 3 half-day boat trips, most gear. **When:** Year-round. **Contact:** Casa Bertmar, P.O.Box 637, Grand Cayman, Cayman Islands, British West Indies; phone 92514.

Photography for Divers: A 7-day course for scuba divers interested in underwater photography is offered in the waters of Grand Cayman. A typical day begins around 7 a.m. with a review of the previous day's photography. Then participants travel to Spanish Bay Reef for an underwater session. After lunch another session is held, then 2 to 3 hours of lecture and discussion follow on various aspects of underwater picture-taking followed by a session on night photography. Topics include composition, photo-biology, strobe work and maintenance of underwater equipment. **Cost:** $689 includes accommodations, meals, tank, backpack, weights, instruction. **When:** February to March. **Contact:** Jim and Cathy Church, P.O. Box 80, Gilroy, CA 95020, USA; phone (408)842-9682.

Biology Course for Divers: A marine biology course on the tropical reef is being offered to divers at Grand Cayman in the British West Indies over the Thanksgiving week. This is a chance for divers with little or no science background to learn about the varied marine life of the reefs. The college-level course, taught by professional marine biologists, combines informal classroom discussions illustrated with slides and guided underwater field trips to Cayman's prolific reefs. The 11-day trip provides ample time for diving and photography. Several summer courses are also offered. **Cost:** $935 includes rooms, meals, diving, instruction, roundtrip airfare from Miami. **When:** November. **Contact:** Sea Life Discovery, 19915-A Oakmont Dr., Los Gatos, CA 95030, USA; phone (408)353-1766. *(M)*

Cayman Diving in the Caribbean: Divers spend 8 days aboard the 83-foot *Cayman Diver* traveling to diving sites around the islands of Grand Cayman that can only be reached by boat. Hosted by professional dive leaders, participants have the advantage of onboard air bank and compressor, a diving platform, gangway and fresh water equipment rinse. Early in the week divers explore the great coral gardens of the south coast, where great forests of antler coral fringe deep clefts in the living coral. Excellent visibility and a wide variety of marine life including eagle rays, sea turtles and grouper make the trip especially suited to underwater photographers. Participants move to dramatic drop-offs where divers view a variety of sponges ranging from huge basket sponges to the brilliant blood-red sponge. In 35 feet of water, divers explore the wreck of the *Balboa;* they attract darting wrasse, sergeant-majors, angelfish and parrotfish with fish food. Participants take night dives, explore shallow caves such as those at Eden Rocks and dive into gigantic canyons with large gorgonian fans. On the final day divers are transported to the airport for the return flight to Miami. **Cost:** $600 from Grand Cayman includes transportation, guides, meals, accommodations, tanks, backpacks, weights, unlimited air refills. **When:** Year-round. **Contact:** See and Sea Travel Services, Inc., 680 Beach St., Suite 340, Wharfside, San Francisco, CA 94109, USA; phone (415)771-0077.   *(M)*

Cuba

Scuba Cuba: Underwater enthusiasts are invited to take 8 days and 7 nights exploring the heretofore unavailable subsurface areas of the Cuban coast. Because of the long ban on Western visitors, the reefs are in virtually undisturbed condition. Beside underwater exploration, other activities are available, including swimming, tennis, racquetball, volleyball, fishing, horseback riding and bicycling. Non-divers are also welcome. **Cost:** $595 for divers, $464 for non-divers includes transportation from Tampa, room, board. **When:** On request. **Contact:** Sport-Treks, 1410 Ave. of the Americas, New York, NY 10019, USA; phone (212)744-6830.

Dominican Republic

Caribbean Scuba Diving: Six full days of diving are offered along the coastal waters of Santo Domingo. Setting out by boat from beachfront accommodations, a maximum of 20 participants dive the warm Caribbean waters in a variety of marine settings. Divers make close observations of colorful tropical fish and underwater scenery. The city of Santo Domingo itself was founded in 1496 and is the oldest settlement by Europeans in the Western Hemisphere. Both divers and non-divers may explore the city, including its ancient cathedral where the ashes of Columbus are reputedly buried. **Cost:** $385 for divers includes boats, tanks, weights, guides, lunches, accommodations; $299 for non-divers. **When:** Year-round. **Contact:** Aquaventures, P.O. Box 1816, Max Henriquez Urena No. 89, Santo Domingo, Dominican Republic; phone 566-7608.

Haiti

Haitian Week: An 8-day trip provides instruction in scuba diving for beginners out of a beach-front dive center. For the most part, participants spend the mornings learning diving; the afternoons are spent on local excursions, sailing trips or individual exploration. Instruction begins in the swimming pool and moves to the beach on the second day, at first with snorkel and then with scuba gear in shallow water over a small reef. After a day off from diving, a full day is provided for exploring the Arcadin Cays. A

Shallow-water dives close to shore are part of an instruction course offered by Kilbrides Underwater Tours in the Virgin Islands. (Carol Baker)

richly coraled area, the cays have exceptional visibility and no strong currents. Finally, on their last full day, participants dive either the wall of Voodoo Heads at Trouforban Point or the long wall of La Gonave. Filled with wide natural aqueducts through the coral and dotted with ancient wrecks, the area offers opportunities for divers of all levels of proficiency. Throughout the trip, evening entertainment ranging from a native voodoo ceremony to disco dancing is offered. **Cost:** $450 for divers includes instruction, accommodations, breakfasts and dinners, all transportation on Haiti, equipment, entertainment; $339 for nondivers. **When:** Year-round. **Contact:** Oceaneers Dive Tours, Inc.,

5555 Hollywood Blvd., Hollywood, FL 33021, USA; phone (305)983-0017 or tollfree (800)327-3810.

Arcadin Diving: Upon arrival in Port au Prince, participants commence an 8-day diving journey to the Arcadin Islands. Individuals board dive boats which transport them to the Arcadin Islands where they explore the 40-foot stands of brightly colored coral rising off the white sand bottoms. Shuttling to and from the hotel and dive spots, divers explore the outer fringes of the coral cays, often inhabited by huge manta rays and other varieties of tropical fish. Night dives are optional. Divers visit the islands of La Gonave to view the huge underwater escarpment abounding in sea

JOIN THE WORLD
OF ADVENTURE TRAVEL

Accept this special charter membership invitation to join the American Adventurers Association, and the world of adventure is yours to enjoy. For $25, you will receive: 1) a year's subscription to *Adventure Travel* magazine, a monthly magazine with spectacular photography and comprehensive information telling you how to find adventure; 2) a year's subscription to *Adventure Travel Newsletter*, a monthly report on the who, what, where and how of adventure travel; 3) the annual edition of *Worldwide Adventure TravelGuide*, a fact-filled guide to more than 3,000 adventure trips you can go on; 4) plus discounts on trips, equipment, books and much more.

For more information on membership in the American Adventurers Association, write to:

American Adventurers Association SUITE 301, 444 NE RAVENNA BLVD., SEATTLE, WA 98115

JOIN THE WORLD
OF ADVENTURE TRAVEL

We trust that you find your **Worldwide Adventure TravelGuide** interesting and useful. We would like to welcome you as a member of the American Adventurers Association.

As a member you will receive: 1) A one-year subscription—12 issues—to **Adventure Travel** magazine, featuring expanded accounts of adventure travel experiences in the world's most exciting places, captured in spectacular color (a $24 newsstand value). 2) The 1980 edition of the annual **Worldwide Adventure TravelGuide** (which sells for $10.95 in bookstores). 3) A one-year subscription—12 issues—to **Adventure Travel Newsletter,** the most timely update on the world of adventure travel (subscriptions are regularly $26 1 year). 4) Discounts on many adventure trips offered by Association organizational members. 5) Special discounts on outdoor equipment. 6) Discounts on film and film processing. 7) A literature service providing discounts of up to 35% on travel books, maps and guides from around the world. 8) An information service listing worldwide trips you can go on. 9) Members-only outings. 10) Membership identification materials including shoulder patch, membership scroll and a permanent Association membership card.

Your $25 Charter Membership dues cover publications valued at over $60, plus the full range of Association services.

☐ **Please enroll me** as a Charter Member of the American Adventurers Association for the period indicated below. I understand that I am entitled to all of the benefits and privileges described in the **Worldwide Adventure TravelGuide.** (Membership dues are normally $35 a year, but I will pay only $25 for Charter Membership.)

☐ One year $25   ☐ Two years $50   ☐ Three years $75
  (Regularly $35)   (Regularly $70)   (Regularly $105)

☐ Payment enclosed   ☐ Please charge my credit card below for $ _____

☐ BankAmericard/VISA   ☐ Master Charge Credit Card No. _____

  Exp. Date/Mo. _____ Year_____ Bank No. (Master Charge only) _____

☐ **Please bill me.** Payment is due only after I have received the materials described above. If I am not satisfied I may return the materials within 10 days after receiving them without further obligation.

☐ All I want is the next edition of the **Worldwide Adventure TravelGuide.** Please place my advance order for the 1980 edition, and bill me later.

NAME _____

ADDRESS _____

CITY _____ STATE _____ ZIP _____

☐ **Make mine the gift of adventure.** Please send Gift Membership in my name to the persons listed below. I am enclosing $25 for each Gift Charter Membership.

NAME _____

ADDRESS _____

CITY _____ STATE _____ ZIP _____

NAME _____

ADDRESS _____

CITY _____ STATE _____ ZIP _____

BUSINESS REPLY CARD

FIRST CLASS   PERMIT NO. 20078   SEATTLE, WA

POSTAGE WILL BE PAID BY ADDRESSEE

American Adventurers ASSOCIATION

SUITE 301, 444 N.E. RAVENNA BLVD.
SEATTLE, WASHINGTON 98115 U.S.A.

NO POSTAGE
NECESSARY
IF MAILED
IN THE
UNITED STATES

life. Participants witness voodoo ceremonies after a full day of snorkeling and skin diving off the village shore. Since no strong currents occur in the Arcadin Cays, divers may leisurely explore the brilliantly lit crystal coral caves. Participants head back to the 45-mile-long wall of La Gonave where they may drift through natural aqueducts worn through the living coral. Participants return by air to Miami. **Cost:** $389 from Port au Prince includes accommodations. **When:** On request. **Contact:** Poseidon Ventures Tours, 359 San Miguel Dr., Newport Beach, CA 92660, USA; phone (714)644-5373.

Jamaica

Jamaican Coral Expedition: A diving project concentrates on one of the last major frontiers of coral reef research—the geology and biology of reef interiors. For periods of 2 weeks, diving teams explore reefs off the coast of Jamaica and Bonaire, taking samples of the many groups of plants and animals that inhabit the internal cavities of reef structure. Divers attempt to discover exactly what animals, which may include sponges, algae, crustacea and mollusks, move in and out of the cavities, what geological traces they left, how they have adapted and how they have affected the evolution of the reefs. Field work in both Jamaica and Bonaire involves short field investigations of coastal, fossilized reef cavities and 2 to 3 daily dives to study living reefs. Diving conditions are agreeable with 80°F water and visibility of more than 120 feet. In Jamaica accommodations are provided at Discovery Bay Marine Labs and in

Bonaire at a private house surrounded by a national park and bird sanctuary. All volunteers must be certified scuba divers. There is ample opportunity for underwater photography, and photographs are always needed to document field work. **Cost:** $775. **When:** July, August. **Contact:** Earthwatch, P.O. Box 127 AG, Belmont, MA 02178, USA; phone (617)489-3030.   **(M)**

Netherlands Antilles

Underwater in the Netherlands Antilles: A marine biologist and NAUI scuba instructor accompany participants to Bonaire for 11 days of diving and snorkeling. Group members meet in Miami, then set up home base in a hotel overlooking the southern Caribbean. For the next 9 days the group dives by day

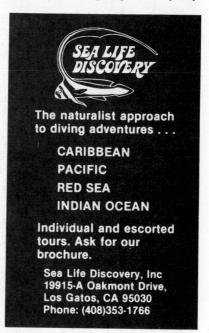

and night amid coral, sponges and schools of friendly fish. Snorkelers follow a similar schedule, though plenty of time is allowed for swimming at white sand beaches, island excursions and photography. On the final day participants have the option of making excursions to Aruba, Curacao and South America or returning to Miami. All trips take a naturalistic approach to diving and offer informal study of marine life with knowledgeable and experienced leaders. **Cost:** $1,115 for divers, $1,025 for snorkelers includes transportation from Miami, meals, accommodations, guides, use of boats, tanks, weight belts, airfills. **When:** June; other times to be announced. **Contact:** Sea Life Discovery, Inc., 19915-A Oakmont Dr., Los Gatos, CA 95030, USA; phone (408)353-1766.   *(M)*

Puerto Rico

San Juan Scuba Sessions: The Caribbean waters around Puerto Rico abound with ancient shipwrecks, hundreds of species of tropical fish and coral beds that divers can enjoy year-round on deep or shallow dives. Participants leave from Puerto Rico aboard a 36-foot charter craft on 5- and 7-day trips to islands such as Vieques, Culebra and the Virgin Islands; none of the islands is very heavily populated, and when the dive boat anchors at night, group members can relax in the secluded setting of a quiet tropical cove. The trips offer a full program of advanced scuba activities including night diving, deep diving and wreck diving, combining fun dives with a loose itinerary of more formal instruction. Participants can upgrade their scuba certi-

fication level during the trips under the supervision of a certified diving instructor. Off the water, divers can experience the night life in San Juan or explore the old sections of the city with a history going back to Columbus. **Cost:** $290 to $390 includes all land and water transportation, accommodations aboard the boat, meals, air, tanks, backpacks, weights. **When:** On request. **Contact:** Caribbean School of Aquatics, Inc., La Concha Hotel, Ashford Ave., P.O. Box 4195, San Juan, PR 00905, USA; phone (809)723-6090, 724-7609 eves.

Puerto Rican Plunge: Scuba lovers spend 7 days exploring coral reefs inhabited by a multitude of tropical fish. The waters of Puerto Rico offer many underwater photographic opportunities, with a visibility factor of 200 feet. Non-divers are also welcome on the trip, and skin diving lessons are available in the hotel pool. Accommodations are in a hotel near La Paguera where 2 meals a day are provided. For scuba divers, the schedule allows 2 dives a day. **Cost:** $490 includes airfare, transportation, entertainment. **When:** July to August. **Contact:** Great Lakes Divers Inc., 244 Niagara Falls Blvd., Tonawanda, NY 14223, USA; phone (716)836-6900.

Submerging in Vieques: Charter diving trips can be arranged with a dive center located on the Caribbean coast of the island of Vieques. Groups of no more than 6 divers set up a home base in the small fishing village of Esperanza, then venture out among growing coral reefs in a 36-foot dive boat. Chances are that the group is the sole scuba expedi-

A diver gears up in a full wet suit before entering the chilly waters of River's Inlet along the rugged British Columbia coast. (Carol Baker)

tion on the island. Participants and instructor/guides determine an itinerary based on the group member's, desires and skills. Diving courses are offered year-round for the total beginner and those at other levels as well. Accommodations are available at 3 guest houses near the beach. **Cost:** $25 for a 2-tank dive, $15 for a single; $10 to $30 a night for accommodations. **When:** Year-round. **Contact:** Vieques Divers, Duffy's Esperanza, Isla Vieques, PR 00765, USA.

West Indies

Caribbean Wreck Diving: Scuba divers spend 7 days exploring old wrecks off the coast of Barbados. Each day divers head out from their onshore accommodations to search for sunken French, English, Spanish and Dutch vessels, using an underwater metal locator. Experienced guides accompany each group; daily itineraries include dives in the mornings and afternoons. Evenings are unscheduled so that participants may explore the island's forts, old plantations, extinct settlements and interior treasure sites. **Cost:** $750 includes room, dinners, airfare from Florida. **When:** June to December. **Contact:**

Adventurers International, 215 E. Horatio Ave., Maitland, FL 32751, USA; phone (305)645-1332. *(M)*

Diving Virgin Waters: Buck Island Reef, a shallow reef 15 to 35 feet down, is one of several locations divers can explore in a number of underwater trips off the waters of St. Croix. U.S. Coast Guard-licensed divers act as guides to various locations with features such as walls, drop-offs, black coral, canyons, ravines, caves and ledges. The crystal-clear waters of the Caribbean offer close-up views of the jacks, snappers, parrotfish, groupers, lobsters and rays which swim here. A basic 3-hour program introduces participants to the area, providing shallow water practice and sufficient experience so that people of any age or physical condition can participate in a supervised reef trip. **Cost:** $23 for guided reef trip, $35 for 3-hour program. **When:** Year-round. **Contact:** Caribbean Sea Adventures, Inc., P.O. Box 3015, Christiansted, St. Croix, VI 00820, USA; phone (809)773-2100, ext. 239.

British Virgin Islands Scuba Dives: A variety of scuba classes and tours is available in the British Virgin Islands for beginning and advanced divers alike. Often divers view schools of amberjack, horse-eye jack, spadefish and glasseye snapper while exploring the warm waters of an ocean area that measures some 30 miles long by 80 miles wide. Although the water is often deep, the distance between some 60 tiny islands is seldom more than a mile or two. Lobsters, turtles and nurse sharks are plentiful, and large rays are also seen frequently in the area. Another attraction for divers is the area's reputation as one of the great undersea graveyards for lost ships. The wreck of the *Rhone* rests here. Temperatures range from 70° to 80°F year-round. Activity is based on Virgin Gorda, which is reached by frequent flights from New York, Miami and other major gateways. Diving/hotel packages are available. **Cost:** $189 to $650 depending on type of accommodation and length of visit. **When:** Year-round. **Contact:** Dive BVI Ltd., Virgin Gorda Yacht Harbor, Virgin Gorda, British Virgin Islands; phone 55513, 55519, 42174.

Diving off St. Vincent: A week-long package provides complete accommodations and daily diving in the Caribbean. The area features clear water and abundant marine life. Non-diving activities available include hiking and visiting the recently active volcano, Soufriere. Diving instruction and certification, from level 1 to level 4, are also offered. All diving equipment may be rented. Trips may also be arranged to nearby islands. **Cost:** From $217 to $243 depending on accommodations and meal plan. **When:** Year-round. **Contact:** Dive St. Vincent Ltd., Box 864, St. Vincent, West Indies. *(M)*

Virgin Islands Scuba Diving: Introductory scuba courses and underwater diving trips in the British Virgin Islands are arranged according to the desires of the divers themselves. The introductory course consists of training on land followed by a shallow-water dive to practice skills. Students dive at over 50 dive sites, including the wreck of

Coral gardens in the mid-Atlantic Bermuda Islands can be explored on snorkel or scuba dives; Dave McLeod's Diving Adventures offers courses and trips for beginning and experienced divers. (Bermuda News Bureau)

the *Rhone,* sunk in 1867. Both underwater photography and marine biology instruction are available by arrangement. Diving tours are conducted under the supervision of certified instructors. In the interest of conservation no spearfishing, lobstering or taking of live coral is permitted. **Cost:** $50 for diving course, $25 to $40 for dive trips includes equipment, boat, guide. **When:** Year-round. **Contact:** Kilbrides Underwater Tours, Box 40, Virgin Gorda, British Virgin Islands; phone 55555 ext. 37. *(M)*

Virgin Islands Scuba Dives: The British Virgin Islands are the setting for scuba tours, instruction and photography. Time spent underwater and locations depend on the experience and desires of divers involved. Depths can vary from 10 to 140 feet in over 60 diving locations, with all activity based on Tortola, British Virgin Islands. Full equipment rentals are available, along with 3-hour instruction periods and underwater photography sessions. For any of the activities available, full gear and equipment are included in package prices. Group rates are available upon request. Dive tours generally last a half day and leave from Road Harbor twice daily. **Cost:** $24 to $40 for scuba tours and instruction; $40 to $475 for photography-oriented trip. **When:** Year-round. **Contact:** Marler Industries Ltd., P.O. Box 108, Roadtown, Tortola, British Virgin Islands; phone 42839.

Diving in Barbados: A wide variety of diving activities is available through a dive center in Barbados. Beginning to advanced level instruction is offered. The trips available range from 1-hour snorkeling trips at a shipwreck and 1-tank dives at nearby reefs to glass-bottomed boat rides. Sailing and water-skiing outings are also available. Most equipment can be rented on location and group rates can be arranged. **Cost:** $2 an hour for snorkeling; $20 for 1-tank dive trips; $5 for glass-bottomed boat trip. **When:** Year-round. **Contact:** Scuba Safari, Hilton Dr., St. Michael, Barbados, West Indies; phone 60621.

St. Thomas and St. Croix Diving: Two trips of 8 and 11 days may be combined into one for a comprehensive Virgin Island experience. The first part centers in and around St. Thomas where travelers stay at a small hillside hotel; from there boat trips can be taken to Sapphire Bay for morning and afternoon boat dives. Time for island sightseeing is provided, as well as an excursion to nearby St. John, a lovely undersea and land park. On the eighth day participants may continue on the second part of the trip to St. Croix. Arriving by seaplane, participants stay in a hotel overlooking the Caribbean. While basic scuba students learn skin and scuba diving skills, experienced divers explore the Cane Bay Drop-off directly in front of the hotel. The underwater park at Buck Island is explored, as is the Frederiksted pier. Photographers may take pictures of a variety of colorful species of tropical fish and sea horses. **Cost:** $855 for divers, $760 for snorkelers for initial 8-day trip; $1,065 for divers, $850 for snorkelers for second 11-day section, less $140 for those participating in first part. **When:** June, July. **Contact:** Sea Life Discovery, Inc., 19915-A Oakmont Dr., Los Gatos, CA 95030, USA; phone (408)353-1766. **(M)**

Above and Below Water: A variety of diving and sailing experiences is offered in Grand Cayman, part of the British West Indies. Basic training is available in both of these sports, as well as expedition equipment for those interested in exploring the surrounding waters. Scuba diving classes last 6 days and offer full certification. Day and half-day trips are available in which divers observe the tropical fish and coral. A 40-foot motor sailboat can also be chartered for a moonlight cruise with dinner served onboard, or for inter-island trips of 3 days or longer. Individual sailboats can be used for individual itineraries. **Cost:** $187 for 6-day scuba course, $8 an hour for sailing instruction; other prices on request. **When:** Year-round. **Contact:** Surfside Watersports, P.O. Box 26, Grand Cayman, British West Indies; phone 9-2724.

Scuba Courses in the Caribbean: Beginning and experienced divers visiting the Virgin Islands can upgrade their scuba techniques and certification levels in courses that cover basic instruction and work up to skills at the divemaster's level. The basic scuba certification course involves 24 hours of instruction spread out over 6 days, with time divided between classroom sessions and actual diving experience near Coki Point. From there, students go on to open water and night diving courses, or they can choose from a variety of guided scuba tours through the coral forests of the reef off St. Thomas or to shipwrecks along the coast. **Cost:** $75 to $300 for courses includes all transportation to dive sites, all equipment. **When:** On request. **Contact:** Virgin Islands Diving School, P.O. Box 9707, St. Thomas, VI 00801, USA; phone (809)774-8687.

CENTRAL AMERICA

Belize

Cruising Belize: Based on a fleet of 3 cruise boats, divers spend 6 days cruising and diving in the clear waters around Belize. Participants are met at the airport in Belize City and transfer to the docks where the cruise boats are waiting staffed with a captain, mate and chef. Tanks, compressors, weightbelts and weights are provided. Diving begins that same day at one of the many sites that have been selected off the second largest barrier reef in the world. Photographers find excellent conditions and specimens at Long Caye on Lighthouse Reef. Turneffe Reef offers shallow water and deep drop-offs and ravines. Time is spent exploring an under-water cavern known as the Blue Hole. The site and its huge stalactites have been made legend by Jacques Cousteau. The last night of the trip is spent onshore, and after a farewell breakfast the next morning, participants depart for the airport. Arrangements can be made for those who want to stay on an extra day to visit the Mayan ruins in Belize. **Cost:** $499 from Belize includes transportation, meals, accommodations, tanks, air, cruiseboats. **When:** June. **Contact:** Atlantis Safaris, P.O. Box 530303, Miami Shores, FL 33153, USA; phone (305)754-7480.

Caribbean Barrier Reef Diving: The world's longest, "living" barrier reef is only a half-mile off Ambergris Cay, a 26-mile-long island in the Caribbean. Here divers can create their own customized diving experience with the assistance of experienced local divers. Adventurers reach the island by small plane or boat from Belize and stay at a comfortable rustic hotel bordered by white beaches and tropical jungle. Certified divers have access to waters with visibility up to 250 feet, reef canyons, holes and special "blue holes" reached by float plane. Participants need only bring lightweight gear since tanks, belts, packs, weights, fins, snorkels and even boats can be rented. Protected snorkeling inside the great barrier reef, underwater photography, beachcombing, deep sea fishing for tarpon, marlin and barracuda and bird watching are other activities which trip members may enjoy. Local guides are available for interests ranging from coastal exploration and jungle trekking to high sea adventures. The nearby ancient fishing village of San Pedro along with the native cuisine reflect the Mayan, Spanish and British influences on the island culture. **Cost:** $35 for single room, $60 for double includes meals. **When:** Year-round. **Contact:** Casa Solana, Rt. 1, Box 40 Palacios, TX 77465, USA; phone (512)972-3314. *(M)*

Gulf of Honduras Scuba: The second longest barrier reef in the world can be explored off the coast of Belize on a series of dives in the Gulf of Honduras. Diving trips for a minimum of 8 divers are offered including a 4-dive trip in local waters and a 2-day trip to the famous Belizean blue hole for 2 compression dives. Caves, drop-offs and wrecks are explored, and an abundance of native Caribbean marine life can be seen and photographed. Opportunities are also available to dive at Turneffe Island and its 250-fathom coral drop-offs. **Cost:** $50 to $65 a day includes 3 meals, tanks, air, backpacks, weights. **Contact:** Club 99 Scuba-Belize, P.O. Box 164, Belize City, Belize.

Cay Aquarius: Divers explore the Caribbean in week-long trips to an island 15 miles from the coast of Belize. A 176-mile-long reef a mile from the island provides a variety of underwater attractions. The water temperature is 85°F year-round. Non-divers may avail themselves of resort facilities, including a sailboat; inland trips to the Mayan ruins of Altun Ha may also be arranged. Diving trips to the Cayman Islands and the Bahamas and scuba lessons from beginning to advanced are also offered. **Cost:**

$620 from New Orleans includes all costs. **When:** August. **Contact:** John the Diver, Inc., Star Rt. 1, Box 459, Table Rock Lake, Branson, MO 65616, USA; phone (417)338-2224.

Offshore Sail and Dive Expedition: After a visit to the recently discovered Mayan ruins of Altun Ha, trip members sail from Belize to explore the world's second longest barrier reef. During the 2-week trip divers explore the famous Blue Hole of Lighthouse Reef and visit the ancient Mayan seaport of Tulum, stopping en route at isolated bays and on the offshore reefs of Banco Chinchorro. On a sail to Key West, participants learn the art of celestial navigation. There are many opportunities for individual explorations of beaches, coves and the underwater terrain. **Cost:** $890. **When:** May. **Contact:** Oceanus, P.O. Box 431, Hohokus, NJ 07423, USA; phone (201)447-0393. *(M)*

Ambergris Cay Underwater Caving: Northeast of Belize City, the small island of Ambergris Cay is the launching point for sailing, snorkeling and scuba diving in warm Caribbean waters. The second largest barrier reef in the world lies a quarter mile off the white sand beaches that extend from the hotel/dive center where travelers stay. Inexperienced divers can snorkel and free dive in shallow, protected waters alive with tropical fish. Visibility is seldom less than 50 feet and caves, cuts, drop-offs and coral forests are all accessible. The fish are easy to approach, and divers equipped with underwater cameras can get close-ups without special lenses. With almost 500 species of birds in Belize, bird watchers have a chance to see some unique forms such as the great curassow, the keel-billed toucan and jabiru stork. Special trips can be arranged for ornithologists. **Cost:** $18 to $35 for accommodations, meals; $55 for full day, $35 for half-day includes boat rental for 4 persons. **When:** Year-round. **Contact:** Paradise House Hotel, P.O. Box 888, Belize City, Belize; phone 2403.

Barrier Reef Sink: Divers spend 8 days in and around the waters off Belize. For 6 nights participants stay at Glover's Reef Village, a simple resort approximately 35 miles off the coast of Belize and removed from the outside world. On the atoll one may find a great deal of freedom, privacy and extraordinary diving opportunities: a 50-foot-deep protected lagoon and a 2,000-foot drop-off from the reef to the deep. The final 2 nights of the journey are spent in Belize City where participants stay at a hotel and may dive near the beaches. The equipment provided includes tank, fills, weights, boat and guide. **Cost:** $319 plus meals, airfare. **When:** Year-round. **Contact:** Scubaplus, 201 E. 34th St., New York, NY 10016, USA; phone (212)689-0035.

(M)

Honduras

Diving the Gulf Stream: Clearwater diving enthusiasts stay at a resort on the island of Roatan off the coast of Honduras and make dives on either side of a barrier reef whose outer edge is washed by Gulf Stream waters. Visitors discover a variety of caves, ledges, passes, tunnels, eel holes, tropical fish and coral species on their scuba explorations, with guides suggest-

Barracuda, dolphins, turtles and tropical fish can be seen on boat dives near reefs in the Red Sea, where the water is warm and clear year-round. (Sea Life Discovery)

ing spots likely to be of interest. The island, largest of the Honduran Bay Islands, was once a hide-out for pirates, and divers are encouraged to watch for signs of undiscovered shipwrecks. Since the barrier reef is still an unspoiled undersea environment, divers are prohibited from coral picking, live shelling or using spear guns when they explore it. Land-based activities on the 33-mile-long island include room, meals, boats, guides, snorkeling equipment, small sailboats, transportation to and from Roatan Airport. **When:** Year-round. **Contact:** Anthony's Key Resort, P.O. Box 18412, Dallas, TX 75218, USA; phone (214)328-4244.

Island Deep: Divers and non-divers alike travel to the island of Roatan for a 7-day scuba diving tour. Located just off the Caribbean shore of Honduras, Roatan has waters from 20 to 130 feet in depth with a visibility range of 100 to 200 feet. Divers travel to such areas as West End Rock, a small, well-protected cove with its own 100-foot wall dropping into the depths. West Bay Reef is also accessible for night dives; it is an area teeming with nocturnal life not seen in most inland waters. Accommodations are provided at Spyglass Hill Resort, where non-divers may play tennis, go horseback riding or go reef fishing. Deep-sea fishing and bone fishing are also available. **Cost:** $599 for divers, $525 for non-divers includes accommodations, meals, airfare from New York, 2 dives a day. **When:** July. **Contact:**

Atlantis Divers World, 500 Ave. of the Americas, New York, NY 10011, USA; phone (212)242-1786 or 242-1757.

Studying Sunlight in Coral Reefs: Members of a research team study the relationship of transmitted sunlight at various depths of reef with photosynthetic rates of several marine algae along the island of Utila, one of 3 inhabited bay islands off the Caribbean coast of Honduras. Participants 16 to 24 years old study tropical marine life for 2 weeks while diving or snorkeling. The research has been in progress for the past 3 years. Expedition members become familiar with the life of the coral reef ecosystem through observation and discussion. **Cost:** $550. **When:** July, August. **Contact:** Expedition Training Institute, Inc., P.O. Box 171, Prudential Ctr. Sta., Boston, MA 02199, USA; phone (617)922-0577. *(M)*

Coral Reef Diving: The exploration of a spectacular variety of coral, sponge and fish life is readily available off the shore of Roatan in the Caribbean. Anthony's Key Resort, where accommodations are arranged for 7 nights, is midway between 20 miles of coral reef. There are at least 30 distinct diving areas within 15 minutes of the resort. Among these is West End Point where there is an abundance of colorful sponges, groupers and angel fish. At Bear's Den, an opening in about 30 feet of water leads to a 200-foot complex of caves and caverns. Each morning, divers and guides meet to pick that day's dive spots. The package also includes a night dive, sailing and horseback

riding. Airfare is not included and participants must provide mask, fins, and regulator. **Cost:** $359 for divers, $269 for non-divers. **When:** March. **Contact:** Go Diving, Inc., 715 Florida Ave. S., Minneapolis, MN 55426, USA; phone (612)544-7168. *(M)*

Diving at Cayos Cochinos: A remote resort on a 1-square-mile island serves as the center for reef diving. The island is surrounded by more than 100 square miles of reefs, coves and drop-offs, most of them unexplored. Usually 2 dives are

556 / UNDERWATER ADVENTURES

made daily, either from boats or the beach. Other activities include excursions to uninhabited keys in the area, night boat trips and barbeques. Reservations should be made 6 months in advance. **Cost:** $35 a day includes accommodations, meals, all dives, equipment, guides, excursions. **When:** Year-round. **Contact:** Plantation Beach Resort, Cayos Cochinos, Apartado No. 10, La Ceiba, Honduras.

Islas de la Bahia Diving: A resort on the Roatan Bay Islands, off the north coast of Honduras, offers scuba and skin diving, snorkeling and swimming opportunities. Divers and non-divers alike may enjoy other activities such as boating, hiking, horseback riding and studying Mayan archaeology. A 32-mile-long reef protects the area, and the islands are virtually free of insects. The average temperature varies between 81°F in the day and 69°F in the night, with the water temperature at 80°F. **Cost:** $30 to $55 a day depending on accommodations and time of year includes meals, equipment. **When:** Year-round. **Contact:** Spyglass Hill, c/o Roseo Affiliates, 630 N. Western Ave., Lake Forest, IL 60045, USA; phone (312)234-2222.   *(M)*

Panama

Panamanian Plunge: Scuba divers explore the waters off the isthmus for 10 days. Starting from Baltimore, the group flies to Panama City for a 2-day stay at the El Panama Hotel. Then 7 days are spent on Isla Grande exploring its coral-filled waters. Starting from around 40 feet below the surface, the reefs run mainly to black coral

areas that teem with tropical fish. Fishing is included, as is a New Year's Eve party and a tour of the Miraflores Locks. Two tank dives a day are scheduled; air refills are unlimited. The group returns to Baltimore on the tenth day. **Cost:** $749 includes airfare, meals on Isla Grande, accommodations. **When:** December. **Contact:** Diver's Den, Inc., 8105 Harford Rd., Baltimore, MD 21234, USA; phone (301)668-6866 or 668-6869.

EUROPE
Yugoslavia

Diving Dubrovnik: Dubrovnik lies on the shores of the Adriatic Sea in southwestern Yugoslavia, a region whose islands, undersea rock formations and marine life have rarely been explored by divers. Visitors depart from New York and fly to Yugoslavia, spending 6 days at a hotel in Dubrovnik; guides and boats are available through the resort for an added fee. Visitors committed to land activities can take sightseeing tours through the area that provide insights into Dubrovnik's history. **Cost:** $629 includes roundtrip airfare from New York, accommodations, continental breakfasts; $27 extra includes boat, guide, diving equipment. **When:** September to October. **Contact:** Scubaplus, 201 E. 34th St., New York, NY 10016, USA; phone (212)689-0035.   *(M)*

INDIAN OCEAN
Maldives

Spice Islands Diving: Living

aboard a 74-foot motor sailboat with a crew of 10, divers have the opportunity to experience the rich diving region of the Maldive Islands off the southwest coast of India. Diving sites include the steep outer slopes where big pelagics drift by, shallow coral gardens resplendent with a myriad of tropical fish, and passes where sharks gather. Land exploration takes place on Sri Lanka, with visits to tea plantations in the mountains, the Sigirya fortress and Polommaruwa, site of a sophisticated civilization 800 years ago. **Cost:** $1,450 plus airfare includes all expenses aboard the boat. **When:** August. **Contact:** See and Sea Travel Service, Inc., 680 Beach St., Suite 340, Wharfside,

San Francisco, CA 94109, USA; phone (415)771-0077. *(M)*

MEXICO

Quintana Roo

Diving off Cozumel: A variety of rates and services is available for diving around Palancar Reef, off the island of Cozumel. Depths from Palancar Reef range from 30 to 2,000 feet along a drop-off, with visibility up to 200 feet. Rising as high as 60 feet from the bottom, coral heads provide the backdrop for the rich undersea life of the Caribbean. Dives are made daily, and all equipment is available for rent. A package rate can be ar-

A diver takes aim with her camera as a gray angelfish poses near the Palancar Reef off Cozumel, Mexico. (Kent Schellenger)

ranged with the local hotel, and group rates are available for 8 or more people. Night dives may be arranged, as well as short expeditions to nearby Mayan ruins. **Cost:** $22 a day covers 2 tanks, lunch, refreshments. **When:** Year-round. **Contact:** Aqua Safari, S.A., Box A.P. 41, Cozumel, Quintana Roo, Mexico; phone 2-01-01.

Yucatan Scuba Trips: Cozumel, on the Caribbean edge of the Yucatan Peninsula, is the setting for 4- to 9-day diving excursions that combine scuba lessons with guided dives along the coastal reefs. Arriving from Houston, enthusiasts dive areas such as Palancar Reef or Santa Rosa Reef, a spectacular wall dive down a steep ocean slope. Water temperatures remain around 75°F, with a 200-foot visibility that provides good conditions for underwater photographers. Novices may take a complete scuba course in Cozumel during trips of 7 days or longer; skills are practiced in Chancanab Lagoon, followed by classroom sessions and beach dives. The last 2 days of the course involve check-out dives off the boat. Divers should bring all their own equipment except for tanks and weights, which are provided. **Cost:** $239 to $325 includes roundtrip airfare from Houston, tanks, weights, lunch on diving days, guide, boat. **When:** April to December. **Contact:** Blue Water Diving School, 910 Westheimer, Houston, TX 77006, USA; phone (713)528-0634.

Sunken Ship Exploration: There are an estimated 200 wrecks in the Mexican territorial waters of the Gulf of Mexico and the Caribbean

Sea. Based on records found in the archives of the Spanish Navy, about 20 wrecks have been found, most of which are located on the Chinchorra Bank Reef. An expedition to further the archaeological work in this area lasts 2 weeks. The expedition visits known wreck sites and engages in excavation, recovery operations and exploration of new sites. The Chinchorra Bank Reef lies just below the surface 25 miles east of Xoalak, a fishing village located at the southernmost tip of Quintana Roo, by the border which separates Mexico from Belize. The easterly rim consists of some of the most beautifully formed coral reefs in the world. Caverns, tunnels and cul-de-sacs created by centuries of coral growths give the reef an unearthly beauty. Headquarters for the expedition is a modern scientific complex at Akumal, Mexico. **Cost:** On request. **When:** July. **Contact:** CEDAM Internlas, TX 75224, USA.

Diving Palancar: Spectacular Palancar Reef, off Cozumel, is explored daily on a week-long dive trip. Staying in a beach-front hotel and taking meals there or in town, participants depart from the dock each morning at about 9:30 and travel out to the reef, which offers a wide variety of diving spots within a short distance. Palancar is a huge reef with giant pinnacles, 100-foot walls covered by sponges and gorgonians and numerous caves and arches; one area of the reef off Santa Rosa Beach is famous for its large schools of rays. Divers can either explore the reef's interior or "drift dive" along its outer edge, being carried gently along by the current. In addition, a few minutes' walk from the hotel is shallow Little Paradise Reef, where wade-in diving reveals a fascinating closed ecological system in an isolated coral outcropping. **Cost:** On request. **When:** On request. **Contact:** Go Diving, Inc., 715 Florida Ave. S., Minneapolis, MN 55426, USA; phone (612)644-7168. *(M)*

Reef Diving off Cozumel: Accommodations are provided at a hotel on the beach during a week of diving in the reefs off the Caribbean island of Cozumel. After a day of snorkeling or swimming, participants meet to discuss with a guide the upcoming diving trips, diving safety, buddy arrangements and boat routine. Divers find coral reef fish and shells in the shallow Palancar Reef and deeper down find dozens of varieties, shapes and colors of sponges. Diving boats anchor at a new section of the reef every day, allowing divers to explore the area of sharply sloping drop-offs. The trip provides excellent opportunities for underwater photography. **Cost:** $600 from Cozumel includes accommodations, guides, meals, boats, tanks, weights, backpacks. **When:** Year-round. **Contact:** See and Sea Travel Service, Inc., 680 Beach St., Suite 340, Wharfside, San Francisco, CA 94109, USA; phone (415)771-0077. *(M)*

Palancar Plunge: Participants fly to the island of Cozumel for 8 days of diving, snorkeling, beachcombing and island roaming. Staying at a beach-front hotel south of the town of San Miguel, divers board dive boats and head out for a day along Palancar Reef. The reef extends along the coast for 7 miles, forming pinnacles that drop into sheer walls covered with sponges and gorgonians. Divers drift along the outer edge or, protected from the currents, find coral formations in 35 to 60 feet of water. Weather permitting, the group journeys across the

A scuba diver makes her way amid tropical fish across an undersea coral field off the coast of Tahiti. (Carl Roessler/See and Sea Travel)

channel to Akumal on the Yucatan mainland for 2 days of diving and the opportunity to explore the wreck of an 18th-century Spanish galleon. An unstructured day for roaming around Cozumel precedes the return flight home. **Cost:** $375 for divers, $339 for non-divers includes transportation from Cozumel, meals, accommodations, daily dive trips. **When:** June to November. **Contact:** Sunland International Tours, 8677 Wilshire Blvd., Beverly Hills, CA 90211, USA; phone (213)657-3472.

Yucatan

Diving the Caribe: The Mexican Caribe from Cancun to Tulun is the location for an 8-day scuba diving trip commencing at Merida. The first day is spent touring Merida's monuments, including the Cathedral, the Casa de Montejo and the Museum, and visiting the ruins at Dzibilchaltun. The next day participants fly to Cancun where they spend 5 days diving. Two tanks are provided for diving each day, and there is also 1 night dive. Accommodations are at a hotel. An optional day trip visits Tulun Ruins and Xel-Ha Cove for snorkeling. **Cost:** $277 to $383 includes all scuba gear, boat accommodations, meals. **When:** Year-round. **Contact:** Kel, S.A. Travel Bureau, Paseo Montejo, No. 470, Merida, Yucatan, Mexico; phone 2-64-53.

MIDDLE EAST

Israel

Gulf of Aqaba Diving: Participants explore coral reefs in the Gulf of Aqaba, north of the Red Sea in either of two 7-day diving trips. These reefs are distinguished by the abundance of large umbrella corals and lavishly colored soft corals, and lionfish are present in large numbers. Both trips start with 2 days diving in the Neviot area, using the facilities of the Neviot Diving Center. From here members of the Ras Abu Galum trip proceed to the reefs of Hibiek, Suchoon, Ras Mamlach and Ras Abu Galum; on the Ras Muhammed trip members dive at Dhabab Oasis, Nabec Oasis, Sharm el Sheikh and Ras Muhammed. **Cost:** $300 for Ras Abu Galum, $330 for Ras Muhammed includes transportation from Elat, accommodations, guides, equipment, most meals. **When:** Year-round. **Contact:** Neviot Diving Center, Neviot Holiday Village, Neviot Post Elat, Israel; phone 059-3667. *(M)*

Red Sea Diving: An 18-day trip to Israel is highlighted by spectacular diving in the Red Sea at Sharm El Sheikh. Coral reefs start just below the surface and drop vertically for thousands of feet. Clouds of wildly colored fish are everywhere, while sharks and an occasional manta pass by. Excellent opportunities exist for photography and undersea life observation. Snorkelers also find the cool waters of the Red Sea rewarding because of excellent visibility. The twice-daily dives are made at varying sites. A few days are set aside for sightseeing in Tel Aviv and Jerusalem. **Cost:** $2,325 includes roundtrip airfare from New York, double-occupancy accommodations, some meals. **When:** October. **Contact:** Sea Life Discovery Underwater Exploration,

A group of divers exploring the wreck of the Woodburn *off Fiji is framed in coral-covered steel girders. Scubahire Ltd. outfits divers for as little as $4 a day for tank rental. (Scubahire)*

19915-A, Oakmont Dr., Los Gatos, CA 95030, USA; phone (408)353-1766. **(M)**

Jordan

Aqaba Aquatics: Divers spend 2 weeks exploring land and sea in the Gulf of Aqaba region of the Middle East. After an overnight stay in the Jordanian capital of Amman, the group flies to Aqaba for a visit to Wadi Rum, once the stronghold of Lawrence of Arabia. Local trips on camelback are taken before return to Aqaba and an orientation meeting. Daily dives begin early in the morning on local fishing boats that anchor in water 20 to 80 feet deep; the dives are long and leisurely, with constant opportunity for underwater photography. A day-long outing is taken to Petra, a rock-cut city with only 1 entrance; riding Arabian ponies, participants pass through a narrow passage to view the carved tombs of the ancient Nabateans, some of which have cliffside facades 200 feet high. The last 4 days of the trip are mostly spent underwater. A final feast, or "Mensel," is held in traditional Arabian fashion. **Cost:** $2,000 includes accommodations, meals, guides, tanks, weight belts, land transportation from Amman. **When:** May, October. **Contact:** See and Sea Travel Service, Inc., 680 Beach St., Suite 340, Wharfside, San Francisco, CA 94109, USA; phone (415)771-0077. **(M)**

PACIFIC
Fiji

Scuba Diving off Fiji: Diving is available on a day-to-day or extended basis in the wide variety of reefs and holes around Fiji. Frequent trips are made to the water surrounding the Beqa Barrier Reef and the Lau Group, renowned for its high visibility, abundance of marine life and uncrowded conditions.

Diving may also be done from the beach. All equipment is available for hire, from tanks and regulators to charter boats and a decompression chamber. **Cost:** $4 a day, $15 a week for tanks. **When:** Year-round. **Contact:** Scubahire Ltd., GPO Box 777, Suva, Fiji; phone 361-241. *(M)*

Diving in the Fiji Islands: For 17 days divers explore the waters around Mana and Taveuni islands, which only recently acquired diving facilities. Participants spend full diving days at Rainbow Reef on Taveuni Island, whose 19-mile-long coral structure remains largely unexplored. The reef face is a precipitous drop-off interlaced with crevices, caverns and large overhangs. Sea life is bountiful, and over the drop-off are found jacks, turtles, groupers and a few sharks. After a crossing to Mana Island, divers lunch in the afternoon and snorkel in the waters offshore. The next 4 days offer opportunities to dive to a dozen or more local reefs that rise to within 15 to 20 feet of the surface and drop to a sandy bottom at about 100 to 150 feet. On the last day participants return by ferry to Lautoka for a dinner and a late night flight back home. **Cost:** $1,500 plus airfare. **When:** On request. **Contact:** See and Sea Travel Service, Inc., 680 Beach St., Suite 340, Wharfside, San Francisco, CA 94109, USA; phone (415)771-0077. *(M)*

French Polynesia

Moorea Plunge: Divers travel to the Tahitian islands on a 7- to 10-day excursion. Starting from Papeete, participants catch a flight to the island of Moorea, where divers explore the deep coves and coral barrier reefs surrounding the island. Above water, activities include hiking to native villages, snorkeling, fishing, sailing and taking glass-bottomed boat tours. Divers should bring a lightweight wetsuit, regulator, fins, mask, snorkel, depth gauge and buoyance compensator. **Cost:** $420 to $595 includes meals, accommodations, 1 dive a day. **When:** May to September. **Contact:** Bay Travel Diving Adventures, 2435 E. Coast Hwy., Corona del Mar, CA 92625, USA; phone (714)675-4321. *(M)*

Society Diving Cruise: A 14-day diving trip begins with an 8-day sailing cruise through the northwestern areas of the Society Islands; the second part of the trip is

spent diving in the Tuamotus. On the third day participants board a 58-foot yacht and set sail, anchoring at dive sites during the day and sailing during the morning and evening. Islands along the route are Huahine, Raiatea, Tahaa, Bora Bora and possibly Maupiti. Dive sites include shallow lagoons and deep outside reefs with high visibility and large ocean fish. The cruise ends in Bora Bora, where participants are flown back to Papeete and then to Rangiroa in the Tuamotus where they spend the remaining 4 days. An unusual feature of the area is a narrow pass through which the incoming tide rushes at speeds of 8 to 12 knots; qualified divers may drift through it at depths of 30 to 70 feet and observe sea life from reef fish to turtles and porpoises. Finally the group flies back to Papeete to connect with a return flight to Los Angeles. **Cost:** $2,000 from Papeete, Tahiti includes transportation, accommodations, meals, tanks, equipment. **When:** June. **Contact:** See and Sea Travel Service, Inc., 680 Beach St., Suite 340, Wharfside, San Francisco, CA 94109, USA; phone (415)771-0077. *(M)*

Hawaii

Diving the Aloha State: A complete, 5-day open-water diving course provides 10 ocean dives including an inter-island boat dive. The clear, warm waters allow a pleasurable learning experience and opportunities to dive the islands of Maui, Lanai, Molokai, Kahoolawe and Molokini. The 42-foot custom dive boat *Odysseus* is available for inter-island charters, which include 3 tanks, backpack, weights, guides and lunch. Also available is a dive to the sunken 311-foot submarine *USS Bluegill*, and snorkeling instruction among Maui's shallow underwater grottos. **Cost:** $43 for inter-island diving, $26 for introductory instruction. $18 for *USS Bluegill* dives. **When:** Year-round. **Contact:** Central Pacific Divers, 780 Front Street, Lanaina, Maui, HI 96761, USA; phone (808)661-4661.

Diving Kauai: Kauai has more unspoiled reefs than any of the other islands of Hawaii. Operating out of Nawiliwili harbor, divers can explore the island's reefs and sea life on a series of dive tours. On a special package tour a group of divers may take their Basic Scuba Diver Course and PADI Ocean Diver and/or NAUI Sport Diver Certifications. Or divers may choose to take private lessons or an intensive scuba diving course lasting 1 to 2 weeks. Charters for fishing and water-skiing are also available. **Cost:** $55 for package tour includes hotel, equipment, dives; $100 to $150 for private lessons. **When:** Year-round. **Contact:** Garden Island Marine, RR Box 180-B, Lihue, Kauai, HI 96766, USA; phone (808)245-6361.

Kona Coast Diving: Scuba divers explore the undersea slopes off the western shore of the island of Hawaii, making either 2 or 3 dives depending on whether half- or full-day boat charters are arranged. Divers have freedom to choose their own spots, but advice on good diving locales is available from guides who try to put divers in places well suited to their interests. Group sizes can range from 1 to 24

Divers often carry underwater camera gear and lights for probing murky waters. (Hong Kong Tourist Bureau)

in a party, with an outfitted Boston Whaler outboard available for smaller groups. Novices are also welcome, either as observers or students; 5-hour and 30-hour instructional courses are offered to those who wish to learn scuba diving. **Cost:** $25 to $45 for boat charters includes diving gear, lunch; $50 to $250 for diving courses. **When:** On request. **Contact:** Havaiki, RR 1, Box 54, Kailua-Kona, HI 96740, USA.

Islands Diving Cruise: Divers visit up to 5 of the Hawaiian Islands on diving trips lasting 2 to 7 days. The islands, including Hawaii, Molokai, Maui and Lanai, are famous for their underwater cathedrals. Molokini, a small uninhabited island, features an extinct volcano suitable for swimming and diving. From an equipped dive boat, participants swim in 15 to 75 feet of water. Experienced divers can take deeper and more technical dives which include exploration of a sunken submarine at 130 feet and underwater caves. **Cost:** $209 to $595 all-inclusive. **When:** Year-round. **Contact:** Pacific Sportdiving Co.,

Inc., 4104 E. Anaheim St., Long Beach, CA 90804, USA; phone (213)433-7485. *(M)*

Diving and Snorkeling off Maui: Scuba orientation programs are designed to introduce beginning divers to the warm and clear waters of the Hawaiian Islands under close supervision by certified diving instructors. Dives are scheduled off the coast of Maui and the other islands of the chain. Snorkeling is available on a daily basis, with instruction provided on both beach and boat trips. All trips last half a day. **Cost:** $30 for orientation program and dives; $10 and $15 for snorkeling includes hotel pickup, equipment. **When:** Year-round. **Contact:** Skindiving Hawaii, P.O. Box 917, Kihei, Maui, HI 96753, USA; phone (808)879-1558.

South Seas Scuba: Beginning and advanced divers take a half or full day to practice underwater work before setting out from the island of Oahu for the waters off various beaches. For beginners Hanauma Bay provides an opportunity to practice the basics in shallow water; instructors review techniques on the beach, then take participants out. The more experienced divers may leave on a boat for deeper waters on a half-day, 2-dive trip to deeper water. A full-day trip is also offered for experienced divers; the boat leaves from Pokai Bay and works its way to the underwater caves at Makaha. Each trip includes free transportation from the divers' hotels. **Cost:** $30 for half-day, $60 for full-day. **When:** Year-round. **Contact:** South Seas Aquatics, 1125

Ala Moana Blvd., Honolulu, HI 96814, USA; phone (808)538-3854.

Underwater Behavioral Studies: Two weeks are spent diving in Kaneohe Bay learning how fish adapt to their environment, with an emphasis on locomotion techniques of various species. Participants collect live specimens for laboratory analyses, including several unusual species captured at lower depths. Underwater behavioral observations and photographs are made on variations and specializations of locomotor activity in selected species. Group members must be experienced scuba divers with their own equipment and qualified for special certification at a depth of 30 feet. A knowledge of underwater photography or marine biology is desirable. Team members are lodged in a rented house on Oahu Island. The assembly point is Honolulu. **Cost:** $750. **When:** July, August. **Contact:** University Research Expeditions Program, University of California, M-19 Wheeler Hall, Berkeley, CA 94720, USA; phone (415)642-6586. *(M)*

Micronesia

South Pacific Plunge: Divers depart from Seattle for 15 days of diving and travel through Guam, Palau and Truk. Escorted by a diving guide, participants stay in hotels and are provided with tanks, air, backpack and weights. For 1 day divers explore the massive submerged mountain and fringed coral reefs that lie off the coast of Guam. Palau offers views of large sea fans, giant clams weighing a half ton, rare species of colorful Indo-Pacific fish and a wide variety of coral.

After 4 days of diving in Palau, the group journeys to Micronesia for another 4 days of wreck diving. The water in Truk Lagoon is 85°F, and its surface is dotted with dozens of palm-laden islands. Divers encounter the legacy of World War II scattered on the sea floor: tankers, planes, battleships and submarines. The journey ends with the return flight to Seattle. **Cost:** $1,633 for divers, $1,214 for non-divers includes transportation from Seattle, accommodations, guide. **When:** June. **Contact:** Lighthouse Dive 'N Ski, 350 Sunset Blvd. N., Renton, WA 98055, USA; phone (206)772-1415.

Micronesia Underseas: Fifteen-day journeys to the diving areas of Palau and Truk islands bring scuba enthusiasts to waters featuring tropical coral reefs, graveyards of sunken Japanese warships, caves and giant clams that weigh nearly a half ton. At Palau, an atoll measuring about 62 miles long and 12 miles wide, participants explore a lagoon filled with 350 tiny islands that form a pattern of waterways, canals and secluded beaches. At Truk divers enter artificial reefs containing more than 40 ships of the Imperial Japanese fleet, including the *Fijikawa Maru*, a 436-foot aircraft ferry. **Cost:** $750 to $900 includes accommodations; airfare extra. **When:** June to September. **Contact:** Poseidon Venture Tours, 359 San Miguel Dr., Newport Beach, CA 92660, USA; phone (714)644-5373.

Micronesian Plunge: Divers spend 15 days exploring the lagoons and open water around the islands of Truk and Ponape in the South Seas region. Truk was the scene of an enormous battle in World War II; over 64 ships and 250 aircraft of the Imperial Japanese Fourth Fleet lie intact beneath the water. The island of Ponape, to the southeast, is surrounded by atolls with deep cuts, black coral and steep submarine walls. In the mangrove swamps participants investigate the ruins of an ancient civilization whose origins and endings remain a mystery; one of the only clues rests in the presence of millions of basalt crystal logs, some of which weigh up to 25 tons. **Cost:** $1,595. **When:** June. **Contact:** Silent World Divers, Inc., 14444 SE Eastgate Wy., Bellevue, WA 98007, USA; phone (206)747-8842.

Island Aquatics: Scuba fans spend 8 or 11 days exploring the underwater reaches of the mid-Pacific islands. The 8-day tour begins with a flight from Los Angeles to Honolulu. The next day travelers press on to Majuro, where 5 days are spent fishing, snorkeling, sailing, kayaking, canoeing and scuba diving. Several of the adjacent islands are explored, and the schedule is kept loose to allow plenty of time for activities. Return is then made to Los Angeles via Honolulu. The 11-day excursions involve either 9 days on Majuro or a twofold journey including 5 days on Majuro and 4 days on Truk. Divers visiting Truk have the opportunity to inspect the over 100 Japanese ships of the Imperial Fourth Fleet sunk off the island during World War II. **Cost:** $490 to $515 for adults for 8 days; $680 to $710 for adults for 11 days; airfare, diving expenses extra. **When:** Year-round. **Contact:** Western River Expeditions, 3639 MacIntosh Ln., Salt Lake City, UT 84121, USA; phone (801)942-6669.

SOUTH AMERICA
Colombia

Colombian Sea Dive: Divers on a tropical venture spend 7 days on the Caribbean island of San Andres. Full accommodations at an inn or hotel provide participants with comfort at night while they spend their days diving in such areas as the Blue Hole or in deep caves and near steep drop-offs. A total of 8 dives is planned in the package, including 1 night dive. The equipment supplied includes a belt, weights, tank, backpack, fills, a boat and a guide. Casinos, restaurants and a variety of night life are available. **Cost:** $239 plus airfare. **When:** Year-round. **Contact:** Scubaplus, 201 E. 34th St., New York, NY 10016, USA; phone (212)689-0035.

(M)

Ecuador

Underwater Archipelago Wandering: Undersea life is as spectacular and unusual as terrestrial creatures seen by divers spending 18 days exploring the Galapagos Islands. After a day in Quito, participants fly to Baltra Island and board the 70-foot staysail schooner, *Encantada.* The diving ranges from shallow reefs to sheer pinnacles rising from the sea floor. Accompanied by a professional dive master and local naturalist, participants

have the chance to investigate it all in 1 to 3 daily dives; they make 1 or 2 shore excursions every day and maximize time ashore and underwater by frequent night sailings. Near Punta Vicente Roca on Isabela Island, divers spot whales and giant ocean sunfish and explore a large cave filled with brilliantly colored gorgonia, sea anemone, coral and a bright yellow species of black coral. Participants spend 1 night ashore and make frequent day trips to hike and visit places such as the Darwin Research Station in Academy Bay which houses giant land tortoises. An overnight stay in Quito concludes the trip. **Cost:** $2,000 from Quito includes transportation, meals, accommodations, guides, tanks, backpacks, weights. **When:** March, June. **Contact:** See and Sea Travel Service Inc., 680 Beach St., Suite 340, Wharfside, San Francisco, CA 94109, USA; phone (415)771-0077.

(M)

UNITED STATES
Alaska

Sub-Arctic Scuba: Diving courses at the University of Alaska and weekend trips to coastal diving locations provide the hardy undersea enthusiast with opportunities to explore Alaska's offshore regions. The best diving is around Seward, but other areas considered good for scuba activities include portions of the coastline around Homer, Juneau, Ketchikan and Whittier. Outfitting for most trips must be arranged through either Anchorage or Fairbanks, where diving shops have been set up to provide essential undersea gear. **Cost:** On request. **When:** On request. **Contact:** Alaska Sub-Arctic Dive Club, SR 3, Box 31136, Fairbanks, AK 99701, USA.

Kenai Scuba: Divers with a taste for cooler waters spend 1 day diving in the area of the Kenai Peninsula near Cook Inlet. The inlet is home to breeding salmon and an occasional gray whale. The diving ship Blueberry leaves from the town of Homer to take participants out into the frigid waters of Kachemak Bay and beyond. One day of diving consists of a 3-tank dive. **Cost:** $30. **When:** On request. **Contact:** Diver's World, 1534 Gambell St., Anchorage, AK 99501, USA; phone (907)274-9421.

Arizona

Diver's Education: Scuba diving classes and organized diving trips are offered to underwater enthusiasts in Arizona. Classes are limited to 10 people and consist of 7 sessions equally divided between classroom and pool. In addition, there are 7 extra pool sessions where students work on building skills and confidence. Included in the course are 2 separate diving trips: a 1-day freshwater dive and a 2-day dive near Guaymas or Sonora, Mexico, or San Diego, California. After graduating from the basic course, divers may take underwater photography courses and advanced diving courses and participate in the school's recreation and dive travel club. Trips are sponsored to places such as Catalina Island, San Pedro Island, San Carlos in Mexico and Belize. **Cost:** On request. **When:** Year-round. **Contact:** Tucson School of Scuba Diving, Scuba Cove, 3575 E. Speed-way, Tucson, AZ 85716, USA; phone (602)795-1140.

Arkansas

Private Island Diving: Located approximately 15 miles off the coast of Belize, a 1,200-acre island is available exclusively to divers. An 8-day stay allows for thorough exploration of the nearby waters which include a 176-mile-long reef a mile off shore. The water temperature is 85°F, the visibility is 200 feet and the diving accommodations are directly at the water's edge. Tropical fish observation, lobster hunting, sightseeing and photography are among the activities that may also be enjoyed. **Cost:** $670 from Little Rock includes transportation, meals, accommodations, tanks, weights, boats, all diving. **When:** Year-round. **Contact:** Cap'n Frogs of Arkansas, Inc., 11401 Rodhey Parnham, Little Rock, AR 72212, USA; phone (501)227-9005.

California

Deep Sea Education: Participants spend 25 to 427 hours learning various aspects of commercial deep sea diving at a school based on a navigable estuary in Oakland. The courses offered prepare trainees for careers in underwater research, construction and diving station work. The basic course is an 11½-week session that trains students in the physics of diving, diving hazards and first aid, advanced diving equipment, underwater welding and cutting, and other topics related to the area of underwater construction, salvage, research and oil field work. Adjuncts to diving such as demolitions, photography, hydraulic and pneumatic tools, televi-

Diving off the Florida Keys reveals an abundance of crusted hulls, anchors and other maritime debris which can be investigated on trips offered by Coral Reef Resort. (Florida Dept. of Commerce)

sion, decompression, robots and submarines are also discussed. A 4-week course in mixed gas-bell-saturation work is also offered, as is a scuba course and a submersible operator course. **Cost:** $1,245 for 11½ weeks; $1,950 for mixed gas course; $50 for scuba course; $575 for submersible operator course. **When:** On request. **Contact:** Coastal School of Deep Sea Diving, 320 29th Ave., Oakland, CA 94601, USA; phone (415)532-4211.

Colorado

Rocky Mountain Diving: A wide variety of scuba courses involving both pool and open water work caters to the divergent needs of diving students. A private comprehensive course includes 6 lectures, 6 pool sessions and unlimited practice at the student's convenience. A similar session is also available for groups. Open water lake diving and advanced scuba diving, ice diving and a basic underwater photography course are other options. Overseas trips are planned from June to November to such locations as San Salvador, the Channel Islands, the Red Sea and the South Caicos. **Cost:** $75 to $300 for cours-

es; $340 to $1,950 for overseas trips. **When:** Year-round. **Contact:** Rocky Mountain Diving Center Ltd., 1920 Wadsworth Blvd., Lakewood, CO 80215, USA; phone (303)232-2400.

Connecticut

Basic Open Water Dive Program: A 6-week course for beginning divers is designed to instill confidence in the student by exposure to several open water dives throughout the course. Each course is taught by an experienced instructor and consists of 42 hours of instruction and 6 dives in New England waters. The limit of students per course is 10. Upon completion of the course, divers receive NAUI certification in Basic Scuba and PADI certification for Open Water Diver. Underwater photography courses and diving trips to the Caribbean are also offered through the operator. **Cost:** On request. **When:** Spring to fall. **Contact:** Innerspace Diving Supply Co., Inc., 598 Center St., Manchester, CT 06040, USA; phone (203)646-2352.

Florida

Underwater Learning: Participants

take part in 5 courses that cover various aspects of scuba diving: the first is an introduction to scuba, consisting of condensed practical instruction on one of Coral Reef State Park's own reefs. The next course is a simple check-out dive for those who have completed a national certification but are in need of an open water dive. Professional Association of Diving Instructors certification, gained via a written examination and a pool check, is available in the third course. The fourth course is a 28-hour, 4-day intensive course designed to qualify students for NAUI certification; participants must be at least 15 years old and be able to swim 200 yards and tread water for 5 minutes. The final course is the same as the latter, but is designed for private certification instead of NAUI. **Cost:** $50 to $150. **When:** Year-round. **Contact:** Coral Reef Park Co., P.O. Box 13-M, Key Largo, FL 33037, USA; phone (305)451-1621.

Key Scuba Adventures: From a resort at Windley Key, divers enjoy waters with temperatures of 70°F in winter and visibility of 60 to 110 feet. Stretching 220 miles, the reef has depths ranging from 12 to 80 feet and is home to more than 600 species of tropical fish and 50 varieties of coral. Groups of 4 to 10 can take 4-day diving trips that include accommodations, 3 half-day dives, tank, weightbelts and air. In addition to various package trips, guided dives with licensed captains, drive-it-yourself dive boats and complete equipment rental and sales are available. Divers may investigate the area's many sunken Spanish galleons and World War II wrecks; more than half of all the gold lost in maritime disasters is estimated to be lying on the ocean floor off of the coast of Florida. Though services are geared toward certified divers, lessons in a freshwater pool are also offered. **Cost:** $16 to $25 a day depending on size of group, duration of stay, type of equipment provided; meals extra. **When:** Year-round excluding holidays. **Contact:** Coral Reef Resort, Box 575, Islamorada, FL 33036, USA; phone (305)664-4955.   *(M)*

Southern Diving: A dive shop in the Florida Keys sponsors a variety of diving-related activities. Group rates and complete diving packages are available for those who want a

trip tailored to the group's desires and abilities. The shop's vessel can carry up to 34 passengers. A 22-foot Aquasport accommodates special dive charters for up to 6 divers with full equipment. Scuba and snorkeling instruction is also available for novice and advanced divers. Among the types of dives featured are regular ledge dives from 50 to over 125 feet, night dives, wreck dives and overnight trips to the Dry Tortugas. **Cost:** On request. **When:** Year-round. **Contact:** Key West Pro Dive Shop, Inc., P.O. Box 580, Key West, FL 33040, USA; phone (305)296-3823. *(M)*

Diving School: Three-week courses begin each month in open water scuba certification, tropical fish collecting, underwater photography and snorkeling techniques. Participants have the choice of taking the 32-hour course in Deerfield Beach or in Pompano Beach. Certified divers may utilize a 30-foot diving boat which is used for daily trips. Divers explore several local reefs and drop-offs, with depths ranging from 30 to 100 feet. Visibility is equal throughout the diving range, and the water contains much tropical sea life including lobsters, snappers and groupers. A complete line of diving gear is available for purchase or rental. **Cost:** $130 for basic scuba course; includes equipment. **When:** Year-round. **Contact:** Professional Diving Schools of Florida, 210 N. Federal Hwy., Deerfield Beach, FL 33441, USA; phone (305)428-0560. *(M)*

Sport Diving and Research: The Florida Keys are the site for 2 snorkeling programs which teach the fundamentals of snorkeling as well as study of coral reefs. Following instruction, a tropical ecology program progresses to different diving sites each day, ending with the Looe Key Reef 7 miles offshore. Major life zones to be explored also include rocky inter-tidal, mangrove fringe, sponge and soft coral communities and tropical hardwood hammock forest. Team members of the coral reef research project assist in data collection of selected fish and invertebrates and the study of other ecosystems. Work is undertaken in small groups with 2 staff members each, with emphasis placed on minimal impact observation and the special conservation problems of the Keys. **Cost:** $175 for tropical ecology program includes food, tents, snorkeling gear; $245 for coral reef research includes meals, most gear. **When:** July, August. **Contact:** Wilderness Southeast, Rt. 3, Box 619-AA, Savannah, GA 31406, USA; phone (912)355-8008. *(M)*

Illinois

Midwest Skin Diving: Distance from warm tropical clime does not prevent this diving club and school from offering some exciting underwater adventures. Underwater enthusiasts may join trips to Grand Cayman and other southern ports in addition to ice dives in Naperville, Racine and Pearl Lake. The ice dive takes place in February and is preceded by formal instruction in the art. Lake Michigan dive trips, a "Great Lakes Dive-In" and various instruction programs are offered, including an 8-session underwater photography class taught by a professional photographer. **Cost:** $8 for ice dive, $60 for underwater photography class. Other trip prices on request. **When:** Year-round. **Contact:** Aqua Center, Inc., 717 Morton Ave., Aurora, IL 60506, USA; phone (312)896-3596.

Michigan

NAUI Sport Diver Course: A diving center in Midland offers a course with 8 different diving activities designed to provide scuba divers with exposure to new types of diving conditions and skills. In the 4 days of the course divers participate in a night dive, wreck dive and underwater mapping and navigation dives. All diving activities count toward fulfilling some of the requirements for advanced certifications. Onshore instruction is given in diving first aid, handling open water emergencies, search and recovery techniques, decompression, air consumption calculations and cold weather diving. Participants make a deep dive with simulated decompression, engage in light salvage activities, make a search and recovery dive and make a recompression chamber dive to 160 feet. Newly certified and inactive divers may find the course particularly helpful. **Cost:** $65 from Midland includes instruction, certification fees, wreck dive fees, 50 percent discount on air fills, equipment rentals. **When:** September, October. **Contact:** Seaquatics Inc., 28 Ashman Circle, Midland, MI 48640, USA; phone (517)835-6391.

New York

Big Apple Dive: Closed charters and weekend dives in search of shipwrecks along the New York coast bring participants to the remains of the ships *San Diego, Oregon* and *Coimbra Lightburne*. A vessel specially equipped for scientific research provides the transportation to reefs that range from 20 to 175 feet in depth. Instruction in underwater photography, instructor training, seamanship and navigation are also available. **Cost:** $10 to $500 depending on the type of dive includes guide, accommodations aboard the research vessel *Black Coral*. **When:** Year-round. **Contact:** Coastal Diving Academy, 106 Main St., Bay Shore, NY 11706, USA; phone (516)666-2127.

Oregon

Open Water Diving Class: Advanced scuba divers may perfect their skills with open water classes at Coos Bay. The course emphasizes navigating underwater, exchanging tanks underwater while sharing air, sharing air vest ascents and computing air consumption. Two hours of instruction in both a classroom and a swimming pool precede the open water dive. Upon completion of the course, students receive the TIC Open Water Card. It contains a microfilm dot which can include the student's diving and training history, medical records and equipment record. **Cost:** $25. **When:** Year-round. **Contact:** Northwest Divers Supply, Inc., 852 S. Broadway, Coos Bay, OR 97420, USA; phone (503)267-3723.

Pennsylvania

Erie Diving: By boat or from the shore divers can reach several shipwrecks in the fairly shallow waters of Lake Erie. Visibility is unpredictable when exploring the old wooden lake freighters, barges and tugs because in Lake Erie a small breeze can cloud things up quickly. An alternative diving spot is the Niagara River. The waters there are no place for a beginner, but experienced divers may find antique bottles, anchors, coins and weaponry. Canadian quarries just across the border usually provide divers with clear water, fish and sometimes old mining equipment to investigate. During the summer longer trips are scheduled to places such as Manitoulin Island in Georgian Bay, Canada. **Cost:** On request. **When:** Year-round. **Contact:** Lake Erie Skin Diving School Inc., 330 Holland St., Erie, PA 16502, USA; phone (814)454-0285.

Washington

San Juan Weekends: Weekend diving trips are offered year-round in the offshore waters of the San Juan Islands. Groups of up to 10 divers embark on a charter boat at Edmonds and enjoy 2 full days of diving. Instruction in skin diving is also available. **Cost:** $75 includes meals, accommodation. **When:** July. **Contact:** Aquarius Skin Diving School, 20801 Hwy. 99, Lynnwood, WA 98036, USA; phone (206)776-7706.

Diving Instruction: Students from ages 18 to 40 receive comprehensive training to become professional deep sea divers. Meeting 5 days a week for 6 months at the Lake Washington Ship Canal in Seattle, the course familiarizes students with all aspects of commercial diving, with special emphasis on safety. Included in the course are such topics as communications, underwater physics and physiology, de-

compression, equipment, underwater work, cutting and welding, salvage, demolition, rigging and boat handling. Students are provided with information regarding employment in deep sea diving. Underwater photography and television, mixed gas diving, scuba, saturation, hot water systems and first aid are further subjects covered. After 25 weeks at 30 hours a week divers receive professional certification. Financial assistance is available, and the program is veteran-approved. **Cost:** $3,200 tuition, $50 application fee; scuba gear extra. **When:** Year-round. **Contact:** Diver's Institute of Technology Inc., P.O. Box 70312, 1133 NW 45th St., Seattle, WA 98107, USA; phone (206)783-5542.

Wisconsin

Water-Filled Wrecks: Divers learn maritime history first-hand by investigating the wooden sailing ships and steamships that lie at the bottom of Lake Michigan and Green Bay. During half-day and day-long dives participants choose from a variety of wrecks including large steamships with machinery still intact. Some wrecks are partially buried in high grade ore or other cargo, and small mouth bass, carp, clams, salmon, perch and salamanders may be found at certain sites. Visibility varies from 12 to 50 feet depending on the site, algae and currents. Not all dives involve wrecks; from Table Bluff divers descend past an avalanche of rock to swim amidst enormous boulders, crevices, caves and outcroppings. Opportunities for underwater photography exist in many spots. **Cost:** $8 to $12 for charters to dive sites; rental equipment extra. **When:** May to October. **Contact:** On the Rocks, Rt. 1, Box 297, Ellison Bay, WI 54210, USA; phone (414)854-2808.

RESOURCES
Clubs and Associations

American Association
of Certified Divers
Dept. Dive 1, P.O. Box 3820
Stamford, CT 06905, USA

Alaska Sub-Arctic Dive Club
Star Rt. 3, Box 31136
Fairbanks, AK 99701, USA

American Littoral Society
Sandy Hook
Ft. Hancock, NY 07732, USA
Phone (201)291-0055

Associated Skin Divers
27 Westbrook Rd.
Rocky Hill, CT 06067, USA

Atlantic Skin Divers Council
7416 Glendora Dr.
Washington, DC 20028, USA

British Sub-Aqua Club
70 Brompton Rd.
London SW3, Great Britain

Club Aquarius
P.O. Box 17067
Long Beach, CA 90807, USA
Phone (213)595-5649

Council for National Cooperation
in Aquatics

51 Clifford Ave.
Pelham, NY 10803, USA

International Divers Association
P.O. Box 6657
Tamuning, Guam 96911, USA

Irish Underwater Council
The Georgian Inn, EMO
County Laois, Ireland

Marine Technology Society
1730 M St. NW
Washington, DC 20036, USA
Phone (202)659-3251

Mid West Council Diving Club
730 Arapaho
Wichita, KS 67212, USA

National Association for Cave Diving
3001 W. Tennessee St.
Talahassee, FL 32304, USA

National Association
of Skin Diving Schools
1757 Long Beach Blvd.
Long Beach, CA 90813, USA

National Association
of Underwater Instructors (NAUI)
Box 630
Colton, CA 92334, USA
Phone (714)824-5540

Professional Association
of Diving Instructors (PADI)
2064 N. Bush
Santa Ana, CA 92706, USA
Phone (714)547-6696

Underwater Adventurers Association
5915½ W. Irving Park Rd.
Chicago, IL 60634, USA

United Divers Association
6330 Woodlawn Rd.
Verona, PA 16147, USA

World Underwater Federation
34 rue de Colisse
75008 Paris, France

Reader Service

Free Information on Request

ADVENTURE TRAVELGUIDE has made it easier for you to obtain information at no cost.Simply circle the number(s) on the adjoining postage-paid card which correspond to the number(s) below for the information you wish to receive.

We also would appreciate your answers to a few questions about yourself and your travel interests on the Reader Service Card. Postage is prepaid so you can drop it in any U.S. mailbox.

1. ADVENTURE CENTER—Adventure travel specialists featuring a wide variety of adventures throughout the world. Includes trekking, overland expeditions, safaris, camping tours, and more. Complete 40-page catalog.

2. ADVENTURE WORLD—Travel agents specializing in unusual and exciting adventure trips. River running, air sports, yacht charters, bicycle tours, X-country skiing, and more. Trip details.

3. ADVENTURERS INTERNATIONAL—Completely guided treasure hunting expeditions to tropical Caribbean islands, plus Central and South America. No experience necessary. Excellent accommodations for singles and families.

4. ADVENTURES INTERNATIONAL—Whale watching trips in Baja and Hawaii. Gorilla safari through Rwanda/Zaire. Kenya wildlife safari, 15 to 21 days. Brochure containing costs, dates and trip descriptions.

5. AEROSTAT RENAISSANCE—Hot air ballooning over California's picturesque Napa Valley. Scenic flights, flight instruction, certification, and aerostatic displays all provided. Complete information.

6. AFRICAN TRAVEL SUPERVISORS—U.S. general agents for travel to southern Africa. Professionally organized safaris to the heart of the wildlife continent. Color information folders.

7. ALASKA WILDERNESS UNLIMITED—Guided wilderness backpacking trek into the heart of Alaska's remote Brooks Range. Descriptive brochure.

8. AMERICAN WILDERNESS EXPERIENCE, INC.—Horsepack **and backpack treks into remote wilderness areas of** the West. Colorful native guides and small intimate groups learn to live in harmony with the wilderness. Color brochure.

9. ANDEAN OUTFITTERS—Explore the fjords of southern Chile; climb the Cordillera Real in northern Bolivia, or trek in Peru. Trips up to 150 days. Itineraries and costs.

10. ARENA TOURS—Explore Iceland. Overland expeditions for all ages. Opportunity to view glaciers, volcanic formations, geysers, boiling clay pits and thundering waterfalls. Trip descriptions and details.

11. AVENUE TRAVEL, INC.—Full service travel agency specializing in Himalayan treks and other adventure tours. U.S. representatives for Sherpa Co-operative Trekking, Ltd. Trip information.

12. BAY TRAVEL DIVING ADVENTURES—Specialize in scuba diving tours. Individuals or groups. Destinations around the world. Australia, Caribbean, Cozumel, Fiji, Tahiti, Micronesia, Seychelles, Hawaii, Mexico. Brochures.

13. BLACK OTTER GUIDE SERVICE—Licensed guides take you to the remote Absaroka-Beartooth Wilderness for trout fishing and excellent photography. Special trips for teenagers. Details on all trips.

14. BLUE WATER CRUISES—Sail on a chartered yacht among the Virgin, Leeward, or Windward islands in the Caribbean. Year-round departures. Help sail one of 50 owner-operated yachts. Complete information.

15. CALIFORNIA MOUNTAINEERING AND TECHNICAL ROCK CLIMBING SCHOOL—Beginning through advanced classes offered year-round, along with guided climbs and expeditions worldwide. Brochure.

16. CANADIAN RIVER EXPEDITIONS LTD.—Ten-day river rafting and camping trips on the Chilcotin and Fraser rivers of western British Columbia. Color brochure with departure dates.

17. CANOES NORTH/CANOES SOUTH—Canoe/kayak trips in wilderness surrounding Hudson Bay. Also canoe safaris in the remote jungles of South America. Brochure.

18. CANYONEERS—River trips down the Colorado, Green, San Juan and Skagit rivers. One to 5 days. Hiking and backpacking trips through the Grand Canyon and along the Baja coast. Color Brochure.

19. CASA SOLANA RESORT HOTEL—Isolated island paradise off the coast of Belize, Central America. Excellent adventure opportunities for trophy fishermen, divers and naturalists. Color brochure.

20. CASCADE RIVER HOLIDAYS LTD.—River raft trips on the Fraser/Chilcotin/Thompson rivers in British Columbia, Canada. One- to 12-day duration. Charter and schedule bookings. Color brochure.

21. CROSSROADS INTERNATIONAL—Small group summer camping, climbing, cycling. Cross-country, England, France, Scandinavia, Yugoslavia. High school students. Booklet includes descriptions, dates and prices.

22. DAMART THERMAWEAR, INC.—Complete line of thermal underwear for men and women. Color catalog.

See facing page for Advertiser Index
For more information on trips, products or services mentioned in this issue, please answer the reader profile questions and circle the appropriate numbers below. Allow 4 to 6 weeks for delivery.

NAME _____

ORGANIZATION _____

ADDRESS _____

_____

(include postal/zip code)

1	2	3	4	5	6	7	8	9	10	11	12	13
14	15	16	17	18	19	20	21	22	23	24	25	26
27	28	29	30	31	32	33	34	35	36	37	38	39
40	41	42	43	44	45	46	47	48	49	50	51	52
53	54	55	56	57	58	59	60	61	62	63	64	65
66	67	68	69	70	71	72	73	74	75	76	77	78
79	80	81	82	83	84	85	86	87	88	89	90	91
92	93	94	95	96	97	98						

Limit: Circle only 10

READER SERVICE CARD

In order to develop a composite reader profile, we request that you answer the following questions. Circle only one answer.

1. **Where did you get your copy of ADVENTURE TRAVEL magazine?**
   1. Subscription 2. Membership in the Association 3. Travel Agency 4. Newsstand 5. Outdoor Recreation Store 6. Friend 7. Airline

2. **What is your age?**
   A. Under 18 B. 18-24 C. 25-34 D. 35-49 E. 50-64 F. 65-over

3. **What is your occupation?**
   1. Professional 2. Manager/administrative 3. Clerical/sales 4. Education 5. Craftsman 6. Other employed 7. Retired 8. Not employed

4. **What activity do you prefer to participate in? (Circle one)**
   A. Skiing B. Bicycling C. Mountaineering D. Backpacking E. Scuba / skin diving F. White water sports G. Overlanding H. Nature study I. Canoeing J. Fishing K. Sailing L. Horsepacking M. Air adventures N. Cruising O. None

5. **What activity in question number four would be your second preference?**
   A   B   C   D   E   F   G   H   I   J   K   L   M   N   O

6. **How many trips have you taken on an airline for business or pleasure in the past 24 months?**
   1. None   2. 1-2   3. 3-5   4. 6-12   5. 13-19   6. 20 or more

7. **Which area do you plan to visit in the next year to participate on an adventure trip? (Circle only one)**
   A. Western U.S. B. Eastern U.S. C. Canada D. Mexico E. Alaska F. Hawaii G. Europe H. Africa I. Caribbean J. Middle East K. Australia / New Zealand L. South America M. Far East N. South Pacific O. Central America P. North Atlantic Q. No travel plans

(This card void after Dec. 31, 1979. Please direct later inquiries to advertiser)

See facing page for Advertiser Index
For more information on trips, products or services mentioned in this issue, please answer the reader profile questions and circle the appropriate numbers below. Allow 4 to 6 weeks for delivery.

NAME _____

ORGANIZATION _____

ADDRESS _____

_____

(include postal/zip code)

1	2	3	4	5	6	7	8	9	10	11	12	13
14	15	16	17	18	19	20	21	22	23	24	25	26
27	28	29	30	31	32	33	34	35	36	37	38	39
40	41	42	43	44	45	46	47	48	49	50	51	52
53	54	55	56	57	58	59	60	61	62	63	64	65
66	67	68	69	70	71	72	73	74	75	76	77	78
79	80	81	82	83	84	85	86	87	88	89	90	91
92	93	94	95	96	97	98						

Limit: Circle only 10

READER SERVICE CARD

In order to develop a composite reader profile, we request that you answer the following questions. Circle only one answer.

1. **Where did you get your copy of ADVENTURE TRAVEL magazine?**
   1. Subscription 2. Membership in the Association 3. Travel Agency 4. Newsstand 5. Outdoor Recreation Store 6. Friend 7. Airline

2. **What is your age?**
   A. Under 18 B. 18-24 C. 25-34 D. 35-49 E. 50-64 F. 65-over

3. **What is your occupation?**
   1. Professional 2. Manager/administrative 3. Clerical/sales 4. Education 5. Craftsman 6. Other employed 7. Retired 8. Not employed

4. **What activity do you prefer to participate in? (Circle one)**
   A. Skiing B. Bicycling C. Mountaineering D. Backpacking E. Scuba / skin diving F. White water sports G. Overlanding H. Nature study I. Canoeing J. Fishing K. Sailing L. Horsepacking M. Air adventures N. Cruising O. None

5. **What activity in question number four would be your second preference?**
   A   B   C   D   E   F   G   H   I   J   K   L   M   N   O

6. **How many trips have you taken on an airline for business or pleasure in the past 24 months?**
   1. None   2. 1-2   3. 3-5   4. 6-12   5. 13-19   6. 20 or more

7. **Which area do you plan to visit in the next year to participate on an adventure trip? (Circle only one)**
   A. Western U.S. B. Eastern U.S. C. Canada D. Mexico E. Alaska F. Hawaii G. Europe H. Africa I. Caribbean J. Middle East K. Australia / New Zealand L. South America M. Far East N. South Pacific O. Central America P. North Atlantic Q. No travel plans

(This card void after Dec. 31, 1979. Please direct later inquiries to advertiser)

BUSINESS REPLY CARD

FIRST CLASS   PERMIT NO. 217   CLINTON, IA

POSTAGE WILL BE PAID BY ADDRESSEE

MAGAZINE

P.O. Box 2693
Clinton, IA 52735, USA

NO POSTAGE
NECESSARY
IF MAILED
IN THE
UNITED STATES

BUSINESS REPLY CARD

FIRST CLASS   PERMIT NO. 217   CLINTON, IA

POSTAGE WILL BE PAID BY ADDRESSEE

MAGAZINE

P.O. Box 2693
Clinton, IA 52735, USA

23. DIRIGO CRUISES—Board the 95' Harvey Gamage, a replica of a Maine trading schooner, for a week of cruising in the Virgin Islands. Maine coast cruises in the summer. Newsletter.

24. EAST AFRICAN TRAVEL CONSULTANTS—Natural history and wildlife conservation camera safaris in Kenya, Zambia and Tanzania. Trips last 1 to 23 days. Itineraries and costs.

25. EASTERN RIVER EXPEDITIONS—Whitewater rafting Maine's Kennebec and Penobscot rivers; West Virginia's Gauley River. Full outfitting, equipment, guides, meals. Brochure.

26. ECHO: THE WILDERNESS CO.—Whitewater rafting: Idaho, Oregon, California and Alaska. Outstanding rapids, beautiful canyons and excellent cooking. Complete brochure.

27. ENCOUNTER OVERLAND—Adventurous camping expeditions in Africa, Asia and South America. Four-wheel drive expeditions range from 3 weeks to 4 months. Details on itineraries and costs.

28. EXODUS—Overland expeditions, 3 to 4 months in Asia and Africa. Himalayan treks and other adventure holidays, 3 to 4 weeks by 4-wheel drive vehicle and foot. Full color booklet.

29. EXPEDITION RESEARCH, INC.—Membership and services organization offering information on scientific and exploratory expeditions around the world. Registrants receive a quarterly newsletter and an annual journal. Information on membership and services offered.

30. EXPLORANDES—One- to 20-day expeditions along the Inca Trail take you through tropical forests, over mountain passes, and into archaeological ruins of the Incas in Peru. Details and itineraries.

31. EXPLORE BEYOND LTD.—Cultural and exploratory expeditions to Yemen, northern Thailand, Mesopotamia, Persia, Nepal, Afghanistan, Pakistan, Sudan, East Africa, Himalayas and Central Sahara. Brochure.

32. FALKLAND WILDLIFE—Weekly nature cruises to the Falkland Islands aboard the MN Tussock Bird. View the unique wildlife habitats of the penguin. Details and itineraries.

33. GEORGIE'S ROYAL RIVER RATS—Grand Canyon River trips in large or small pontoon rafts. Four-, 6, and 9-day trips. Descriptive literature.

34. GERHARD'S BICYCLE ODYSSEYS—Bike Europe. Two-week cycling experiences with sag wagon, hotels, and experienced leader. Ireland, Holland and Germany; or Germany and Austria. Brochure.

35. GLAD TIDINGS—Sail to the spectacular and isolated fjords of Newfoundland aboard the 46' brigantine Glad Tidings. Private charter cruises for four. Itineraries and costs.

36. GOLDEN BEAR ENTERPRISES—Hot air balloon rides in the scenic desert area near Los Angeles. Flights begin at dawn year-round. Reservation information.

37. GOWAY TRAVEL, LTD.—Toronto-based trip wholesaler specializing in promoting overland camping tours and expeditions. Camping tours in Canada, U.S.A., Europe, and Australia. Overland expeditions across Africa, Asia, and South America. Information booklet.

38. GUERBA—Buy/hire expedition motor home for use in remote areas of Africa, Asia or South America. No experience necessary. Excellent accommodations for singles and families.

39. HIGH HORIZONS—Mountain programs and camps for juniors, teenagers, and adults in the Canadian Rockies. Programs include hiking, mountaineering, backpacking and leadership training. Complete information.

40. HIKE-SKITOUR VERMONT—All ski levels. Tepee ski tour. Inn to inn skiing. Multi-media tour combines hiking, horseback riding, bicycling and canoeing. Also European wine tours by bicycle. Full details.

41. HIMALAYA—Explore and experience the remote places and cultures of the Himalayas with experienced guides. Trekking and wilderness expeditions to Kashmir, Ladakh and Nepal. Brochure describing the 1979 treks.

42. HOLBROOK TRAVEL—Follow the steps of the Inca to Machu Picchu on a natural history, archaeology, anthropology, and wildlife trip. Other trips available to South America, East Africa, Australia, and other exotic destinations. Complete information.

43. HORIZONS UNLIMITED—Mountaineering, backpacking and rock climbing school offers 5-, 10-, 18-, 24-day courses or guided tours to Idaho Primitive Area. Complete details and brochure.

44. IDAHO ADVENTURES—Whitewater river rafting trips on the Salmon, Owyhee, Snake, and Middle Fork rivers of Idaho. Trip durations of 1, 2, 3, or 6 days. Information and brochure.

45. INFINITE ODYSSEY—North American adventure program featuring unique learning experiences in climbing, ski touring, kayaking, sailing, and more. Brochure and application.

46. INTERNATIONAL BACKPACKERS ASSOCIATION, INC.—Assist in building and preserving non-motorized trails. Membership entitles you to discounts, trail information, club activities and more. Membership information available.

47. INTERNATIONAL SCHOOL OF MOUNTAINEERING—Introductory, classical, and modern alpine climbing with instructors of international reputation. Information on course offerings.

48. IRISH TOURIST BOARD—Ireland: Land of youth—land of learning. The least expensive airfare to Europe lands you in

Ireland. Enjoy the countryside, cruise the Shannon, pony tracking, cycling. Adventure travel packet.

49. JESS RANKIN—Working dude ranch with chuck wagon rides, fishing, cook-outs, and cabins. Rates available.

50. JOURNEYS—Trek the Himalayas in Nepal or Kashmir/Ladakh. Other journeys available to Sri Lanka and Colombia. Trip itineraries.

51. KACHEMAK BAY WILDERNESS LODGE—Set in Alaska's spectacular and remote Kachemak area, this lodge provides excellent fishing, guided trips for naturalists, and other wilderness offerings. Booklet.

52. KENAI GUIDE SERVICE—Alaska's finest backpacking. Three-day trips to a fully guided 9-day expedition into the Kenai mountains and Harding Ice Field. Brochure.

53. MACKAY BAR—Float the famous "River of No Return" on a 5-day trip with licensed river runners, or combine a 3-day river trip with a 2-day pack trip in Idaho's wilderness. Brochure.

54. THE MOUNTAIN MEN—Four-wheel drive trips year-round into the remote areas of the Colorado Rockies. Includes X-country skiing in the winter. Details and itineraries.

55. MOUNTAIN PEOPLE SCHOOL—Adventure-oriented courses offered in rock climbing, wilderness skills (7- or 14-day adventures), and snowshoeing. See the California Sierra Nevada. Complete information.

56. MOUNTAIN RIVER TOURS INC.—Whitewater rafting on the New and Gauley rivers. One-day trips cover 15 miles and 21 major rapids. Two-day trips also available. Brochure.

57. MOUNTAIN TRAVEL—The oldest and largest adventure travel outfitter in the world. Offers over 80 high-quality expeditions and outings on 5 continents and outfits everything from country walks to major expeditions. Color brochure.

58. MUSEUM OF COMPARATIVE ZOOLOGY—HARVARD UNIV.—Natural **history trips to Baja, Hawaii, Ecuador, the Galapagos** Islands and Peru. Expert guides, conservation-oriented. Detailed itineraries.

59. NATURE EXPEDITIONS INTERNATIONAL—Nature, cultural and photography expeditions from Afghanistan to Yucatan. Expert leadership; small groups. An in-depth travel experience. 1979 Expedition Preview.

60. NEVIOT—Desert safaris and camel trekking in the Sinai Desert. Diving exploration along the Red Sea's coral reefs. Brochure with full details.

61. NORTHERN WILDERNESS COMPANY—Guided river trips down the wildest and most scenic rivers of the Pacific Northwest and Alaska. Trip descriptions and brochures.

62. NORTHWEST OUTWARD BOUND SCHOOL—Pacific Northwest wilderness experience courses for men and women 16½ years and older. Learn mountaineering, river running, backpacking skills, and much more. Complete information on courses and costs.

63. NORTHWEST WATERS—Explore the west coast of Vancouver Island by canoe. Twelve-day guided expedition. Complete information.

64. OCEANIC SOCIETY EXPEDITIONS—Explore the ocean world on a sailing ship. A variety of trips and itineraries available from the North Atlantic to the South Pacific. Booklet describing 1979 expeditions.

65. OCEANUS—Voyages of discovery which combine adventure sailing vacations with a learning experience. Skippered yachts travel to unique destinations in the Caribbean and the Atlantic. Information on 1979 expeditions.

66. OPERADORES TURISTICOS—Peruvian trekking adventures to the Cordillera Blanca, along the Inca Trail, and other Andean destinations. Itineraries and costs.

67. OSPREY RIVER TRIPS INC.—River spirit: Whitewater rafting and kayaking trips in Oregon and California. Small groups only. Special trips and workshops for women. Brochure.

68. OUTDOOR LEADERSHIP TRAINING SEMINARS—Specialized **outdoor training for educators, outdoor leaders and** general public. Courses in rafting, horsepacking, kayaking, ski touring, rock climbing and mountaineering. Brochure containing costs and details.

69. OVERLAND ROLLS—Week-long, fly-in ski tours to the wilderness of northern Maine. Bicycle tours along the Maine seacoast and its islands. Brochures and costs.

70. PRIMITIVE AREA FLOAT TRIPS—Oar-powered trips using neoprene inflatable rafts. Custom whitewater trips running 3 to 11 days. Color brochure.

71. QUESTERS TOURS—Camp and trek through a multitude of environments such as Nepal, Ladakh, Kashmir, Death Valley, Baja coast and much more. Custom-made trips take the naturalist approach to adventure. Directory of worldwide nature tours.

72. REI ADVENTURE TRAVEL—Three- to 7-week treks in Nepal and Pakistan through the rugged Himalayas. Cross-country skiing in Norway. Sailing in the Greek Isles and Hawaii. River running in Ecuador, Alaska and Washington. Brochure with details.

73. ROGUE RIVER OUTFITTERS—Specialize in outfitting whitewater paddlers and cross-country skiers. Rafting and skiing instruction or trips offered in southern Oregon. Brochure.

74. SACRED MONKEY EXPEDITIONS—Wilderness adventure trips to the remote corners of North America. Includes river expeditions down the Usumacinta River in southern Mexico, jungle trekking, and rafting trips in British Columbia. Booklet.

75. SEA LIFE DISCOVERY—Scuba and snorkel vacations to the Caribbean, Hawaii, Micronesia, Red Sea. Group or individual tours arranged. Brochures describing each itinerary.

76. SEE & SEA TRAVEL SERVICE, INC.—Worldwide diving adventure offered through this long-established diver's travel agency. Booklet includes information on trips and costs.

77. SHENANDOAH RIVER OUTFITTERS—Day, weekend, and week-long canoe trips on the beautiful Shenandoah River. Completely outfitted. Brochure.

78. SLICKROCK KAYAKS—Kayak adventures for beginners to advanced boaters on Utah/Colorado's magnificent rivers. Support, instruction, equipment and transportation included. 1979 trip schedules.

79. SOUTH AMERICAN WILDERNESS ADVENTURES—Three- to 5-week treks in South America to places such as Patagonia, the Cordillera Blanca in Peru, the Inca Trail and Ecuador. Wildlife safaris, nature expeditions. Brochure.

80. SOUTHWEST SAFARIS—Natural history expeditions through New Mexico, Colorado, Utah, Arizona. Bush flying, jeeping, rafting, hiking. Geology, Archaeology, Botony. Brochure.

81. SPYGLASS HILL—Honduras. Diving adventure on Roatan's barrier reef. Villa accommodations. Superb meals. Complete diving facilities. Complete information.

82. TELLURIDE MOUNTAINEERING SCHOOL—One of the finest summer leadership schools for students 13-18 years old. Nineteenth year of operation. Kayaking, rafting, mountain climbing, backpacking in the San Juan Mountains and Utah canyon country. Brochure.

83. TRACKS TRAVEL LTD.—Overland adventures from London to Johannesburg or Nairobi. European camping vacations from 3 days to 9 weeks covering 28 countries. Complete brochure.

84. TRAVELTRENDS, INC.—Adventure travel with Holubar to the remote corners of the world. Trips to the Amazon, Alaska wilderness, Nepal, Kenya, Europe and more. Brochure.

85. TREK ADVENTURES—See the world through an incredible variety of overland trips. European camping tours from 21 to 62 days. Transcontinental expeditions, from a 15-day mini-trek to a 3½-month journey. Complete details provided.

86. TX RANCH—Working cow ranch on the Wyoming-Montana border. Trail cattle, ride herd, rope calves alongside the cowboys. Brochure.

87. UNIVERSITY OF THE WILDERNESS—Environmental adventures: mountain, desert, snow country, seashore. Backpack, canoe, ski field trips. Explorations, nature study, birding, archaeology, wilderness photography. Catalog.

88. V.I.P. TRAVEL—Full service travel agency, specializing in the unique requirements of the adventure traveler. Brochure.

89. WANAPITEI—Wilderness canoe adventures in the Canadian north woods. One week to 3 weeks. Brochure gives full details.

90. WESTERN ADVENTURE SAFARIS, INC.—River trips from 1 to 6 days on the Colorado and Green rivers. Family and group rates. Brochure.

91. WILDERNESS ENCOUNTER—A variety of programs offered in wilderness and underwater photography, backpacking, rafting and canoeing. College credit available. Complete information.

92. WILDERNESS INSTITUTE—Spring, summer and fall backpacking, canoeing and special wilderness survival and mountaineering courses in the Rocky Mountain States. Ski touring in winter. Full details and costs in brochure.

93. WILDERNESS SOUTHEAST—Naturalist-led adventures; exciting, easy learning. Okefenokee, Smokies, Keys, wild islands, 'Glades, Guatemala. Backpacking, canoeing, snorkeling. Schedule and trip descriptions.

94. WILDERNESS TRAILS—Guided backpacking trips into the Idaho Primitive Area. Six-, 10-, and 15-day trips offered in the spring and fall as well as throughout the summer. Brochure and costs.

95. ZAMBIA AIRWAYS—Game-viewing and photographic tours in Zambia and Botswana by Land Rover and on foot. Colorful brochure and details.

96. ADVENTURE TRAVEL NEWSLETTER—First monthly newsletter in adventure travel field. Sixteen pages of information on worldwide adventure trips open to everyone. Regularly $22, now half-price at $11 for 12 issues. Free issue. No obligation.

97. AMERICAN ADVENTURERS ASSOCIATION—An association for individuals and travel organizations interested in adventure travel. Members receive subscriptions to ADVENTURE TRAVEL Magazine, WORLDWIDE ADVENTURE TRAVEL-GUIDE and ADVENTURE TRAVEL NEWSLETTER. Plus equipment, literature and photo processing discounts. Information referral service for worldwide adventure. Extensive promotional benefits for travel organizations. Information and membership application.

98. HARVARD'S FRIENDS OF THE MCZ (Museum of Comparative Zoology)—Natural history trips to Baja, Hawaii, Ecuador, the Galapagos and Peru. Expert guides, conservation-oriented. Detailed itineraries.

APPENDIX

ORGANIZATIONAL MEMBERS

The following is a list of the American Adventurers Association's organizational members—those organizations, trip operators and businesses directly involved in the adventure travel field. Many operate the trips described in this guide, and all are excellent sources of adventure travel informaton.

Aardvark Expeditions
14 Coleridge Rd.
London N8, Great Britain
Phone 01-340-7598

Adventours—Wet and Wild, Inc.
Box B
Woodland, CA 95695, USA
Phone (916)662-6824

Adventure Africa
Stablings, 34b High St., Ramsbury
Marlborough, Wiltshire, Great Britain
Phone Ramsbury (06722)569

Adventure Bound, Inc.
6179 S. Adams Dr.
Littleton, CO 80121, USA
Phone (303)771-3752

Adventure Center
5540 College Ave.
Oakland, CA 94618, USA
Phone (415)654-1879

Adventure Cruises, Inc.
P.O. Box 22284
Ft. Lauderdale, FL 33316, USA
Phone (305)735-4045

Adventure River Expeditions
4211 Mars Wy.
Salt Lake City, UT 84117, USA
Phone (801)278-1867

Adventure River Tours
2101 Arnold Dr.
Martinez, CA 94553, USA

Adventure Tours
Hotel Shaheen, 4-Gupkar Rd.
Srinagar 190001, Kashmir, India
Phone 5248

Adventure Tours & Travel Unlimited
Suite 414, Airport Plaza Bldg.
19415 Pacific Hwy. S.
Seattle, WA 98188, USA
Phone (206)824-2192

Adventurers International
215 E. Horatio Ave.
Maitland, FL 32751, USA
Phone (305)645-1332

Adventures International
4421 Albert St.
Oakland, CA 94619, USA
Phone (415)531-6564

Aerostat Renaissance
1644 Silverado Trail
Napa, CA 94558, USA
Phone (707)255-6356 or 255-6863

Africanus
15 Central Chambers, Cooks Alley
Stratford-on-Avon, Warwickshire
Great Britain
Phone (0789)5033

Afro Ventures
P.O. Box 10848
Johannesburg 2000, South Africa

Aigas Field Centre
Highland Wildlife Enterprises
Aigas House
Beauly, Inverness-shire 1V4 7AD
Great Britain
Phone (0463 71)2443

Alaska Discovery Enterprises
P.O. Box 337
Juneau, AK 99802, USA
Phone (907)586-6245

Alaska Raft Adventures
Box 73264
Fairbanks, AK 99707, USA
Phone (907)452-1465

Alaska Wilderness Expeditions, Inc.
P.O. Box 7814
Ketchikan, AK 99901, USA

Alaska Wilderness Unlimited
Drawer 8M
Anchorage, AK 99509, USA
Phone (907)277-0197 or 863-7284

Alaska Wildwater and Mountaineering
Box 3555
Anchorage, AK 99510, USA

Alaskan Adventure
P.O. Box 18
Hope, AK 99605, USA

Alatna Guide Service
P.O. Box 80424
Fairbanks, AK 99708, USA
Phone (907)479-6354

Allagash Wilderness Outfitters
Frost Pond, Star Rt. 76
Greenville, ME 04441, USA

American Institute for Exploration
1809 Nichols Rd.
Kalamazoo, MI 49007, USA
Phone (616)381-8237

American Safari
386 60th St.
Oakland, CA 94618, USA
Phone (415)652-7825

American Sportsman's Safari Co.
P.O. Box 33240
Northglenn, CO 80233, USA

American Trails West
92 Middle Neck Rd.
Great Neck, NY 11021, USA
Phone (516)487-2802

American Wilderness Experience
P.O. Box 1486A
Boulder, CO 80306, USA
Phone (303)499-5703 or 499-0050

AMTREK-Overland Expeditions
P.O. Box 206
Santa Clara, CA 95052, USA

Andean Outfitters
P.O. Box 4547
Aspen, CO 81611, USA
Phone (303)925-3371

Arena Tours
Hvasseleiti 26
Reykjavik, Iceland

Arizona Soaring, Inc.
P.O. Box 27427
Tempe, AZ 85282, USA
Phone (602)568-2318

Atamiskow Lodge
P.O. Box 1438
The Pas, MB Canada R9A 1K8
Phone (204)624-5429, winter 623-7316

Aurora Borealis Expeditions
132 Eileen Circle
Burnsville, MN 55337, USA

Ausventure
P.O. Box 54
Mosman, N.S.W. 2088, Australia
Phone 960-1677

Bahama Sailing Camp
480 W. 246th St.
New York, NY 10471, USA
Phone (212)548-1184

The Balloon Ranch
Star Rt., Box 41
Del Norte, CO 81132, USA
Phone (303)754-2533

BAR-BQ Ranch
P.O. Box 173
Harrison, ID 83833, USA
Phone (208)689-3528

Bay Travel Diving Adventures
2435 E. Coast Hwy.
Corona del Mar, CA 92625, USA
Phone (714)675-4321

Beamer Expeditions
P.O. Box 285
Canoga Park, CA 91305, USA
Phone (213)883-3522

BelAir Travel Agency
P.O. Box 16
Belize City, Belize
Phone 2999

Belize Diver's World
711 Fannin #1222
Houston, TX 77002, USA

Bell Island Hot Springs, Inc.
Bell Island. AK 99950, USA
Or: P.O. Box 66311
Seattle, WA 98166, USA
Phone (206)242-0466

Big Island Adventures
P.O. Box 2639
Kailua-Kona, HI 96740, USA
Phone (808)329-2676

Bike Dream Tours, Inc.
P.O. Box 20653
Houston, TX 77025, USA
Phone (713)771-1172.

Bikecentennial
P.O. Box 8308
Missoula, MT 59807, USA
Phone (406)721-1776

Black Forest Gliderport
9990 Gliderport Rd.
Colorado Springs, CO 80908, USA
Phone (303)495-4144

Black Otter Guide Service
P.O. Box 93
Pray, MT 59065, USA
Phone (406)333-4362

Black Tusk Touring and
Guide Service Ltd.
3064 St. Kildas Ave.
North Vancouver, BC Canada V7L 2A9
Phone (604)985-9223

Blue Hole, Inc.
4817 W. Farmington Rd.
Peoria, IL 61604, USA
Phone (309)676-1852

Blue Water Cruises
Box 758-AX
St. Thomas, VI 00801, USA
Phone (809)774-0650

Bob Crick High Country Outfitters
Rt. 1, Box 99A
Victor, MT 59875, USA
Phone (406)642-3233

Boothy's Safariland Tours
P.O. Box 40058
Casuarina N.T., Australia
Phone 85-3023

CAF Industries, Inc.
101 S. 30th St.
Phoenix, AZ 85034, USA

California Mountaineering and
Technical Rock Climbing School
6121 Prescott Ave.
Yucca Valley, CA 92284, USA
Phone (714)365-1152
Summer: P.O. Box 1576
Idyllwild, CA 92349, USA
Phone (714)659-4801

Camp Denali
McKinley Park, AK 99755, USA
Phone (907)683-2290
Winter: (907)683-2302

Canadian River Expeditions Ltd.
1005 Highland Dr.
West Vancouver, BC Canada
Phone (604)926-4436

Canatrek Mountain Expeditions
P.O. Box 1138
Banff, AB Canada T0L 0C0
Phone (403)762-3143

Canoes North/Canoes South
Box 5656
Armstrong, ON Canada P0T 1A0
Phone (807)583-2055

Canyoneers, Inc.
P.O. Box 2997
Flagstaff, AZ 86003, USA
Phone (602)526-0924

Capricorn Travel and Tours
21 Ebury Bridge Rd.
London SW1W 8QX, Great Britain

Casa Solana
Rt. 1, Box 40
Palacios, TX 77465, USA
Phone (512)972-3314

Cascade Corrals
Stehekin, WA 98852, USA
Phone (509)663-1822

Cascade River Holidays
P.O. Box 65
Yale, BC Canada V0K 2S0
Phone (604)863-2332

Centaur Overland Travel Ltd.
146 Halfway St.
Sidcup, Kent DA15 8DF, Great Britain
Phone 01-302-5959

Centrotourist International Inc.
509 Madison Ave.
New York, NY 10021, USA

Challenge/Discovery
Box 229
Crested Butte, CO 81224, USA
Phone (303)349-5432

Churchill House Inn
RFD #3, Rt. 73E
Brandon, VT 05733, USA
Phone (802)247-3300

Club Andino Peruano
Las Begonias 630 #11
Lima 27, Peru

Colorado Rocky Mountain Hiking
Box 376
North Conway, NH 03860, USA
Phone (603)356-3594

Colorado WET, Inc.
2912 Aspen Dr.
Durango, CO 81301, USA
Phone (303)247-1159

Consolidated Tours Ltd.
550 Sherbrooke St. W., #480
Montreal, PQ Canada H3A 1B9
Phone (514)849-1259

Coral Reef Resort
Box 575
Islamorada, FL 33036, USA
Phone (305)664-4955

Court's White Water Trips
Box 1045
Gold Beach, OR 97444, USA
Phone (503)247-6504

Crossroads International
Hillsboro, NH 03244, USA
Phone (603)478-5251

Desert Dance
Box 77
Terlingua, TX 79852, USA
Phone (915)371-2211

Desert Expeditions, Inc.
P.O. Box 1404
Palm Desert, CA 92260, USA
Phone (714)346-6927

Dirigo Cruises
Schooner *Harvey Gamage*
39 Waterside Ln.
Clinton, CT 06413, USA
Phone (203)669-7068

Discovery Tours International
628 NW 6th Ave.
Portland, OR 97209, USA

Dive St. Vincent Ltd.
Box 864
St. Vincent, West Indies

Early Winters Ltd.
110 Prefontaine S.
Seattle, WA 98104, USA

Earth Journeys
3400 Peachtree Rd.
Atlanta, GA 30326, USA
Phone (404)231-0073

Earthwatch
P.O. Box 127 AG
Belmont, MA 02178, USA
Phone (617)489-3030

East African Travel Consultants Inc.
33 Bloor St. E., Suite 206
Toronto, ON Canada M4W 3H1
Phone (416)967-0067

Eastern River Expeditions, Inc.
824 Petem Rd.
Kingsville, MD 21087, USA

ECHO: The Wilderness Company, Inc.
6505 Telegraph Ave.
Oakland, CA 94609, USA
Phone (415)658-5075

Eddie Bauer
15010 NE 36th
Redmond, WA 98052, USA

EE-DA-HOW Mountaineering
P.O. Box 207
Ucon, ID 83454, USA
Phone (208)523-9276

Encounter Overland
369 Pine St., Suite 516
San Francisco, CA 94104, USA
Phone (415)421-7199

Exodus Expeditions
167 Earls Court Rd.
London SW5, Great Britain
Phone 01-373-7895

Expedition Research, Inc.
P.O. Box 467
Annapolis, MD 21401, USA
Phone (301)268-3222

Expedition Training Institute, Inc.
P.O. Box 171, Prudential Ctr. Sta.
Boston, MA 02199, USA
Phone (617)922-0577

Explorandes
Nicolas de Pierola 672, Of. 205
Lima, Peru
Phone 23-6992

Explore Beyond Ltd.
1 Ludgate Circus Bldgs.
London EC4M 7LQ, Great Britain
Phone 01-248-9082 or 01-236-4395

Falkland Wildlife
c/o Drifts, Chinnor Hill
Oxford, OX9 4BS, Great Britain

Flying Dutchman Yachts
2727 Fairview E.
Seattle, WA 98102, USA

Forum Travel International
2437 Durant, No. 208
Berkeley, CA 94704, USA
Phone (415)843-8294

Galapago Inn
Apartado Postal 289
Cozumel, Quintana Roo, Mexico

Galapagos Yacht Charters
Casilla 9481
Guayaquil, Ecuador

Garden Island Marine
RR Box 180-B
Lihue, Kauai, HI 96766, USA
Phone (808)245-6361

Geneva Spur Ltd.
1109 Lakewood Dr.
Vienna, VA 22180, USA
Phone (703)281-3316

Georgie's Royal River Rats
Box 12489
Las Vegas, NV 89112, USA
Phone (702)451-5588

Gerhard's Bicycle Odysseys
1137 SW Yamhill
Portland, OR 97205, USA
Phone (503)223-5190

Glacier Guides, Inc.
205 S. 300 W.
St. George, UT 84770, USA
Phone (801)673-3697

Glad Tidings
Box 394
Oakland, ME 04963, USA

Globe Treks
410 Fifth Ave., Suite 10
Hendersonville, NC 28739, USA
Phone (704)692-4294

Globetrek, Inc.
226 W. Prien Lake Rd.
Lake Charles, LA 70601, USA

Go Diving, Inc.
715 Florida Ave. S.
Minneapolis, MN 55426, USA
Phone (612)544-7168

Government of Yukon Territory
Dept. of Tourism
P.O. Box 2703
Whitehorse, YT Canada Y1A 2C6

Goway Travel Ltd.
53 Yonge St., Second Floor
Toronto, ON Canada M5E 1J3
Phone (416)863-0799

Guerba Expeditions Ltd.
Stokehill Farm
Erlestoke, Devizes, Wiltshire SN10 5UB
Great Britain
Phone Bratton 476

Gunflint Northwoods Outfitters
Box 100-AD
Grand Marais, MN 55604, USA
Phone (218)388-2296

H & M Landing
2803 Emerson St.
San Diego, CA 92106, USA
Phone (714)222-1144

Hann Overland
17 Stanthorpe Rd.
London SW16, Great Britain
Phone 01-769-6659

Haron—Sinai Tours Division
c/o Neot Hakikar
28 King David St.
Jerusalem, Israel
Phone (02)221624

Hells Canyon Navigation Co.
P.O. Box 145
Oxbow, OR 97840, USA
Phone (503)785-3352

High Country Adventures
P.O. Box 176
Helena, MT 59601, USA
Phone (406)443-2842

High Country Outfitters
RR 1, Box 1
Donnelly, ID 83615, USA

High Horizons
P.O. Box 1166
Banff, AB Canada T0L 0C0
Phone (403)762-2868

High Mountains Helicopter Skiing
Box 2217
Jackson, WY 83001, USA
Phone (307)733-3274

Hike-Skitour Vermont
RFD 1
Chester, VT 05143, USA
Phone (802)875-3631 or 875-3613

Himalaya
3023 Franklin St.
San Francisco, CA 94123, USA
Phone (415)441-2933

Himalayan Journeys
P.O. Box 989
Kathmandu, Nepal

Hondo Rast and Co.
P.O. Box 231
Hamilton, MT 59840, USA
Phone (406)363-3440

Hondoo Rivers and Trails
P.O. Box 377
Ferron, UT 84523, USA
Phone (801)384-2961

Horizons Unlimited
P.O. Box 147
Pocatello, ID 83201, USA
Phone (208)233-9428

Horsehead Pack Trips
P.O. Box 68
Monticello, UT 84535, USA
Phone (801)587-2929

Icelandic Airlines
630 Fifth Ave.
New York, NY 10020, USA
Phone (212)757-8585

Idaho Adventures
P.O. Box 834 AD
Salmon, ID 83467, USA
Phone (208)756-2986

International Alpine School
Eldorado Springs, CO 80025, USA
Phone (303)494-4904

International Aquatic Adventures, Inc.
2047 Broadway
Boulder, CO 80302, USA
Phone (303)444-5829
Or tollfree (800)525-2545

International Bicycle Touring Society
2115 Paseo Dorado
La Jolla, CA 92037, USA

International School of Mountaineering
Club Vagabond
1854 Leysin, Switzerland
Phone (025)6-23-21

Iowa Mountaineers
30 Prospect Pl., P.O. Box 163
Iowa City, IA 52240, USA
Phone (319)337-7163

J Box Dot Guest Ranch
Box 616
Afton, WY 83110, USA
Phone (307)886-5565

Jerrycan Expedition
Ave. Legrand 86
1050 Brussels, Belgium
Phone (02)648-22 69

Johann Mountain Guides
P.O. Box 2334
Lincoln City, OR 97367, USA

K.E. Schultz Guide
and Outfitting Service
0010 Ponderosa Dr.
Glenwood Springs, CO 81601, USA

Keewaydin Camp and Ojibway of Keeway-
din
4242 Brookdale St.
Jackson, MS 39206, USA
Phone (601)353-6233
Summer: Timagami, ON Canada P0H 2H0

Key West Pro Dive Shop, Inc.
P.O. Box 580
Key West, FL 33040, USA
Phone (305)296-3823

Kilbride's Underwater Tours
Box 40
Virgin Gorda, British Virgin Islands
Phone 55-555, ext. 37

Killington Adventure
Killington, VT 05751, USA
Phone (802)422-3333

Klondike Safaris
P.O. Box 1898
Skagway, AK 99840, USA

Kobe Safaris
167 Earls Court Rd.
London SW5, Great Britain

Kumsheen Raft Adventures Ltd.
Suite 116, 525 Seymour St.
Vancouver, BC Canada V6B 3H7
Phone (604)669-0415

L.D. Frome, Outfitter
RFD
Afton, WY 83110, USA
Phone (307)886-5240

Larry Dean Olson Survival Assoc.
Box 1301
Salt Lake City, UT 84101, USA

Leonard Expeditions
P.O. Box 98
Stanley, ID 83278, USA
Phone (208)774-3656

Lowry's Lodges Ltd.
Box 40
Horsefly, BC Canada V0L 1L0

Lute Jerstad Adventures
P.O. Box 19527
Portland, OR 97219, USA
Phone (503)244-4364

Mackay Bar
Business Office Drawer F, Rm. 1010
1 Capital Ctr.
Boise, ID 83702, USA
Phone (208)344-1881

Mark Miller
Skwentna, AK 99667, USA

Missouri River Cruises, Inc.
Box 1212
Ft. Benton, MT 59442, USA
Phone (406)622-3295

Moose Lake Wilderness Canoe Trips
Box 358
Ely, MN 55731, USA
Phone (218)365-5837

Mt. Adams Wilderness Institute
Flying L Ranch
Glenwood, WA 98619, USA
Phone (509)364-3511 or 364-3488

Mt. Baker Guide Service
1212 24th St.
Bellingham, WA 98225, USA
Phone (206)671-1505

Mountain Meadows Ski Touring Center
Killington, VT 05751, USA
Phone (802)775-7077

Mountain People School
157 Oak Spring Dr.
San Anselmo, CA 94960, USA
Phone (415)457-3664

Mountain River Tours Inc.
Box 88, Sunday Rd.
Hico, WV 24854, USA
Phone (304)658-5817

Mountain Travel Inc.
1398 Solano Ave.
Albany, CA 94706, USA
Phone (415)527-8100

Museum of Comparative Zoology
The Agassiz Museum
Harvard University
Cambridge, MA 02138, USA
Phone (617)495-2463

Nantahala Outdoor Center
Star Rt., Box 68
Bryson City, NC 28713, USA
Phone (704)488-6407

Nature Expeditions International
599 College Ave.
Palo Alto, CA 94306, USA
Phone (415)328-6572

Neviot Diving Center
Neviot Holiday Village
Post Elat, Israel
Phone 059-3667

New England Divers Inc.
Mail Order Warehouse, Tozer Rd.
Beverly, MA 01915, USA

Norm McDonough and Sons
R Rt.
Wolf Creek, MT 59648, USA

North Country Mountaineering, Inc.
P.O. Box 951
Hanover, NH 03755, USA
Phone (603)643-3299

North Woods Canoe Trips
2659E S. Xanadu Wy.
Aurora, CO 80014, USA
Phone (303)750-8438

Northern Lights Alpine Recreation
Box 399
Invermere, BC Canada V0A 1K0
Phone (604)342-6042

The Northern Wilderness Company
P.O. Box 25795
Seattle, WA 98125, USA
Phone (206)633-3946

North-West Expeditions
P.O. Box 1551
Edmonton, AB Canada T5J 2N7

The Northwest Outward Bound School
0110 SW Bancroft
Portland, OR 97201, USA
Phone (503)243-1993

OARS Inc.
P.O. Box 67
Angels Camp, CA 95222, USA
Phone (209)736-2924 or 736-2661

Oceanus
P.O. Box 431
Hohokus, NJ 07423, USA
Phone (201)447-0393

Oldfather Canoe and Kayak Center
60390 Star Rt. 15
Goshen, IN 46526, USA
Phone (219)533-2295

Orient Tours
81 Cadogan Sq.
London SW1X 0DY, Great Britain

Osprey River Trips, Inc.
11468 Redwood Hwy.
Wilderville, OR 97543, USA
Phone (503)479-4215

Outdoor Adventures
3109 Fillmore St.
San Francisco, CA 94123, USA
Phone (415)567-9938

Outdoor Leadership Training Seminars
2220 Birch St.
Denver, CO 80207, USA
Phone (303)333-7831

Outdoors Unlimited
2500 Fifth Ave.
Sacramento, CA 95818, USA
Phone (916)452-1081

Outlaw Trails Inc.
P.O. Box 336
Green River, UT 84525, USA
Phone (801)564-3477

Overland Rolls
P.O. Box 4134, Sta. A
Portland, ME 04101, USA

Pacific Northwest Float Trips
829 Waldron St.
Sedro Woolley, WA 98284, USA
Phone (206)855-0535 or 855-0417

Pacific Northwest Sea Trails, Inc.
13062 Caminito del Rocio
Del Mar, CA 92014, USA
Phone (714)481-9540

Pacific Sportdiving Co., Inc.
4104 E. Anaheim St.
Long Beach, CA 90804, USA
Phone (213)433-7485

Penn Overland Tours Ltd.
330 Sutter St.
San Francisco, CA 94108, USA
Phone (415)391-5728
Or: 122 Knightsbridge
London SW 1, Great Britain
Phone 01-589-0016

Price Canyon Ranch
P.O. Box 1065
Douglas, AZ 85607, USA
Phone (602)558-2383

Primitive Area Float Trips, Inc.
P.O. Box 585
Salmon, ID 83467, USA
Phone (208)756-2319

Professional Diving Schools of Florida
210 N. Federal Hwy.
Deerfield Beach, FL 33441, USA
Phone (305)428-0560

Quest 4 Ltd.
Aston Wold
Peterborough PE8 5LZ, Great Britain

Questers Tours and Travel, Inc.
257 Park Ave. S.
New York, NY 10010, USA
Phone (212)673-3120

Rainbow Travel
71A Trapelo Rd.
Belmont, MA 02178, USA

REI Adventure Travel, Inc.
1525 11th Ave.
Seattle, WA 98122, USA
Phone (206)322-7800

River Trips Unlimited
900 Murphy Rd. W.
Medford, OR 97501, USA
Phone (503)779-3798

Rivers Northwest
141 Eagle St. NE
Winslow, WA 98110, USA
Phone (206)842-5144

Rocky Mountain Backpack Tours
P.O. Box 2781
Evergreen, CO 80439, USA
Phone (303)674-0519

Rogue River Outfitters
8890 Rogue River Hwy.
Grants Pass, OR 97526, USA
Phone (503)582-1672

Royal Gorge Nordic Ski Resort
P.O. Box 178
Soda Springs, CA 95728, USA
Phone (916)426-3793

Sacred Monkey Expeditions
Box 363
Jerome, AZ 86331, USA
Phone (602)634-5711

Safaris Equatorianos
Casilla A-122
Quito, Ecuador
Phone 529-963

Schweizer Aircraft Corp.
P.O. Box 147
Elmira, NY 14902, USA
Phone (607)739-3821

Scorpion Productions
Box 1147
Perris, CA 92370, USA

Scubahire Ltd.
GPO Box 777
Suva, Fiji
Phone 361-241

Scubaplus
201 E. 34th St.
New York, NY 10016, USA
Phone (212)689-0035

Sea Life Discovery, Inc.
19915-A Oakmont Dr.
Los Gatos, CA 95030, USA
Phone (408)353-1766

Sea Us Corp.
Box 12, NAUSTA
FPO San Francisco, CA 96651, USA

Seawind Sailing School
6535 Seaview Ave. NW
Seattle, WA 98117, USA
Phone (206)246-7245

See and Sea Travel Service, Inc.
680 Beach St., Suite 340
Wharfside
San Francisco, CA 94109, USA
Phone (415)771-0077

Semjon Lass Associates
Action Tours
Box 1000
Lowell, MA 01854, USA
Phone (617)459-2104
Or: Talisman Travel Service
3440 Geary Blvd.
San Francisco, CA 94118, USA
Phone (415)668-2956

Shenandoah River Outfitters, Inc.
RFD 3
Luray, VA 22835, USA
Phone (703)743-4159

Sherpa Expeditions
3 Bedford Rd., Chiswick
London W4, Great Britain
Phone 01-994-7668
Or: Durbar Marg
P.O. Box 1519
Kathmandu, Nepal
Phone 12422

Skinner Brothers Mountaineering
Box B
Pinedale, WY 82941, USA
Phone (307)367-2270

Society Expeditions
P.O. Box 5088, University Sta.
Seattle, WA 98105, USA
Phone (206)324-9400

Sourdough Outfitters
Bettles, AK 99726, USA
Phone (907)692-5252

South American Wilderness Adventures
1760 Solano Ave.
Berkeley, CA 94707, USA
Phone (415)524-5111

Southwest Safaris
P.O. Box 945
Santa Fe, NM 87501, USA
Phone (505)988-4246

Special InteresTours
P.O. Box 37
Medina, WA 98039, USA
Phone (206)455-1960

Spirit Waters
5375 Eureka Rd.
Excelsior, MN 55331, USA
Phone (612)474-5190

Spyglass Hill
c/o Roseo Affiliates
Roatan Island, Honduras

Sundance Expeditions
14894 Galice Rd.
Merlin, OR 97532, USA
Phone (503)479-8508

Sunrise County Canoe Expeditions, Inc.
Cathance Lake
Grove Post Office, ME 04638, USA
Phone (207)454-7708

Sunrise Scenic Tours
P.O. Box 447
Klamath Falls, OR 97601, USA

Taku Outfitters, Ltd.
Box 30, Klahanie Dr., RR 2
Powell River, BC Canada V8A 4Z3
Phone (604)483-9238

Telluride Mountaineering School
Box 67
Telluride, CO 81435, USA
Phone (303)925-3603

Tracks
165 Kensington High St.
London W8 6SH, Great Britain
Phone 01-937-5964

Transcontinental Safaris
Douglas Scrub
McLaren Flat, South Australia
Phone Adelaide 3830230

Travelsur Tours, Inc.
551 Fifth Ave., #922
New York, NY 10017, USA

Treasure Treks Ltd.
Third Floor, Panton House
25 Haymarket
London SW1Y 4EN, Great Britain
Phone 01-839-4267

Trek Adventures
3 E. 54th St.
New York, NY 10022, USA
Phone (212)751-3250

Trekamerica, Inc.
62 Kenway Rd., Earls Court
London SW5 ORD, Great Britain
Phone 01-370-4013

Trekking Percy Tapia
P. O. Box 3074
Lima 106, Peru

Triumph Travel Corp.
914 Second Ave.
Seattle, WA 98104, USA

TX Ranch
P.O. Box 453
Lovell, WY 82431, USA
Phone (406)484-2583

Ultimate Experience, Inc.
P.O. Box 2118
Santa Barbara, CA 93120, USA
Phone (805)965-0096

United Touring Co.
P.O. Box 42196
Nairobi, Kenya
Phone 331960, ext. 266

University Press of Hawaii
John Kooistra
2840 Kolowalu St.
Honolulu, HI 96882

University Research
Expeditions Program
University of California
M 19 Wheeler Hall
Berkeley, CA 94720, USA
Phone (415)642-6586

University of the Wilderness
27654 Hwy. 74, No. 1687
Evergreen, CO 80439, USA
Phone (303)674-4695

VIP Travel
P.O. Box 157
Sierra Madre, CA 91024, USA
Phone (213)355-1438

Vail Guides Inc.
P.O. Box 1474

Vail, CO 81657, USA
Phone (303)476-5387

Vermont Bicycle Touring
RR 2
Bristol, VT 05443, USA
Phone (802)388-4263

Vic McLean's Outdoor Adventures
21666 Arbor Ct.
Hayward, CA 94541, USA

Virian J. Wadford
P.O. Box 173
Elk Grove Village, IL 60007, USA

Wagons Ho
P.O. Box 1879
Quinter, KS 67752, USA
Phone (913)754-3347

Walkers Tours & Travels Ltd.
P.O. Box 1048, 11 York St.
Colombo 1, Sri Lanka
Phone 22553

Wanapitei
7 Engleburn Pl.
Peterborough, ON Canada K9H 1C4
Phone (705)743-3774
Summer: Camp Wanapitei
Timagami, ON Canada P0H 2H0
Phone Timagami Island 1-R-13
(New Liskeard)

West Ridge Manufacturing
11920 W. Olympic Blvd.
Los Angeles, CA 90064, USA

Western Adventure Safaris, Inc.
P.O. Box 1732
Grand Junction, CO 81501, USA
Phone (303)242-6621

Western Charters
Westport, WA 98595, USA

Western Outdoor Adventures Ltd.
16115 32nd Ave.
White Rock, BC Canada V4B 4Z5
Phone (604)531-3969

Western Rivers of Idaho
P.O. Box 7129, University Sta.
Provo, UT 84602, USA
Phone (801)377-9750
Or tollfree (800)453-1482

Western Safaris Inc.
3379 Wedgewood
El Paso, TX 79925, USA
Phone (915)592-5984

WEXAS International Inc.
Suite 354, Graybar Bldg.
420 Lexington Ave.
New York, NY 10017, USA

Whitewater Adventures Ltd.
P.O. Box 46536
Vancouver, BC Canada V6R 4G8
Phone (604)736-2135

Wild & Scenic Inc.
P.O. Box 2123A
Marble Canyon, AZ 86036, USA
Phone (602)355-2222

Wilderness Associates of North America
P.O. Box 109
Monterey, CA 93940, USA
Phone (408)649-4868

Wilderness Encounter
720 Grand Ave.
Glenwood Springs, CO 81601, USA
Phone (303)945-8365

Wilderness Experience, Inc.
20120 Plummer St.
Chatsworth, CA 91311, USA
Phone (213)993-1191

Wilderness Experiences
Jan Jacobson
Rt. 1, Box 12
Thonotosassa, FL 33592, USA

The Wilderness Institute
333 Fairfax
Denver, CO 80220, USA
Phone (303)393-0400

Wilderness Southeast
Rt. 3, Box 619 AA
Savannah, GA 31406, USA
Phone (912)355-8008

Wilderness Wildlife Camps
c/o El Rancho Motel
SR 60338
Fairbanks, AK 99701, USA
Phone (907)488-2983

Wilderness World
1342 Jewell Ave.
Pacific Grove, CA 93950, USA
Phone (408)373-5882

Wildernorth, Inc.
Mile 102, Glenn Hwy., SRC Box 92E
Palmer, AK 99645, USA

Wildlife Outfitters
Rt. 1, Box 99B
Victor, MT 59875, USA
Phone (406)642-3262

Wildwater Expeditions Unlimited Inc.
P.O. Box 55
Thurmond, WV 25936, USA
Phone (304)469-2551

Wrangell Mt. St. Elias Outfitters
Dan Creek
VIA Glenallen, AK 99588, USA

Yak Works
10706 12th Ave. NW
Seattle, WA 98177, USA

Yellowstone Wilderness Guides
Box 446
Red Lodge, MT 59068, USA

Yonkers Travel Bureau
180 S. Broadway
Yonkers, NY 10701, USA

Young Abroad Club
Kowa Bldg., Fourth Floor
2-3-12 Shinjuku
Shinjuku-ku, Tokyo, Japan 160

Zambia Airways
1 Rockefeller Plaza
New York, NY 10020, USA
Phone (212)582-6637

Zephyr River Expeditions
P.O. Box 529
Columbia, CA 95310, USA
Phone (209)532-6249

Zig Zag River Runners
REI Adventure Travel
1525 11th Ave.
Seattle, WA 98122, USA
Phone (206)322-7800

INDEX I—GEOGRAPHY

Jordan, diving, 562; overlanding, 261, 287, 289; trekking, 102.

K

Kansas, caravanning, 152.

Kashmir, see India.

Kentucky, bicycle touring, 332, 334; houseboating, 510; nature trips, 145.

Kenya, archaeology/anthropology, 240, 241; backpacking, 188; ballooning, 364, 365; canoeing, 438; diving, 532; mountaineering, 14; nature trips, 124; overlanding, 254, 257; research expeditions, 306; trekking, 89; wildlife safaris, 109-15.

L

Lapland, see Finland, Norway, Sweden.

Lesotho, backpacking, 188.

Louisiana, overlanding, 298.

M

Madagascar, cruising, 502.

Maine, backpacking, 215; bicycle touring, 336, 337; canoeing, 450, 451; kayaking 463; mountaineering, 29; nature trips, 145; research expeditions, 424; river rafting, 424; sailing, 469, 483, 484; skiing, 61; wilderness survival, 354; windjamming, 490-3.

Malaysia, nature trips, 125; overlanding, 262, 267, 268; sailing, 469.

Maldive Islands, diving, 556.

Mali, overlanding, 256, 258.

Manitoba, nature trips, 128.

Marquesas Islands, see French Polynesia.

Maryland, houseboating, 510; sailing, 469, 484.

Massachussetts, nature trips, 528; overlanding, 298; research expeditions, 518; sailing, 485; windjamming, 494.

Mauritania, trekking, 89.

Mexico, trans-, nature trips, 134; overlanding, 276, 286, 296; river rafting, 407, 408; see also by state.

Mexico, DF, overlanding, 286.

Michigan, bicycle touring, 337; diving, 573; hang gliding, 386; parachuting, 393; research expeditions, 316; skiing, 71.

Micronesia, diving, 566, 567.

Middle East, trans-, overlanding, 287; see also by country.

Minnesota, backpacking, 216; canoeing, 452, 453; dogsledding, 85; hang gliding, 387; houseboating, 511; nature trips, 146; river rafting, 424; skiing, 61; soaring, 373; wilderness survival, 354.

Mississippi, bicycle touring, 338.

Missouri, houseboating, 511.

Montana, backpacking, 225, 226; ballooning, 368; bicycle touring, 339; canoeing, 453; cattle driving, 184; cruising, 504; hang gliding, 388; horsepacking, 170, 171; overlanding, 296; skiing, 61; soaring, 374; wilderness survival, 355.

Mongolia, archaeology/anthropology, 242.

Morocco, horsepacking, 156; overlanding, 254, 257, 259, 284; parasailing, 391; trekking, 89.

N

Nebraska, canoeing, 453; hang gliding, 388.

Nepal, backpacking, 190; overlanding, 260, 261, 262, 264; river rafting, 400; trekking, 95-9, wildlife safaris, 119.

Netherland Antilles, diving, 545; sailing, 473.

Netherlands, bicycle touring, 329, nature trips, 522; overlanding, 278, 283; sailing, 476.

Nevada, overlanding, 300; soaring, 375.

New Caledonia, nature trips, 137; research expeditions, 312.

New England, see by state.

New Guinea, see Papua New Guinea.

New Hampshire, backpacking, 226; bicycle touring, 332, 339; hang gliding, 388; mountaineering, 29, 34; skiing, 61, 62; soaring, 375; wilderness survival, 356.

New Hebrides, nature trips, 137.

New Jersey, hang gliding, 389; parachuting, 393.

New Mexico, backpacking, 227; flying, 381; horsepacking, 171; overlanding, 294; river rafting, 425.

New York, bicycle touring, 339; canoeing, 454; diving, 573; horsepacking, 172; houseboating, 511; nature trips, 146; overlanding, 296, 298; parachuting, 393; sailing,

INDEX II—TRIP OPERATORS

A

D

E

Oceanus, 472, 474, 528, 552.
Odyssey, 202.
Offshore Sailing School, Ltd., 474, 475, 485.
On the Rocks, 574.
Orange Torpedo Trips, 462.
Oregon Museum of Science and Industry, 316.
Osprey River Trips, Inc., 427.
Otis B. Driftwood Adventures Unlimited, 84.
Outdoor Adventures, 412, 416.
Outdoor Leadership Training Seminars, 248, 352.
Outdoor Seminar Retreats, 358.
Outdoors Unlimited, 416.
Outlaw Trails Inc., 174, 431.
Outward Bound Loch Eil, 24.
Overland Rolls, 336, 337.

P

Pacific Marine Institute, Inc., 519.
Pacific Northwest Float Trips, 432.
Pacific Northwest Sea Trails, Inc., 197.
Pacific Sportdiving Co., Inc., 565.
Palisade School of Mountaineering, 22.
Panamundo Guatemala Travel Service, 246.
Papillon Helicopters, 381.
Paradise Guest Ranch, 184.
Paradise House Hotel, 552.
Paradise Houseboat Rentals, 509.
Parke County, Inc., 334.
Penn Overland Tours Ltd., 267, 268, 281, 285.
Penobscot Raft Adventures, 424.
Peregrine Holidays, Town and Gown Travel, 136.
Philbrick, Capt. Gilbert E., 493.
Philippine Airlines, 533.
Phillips, Dick, 191.
Pittman's Boat Tours, 498.
Plantation Beach Resort, 555.
Plaza Travel Centre, 364.
Pollman's Tours and Safaris, Ltd., 114.
Poplar Bluff Stock Farm, 182.
Popplewell's Alligator Dock No. 1, 510.
Poseidon Circumnavigations, 487.

Poseidon Ventures Tours, 543, 567.
Price Canyon Ranch, 166.
Primitive Area Float Trips, Inc., 423.
Professional Diving Schools of Florida, 572.
Ptarmigan Tours, 52.
Pruckl Ranch, 182.
Putney Student Travel, Inc., 325.

Q

Questers Tours and Travel, Inc., 124, 126, 130, 143.

R

REI Adventure Travel, Inc., 15, 38, 54, 55, 94, 97, 101, 320, 329, 400, 476.
Railtours, 268.
Railway Travel Centres, 125.
Rainier Mountaineering Inc., 26, 30, 38.
Rawhide Harris Ocean Sailing School, 478.
Red's Meadow Pack Stations, 167.
Red Baron Soaring, 374.
Rick Horn Wilderness Expeditions, 72.
Ridge Soaring, Inc., 376.
Rimrock Ranch, 177.
Rio Bravo River Tours, 425.
Ripcord Paracenter Inc., 393.
River Trips Unlimited, 427.
Rivers Northwest, 432.
Rock Creek Pack Station, 167, 182.
Rocky Mountain Diving Center Ltd., 570.
Rocky Mountain Raft Tours, 402.
Rocky Mountain Ski Tours and Backpack Adventures, 223.
Rocky Mountain Trail Rides, 157.
Rogue River Outfitters, 65.
Root, Alan, 365.
Routeburn Walk Ltd., 194.
Rowand's Reef, 536.
Royal Gorge Nordic Ski Resort, 31, 50, 54, 56, 72.
Rust Flying Service, 383.

S

SAS Ski Desk, 83.

Student Hosteling Program of New England, Inc., 322, 324.
Study Tours, 326.
Sugar Mill Inn, 200.
Sun Mountain Lodge, 71.
Sundance Expeditions, 463.
Sunland International Tours, 559.
Sunrise County Canoe Expeditions, Inc., 451.
Sunrise Scenic Tours, 427.
Surfside Watersports, 550.

T

TH Guest Ranch, 52.
TVA-Land Between the Lakes, 145.
TX Ranch, 185.
Tag-A-Long Tours, 302.
Taku Outfitters, Ltd., 160.
Tallman Tours, Ltd., 243.
Tauck Tours, 126.
Tecumseh Parachuting Service, 393.
Telluride Mountaineering School, 33.
Tentrek Expeditions, Ltd., 282, 284.
Te Rehuwai Safaris Ltd., 156.
Terres d'Adventure, 53, 78, 190, 202, 204.
Thomas Cook Ltd., 207.
Three Bar J Ranch, 182.
Three Eagles Expeditions, Inc., 223.
Tonquin Valley Trail Trips, 158.
Topkapi Safari, 290.
Touch of Nature Environmental Center, 414.
Tour-East, 262.
Tracks, 256, 278, 284.
Trail Riders of the Canadian Rockies, 159.
Trailfinders, 266.
Trailside Country School, 141.
Transcontinental Safaris, 100, 272.
Transit Travel Ltd., 264, 278.
Traveling Taj, Inc., 56.
Treasure Treks Ltd., 98, 287, 293, 296.
Trek Adventures, see NAT Eurotours Ltd., Treasure Treks, Ltd.
Trekamerica, Inc., 286, 298.
Trekking Percy Tapia, 105, 236.

Trinity Pack Trains, 167.
Tucson School of Scuba Diving, 569.
Tu-Kay Renegades, 229.
Twickenham Travel Ltd., 522.

U

UCLA Extension, 136, 527.
UCSB Extension, 518.
Underwater Safaris, 539.
University of the Wilderness, 79, 227, 228, 455.
University Research Expeditions Program, 241, 307, 310, 312, 566.
Up-It, 390.

V

VIP Travel, 380.
Vail Guides Inc., 300, 419.
Valley Ranch, 178.
Veach, Don and Judy, 147.
Venturetreks Ltd., 194.
Ven-Turs, 214.
Vermont Bicycle Touring, 341.
Victor Emanuel Nature Tours, 134.
Vieques Divers, 546.
Villa de la Mina, 430.
Virgin Islands Dive School, 550.
Visitours Tour Service, 273.
Voyage, 487.
Vuelo Libre, 385.

W

WEXAS International Inc., 89, 94, 99, 102, 119, 161, 468, 532.
Wadloop Centrum, 532.
Wagons Ho, 152.
Wahweap Lodge & Marine, 508.
Wales Tourist Board, 163.
Walkabout International, 211.
Walkers Tours & Travels Ltd., 125, 190, 243.
Wanapitei, 444.
Warner and MacKenzie Guiding and Outfitting, 159.
Warrenton Soaring Center, 377.

Waymark Holidays, 188, 204, 205, 206, 209.
Welcome Swiss Tours, 162, 330.
West Himalayan Holidays, 94.
Western Adventure Safaris, Inc., 431.
Western Outdoor Adventures Ltd., 198, 440.
Western River Expeditions, 567.
Western Rivers of Idaho, 424.
White Bear Gliding, 373.
White Water Adventurers, 429.
White Water Sports, 456, 464.
Whitewater Adventures Ltd., 471.
Whitewater Voyages/River Exploration Ltd., 406, 480.
Wild & Scenic Inc., 229, 431, 464.
Wild Places, Inc., 453.
Wilderness Adventure, 147.
Wilderness Adventures, Inc., 169.
Wilderness Associates of North America, 416.
Wilderness Bound, Ltd., 29, 41, 216.
Wilderness Encounter, 352, 419, 528.
Wilderness Expeditions, 73.
The Wilderness Institute, 73, 218, 231, 355, 444.
Wilderness Experiences, 385.
Wilderness Experts Inc., 199.
Wilderness River Outfitters and Trail Expeditions, 60.
Wilderness Southeast, 145, 201, 224, 316, 356, 449, 450, 572.
Wilderness Studies, 142, 441.
Wilderness Tours, 405.
Wilderness Trails, Idaho, 225.
Wilderness Trails, Ohio, 64, 359.
Wilderness Trails, Wyoming, 179.

Wilderness Trails Ltd., 117.
Wilderness Walks, 138, 148.
Wilderness Wildlife Camps, 351.
Wilderness World, 287, 406.
Wildernorth, Inc., 218, 219.
Wildlife Outfitters, 171.
Wildwater Expeditions Unlimited Inc., 434.
Wildwater Ltd., 429.
Wilson Outfitters, 453.
Wind Over Mountain, 26, 156.
Wind Works, 487.
Windblown, 62.
Wonder Bird Tours, 128, 140.
Wolfcreek Wilderness, 224.
Wrangell Mt. St. Elias Outfitters, 57, 219.

Y

YHA Adventure Holiday, 23, 163, 209, 328, 370, 475.
Yankee Schooner Cruises, 493.
Yellowstone Nordic, 73.
Yellowstone Park Co., 74.
Yellowstone Wilderness Guides, 41, 232.
Yosemite Mountaineering, 58.
Yosemite Natural History Association, 142.
Youth Adventure, Inc., 494.

Z

Zambia Airways, 118.
Zeilinstituut "De Bird", 476.
Zephyr River Expeditions, 417.
Zig Zag River Runners, 433, 446.